VATICAN II
The Theological Dimension

VATICAN II

The Theological Dimension

EDITED BY

ANTHONY D. LEE, O.P.

WITH INTRODUCTION BY

FERRER E. SMITH, O.P.

THE THOMIST PRESS

1963

Originally published as a

SPECIAL ISSUE OF

THE THOMIST
Volume XXVII (complete)
April, July, October
1963

WITH

Introduction by FERRER E. SMITH, O. P.

THE THOMIST PRESS
PRINTED IN U. S. A.

CONTENTS

_____

v

EDITOR'S PREFACE

Caritas Christ urget nos (2 Cor. 5:14). The whole world has been witness to the charity of Christ in the heart of the late Pope John XXIII. In the few but full years of his pontificate, the charity of Christ urged him, not only to bring to the people of Rome his personal warmth, but to communicate to and share with the modern world the universality of Christ's love for mankind. He chose a most fruitful and universal way to renew in this world the Christian spirit in his heart: The Second Ecumenical Council of the Vatican. Through this initiative, the vision, zeal, and charity within him were communicated to and shared with the bishops of the world. Continued in the same spirit by Pope Paul VI, the Council, in turn, promises to bring, through the deliberations of the Conciliar Fathers, the charity of Christ to all the faithful and to all men of good will attentive to its counsels.

The prospect of editing a work on the theological dimension of this momentous Council was awesome; yet the actual preparation of this volume has been a joy, since it has been a personal experience of the renewal of Christian vision, zeal, and charity inspired by Pope John XXIII and continuing under the benevolence of Pope Paul VI.

The response of eminent theologians from all parts of the world to our request for articles was immediate and enthusiastic. As the manuscripts were read it became clear that their understanding of the issues of the Council and their theological skill in presenting their views were as profound as their zeal was spontaneous. Each study stands on the merit of the author's own competence and of the quality of his presentation. Because of this, and because of the technical nature of many of the studies, the editor has viewed his task simply as one of reproducing faithfully the manuscripts offered by the authors. While such a procedure permits a variety of opinion, it has the advantage of presenting, without editorial intrusion, the exact thought of many authors; and while it permits marked differences in style, it has the advantage of preserving, without editorial interference, the international flavor of the volume.

Even in this one appointed task, the editor must personally acknowledge the immense assistance he has received from generous and zealous colleagues and friends. The volume is first and foremost the work of the editorial staff of THE THOMIST upon whose collective knowledge, experience, and skill I have constantly depended. Particularly, I am indebted to the members of the staff who have contributed articles to this volume.

Although translators are said to perform a thankless task, my thanks are certainly due to Mr. Francis Turpin, to T. C. O'Brien, O. P., and especially to F. C. Lehner, O. P. who carried the burden of translations for this volume. The generous assistance of Edwin M. Rogers, O. P., Business Manager of The Thomist Press, in many office duties was most valuable. For typing and manuscript preparation I extend my appreciation to Miss Nancy Caldwell and to Helena Maxfield.

To Very Reverend E. F. Smith, O. P., Regent of Studies of the Province of St. Joseph, who encouraged the work at every turn and provided the Introduction to the volume, I offer sincere and lasting gratitude. For the solicitude and support which has made possible, not only this volume, but the continued work of THE THOMIST and The Thomist Press, I acknowledge my filial indebtedness to Very Reverend W. D. Marrin, O. P., Provincial of the Dominican Fathers, Province of St. Joseph.

ANTHONY D. LEE, O. P.

INTRODUCTION

E VERY age seeks self-understanding, insight into its
sources of strength and its areas of weakness, clarification of the direction it is taking in reality as well as
in intent. Ages past have, in the perspective of time, been
called " golden " or " dark "; an era, a century, a reign, or a
decade has been characterized as renaissance, revolutionary,
glorious, or uproarious. How should the twentieth century
understand itself? How will the twentieth century appear in
the pages of history? Some would see it already characterized by the mushroom cloud of the atom bomb: a century of
fear, of anxiety. For others, despite the tremendous technical
advance in transportation and communication, or perhaps
because of this, the twentieth is the century of loneliness in
which man is estranged from his fellow man; or of emptiness
in which the control over the earth, maybe the stars, has
served to reveal a tragic impoverishment of the human spirit.

God gave to this twentieth century Pope John XXIII and
John gave to it a new meaning. He saw himself as an optimist and as an optimist he appeared and appealed to men
everywhere. His words were many and of them many were
powerful. Yet what he was, what he did, more than what he
said, entranced a world. He gave hope in being hopeful, con-
fidently reaching for goods long since abandoned in despair.
He preached love most effectively in the daily, generous exercise of his own universal fatherhood. He lived through many
wars, two of which were rightly called "world"; they effected
in him a profound vision of "peace on earth." Paradoxically
he restored a warm hope of unity and peace while nations still
chose sides in a cold war; he restored man to personal dignity
by personifying the inestimable value of simplicity. In all, a
rich interior goodness overflowed as most vigorous, robust,
triumphant living. John was, in the phrase of St. Catherine

of Siena, " Christ on earth " and all men seeing Christ in him
were in some measure, small or great, renewed in themselves.

" Renewal " early became the watchword of the Council
called by Pope John. Thus on October 20, 1962, the Conciliar
Fathers declared: " Under the guidance of the Holy Spirit,
we intend in this assembly to seek the most effective ways of
renewing ourselves and of becoming increasingly more faithful
witnesses of the Gospel of Christ. We will strive to propose
to the men of our time the truth of God in its entirety and
purity so that they may understand it and accept it freely." [1]

The hope and love, the quest for peace and simplicity, the
witness to Our Lord characteristic of Pope John have animated the Council. The reason for the Christian vitality of
both Pope and Council is the one Holy Spirit, font of light
and love for the Church of Christ, abiding in the Holy Father
and the Fathers of the Second Vatican Council. The Church
renews herself from within and deep within her is God's Spirit.
Through John He manifested, even dramatically, His power
to draw the hearts of men. Through the Council He would
change those hearts, fill them with His love.

From the first moment of planning, the perspective of the
Second Vatican Council has been pastoral, not polemic. Holy
Mother Church is engaged, not primarily in forging weapons
for combat, but in opening wide the arms of love to embrace
all men in Christ. She seeks to deepen and intensify the inner
life of her children, to bring all men to partake of that life.
"We humbly and ardently invite all," affirmed the assembled
Bishops, "not only those brothers whom we serve as pastors,
but all our brothers who believe in Christ and all men of good
will . . . to collaborate with us in establishing a more ordered
way of living and greater brotherhood." [2]

The way must be His way, the way of truth. Life is ordered,
love is nourished, men are drawn one to another in unity and

---

[1] " The Council Fathers Speak to the World " *The Pope Speaks*, Vol. 8, No. 3
(1963), p. 302.

[2] *Ibid.*, p. 303.

peace by truth. The pastoral concern of the Council presents to the world the Church drawing upon the innermost well-springs of her living wisdom, reaching ever more deeply into her life with God, in God, into her possession of Christ, by Christ. In previous Councils, those especially of modern times, the Church was confronting error with truth, manifesting therein a profundity beyond the ken of error, but nevertheless limited to a context occasioned by error. In the present Council the Church "will strive to propose to the men of our time the truth of God in its entirety and purity." The infinite richness of that truth enforces a demand for precision and accuracy, for clarity and felicity of expression, for a simplicity possible only to a firm grasp of principle. Only so can life and love and universal brotherhood be established solidly, with ever expanding fruitfulness.

The Spirit of truth has provided the Church in Council with the resources proportioned to the demand upon her. She is a living organism, the body of Christ besouled by His Spirit, assimilating what the world at any time may offer, giving to all thus drawn to herself a new life, her own. The past to her is not a succession of dead monuments but part of her living mind giving understanding of the present and wisdom for the future. The historian, Dr. Ernest Colwell, has said: "Historians believe in the unbroken continuity of human experience in historic time, but a continuity which is constantly modified by change."[3] The two attributes, continuity and change, have provided historical inquiry with antithetical poles of interpretation and evaluation and have contributed to daily life, individual and societal, the tensions constitutive of vitality. Dedicated to continuity without change civilizations have atrophied and perished; breathless pursuit of novelty without continuity has equally expired, only more quickly and with less impact. The Church achieves a vital balance in transcending time, in lifting the human and mundane to the divine, in

[3] Colwell, Ernest C., *Jesus and the Gospel*, Oxford University Press, New York, 1963, p. 6.

showing the role of man within the plan of God, in giving purpose to continuity and meaning to change, in measuring the existence of man by the eternity of God. Thus the moment in her life that is the Council is enriched by the holiness of her saints, by the wisdom articulated by every doctor and theologian, by the experience absorbed into practice from Peter to Pope Paul VI.

History as caught up in the life of the Church prepares her for the work of renewal. Proximately and also providentially history as a field of human inquiry contributes to the deliberations of the Conciliar Fathers. In fact, the loving hand of God may be perceived awesomely in the immediate preparation of the minds of men to the pastoral orientation of the Council. Not only history but also Biblical studies, liturgy, philosophy, social research, and non-Catholic thought have been in recent decades the object of intensive scholarly research and popular interest within and without the Church— all in ways most apt to the needs of the Council. Philosophical trends have sharpened attention upon the person, the existent situation, phenomenological concerns; Biblical studies have offered insights promising an ever expanding grasp of divine revelation; contact with non-Catholic thought has led to a deeper penetration of the Church's wealth of wisdom as well as the exploration of other minds and the understanding of other vocabularies; the resurgence of ancient cultures and the rise of new nations have given both impetus to apostolic activity and release to the capacity of the Church to assimilate the most diverse ways of human life to a way of life divine. All these factors, and more, seek expression in the liturgy; all seek meaning in theology; all find their true value in the Council.

Within this context the present volume of essays on the theological dimensions of the Council finds its own meaning. The reason for the choice of topics is obvious; they are those of concern to the Conciliar Fathers. Study reveals the treatment of these topics to be fully in the spirit of the Church in Council.

These articles are not surveys of battle lines drawn up in the clash of opinion nor are they polemic volleys hurled at opponents. Each in its own way strives to make positive contribution to the design of the Conciliar Fathers " to propose to the men of our times the truth of God in its entirety and purity." The motivating quest for renewal, the animating spirit of confident hope and fraternal charity are everywhere evident. The authors from ten nations include theological experts (*periti*), private consultors to the hierarchy of several nations, advisors on special commissions, an observer-delegate —all of whom were present at the first session of the Council —and distinguished scholars whose contributions to theological thought have had international impact.

As theologians the writers of this volume draw upon all divine revelation, all human knowledge, all experience. As theologians of the Church they refer to her constantly for guidance as well as inspiration. In common they search for synthesis, not to close a question nor to elaborate a system, but to afford variety of insight, to achieve balance through analogy, to give deeper meaning and wider dimension to truth possessed. Genuine and solid thought gives birth to ever more profound thinking, generates new problems, elevates perspective. Wisdom has long since proved that only so will simplicity be earned, a simplicity of infinite richness.

The other traits of these articles are implicit in these basic characteristics. Definition is a goal, not to remove reality to the realm of abstract discourse or make it a matter of merely verbal concern for scholarly discussion, but to grasp it in its innermost actuality, to release its impact upon life, to unfold new values to living. Then only is synthesis an insight into existence reentering that existence to enrich it. Thus the efforts, constant within the volume, to be theologically precise and accurate neither hamper nor restrain felicity of expression with unnecessarily technical or outmoded jargon, but liberate thought for clarity of communication, readiness of grasp and aptness of application. Precision and accuracy are themselves guaranteed by the omnipresent concern with principle and the dependence of the most particularized and remote conclusion upon principle. So these are essays in theology, at once a science and a wisdom.

In sum, wisdom is the focus of these considerations of the theological dimensions of the Second Vatican Council. The most recent deliveries of Biblical studies, history, philosophy, social research and experience blending with the ancient treasures of Augustine and Aquinas equip the theological mind to grapple with the challenge to renew the Church in the twentieth century. The old is not slavishly repeated, the new is not thoughtlessly parrotted, but a genuine effort is made to draw upon the truth from every source, to point the way to a unity rich with pulsating life, that the men of our time "may understand and accept freely." For the twentieth century cannot understand itself save as it is seen in the entire and pure truth of God. Then will the hope that animates the Church and her Council animate the world.

FERRER E. SMITH, O. P.

THE PASTORAL CHURCH IN THE
NEW TESTAMENT *

ఌ

I F true Christian life consists in the practice of the virtues of faith, hope and charity (1 Thess. 1:3; 4:9; 1 Cor. 13:13), it behooves us to make good use of God's grace in the most varied circumstances of human existence (1 Pet. 4:10): "Who is wise and instructed among you? Let him by his good behaviour show his work in the meekness of wisdom" (Jas. 3:13; cf. Eph. 4:15). This instruction is the immanent work of God the Father, of Christ the Teacher (Mt. 23:8-10), of the guiding Holy Spirit (Jn. 16:12-15; cf. 14:17, 26), as well as of the leaders of the Church, whose mission it is to see to the moral formation of the faithful.

Peter, like his master (Jn. 10:1-15), is responsible for the conduct, nourishment and health of the flock (Jn. 21:16-17). Paul, "God's collaborator" (1 Cor. 3:9-12), the "wise architect" who lays the foundation of the local Church, supervises the building process very closely. He admonishes and instructs ". . . in all wisdom, that we may present every man perfect in Christ Jesus" (Col. 1:28). All the Apostles must teach the converts to live by the morality of the Gospel (Mt. 28:19). The leaders, mentioned in Heb. 13:7, watch over the souls entrusted to them and have the right to expect obedience and submission to their practical advice (cf. 1 Thess. 5:12-13). Finally, after Timothy, every Church leader devoted himself to the education of the faithful with a program furnished by St. Paul's testament: "Preach the word, be urgent in season, out of season; reprove, entreat, rebuke with all patience and teaching (2 Tim. 4:2; cf. Tit. 2:13). All these doctor-pastors announced and handed on "the wisdom of God" (1 Cor. 2:6-7). What was their method? [1]

---

* Translated by Francis J. Turpin.

[1] This theme is not treated in the "Morales du Noveau Testament"; however,

Just as the Lord, while teaching and preaching in the cities (Mt. 11:1), gave special instructions to his Apostles, they in turn elaborate plans (Acts 20:13), settle questions of detail (1 Cor. 16:1), finalize certain usages or the application of principles which assure the peace of souls and the good order of liturgical assemblies (1 Cor. 11:34). Left at Crete to complete the organization of the urban communities, Titus will only have to conform to the arrangements made by St. Paul himself (Tit. 1:5).

A similar task is entrusted to Timothy at the head of the Church of Ephesus (1 Tim. 1:3), a task summarized as the exercise of authority and the teaching of doctrine (1 Tim. 4:11). In some circumstances it will include opposition to the propaganda of unorthodox doctrines (1:3); laying down regulations to advance religious life (4:11); reminding widows of the obligations of their state (4:7) and the rich to be generous with their worldly goods (6:17); reiterating the injunction to those who are lazy that they must work (2 Thess. 3:10); giving observations on good behaviour and reprimands for the lack of decorum (1 Cor. 11:17); exhorting all to progress in saintliness, to live in complete wisdom (1 Thess. 4:11), to be faithful to the solemn obligations of baptism (1 Tim. 6:13-14). In all cases, the pastor prescribes and delivers the watchwords, but more exactly he informs and announces; he is only an intermediary. The reserve and discretion shown by the Apostles in their prescriptions is quite remarkable. The Lord alone has the authority to command, they merely convey his instructions (Mt. 28:20), and they ceaselessly remind us that they impose nothing in their own right (1 Cor. 7:10; cf. 2 Thess 3:3-4).

To be sure, they issue directives (Acts 18:15; Col. 4:10), and even precepts, but they are instructions as well as commands, and they always recall their divine origin.[2] It is with

valuable indications may be found in W. Schrage, *Die Konkreten Einzelgebote in der Paulinischen Paranese*, Gutersloh, 1961.

[2] 1 Cor. 14:37: "If anyone thinks that he is a prophet or spiritual, let him

extreme reluctance that St. Paul formulates orders in the strictest sense of the term. It is easy to conceive, since the aim of any instruction or *paraggelia* is to inculcate charity (1 Tim. 1:5), and a spiritual love can only be aroused by "the language of the Spirit," not by that of the law (1 Cor. 2:13). This is precisely the goal of the pastoral ministry, the formation of a pure heart, a good conscience and a strong faith, which are the indispensable conditions of the true *agape* (1 Tim. 1:3-4; cf. Heb. 10:22-25) inspired by the Holy Spirit.

The role of teaching cannot be overemphasized in the origins of Christianity. The whole life of Jesus was a preaching ministry (Mt. 4:23; 9:35; Lk. 13:22). He entrusted his Apostles with the task of instructing the disciples (Mt. 28:20; cf. Mk. 6:30), and ever since that time the Church's role has been that of a teacher (1 Tim. 3:15), the pastors are the ones who teach, and the faith and Christian education are the realities which are taught. It is a formation which is both doctrinal and practical (1 Cor. 4:17; 2 Tim. 2:2; 3:10). When the convert has accepted the apostolic message (Acts 4:2; 28:31), he receives a *didaché* or elementary instruction regarding baptism, the imposition of hands, the resurrection of the dead and eternal judgment (Heb. 6:2; cf. 1 Cor. 15), all of which summarize the essential elements of his solemn profession of faith. Later it is explained that he must resist scandals (Rom. 16:17), and that he must not allow himself to be contaminated by the Jewish practices (Acts 21:21, 28). The emphasis is on the reform of morality, the casting off of the "old man" (Eph. 4:21-23), "everything that is expedient" for a genuine Christian living (Acts 20:20). Obviously, young people and slaves

recognize that the things I am writing to you are the Lord's commandments"; 2 Peter 3:2: ". . . wherein I stir up your pure mind to remembrance that you may be mindful of what I formerly preached of the words of the holy prophets and of your Apostles which are the precepts of the Lord and Saviour"; 1 Jn. 2:7: ". . . no new commandment I am writing to you, but an old commandment which you had from the beginning"; 1 Jn. 4:21: "This commandment we have from him"; 2 Jn. 4: "I rejoiced greatly that I found some of your children walking in truth, according to the commandment that we have received from the Father."

are subjected to a more detailed instruction, *didaskalía* (Tit. 2:6-10; cf. 1 Tim. 6:1).

Little by little the neophyte becomes an adult in his faith and is in a position to become an instructor to his brothers (Heb. 5:12). St. Paul encourages this zeal,[3] but St. James is suspicious of the interference of these teachers, who are often incompetent and spurred on by vainglory.[4] In fact, there is an extreme infatuation within the Church with everything that is knowledge and speculation; no title is more highly valued than that of teacher; and both men and women [5] may be seen going from house to house (1 Tim. 5:13) or speaking at meetings, proposing a *didaché* (1 Cor. 14:26), " advancing " (2 Jn. 9), and " teaching things that they ought not " (Tit. 1:11). The results of doctrinal deviations are so gross [6] that St. Paul and St. John are forced on the one hand to specify the criteria of orthodoxy,[7] and on the other hand to accredit the truly inspired

[3] Col. 3:16: ". . . in all wisdom teach and admonish one another. . . ." 1 Cor. 12:31; 14:1, 39; cf. Heb. 10:24; 12:15. This catechist is not a doctor, but a teacher, instructor-educator, in conformity with the phrase "teacher of children" (Rom. 2:20), with the later honorary Jewish title of *Hakam*, head of the *Bet ha-Midrash* (cf. H. Mantel, *Studies in the History of the Sanhedrin*, Cambridge, Mass., 1961, pp. 132 ff.), and with the usage of the papyri which designate by this term the relationships of patron and apprentice in apprenticeship contracts (cf. J. H. Moulton, G. Milligan, *The Vocabulary of the Greek Testament*, London, 1949, on this word).

[4] Jas. 3:1: "Let not many of you become teachers." There are so few candidates for the administrative tasks of the Church because so many are seeking the teaching positions; thus the rehabilitation of the administrative positions in 1 Tim. 3:1 (cf. C. Spicq, "Si quis episcopatum desiderat," *Revue des Sciences Philosophiques et Theologiques*, 1940, pp. 316-326).

[5] Acts 15:1; 1 Cor. 14:34; 1 Tim. 2:12; Apoc. 2:20.

[6] The Lord had already asked his followers to be on guard against the teaching (*didaché*) of the Pharisees and Saducees, denouncing the *spirit* of their religious formation as being similar to a leaven (Mt. 16:12). St. Paul was indignant with the vagaries of those "tossed to and fro and carried by every wind of doctrine devised in the wickedness of men" (Eph. 4:14; cf. Heb. 13:9). There is already a multitude of teachers (2 Tim. 4:3) who "understand neither what they say nor the things about which they make assertion" (1 Tim. 1:7), proposing "doctrines [*didaskalía*] of devils" (1 Tim. 4:1), creating "destructive sects" (2 Pet. 2:1) which will exist at Pergamum and Thyatira (Apoc. 2:14, 15, 24).

[7] Every believer is a disciple, that is, one taught (2 Thess. 2:15; Gal. 1:12; Eph.

and the members of the hierarchy as teachers. These two categories are not opposed to each other, since "the spirits of the prophets are under the control of the prophets," and also the head of the community regulates its manifestations (1 Cor. 14:32 ff.). In Antioch, the prophets and teachers are ministers of the cult, and the Church ordains them to send them officially on mission (Acts 13:1-2). The Council of Jerusalem acts in the same way with regard to "leading men among the brethren" who are also charismatic (Acts 15:22, 32). Timothy will receive his *charisma*, granted "by reason of prophecy with the laying on of hands of the presbyterate."[8] The bishops and presbyters, who must be qualified to teach (1 Tim. 3:2; 2 Tim. 2:24), are simultaneously chosen by the Apostle's delegate

4:21; Col. 2:7). He is defined by his relationship to a Master and to the reception of his doctrine, "the teaching of God our Saviour" (Tit. 2:10), the only one worthy of blind adherence (1:9). Transmitted by the Apostles (cf. Heb. 4:2), it is in fact true, "as truth is in Jesus" (Eph. 4:2). Faith is essentially obedience to "that form of doctrine into which you have been delivered" (Rom. 6:17; cf. A. Seeberg, *Der Katechismus der Urchristenheit*, Leipzig, 1903, pp. 1 ff.; 193 ff.; S. Lyonnet, *Exegesis Epistulae ad Romanos V-VII*, Roma, 1961, pp. 48 ff.), in harmony with the common object of faith (Rom. 12:6; Tit. 1:4), "according to the gospel of the glory of the blessed God" (1 Tim. 1:10-11; cf. Tit. 2:1). It is this exact relationship with "the doctrine of Christ" (2 Jn. 9) which defines "the good doctrine (1 Tim. 4:6) or the "sound doctrine" (1 Tim. 1:10; 6:3; Tit. 1:9; 2 Tim. 4:3). On the soundness of doctrine cf. C. Spicq "Pastorales" in *DBS* VII, 95). Doubtless each Apostle has his personal "methods," his own way of presenting the message and of accentuating certain rules of life (1 Cor. 4:17; cf. 2 Tim. 1:13); thus there will be Paul-, James-, John- and Peter-type spiritualities, whose legitimacy the Lord implicitly recognized (Lk. 7:31-35). Preserving the trust unchanged (1 Tim. 6:20) does not mean the stagnation of the teaching. Again, we must cite St. Vincent of Lerins: "Guard the trust, that is, what was entrusted to you, not what you invented; what you received, not what you thought up. . . . You are not an author but a guardian, not a founder but a disciple. . . . You received gold, return gold. . . . O Timothy, because of your explanation we now believe in a clearer way what we used to believe in a more obscure way. . . . Teach the same things you were taught. Speak in a new way, but do not speak of novelties: *cum dicas nove, non dicas nova*" (*Commonitorium*, 22; PL, L, 667). The important thing is fidelity to the spirit of Jesus Christ.

[8] 1 Tim. 4:14. The laying on of hands transmits the Spirit (cf. C. Spicq, *Les Epîtres Pastorales*, Paris, 1947, pp. 320 ff.; E. Lohse, *Die Ordination in Spatjudentum und im Neuen Testament*, Gottingen, 1951; M. Black, "The Doctrine of the Ministry," *Expository Times*, LXIII, pp. 112-116.

(Tit, 1:5; 1 Tim. 3:2) and " established by the Holy Spirit " (Acts 15:28). Thus, as regards either missionaries or local ministers, we may say that the doctrinal capacity and authority come from God, who "established" the Apostles, prophets, evangelists, teachers and pastors in the Church.[9] They all have the duty of faithfully accomplishing this teaching task [10] if they desire their own salvation and that of others (1 Tim. 4:16). They are but the organs of an uninterrupted tradition, exposing a Church doctrine " according to piety " (1 Tim. 6:3; cf. 3:15-16), and which they in turn will transmit to qualified believers [11] without it being possible for them to modify the purport (1 Pet. 1:20; 1 Tim. 6:20).

The activities of these teachers are extremely different in both nature (genre) (1 Cor. 12:4-6, 10-11) and quality.[12] The

[9] I Cor. 12:28 (Eph. 4:11); 1 Tim. 1:12; 2 Tim. 1:11; Acts 20:28 (cf. C. Claereboets, " In quo vos Spiritus Sanctus posuit episcopos," Biblica 1943, pp. 370-387). It is to be observed that the names of the charisms usually place stress on delegation: the apostle is sent (envoyé) (Rom. 10:15), the prophet speaks in the name of God, announces what God told him to say (Jas. 5:10; 1 Pet. 1:21; cf. Fl. Josephus, C. Ap., I, 7-8; J. B. Frey, " La Révélation d'après les conceptions juives au temps de Jésus Christ," RB, 19616, pp. 494 ff.; cf. Act. 21:10-11); the prophet Agabus presents his message, " Thus says the Holy Spirit "; the evangelist exposes and comments on the good news promulgated by Jesus (Heb. 2:3; 4:2; 1 Pet. 1:25; 2 Tim. 4:5); the teaching instructor gets his doctrine from Scripture (2 Tim. 3:16), from apostolic tradition (1 Tim. 4:6; 6:3; Tit. 1:9; 2 Tim. 3:10), and finally from Jesus' message itself (1 Tim. 2:7; 2 Tim. 1:11), the pastor feeds Christ's sheep (Jn. 21:15-17; cf. Acts 20:28).

[10] Rom. 12:7. This explains the insistence of the pastorals in recommending to Timothy, Titus, the bishops, the presbyters: " speak, teach, persevere in instruction," the eminent task of " the good minister of Jesus Christ " (1 Tim. 4:6, 16, 17; 6:3; Tit. 1:9; 2:1; 2 Tim. 4:2); the most explicit text is 1 Tim. 4:13: " Until I come, be diligent in reading, in exhortation and in teaching."

[11] 2 Tim. 2:2: " Therefore . . . be strengthened in the grace which is in Christ Jesus; and in the things you have heard from me through many witnesses, commend to trustworthy men who shall be competent in turn to teach others "; cf. 1 Tim. 5:22.

[12] One of St. Paul's great preoccupations was to control and organize the charismatic manifestations in church. He requires on the one hand that they have a maximum of intelligibility (1 Cor. 14:7-20), and on the other hand that they be useful to the listeners (v. 6; 12:7); that is, something completely different from a marvel or a craze, but rather a solid construction: edification (1 Cor. 14:4-5, 12, 26). A speech is " edifying " only if it instructs, encourages and finally strengthens what is good and pushes towards its realization (v. 3; 2 Cor. 12:19; 13:8-11; Eph. 4:29).

best [13] and most widely accepted [14] is unquestionably *prophecy*, directed " not to unbelievers but to believers " (1 Cor. 14:22), and whose modes are also very diverse. In fact, the prophet is like a " lamp, burning and shining " (Jn. 5:35; cf. 2 Pet. 1:19), able to predict the future (Acts 11:28; 21:10) and to discern the *mirabilia Dei* (Lk. 2:25, 36), and fervent to sing them (Lk. 1:67; Acts 19:6); he is also keen in penetrating the secrets of hearts (Jn. 6:19; cf. Heb. 4:12-13) and thus bring about their conversion (1 Cor. 14:24-25). But, after John the Baptist, his principal duty is to prepare the arrival of the Saviour into souls (Jn. 1:23, 26; Apoc. 19:10; cf. 3:20); he is a herald who proclaims salvation and interprets God's revelation made by his Son. He corresponds to our conception of a preacher, whose triple role is to instruct, exhort and encourage or console the faithful (1 Cor. 14: 3,6,31). He is a " paraclete " who teaches,[15] convinces (1 Pet. 5:2-3), enriches and changes the spirit of his listeners. Thus his sermon on *paraklesis* is at first a *didaskalía* or *didaché*, but in an animated style [16] which will distinguish clearly the voice of an apostle from that of a professor (1 Cor. 14:3), because it will edify, and it is God who exhorts through him.[17]

This aspect of pressing invitation and stimulation is so preponderant that the apostolic sermon—whose best definition is an exhortation— commands all the practical morality of the New Testament: the evangelic doctrine is presented, and the servants of the Word insist most emphatically on the adherence

---

[13] Recall the charisms of knowledge (1 Cor. 13:2), wisdom (12:8), teaching (v. 28), revelation (14:6), interpretation (v. 26); cf. H. Karpp, " Prophet oder Dolmetscher? ", *Festschrift G. Dehn*, Neukirchen, 1957, pp. 103-117. St. Paul counsels: " Aim especially that you may prophesy " (1 Cor. 14:1, 5).

[14] Acts 2:17; 21:9; 1 Cor. 14:31; 2 Cor. 13:11; 1 Jn. 4:1-2; Apoc. 22:9, etc.

[15] Cf. Jn. 14:26; 15:26; 16:13; Rom. 12:8.

[16] Lk. 3:18; 1 Thess. 2:3; 1 Tim. 4:13; 6:3.

[17] 2 Cor. 5:20. The sermon, an apostolic function, is necessarily an act of God (2 Thess. 2:16; Heb. 12:5), of the Holy Spirit (Acts 9:31), of inspired Scripture (Rom. 15:4). C. Ryder Smith sees there the constant help of God stimulating Christian life, hence a quasi-synonym of grace (*The Bible Doctrine of Grace*, London, 1956, pp. 81 ff.).

of the heart and its application in one's conduct; that is, not to
receive the grace of God in vain (2 Cor. 6:1; Heb. 3:7; 4:11),
remain attached to the Lord with all one's soul (Acts 11:23),
be steadfast in the faith (Acts 14:22; Jude 3), give all one's
life in sacrifice to God,[18] observe the " commandment " of how
one must walk so as to please God,[19] pray (1 Tim. 2:1), be
obedient, charitable, and peaceful,[20] guard against carnal covet-
ousness (1 Pet. 2:11), not to become inured to sin (Heb. 3:13).
Sometimes the sermon will revive, encourage, strengthen,[21] at
other times it reassures one of the authenticity of the Christian
life (1 Pet. 5:12) and consoles anxious hearts.[22]

   In the beginnings of the Church, temptations of lassitude
and inertia menaced the travellers to the celestial city. Certain
ones already have " hands that hang down and tottering
knees," [23] and deviate from the straight road. The teaching
of the *didaskalía* strives to bring a remedy [24] by bringing them
back and guaranteeing their stability.[25] They appeal to Scrip-

---

[18] Rom. 12:1, introducing the whole exhortatory part of the Epistle (cf. the
perfect commentary of H. Schlier, *Le temps de l'Eglise*, Tournai, 1961, pp. 85-99).
Written by a prophet or an inspired teacher, exposing a doctrine which is instructive as well as encouraging and consoling, the Epistle to the Hebrews presents itself
as a " word of exhortation " (13:22). I Peter has the same character (5:12).

[19] I Thess. 2:12; 4:1-2, 10-11; 2 Thess. 3:12; Eph. 4:1.

[20] I Thess. 5:14; Rom. 16:17; 1 Cor. 1:10; 4:16; 16:15-16; 2 Cor. 10:1; Phil. 4:2;
Philemon. 9.

[21] 1 Thess. 4:18; 5:11; 2 Cor. 2:7; 1 Tim. 5:1; Heb. 3:13; 6:18.

[22] This acceptation of the paraclesis-consolation during the trial of life, constant
in the Old Testament, is known from Paul who attributes this comfort to God (cf.
2 Cor. 1:3-7; 7:4-13), providing renewed hope (Rom. 15:4). Liberated from
prison, the Apostle and Silas do not want to leave Philippi without having reassured
and consoled the brethren with a visit (Acts 16:40; cf. 1 Cor. 4:13; Eph. 6:22;
Col. 4:8).

[23] Heb. 12:12 (Is. 35:3); cf. recalling these waverings in Spicq, C. " La parabole
de la Veuve obstinée," *RB* 1961, pp. 88 ff.; the *Guerre des Fils de Lumière* . . . X,
5: les fondus de coeur; XI, 10: les abattus d'esprit; XIV, 5: les chancelants; XIV,
6: les mains défaillantes, les ondoyants de genoux; XV, 7.

[24] Heb. 12:12 [13]: " . . . that no one who is lame may go out of the way, but
rather be healed "; cf. 1 Kings 18:21.

[25] Heb. 12:12; the verb *anorthoō*, " to straighten " what is bent, deviated (Lk.
13:13) or collapsed, has the sense of consolidating and stabilizing a dynasty (Acts
15:16; cf. 2 Sam. 7:13, 16, 26). It is part of the technical vocabulary of the

ture, which is so effective in denouncing errors of orientation, in obviating failures, in assuring the uplifting and correction of morals (2 Tim. 3:16). Thus, the punishment of the unfaithful Israelites constitutes one of the warnings (1 Cor. 10:11) which Providence wreaks on those who would follow "the same example of unbelief."[26] If every child is educated by the rude discipline of the traditional *paideia*, the adult is especially in need of instructions and admonitions which will develop his insight and familiarize him with wisdom. Charity requires of every good Christian to give his brothers this opportune advice and even to repeat it;[27] but it is the duty of the community leaders especially to reprimand, even to censure (Tit. 3:10). If they summon and command, it is to obtain irreproachable conduct from the faithful, and that implies a recall to order, repeated admonitions (Col. 1:28)—1 Thess. 5:12 summarizes their entire service.

In reality, a master is led not only to scold his disciples and inflict blame on them (Lk. 19:39), but also to reprimand them for their omissions and to punish them (Jude 9). Now, it is remarkable that the pastors never apply punishments—only God punishes.[28] They are only required to denounce evil in all its forms and to correct the delinquents, an element which is just as essential to the Church's teaching as the teaching of what is good and the exhortation of the faithful.[29] First this

Sapiential Books: "You have given me your saving shield; your right hand has upheld me" (Ps. 17 [18]:36); "Though they bow down and fall, yet we stand erect and firm" (Ps. 19:9). This re-establishment is the function of religious insight: "By wisdom is a house built, by understanding is it made firm" (Prov. 24:3; cf. Jer. 10:12; 33:2), but first a gift of God: "The Lord raises up those that were bowed down" (Ps. 146:8; 145:17; Sir. 11:12).

[26] Heb. 4:11; The Apocalypse of Baruch: "Do not stray from the road of the Law, but watch and admonish the rest of the people, lest they stray from the precepts of the Almighty (44:2-4; *Patrologie Syr.* II. 1132-35).

[27] Rom. 15:4; 1 Thess. 5:14; 2 Thess. 3:15; Col. 3:8.

[28] 2 Pet. 2:9 (cf. Mt. 25:46). Neither punishment (cf. 1 Jn. 4:18) nor pain (Heb. 10:29; cf. 2 Mac. 4:38; Wis. 19:4), required as the vengeance of evil (cf. Acts 22:5; 26:11), belong to the vocabulary of the New Testament teaching. 1 Cor. 4:21 is but a threat: "Shall I come to you with a rod?"; this as opposed to the iron rod of Apoc. 2:27; 12:5; 19:15.

[29] 2 Tim. 3:16; 4:2; Tit. 2:15. The presbyter must be capable of exhortation by a

implies that they enlighten consciences, bring errors and wrongs to light, not hesitating to label what is wrong as wrong, and to specify in what it consists; [30] since they define guilt (Jas. 2:9; 2 Pet. 2:16), they should have the courage and frankness to accuse and confound the delinquents (Jude 15). Regardless of what kind it is, the sin of the sinner must always be denounced and corrected (Mt. 18:15; 1 Tim. 5:20): all who do evil (Jn. 3:20) and the works of darkness (Eph. 5:11), those who break the Law (Jas. 2:19), adulterers (Lk. 3:19), the impious (Jude 15) and the unorthodox. . . . [31]

Thanks to this vigilance and insistence of the pastors (1 Tim. 4:15-16; 2 Tim. 4:2), the faithful are assured of being linked to the authentic Word of Christ and that there will be no deviation in the uprightness of their lives. They benefit from all the help of a Church which carries the divine seal: " Let everyone depart from iniquity who names the name of the Lord " (2 Tim. 2:19).

CESLAUS SPICQ, O. P.

Albertinum
Fribourg, Switzerland

sound *didaskalía* and of refuting contradictors (Tit. 1:9; cf. v. 13; Epictetus: " He is skilled in reasoning and he knows how to refute and convince; he is capable of showing each contradictor the cause of his fault and to point out clearly how he is not doing that which he wills but doing that which he does not will," II, 26, 4). In the divine *paideia*, the sinner is reinstated by the word of God (Heb. 12:5).

[30] Those who do evil are fleeing from the light, for fear that their deeds will be denounced and condemned (Jn. 3:20; cf. Epictetus, I, 26, 17: " In everyday life we are not willingly receptive to censure and we detest the one who censures "; II, 1, 32; XIV, 20). The prophets have a real gift for discerning the secrets of conscience and for persuading the accused and to bring about his confession (1 Cor. 14:24; cf. Heb. 4:12-13). In fraternal correction, according to Mt. 18:15, every Christian must enlighten his brother as to the seriousness of his faults and reprimand him. Thus Eph. 5:11-13: " Have no fellowship with the unfruitful works of darkness, but rather expose them. For of the things done by them in secret it is shameful even to speak." Compare Qumrân, I QS V, 2h-VI, 1; IX 17; C. D. VII, 2; IX, 6-8.

[31] Tit. 1:9-13. G. Bornkamm (" The History of the Origin of the So-Called Second Letter to the Corinthians," *New Testament Studies*, 1962 pp. 261 ff.) reminds us that the warnings against false teachers are most often placed at the end of the sermons, letters or New Testament writings (Mt. 7:15 ff.; Acts 20:29-30; Rom. 16:17-20; Gal. 6:11 ff.; 1 Cor. 16:22; 1 Pet. 4:17; 5:2; Jude 17 ff.; *Didaché* 16:3 ff.).

TOWARDS AN ADEQUATE CONCEPT OF CHURCH

∽

I T is sometimes asserted that modern ecclesiology needs to elaborate a more spiritual concept of Church to replace one which has been too juridic and sterile. Such a perspective, however, seems superficial. It does not touch the fundamental reality of the Church. The need of the present moment is not for substitution but synthesis. It is possible now to recapture the Pauline synthesis which was lost when apologists and polemicists concerned themselves exclusively with the visibility of the Church. The need is to take up this synthesis once again and restate it in terms for our times.

An adequate concept of Church must explain the Church's theandric character. Recognizing the Church as a reality which is at once visible and invisible, it must accept the Church as both a society and a life; a society which manifests in a public way Christ's triumph over Satan; a life which establishes a totally new relationship between redeemed humanity and God. The members of the Church possess a unique relationship to Christ and the Holy Spirit. The communion among those possessing these relations constitutes the precise reality which imparts to the Church its specific *esse*, viz. a mystico-visible sharing in the life of Christ.

The present article will not attempt to present an adequate concept of Church. Rather its aim is to establish what seems to be an antecedent necessity: that only through a synthesis of the juridic and spiritual viewpoints can we arrive at a truly adequate concept of Church.[1] It will do this by reviewing the synthesis which is present in St. Paul. It will then explain how this synthesis was lost and offer some suggestions relative to the restatement of this synthesis today.

[1] Although this was recognized in the last century by Scheeben, it has not received the consideration it merits. Cf. B. Fraigneau-Julien, *L'Eglise et le caractère sacramentel selon M.-J. Scheeben*, (Paris, 1957).

So rich and complex is the concept of Church that St. Paul uses a multiplicity of biblical images to describe it: Body of Christ, People of God, Bride of Christ, Kingdom of God, Temple of God.[2] Each image expresses some element or some consequence of the union of men with Christ. We do not have to seek the origin of St. Paul's thought in the Stoic metaphor which saw the whole cosmos as a body animated by a divine *Pneuma*; or in the gnostic myth of Urmensch.[3] These certainly influenced the evolution of Paul's expression, but his thought concerning the Church was already fully contained in his awareness of our oneness " in Christ." The words which he heard on the road to Damascus had given him this awareness which he never lost. The heavenly voice's identification of the Christian community with Jesus was without doubt the source of Paul's thought and it was this he sought to express by a variety of images. Among these there are two which stand out: People of God and Body of Christ.

From the time when God first made a special intervention in human affairs and called to Himself a special group of men, there was always a People of God on earth. The divine election effected on Mt. Sinai made the Jews God's own people. The desert community was thus set aside from the rest of humanity. They became, as a race with an existence and a unity of their own, the heirs of Abraham and of the promises made to his seed. They were also raised up as a sign to all nations that God had determined upon a definite plan for the world and its salvation. At the very beginning of this covenant between God and his people, there was foreshadowed Israel's sin and unfaithfulness.[4] God's plan for Israel would never be fulfilled. In time the prophets would announce a

---

[2] Space limitations make it impossible to treat this very important image of temple. It is well treated by J. C. Fenton, " The New Testament Designation of the True Church as God's Temple," in *American Ecclesiastical Review*, 140 (1959), 103-117.

[3] This is the judgment of Pierre Benoit, O. P. Cf. " Corps, Tête et Plérôme," in *Exégèse et Théologie*, (Paris, 1961), II, 109.

[4] Lev. 26, 14; Deut. 28, 15.

renewed, spiritual kingdom not subject to any disintegration: a remnant of the old people would be saved and a new people formed from it.

From the beginning, the Christians were for St. Paul the "new people of God." He saw in them the fulfillment of Osee's prophecy [5] and he thus transferred to them the Old Testament concept of *laos periousious*.[6] In the Old Testament this people was formed from a national community, through a religious obedience. In the New Testament, the concept is stripped of its nationalistic orientation. The people is exclusively religious. There is no longer Jew or Greek.[7] In the second epistle to the Corinthians, St. Paul applies to this people the words spoken by Yahweh to the community in the desert: " I will be their God and they shall be my people." [8] Nor is the image of " people " exclusively Pauline. It is found in the first epistle of St. Peter,[9] and in the fifteenth chapter of the Acts of the Apostles both James and Peter refer to the new Christians as a " people." [10]

This image certainly has its foundation in the teaching of Jesus. It is found in his words and deeds concerning the Kingdom of God, especially in his prediction that the kingdom shall be given to another people. At the Last Supper he inaugurates a new sacrifice to commemorate his passage to the Father and to seal the new covenant in his blood. Those with whom he makes this covenant and to whom he gives this sacrifice are the apostles. They are to pass out of the old people as the Jews passed out of Egypt and so become a people in themselves. Perhaps the most significant passage is found in St. John's explanation of the prophecy of Caiphas that one man should die for the people: "This, however, he said not of himself; but being high priest that year, he prophesied that

[5] Rom. 9, 23-26.
[6] Ex. 19, 5 ; 23, 22. Deut. 7, 6; 14, 2.
[7] Gal. 3, 26.
[8] 2 Cor. 6, 16.
[9] I. Peter, 2, 9.
[10] The event was the Council of Jerusalem; the context, the calling of the Gentiles.

Jesus was to die for the nation; and not only for the nation, but that he might gather into one the children of God who were scattered abroad." [11] This passage is invaluable for the insight it gives us into the mind of St. John. For him, the concept of people lay at the very heart of the new order. He expresses the efficient cause of the new people: the dynamic divine intervention in human affairs. This forms a new dispensation inaugurated through the redemptive shedding of Christ's blood. This new people is also a purchased people. The term has a qualitative significance. It is the people assembled through a divine call. This idea of calling is essentially bound to St. Paul's thought concerning the Church.[12] In his farewell to the presbyters of Ephesus he calls it " the Church of God, which he has purchased with his own blood." [13]

It is clear that for St. Paul the Christian communities formed the new people of God. They were both the rejection and the fulfillment of the desert community whereby the people first came into being. As God's people the Christians already shared in a limited manner in the union with God in Christ which would be perfectly realized only when Christ returned again to gather all things to himself in a manner which would be perfect. This forward dimension was imparted to the concept of Church by Paul's theory of realized eschatology and the tension this posits between the indicative and the imperative; this is, between present participation and future fulfillment.[14] They were the people of God and they had to become the people of God. They were holy and they had to become holy. The people was always to be built up until the *parousia* when it would receive its final and perfect fulfillment in the heavenly kingdom of the fully realized return of man to God in Christ.

This notion of the people of God is without doubt an insti-

---

[11] Jn. 11, 51-53.

[12] Cf. L. Cerfaux, *The Church in the Theology of St. Paul*, (N. Y., 1959), 183ff.

[13] Acts, 20, 28.

[14] On this paradox of realized eschatology cf. Benoit, *art. cit.*, 112-3.

tutional and a juridical one. The ancient and venerable assembly raised up by God in the desert under the leadership of Moses and Aaron was compact and socially structured. It was formed by a divine call which gave it a specific existence of its own. This same community was raised up by God again as a messianic community gathered around Jesus. The local assembly in Jerusalem was the first to assume this character. Later with the multiplication of communities, it was the universal Church which appeared as the new people of God, scattered throughout the world, but retaining its specific character through its unique essence and its own proper existence within the totality of the human race.

For St. Paul the Church is also the body of Christ. This is based upon a physical realism which views the resurrected body of Christ as the source of all spiritual life. Individual Christians partake of this life through faith and baptism. Consequently all are one because all possess the same life which animates the body of Christ. It seems that St. Paul never had any concept of a union between Christ and the Christian except under the form of a physical (i. e., sacramental) union of the Christian with the individual resurrected body of Christ.

This theme is found in the epistle to the Romans and the first epistle to the Corinthians. Here Christians are given a mystical identity with the one physical body of Christ. The *en soma en Cristo* of Romans 12, 5 and the *soma Cristou* of I Corinthians 12, 27 express the same idea. This idea " brings together in its imprecision the Hellenistic simile and a mystical identification of all Christians with the body of Christ."[15] In the epistles of the captivity this theme receives some new qualifications, but is substantially the same and has essentially the same foundation: Paul's deep personal awareness of the unity of all Christians " in Christ."[16] In the epistle to the

[15] Cf. Cerfaux, *op. cit.* 277-8.

[16] Cerfaux believes that *soma* never meant a moral body in Romans or I Corinthians (cf. 266-282). However we have followed Benoit's interpretation which sees the theme " body of Christ " essentially the same in the major epistles of the captivity. Cf. Benoit, *art. cit.*, 116-123.

Ephesians, it is a living organism hierarchically structured, which is continually growing.[17] In the epistle to the Colossians the body is " supplied and built up by joints and ligaments " and " attains a growth that is of God." [18] In these epistles, the body of Christ is the Church and is personified and distinguished in a more explicit fashion from the individual Christ. The Church as body of Christ is constituted by personal religious experience effecting a transfigured natural existence through the communication of the life of Christ. The Church is conceived as life rather than institution.

This theme of body is related by St. Paul to the images of headship and *pleroma*. The image of Christ the head first appears in relation to the heavenly Powers and not in relation to the Church. Paul is led to a new level by the necessity of refuting the errors of the Colossians. He has to show that Christ is above all the Powers and Principalities. He does this by stating that Christ is the " head of every Principality and Power.[19] By his resurrection he has been set " above every Principality and Power and Virtue and Domination." [20] This original concept of headship expresses a principle of authority. Christ is superior to all the Principalities and Powers because he has supreme authority over them and thus is their head.

When this image is applied to the Church, Christ is its head because he possesses supreme authority over it. Later, Christ's headship in regard to the Church came also to signify that he is the source of life, motion and nourishment. Here St. Paul is drawing upon Hellenistic and not Semitic science. When we find the combination of Christ-Head and Church-Body, we cannot overlook the fact that the image of Christ-Head is a development of the image of Christ as supreme over the Powers.[21] It is not a development of the image of the Church as the body of Christ. The consequences of this are decisive for the concept of Church. The Powers are in no way

---

[17] Eph. 4, 15-16.
[18] Col. 2, 19.
[19] Col. 2, 10.

[20] Eph. 1, 21.
[21] Benoit, *art. cit.*, 130.

integrated into the Church-Body. The body remains always
those men possessing life through a physical union with the
dead and resurrected body of Christ. Only men can exist in
this body—men united to Christ by faith, baptism and the
Eucharist. It is absolutely impossible for the Powers to form
any part of the body of Christ. Since they pertain to the
world they are under the headship of Christ and thus pertain
to the new creation effected by Christ, but nothing more.
Paul does not give a fully developed treatment of them; it is
not even clear who they are; but it is evident that they look
upon the Church from the outside. Paul is giving a cosmic
extension to the salvific activity of Christ, not to the Church.
All creation—animate and inanimate—will be made new. Thus
the Powers also. This effectively places them under the dominion of Christ and this is all Paul seeks to do.

Paul sedulously reserves *soma* for regenerated humanity.
The cosmos for him is merely the frame of this humanity. He
is not interested in it directly. Having been brought to a new
level of observation by his refutation of the errors at Colos-
sae, he finds himself in need of a new word to designate this
cosmic frame. The word he uses is *pleroma*. The *pleroma* is
only indirectly attached to Christ, but it does participate in
some fashion in his work of salvation. The *pleroma* of Christ
is a plenitude of being, of divinity and of the cosmos. The
plenitude of divinity is his by nature. The plenitude of the
whole world is his by his redemption which subjects all things
unto himself. The plenitude of the Church is his because he
is its head (source of nourishment); the fullness of the Powers
is his because he is their head (source of authority). Paul
found a ready background for this concept of *pleroma* in both
the Stoic philosophy and biblical thought.[22]

The fundamental Pauline idea of *pleroma* is not transferred
to Church-Body without alteration. In the epistle to the
Ephesians 1, 23 and again in 4, 13 the *pleroma tou Cristou*
is clearly coextensive with the *soma*. This does not extend the

---

[22] *Ibid.*, 138-153.

Pauline concept of *soma*. Rather it applies to Church-Body the concept of growth—a concept which is at least fundamentally contained in *pleroma*. The *pleroma* of Christ, although it is a fact, must find its achievement in the time between Christ's resurrection and his second coming. This is accomplished through the growth of the Church. This plenitude is an achievement which will be realized only gradually, but there is no doubt it will be realized only in the Church for only here do we find the sacramental, physical union of the saved with the resurrected and glorified body of Christ. Again, Paul's theme of realized eschatology is very strong. The richness of Paul's thought here emphasizes the dynamic nature of the Church-Body. Its life must be a growth. This rethinking of things on the cosmic plane served Paul well in his search for a solution to the union of Jews and Gentiles. It did nothing to alter his understanding of Church-Body as regenerated humanity: the unity of those who are one because they possess the life of Christ through their sacramental union with the resurrected body of the Saviour.

From this understanding of body, head and *pleroma*, it is evident that we must avoid giving a cosmic extension to the Church-Body. Such a thought would not be Pauline. Paul did not know a Church which embraced the Powers as well as regenerated humanity. He did not know a Church which embraced the whole universe. This becomes clear once we understand the original meaning of Christ-Head and *pleroma* and the precise manner in which they are predicated of the Church. They are used by Paul merely to clarify one or more qualities of the Church-Body. They do not extend that body in the least.

It is time now to compare the two fundamental Pauline concepts: People of God and Body of Christ. At the heart of St. Paul's ecclesiology lies the identification of these two concepts. One did not replace the other. There was no metamorphosis in Paul's thought from a visible, societal concept of Church to a spiritual concept; nor are *people* and *body* re-

lated to one another as container to contained or as signification to thing signified. There is only one reality which is at
once visible and spiritual. *Body* thus qualifies and comple-
ments *people*.

Whether we begin our comparison with the community or
the life communicated, our conclusion is the same: there is
no dialectic in Paul's ecclesiology. He does not know two
churches. The one Church he acknowledges cannot be adequately present unless there is a union with Christ which is
a mystico-juridic one. This union forms a people who, according to the positive desire of Christ, comprises a visible, living
organism and not just a sociological unit.

If we consider first the community, we see that the people
of God is not just an amorphous mass. Nor is it " a riotous
horde of people who chanced to be travelling together in the
same direction." [23] It is no longer a racial unit but a society
called out from mankind, the new people, the *tertia gens*. Its
very existence is a public and continual sign of God's new
covenant with humanity. This new people continues the mission of Christ. It possesses a unity which is societal.

First, it continues the mission of Christ. Christ is the one
Redeemer, the one mediator between God and man. He is the
only Apostle, the only teacher, the only Priest. The Church
as the prolongation of Christ must become itself the only
apostle, teacher and priest. It does so through an extension
of Christ's mission: " As the Father has sent me, I also send
you." [24] The Church becomes the teacher who is to make
disciples of all nations. It becomes the priest who continually
offers the eternal sacrifice to God the Father. Some among
the faithful are set aside by the will of Christ (not the community) exclusively " for the work of the ministry." This does
not remove the functions from the whole community. This
group becomes the divinely established and visible authenti-

[23] A. De Bovis, *What is the Church?* (N. Y., 1961), 75.
[24] Jn. 20, 22.

cation of the communal functions.[25] These functions themselves have a necessary visible aspect and the concentration of them in a divinely established group of ministers makes the community all the more necessary. In fact the communal activity has no legitimacy apart from this group. It is the visible source of all the community's ministry.

This community posseses a unity which is caused first by its organization. It is found upon the apostolic administration. Paul, as an apostle, possesses full authority over the communities which he established. There is no evidence that he was reluctant to exercise this authority.[26] The unity of the Church is caused also by traditions, including customs and rites as well as teaching;[27] this unity gives the Church an order and a cohesion,[28] and is founded also upon " one Lord, one faith, one baptism." [29] Profession of faith and reception of baptism are the necessary requisites for admission. The reception of the one bread is the badge of perseverance. It is true that during the ministry of St. Paul the organization of the Church did not achieve full maturity; yet the basic hierarchical structure and corporate form are both present in primitive fashion. This organization was not something accidental either in fact or in Paul's thought. His exhortation to the presbyters of Ephesus, his excommunication of the incestuous Corinthian, his instruction to Titus and Timothy, his references to those " who are over you in the Lord "—all these provide us with insights into the value he assigned to the Church's organization.

The ministry which the community prolongs and the unity which it possesses are not exclusively visible and societal. The community continues also the life of Christ by communicating it through a sacramental dispensation. The ministry of apos-

[25] Jean Colson, *Les fonctions ecclesiales*, (Paris, 1954), 163ff.

[26] Cf. I Cor. 1, 1; 4, 20; 11, 16; 14, 37; 2 Cor. 1, 1; Gal. 1ff; Rom. 1, 1-6.

[27] Cf. The eleventh chapter of first Corinthians. Also: I Thess. 4, 1-3; Col. 2, 6.

[28] Eph. 4, 11-16; Col. 2, 19.

[29] Eph. 4, 5-6.

tle, teacher and priest is an effect of the Holy Spirit poured out upon all, but especially upon those set aside exclusively for the work of the ministry. The spiritual gifts and the charisms which the Spirit imparts give to these functions the same supernatural dimension possessed by the one Mediator himself and they bring about the same result: union of man to God through and in Christ.

The unity which is caused by the apostolic foundation and the ecclesiastical organization, by the profession of faith, and the reception of baptism and the Eucharist is also founded ultimately upon the life " in Christ " which these functions confer. This life is sacramental in its inception and societal in its existence. Thus the social reality which has an articulated institution is also a spiritual reality which is the common possession of life " in Christ." St. Paul clearly indicates that the mystery of the Church actually lies precisely in its theandric nature. If we allow any separatism to be introduced here, we destroy the Pauline synthesis.

The same conclusion is reached if we start out with a consideration of the life which is communicated. The unity of Christians is rooted ultimately in the common possession of the life of the resurrected Christ. But this does not mean that St. Paul recognized any society of the justified, or the predestined, or the elect by themselves. He never applied the term body of Christ to such a group. The life of Christ which is shared by his followers is not simply a personal, individual regeneration. This life has a corporate aspect; it is received through faith and baptism. These two form a contract between the individual and the community. This life is to be lived as a member of the new people of God, the individual thus giving public testimony to God's plan of salvation as well as rendering service to the community through the fulfillment of a ministry which is either general or particular. This visibility is not simply an external manifestation of the life which is present, rather, it pertains to the very substance of the new life in Christ. For Christ has willed that his new people should not only possess life, but that this life should be manifest to the world, that the world might believe. His people are a sign raised up, as he himself was, to draw all nations to itself.

The corporate aspects of the life " in Christ " are clearly manifest in the manner in which an individual comes to participate in this life. For St. Paul this is not simply a spiritual reality effected by baptism; such a view does violence to the integrity of St. Paul's ecclesiology. The context is always a communal one. The community preaches the gospel; the individual responds with a profession of faith and is accepted by the community through the rite of baptism; the whole process being ratified by the outpouring of the Holy Spirit. This is how one comes to live " in Christ." [30]

Thus visibility is not merely the external manifestation of a union with a Church which remains essentially invisible and spiritual; it pertains to the very union itself. The union with Christ which gives rise to the Church is not a mystical union which is given a visible manifestation, but a union which is itself mystico-visible. It is this mystico-visible union which constitutes the Church. This concept clearly expresses the incarnational character of the Church and in so doing justifies the assertion that the Church is the prolongation of Christ. It also directs our attention toward the upward dimension of the Church. The Church exists not only to reconcile men to God, but to provide before all mankind a public testimony to God's triumph over the forces of darkness.

St. Paul did not give a complete, orderly exposition of his awareness concerning the Church. From a consideration of his principal images, however, it appears that he understood the Church as a reality which is at once visible and invisible. It is a reality which can not be considered apart from Paul's theme of realized eschatology. There is a constant tension between the ideal, the Church as it should be, and the real,

[30] Cf. the second, third and fourth chapters in the Acts of the Apostles. For this concept in St. Paul, cf. Cerfaux, *op. cit.*, 161-175.

the Church as it actually exists in the world. One is the actual but imperfect realization of the other.

The complexity and the incompleteness of Paul's ecclesiology do not obscure the synthesis he effected between the visible and invisible elements. The people of God is not only an identifiable corporeity but also an organism alive with the life of Christ. The body of Christ is composed of those who are one in Christ through the sharing of his life; but this is not just an individual, invisible sharing but one which possesses a corporate aspect.

We cannot consider here the patristic evidence for this view of the Church. Certainly it is found in St. Augustine.[31] It was obscured by the juridicism of the Middle Ages and lost in the agitation of the counter-reformation. Theologians became preoccupied with the externals of the Church because of the necessity of identifying the Roman Catholic Church with the true Church of Christ. St. Robert Bellarmine spoke of union between the individual and the Church rather than between the individual and Christ.[32] The union was not in Christ but in the visible society. This Bellarminian view of the Church is perfectly accurate if we understand the context within which it was elaborated.[33] It remains, however, only a partial view of the Church.

From the sixteenth century on, the treatise *De Ecclesia* became more and more narrow in scope.[34] For a variety of reasons the external and institutional aspect of the Church comprised almost the entire treatise. So obscure did the Pauline

[31] For the thought of St. Augustine, cf. S. Grabowski, *The Church: An Introduction to the Theology of St. Augustine.* (St. Louis, 1957). 209-230. For a general view of the Fathers, cf. J. N. D. Kelly, *Early Christian Doctrines,* (N. Y., 1959), 189-223 and 401-422.

[32] *De eccl. mil.* c. 1.

[33] Cf. J. C. Fenton, "St. Robert's Definition of Church," *AER,* III (1945), 131-45. For more on this subject by the same author, cf. *AER,* 124 (1951) 213-21 and 127 (1952), 370-72.

[34] Y. Congar, O. P.., "L'Ecclesiologie de la revolution française au Concile du Vatican sous le signe de l'affirmation de l'autorité," in *L'Ecclesiologie au XIXe siècle,* (Paris, 1960), 77-114.

synthesis become that at the time of the First Vatican Council, the Fathers refused to call the Church the mystical body because that term was too vague and might seem to favor the notion of an invisible Church. A beginning had been made, however, and in the period between the two great wars, there developed a whole doctrine of the mystical body which brought to the fore once again the spiritual reality of the Church.[35] Unfortunately, this theology remained isolated from the continuing theology of the Church as a visible institution. These two perspectives were finally brought together by Pius XII in *Mystici Corporis* when he identified the Roman Catholic Church and the mystical body. So strong had been the theological reaction to the excessively juridic treatment of the Church that this identification encountered some reluctance and Pius XII had to insist upon it again in *Humani Generis*. Even today ecumenial interests incline some to extend the mystical body beyond the Roman Catholic Church in order to include, at least, all baptized Christians.

It would seem that this renders it extremely difficult to recapture the Pauline synthesis. It would help to recognize that the post-reformation ecclesiology was not without its advantages. It did clearly delineate the external, social, juridic nature of the Church. This was necessary because of the Protestant doctrine of an invisible Church. When later generations confused this counter-reformation apologetic with an integral theological treatise, the concept of Church became one-sided and thus distorted. This distortion isolated one element which can be properly viewed only when integrated into a comprehensive consideration of the complex reality of the Church. We must be careful today that we do not repeat this error in the opposite direction by isolating the spiritual element of the Church. Our greatest need is not to replace the juridic treatment with a spiritual one, but to restore the juridic element to its proper place within the Pauline under-

---

[35] Cf. Jaki, *Les Tendences nouvelles de l'ecclesiologie*, (Rome, 1957), 154-204.

standing of the Church as the theandric reality which prolongs the Incarnate Word through space and time.

This would emphasize the corporate nature of the new dispensation. Man is saved not through the private possession of life in Christ, but through possession of this life as a member of God's new people. He has received a call to come out of the world, not individually, but as one of the group which itself has been called out of the world by Christ. This people is to bear witness between God and redeemed humanity. It is to give service to the whole of humanity by continuing the general ministry of the word, common to all the members of the society, and by the particular ministry exercised by those who have been set aside by the sacrament of Orders, as Moses and Aaron were set aside in the original desert community.

Within this framework we can set about restating the synthesis of St. Paul according to our modern theological and ecclesiastical structures. For this, the concept of communion seems to hold more promise than that of sacramentality.[36] The Church is a communion because it is a solidarity based upon faith, the sacraments and authority. It is a solidarity which, in an even more fundamental sense, grows out of a common possession: life in Christ. Because we are all individually united to Christ through possession of his life, we are united to one another. This solidarity gives rise to a common activity which is the life of the new people of God and which prolongs the three-fold mission of Christ. All of this is contained in the notion of communion. The Church is a communion in being as well as in action. It is an unique existence based upon the common life shared by all. This common life includes a two-fold relation: one between the members and God, the other among the members themselves. Because these relations are unique they are characteristic of the Christian collectivity.

The uniqueness of our relation to God is the more difficult

[36] For the notion of communion, cf. J. Hamer, *L'Eglise est une communion*, (Paris, 1962).

to grasp. A partial understanding is found in Cajetan's commentary on II-II, q. 39, a. 1. In this article, St. Thomas says that schism is a special sin because it is opposed to that unity of the Church which is effected by charity. This unity not only gathers the members together by a bond of spiritual love but it gives the whole Church a unity in spirit. Considering this, Cajetan asks two questions which are of interest to us. First, he asks what is the unity of the Church to which schism is opposed. Further, in the light of the principle, *unum sequitur esse*, schism must be opposed to some *esse ecclesiae*. What then is the *esse ecclesiae* which schism destroys? Secondly, he asks how unity can be the effect of charity since it can exist without charity.

In answering the first question, Cajetan rules out faith, hope, charity, the sacraments, subjection to the one head. Faith, hope and the sacraments can remain with schism; charity can be lost without schism. Subjection of all members to one head cannot be the *esse ecclesiae* which schism destroys since this subjection is not sufficient to constitute the Church a numerical whole, but merely to constitute it under one head. Cajetan considers the Church as a " *unitas collectionis universorum fidelium.*" Each member receives from this an *esse relativum*, first to be part of the whole, then to be dependent upon that whole. He receives also a specific *actio* and *passio* in as much as this relation to the whole brings him under the special influence of the Holy Spirit. Cajetan states that the Holy Spirit influences not only the substance of his actions but also the mode. By this he means that the Spirit moves him not simply to act but to act as part of a corporate totality. Thus he believes as one possessing a corporate unity with others who believe. He receives the sacraments as one who is part of a group which receives the sacraments. The Spirit moves the whole body. He must necessarily impart not only the same motion to each member, but he must further move each member precisely in as much as he is part of the whole.

There is no reason for this beyond the desire of the Spirit that there be but one Church. He wills that men be saved as parts of a corporate whole. Since there is one Spirit imparting one influence, the Church must necessarily be numerically one and Cajetan has found the *esse ecclesiae* to which schism is opposed: "*est ipsum esse Ecclesiae ut unius totius rationem habet.*" A schismatic withdraws himself from this unity and consequently from the specifically ecclesial subjection to the Holy Spirit. It does not make any difference why he does this. He makes of himself a quasi-whole and thus negates the salvation within the Church-whole which is willed by the Spirit. To the second question, Cajetan answers that the effects of charity may be formed or unformed; unity, as an effect of charity, is always formed in the Church herself since the Church is always spotless. But as possessed by an individual, unity can be unformed, and thus there is no difficulty in saying that unity is an effect of charity.

It does not seem that Cajetan has really found a solution to this first question. To say that the *esse Ecclesiae* to which schism is opposed is the Church's characteristic of being an undivided whole is not really to progress beyond the concept of unity. Nevertheless, even with this reservation, the text is rich in its ecclesiological insights and the parallel it possesses with the teaching of St. Paul. Cajetan has stated the problem of the Church's nature in terms which are exact. He has arrived at the most fundamental consideration with his treatment of the members' relation to the Holy Spirit. This relation, together with subjection to the visible head, makes one a member of the Church. The reality which schism destroys is not just subjection to a visible head but the unique relation to the Spirit which accompanies it.

So the Church is a reality at once spiritual and societal. The spiritual aspect is described as a modal influence exerted by the Holy Spirit. Some will object that this can only be something accidental and as such is not fittingly taken as the constitutive element of the Church. To this it could be said that the will of God is decisive here. He has willed that his people have a corporate form to which this unique relation to the Holy Spirit is a correlative. That which God directly wills cannot be viewed as accidental. In moral matters it is the will of the individual which determines what is substantial and what is accidental. We must admit, however, that we are not able adequately to describe this relation and, until we can, an adequate concept of Church will elude us. But without hesitation we affirm that this outpouring of the Spirit actualizes, formalizes the Church. It provides the spiritual reality which renders intelligible the concept of Church as body of Christ.

Let us, then, say what can be said about this relation, leaving to others the completion or correction of what we say. This relation is not one of charity and so the Church is not the society of those in sanctifying grace. This relation is an effect of charity. The Holy Spirit always moves and informs the Church and so she remains holy with a holiness no man can sully. The individual, on the other hand, can react to the justifying act of the Spirit in varying degrees. He can possess charity but not the effect of charity which is external union with the Church. Consequently he is not uniquely related to the Holy Spirit and is not a member of the Church.[37] He can be bereft of charity and external unity with the Church. For even greater reasons he is not a member of the Church. He can lose charity but still remain subject to the visible head and thus retain a unique relation to the Spirit—Cajetan would say he is still moved as part of a whole. We say then that membership in the Church is an effect of charity—but an effect which can be formed or unformed. This sheds much light upon the understanding of the Church's nature since the Church is the communion of those possessing this unique relationship.

With this we are brought back to St. Paul's realized escha-

---

[37] Such an individual is not, of course, completely separated from the Church. He preserves some union, which however, is not membership. Cf. J. King, *The Necessity of the Church for Salvation*, (Washington, 1960), 289-339.

tology and the attainment of the *pleroma Christi* in the growth
of the Church. There must be a constant, dynamic activity
moving the Church ever closer to the perfect realization of
her ideal existence; this ideal is already realized in the present time but only in a limited manner. The life of Christ
which is shared is not necessarily sanctification—although it
is meant to be this in its fullness. But because it is not, the
Church is not the communion of those in sanctifying grace
but the communion of those who are subject to the visible
head and to the Holy Spirit in a unique way. Although this
subjection may be imperfect because it is unformed, it is a
relationship and thus a life [38]—a life which is not attainable
by those who separate themselves from the whole. So the
Church must be constantly built up not merely by being extended but by bringing about among the members a more
perfect sharing of the life of Christ through a more perfect
submission to his Spirit. Thus, in order to restate the Pauline
synthesis in our day, we must first recognize the Church as
a complex reality which is at once visible and invisible. We
must recognize the Mystical Body and the Roman Catholic
Church as one and the same reality. Secondly, we must weigh
well the effect of Paul's notion of realized eschatology upon
the concept of Church. Thirdly, we must inquire into the nature of the unique relation which exists only between the Holy
Spirit and the members of the Church. These hold the only
promise of developing a truly adequate concept of Church.

JOHN J. KING, O. M. I.

Oblate College,
  Washington, D.C.

[38] It may seem, at first, that such a relationship should not be called "life."
But there is a strong basis for such a terminology. To mention only one, we quote
the following from Pius XII:
For not every sin, however grave it may be, is such as of its own nature to sever
a man from the Body of the Church, as does heresy or apostasy. Men may lose
charity and divine grace through sin, thus becoming incapable of supernatural
merit, and yet not be deprived of all life, if they hold fast to faith and Christian hope, and if, illumined from above, they are spurred on by the interior
promptings of the Holy Spirit to salutary fear and are moved to prayer and penance for their sins. *Mystici Corporis*, par. 23.

THEOLOGY OF THE CHURCH

∽

Introduction

D IFFICULT as it is to present an adequate picture of the present-day world, no one could deny that one contour which characterizes this age is the general feeling of estrangement among men. Because of this general feeling, the existential philosophers, so solicitous for personal integrity and inter-personal communication, have gained a wide-spread and sympathetic audience. It is also the reason the theology concerning the Church of Christ—a communion of love initiated by God to be shared in by all men through his Son—is especially important and relevant today.

The great inner renewal which the Church herself is presently undergoing can also be cited as justifying a theological essay on the nature of the Church. Some degree of insight into the mysteries involved in this study is really the key to an understanding of the direction and potentials of this renewal. At least a rudimentary introduction into ecclesiology is, therefore, a quasi-necessity for every informed member of the Church.[1] It is also true that, especially since the Protestant Reformation, tracts entitled *de Ecclesia* have frequently been written. These, however, have been mostly in the field of apologetics. Authors who have modelled their works on that of St. Robert Bellarmine have intended principally to defend the right of the Roman Catholic Church to call herself the " one, true Church," as distinguished not only from pagan religious bodies, but also from the various Christian denominations.

---

[1] Despite the quantity of current literature in the field of ecclesiology, it is generally admitted that the masterful guides to be had in other spheres of theological study are lacking in this area. In the past fifty years, for example, excellent works have appeared on the subject of the Church as the Mystical Body of Christ—all of which have been surpassed in excellence and authority by the encyclical, *Mystici Corporis*, of the late Pope Pius XII.

One serious difficulty in the writing of such an essay is the amount of material involved in a complete treatment of ecclesiology. A full vision of the Church is a sort of synthesis of many elements taken from the entire theological discipline and welded together in a somewhat different form. If one reflects, for example, that ecclesiology is a study of the Church of Christ, it is evident that it must be based on a correct understanding of the mystery of the Incarnation. Again, this Church is composed *of men*; so the study of it depends, in a certain measure, on an understanding of the potentialities of human nature created in God's image. The Church is, moreover, organized in a hierarchial way; and its activity is sacramental. To this extent ecclesiology is connected with the theology of the divine government of the universe and that of the sacraments instituted by Christ. Since this is the case, the *theology* concerning the Church should not be the first subject taken up by a student of sacred doctrine.

No less a theologian than St. Thomas apparently omits to treat explicitly of the mystery of the Church, at least in his great theological synthesis, the *Summa Theologiae*. Still this apparent lacuna in the works of St. Thomas does not mean that the Angelic Doctor fails to furnish the principles for developing a balanced ecclesiology. The contrary is true; and perhaps the text which is most relevant to the organization of this subject matter is the following:

Even as in the order of natural things, perfection, which in God is simple and uniform, is not to be found in the created universe except in a multiform and manifold manner, so too, the fullness of grace, which is centered in Christ as head, flows forth to His members in various ways, for the perfecting of the body of the Church. This is the meaning of the Apostle's words: " He gave some apostles, and some prophets, and other some evangelists, and other some pastors and doctors for the perfecting of the saints " (Eph. 4 : 11-12). (*Summa Theologiae*, II, II, 183, 2, c.)

It is clear that St. Thomas here compares the dependence of the Church on Christ with the dependence of the created universe on God. It is clear also that certain distinctions must be made in order that this comparison be admitted as valid. The most important is based on the truth that there is, strictly speaking, only one creation, of which God is the sole author. As man, Christ himself is not able to create; because this activity is defined as the production of being in its entirety, from absolutely nothing (cf. *Summa*, I, 45, 1 and 5).

When, therefore, the Church is designated as a New Creation, the meaning is simply that everything in the Church proceeds from Christ and returns to him. This truth, however, is itself pregnant with consequences; because it means that the study of the Church can validly be organized on the model of theology as a whole. It may be recalled that St. Thomas' synthesis of sacred doctrine is based on the affirmation that God is the subject of all theology. Therefore, a study of the divine mysteries in themselves has primacy. St. Thomas treats consequently all that proceeds from God, but especially the being made in his image. Finally, he considers the movement of the rational creature, God's image, toward the fulfillment of that for which he was made, the face to face vision of God himself.

Since the Church is fashioned in the image of Christ, much of the order of theology described so briefly here can be transferred to the study of the Church. Such an ecclesiology should be a just presentation of the reality. In the first place, it appears that the entire study must be divided into two great units. The first might be described as the *exitus* or going forth of the Church, as she proceeds from Christ. Perhaps no more appropriate text from the Bible might be cited in this connection than the opening phrases of the ninth chapter of the book of Proverbs: " See, where *wisdom* has built herself a house, carved out for herself those seven pillars of hers " (cited according to the translation of Msgr. Knox). Every element of the structure of this New Creation has as its cause Christ, who, as the Son of God, is *Sapientia genita*. The second part of ecclesiology will be concerned with the *reditus* or return of the Church to Christ, her Author and Head. Whereas the former part of this study may be called the dogmatic consideration of the structure of the Church, the latter part may be designated as the "moral theology concerning the Church." It will deal with the life or activity proper to the Church, itself determined by the structure articulated according to the wisdom of Christ.

Within both of these large divisions, which spell out the structure and the life of the Church respectively, other obvious distinctions are to be made. Briefly, the structure may be described through the three categories of creation (or birth), order, and government; while the life of the Church may be understood according to the final consummation, the activity through which this perfection is reached, and the principles from which such activity proceeds.

I. THE STRUCTURE OF THE CHURCH, BASED ON THE WISDOM OF CHRIST

A. *The birth of the Church*

From all eternity the Son of God was predestined to be the Founder and Head, Savior and Support of a gathering which would be called his Church. This is the mystery which St. Paul announces in the very beginning of his epistle to the Ephesians: "[God] has chosen us out, *in Christ*, before the foundation of the world, to be saints, to be blameless in his sight, for love of him; marking us out beforehand (so his will decreed) to be his adopted children through Jesus Christ " (1:4-6). This is the justification for calling the Church, the Church *of Christ*; and the first task in ecclesiology is to delineate the senses in which this is true.

The first, most obvious sense of Christ's principality is verified in the order of his *effective* lordship. St. John represents him as " full of grace and truth," and adds, almost immediately; " Yes, of his fulness we have all received " (John 1:14b, 16a). The Incarnate Word of God is the agent cause to which every existing element of the Church's structure can be traced. All the gifts of God which are present effectively in the Church are due directly to the work of Christ.

The same reality, moreover, which depends effectively on

Christ tends toward him as toward its final cause. Since the
Lord is full of grace and truth, i. e., since every perfection of
the Church does exist in him, simply and uniformly, the perfecting of the Church herself must consist in attaining perfect
union with her Author and Head. This is a process which is
verified in history, but in a mysterious and hidden way. Its
consummation is described by St. Paul as follows: " When all
things will have been subjected to [the Son], then the Son will
subject himself to him who has subjected all things to [the Son],
in order that God may be all in all " (I Cor. 15 : 28) .

From this it follows too that Christ is the exemplar in whose
image the Church is fashioned, and against which everything
in the Church is measured. The idea is, again, Pauline. " Those
whom [God] has discerned beforehand, he has also predestined
to reproduce the image of his Son, in order that he may be the
first-born of many brothers " (Rom. 1 : 20) .

As Author of the New Creation, therefore, Christ is the
effective, final, and exemplar cause of the Church in her
entirety.

When was the Church created? Some would answer this
question with reference to the Old Testament, showing that
even in pre-Christian times the Church existed, at least in
nascent form, in the gathering of God's chosen people, Israel.
This is true, of course, and understanding the mystery of the
Church does depend in some degree on seeing how the Church
of the New Testament is a fulfillment of the covenant that God
made with Abraham and his seed. Still, it is perhaps better to
consider how the Church *actually* came into being through the
historical mystery of the Incarnation of the Word of God.

There is a sense, then, in which the coming into being of the
Church coincides with the taking of a human nature by the
Word of God in the womb of Our Lady. From the moment the
Sacred Heart of Jesus begins to beat with love for all men the
Church exists. At that moment the design of the Church is
already revealed and its life of love has begun. This is the
Church in Christ, for in his Heart dwelt the fullness of the
godhead; and from it would flow one day the blood and water

which are, in the Church, the sources of the power of the sacraments of rebirth and renewed life.[2]

Christ himself planned, however, that the divine gifts which constitute the structure of his Church should be revealed and, in a sense, ratified during the entire time of his earthly life. While he was exercising his ministry of preaching and doing good, the Lord chose a group of men to whom he committed the responsibility of being the foundation stones of his temple, to whom he also communicated the powers by which they might effectively acquit themselves of this superhuman task. Within this group of Apostles, he singled out one, Simon Peter, to whom he committed the responsibility of being the universal Father and Shepherd of his flock, and to whom he communicated the powers which one day would be described as episcopal, supreme, and altogether independent of any other authority, within or without the Church.[3] He also indicated to this group of twelve his will concerning the sacraments, through which the life of God should henceforth be communicated in the Church. In other words, he *instituted* these sacraments and committed them to the Church in the person of his envoys and ministers.

Two other moments are crucial in the foundation of the Church. The first is the passion and death of the Lord on the cross. No better description of what this event means to the Church can be found than that of St. Ambrose (cited in *Mystici Corporis* by Pius XII): " It is now that it is built, it is now that it is formed, it is now that it is . . . molded, it is now that it is *created* . . . Now it is that arises a spiritual house for a holy priesthood." The venerable doctor of the fifth century is saying that all the gifts which Christ had revealed during his public ministry were confirmed and given their efficacy by the power of the cross. " It was on the tree of the cross," says Pius XII in this same passage, " that he entered into possession of his Church." The final moment of the Church's creation was

[2] See Durrwell, F. X., *The Resurrection* (N. Y.: Sheed and Ward, 1960), pp. 79-91.

[3] *Constitutio Dogmatica de fide catholica* of the First Vatican Council (D. 1827).

Pentecost, when the Holy Spirit appeared in the form of tongues of fire that rested above the heads of the chosen Apostles. In this way Christ proclaimed from his throne in heaven the glory of his Spouse, the Church; and he set the seal of his approval upon her supernatural mission and task.[4]

B. *Order and distinction in the Church*

This seems to be the proper place to point out that the theology concerning the Church is derived largely from symbolic representations of this mystery contained in the Bible. The theologian's first task is to collect these figures from the pages of Sacred Scripture. They must then be seen in their various stages of development throughout the history of salvation and be compared one with the other. Finally, they should be converted into language which is more proper, insofar as this is possible. For an ever more adequate penetration of the mystery of the Church, the theologian must have constant recourse to these figures, in their biblical context. He interprets them, of course, according to the " analogy of faith," i. e., against the background of the living teaching of the Church, and in relation to all the revealed mysteries of the Catholic faith.

The more important figures in question are very familiar, because they are the basis of all ordinary preaching and teaching concerning the Church. St. Paul calls the Church the body of Christ (see especially Rom. 12:4 ff. and I Cor. 12:12 ff.; also Eph. 1:22-23 and Coloss. 1:18, 24); and Pius XII affirms that to describe the Church " we shall find no expression more noble, more sublime or more divine." [5] Other symbolic expressions do complement and supplement, to a certain degree, what is implicit in that foremost figure. For example, in the passage which he devotes to the mutual relation of husband and wife in the Christian family, St. Paul makes the model of this rela-

---

[4] For Pius XII's development of the foregoing points, see *Mystici Corporis* (Eng. transl., America Press), para. 32-41.

[5] Cf. Hamer, J., *L'Eglise est une communion* (Unam Sanctam, 40) (Paris: du Cerf, 1962), pp. 50-66, 95-100.

tion the loving dominion of Christ over his *Spouse*, the Church
(Eph. 5:21 ff.). Christ himself had made the theme of his
preaching still another symbol, that of the *Kingdom*; and this
too may be applied to the Church. St. John's gospel contains
two other descriptions based on the words of Christ: the Church
as the *Flock* over which the Good Shepherd keeps constant
watch (John 10:11 ff.); and the Church as the union of vine
and branches, Christ being the vine without whom we can do
nothing (John 15:5). Another Pauline figure of the Church
is contained in the epistle to the Ephesians, wherein the Apostle
speaks of the Church as a *temple* (2:20-22). This theme is
alluded to in other places, and by other inspired writers (cf. I
Petr. 2:5); but this is also true of the other figures. Finally,
there are places in the New Testament in which the Church is
spoken of as a *city* (cf. Apoc. 21, where the reference is primarily to the consummation of the mystery of the Church in
heaven); or as a *household* (cf. Luke 12:42).

The aspect of the mystery of the Church to which meditation on the ensemble of these biblical figures draws our attention is the various kinds of ecclesial order or distinction. In
the present context this means merely that the biblical figures
are the starting point from which may be derived a more or
less perfect understanding of the *catholic unity* of the Church;
because the articulated distinction of the Church's constitution
makes her to be one and catholic. Her unity is both organic,
i. e., that of a living and growing organism, and ordered, i. e.,
related to a single principle and source of power or authority.

That distinction or order in the Church which furnishes the
best insights into the Church's catholicity may be called a
distinction or order of perfection. Under this heading it is
possible to touch briefly on the subject of the conditions of
membership in the Church, and to discuss the import of the
dogmatic axiom, " outside the Church, no salvation."

A good starting point would seem to be St. Paul's doctrine
concerning the distinction of the Church, as a whole, from
another gathering, which is her enemy. Speaking to the Colossians of God's largesse, he says: " He has, in fact, rescued us

from the empire of darkness and has transferred us into the kingdom of his well-beloved Son, in whom we have redemption, the remission of sins" (1:13-14). The Apostle is saying simply that the Church, a kingdom of goodness and holiness, is distinguished by an action of God from another kingdom in which Satan has hegemony. The citizens or members of the former kingdom are, therefore, distinguished or marked as belonging to God in and through Christ. This is a rather elementary way of expressing the idea of membership in the Church, for it is really a response to a divine vocation, in virtue of which a man passes from darkness to light.

A two-fold question arises in consequence: what do the members of the Church have in common one with another, and how are they distinguished among themselves, precisely as members of the Church? These questions must be discussed in order.

The Catholic doctrine on the common conditions for membership in the Church are succinctly expressed by Pius XII in *Mystici Corporis:*

Only those are really to be included as members of the Church who have been baptized and profess the true faith and who have not unhappily withdrawn from the body-unity or for grave faults been excluded by legitimate authority. . . . those who are divided in faith or government cannot be living in one body such as this, and cannot be living the life of its one divine Spirit.

Real or actual membership, therefore, requires an initial introduction into the kingdom of light through the sacrament of faith, which is baptism. This is, as it were, the door to the Church. To this sacrament there is bound up intimately the profession of the true faith. Furthermore, being washed in this bath of redemption also implies the willingness to live in what Pius XII calls the " body-unity," i. e., in loving submission to the hierarchical order which Christ himself has established in his Church.

Once a person has been introduced through baptism into the kingdom of light, the possibility of a withdrawal or separation is real, though not according to God's will. This may happen through heresy, for example, when the faith suffers corruption. It may happen through schism, when a member or group of members become unwilling to live in communion with and under the authority of Christ communicated to the hierarchy, especially to the Roman Pontiff. Finally, it may happen through excommunication, when the Church herself takes action against a member whose life does not correspond to the vocation of the children of light.

It is according to these principles that the saying, " outside the Church, no salvation," must be understood. Since incorporation into Christ is accomplished really through the conditions outlined above, and since Christ is the only way that men have to return to God, necessarily these conditions must, in some sense, be verified in order that a man be saved. This is not to say, however, that they are always verified in exactly the same way. As a matter of fact, it is the constant teaching of Catholic tradition that men may be related to the Church, though not members in a full sense, in a hidden or latent way. As far back as the fifth century St. Augustine had this to say about a situation which seems often to be verified in our own day:

A person who defends his own opinion [in matters of faith], even though it be erroneous and perverse, but who defends it without obstinacy, especially when the [opinion] is not the fruit of his own perverse presumption, but is rather inherited from parents who have fallen into error; who, furthermore, is searching diligently for the truth, ready to surrender to it when he comes to know it—such a person is not to be counted among the heretics (Epist. 43, 1 [ML 33, 160]).

Today we would say that some men are related to the Church by an unconscious wish or desire, which may even be implicit. This means that when a man, through no fault of his own, does not have the opportunity to make use of the ordinary channels of salvation, and when he acts in accord with the conscience that speaks within him as the voice of God, his Creator; then God will give him grace, and he will be able to be saved. Such a man *is* related to the Church.

When such a situation is actually verified is difficult, if not impossible, to determine; still, there seem to be certain " rules of thumb " that are applications of the principles of the necessity of grace. If it be true that in his present condition man is incapable, without grace, of accomplishing even the good which is connatural to him (cf. *Summa*, I, II, 109, 2), and if the moral good that man does is measured, in a certain way, according the perfection of his communion with others, then it would seem to follow that real inter-personal communication among men is a sort of sign of the presence, to one degree or another, of the mystery of the Church. This seems to be what Father M. J. Congar, O. P. is referring to in the following passage:

A love before charity must be a true love if it is to lead to charity; it must be a self-giving love, otherwise it cannot be charity's first matrix, its preformation or anticipation. Contrarily, when a man goes out of himself, when he gives himself to some good that surpasses himself, when there *really* is love, then there is the possibility of meeting, in the form of an absolute, the hidden God who wants to draw us to himself and save us. . . . God can be " aimed at " through very inadequate representations and even under other names than his. That is the case with men—whole peoples!— brought up in other religions, which may be monotheistic, like Islam, or wholly heathen (*The Wide World My Parish*, London, 1961, pp. 121-123).

Such a statement of the case leads naturally to a discussion of the second question: how are members of the Church distinguished among themselves? Is it possible that *love* has something to do with the distinction?

First of all, it is clear that love, of itself, is not an absolute requirement for membership in the Church. If it were, sinners would be excluded from membership; and this is an idea alien to tradition. This tradition is based, moreover, on such solid ground as the parable of the Lord concerning the field planted with wheat in which the tares are allowed to grow until harvest time. It would, however, be a gross misunderstanding to suppose that love or charity had nothing at all to do with membership in the Church. In reality, all the conditions—baptism, profession of the true faith, and submission to lawful authority in the Church—bespeak or point to love. Love is the normal fruit or expression of all of them, so much so that St. Thomas speaks of schism as a sin which is directly contrary to divine love (cf. *Summa*, II, II, 39, 1). Therefore, in the Church there is an order or distinction of the members according to the degree in which the gifts of God do bear fruit in true charity. This order or distinction has no necessary connection with the exterior or visible order which will be discussed shortly; although it is manifest in this, that a man really takes his place in the Church to the degree that he is possessed by charity.

The catholicity of the Church, therefore, insofar as it is considered qualitatively, consists in this marvelous exchange of divine gifts, whereby the entire membership of the Church images the head, Christ. Each member holds an unique place, which no other member can fill—and this regardless of the office or function which he may be called to exercise. Filling one's place in the Church means giving oneself to the healing and elevating grace of Christ, so that *this* human nature, transformed by grace, may operate for the good of the entire body. "Does one member suffer? All the other members suffer with him. Is one member honored? Then all the members share in his joy" (Cor. 12:26). On the other hand, to the extent that a member refuses to take part in the communion which proceeds from God through Christ in the Church, to that extent does he withdraw his possible contribution to the catholicity of the Church. The Church is always capable of embracing him in her universality; thus she is always catholic, as is Christ, her Spouse. God wills, however, that the members of the Church in a mysterious way fill up those things which are lacking to the sufferings of Christ.

The second great category or type of order or distinction in the Church may be called an order of office or function. In its broadest terms it is expressed through the terms, hierarchy and laity. Since, moreover, to every office or function there corresponds a certain specified power to act, the hierarchy and the laity in the Church must be distinguished, in the concrete, by the distinct powers they have.

Here the link with the theology of the sacraments is intimate, for the Catholic doctrine concerning the " sacramental characters," one of the effects of some of the sacraments, shows that these characters are powers or certain participations in the priesthood of Christ. Possibly, then, a layman in the Church may be defined as a person whose activities proceed from those powers which are the sacramental characters of baptism and confirmation. A " hierarch," or member of the hierarchy, would be defined as a person whose activities in the Church proceed from the sacramental character of orders, or at least from something which is analogous to it.

What does this mean, in the concrete? The answer to this question is implicit in St. Thomas' explanation of these sacramental characters. To the first two he gives the name " passive powers "; while the sacramental character of orders he calls an " active power." This means simply that in the Church laymen depend on the hierarchy somewhat as a wife depends on her husband. St. Thomas affirms, in fact, that the bishop, who is a member of the hierarchy par excellence, is called, in a special way and in dependence on Christ, the Church's Spouse.[6]

---

[6] The precise manner in which the activity of the hierarchy and that of the laity are distinct, and how they mesh together for the constant building up of the body of Christ, will be discussed later in the section on the principles by which the Church is governed. One possible misunderstanding is to be excluded, however, in order that this summary explanation be as accurate as possible. To say that the powers of the laity are " passive " does not mean that the place of the laity in the Church is altogether *passive*, in the ordinary sense of the word. The term here, which is technical, designates a power the activity of which is ordered specifically to the transformation or perfection of the subject itself; while an active power is ordered to the transformation or changing of a subject which is outside the agent, or distinct from it. Therefore, the primary function of the laity is, through the activation of the passive powers which are theirs, and this in dependence upon the hierarchy, to grow in perfection and to enter into more perfect communion with the Church. On the other hand, by its active powers the hierarchy is fit to deal with the body of Christ, both the sacramental body and the mystical body, and this in order that Christ's sacramental body be received worthily and fruitfully in the mystical body. Thus it is that the distinction of office or function in the Church reveals a primary aspect of the Church's unity; for everything in this order is made for more perfect eucharistic communion, of which the final term is the unity of the Church.

C. *The means through which the Church is maintained and governed.*

The distinction of members in the Church according to office or function, while being a concrete manifestation of the Church's unity, is also the foundation of the theology of the Church's government. St. Thomas observes:

[In the universe] inferior things are governed by that which is superior, and this not because of any defect in God's power, but rather on account of the abundance of his goodness. This is such that he communicates even to creatures the dignity of causality (*Summa*, 1, 22, 3, c.).

When this dictum is applied to the New Creation, which is the Church, it means that Christ has communicated his governing power to those in the Church who act as superiors. This is not because of a lack of perfection in Christ; in fact, just as God governs the entire universe in an altogether transcendent way, so too does Christ govern the Church as her invisible head.

Our divine Saviour governs and guides his community also directly and personally. For it is he who reigns within the minds and hearts of men and bends and subjects to his purpose their wills even when rebellious. " The heart of the king is in the hand of the Lord; whithersoever he will, he shall turn it." By this interior guidance the " Shepherd and Bishop of our souls " not only watches over individuals, but exercises His providence over the universal Church as well, whether by enlightening and giving courage to the Church's rulers for the loyal and effective performance of their respective duties, or by singling out from the body of the Church— especially when times are grave—men and women of conspicuous holiness, who may point the way for the rest of Christendom to the perfecting of his Mystical Body (Pius XII, *Mystici Corporis*).

The superiority and inferiority involved here do not imply that the governed are mere pawns who are lorded over by the governing superiors. The words of Christ himself are very clear on this point:

The kings of the Gentiles lord it over them, and those who bear rule over them win the name of benefactors. With you it is not to be so; no difference is to be made, among you, between the greatest and the youngest of all, between him who commands and him who serves. Tell me, which is greater, the man who sits at table, or the man who serves him? Surely the man who sits at table; yet I am here among you as your servant (Luke 22:25-27).

In other words, the principle of mediation in the working out of Christ's plan for the Church is applied in such a way that the dignity of all the members of the Church, the governing hierarchy and the governed laity, is enhanced.

This contact of Christ with his Church through mediation has, in general, two effects. The first is that the Church is maintained or supported in the good which is proper to her, even while she is undergoing growth and perfection. This good is, of course, the Church's holiness, a quality by which she is distinct from any other society. The second effect of this government is a sort of movement by which the Church is ever directed toward a better fulfillment of her vocation to be the spotless Bride of the Savior. This movement more clearly manifests how the Church is apostolic. These two general effects need to be the subject of a more detailed analysis.

When holiness is designated as the good proper to the Church, the meaning is that the life of the Church is the grace of Christ, in virtue of which all the members of the Church, the adopted sons of God, are fashioned according to the image of Christ. No other society has such an intimate principle of cohesion, for all other groups of men are bound together only in virtue of natural ties, e. g., the blood ties in a family or the common good of the body politic. Now is there any factor in the Church herself to which this conservation of the Church's holiness, i. e., the maintenance and nourishment of grace, is related as to its cause?

A simple answer to this question is difficult to formulate; yet one thing seems to be certain. The grace which is the Church's life—the grace of Christ—is *sacramental* grace. This means that it is communicated in the Church through the sacraments.

Therefore, the persons in the Church who are responsible for the sacraments constitute, it seems, a collective instrument for the conservation of the Church's holiness. Of course, these persons are none other than the Church's priests, for they are the ministers of the sacraments. The sacraments of the Church are committed, as it were, to the Christian priesthood. Therefore, this priesthood is the means whereby Christ maintains his Church as holy.

Even prior to any mention of the Church's ruling power, properly so-called, it is altogether right that the principality of the Roman Pontiff, and, around him, of the college of bishops, should be emphasized. The very fact that the Pope is called the *Summus Pontifex*—the Supreme Pontiff—is very significant. *Pontiff* is a term which seems to refer directly to priesthood; for the priest is, most of all, a bridge or mediator (cf. *Summa*, III, 22, 1). In the universal Church, therefore, the bishop of Rome is the High Priest, under Christ and in dependence on him; and, *servatis servandis,* the same is true of the bishop in his own diocese. Although it is true that all ordained priests in the Church are able autonomously to offer the sacrifice of the Eucharist—the power to do so is theirs—still any priestly activity which they exercise with respect to the preparation of the mystical body for the reception of the eucharistic body of Christ is done in strict dependence on the bishop, who is, as has been said, especially the Spouse of the Church.

Even while the Church lives by the grace of the sacraments, always available in virtue of the priesthood; there are other instrumental factors by which the Church is governed and through which the interior good of the Church can be promoted and the boundaries of the Church can be extended. These are the hierarchical powers to *teach* infallibly the revelation of God's love and to *rule* in accord with the New Law.

The infallibility of the Church in the transmission of those supernatural truths which are called the " deposit of faith " is not something which needs to be demonstrated; for it can be taken as itself part of that deposit. Some explanation of the meaning and the extent of this infallibility is, however, called for.

The first point that needs to be made is, simply, that the remote subject of this endowment is the Church herself.[7] When infallibility is predicated of the Pope (and this according to the definition of the First Vatican Council), or when a similar predication is made concerning an Ecumenical Council or the college of bishops teaching Catholic truth in concert with the Holy See, the meaning is that the Pope or the Council, and the bishops teaching together are active organs of the Holy Spirit in the Church by which the deposit of faith is preserved from error in its propagation. The conditions under which the Roman Pontiff acts as an infallible teacher of Catholic truth are carefully defined: ". . . when he speaks *ex cathedra*, i. e., when he is exercising the office of pastor and teacher of all Christians and is defining by his supreme apostolic authority a doctrine which pertains to faith or Christian living to be held by the universal Church" (D. 1839). Nevertheless, neither the Pope nor the bishops depend on any other authority, or even on the subsequent approval of the Church as a whole, in the exercise of this office. Such is the explicit teaching of the Church as regards the Roman Pontiff; and it follows rigorously that the same may be said of the bishops' authority.

What, then, are the limits of this teaching authority in the Church? If the Pope and the bishops are autonomous in their transmission of Catholic truth, how are they guided? The answer, of course, is that the gift of infallibility is itself exercised on that which is *given* to the Church by Christ and the Apostles. The living magisterium of the Church, which is exercised in every age of the Church's life to one degree or another, is a re-expression and development of a revelation that was given, once and for all, in apostolic times. According to Catholic doctrine, public revelation ceased with the death of the last of the Apostles; and from that time on the Church

---

[7] See the article of W. Bartz, "Le Magistère de l'Eglise d'àpres Scheeben," in *L'Ecclesiologie au 19ᵉ siècle* (Unam Sanctam, 34) (Paris: du Cerf. 1960), pp. 309-327.

has been guided by the Holy Spirit precisely in this: not to make a mistake concerning this revelation.

It is generally said that the revelation is contained fully in the Scriptures and Tradition, and that the function of the teaching Church is merely to " guard and infallibly declare [the meaning of] the divine deposit committed to the Spouse of Christ " (D. 1800). The Fathers of the First Vatican Council went on to define, moreover, that " precisely that sense of the holy dogmas is forever to be retained which is once declared as such by Holy Mother Church; nor ought that sense to be abandoned on the pretext or under the species of a higher understanding [reference to a sort of false gnosis]. Therefore, the understanding, the knowledge, and the wisdom of all—both of single members and of the entire Church, and this under all conditions and in all ages—ought to grow and see great progress: yet on the condition that the genus remain always the same, i. e., that exactly the same understanding and penetration of the dogma always prevail " (ibid.).

One obvious difference between the Church's teaching power and her ruling power, properly so-called, is that, whereas the Church's teaching involves not only a *didascalia* (an instruction that takes place within the Church in order that the Gospel be better understood), but also a *kerygma* (a proclamation of the Gospel ordained to draw into the communion of the Church those who are still subjects of the empire of darkness); her rule is exercised almost exclusively over those who have already made the transferral from one kingdom to another. It becomes evident, therefore, that there is an intimate relation between these two powers; and that they are both designed to move the Church toward greater perfection according to a pre-established order. The outline of this order is drawn by Christ as he is about to ascend to his Father: " All power is given to me in heaven and upon the earth. Go, therefore, make disciples of all nations, baptising them in the name of the Father, Son and Holy Spirit, and teaching them to observe all the things that I have prescribed to you " (Matt. 28:18b-20).

The New Law is primarily one written upon the hearts of

those who take part in the New Covenant. It is, as St. Thomas teaches, identical with the " grace of the Holy Spirit, given through the faith of Christ " (*Summa*, I, II, 106, 1, c.) . This law is, of course, divine; and it may be expressed in the concrete as the universal impulse of all those who are incorporated into the Church, or are related to her in some way, to enter into the communion of love with God and other men.

Ecclesiastical law, however, which is the expression of the ruling power of the Church, is made, executed and sanctioned in an exterior way, simply because the Church herself is a visible society, with a visible articulation of parts or members. This is not to say that ecclesiastical law—the "laws of the Church"— are not related to the inner law of love; to think thus would be to misunderstand completely the governing function of the Church. In reality, the Church exercises jurisdiction over her members in order that the law of love may be more perfectly observed. St. Thomas expresses this very well when he points out that the proper function of the bishops in the Church, to whom this jurisdiction is committed by divine right, is to prepare the faithful for the worthy or fruitful reception of the sacrament of the Eucharist (cf. *Suppl.*, 40, 4, 1, in c.) . Elsewhere, moreover, it is his contention that the effect or term of the Eucharist is the actual unity of the Church, unity itself being a primary effect of love (cf. *Summa*, III, 73, 1, arg. 2, and ad 3; 73, 2, s. c.; 73, 3, c.; 73, 6, c.; 79, 4, c.) .

As to the manner of exercising this ecclesiastical or canonical jurisdiction, the primacy of the bishop of Rome must be set forth, and in addition, a balanced judgment must be made concerning the pontiff's relation with the college of bishops throughout the world. In reality, of course, this primacy and the relations that follow from it reproduce the primacy of St. Peter, conferred on him by Christ, and the relation of the Prince of the Apostles to the apostolic college. It is certainly true that the Church's consciousness of the implications of Peter's position in the Church has evolved throughout the centuries, and that the manner in which this position is exteriorly expressed has undergone great change. The evolution, however, has been homogeneous; and the changes have not affected what is essential to the structure of the Catholic hierarchy.

Certain attributes relating to ruling power are common to all the bishops, including the bishop of Rome. All the bishops hold *ordinary, episcopal,* and *immediate* jurisdiction. These attributes may be understood better through a distinction of a threefold relation. The bishop's power is *ordinary* insofar as it is attached to the very office of bishop itself; *episcopal* insofar as it is a vicarious exercise of the power of Christ himself (this is to say that it is, in a certain sense, divine); *immediate* in relation to the flock committed to the bishop insofar as he needs to go through no intermediary in order to exercise his power over each and every member of the Church committed to him.

The ways in which the ruling power of the Pope differs from and excels that of the rest of the bishops in the Church is expressed as follows: (1) his power is *supreme,* while theirs is subordinate; (2) his is *universal,* while theirs is particularized or localized; (3) his is altogether autonomous, independent, or *sui juris;* while theirs is not. This means that even all the bishops of the Church belong in a certain sense to the flock, the pastor of which is the bishop of Rome. They are, therefore, both his brothers, insofar as they share with him the episcopal office, and his sons, insofar as they exercise this office in accord with his direction. It means also that every member of the Church is subject *immediately* to the Pope. Neither does he have to pass through another bishop to exercise his power over any member of the Church. Finally, it means that the very power of the episcopate, held by all the bishops of the Church, is dependent on the Roman Pontiff. In a certain sense, the entire apostolate of the Church rests on his shoulders. This is the sense in which the see of Rome is called the " Apostolic See." [8]

[8] Very apropos of these relations are the words of Pope Leo XIII, contained in an encyclical (*Satis cognitum*) which was devoted to the unique character of the Roman Catholic Church:

   That there be a twofold authority [over the faithful] does not make for confusion in administration. It is impossible, in the first place, even to suspect

These two brief discussions of the order and distinction in
the Church and of the principles according to which the government of the New Creation is accomplished have resulted in
an elucidation of the four qualities, properties or marks of the
Church herself, to which the Creed bears witness: *unam, sanctam, catholicam et apostolicam.* The Church is one and catholic according to the twofold distinction to be discerned in the
mystery. Her catholicity is best expressed, it seems, in terms of
the distinction according to perfection; insofar as all the members of the Church mirror in some way the catholic perfection
of Christ, the Head. Her unity is both signified and caused by
the distinction of office, according as the hierarchy receives
from Christ the power to prepare the laity for eucharistic communion. The holiness and apostolicity of the Church, insofar
as they *really* belong to her, seem to be brought out quite clearly
through a consideration of the various principles of the Church's
government. Her holiness is intimately connected with the
priesthood, a power which is directly ordained to the communication and maintenance of the life of grace in the Church.
Her apostolicity is bound up with the teaching and ruling functions, which are possessed and exercised principally by the hierarchical members of the Church, all in subordination to the
Vicar of Christ, the Pope. Thus are verified the words of St.
Paul: " Apostles and prophets are the foundation on which you
were built, and the chief-cornerstone of it is Jesus Christ himself. In him the whole fabric is bound together, as it grows into
a temple, dedicated to the Lord; in him you too are being
built in with the rest, so that God may find in you a dwelling-
place for his Spirit " (Eph. 2 : 20-22) .

this; for it is by the wisdom of God himself that this regime is organized.
Furthermore, it is to be noted that the order of things and their mutual relations are only disturbed if two authorities ruling over a people are of the
same grade, and neither is subject to the other. The power of the Roman
Pontiff, however, is supreme, universal, and altogether *sui juris*; while [the
power of] the bishops is circumscribed by definite boundaries and is not altogether *sui juris* (D. 1961, *in fine*) .

II. The Life of the Church, Expression of the Love of the Holy Spirit

The whole structure of the Church bespeaks activity and growth; and this is brought out particularly well by St. Paul in the text just cited. Up to now, however, we have been concerned almost exclusively with the static or constitutional aspects of the mystery, i. e., with the manner in which the Church is dependent upon Christ and with the various ways (distinction, order, and mediating factors of government) in which she mirrors the perfection of him according to whose image she is made. Turning, then, from this consideration of the *wisdom* of the Church's *exitus*, we are now in a position to take a brief look at the plan of her *reditus*, or return—a return which is synonomous with ecclesial activity, the impulse of which is divine *love*.

Just as the activity of man is understood best in terms of his destiny, so the growth and activity of the Church may be known more perfectly in the light of her final term. Therefore, the order to be followed here is: (1) to discuss briefly the meaning of the " beatitude " of the Church; (2) to outline the nature of the activity which belongs properly to the Church with a view to this beatitude, and to indicate the principles of this activity.

A. *The New Jerusalem*

At least two passages in the New Testament may serve as a basis for a study of the Church's beatitude. The first is a few verses in St. Paul's discussion of the resurrection from the dead (I Cor. 15). Here he speaks of the coming of Christ (*parousia*) in this wise: " The end will take place when [Christ] renders the kingship to God, the Father; after he himself has destroyed every principality, dominion, and power. For it is necessary that he reign right up until the time that he has put all his enemies under foot. And the last enemy to be destroyed is death itself. Thence everything will be in a state of submission—with the exception, of course, of him who has given all things to be under [Christ's] dominion. Finally, when all things will have been made subject to him, then the Son will subject himself to the one who has given all things to be subject to him, in order that God may be all in all " (vv. 24-28). The other passage is the last two chapters of St. John's apocalyptic visions, which begins: " Then I saw a heaven and a new earth—in fact the first heaven and earth disappeared; nor was there anything left of the sea. And I saw the Holy City, the *New Jerusalem*, which came down from heaven, i. e., from God. She was beautiful, as a young bride adorned for her husband " (Apoc. 21 : 1-2).

Now there seem to be considered in this mystery of the consummation of the Church's activity: (1) the similarity or homogeneity of the Triumphant Church and the Militant Church; (2) the difference between the two.

It ought to be understood that at the present time the Church Triumphant exists simultaneously with the Church Militant (and the Church Suffering); the perfect state, moreover, will not obtain until Christ returns for the last judgment of all things. The existence of the New Jerusalem began with the triumph of Christ himself over death; and these latter times in which the Church Militant herself lives are described by St. Paul (*vide supra*) as the process of all things coming under the actual dominion of the Word Incarnate, in order that he may finally deliver his Church into the hands of his Father.

How, then, is the Church Militant like the Church Triumphant, and even one with her? The answer must be in terms of the adage: " grace is the seed of glory." The life of God, or, more precisely, participation in the life of God is common to both. On this earth it is according to faith; in heaven it is by vision. In both cases, however, the participation is real and specifically the same.

To have said this, moreover, is to have suggested the difference between the two. In the Church Militant, the life of God is communicated in a sacramental way; and in order that this be effected the Church Militant contains a distinction of office or function, whereby certain members of the Church are actually empowered to share in the causality of Christ, the Author and Head of the Church. In the final state, however, such sacramental communication will not be exercised; and in this sense the hierarchy will have ceased to exist. As St. Paul puts it: " God will be all in all! " The principle of mediation will have ceased to be operative in this way; although Christ himself will be supremely the Head of the Church, since the redemption and renewal of all things depend upon him, and this for all eternity. God will show his face forever to all those who belong to Christ.

B. *The activity of the Church in view of her destiny*

The principle, of course, for any consideration of activity is that all those are good actions which are in accord with the nature of the being from which they proceed. Activity, therefore, which is perfective of the Church, i. e., which actually promotes her advance toward the New Jerusalem, is that which is in accord with *her* nature. This means that it involves those elements which have been delineated as *natural* to her: the various kinds of order and distinction and the principles of government.

Perhaps an even easier way to approach the question is to ask: since Christ is the author of this New Creation, what activity did he *give* to it? And the answer is, obviously, indicated by the words of the Lord to the Apostles on the eve of his death: " *This do* in a memorial of me. "

The truth of the matter is that the sacrifice of the Eucharist is the activity which is, most of all, according to the nature of Church; and all other activity which takes place in the Church is ordered to it. This is true not only of all the other sacraments, each of which has a more or less intimate relation of order to the Eucharist, but also of any other action taken by members of the Church *as such*, whether they be of the hierarchy or of the laity. It has been pointed out that the function proper to the bishops of the Church is to prepare the faithful for the worthy or fruitful reception of the sacrament of the body of Christ. This means that the teaching power and the ruling power of the bishops, as it is exercised and as it is shared in a certain measure with priests, and even sometimes with members of the laity, is ordered to the Eucharistic celebration. It means also that the supreme function of the bishop is to gather around himself his people to pontificate the Mass. The words of St. Ignatius of Antioch (+ c. 110) are pertinent here: " Let no one do anything touching the Church apart from the Bishop. Let that celebration of the Eucharist be considered valid which is held under the bishop or anyone to whom he has committed it " (*ad Smyrn.* 8, 1) .

It is not at all strange, therefore, that the form of celebration of the Eucharistic sacrifice has evolved in the way it has. The first part of the Mass, sometimes called the Mass of the Catechumens, consists of a service which is, for the most part didactic. Ideally, it culminates in a sermon or homily, which, if it be true that this is the bishop's service, offers the Shepherd of the flock the opportunity to exercise his power to teach his people and to promulgate for them the law of love of the New Government. Then the sacrifice itself accomplishes the perfecting of the unity of the entire Mystical Body. The whole Church acts most perfectly in the Eucharist (although to a certain extent, the whole Church acts in the entire liturgy, insofar as the priesthood of Christ himself is exercised in every liturgical act) , because it is Christ, Head of the Church, who presents through his priest the gift of his body and blood to the eternal Father.

The truth that all activity of the Church leads to Eucharistic worship can be extended to include even that activity which is called " missionary." When the Church extends herself, as it were, and embraces new peoples, it is said that the primary aim of the work of the missionaries is to establish the hierarchy among these peoples. The hierarchy, however, has as its function in the Church either the celebration of the Eucharist or the preparation of the Christian people for worthy participation in this mystery of unity.

If this were the entire story, however, it would be difficult to see how are verified the words of Christ: " Do you believe that I came to establish peace on the earth? No, I say to you, rather division " (Luke 12:51). As a matter of fact, he did establish the Church as a " perfect society," i. e., as having within herself all the means necessary for the attainment of that to which she is destined—the New Jerusalem. Because she is of an entirely different order than any other society, however, it is not surprising that conflicts arise between Church and societies such as the various *states*. This is not because there is any discrepancy between the principles of the supernatural order and those by which political society, for example, is guided. The reason for the conflict is the difficulty involved in understanding the ways in which the principles are to be harmonized in a concrete situation. Thus, at different times and circumstances in history, the Church has carried on that life and activity which is proper to her either with the positive protection of the state, with its indifference, or in the face of positive hostility. The field of Church-state relations is one of those which, at the present time, is the object of most intense study; and a brief essay such as this can hope to do no more than to indicate the locus of the problem in the theology concerning the Church.

C. *The interior or spiritual principles of the Church's activity.*

In the very beginning of this essay reference was made to the possibility of a *balanced* ecclesiology on the basis of principles furnished by St. Thomas. In the actual working out of these principles, moreover, it becomes quite evident that this balance consists in the harmony of the visible with the invisible in the Church, the static with the dynamic, the structure with the life. It is not without reason, therefore, that the essay be designed to end with a short discussion of that principle which enlivens every element of the Church—giving life to her members, vivifying those to whom any office whatsoever is committed. This principle is the indwelling Holy Spirit, who is rightly called the *soul of the Church.*

At the very foundation of this attribution is the truth that, even as he who is the author of the Church is, in his divine personality, *Sapientia genita*; so he who is the soul of the Church is, under the same formality, *Amor procedens*. In the life of the blessed Trinity the Holy Spirit *is* Love, because his procession is the fruit, as it were, of the love of the Father and the Son. Therefore, he is sometimes also called the *nexus* between the Father and the Son. Therefore, too, everything that is an effect of God's love in the universe—and among the effects of his love the Church is, after the hypostatic union, the most astounding of all—is attributed to him.

How is this animation of the mystical body of Christ verified? What does it actually mean? The Holy Spirit enlivens the Church in two ways: (1) as the principle of every movement in the life of the Church; (2) as present in the Church as a single *indwelling* soul.

The first mode of the Holy Spirit's animation of the Church can be explained concretely in reference to elements pertaining to the structure of the Church. For example, all the grace which is given with a view toward the perfection of the Church, is a gift of the Holy Spirit. This is true both of the habitual grace which is present in the souls of those who love God; and of the so-called actual grace, by which men are drawn toward God's love and toward a greater immersion in it. All the other gifts in the Church, which contribute in any way toward her movement in the direction of the New Jerusalem, are also gifts of the Holy Spirit. That the Church is infallible, and that this infallibility is exercised under certain conditions by the Pope, is due to the Holy Spirit's protective guidance. That the ruling power of the hierarchy has force in the Church is due to the fact that the Holy Spirit ratifies the exercise of this power. To the degree, then, that members of the Church, either hierarchical or lay, submit to the sweet movement of the Holy Spirit, to that degree are they cooperating in the progress of the Church in the life that is proper to her. To the degree that they withdraw from the Holy Spirit's influence, to that degree they are an encumbrance to the movement and progress of the Church.

The second mode by which the Holy Spirit animates the Church is called the indwelling presence, and it has no direct reference to movement or activity. The explanation of it is based on the theology of the indwelling presence of the Holy Spirit in the souls of the just. It is the common teaching of Catholic theologians that this mystery takes place in virtue of the grace by which every just person is elevated to share in the life of God. In other words, habitual grace disposes a person to be a host, by knowledge and love, to the Spirit of God. God dwells in such a person as one who is known intimately and with whom real love can be exchanged.

Now it is according to God's plan that all souls of whom this is verified be members of the Church—and, indeed, all such souls are either actual members or are related to her by the unconscious will and desire spoken of previously. Therefore, this indwelling takes place *in the Church*; and, since the Spirit who dwells in these souls is not divided, but one, it is said that the Spirit of God dwells in the Church. As a matter of fact, it is this selfsame Spirit through whom the members of the Church are in living contact one with the other.

Conclusion

The encyclical of Pius XII on the Mystical Body closes, significantly, with a paragraph or two on the role of Our Lady in the Church. This seems to signify that no ecclesiology is complete without some consideration of what Mary is to the Church. It would be possible, of course, to make her role explicit all along the line. The sum of it will, however, be the same. The whole of Our Lady's relationship to the Church is implicit in the truth of her divine maternity. She is the mother of the Incarnate Word, who is the Author and Head of the Church. She is, therefore, the New Eve, as he is the New Adam.

This august dignity is such that, when it is said, with truth, that Our Lady has absolutely no hierarchical status in the Church, this does not derogate in any way from her sublimity. As to the structure of the Church, it would seem that no special place can be assigned to Our Lady, provided that it be maintained that she is the most perfect of the Church's members.

Her Immaculate Conception, which was the foundation of a life which developed in perfect consonance with the interior inspiration of the Holy Spirit, soul of the Church, is the type, as it were, of baptismal purity. Our Lady's correspondence with grace made love bear such fruit that at the moment of the Annunciation the angel could say: "Hail, *full* of grace." As to the life of the Church, however, she is the queen through whom all grace flows into the Church Militant. She is the Mother of the Mystical Body of her Son; and her delight is to be with the sons of men (Prov. 8:31).

MAURICE B. SCHEPERS, O. P.

Dominican House of Studies
Washington, D. C.

THE SIN OF SCHISM:

A CONTRIBUTION TO THE DISCUSSION OF MEMBERSHIP
IN THE CHURCH

∽

A CURRENT definition of the sin of schism goes like this: the external rupture of the unity of the Church by refusal to obey the lawful authority, but without denial of any truth of faith.[1] How adequate is such a definition? The mind is caught by the expressions, "external rupture" and "refusal to obey," and wonders whether this is all that Canon Law means by its definition of a schismatic (allowing for the distinction of the *definita*, viz., " schism " and " schismatic "): " if one, after the reception of baptism . . . refuses submission to the Supreme Pontiff or rejects communion with the members of the Church subject to the latter, he is a schismatic."[2] This canon is taken almost literally from the *Summa Theologiae*: " Wherefore schismatics are those who refuse submission to the Supreme Pontiff and reject communion with those members of the Church who are subject to him."[3] There is only one difference: the canon joins the two clauses with an " or," the *Summa* with an " and." Is this significant? Perhaps the canonical formula reflects the modern way of conceiving the distinction between the visible and juridical aspect of the Church and the invisible and gracious aspect of it, which may not be the same as St. Thomas'. However, since the two formulas are basically identical, it will be profitable to study that of St. Thomas in the context of the question he devotes to schism. This is the first aim of this paper.

The more important aim is to apply the results of this

[1] Bernard Häring, *The Law of Christ* II, (Westminster, Md.: Newman Press, 1962) p. 525, no. 46.
[2] *CIC*, c. 1325, II. 2.
[3] *Summa Theol.*, II-II, q. 39, a. 1.

investigation of the sin of schism (with the help of Cajetan's extraordinary commentary on it) to the much discussed contemporary question of who is a member of the Church.

It is obvious that there is a fruitful tension of opinion among Catholic scholars on this latter question. Sincere students, inspired by a deep love both of the Church of Christ and of all those Christians who are, in fact, not in communion with the bishops and faithful throughout the world who are in union with the See of Peter, are pulled, as it were, some to the side of the Church, others to the side of the non-communicating brethren. The debate centers around the ratio [4] of *member of the Church, member of the Mystical Body of Christ*. The first group are impelled to adopt a ratio of *member* which is quite precise in order to preserve the unique identity of the Mystical Body, the Church of Christ. The second group prefer a less precise ratio of *member* in order to embrace all (or most) of those who do accept Jesus as Lord and Savior and are validly baptized.

Both sides seem to agree on one note in their ratios of *member* as crucial—the note of visible, juridical subjection to the See of Peter. The first group tend to see this note as essential to the ratio of *member*, so that without it a person, even though validly baptized, is not a member of the Church, but only related to it by desire. The second group seem to consider the visible juridical note, as essential, not to the ratio of *member*, but of *perfect member*.

This divergence of emphasis is sometimes presented in the following terms: [5] the first group have a univocal ratio of *member*, the second an analogical ratio, meaning that the first group admits of no degrees of membership, while the second does. This is a tricky distinction and it may help to clarify later discussion if we explore its implications a bit.

First of all, no one really questions the fact that the ratio

---

[4] This term is used throughout the paper to refer to the concept, idea, meaning of a name, which will always be italicized.

[5] Cf. *GB* " Who belongs to the Church? " in *The Ecumenist* I (April-May 1963) 4.

of *member of the Church* is inescapably analogical (whether
proper or improper is still discussed; here it is taken as proper). Other analogates are *member of a physical body* and
member of a social body. The common note is that of an intimate, integral part of a whole, like a hand of a human body,
a citizen of a state, a believer of a Church.

To speak, then, of a univocal and an analogical ratio of
member of the Church does not exactly clarify the discussion.
Perhaps it would be well to adopt the terminology of St.
Thomas in a similar case, the ratio of *person*. This is certainly
an analogical ratio, of which the analogates are divine person,
angelic person and human person. St. Thomas, in discussing
the reference of the ratio of *person* to these three analogates,
distinguishes, quite deliberately, between the more common
ratio of *person* and the less common ratios of *divine person*,
angelic person and *human person*. The more common ratio of
person is: something distinct, complete, subsisting in an intellectual nature. This ratio is verified in each being that may
be called a person. Yet, obviously, the common ratio is verified diversely in the three analogates, just as the common ratio
of *member* is realized diversely in the hand, the citizen and
the believer.

Now a further question presents itself: could the less common ratio of *member of the Church* be realized diversely in
still less common ratios, in other words, are there diverse ways
of realizing the ratio of *member of the Church?* There could
be, if a certain condition were verified. To specify this condition, let us return to our ratio of *person*.

Is the less common ratio of *human person* realized analogously in its inferiors? Our cherished doctrine of the equality
of every human person is evidence that it is not. Is the less
common ratio of *divine person* realized analogously in the
Father, the Son and the Holy Spirit? It is a matter of faith
that it is not. If we follow St. Thomas' notion of the angels
as specifically distinct from each other, then the ratio of
angelic person is in itself realized analogously in each angel.

To apply all this to the less common ratio of *member of the Church*, we must first admit that the ratio itself must include the whole—the ratio of *member* is " part of a whole." Hence, to determine whether the ratio of *member of the Church* is realized diversely in the human beings of which it is predicated, we would have to determine whether the ratio of *Church* or of *Mystical Body of Christ* is realized diversly. That is, we would have to admit the existence of a more common ratio of *Church* or *Mystical Body*, that would be verified in, for example, 1) all the Churches united to the See of Peter; 2) all the Orthodox Churches in communion with each other; 3) all (or many) of the Protestant Churches, whether in communion with each other or not; 4) (perhaps) all non-Christians actually possessing the life of grace. If these (or, at least, those who have valid baptism) can be truly called, in diverse ways, that is, more or less perfectly, the Church of Christ, the Mystical Body of Christ, then the ratio of *member* would have an analogical meaning. This would mean that there must be a Church or Churches outside that Church which is the communion of bishops and faithful in union with the See of Peter. Is there? It is not convincing to point to the obvious fact that there are outside the Catholic Church ecclesiastical groupings that possess visible elements similar to those possessed by the Church. It is precisely the presence of these elements that is the scandal of Christian disunity. If our Orthodox and Protestant brethren did not possess common visible elements of Catholicism, they would not be in agony over their own divisions.

The reader will bear with me, if I engage him in one more preliminary discussion. I think that the explicit intention of the Enclyclical *Mystici Corporis* [6] was to answer the question of the previous paragraph with a clear-cut, " No—there is no Church outside the Church." This Enclycical was not a statement of the extraordinary magisterium of the Roman Pontiff.

---

[6] References to this Encyclical are taken from *Four Great Encyclicals of Pope Pius XII* (New York: Paulist Press, 1961).

Yet, I am convinced that in the precisely determined context of the Enclyclical,[7] the doctrine it proposes on the complete identification of the Mystical Body of Christ in its earthly, historical phase with the Church of the bishops and faithful throughout the world in union with the See of Peter, is a statement of the indefectible ordinary teaching of the Church.

It is understandable that in the discussions on the ratio of *member of the Church*, passages of the Encyclical explicitly referring to it should be cited. Two are of upmost importance. The first is explicitly concerned to clarify the ratio of *member:*

> Actually only those are to be included as members of the Church who have been baptized and profess the true faith, and who have not been so unfortunate as to separate themselves from the unity of the Body or been excluded from it by legitimate authority for serious faults committed.[8]

From its position in the Encyclical, it is clear that the Holy Father in this passage is listing the notes of the ratio of *member of the Church* in the fullest and most obvious sense. He is not dealing with those who are obviously " outside " the Church. They are in his mind, when he later refers to " those who do not belong to the visible Body of the Catholic Church " in the following words:

> For even though by an unconscious desire and longing they have a certain relationship with the Mystical Body, they still remain deprived of those many heavenly gifts and helps which can only be enjoyed in the Catholic Church. Therefore, may they enter into Catholic unity and, joined with us in the one, organic body of Jesus Christ, may they together with us run on to the one Head in the society of glorious love.[9]

---

[7] *Ibid.*, p. 8. " For this reason, We deem it fitting to speak to you on this subject through this Encyclical Letter, developing and explaining, above all, those points which concern the Church Militant."

[8] *Ibid.*, p. 14, n. 22.　　　　　　　　[9] *Ibid.*, p. 46, n. 103.

Of special significance are the two phrases: "enter into Catholic unity" and "joined with us in one organic Body of Jesus Christ." As mentioned above, the ratio of *member of the Mystical Body* depends on the ratio of *Mystical Body*. What the Holy Father means by *members* and *those who do not belong to the visible Body of Jesus Christ*, depends on what he means by *Mystical Body of Jesus Christ*.

It is a fact that the Pontiff devoted considerable space to developing the ratio of *Mystical Body of Christ*.[10] Taking the name *Body* first, he developed a strong case for the visible and organic nature of the Church. Next, he explored the multiplex relations of Christ to his Body. Finally, he comes to a profound exposition of precisely the analogical ratio of *Mystical Body*, by analysing the ratio of *Mystical*.

The Pontiff carefully justifies the use of the name *Mystical* as a suitable means of distinguishing the Church from 1) Christ's physical body, enthroned in glory at the right hand of the Father and hidden under the Eucharistic veils (It is well known that in antiquity the name *mystical* was used to designate the Eucharistic Body of Christ); 2) from any physical body: in the physical body, the parts, the members, have no individual subsistence and no perfection proper to them, independently of the whole; 3) from any merely moral body: in such a body, the principle of union is nothing else than the common end and the common co-operation of all under the authority of society for the attainment of that end.

Unlike the physical body, "the church exists both for the good of the faithful and for the glory of God and Jesus Christ whom He sent." Undoubtedly, according to the traditional view in the Church, the glory of God and of Jesus is the principal end of the Church. It might be asked does the Church manifest the glory of God more perfectly by what she is or by what she does? A parallel question would be: Does Jesus Christ manifest the glory of his Father more by what he is

---

[10] *Ibid.*, pp. 29-30, nn. 60-63.

than by what he does? The answer to both, I think, is: by what he is; by what she is. But what is she?

The Pontiff reaches for the ultimate answer to this question by distinguishing the Church from a merely moral and juridical body. This Church is such a body, but it is mysteriously, incredibly more than this. In the Church there is moral and juridical collaboration for a common end; yet " this collaboration is supplemented by another internal principle, which exists effectively in the whole and in each of its parts, and whose existence is such that of itself it is vastly superior to whatever bonds of union may be found in a physical or moral body. As we said above, this is something not of the natural but of the supernatural order; rather it is something in itself infinite: the Spirit of God, who, as the Angelic Doctor says, " numerically one and the same, fills and unites the whole Church."

At first glance, this sentence might be disappointing to anyone looking for a revelation of the profound reality of the Church, the Mystical Body of Christ. We acknowledge the intimate role of the Holy Spirit in the life of the Church; He is the soul of the Church, and yet He is not the Church, not the Mystical Body of Christ in its created reality. Is the Holy Father suggesting that the whole reality that is called Mystical Body is simply dependent on the moment-to-moment unifying action of the Spirit? Yet what he says is clearly true— whatever reality the Church has, flows from the all-pervasive presence of the Spirit. The Holy Father closed with a quotation taken from St. Thomas; [11] in fact, the whole point he is making is taken from St. Thomas. While I do not wish to presume that the following developments are cloaked in the authority of the Holy Father, on the basis of this one quotation, I do think that it may be profitable for our present discussion if I expand on one word in that quotation, " unites," " he unites the whole Church."

In his writings, St. Thomas approaches the unity of the

[11] *Summa Theologiae*, II-II, q. 39, a. 1.

Church from three distinct, yet not completely separable elements in the reality of the Church. In his Exposition of the Creed,[12] he places the cause of unity within the Church as one Body, of which the Spirit is the soul, in the three theological virtues: in the unity of faith, for all Christians who are of the Body of the Church believe the same; in the unity of hope, for all stand firm in the one hope of attaining eternal life; in the unity of love, for all are linked in the love of God and in love for one another, which when genuine manifests itself in a solicitous and compassionate service of one another.

In this passage, St. Thomas is touching the inner being of the Church, the intrinsic form that gives vitality to the Church, the principal formal effect of the indwelling Spirit; the life of faith, hope and love is God's life shared by men. But is he touching the unique being of the Church as the Mystical Body of Christ on earth. We willingly acknowledge that true faith, hope and charity exist in men, who are not baptized, likewise in men, who are baptized and yet are not in the unity of the Church.

One further point: although St. Thomas is presenting the most hidden aspect of the being of the Church, there is a strong suggestion in the text that this must be made visible, that it is visible in the open profession of one faith and one hope, in the mutual service of all the members.

With regard to the last point, there is a possibly significant statement by St. Thomas in this same work, in the article, "the communion of saints," or rather, as he understands it, the "communion or communication of holy things." [13] It reads: "And because all the faithful are one body, the good of one is communicative to another. . . . Among other members of the Church, Christ is the principal member, because he is the Head, according to Ephesians 1.22: 'And him he gave as head over all the Church, which indeed is his body.'" To the mind of St. Thomas, the reality of the Church, as the

---

[12] *Opuscula Omnia*, ed. Mandonnet. Vol. IV, pp. 378-9.
[13] *Op. cit.*, p. 381.

Mystical Body of which Christ is Head and the faithful are the members, is presupposed to the communication of spiritual goods and is not constituted by such interchange; the Church " is " before she " does." There is, then, a profound " communication," below the level of giving and receiving, of action and passion.

The second approach to the unity of the Church is found in the *Contra Gentiles*. It is an extraordinary presentation of an aspect of the Church that is causing so much reflection today—the juridical aspect. The context is the four chapters on the sacrament of Orders, immediately, the nature of episcopal power and especially the primacy of one bishop in relation to the unique oneness of the Church.

Clearly, then, the chief direction of the faithful belong to the bishops. But this, too, is clear: Although people are set apart according to differing dioceses and states, yet, as the Church is one, so must the Christian people be one. Therefore, as for the specific congregation of one Church one bishop is called for who is the head of that Church; so for the entire Christian people there must be one who is the head of the entire Church.

Then, too, the unity of the Church requires that all the faithful agree as to the faith. But about matters of faith it happens that questions arise. A diversity of pronouncements, of course, would divide the Church, if it were not preserved in unity by the pronouncement of one. Therefore, the unity of the Church demands that there be one who is at the head of the entire Church. . . .

No one should doubt, furthermore, that the government of the Church has been established in the best way, since He has disposed it by whom " kings reign, and lawmakers decree just things " (*Prov.* 8:15). But the best government of a multitude is rule by one, and this is clear from the purpose of government, which is peace; for peace and the unity of his subjects are the purpose of the one who rules, and one is a better constituted cause of unity than many.[14]

We must beware of dismissing this notion of St. Thomas too lightly. I do not think that anyone will seriously main-

---

[14] The citations from the *Contra Gentiles* are from the series *On the Truth of the Catholic Faith*, Bk. IV, c. 76, pp. 290-291.

tain that anarchy is the rule in the Church of God. There is
some form of government and we can understand it only in
terms of our historical experience. There is no question but
that the concept of a monarchical episcopate has been accepted in the Church since before the time of Ignatius of
Antioch. Above all, we must not allow the historical modes
in which authority in the Church has been used and abused
to distort our consideration of it. A kingdom established by
Christ and ruled by his Spirit should be able to preserve order,
unity and peace through the exercise of authority, and excellence through the opportunities for all to rise to the challenge of Christian idealism—freedom through love.

The militant Church, moreover, derives from the triumphant
Church by exemplarity. . . . But in the triumphant Church one
presides, the one who presides over the entire universe—namely,
God—for we read in the *Apocalypse* 21:2: 'They shall be His people and God Himself with them shall be their God.' Therefore, in
the militant Church, also, there is one who presides over things
universally.[15]

Today, we would prefer to speak of the Church as the
eschatological ikon of the heavenly Church.

While the papal power is the vital organ of the visible, historical unity of the Church, it is obviously only an organ
and not the one body of the Church. Have we exhausted St.
Thomas' thought? By no means. The final key is found in
his notion of the sin of schism.[16] We should be alerted to
something special by the fact that St. Thomas places schism

---

[15] Cf. Stephen E. Donlon, S. J., "The Monarchical Episcopate: Its Development
and Significance," in *Chicago Studies* II (Spring, 1963) 1. Summarizing the conclusions of Jean Colson in his *Les Functions ecclesiales aux deux premiers siècles,*
the author writes: "The union between bishops and community, says Colson, is
so strict that the bishop is, so to speak, the incarnation of his church. He sums
it up; he is the image of its living unity which he creates around him. . . . He
is the pole of unity about which all is solidly centered and ordered and unified:
one God, one Christ, one temple, one altar, one Eucharist, one Spirit and Body,
one faith, one hope, one love. To achieve this unity one bishop stands at the head
of the corona of priest and of the community." p. 73.

[16] *Loc. cit.,* aa. 1, 2.

among the sins against charity, as opposed precisely to peace. "Peace" is traditionally almost a technical name for the oneness of the Church, which the faithful have always looked upon as one of the most precious elements in the reality of the Church.[17]

St. Thomas immediately identifies "peace" with "unity"; schism is a special kind of sin by which one intends to separate oneself from unity which charity realizes. The phrasing is important; St. Thomas never says simply that schism is opposed to charity.

In the first article he says that it is opposed to the unity of ecclesiatical unity.[18] In the body of the article, he explains that it is not just a question of personal relationships, which should unite the faithful with the bond of spiritual love, but the charity which binds the whole Church in the unity of the Spirit. In other words, it is a unity that is produced by the Charity who is the Holy Spirit himself. This is "the principal union," since all particular unions within the Church are ordered to the unity of the Church.

This unity of the Church, he continues, is realized: 1) in the linking of the members of the Church to each other, in "communication"; 2) and in the ordering of all the members to one head; this Head is Jesus Christ, whose vicar in the Church is the Supreme Pontiff. This article concludes with the words we cited at the beginning of this paper, which are echoed in Canon Law. From what we have seen of St. Thomas' thought, we can appreciate why he joins the two elements with an "and." Schismatics are rebellious against the Church in its hidden and most profound reality as well as against its visible manifestation and protective organ.

Having determined that schism is a special kind of sin, St. Thomas, in the second article, brings up a question that recurs

[17] "The reward for those 'in peace' can never come to men who have broken the peace of the Lord by the frenzy of dissent." *The Unity of the Catholic Church.* Trans. by M. Benevot, S. J. *Ancient Christian Writers,* No. 25 (Westminster, Md.: Newman Press, 1957), p. 54. Cf. n. 96.

[18] *Op. cit.,* a. 1, ad 3um.

whenever he discusses virtue and vice. His concern for the dignity of a virtue or the malice of a vice may seem academic to some, but the fact is that such discussion throws considerable light on the precise nature of the virtue or vice. This is especially true in regard to vices, for, since they are privations, losses, they can be understood only in terms of the good which is lost.

St. Thomas discusses the comparative malice of the sins of infidelity and schism. His discussion is, incidentally, a good example of his concern to include both essential and existential considerations. The principle he uses here and elsewhere is that the gravity of a particular sin may be judged both according to its specific malice, that is, according to the precise good it opposes and according to the existential circumstances in which it is committed. Now, since circumstances are particular and can vary infinitely, when one asks in a general way about the comparative gravity of two sins, the question must be taken to refer to the specific character of the sins in question. Under this distinction, one could include the case of anyone, who, in virtue of the circumstances of complete good faith, is entirely free of the malice of the sin of schism and yet the victim of its formal effect—separation from communication with the members of the Church in union with the See of Peter. Here it would not at all be a question of the sin of schism, but of a state or condition of schism.

Getting back to a comparison of the specific malice of infidelity and schism, infidelity is clearly a graver sin, since it is opposed to the greater good. There are two goods involved: God himself, as First Truth, who is the object of faith; the participated good which is ecclesiastical unity. There can be no question but that the privation of a divine good is greater than the privation of a created good. The created good involved is a common good, *bonum multitudinis*, yet it is infinitely inferior to the divine Common Good itself. On the other hand, of *all* created goods, the good of ecclesiastical unity is the greatest good of men, hence schism is the greatest sin against love of neighbor (and, may we add, the state of schism is the greatest evil that can befall men who believe in and love God and the Lord Jesus Christ).

In view of the importance of this question for our contemporary concerns, we feel justified in reproducing somewhat in detail the reflections of Cardinal Cajetan on this teaching of St. Thomas.[19]

That he recognizes the importance of what St. Thomas is saying is clear from his initial statement: here we are dealing with the very being of the Church, for *unum sequitur ens*, one follows upon being, that is, in reality one and being are identical; the ratio of *one* adds nothing to the ratio of *being* except a negation of division. There is no being that is not one; each kind of being has its own kind of oneness. So to ask about the oneness of anything is to ask about its very being.

Cajetan approches the unity of the Church with three questions prompted by facts in the life of the Church admitted by all.

The Questions:

1. What precisely is the unity that schism opposes? Is anything destroyed by schism except the relation of subjection to one head? It would seem not. The being (*esse*) of faith, of hope, of sacraments and worship can coexist with schism. On the other hand, the being of charity is destroyed, indirectly by any mortal sin, directly only by hatred or contempt, neither of which is the sin of schism.

2) Nevertheless, schism is looked upon as a sin against charity; but how can it be? Schism seems to destroy something that does not depend upon charity: anyone in the state of mortal sin can also commit the sin of schism. Perhaps, after all, schism is simply a sin of disobedience, a refusal of submission to the Holy See.

3) Besides, how can schism destroy the unity of the Church? The unity of the Church cannot be destroyed, unless there

---

[19] *Commentarium in Summam Theol.*, II-II, q. 39.

can be many Churches, or the Church of Christ can cease to
exist before the end of the world, for the unity is the being
of the Church.

The Answers:

In seeking to determine as carefully as possible the mysterious being of the Church, Cajetan passes swiftly through
the traditional categories of created being, easily dismissing
substance, quantity, quality and the other five that close the
list. That leaves: 1) action and passion; 2) relation. In other
words, he is left with the question: is the reality of the Church
in the category of action and passion or in the category of relation? Since we are contemplating (however analytically) a
reality that embraces the God-Man, Jesus Christ and the
human persons who are one body with him, perhaps we may
be permitted to translate Cajetan's terminology as follows:
does the reality of the Church consist solely in intersubjective
relations or in relations that are objective, binding the Head
and the members in one being, independently of the subjective relations existing at any one moment? [20]

Cajetan points out that there is a kind of unity among
the faithful insofar as they all believe one truth, hope for one
good, love one Being, the Triune God, and possess the same
sacraments. But this is a unity of likeness, not of being. (We
pointed out earlier that this likeness is shared by those who
are not united to the Church.)

There is also the unity of headship, Christ in heaven, his
vicar on earth. By virtue of the relation to one Head and his
vicar, and the interaction between them and the members,
there is a unity; all are under one, like several kingdoms under
one sovereign; but they are not thereby one being. (In this
connection, we should note that simple disobedience to the Supreme Pontiff is not necessarily a sin of schism.)

As he approaches the final unity in which he discerns the
radical being of the Church, Cajetan, in an almost uncon-

---

[20] Cf. *supra* pp. 194-195.

scious witness to the mystery of the reality, shifts his attention to a single member of the faithful, in order to show that the reality of the Church is the interrelation of all the faithful. Accordingly, each one of the faithful is the subject of a relation (*esse relativum*—a predicamental relation), which is real and objective. This relation constitutes him a part of a numerically one people, city, house; through this relation he is dependent for his existence as a member upon the whole.

The Holy Spirit, the all-pervading soul of this whole, moves each of the faithful to works that are interior or exterior as parts of one reality, for the sake of the one reality, according to the requirements of that one reality, which is the Church of God. Each of the faithful believes that he is a member of the Church and as a member of the Church he believes, hopes, loves, administers and receives the sacraments, teaches, learns, etc.; he does all things for the Church, as a part of the whole (*cujus est quidquid est*); and he does all things according to the faith and tradition of the Church.

This unity is a supreme good (*summum bonum*), not absolutely, but in the order of good for our neighbor and ourselves; it is a good of the whole world, a spiritual good, essential, principal; it is the very being of the Church as it is one thing.

And, he adds, the most perfect sign of this reality of the Church is a General Council!

There were two other questions that Cajetan raised at the beginning of his reflections, the answers to which may be of help to those of our contemporaries who are pulled between their love of the Church and their love for those outside the Church.

Is schism a sin against charity? No, it is a sin against an effect of charity. To understand this, we will have to be more explicit than Cajetan is in this passage. The unity of the Church is not the effect of charity in the hearts of its members; it is an effect of the Charity who is the Spirit of Love himself; unity is the primary formal effect constituting the Body of Christ as numerically one reality. But is not every effect of the Spirit in the Church an effect of Charity? Of course, but this effect, the unity of the Body, the *pax* of the Church, is brought into being for the sole purpose of being the image of the oneness of the Father, Son and Holy Spirit, of the love of the Father for Jesus Christ, of the love of Jesus Christ for all men. If the one Body, the one Church is a common good, if it is the supreme good, that apart from God himself, God has prepared for men, then it is, in an unique way, an effect of the Spirit of unitive Love and Loving Union.

This fact is behind the point that Cajetan is making when he states that the preservation of union within the Church can be an " unformed " effect of charity; that is, a man who commits a mortal sin, say, of theft, does not thereby commit a sin against the unity of the Church, just as a husband who commits a mortal sin does not become unfaithful to his marriage union. The good of unity, either of the Church or the marriage, though intrinsically supernatural, can be effectively embraced and maintained by someone who is in the state of serious sin. Again going beyond Cajetan, we may say that the good of unity may be lacking in one who has charity but is not in common with the bishops and faithful of the Catholic Church.

In answer to the third question, Cajetan replies that, although the formal schismatic intends to destroy the unity of the Church, all he accomplishes is to separate himself and his followers from that union.

What then is the ratio of *member of the Church, of the Mystical Body of Christ?* It is a human being in whom there inheres by power of the Holy Spirit a real relation whereby he is objectively linked to Jesus Christ as Head and to all other human persons who are of the Mystical Body of Christ. Note that, insofar as Jesus Christ is a member of the Mystical Body, namely, the Head, therefore, as man, He is really related to all His members. The foundation of this real relation is the action of Christ, as the human instrument of the divinity, in Baptism, incorporating a man into himself by imprinting the character of his priesthood upon him and at the same time causing the real relation that constitutes the reality of his Mystical Body and infusing regenerative grace into the soul. In the administration and reception of Baptism in the way fully intended by Christ, there are three effects produced— the character, the real relation, the grace. From all that we have said above, it is clear that these three effects are separable. An adult receiving Baptism in the Church with an attachment to serious sin, would receive the character, the real relation, but not the grace. A baptized Catholic who committed a formal sin of schism would lose grace and the real relation, but retain the character.

Would it be correct to maintain that a person baptized in a schismatic sect would, if in bad faith, receive the character, but not the relation nor the grace? If in good faith, would he receive the character and grace, but not the real relation? This is the position of St. Augustine.[21] As there can be valid baptism without the Spirit, that is, without grace, so there can be valid baptism without the Church.

What, in the final analysis, is involved here is the sacramentality of the Church. We are well aware of the fact that we have been using the word " sacrament " much too narrowly, confining it to the sacremental rite. We are beginning to appreciate the " sacramentality " of the presence on the altar of the Victim Christ under the species of one bread and one cup that may be shared by the many who are one body. The sacramental grace of the Eucharist is precisely ordered, not just to nourishing the individual Christian, but to preserving and making more and more visible the one Mystical Christ. The bond of matrimony is the " sacrament " of the union of

---

[21] " Quemadmodum autem Spiritum Sanctum habent filii dilecti, non habent filii maligni, et tamen Baptismum habent; sic et Ecclesiam sicut habent catholici, non habent haeretici et tamen Baptismum habent . . . Itaque sicut potest Baptisma esse et unde se aufert Spiritus Sanctus; ita etiam potest esse Baptisma, ubi non est Ecclesia." *De Baptismo,* I, 5, PL 43, 193; cited in *Enciclopedia Cattolica,* III, c. 756.

Christ and his Church; the sacramental grace of matrimony is ordered to making this bond visible.[22]

So everything in the Church is " sacramental," including the juridical relations between the members. How else, by what other kind of being, could men be visibly joined together except by juridical bonds? This sacramentality of the major juridical bond—submission of all the bishops and their faithful to the vicar of Christ on earth is magnificently stated by St. Thomas:

> But let one say that the one head and the one shepherd is Christ, who is one spouse of one Church; his answer does not suffice. For, clearly, Christ Himself perfects all the sacraments of the Church: it is He who baptizes; it is He who forgives sins; it is He, the true priest, who offered Himself on the altar of the cross, and by whose power His body is daily consecrated on the altar—nevertheless, because He was not going to be with the faithful in bodily presence, He chose ministers to dispense the things just mentioned to the faithful. . . . By the same reasoning, then, when He was going to withdraw His bodily presence from the Church, He had to commit it to one who would in His place have the care of the universal Church. Hence it is that He said to Peter before His ascension: " Feed my sheep " (Jn. 21:17) ; and before His passion: " Thou being once converted confirm thy brethren " (Luke 2:32) ; and to him alone (i. e., as an individual) did He promise: " I will give to thee the keys of the kingdom of heaven " (Matt. 16:19), in order to show that the power of the keys was to flow through him to others to preserve the unity of the Church.[23]

[22] Vd. " The Sacramental Grace of Matrimony," James M. Egan, O. P. in *Proceedings CTSA*, 1956.
[23] *The Truth of the Catholic Faith*, Bk. IV, pp. 291-292.

This is in line with the strong words of St. Cyprian (who did not always strongly adhere to their implications):

> God is one, and Christ is one, and His Church is one: one is the faith, and one the people cemented together by harmony into the strong unity of a body. That unity cannot be split; that one body cannot be divided by any cleavage of its structure, nor cut up in fragments with its vital elements torn apart.

JAMES M. EGAN, O. P.,

St. Mary's College
  Notre Dame, Ind.

THE MEMBERS OF THE CHURCH *

∽

THE word " church " does not always convey the same meaning in Sacred Scripture. At times it is applied to the people of Israel wandering through the desert,[1] at other times to a Christian society of domestic characteristics[2] or, of greater extension, to that of a city[3] or a region.[4] The term is also applied to the society of all the children of God redeemed by Jesus Christ and established on the foundation composed of the apostles.[5] Frequently in the Sacred Books allusion is made to the reality signified by " church " through the use of a considerable number of metaphors: flock,[6] vineyard,[7] house of God,[8] heavenly Jerusalem,[9] spouse.[10] We cannot make an indifferent attribution of all these names to the Church without falling into complete theological nominalism. Yet this is a matter of metaphor, and metaphors necessarily have a *partial* content:[11] each metaphor sets in relief a particular detail about the true Church.

Among such metaphors is that of *body*, possibly the most frequently employed by St. Paul. Men united with Christ constitute a body of which He is *the head* and we, *the members*. With this we are already interpreting the terms in the title of this article. Speaking of the members of the Church is the same as speaking about parts of the Church by reason of its existence as a body. And since the Church is a *mystical* and *social* body, to give an adequate answer to any question about members of the Church, it will be necessary to speak about

---

* Translated by C. F. Lehner, O. P.

[1] *Acts* 7:38.
[2] *Rom.* 16:4-5.
[3] *Acts* 8:1.
[4] *Acts* 9:31; *1 Cor.* 16:19.
[5] *Acts* 20:28; *1 Cor.* 12:28.
[6] *John* 10:9 sq.
[7] *John* 15:1-6.
[8] *1 Peter* 2:5; *1 Tim.* 3:15.
[9] *Gal.* 4:26-31.
[10] *Ephes.* 5:25-27.
[11] *Summa Theol.* Ia, q. 33, a. 3; IIIa, q. 8, a. 1, ad 2um.

those who belong to it inasmuch as it is a mystical body as well a social body.

A further determination is also necessary. The expression "mystical body," which nowadays entails the twofold characteristic of being *mystical* and *social*, that is, vital and intimate on the one hand, and external and visible on the other, has had another meaning when applied to the Church of Peter in the patristic and theological tradition. Again when speaking about the members, one must determine the meaning which "body" has with regard to both attribution and predication.

First of all, here on earth during the centuries preceding the coming of Jesus Christ, the mystical body was a reality having only an intimate and recondite character. Even now it continues to be this reality in a way which transcends the earth. It is the body made up of all those who are in vital union with Christ through the grace which comes from Him and through Him without the mediation of an institutional organism. This body had on the earth, and today has beyond this earth, broader limits than those which we shall presently indicate for the Church of Peter.

Secondly, the mystical body is circumscribed in both space and time—the space being that of earth and the time extending from Jesus Christ until the end of the world. In addition to being intimate and recondite, or supernaturally alive, it is also social. Thus, to belong to it, one needs something besides union with Christ through grace. To attain social incorporation in Christ, one needs the mediation of the ecclesiastical society; therefore, no one can be a member in this second sense of mystical body without being also a member of the society in which this mystical body is, as it were, incarnate.

From what has been said it should be clear that the problem of membership in the Church, or in the mystical body of Christ, has two distinct perspectives which permit of their own proper solutions.

The Members of the Church in the First Sense. To make a proper confrontation and resolution of the problem about these members, we must not lose sight of the following truths: first, the redemption accomplished by Christ is universal and reaches all men, from Adam to the last of his descendants; secondly, in the present order of providence, there is no grace coming to men from heaven which is not Christian, which does not come through Christ, and which is not related to Him; thirdly, all grace is sanctifying or supernaturally vivifying in some way or other. Some graces have this characteristic in the plan of preparation: they do not sanctify, but they prepare the way for other graces to sanctify. We refer to charisms, the graces *gratis datae*, actual graces. Other graces, however, have this characteristic in the scheme of accomplishment: they sanctify in fact. We refer to habitual grace and the infused virtues.

If all of this is due to Christ, if all is sanctifying or vital and, therefore, elevates the implied capacity, and incorporates in a vital way, and if, on one or another level, it reached all of the just persons of the Old Testament and reaches all of those who today are not on earth, there is an easy explanation for the usual statements found in Scripture, in patristic and theological tradition, and in the ordinary language of the faithful. In fact, St. Paul speaking of a headship in Christ referred, not only to the just who now live here on earth, but to all men wherever they live and of whatever time they may be. This is not only a headship of order and perfection, but it is also one in the communication of redemptive grace.[12] The Apostle also notes the comparison between the second Adam and the first, while affirming the superabundance of good granted by Christ.[13]

Agreeing with these affirmations of the Apostle, the Fathers speak about the *universal* Church or the Church *which begins in Abel*.[14] The whole human race has belonged to this Church from the very beginning. Such a teaching is also supported

[12] *Col.* 1:18 sq.
[13] *Rom.* 5 passim.
[14] S. Gregory, M., PL 76, 1154.

by this statement of St. Thomas Aquinas: " Like us, the ancient Fathers belonged to the body of the Church." [15] The faithful do not merely recognize one Church, namely, that established here on earth by Christ, which they call " militant." They also speak of the " Church suffering " and the " Church triumphant." In purgatory there is grace, and it comes from Christ. In heaven there is glory, and it comes from Christ. In both places there is vital incorporation with Him. The souls and the blessed are His members.

On the basis of this statement, we must conclude that all the men living on earth before the establishment of the present Church were members of a *universal* Church, or mystical body, the members of which are incorporated into Christ without the mediation of the social institution which is the Church of Peter. Even today all those in heaven and in purgatory are its members.

To understand this truth, we must resort to a teaching of classical theology. In so doing, we would observe that there is a tendency not to use the great teachers of the past in the measure of their value. In the present case, St. Thomas has left us in an article of the *Summa* a teaching which has not become outmoded. Rather it has a profound content of perennial value. We refer to his distinction between *actual* and *potential* members.

The expression " potential member " does not mean that this is a matter of mere logical or objective potency, a non-repugnance or non-impossibility. It means that one possesses a real, authentic principle the fulfillment of which is nevertheless potential. A *potential* member is one who, although not having supernatural life whereby he is vitally incorporated, yet has *something* which, when used well, will lead him to achieve this incorporation. This *something* is the potency. And, according to St. Thomas, it embraces several elements of which we shall speak later.

The blessed are *actual* members of this universal Church or

[15] *Summa Theol.* IIIa, q. 8, a. 3, ad 3um.

mystical body. They are those most intimately incorporated with Christ; from Him they receive the supernatural element which makes them blessed. The souls in purgatory and just persons living on earth before Christ's coming, as long as they lived on earth, were also actual members of the Church. All others are potential members. Each person possesses at least a juridical title, a moral title, and an ontological title—three realities ordering them to the possession of sanctifying grace, whereby they would be changed into actual members provided they used these well. We refer to the *right* to grace which all possess by the very fact of being redeemed. (Those living before Christ were already redeemed in divine acceptation, although Christ had not yet come.) We refer also to the *ordination* of all their ethically good acts to their supernatural end, namely, salvation.[16] They were ignorant of this destiny, but God was not ignorant of it. Since in actual providence there is not a natural but only a supernatural end, and since God never prescinds from the ultimate end, it follows that He ordered such good acts of pagans to this end. Finally, we refer to the *divine impulse* which moved them to perform ethically good acts, an impulse which was an actual grace proportionate to the end to which God ordained their acts. Thus we have three titles: juridical, which we have called " right "; moral, which we have called " ordination "; and ontological, which we have called " impulse." These were authentic realities which, well utilized, could have brought the person to the possession of habitual or sanctifying grace. Therefore such a person can be regarded as a potential member of the Church.

The Members of the Mystical Body in the Second Sense. With the establishment of the Church of Peter, however, a modification is introduced. From that time on, what has just been indicated becomes insufficient for membership in the mystical body here on earth. For incorporation with Christ and membership in His mystical body, putting oneself in direct communication with Christ is not enough. This must rather

---

[16] St. Thomas, *In I Sent.*, dist. 46, q. 1, a. 1.

be done through the social institution in which He sought to incarnate supernatural life. To be an actual member, or to have sanctifying grace, men must belong, in some way, to the society of Peter. And this is true even if they are only potential members, since they must bear some relation to this society.

All this follows because Christ willed that, once the Church of Peter was established, it would be the depositary and administrator of two divine elements which give supernatural life to men on earth. Divine truth and grace are in this Church, and this Church administers them. From this it also follows that, to be incorporated into Christ, one must belong to this Church. The affirmation is serious, but certain. It is based upon the teachings of the Gospel, repeated by a constant tradition, and insistently recognized by the magisterium.

Peter is the rock upon which the Church is built,[17] and the apostles are with him.[18] Moreover, concerning this Church of Peter, the Lord says that it has His presence for guaranteeing divine truth,[19] and that it is the possessor and administrator of grace.[20] Without Peter there is no guarantee of divine truth nor is there divine, sanctifying grace. This is equivalent to saying that, without him, there is no mystical body, inasmuch as the reality of this body consists in union with Christ through the direction (knowledge) and the motion (charity) which goes down into the members from the head.

Two pontifical documents have recently brought this revealed and traditional truth to mind.

For the definition and description of this true Church of Christ, which is the holy, Catholic, apostolic, Roman Church, there is nothing nobler, nothing more excellent, nothing more divine than that phrase whereby it is called the mystical body of Christ—an expression which springs and, as it were, germinates from what is frequently taught in the Sacred Writings and the writings of the Holy Fathers.[21]

[17] *Matt.* 16:18.   [18] *Ephes.* 2:20.   [19] *Luke* 22:32.
[20] *Matt.* 16:19; *Luke* 10:16.
[21] *Mystici Corporis*, AAS. XXXV (1943), 199.

Thus speaks the Encyclical Letter *Mystici Corporis*. And *Humani generis* insists upon this, since, among the dangerous fruits of new currents in theology, Pius XII includes:

[Persons who] do not deem themselves obligated to embrace the teaching which we expounded in an encyclical some years ago and which is based on the sources of revelation, according to which the mystical body of Christ and the Catholic Church are one and the same thing.[22]

Yet, what type of identification is involved here? It is very clear that this is not a matter of *formal* but of *material* identification. It does not involve inseparable conjunction in one identical subject. In other words, what is mystical or vital in the Church, namely, the graces of Christ, and what is social, that is, characteristic of the Church of Peter, are not two elements which are really the same, since grace also existed in the universal Church of which we have just spoken. This matter is clear. Yet these two elements are, in an inseparable manner, in one identical collective subject, namely, the Church of Peter, in such a way that this Church alone possesses the two characteristics. There is, then, an identity of subject (material identity) with a distinction in value (formal distinction.) This interpretation is demanded by the very theological data which are involved: graces, which constitute the first characteristic; and social elements, which constitute the second characteristic. Moreover, this interpretation is confirmed by the structure of the first two parts of the encyclical *Mystici Corporis*, as well as by the very words of this encyclical, which condemn a distinction of opposition, but not a distinction of coincidence.[23]

This means that the problem about membership in this mystical body on earth can be approached from two points of view. Since the body is mystical or recondite inasmuch as it possesses grace, and social or visible inasmuch as it possesses an institutional character, it follows that incorporation can be

---

[22] *Humani generis, AAS.* XLII (1959), 571.
[23] AAS. XXXV (1943), 224.

appreciated from the first point of view (namely, that of grace) or the second (namely, that of the social aspect Understand that we are not resolving the problem by saying that some are members of the soul of the Church and others of its body. We are speaking of the members of the mystical body of Christ here on earth; and this body is the Church of Peter, such as the Lord established it. He established it as mystical and social, and whoever does not belong to it with these two specific notes does not belong to the Church of Peter. Consequently, whoever pertains to it in the mystical aspect belongs also to the social part; otherwise they would not be members of the mystical body of the Lord, which is precisely social. And since this is the only mystical body possessing grace, it follows that they would not belong to any mystical body. Moreover, whoever belongs to it through the social part in any way belongs also to the mystical part. Summarily, one is simultaneously a member of the recondite and visible, or one is not a member at all.

Here it is opportune to recall the theological doctrine on the *votum*, the desire, tendency, or ordination. This is a teaching which has many applications in theology. At times, this desire or ordination is *personal*, because it consists in an explicit act of the will or because it is implied in another act of the same potency. For example, the catechumen who wants to be baptized has an explicit personal desire. The pagan who wants to fulfill God's will completely has an implicit and unconscious personal desire for baptism, since it is God's will that he be baptized. At other times the desire or ordination is only *real*. This is not associated with the personal will of the person to whom it is attributed, but *with things within him*. Since things, too, can have an ordination or tendency to something, they can have a *votum*. Thus, for example, in the actual order of providence, healing grace has a *votum* for elevating grace, since the former is not separated from the latter; baptism has a *votum* for the Eucharist; the real presence of the Lord's Body in virtue of the words of the consecration of the bread has a *votum* for the presence of His Blood, etc.

On the basis of the foregoing explanations, we can classify the members of the mystical body of Christ here on earth, and explain how each of the members about whom we shall speak is a member.

Some are *real and perfect* members of the mystical body according to the two aspects of which we have just spoken. They are perfectly incorporated into Christ in a vital manner, since they live in grace; and this they have done through a real and perfect incorporation with the social body which, here on earth, possesses and administers grace, since they make the profession of faith, receive the sacraments, and are subject to the hierachy of Peter and the bishops.

Some are *real* members of the mystical body under the first aspect, since they possess grace, but are intentional or *in voto* members under the second aspect, since they have the social aspect merely by way of desire. This desire is conscious in some, namely, catechumens, and unconscious in others, namely, those pagans who, fulfilling the natural law and being disposed to fulfill God's will in all matters, have received sanctifying grace from Him.[24]

Some are *real* members of the mystical body under the social aspect, and only intentional or *in voto* members under the vital aspect, namely, those who live within the Church, but not in the state of grace. They possess the sacramental character, for example, as a divine reality which, although not sanctifying them, is ordered to grace actuating it in its proper domain. Submission to the hierarchy and the profession of faith likewise have an ordination to grace.

Some are *real* members of the mystical body in a *perfect* manner under the vital aspect, since they live in grace, and in an *imperfect* manner under the social aspect, since they possess something of this, but not everything. Through what they have, they belong really, too; as regards what they lack, they belong only *in voto*. We refer to the separated brethren.

---

[24] Denz. 1677; *Mystici Corporis,* AAS. XXXV (1943), 243.

Some of these have a partial external profession of faith, and some of the sacraments. Others have the complete faith and all the sacraments, as well as a hierarchy, although this is truncated. In the measure wherein they possess these things, they are real members; in the measure wherein they are lacking, they are intentional members, since what they possess tends to and is ordered to completion regarding what is lacking.

In short, there is no longer any church other than that of Peter. There is no longer any mystical body on earth other than the Church of Peter. It is the possessor and administrator of grace. Yet grace lives in many persons who are separated from this Church. It lives in them because, consciously or unconsciously, they are related to the one Church.

EMILIO SAURAS, O. P.

Real Convento de Predicadores
Valencia, Spain

ST. THOMAS ON THE MEMBERSHIP
OF THE CHURCH

∾

IN assessing the influence of the encyclical *Mystici cor-*
poris it appears particularly worthy of note that, whereas
theologians have had no difficulty in recognizing the
major theme of the letter as common teaching, one detail has,
on the contrary, had the positive effect, not merely of controlling theological development, but of actually changing its
direction, as far as a large number of theologians are concerned. The encyclical's statement on membership of the
Church and on the conditions in which such membership is
realized has led to a wide-scale revision of theological views.
What is curious about this is not, of course, the fact that
theologians take their lead from what they judge to be papal
teaching. But the paradoxical situation has arisen in which
common theological principles concerning the nature of the
Church have been seen to be confirmed by the encyclical and,
at the same time, what was held by a sizeable number of theologians to be an application of these principles now appears
to stand in need of revision. To Thomists it cannot but seem
curious also that the teaching of St. Thomas appears, at least
to some, to fall within the area ear-marked for revision. The
assumption which has given rise to this situation is, as is well
known, that Pius XII defined membership in purely juridical
terms: external profession of the Catholic faith, reception of
the sacrament of baptism and submission to the Vicar of
Christ.[1] Taken in conjunction with the clear affirmation of
the identity which exists between the Roman Catholic Church
and the mystical body of Christ, this definition has been interpreted as restricting membership of the mystical body of

[1] Denz-Schönmetzer 3802 (=Denz 2286).

Christ to those recognized as Roman Catholics who have not left the Church and have not been excommunicated.

While it may legitimately be urged that theologians ought to abandon presuppositions arising from particular theological systems when they are confronted with plain statements of the teaching authority, it is no less mandatory for them to attempt to uncover the inner coherence of such statements. In the present case the paradox is not one which affects only the situation of individual theologians; it is one which, on the supposition that the definition of membership is indeed exclusively juridical, is inherent in the text of the encyclical itself. The principal thesis of the letter is that the Church or mystical body is not a purely juridical entity, that it is animated by a spiritual life which derives from the Holy Spirit. It is from this principle that the theologian must demonstrate that the particular conclusion concerning membership derives. Because it appears particularly difficult to discover a logical connection between a definition of the Church which, to be adequate, must include both spiritual and external elements, and a description of the conditions of membership which takes account only of external factors, an obvious methodological procedure is to raise the question whether Pius XII did in fact define membership in purely juridical terms. It is common knowledge that St. Robert Bellarmine did propose such a definition. If it could be established that Pius XII adopted his teaching then our methodological doubt at least would be solved; but, in spite of the assertions of St. Robert's school, no hint is given in the encyclical itself that this is the case.

One account of Church membership which formerly enjoyed favour among theologians was specifically ruled out by *Mystici corporis*. The distinction between soul and body of the Church, understood in such fashion that the soul is of wider extension than the body, may no longer be maintained. Though the distinction was certainly not one used by St. Thomas in these terms, it had been widely adopted by Thomists for, on its face value, it appeared to express his teaching

on membership. The fact that this terminology has had to
be abandoned as failing to do justice to the reality of the
Church does not necessarily mean that all of what Thomists
were trying to express with terms now seen to be defective
was itself untenable. It has been too quickly concluded by
some writers that to affirm that soul and body are co-terminous is equivalent to affirming that only those whose membership of the body is juridically verifiable belong to the organism. The first statement may equally well be interpreted in
the sense that those formerly thought of as belonging to the
soul of the Church and not to the body must now be regarded
as belonging in some fashion to the body.

Whether such an interpretation is justified is a matter for
theological discussion. If such discussion is to be feasible there
must be a preliminary understanding that necessary insistence on the juridical aspect of the Church and on the juridical qualifications for membership is very far from being the
same thing as adopting purely juridical criterions for deciding
who in fact is a member. It is quite open to anyone to argue
that membership of a juridically constituted society must be
juridically verifiable; but it should also be admitted that
others have a right to think that such an argument when
applied without modification to the unique society of the
Church of Christ falls into the sin of univocal reasoning. The
human societies which we know and understand and which
can be circumscribed by neat legal concepts are only the start-
ing-point for our analogical knowledge of the mystery of the
Church.

The fact that several writers, particularly in the English-
speaking world, are unwilling to admit even the permissibility
of discussing the question of membership would appear to be
an indication that study of the problem in the context of the
recent papal and curial statements is still in the initial stages.
If this is so, it hardly appears likely, as far as human judgment goes, that the Council will pronounce definitively on the
matter. The effort must be made to use Pius XII's formula-

tion of Church teaching, not as a ready-made resolution of a complex problem, but as a guide for fruitful theological penetration. Here the Thomist tradition has a very positive contribution to make. In what follows the attempt is made to suggest what the general orientation of this contribution might be. I have preferred to rely exclusively on the text of St. Thomas, leaving aside the commentators, ancient and modern. I hope to show that St. Thomas' concept of membership of the Church, "spiritual" though it is in its essentials, takes full account of the juridical structure of the Roman Catholic Church and thereby qualifies for admittance to contemporary ecclesiology. In order to reach this conclusion the following ideas, as they are treated by St. Thomas, will be examined in turn: the Church; the Church as body of Christ; membership. This will be followed by a brief discussion of the notions of visibility and unity of the Church in the light of the conclusions on membership.[2]

I. St. Thomas' Concept of the Church

The first section of this part takes note of the principal ways in which St. Thomas uses the term " church." The second section attempts to indicate, in so far as the present question requires, St. Thomas' view of the Church of Christ.

A. *Uses of the term " church "*

Although there are places where St. Thomas uses "church" of local assemblies of the faithful, grouped under the bishop,[3] the term has for him three principal significations.

(i) *The heavenly Church.* There are two remarkable texts in which heaven is spoken of as the " true " Church (as con-

---

[2] No attempt is made in this paper to give a detailed exegesis of papal and curial documents. For this, cf. " Members of the Church: *Mystici corporis* and St. Thomas," *American Ecclesiastical Review* 148 (1963), pp. 113-128, 167-184. In the present paper I have modified the conclusions of the AER article on the baptismal character.

[3] E.g., *Summa theol.*, II-II, q. 63, a. 2, ad 4; *Ad Galatas*, cap. 1, lect. 3 (Marietti ed., [=M.] n. 33; lect. 5 (M. n. 50); cap. 2, lect. 1 (M. n. 52).

trasted with figure and image). The first occurs in the *Commentary on Ephesians*, 3:10. The mystery of Christ will be revealed to the Principalities and Powers through the Church: "not through the earthly Church, but through the heavenly, for it is there that the true Church exists, that which is our mother, towards which we are advancing, and on which our Church Militant is modelled." [4] The second text, in the *Commentary on Galatians*, 4:26, develops the idea of motherhood. The Jerusalem which is above and which is our mother "may be interpreted in two ways according as we understand this mother either as that one through whom we are born, and this is the Church Militant, or as the mother of whom we are born sons, and this is the Church Triumphant." [5]

(ii) *The Roman Catholic Church*. It is particularly important to notice that the sense in which St. Thomas most frequently uses the term "church" is the sense commonly attached to it by contemporary ecclesiologists. It is necessary to insist on this fact, obvious enough in itself, because it is of common occurrence to find St. Thomas' teaching dismissed as irrelevant on the grounds that it envisages some kind of assembly of grace, not identified with the Roman Catholic Church. The likelihood of a medieval papal theologian conceiving of the Church on earth as other than a very clearly identifiable, juridically constituted organization is remote in the extreme. St. Thomas, in any event, has expressed himself with unequivocal clarity.

He speaks of the Church as a distinct community,[6] taught by Christ,[7] founded on the Apostles.[8] This theology of office

[4] *Ad Ephesios*, cap. 3, lect. 3 (M. n. 161).

[5] *Ad Galatas*, cap. 4, lect. 8 (M. n. 264): ". . . per quam generamur [. . .] in cuius filios generamur . . ." Cf. *Summa theol.*, I-II, q. 117, a. 2, ad 1; *Ad Ephesios*, cap. 1, lect. 8 (M. n. 69).

[6] *Summa theol.*, II-II, q. 10, aa. 9, 10, 12; I-II, q. 102, a. 5, ad 2; *Ad Ephesios*, cap. 4, lect. 2 (M. n. 197).

[7] *Summa theol.*, II-II, q. 11, a. 4.

[8] *Ibid.*, I, q. 43, a. 7, ad 6; *Ad Galatas*, cap. 1, lect. 4 (M. n. 41). On the authority of the Apostles: their office of government and teaching: *I ad Cor.*, cap. 12, lect. 3 (M. n. 755) ; their authority in regard to faith: *Summa theol.*, II-II, q.

refers again and again to the Roman hierarchy,[9] noting in particular the authority of the pope in matters of faith [10] and of general discipline,[11] and the function of bishops [12] and the lower clergy.[13] The authority of the Church as a whole in teaching is likewise insisted upon,[14] as is also its general directive power.[15] It is admitted that the judgment of the Church may differ from that of God in respect of an individual's culpability.[16] In addition there is all that St. Thomas has to say on the sacraments, on the charisms,[17] on excommunication,[18] and his stray references to Church history.[19] That the organization so described should contain sinners appears sufficiently demonstrated from the very description; but St. Thomas adverts in specific terms, though rarely, to the presence of sinners in the Church.[20]

(iii) *Eadem Ecclesia.* In his commentary on *Col.*, 1:18, St. Thomas notes that the Church has a two-fold state, that of

---

174, a. 6; I-II, q. 106, a. 4, ad 2; q. 107, a. 4; *Ad Ephesios*, cap. 2, lect. 5 (M. n. 120); lect. 6 (M. n. 131).

[9] Esp. *Summa theol.*, II-II, q. 183, aa. 2, 3; q. 184, Prol.

[10] *Ibid.*, II-II, q. 1, a. 10, ad 3; q. 11, a. 2, ad 3.

[11] *Ibid.*, II-II, q. 39, a. 1; q. 88, a. 12, ad 3; q. 89, a. 9, ad 3; ad 4; q. 100, a. 1, ad 7; III, q. 35, a. 7, ad 3; q. 72, a. 11 ad 1; etc.

[12] *Ibid.*, II-II, q. 185, aa. 3, 4; q. 177, a. 2; III, q. 82, a. 1, ad 4: " princeps totius ecclesiastici ordinis "; *I ad Cor.*, cap. 12, lect. 3 (M. n. 738 f.); etc.

[13] *Ad Philip.*, cap. 1, lect. 1 (M. n. 6); *I ad Cor.*, cap. 12, lect. 3 (M. n. 756).

[14] *Summa theol.*, II-II, q. 1, a. 4, sed contra; a. 9, sed contra; q. 5, a. 3; q. 10, a. 12.

[15] *Ibid.*, II-II, q. 10, a. 10; q. 100, a. 2; q. 147, a. 3; a. 4, ad 1; a. 5.

[16] *Ibid.*, II-II, q. 11, a. 4, ad 1; q. 184, a. 4; cf. q. 189, a. 5: " Ecclesia respicit id quod in pluribus est."

[17] E.g., *ibid.*, II-II, q. 172, a. 4; q. 177, a. 1.

[18] E.g., *ibid.*, II-II, q. 10, a. 9; q. 11, a. 3; *Ad Galatas*, cap 1, lect. 2 (M. n. 24).

[19] *Summa theol.*, II-II, q. 1, a. 9, ad 6; q. 12, a. 1, ad 1; q. 184, a. 6 (ref. to the Western Church); I-II, q. 106, a. 4, ad 4.

[20] *Ibid.*, II-II, q. 1, a. 9, ad 3; *IV Sent.*, d. 4, q. 2, a. qla. 5; *I ad Cor.*, cap. 11, lect. 7 (M. n. 691).These three texts employ—tacitly in the third case—the important distinction: belonging to the Church *numero* and *merito*. Cf. also *I ad Cor.*, cap. 12, lect. 2 (M. n. 725); lect. 3 (M. n. 748); *Ad Col.*, cap. 1, lect. 1 (M. n. 6); *II ad Tim.*, cap. 2, lect. 3 (M. n. 73); *Ad Titum*, cap. 1, lect. 2 (M. nn. 15, 19); lect. 4 (M. n. 45); cap. 3, lect. 1 (M. n. 81); *Summa theol.*, II-II, q. 4, a. 5, ad 4; III, q. 68, a. 5, ad 1.

grace existing at present, and that of glory which is in the future; and " it is the same Church." [21] He goes on in the same place to speak of the " whole Church " of grace, which includes, besides present-day Christians, those in the Old Testament justified through faith in Christ; this is a point he returns to in his discussion of Christ's capital grace, in the *Summa theologiae*:

The ancient Fathers, by observing the sacraments of the law, were brought towards Christ through the same faith and love by which we are still brought towards him. For this reason the ancient Fathers belonged to the same body of the Church to which we belong.[22]

It is such texts as these, taken in conjunction with those which state that those who were justified before the coming of Christ belong to the New Testament,[23] which have given rise to the impression that St. Thomas sees the Church simply as an assembly of grace. That such an impression is false is clear from the preceding sub-section. The Church to which " we " belong is without doubt the Roman Catholic Church; but the texts remain a problem. It is by resolving this problem that an authentic understanding of St. Thomas' teaching is to be found.

B. *St. Thomas' View of the Church*

Our purpose is not so ambitious as to present an account of St. Thomas' ecclesiology, even supposing such a thing were possible. It is sufficient for the present problem to seek an answer to the question: what can we learn concerning the structure of the Roman Catholic Church from the fact that St. Thomas could say that it is the same Church as that of heaven and that of those who were justified before the Incarnation? St. Thomas' own answer is to be found principally in his tract on the Old and the New Law; from this appears his

[21] *Ad Col.*, cap. 1, lect. 5 (M. n. 48).
[22] *Summa theol.*, III, q. 8, a. 3, ad 3.
[23] E.g., *ibid.*, I-II, q. 106, a. 1, ad 3; a. 3, ad 2; q. 107, a. 1, ad 2; a. 3, ad 1.

concern both to preserve an historical perspective and to construct a theological synthesis of the history of salvation.

(i) *The history of salvation.* St. Thomas distinguishes three historical periods in the earthly revelation of God.

Before the Law individual persons or families were, in prophetical fashion, instructed in faith in the one God and in His omnipotence. *Under the Law* the whole people, through the prophets and primarily through Moses, received a fuller revelation with special emphasis on the divine simplicity. Finally, " in the *time of grace* the mystery of the Trinity was revealed by the Son of God Himself." [24]

Man's response to divine revelation falls into a corresponding historical pattern; and this is true of both his interior and his exterior worship of God. This emerges from St. Thomas' discussion of the ceremonial percepts of the Old Law. Here he takes a broader view of divine revelation, extending it to include the beatific vision.[25]

Interior union with God is achieved in two consecutive stages in each individual: in the present life, where divine truth shines upon us only through the medium of sensible figures, and in the beatific vision, where the human intellect will have direct knowledge of divine truth. But historically a development is discernible in the form of union which has been or is possible. This development falls into two historical periods or states. In the *Old Law* " neither was the divine truth manifested directly nor was the way of attaining it laid open." " In the *state of the New Law,*" on the contrary, while direct knowledge of divine truth is still in the future, "the way to it is now revealed." [26] Being concerned here with correlating ceremonial precepts with the historical development of interior union with God, St. Thomas leaves out of the consideration

---

[24] *Ibid.*, II-II, q. 174, a. 6, where revelation of the Incarnation is said to center on the time of realization of the mystery and on Pentecost (*Eph.*, 3:5).

[25] *Ibid.*, I-II, q. 101, a. 2, where the principle is formulated; cf. q. 103, a. 3, where it is specified that interior worship consists in faith, hope and charity.

[26] *Ibid.*, I-II, q. 101, a. 2.

the *pre-law period* in which no liturgy was divinely prescribed. In another place, however, he takes account of this period, so completing his survey of mankind's historical response of faith to the three stages of earthly revelation.[27]

Corresponding to the heavenly and to the three states of earthly union with God are four diverse liturgies. In heaven external worship will have nothing figurative about it but will consist simply in praise of God, directly expressing the inward union. On earth, however, three liturgies have succeeded one another, each of them incorporating ceremonies figurative of the divine gifts not yet given at the period in which it was legitimately used. Before the Law and under the Law the ceremonies pre-figured not only heaven but Christ also and the means he provides for entering heaven. In the " state of the New Law " only heaven is symbolized as something which exists solely in hope; the Way there is " commemorated as one who was in the past and who is now present." [28]

What is noteworthy for our present question is the clear historical distinction that St. Thomas makes between the liturgy of the Old Law and that of the New. This is our first indication of what he means by the " *state* of the New Law." As will appear below, this phrase has not the same signification as the term " the New Law."

The point of transition from the Old Law to the " state of the New Law " is the Incarnation. There could not be a visible mission of the Spirit to the justified before Christ because the visible mission of the Son was not yet accomplished.[29] The Spirit is given visibly, as at Pentecost, only after the Resurrection and Ascension; [30] and for this reason it is only after Christ's coming that there can be a " law " capable itself of introducing all men into salvation.[31] Christ the Priest, by ful-

[27] Cf. *ibid.*, I-II, q. 103, a. 1.
[28] *Ibid.*, I-II, q. 101, a. 2; cf. q. 103, aa. 1, 3.
[29] *Ibid.*, I, q. 43, a. 6, ad 7.
[30] *Ibid.*, I-II, q. 106, a. 4, ad 2.
[31] *Ibid.*, I-II, q. 91, a. 5, ad 2.

filling the Law [32] and displacing the priesthood of Aaron, thereby effects the transition from the Old Law to the New, so that
now the state of the Chosen People has changed and there is
no longer distinction between the nation of the Jews and the
Gentiles.[33]

Once again what is to be noted is the historical character
of the introduction of the state of the New Law. The difference in the new state is clearly discerned in the sacraments.
It is the historical reality of the mystery of the Incarnation
and passion of Christ which gives the sacraments of the New
Law power of justification and sanctification, whereas those
of the Old Law did not contain grace or the power of the mysteries of Christ or Christ himself.[34] The Old-Law ceremonies
had their own validity as external worship during the period
in which they were prescribed,[35] but they were not " spiritual "
as are those of the New Law, which can cause grace,[36] and
consequently they were superseded when Christ's mysteries
were realized.[37]

What is true of the sacraments is true, due proportion being
preserved, of the whole law in its two states. Old and New
Law are not wholly diverse, since it is the same God who gives
both of them and both are directed towards the same end,
namely, the submission of man to God. They are distinct in
the manner that two parts of the same motion are distinct,
according as one part is nearer to the term than the other,
which is to say that the relation of the New Law to the Old
is that of what is perfect to what is imperfect in the same
genus. It becomes clear, however, that the term " law " is
used analogically in the phrase " the New Law " when St.
Thomas goes on to describe the Old Law as " a pedagogue of

[32] *Ibid.*, I-II, q. 107, a. 2; q. 102, a. 4, ad 2.
[33] *Ibid.*, I-II, q. 104, a. 3, ad 3; cf. q. 91, a. 5, sed contra.
[34] *Ibid.*, I-II, q. 103, a. 2; q. 102, a. 2; q. 101, a. 4, ad 2; etc.
[35] *Ibid.*, I-II, q. 102, a. 2. Throughout his discussion of the ceremonial law St.
Thomas distinguishes the " literal " and the " figurative " causes.
[36] *Ibid.*, II-II, q. 100, a. 2; I-II, q. 102, a. 5, ad 8 et 9.
[37] *Ibid.*, I-II, q. 104, a. 3.

children " (*Gal.*, 3:24) and the New Law as " the law of perfection, as being the law of charity [. . .] the bond of perfection." [38]

A new concept has now come to the fore in the connotation of " the New Law," that of grace; and it is this which enables St. Thomas, while preserving his strictly historical view of the development of divine revelation and of man's interior and external response to it, to introduce a supra-historical consideration into his theology of salvation. A brief examination of this new idea will prepare the way for an explanation of St. Thomas' description of the justified, whether before or after Christ, as "the same Church."

(ii) *The supra-historical extension of the New Law.* Though for St. Thomas, following the teaching of St. Paul, the Old Law as such was a purely external indication of the divine will regarding the conduct of the Chosen People and contained no proximate or spiritual help for fulfilling its prescriptions, the way of salvation was not closed to pre-Christian Jews or indeed to those excluded from Jewish citizenship.[39] This was because there was " another help for men from God, accompanying the Law, by which they could be saved; this was faith in the Mediator, through which the Fathers of old were justified in the same way that we are justified." [40] In so far as they received sanctifying grace, given in virtue of the merits of Christ, they belonged to the New Law [41] and looked for spiritual and eternal fulfillment of the promises.[42]

It is, as has been remarked, this element of St. Thomas' teaching which has caused confusion concerning his concept of the Church. Because he affirms that the justified who lived before Christ belonged to the New Law and even that they belonged to " the same Church " as we, it has been concluded that he considers the Church purely as a supra-histor-

---

[38] *Ibid.*, I-II, q. 107, a. 1.

[39] For non-Jews, cf. *ibid.*, I-II, q. 105, a. 3, ad 1.

[40] *Ibid.*, I-II, q. 98, a. 2, ad 4.

[41] *Ibid.*, I-II, q. 106, a. 1, ad 3; a. 3, ad 2; q. 107, a. 1, ad 2; a. 3, ad 3; etc.

[42] *Ibid.*, I-II, q. 107, a. 1, ad 2. Cf. I-II, q. 91, a. 5: the *direct* or immediate end of the Old Law consisted in earthly benefits.

ical assembly of grace. Those who have come to this conclusion have claimed support for their opinion in the well-known
article of III, q. 8, on the headship of Christ. Yet, as we have
seen, St. Thomas has as clear a notion at least of the fact of
the juridical structure of the Roman Catholic Church as any
modern theologian and is quite well aware that it came into
existence only after the Incarnation.

The truth of the matter is that for St. Thomas the New
Law is of wider extension than the Roman Catholic Church.
The latter is a clearly identifiable historical entity, whereas
the New Law exists as the mystery of salvation at work in
the world from the time of the restoration of man to grace.
Yet, though the New Law thus transcends historical periods,
the *state* of the New Law does not. For the state of the New
Law is precisely that third state of revelation and faith which
was initiated in the Incarnation and in the mysteries of Christ;
and it is the Roman Catholic Church which provides that
stable disposition pertaining to grace which is required for a
" state." [43]

(iii) *The State of the New Law.* More is implied in the
state of the New Law than in the *New Law as such.* This is
made clear by St. Thomas in several places and provides the
key to understanding his teaching on the Church. The *state*
of the human race with respect to the divine law, he indicates in one place, varies according to historical succession.
Accordingly, although at all times there have been men who
belonged to the New Law by faith in Christ, the New Law
has not always been *proposed* to men.[44] It is precisely the
proposal of the New Law which characterizes the period after
Pentecost. This is the time when revelation is taught explicitly and stripped of the figures which cloaked it in the Old
Testament.[45] The sacraments of the New Law likewise form
part of the dispositions made by Christ when he inaugurated

---

[43] Cf. *ibid.,* II-II, q. 183, a. 1.
[44] *Ibid.,* I-II, q. 106, a. 3, ad 2.
[45] *Ibid.,* I-II, q. 107, a. 3, ad 1.

the new state of the Chosen People. It is characteristic of the
new state that its sacraments, besides containing Christ or the
power of his mysteries, also, in accordance with the nature of
external worship, are adapted to give expression to explicit
faith in the Christian revelation, whereas those of the Old Law
could give only figurative expression to the same faith.[46] The
judicial precepts of the Old Law, since their purpose was to
maintain good order in the Jewish nation, have lost their binding force because, with the coming of Christ, the state of the
people has been changed.[47] As to the moral precepts, the
teaching of Christ has provided a new understanding of their
meaning and has established an ideal of perfection in the
counsels.[48] Finally, the state of the New Law will give way
to the state of heaven when the Gospel of Christ has been
preached throughout the world with full effect, in such fashion that the Church is founded in every race.[49]

If, then, we wish to discover St. Thomas' teaching on the
Church we cannot simply extract what he says about the New
Law and go on to assert that he has a vague idea of the
Church as an assembly of grace, indifferent to juridical structure. His teaching on the nature of the Roman Catholic
Church is to be found in his analysis of the *state* of the New
Law, for it is precisely the structure of this Church which he
envisages when he describes this state. It is here that St.
Thomas makes his decisive contribution to ecclesiology for he
is not content merely to enumerate the elements which constitute the Church; he gives a theological account which establishes a hierarchy of values within the constitutive elements
and provides thereby a comprehensive criterion for resolving
the problem of membership. The principal place to be consulted is I-II, q. 108.

The basis for q. 108 is laid in q. 106. In reply to the
question whether the New Law is a written one, St. Thomas
replies:

[46] *Ibid.*, I-II, q. 103, a. 2; ad 2.   [48] *Ibid.*, I-II, q. 107, a. 2.
[47] *Ibid.*, I-II, q. 104, a. 3.   [49] *Ibid.*, I-II, q. 106, a. 4, ad 1; ad 4.

The Philosopher points out in *Ethics,* IX, that " each thing is seen to be what is primary in its constitution." Now the primary element of the law of the New Testament, that in which its whole worth lies, is the grace of the Holy Spirit which is given to those who believe in Christ. This appears clearly in St. Paul, *Rom.* 3:27 [. . .] where it is the grace of faith which is termed " the law "; and even more clearly in *Rom.,* 8:2 [. . .].

The New Law has, however, certain elements the function of which is to dispose for the grace of the Holy Spirit and [others] which are related to the use of this grace. These are in the New Law as secondary elements, and the Christian faithful must be instructed about them both orally and in writing in so far as they concern both belief and action. Our reply, accordingly, is that the New Law is primarily interior but that secondarily it is a written law.[50]

In q. 108, a. 1, the distinction between primary and secondary elements is developed in terms of the Incarnation, insofar as this mystery affects the believer. After recalling that the principal element (*principalitas*) of the New Law is the grace of the Holy Spirit, revealed in faith active through charity, St. Thomas goes on:

Now men obtain this grace through the Son of God made man whose *humanity* grace first filled and has thence been brought to us. This is expressed in *Jn.,* 1:14: " The Word was made *flesh,*" and then is added: " full of grace and truth "; and later [v. 16]: " of his fullness we have all received, and grace for grace." Consequently it is added [v. 17] that " grace and truth came by Jesus Christ." *It is for this reason* that there is discoverable a theological harmony in the fact that it is through *external realities, perceptible to the senses* that the grace flowing from the *Incarnate* Word is brought to us, and in the fact that certain *external actions, perceptible to the senses* should be performed under the influence of this interior grace through which the flesh is brought under the control of the spirit.

It is because grace has this incarnational aspect—deriving from its source and its function—that St. Thomas is able to account for the sacramental and juridical structure of the

---

[50] *Ibid.,* I-II, q. 108, a. 1; ad 2 clarifies the notion of " interior " (*indita*); " quasi naturae superadditum per gratiae donum."

Roman Catholic Church. For, in fact, he goes on to explain
the necessity of the sacraments, "baptism, the Eucharist and
the like," [51] in terms of the derivation of grace from the Incarnate Word; and he accounts for the written law and the
exercise of jurisdiction, whether ecclesiastical or civil, as a
consequence of man's need to "incarnate" grace in external
actions, this being a logical necessity derived, not simply from
man's nature, but also from the mystery of the Incarnation
itself. Thus whatever external action is necessarily implied by,
or contrary to, grace falls under precept or prohibition. Whatever, on the contrary, has not such a necessary connection
with grace is left by the legislator, Christ, to whoever has the
responsibility for controlling such matters, whether it be the
individual exercising his freedom or the ruler governing his
subjects.

The following article, q. 108, a. 2, develops this outline in
order to solve the question whether the New Law has made
adequate provision for external acts. The *sed contra* refers to
the Church as a house:

Our Lord says, *Matt.*, 7:24: "Everyone that heareth these my
words and doth them shall be likened to a wise man that built his
house upon a rock." [52] But a wise builder neglects nothing that is
necessary for the building. Consequently, whatever is related to
salvation has been adequately provided for in the words of Christ.

The *corpus* details the provisions. First are the sacraments
"through which we are led into grace and which had to be
instituted by Christ himself since it is from him alone that we
can obtain grace"; the list of seven includes "the order of
ministers of the New Law, [instituted by Christ] when he
appointed the Apostles and the seventy-two disciples." Second is what concerns the correct use of grace through works of
charity: what is absolutely necessary for virtuous life has al-

[51] The list is completed in the following article.
[52] Cf. *Comment. in Matt.*, cap. 7, lect. 2 (M. n. 671): "Vel potest [haec simi-
litudo] intelligi spiritualiter: et sic iste vir est Christus [. . .] Domus Christi est
Ecclesia. . . ."

ready been provided for in the moral precepts of the Old Law
so that the New Law need make no additions in this respect.
But the more specific determination of these precepts, in matters of justice and worship, is not concerned with what is in
itself necessarily bound up with grace and, consequently, such
determination is left to human choice, either of individuals or,
when the common good is at stake, of " prelates, temporal or
spiritual." [53]

A very clear statement of St. Thomas' view of the Church
of the New Testament emerges from these articles. The Church
is precisely the *state* of the New Law, primarily an assembly
of grace, but provided, as a secondary element in its constitution, with a sacramental system administered by a sacramental priesthood deriving from the Apostles, and with a hierarchy empowered to bind its subject to the fulfillment of laws
promulgated as determinations of the general moral principles
for the common good of the spiritual society. Here St. Thomas
simply sketches the outline of his ecclesiology, filling in the
details as occasion arises. From the texts already cited it is
evident that the function of the hierarchy includes, not only
administration of the sacraments and government of Christian morals, but also teaching the faith.

In all of this there is nothing very startling for the contemporary ecclesiologist; but this is just the point which has to
be made. When St. Thomas speaks of " the Church " without
any further qualification, either explicit or implied in the context, he is referring to exactly the same institution as Pius
XII in *Mystici corporis*. What may be called specifically
Thomistic is the distinction between primary and secondary
elements and the hierarchy of values thus established. It is
this distinction which leads to an understanding of the inclusion of the justified of the Old Testament and the blessed of
heaven in " the same Church " as ourselves.

(iv) *The extension of the Church*. There is no difficulty in

---

[53] The climate of thought in which this question is placed appears also in the
objections, esp. a. 2, obj. 3, a. 4, obj. 3. The Roman Church is clearly envisaged.

determining the historical extension of the Church when this is understood in its strict sense as the Church of the Apostles and the sacraments. This Church depends wholly on the intervention of the divine Word made flesh in human history. Its secondary elements—sacraments and hierarchy—draw their validity from the revelation, the mysteries and the dispositions of Christ; its primary element depends on the secondary elements for its existence and its activity. It is the New Law in its historical, material setting; it is, one might say, developing St. Thomas' hint, the New Law incarnate—grace, that is, depending on material things for its existence in man and manifesting itself in external action under the direction of individual prudence and juridically constituted authority. The difficulty concerns those who received grace before the coming of Christ. Though, to the extent that they were in grace, they belonged to the New Law, there is no question of their having used its secondary elements which, nevertheless, form an integral part of the New Law as it is realized in the Roman Catholic Church. They did not belong, that is, to the Roman Catholic Church. And yet they belonged to "the same Church" as we do.

As has been seen, St. Thomas explains the historical continuity between the Old Law and the New in terms of motion towards one end, the submission of man to God, so that the two laws are related as imperfect and perfect in the same species.[54] The union that he affirms between the justified who lived under the Old Law and the present Church is very much closer than this. Its basis is the grace of the Holy Spirit which, though given before Christ, is the special possession of the present Church, constituting its primary element. It is the same gift of the Holy Spirit, grace and glory, which unifies the present Church and heaven. In respect of this gift St. Thomas distinguishes, in fact, only two states of man, denominated, in conformity with his theology of beatitude, in terms of knowledge of God. Man's fundamental supernatural link

[54] Cf. Summa theol., I-II, q. 91, a. 5.

with God is either vision or faith.[55] Vision is the end of both laws and it can be attained only through faith in Christ which is active through charity. In accordance with this, the fundamental rôle of Christ's redemptive mission is to "make manifest the way of *truth*." [56] Because the just who lived under the Law had faith in Christ perfected by charity they enjoyed the primary reality of the Catholic Church. The unity of faith of the two testaments bears witness to their unity of purpose.[56a]

If, however, the faith of the justified Jews is the same as that of the Church in respect to its object, there is a difference in historical perspective " because they preceded Christ whereas we follow him." Consequently, " the same faith is expressed in different ways by them and by us " since they spoke of future events and we of what is past.[57] Similarly, faith in the divine promises calls for distinct ceremonial signs before and after the fulfillment of the promises. " Consequently, while [fulfillment] was still future the faith of Abraham had to be proclaimed in circumcision. But after it has been achieved the same reality must be declared by another sign, namely, baptism which succeeds circumcision in this respect." [58] It is apparent that as far as the external organization of the community of the faithful goes there is not discernible the same unity between the Jews and the Church as exists in their common faith. There is, nevertheless, a certain unity even at this external level, based on two factors.

First, considering the organization as such, as it includes liturgical ceremonies and the teaching of revelation, the ceremonies of the Old Law were *figures* of the mysteries realized in Christ and commemorated in the Church; and the *same revelation* is proposed in both states, implicitly and in figure in the Old Law, explicitly and openly in the Church.

---

[55] Cf. *ibid.*, I-II, q. 101, a. 2.
[56] *Ibid.*, III, Prol.
[56a] *Ibid.*, I-II, q. 107, a. 1, ad 1.
[57] *Ibid.*, I-II, q. 103, a. 4.
[58] *Ibid.*, I-II, q. 103, a. 3, ad 4; cf. esp. III, q. 68, a. 1, ad 1.

This divinely conceived harmony between the externals of
the two states makes possible the second factor in visible
unity. When used with faith the ceremonies of the Old Law
made visible the People of God in the same way that the liturgy of the Catholic Church does today. The form of unity
spoken of here is confined strictly to the fact of *proclamation
of faith in Christ* through prescribed ceremonies. The sacraments of the New Law imply more than this; they contain the
power of Christ's mysteries, something which was impossible
for the Old-Law sacraments. Though for this reason unique
professions of faith, yet, the sacraments of the Church incorporate all the cult values of the Old-Law ceremonies and
to this extent the latter are anticipations of the former.[59] St.
Thomas concentrates his attention on the ceremonial aspect
of external union between the believers of the Old Testament
and the Church precisely because it manifests the union of
faith, implying the teaching of a common revelation. He does
not appear to be concerned to discover any form of unity of
jurisdiction, preferring to consider the judicial precepts as
social regulations adapted to the state of the Jewish people.

Our conclusion, then, is as follows. For St. Thomas the
present Church is the Roman Catholic Church which takes its
historical origin from the Incarnation and the mysteries of
Christ. When he says that the just of the Old Testament
belonged to the same Church as we do he does not mean that
the present Church is purely an assembly of believers or of
the justified. He means that the present Church existed in
another form before Christ. The diversity of form is not to
be attributed to a difference in faith, for, in spite of accidental
differences, this is the same before and after Christ. The difference is to be sought in the secondary elements which serve
faith and which constitute the two historical states of the
congregation of believers.[60] For, whereas the sacraments of
the Church commemorate the mysteries of Christ and con-

---

[59] Cf. *ibid.*, III, q. 70, which applies the principles established in qq. 60, 61.

[60] The phrase appears in *Summa theol.*, III, q. 8, a. 4, ad 2; q. 70, a. 1; etc.

tain their power, the sacraments of the Old Law were no more than figures of the mysteries so that their religious value depended wholly on the faith of those who used them. For this same reason it was not the Jewish people as such or the Old Law as such which constituted the pre-existence of the Roman Catholic Church. The present Church existed in a preliminary, provisional form in the Remnant of Israel, those who possessed the grace of the Holy Spirit, believing in Christ as revealed by the prophets, and expressing their faith by means of the Jewish liturgy and by obedience to the judicial precepts of the law. The essential factors constituting them the pre-Church—essential because implying the other factors —were living faith and use of the Jewish sacraments. They used these sacraments precisely as " images and shadows of what was to come." And since " motion to an image, formally as an image, is the same as motion to the thing imaged " the religious Jews " were brought through their liturgy to Christ by the same faith and love as that by which we are brought to him." And for this reason they belonged " to the same body of the Church as that to which we belong." [61] They belonged to the *body* of the Church precisely because they used their *sacraments* with faith. The body that they formed could only be a shadow of the body of the Roman Catholic Church because the personal body of Christ was not yet formed in the womb of their supreme representative. With the Incarnation the body of the divine Word appears in Israel as the source of a wholly new sacramental system which will give rise to the perfect body of the faithful.

Sacraments are the decisive factor. They give the congregation of believers its basic visibility, make it, that is, a body. They distinguish the Roman Catholic Church from the Remnant of Israel and from those other members of Christ who lived before the Incarnation and yet were saved by living faith and by whatever natural sacraments they chose to ex-

[61] *Ibid.,* III, q. 8, a. 3, ad 3; cf. objection.

press their faith.[62] Sacraments too, insofar as through their historical development they express the same faith in more or
less perfect symbols of the same reality, unify all believers
in a body which is one, not juridically, but one in being
directed to one end under the influence of one person who possesses the end by right. Further, it is the need to use sacraments
as expressions of faith which distinguishes all the successive
earthly assemblies of believers from the heavenly consummation of the Church; and, at the same time, sacraments give to
our present knowledge of God that corporeal expression which
will be perfected in the beatific vision and in the consequent
glory of the risen body.

Thus the Church, accordingly, existed before the Incarnation in a preliminary state; it will exist after the parousia
in its consummation. But in the present intervening period
it is identified with the Roman Catholic Church. This is certainly the teaching of St. Thomas.

II. THE CHURCH AS THE BODY OF CHRIST

St. Thomas, adopting the lead of the Scriptures, uses several metaphors of the Church. It is, for example, a house or
a city.[63] It is the unique spouse of Christ.[64] Most commonly,
with St. Paul, he uses the metaphor of a human body. We
shall consider the sense in which he uses " body " in this context, noting the realities to which he applies it. A second section will be concerned with the nature of the body of Christ
in St. Thomas' writings.

A. *Sense of " body "; its extension*

It is not necessary for our purpose to investigate exhaus-
tively the manner in which St. Thomas exploits the metaphor
of the body. In general, he develops two ideas suggested by

---

[62] Cf. *ibid.*, III, q. 68, a. 1, ad 1.

[63] E.g., *Ad Ephesios*, cap. 2, lect. 6 (M. n. 124).

[64] *Ad Romanos*, cap. 7, lect. 1 (M. nn. 526, 522); cf. *Summa theol.*, I-II, q. 102,
a. 5, ad 3; III, q. 61, a. 2, ad 3.

the analogy. He contrasts Christ, the Head, with the Church, the body, and analyzes the relations between the two.[65] Or else he illustrates the theme of diversity of gifts and offices within the unity of the Church by appeal to the diversity of members in one body.[66] These two ideas are not rigorously separated—Christ is seen, for example, to influence the members through the intervention of office-holders[67]—but the first is developed in terms of the gift of grace made by the Head to his members, while the second is concerned with the external organization of the Church.

The text of *Ephesians*, 1:3, is sufficient for St. Thomas to make the equation between the Church and the body of Christ; but he is quite willing to take advantage of the evident ambiguity of the term "church" in this context. The outstanding example is the central text, III, q. 8, a. 3, where St. Thomas explicitly adopts the point of view which encompasses "the entire history of the world" (*totum tempus mundi*) and where he speaks of "the body of the Church constituted of men from the beginning of the world to its end"; and in fact the saints and even angels are included also, so that in the following article (a. 4) the term "church" is applied to all who benefit from Christ's influence, whether on earth or in heaven, and all are said to form one body of which Christ is the Head. For a comprehensive account of the unique body of Christ such a broad view is necessary. That this body of Christ takes on a particular sacramental and juridical form in the period between the fulfillment of the mystery of the Incarnation and the parousia remains a truth already estab-

---

[65] *Summa theol.*, III, q. 8; *Ad Ephesios*, cap. 1, lect. 8 (M. nn. 69, 70, 71): "Et quia Ecclesia est instituta propter Christum, dicitur quod Ecclesia est plenitudo eius, scilicet Christi, id est, ut omnia, quae virtute sunt in Christo, quasi quodam modo in membris ipsius ecclesiae impleantur, dum scilicet omnes sensus spirituales, et dona, et quidquid potest esse in ecclesia, quae omnia superabundanter sunt in Christo, ab ipso deriventur in membra Ecclesiae et perficiantur in eis."

[66] E.g. *Suppl.*, q. 37, a. 1, sed contra; *Ad Romanos*, cap. 12, lect. 2 (M. nn., 972, 973); *Ad Ephesios*, cap. 4, lect. 5 (M. n. 225); *Ad Col.*, cap. 1, lect. 5 (M. n. 46).

[67] E.g., *Summa theol.*, III, q. 8, a. 6; q. 82, a. 1, ad 4; and all that is said on the minister of the sacraments.

lished in the *Prima-Secundae*: and St. Thomas does us the compliment of expecting that we will remember this. In III, q. 8, where he is meditating on the mystery of Christ, " the universal principle in the genus of those who possess grace," [68] the idea foremost in his mind is that " men could at no time be saved, even before the coming of Christ, unless they became members of Christ," being incorporated into him.[69] Historical details of external organization necessarily take, in this theological synthesis, the secondary place which he has already demonstrated is their due; they have been or will be given full consideration in other sections of his *Summa*. Sufficient notice is taken of the present state of the mystical body in q. 8, a. 6, where the function of the pope and the bishops is very precisely outlined: while Christ is " Head of all those who belong to the Church according to all times, all places and all states," the pope is " head of the whole Church according to a determined time, during the time, that is, of his pontificate; and according to a determined state, that namely of wayfarers "; and bishops are heads of their local churches.

Our conclusion is parallel to that of the preceding section. For St. Thomas " (mystical body) of Christ " is equivalent to " (whole) Church," to which term it adds a clearer reference to Christ as the cause of the existence and the unity of the congregation of the faithful. While the term may be employed with the same freedom as " the Church," after Pentecost the body of Christ on earth is the Roman Catholic Church. This body the bishops or their delegates " dispose." [70]

To this conclusion a further consideration may be added. Commenting on *Eph.*, 4:13, St. Thomas goes beyond the normal comparison of the Church to a human body. He interprets the text as referring to the state of heaven, and comments:

Secondly he indicates the exemplar cause of this perfection when he says "unto the measure of the age of the fullness of Christ."

---

[68] *Ibid.*, III, q. 7, a. 9; a. 11.

[69] *Ibid.*, III, q. 68, a. 1, ad 1.   [70] *Ibid.*, III, q. 82, a. 1, ad 4.

Notice here that *the true body of Christ* is the exemplar of the mystical body; for both are formed of several members gathered into one.[71]

The conclusion drawn—that the age of the saints will be thirty-three—is of less importance than the principle leading to it and the implied application to the mystical body of the text quoted in confirmation: " Who will reform the body of our lowness, made like to the body of his glory " (*Phil.* 3:21). Possibly St. Thomas, as reported here, is interested simply in discovering a material resemblance between Christ's body and those of his glorious members; but the suggestion of a wider significance to the analogy cannot be ignored in the light of St. Thomas' understanding of the instrumental use in salvation of Christ's humanity—of his body, as he puts it in III, q. 8, a. 2. If the Church is to be thought of as the fullness of Christ's true body, as some exegetes propose, then the Church founded at the Incarnation and consummated at the parousia has a special title to be called the mystical body. This accords admirably with St. Thomas' theology. It is the reality of the humanity of Christ which gives the present Church its excellence, as manifested primarily in the sacraments. The continuity of efficient causality that now exists between the glorified body of Christ and the sacraments of the Church lends a new realism to the denomination of the Church as the body of Christ. As dependent on the true body for the efficacy of its sacraments and its grace, it constitutes the fullness of the true body and for this reason it is to be seen, together with its heavenly consummation, as the mystical body *par excellence*, more truly the mystical body than the Remnant of Israel which was united to the future Christ by faith and purely ceremonial sacraments. But if, in these terms, we might distinguish between a mystical body before the Incarnation and the true mystical body after, it is unthinkable that there should be a multiplicity of mystical bodies at the present time. For, in addition to the fact that

[71] *Ad Ephesios*, cap. 4, lect. 4 (M. n. 216).

the metaphor was chosen by St. Paul precisely in order to emphasize the union of many in one association, the uniqueness of Christ, the Head, and of his true body demand that the mystical body be one; and of this the Roman Catholic is the present earthly guarantee and realization.

B. *Nature of the mystical body*

Since "mystical body" and "Church" are synonyms, applicable to each or all of the various states of those who receive the influence of Christ, it is clear that what has been said about the nature of the Roman Catholic Church is valid also for the present state of the mystical body. It is useful, however, to relate certain statements that St. Thomas makes about the mystical body to the account given of the structure of the Church in the discussion of the New Law.

As with the Church, there are to be distinguished in the mystical body primary and secondary elements. The primary element, grace, is now conceived explicitly in terms of union with Christ. It is according to this union that Christ is Head; and here there are three degrees of perfection: union through glory, through charity and through unformed faith.[72] Without faith there is no supernatural union with Christ on the part of men; the sin of infidelity "radically separates a man from the unity of the Church."[73] On the other hand, the universality of Redemption gives Christ the right to the title of Head even of unbelievers, as long as they retain the power of freely submitting to him.[74] While effective exercise of headship is attributed to Christ in respect to the man who possesses only unformed faith, the primary element of the mystical is grace in the full sense of the word. Charity is indispensable for perfect union with Christ and such union, insofar as it can be achieved here, is the ideal state of the mystical body on earth. Accordingly St. Thomas can say, when

[72] *Summa theol.*, III, q. 8, a. 3.
[73] *Ibid.*, III, q. 80, a. 5, ad 2.
[74] *Ibid.*, III, q. 8, a. 3, ad 1.

speaking of the Eucharist: ". . . the mystical body of Christ . . . is the society of those who are holy." [75] Unformed faith is no more than initial union with Christ; but, as a participation in the primary element of the mystical body, it prevents total separation from the unity of the Church insofar as this is achieved by charity.

The secondary elements of the mystical body, which at the present time give it that organization which constitutes it the Roman Catholic Church, are to be considered relevant to the explanation of the metaphor to the degree that they serve union with Christ and the unity of the faithful in charity. This primacy of the spiritual over the material and the juridical is vigorously asserted in every place where St. Thomas speaks of the Church or the mystical body. Among the secondary elements the chief place, in such a perspective, must go to the teaching office of the Church and to the sacraments. Moreover, while the proposition of revealed truth by the Church is no more than a condition for the exercise of faith, the sacraments are causes of grace in subordination to the humanity of the Word. The sacraments are, accordingly, the principal secondary element of the mystical body so that use of them implies acceptance of all the other secondary elements. Union with Christ by faith and by sacraments—the phrase which occurs so often in the *Tertia Pars*—is, therefore, an accurate description of the mystical body as it is identified with the Roman Catholic Church in the present period of the history of salvation.

Two sacraments, baptism and the Eucharist, contribute decisively and directly to the realization of the primary element of the mystical body so that both of them are necessary for the existence of the primary element. In St. Thomas' theology of these two sacraments is to be found the application of his teaching in III, q. 8, to the present post-Incarnational state. He writes of them:

[75] *Ibid.*, III, q. 80, a. 4: *societas sanctorum.*

Baptism is the origin (*principium*) of the spiritual life and the way of entrance to the sacraments. The Eucharist, on the contrary, is a form of [*quasi*—i. e., in the present life] perfection of the spiritual life and the term of all the sacraments. [. . .] Accordingly, reception of baptism is necessary for beginning the spiritual life, whereas reception of the Eucharist is necessary for perfecting it, not for the simple fact of possessing it. . . .[76]

The social and juridical implications of baptism are most clearly noted in St. Thomas' discussion of circumcision, III, q. 70. The two sacraments have in common the fact that they were instituted as professions of faith and means of entry into the congregation of the faithful.[77] To this extent what is said of circumcision is true of baptism:

The nation of believers had to be brought together by means of a visible symbol; for this is necessary for the grouping together of men in any religion, as Augustine remarks in his *Contra Faustum*.[78]

Baptism, in common with all the New-Law sacraments, is more than a profession of faith; it " contains the perfection of salvation ";[79] consequently it is clearly distinguished from circumcision:

For in baptism grace is given from the power of baptism itself, which it possesses by reason of being an instrument of the passion of Christ, now accomplished. Circumcision, on the contrary, gave grace in so far as it was a sign of faith in the future passion of Christ; that is to say, the person who submitted to circumcision made profession that he accepted this faith, whether it was an adult who did this personally or it was someone else who did it for infants [. . . *Rom.*, 4: 11]. What was signified was justification which comes from faith, not from the symbol of circumcision itself.[80]

Baptism, accordingly is a symbolic profession of faith, aggregating the recipient to the society of believers; at the same

---

[76] *Ibid.*, III, q. 73, a. 3.

[77] *Ibid.*, III, q. 70, a. 1.

[78] *Ibid.*, q. 2, ad 2. References to the *Contra Faustum* are frequent wherever St. Thomas discusses the sacraments of the Old and New Laws.

[79] *Ibid.*, III, q. 70, a. 2, ad 3.

[80] *Ibid.*, III, q. 70, a. 4.

time, and by priority of nature, it is the cause of justification and therefore of faith.[81] By receiving this sacrament of faith the believer submits to the entire regime of the Church:

Whoever presents himself for baptism, by this very fact proclaims that he has the true faith of Christ, and that he venerates this sacrament, and that he wishes to conform to the Church, and that he wishes to renounce sin.[82]

This text is of special importance for the question of membership. Its significance will be developed below.

What is begun by baptism is brought to fulfillment by the Eucharist. The mystical body on earth perfects its union with Christ, and so its own unity, through acts of charity. The Eucharist is " the sacrament of Church unity, which consists in many being ' one in Christ ' (*Gal.* 3:28)." [83] It contains, under the symbol of unity, Christ himself the source of unity through charity so that its effect (*res significata et non contenta*) is the mystical body [84] in, that is to say, its perfect earthly state. The Eucharist is the supreme sacrament because it constitutes the limit case of the distinctive characteristic of the New-Law sacraments; it contains *Christus passus* himself. Thus a secondary element of the mystical body has become symbol and cause of the fullness of the primary element; the Roman Catholic Church is essentially eucharistic. The other sacraments are subordinate to this one and draw their significance as elements of the mystical body from it. Their function is to give visible structure to the body by conferring status or office in the Church (baptism, confirmation, orders, matrimony) and to give the graces, sanctifying and actual, corresponding directly to their limited purpose; like the body itself, their immediate purpose is perfected in charity, the special effect of the Eucharist.[85]

---

[81] Cf. *ibid.*, I-II, q. 114, a. 5, ad 1: "*dum iustificatur, credit.*"

[82] *Ibid.*, III, q. 69, a. 9, ad 3.

[83] *Ibid.*, III, q. 82, a. 2, ad 3; cf. St. Augustine, *In Ioann.*, tr. 16, n. 13.

[84] *Summa theol.*, III, q. 80, a. 4, ad 1.

[85] Cf. *ibid.*, III, q. 65, a. 3.

Within the limits of the present enquiry the following conclusion may be drawn concerning St. Thomas' teaching on the
nature of the mystical body in its present state. The primary
element of the body is charity; the believer who is in sin participates only imperfectly in this inner reality of the body, but
sufficiently not to be radically separated from the unity of
the whole. The secondary elements may be arranged in relation either with baptism or with the Eucharist. Baptism is for
the individual the necessary means of receiving from Christ
a share in the primary element of the body and is the ritual
of admittance and of submission to the visible organization
of the Church. The Eucharist, because it brings the primary
element to perfection, is the end towards which all the other
sacraments and offices of the Church are directed. The Eucharist, in its turn, is directed towards the enjoyment of Christ
in heaven, serving meanwhile as the necessary complement to
faith.[86]

III. Membership of the Mystical Body and of the Roman Catholic Church

A. *Membership and salvation*

The correlative notions of Head and member are essential
to St. Thomas' theology of salvation. The satisfaction and
merit of Christ have significance for others only because these
others form one mystic person with him. " Head and members are as one mystic person. *Consequently*, Christ's satisfaction belongs to all the faithful as to his members." [87] If the
validity of this concept were to be denied, it does not appear
that the Thomistic—or, for that matter, the Pauline—Christ-
ology could survive.

St. Thomas' view of incorporation into, and membership of,
Christ derives from his theology of man's predestination in
Christ. Divine permission of Adam's sin, which entails de-

[86] *Ibid.*, III, q. 80, a. 2, ad 1; ad 2.
[87] *Ibid.*, III, q. 48, a. 2, ad 1.

privation of grace for all mankind and consequent absorption
in material things, conditions the decree of salvation through
the Incarnate Word, the new Head of mankind, whose fleshly
mysteries will be valid as satisfaction and as merit for all men.
Christ, through his human mysteries, is established as the
universal efficient cause of salvation. The gift of grace to individual men remains a divine prerogative, something which
is determined solely by divine choice; but it is now given in
such fashion that, in the very reception of grace, the individual is associated with Christ in his mysteries, sharing thereby
in his satisfaction and his merits. This association with Christ
is achieved primarily by faith—a gift of God as well as disposition for grace—whereby the individual believes that " God
is [his] justifier through the mystery of Christ." [88] By this
faith the individual acknowledges the mystery of Christ's
Headship and, by acknowledging it, makes that Headship personally effective for himself so that, being in this way actually incorporated into Christ as a member, Christ's satisfaction and Christ's merit are *his* in the measure determined by
God and by his own free will. On St. Thomas' principles, to
say of a person that he is not a member of Christ is to say
that he is excluded from grace and salvation; for the communication of Christ's satisfaction and merits to men is possible *only* on the basis of a mystic identification with Christ.
The personal association with Christ achieved under the influence of sanctifying grace constitutes the proximate disposition
for justification, so that, while membership of Christ is a gift
of God, it is also achieved by the free act of the adult believer.
This is simply an application of the normal Thomistic teaching on the justification of the sinner.

It must, however, be further observed that in the incarnational economy willed by God the gift of grace is always given
at the present time through the efficient instrumental intervention of the humanity of Christ. And, in the logic of this
materialization of active salvation, it is regularly given through

[88] *Ibid.*, I-II, q. 113, a. 4, ad 3.

the subordinate efficient instrumental intervention of the sacraments. In this fashion, not only is fallen man's absorption
in material things orientated towards the spirit, but in addition the system of worship centered on the sacraments is raised
to a wholly higher level of sanctity by reason of the entry into
it of Christ himself, worshipping the Father and bringing
grace to the faithful. By using the sacraments of faith the
individual is associated in a new way with Christ the Head;
his association by faith finds external expression in a ceremonial which symbolizes, in one way or another, the saving mysteries of Christ's flesh and contains the saving power of those
mysteries. The purpose of this symbolic and causal association
is the same as that of the association by faith. It is integrated
with association by faith, rendering it human, as body does
soul, and thereby incorporates the believer *corporeally* as well
as spiritually into Christ. In other words, Christ's satisfaction
and merit are made effective for the believer because he forms
a single mystic person with Christ; and when sacraments are
used, the fact of being, through faith, one mystic person with
Christ is expressed in symbolic actions which procure a causal
contact between Christ and his member.

Incorporation into Christ has, accordingly, for its precise
purpose the actualization in respect to the individual of that
mystical identification of all men with Christ which is implied
in the divine decree of Christ's predestination as Head, and
which permits the attribution of Christ's satisfaction and merit
to others. In the present economy, grace cannot be given to
an individual unless he is a member of Christ, unless he is
incorporated into that mystical person to whom the merits of
Christ belong. Or, to put it in another and more theological
way, the fact that God gives His grace to an individual necessarily entails incorporation into Christ, at least by faith, and,
if sacraments are used, also corporeally. " Body," " Head,"
" member " are metaphorical terms, revealed in the Scripture
as analogical ways of expressing what is involved in the communication of the moral value of Christ's mysteries to other
persons.

B. *Dynamic incorporation*

In accordance with the basic formulation of the mystery just outlined, St. Thomas frequently gives to the notion of incorporation what might be called a dynamic perspective. Incorporation is then conceived, not so much as a stable relationship to Christ, but rather as an action by which man is inserted or, under divine grace, inserts himself into the savings acts of Christ's earthly life, thereby establishing the mystic, active union which makes possible the communication of the saving value of Christ's actions. Citing *Rom.*, 6:8, St. Thomas says:

By baptism a person is *incorporated into the passion and death* of Christ. [. . .] This makes it clear that the passion of Christ is communicated to everyone who is baptized, as a remedy, *just as though it were he who had suffered and died;*

and he adds in a response:

The penalty of Christ's passion is communicated to the person baptized—by reason of the fact that he becomes a member of Christ —*as though it were he who had borne that penalty.*[89]

It is in this " dynamic " sense that he can say, in III, q. 62, a. 1: " It is clear that through all the sacraments of the New Law a man is incorporated into Christ . . ." And it is in this sense also that he continues in the same article: " A man does not become a member of Christ except through grace." In the dynamic perspective he adopts here St. Thomas understands incorporation as the necessary condition for the communication of Christ's merits to the individual. The sacraments are the corporeal means of achieving association with Christ's passion so that the believer may benefit from the merits of Christ as belonging to, and acting in, the same mystic person. Only grace can procure this active saving incorporation; indeed such incorporation—*ad Christum* or *Christo* —may be said to consist in " acts of virtue." [90]

---

[89] *Ibid.*, III, q. 69, a. 2, ad 1; cf. a. 7, ad 1; q. 68, a. 5, ad 1.
[90] Cf. *ibid.*, III, q. 69, a. 5, Title.

There is, however, a stable form of incorporation into Christ, related to dynamic incorporation as effect to cause or as *actus primus* to *actus secundus*.

C. *Stable incorporation*

Taking into account St. Thomas' identification of the mystical body with the Church—after the Incarnation and on earth, with the Roman Catholic Church—and his admission that unformed faith suffices to maintain membership, however imperfect, of Christ, it may be stated that for him stable incorporation into Christ is achieved by possession of faith and reception of baptism. These two correspond to the primary and secondary elements respectively of the New Law in its present state. Hence there are two grades of incorporation which we shall consider separately. This methodological division is not to be taken as an assertion of the possibility of real division.

(i) *Mental incorporation*. Faith, whether the act or the habit, is the foundational bond with Christ because it implies intellectual acceptance of the mystery of salvation being achieved by the Blessed Trinity through Christ and through the Church. Of itself this is not a personal union involving full commitment of the will, but it provides sufficient incorporation into the mystic person of the Redeemer to serve as a human basis for obtaining the life of grace.[91] Such mental incorporation is perfect only when there is charity. "Mental incorporation" is therefore an analogical term applicable primarily to the result of living faith, secondarily to that of unformed faith; or, if the heavenly Church is taken into consideration, the prime analogue is union with Christ in vision and enjoyment of God. What is common to all analogues is knowledge of the mystery of God, revealed in Christ. In the present state such knowledge presupposes in adults the proposition by teachers of its object, normally by the teaching authority of the Church.

[91] *Ibid.*, III, q. 8, a. 3, ad 2.

(ii) *Sacramental incorporation.* The sacraments complement faith, providing a form of incorporation which St. Thomas contrasts with that provided by faith in the following terms: sacramental, mental;[92] bodily, mental;[93] sacramental, "real";[94] in body, in heart;[95] by number, by merit;[96] and by the signs of faith and by faith.[97]

The original "dynamic" incorporation is procured by the *sacramentum tantum* or the "visible sacrament" of baptism,[98] which serves as the efficacious symbol of Christ's passion and death as communicated to the recipient. This is a transposition into symbolism, which is efficacious, of the mystical identification with Christ achieved by faith. St. Thomas also speaks of it as "configuration" to Christ, the sense being that the believer engages in external action which symbolizes the external action of Christ in his passion. A similar configuration, this time "real" rather than symbolic, is achieved by bearing actual suffering as satisfaction for sin.[99] While the Church guarantees faith for infants, it is clear that without true faith in an adult who receives baptism the symbolism of the visible sacrament is falsified, for the person is not personally associated with Christ in his passion; consequently, in spite of external configuration, dynamic incorporation at least is not achieved.

Granted, however, that the sacrament is valid, it produces as its effect a permanent reality, the baptismal character, and it is in virtue of this reality that stable sacramental incorporation is *possible.* Whether it is in fact achieved depends on whether or not the person is mentally incorporated. This calls for more detailed explanation.

The part played by the character in sacramental incorpor-

[92] *Ibid.*, III, q. 68, a. 2.
[93] *Ibid.*, III, q. 69, a. 5, ad 1.
[94] *Ibid.*, III, q. 80, a. 4, ad 4.
[95] *Ibid.*, III, q. 68, a. 2, ad 1.
[96] *IV Sent.*, d. 4, q. 2, a. 2, qla. 5; *Summa theol.*, II-II, q. 1, a. 9, ad 3.
[97] *Summa theol.*, III, q. 61, a. 3; a. 4; q. 70, a. 1; a. 2, ad 2.
[98] *Ibid.*, III, q. 69, a. 5, ad 1.
[99] *Ibid.*, III, q. 49, a. 3, ad 2.

ation is best understood in terms of the comparison, suggested by St. Thomas, with circumcision.[100] The Old-Law rite of initiation introduced the Jew into the congregation of the Chosen People, dedicated to the worship of the true God. Because the sacraments of the Jewish liturgy were nothing more than symbolic ceremonial, the sign of aggregation to the People was itself purely external. In the New Law, on the contrary, the sacraments contain the power of Christ's passion which inwardly affects the worshipper. To participate sacramentally in this liturgy-*par-excellence* of Christ's passion a special power is needed and this is supplied by the character. While thus enabling the worshipper to act in the sacraments, the character of baptism still fulfills the rôle, formerly assigned to circumcision, of distinguishing the worshipper in the Christian liturgy from those unable to take part in it. The baptismal character is consequently not only a liturgical power but also a sign distinguishing the person who possesses the right and the duty of taking part in that worship in which Christ is the principal agent [101] and in which the individual is associated with others who bear the character.[102]

The baptismal character is, consequently, an element in incorporation into Christ, first, insofar as it is a faculty or *power* providing that participation in Christ's priesthood which enables its bearer to take part in the sacraments and thereby to be further incorporated into Christ sacramentally and dynamically; and secondly, insofar as it is a permanent *sign* of the believer's sacramental association with Christ the Priest and with his fellow worshippers. For these two reasons St. Thomas can describe the baptismal character as " incorcorpating a man into Christ ".[103] It must, however, be observed that the character does this only for the person who has faith, a situation envisaged in the place just quoted; for

[100] Cf. *ibid.*, III q. 70, a. 4; q .63, a. 1, ad 3.
[101] *Ibid.*, III, q. 63, a. 3. For the character as sign, cf. q. 63, a. 2, ad 4.
[102] *Ibid.*, III, q. 68, a. 1, ad 3.
[103] *Ibid.*, III, q. 70, a. 4.

the character is no more than an executive power subordinated to faith, enabling the believer to make those signs of faith which constitute his part in the sacraments.[104] It is quite true that the character may be used and sacraments thereby rendered valid simply through an intention, even without faith; but the baptismal character is given for the service of the individual's faith and only as long as faith is preserved can there be any question of incorporation. The character makes sacramental the stable mental incorporation of faith. Lacking faith, one who has received baptism may be said to have " put on Christ as being configured to him by the character, but not conformed to him by grace." [105] The term " configured " is here to be understood by analogy with the sense it has when used of the person receiving the *sacramentum tantum*: the character is a permanent sign indicating that a person has been deputed to take part in sacramental actions symbolic of Christ's mysteries and containing the power of those mysteries; it is a power which makes further dynamic sacramental incorporation possible. When combined with faith, the character provides true stable sacramental incorporation into Christ and makes possible dynamic sacramental incorporation. When faith is absent the fundamental union of Christ and the individual in one mystic person is also absent, with the result that the sacramental association procurable through the character is meaningless. This point must be insisted on against several Thomists who ascribe incorporation —often without any further qualification—to the baptismal character. Not only is the unqualified statement explicitly contrary to St. Thomas' teaching on the possibility of incorporation without the character; it logically implies as well that even the damned, if they have the character, are incorporated into Christ. Simply to assert that the character incorporates the living, but does not incorporate those in hell, looks un-

---

[104] Cf. *ibid.*, III, q. 63, a. 4, ad 3—perhaps the most illuminating of all St. Thomas' remarks on the character.

[105] *Ibid.*, III, q. 69, a. 9, ad 1.

pleasantly like a covert use of the principles of a voluntaristic theology. There is an ontological reason if the baptismal character does not incorporate, namely, the absence of faith, the principle of all incorporation.

For the sake of clarity our conclusion—which includes elements from previous sections—is cast in tabular form:

Stable sacramental incorporation:

— *presupposes* mental incorporation by faith
— *is obtained* by sacramental baptism
— *is maintained* by the baptismal character
— *implies* (by reason of baptism accepted with faith):
    — acceptance of the magisterium
    —acknowledgment of the binding force of the hierarchy's directives
—*is exercised* in acts "proper to the present Church" [106] (all Christian action, whether directly sacramental or not)
—*is perfected* by charity obtained through the Eucharist.

It is evident that the external obligations of sacramental membership are adequately proposed, and the opportunity of fulfilling them integrally is presented, only to those commonly known as Roman Catholics. For this reason we may denominate them "integral sacramento-juridical members." The term is admittedly tautologous; it being sufficient to say "integral sacramental members" since integrity in sacramental incorporation implies acknowledgement of juridical obligations. Nevertheless the longer term is to be preferred so as to avoid ambiguity. For such members as these, charity not only perfects mental membership but also ensures the fulfillment of the external obligations, constituting integral and perfect sacramento-juridical membership. The inclusion of mental membership in sacramental membership means that the term "member" is applied by analogy to Roman Catholics in the state of grace and to those in sin. The use of a common term is justified by the characteristic common to the two groups: faith and integral sacramental incorporation, the latter de-

---

[106] Cf. *ibid.*, III, q. 63, a. 1, ad 1.

noting the state in which all the external obligations of baptism may be fulfilled.

C. *Other forms of membership*

While integral sacramento-juridical membership is confined to believers known as Roman Catholics, the possibility of others than those being saved entails, according to St. Thomas' concept of salvation, that membership of Christ and therefore of the Church may be achieved in a fashion which is not integrally sacramento-juridical. As has been pointed out, the gift of sanctifying grace presupposes and grants mental incorporation into Christ, unique Head of redeemed humanity. Such incorporation cannot be maintained unless supernatural faith is preserved. Here it will be assumed, without discussion of the problems involved, that both faith and charity may be given to those not known as Roman Catholics; since the Church teaches as much our assumption is justified.[107] What follows concerns the nature of the membership which results from the possession of these gifts, first by baptized non-Catholics, secondly by those not baptized. The problem consists essentially in determining the relationship which exists between the mental membership of such persons and the visible elements of the one Church. The principle of solution lies in St. Thomas' distinction between the primary and secondary elements of the New Law in its present historical state.

(i) *Baptized non-Catholics.* Baptism, validly administered, is the baptism of the one Church.[108] Validity requires, on the part of the minister, an intention to do what the Church does,[109] and, on the part of the adult recipient, an intention to receive what the Church gives.[110] Fruitful reception of baptism requires either the personal faith of the adult recipient [111]

---

[107] A useful summary of contemporary discussion of these problems is to be found in M. Eminyan, S. J., *The Theology of Salvation*, Boston, 1960.

[108] *Summa theol.*, III, q. 68, a. 8, ad 2.

[109] *Ibid.*, III, q. 67, a. 5, ad 2.

[110] *Ibid.*, III, q. 68, a. 9, ad 3.

[111] *Ibid.*, III, q. 68, a. 8; cf. a. 39, a. 5.

or, for infants and others in similar condition, the faith of the
Church, always supplied with valid baptism.[112] In the latter
case, baptism, wherever administered, has equal effect; perfect and integral sacramento-juridical membership of the one
Church is obtained, though it evidently cannot be fully exercised. What is the position of adult believers who receive valid
baptism from a non-Catholic minister?

St. Thomas envisages such a case in the more general terms
of acceptance of a sacrament from an heretical or excommunicated minister. Granted that the minister has power to
administer the sacrament—and about this there is no difficulty in the case of baptism—the recipient receives it fruitfully in two circumstances; if the minister is not manifestly
cut off from the Church, and if the recipient is ignorant of
the minister's condition.[113] Assuming, then, good faith on the
part of the recipient, valid baptism in a non-Catholic religious group is fruitful, either procuring mental and sacramental incorporation for the first time or making mental incorporation sacramental. Such a person maintains a stable
sacramental incorporation by faith and possession of the baptismal character.

To determine the nature of this sacramental incorporation
its elements must be examined. By reason of the faith of the
person it involves implicit acceptance of the divinely-insti-
tuted magisterium (which itself constitutes a material object
of faith). This is so even if, as may be assumed to be the
case, the individual explicitly rejects the teaching authority of
the hierarchy; for, faith, granted that it is possessed, is infallible and embraces the whole of revelation, attaining every
truth at least implicitly; and faith is unaffected by false ideas
entertained on "human conjecture" or because of misguid-
ance by teachers.[114]

Faith also implies belief in the general authority of the

---

[112] *Ibid.*, III, q. 68, a. 9.
[113] *Ibid.*, III, q. 64, a. 9, ad 2; ad 3.
[114] Cf. *ibid.*, II-II, q. 1, a. 3, ad 3; q. 2, a. 6, ad 3; q. 5, a. 4.

hierarchy; and acceptance of baptism carries with it juridical acknowledgement, at least implicit, of this authority. A comparable submission to superiors who are not consciously acknowledged cannot be realized in a purely human society. It is once again the universality of infused faith which adheres without reserve to the truth revealed by God that makes it possible in the Church. By reason of faith, ratified juridically by the *sacramentum-tantum* of baptism, there is achieved sacramento-juridical union with the pope and the episcopate. It is imperfect in its juridical aspect, not objectively, but subjectively, by reason, that is, of the lack of consciousness on the part of the recipient of the full consequences of his engagement. His situation in this respect is not that of a responsible adult, but is comparable rather to that of a child presented to baptism by the faith of the Church.

The union with the Church acquired in baptism is maintained by faith and the baptismal character; but the non-Catholic cannot exercise fully his sacramental membership in acts " proper to the present Church." External acts of virtue are possible and serve, as do those of recognized Catholics, to give testimony to the mystery of Christ in the world, though in official fashion only when valid confirmation has been received. Strictly sacramental activity varies according to the religious body in which the individual worships; but all baptized believers can share in the sacrifice of the Mass in virtue of the baptismal character; all too are sacramentally directed by baptism towards reception of Communion.[115] In no case, however, is there implementation of the implicitly accepted juridical consequences of baptism, so that submission to the hierarchy remains in an habitual, implicit state. Nor is the magisterium of the Church directly effective in proposing the object of belief. Nevertheless, some part of the authentic Christian revelation is proposed to the non-Catholic through the Scriptures and through the teaching of his religious group. Though such truth is mingled with error and is not taught

[115] *Ibid.*, III, q. 73, a. 3.

with the divine authority of the Church, which alone can objectively justify assent, it might be said to be a participation in the content of the magisterium.

By reason of these imperfections in exercise, the membership of baptized non-Catholics may be termed partial sacramento-juridical membership, it being understood that only when membership is integral are juridical obligations fulfilled by conscious submission to the hierachy in its teaching and directive office. Partial sacramento-juridical membership is not lost with charity but only with faith; for baptism actually received entails a positive act of will binding the individual to Christ and the Church sacramentally and juridically; and this can be withdrawn only by a contrary act such as is involved in formal heresy or schism. Accordingly, the baptized non-Catholic may be either a perfect partial sacramento-juridical member—if he has charity, which means desire of the Eucharist—or an imperfect partial sacramento-juridical member—if he has unformed faith. "Perfect" and "imperfect," it will be seen, refer directly, not to sacramental membership, but to mental. To compare the status in the Church and in the mystical body of a non-Catholic and a Catholic requires comparison at the level of both forms of membership.

(ii) *The non-baptized*. It is evident that the non-baptized are not incorporated into Christ sacramentally, either dynamically or in stable fashion. On St. Thomas' principles it is evident too that if the non-baptized are to be saved they must be incorporated into Christ mentally; and St. Thomas says as much explicitly.[116] When speaking of mental incorporation in these circumstances St. Thomas normally envisages it as being achieved by "faith working through charity" (*Gal.*, 5:6); but in III, q. 8, a. 3, he admits in quite general terms that unformed faith is adequate for (mental) incorporation, though he qualifies such membership as *secundum quid*—not, that is, affecting the individual in his complete person. Lacking the juridical and sacramental stability of personal engage-

---

[116] Cf. *ibid.*, III, q. 68, a. 2; *Qdl.* 4, q. 7, a. 1.

ment procured through baptism, such a person might be thought to have lapsed from membership; but if St. Thomas' cautious reservations are noted there is no reason to refuse his opinion.[117]

Seen against the background of St. Thomas' theology of salvation his attribution of membership to the non-baptized person who possesses infused faith must be recognized as inevitable; and it is for this reason that his position is urged with such insistence. The difficulty is, of course, to reconcile this position with the teaching of the magisterium that the mystical body is identified with the Roman Catholic Church. To avoid this difficulty by the assertion that St. Thomas meant that the non-baptized believer is incorporated in some other mystical body than that which is the Roman Catholic Church is to ignore his very clear teaching that the mystical body in its present earthly state is precisely this Church—to say nothing of the violence done to the formal point of the scriptural metaphor. In other words the difficulty is not one that has arisen since the publication of *Mystici corporis*; it is one that is already to be found in the text of St. Thomas; and it is here that a solution must be sought.

The principle of the solution offered by St. Thomas, as has already been suggested, is his distinction between the primary and the secondary elements in the present state of the mystical body on earth, the Roman Catholic Church. The primary element is grace; the secondary elements, whatever externals are presupposed by grace or required for its full development. Since the Incarnation grace is *caused* through the humanity of Christ and through the sacraments of the Church; and the *use* of grace presupposes the directive authority vested in the hierarchy. At the present time, in other words, sanctifying grace necessarily bears a relation to the visible organs of the

---

[117] There is nothing contrary to this opinion in the letter of the Holy Office, *Suprema haec sacra*, 8 August, 1949. This requires that the desire by which the non-baptized are "ordered to Christ" be informed by charity: "ut homo salvetur" (Denz-Schönmetzer 3872), which is evidently true, but abstracts from the problem of present membership in the Church.

Church. The necessary function of the secondary elements of the Church being thus affirmed as a consequence of the *Incarnation,* the solution to the abnormal—though possibly frequent—case that we are now considering may be sought by directing attention to the *secondary* character of these elements. This is what St. Thomas does; he is content to restrict his explanations to the problem of the necessity of the sacraments. Contemporary Thomists must develop the implications of his solution in order to satisfy all current difficulties.

In the first place, St. Thomas relates all justification from original sin to baptism. Those who neither receive actual baptism nor have at least an implicit desire for it cannot be saved, " for neither mentally nor sacramentally are they incorporated into Christ through whom alone is there salvation." [118] The concept of " baptism *voto* " has become so much a commonplace of theology that its full significance for the problem of membership may easily be overlooked. It is proposed by St. Thomas precisely as a solution to this problem, so that it is worth while to analyze its sense.

The *votum baptismi* is not, in the first place, a desire for baptism as an instrumental efficient cause of justification, for the hypothesis is that justification has already been granted. St. Thomas specifically rules out the absolute necessity of sacraments as efficient causes of grace with the phrase: " the power of God is not restricted to the sacraments." [119] Baptism is not desired, accordingly, as a means of mental incorporation, for this is presupposed to the *votum*; it is desired as the means of sacramental incorporation. That is to say, it is desired first as a means of dynamic sacramental incorporation into Christ's passion, which commmunicates a fuller share in his satisfaction, and as the prescribed ceremonial of profession of faith and of entry into the congregation of believers.[120] It is desired secondly as the efficient instrumental cause of the char-

---

[118] *Summa theol.*, III, q. 68, a. 2; cf. q. 69, a. 4, ad 2.

[119] *Ibid.*, III, q. 68, a. 2.

[120] Cf. *ibid.*, III, q. 69, a. 4, ad 2.

acter which gives stable sacramental incorporation. What is desired is not yet possessed; consequently there is no sacramental incorporation. There is already, however, as a necessary condition of mental incorporation, implicit submission to the Church and acknowledgement of the Roman hierarchy, together with a readiness to undergo the ceremony of entry to the Church. Such incorporation, which is equivalent to first justification, can be achieved only by charity which includes a readiness to fulfill all the obligations contained in divine revelation. Once achieved, a vestigial mental membership may remain through faith if charity is lost.[121] Restoration to grace after personal sin can be achieved only through a desire of the sacrament of penance; [122] this *votum* has a similar significance to that of baptism.

St. Thomas further relates mental membership of the non-baptized to the Eucharist; and it is in this context that he explains the phrase: *Nulli patet aditus salutis extra Ecclesiam*. The unity of the mystical body is the effect (*res*) of the Eucharist; accordingly there can be no salvation for anyone who does not receive this effect, through reception of the sacrament actually or in desire.[123] Spiritual eating of the Eucharist is equivalent to receiving the sacrament fruitfully, to incorporation into Christ, and is achieved by actual worthy reception or by desire.[124] Once again, the term "*votum*" is introduced in order to state clearly the sacramental reference included in charity given after the Incarnation. The act of charity is the sacramental grace of the Eucharist and is ordained towards finding expression in the *convivium* of the Eucharistic sacrifice and Communion. In absence of the baptismal character such expression is impossible for the person concerned.[125] Nevertheless his grace is an effect of the Mass

---

[121] It is to be noted that here we are abstracting from the question whether such a situation could arise in fact. The possibility at least may be envisaged.

[122] E.g., *Qdl.*, 4, q. 7, a. 1, ad 3.

[123] *Summa theol.*, III, q. 73, a. 3.

[124] *Ibid.*, III, q. 73, a. 3, ad 2; q. 80, a. 1, ad 3; a. 11.

[125] If the phrase "to offer the Christian sacrifice through Christ" is understood

and is symbolized by the Eucharistic species and to this extent is signified and caused by a sacrament.

It is necessary to insist on this sacramentalizing through the Eucharist of the grace of the non-baptized. It is the sole actual relation of such persons to an element in the sacramental structure of the Church. Baptism *voto* has reference to a sacrament which does not yet exist, which may never exist, for baptism is evidently real only when actually received by an individual. The Eucharist, on the contrary, is actually related to all those who are incorporated into Christ on earth, whether sacramentally or simply mentally. It is precisely the *sacramentum ecclesiasticae unionis*. This is not to suggest that Eucharistic union by itself is adequate for the present state of the mystical body, or even that if all those whose membership is partially sacramental were to be brought into the condition where they could actually receive the sacrament, the unity and visibility of the Church would leave nothing to be desired. Such a position might represent the objective of the Eastern Orthodox Church. The Catholic theologian must insist that full Eucharistic communion presupposes baptism and consequently all the juridical consequences of baptism, foremost among them submission to the Vicar of Christ.

Our conclusion, accordingly, is that there is no such thing as exclusively mental membership of Christ. What is termed mental membership is sacramental at least to the extent that it is caused and symbolized by the Eucharist, sacrifice and communion, the sacrament of that body of Christ which, being united to the divine Word, is the created source of all grace.

If terms are to be found which will express the difference between Orthodox Christians, other baptized non-Catholics, and the non-baptized, it might be suggested that the first be denominated " partial sacramento-juridical members," (thus

to refer to Christ's status as the Head who offers in the name of all men, and if " to offer with Christ " is understood of the sacramental offering of the Eucharist possible for each of the baptized, then the non-baptized in grace may be said to offer the Mass through Christ, but not with him.

reserving to them a term previously used of all baptized non-Catholic believers), the second, " partial baptismo-juridical members," and the last, " partial Eucharistic-non-juridical members"—what is lost in elegance of expression being compensated for by accuracy of description. If it is granted, that unformed faith is sufficient for rudimentary membership, a further distinction must be made between perfect and imprefect Eucharist-non-juridical members. It is more important, however, that the reality signified by the terms be understood than that there be agreement on the terms themselves.

*   *   *   *

To use the single term " member," however qualified, of all those who have been raised to the supernatural life clearly involves analogy. The purpose of the employment of a common term is to express, by means of the revealed metaphor, the fact that grace can be received only on condition that the individual man is so associated with the person of Christ, that Christ's merits and satisfaction are communicated to him as his own. Such association may, however, be achieved in a variety of ways. Of its essence it requires faith in the mystery of divine predestination in Christ, for without such faith Christ's headship is not efficacious in regard to the individual. Moreover, man's enslavement to material things because of sin, and the consequent assumption of a material body and a human soul by the divine Word, have made it necessary that faith in Christ be expressed externally in bodily ceremonial symbolic of man's interior association with the Redeemer. The term "member of Christ," when applied to men on earth, thus signifies union with Christ by faith and by the signs of faith. Yet, if this is what is common to all those on earth denominated " members," quite distinct realities correspond to the them in the various classes of individuals concerned. Faith may be either formed or unformed. Union by the signs of faith ranges from that which was available even before the Old Law to that which is obtained through the sacramental signs of the Church, which contain the power of Christ and which imply conformity to the way of life in a highly organized religious society. At the present time union with Christ by faith must be complemented by union through the necessary sacraments of the Church with all their juridical consequences. Since these conditions may be fulfilled either *re* or *voto* (as regards sacraments), either explicitly or implicitly (as regards juridical consequences), the use of the term "member" remains analogical by analogy of strict proportionality. Each individual so denominated is united to Christ by faith and sacraments in the manner consonant with his explicit knowledge of revelation.

When the term "member" is extended to the saints in heaven the reality expressed is beatific vision and corporeal union with Christ. This further modifies the proportional similarity denoted by the analogical term; we are now given "supernatural knowledge of God, given by Christ, expressed externally according to ones' condition in respect of the Incarnation." If, with St. Thomas, we include the angels in the mystical body in so far as they are influenced, though not sanctified, by Christ, the similarity between the classes denominated as members becomes less definite—perhaps: "supernatural knowledge of God and receptivity in respect of Christ."

A final problem must be noticed. If membership of the mystical body on earth is to be extended not only to non-Catholic Christians but also to the non-baptized, what has become of the visibility and the unity of the Church?

IV. Visibility and Unity of the Church

A. *Visibility*

The problem of the visibility of the Church is treated in apologetics with the purpose of proving that the society founded by Christ is discoverable as such and thereby distinguishable from other societies claiming this title. Further development of the theology of the Church may presuppose the conclusion of apologetics that the Roman Catholic Church is the true Church founded by Christ and preserved indefectibly.

This we have seen to be St. Thomas' assumption when he takes it for granted that the New Law in its present state is the Church of Rome. Granted, then, that the sincere and intelligent enquirer can be led to a judgment affirming the credibility of the claim of the Church, and granted that, given grace, such a judgment should lead to conscious submission to the Church, the question may still be asked whether the visibility which is a property of the Church can be realized exclusively by full, open adherence to the society known to all as the Roman Catholic Church. It may be replied at once that only in this way may full visibility be realized and that there is a very clearly defined portion of the human race which does in fact realize such full visibility. It may also be granted that membership of a visible society must be visible. But, since there are in fact in the Church several factors which contribute to such membership, is it possible that these factors are separable in such wise that individuals may satisfy certain requirements of visibility and not others? Should an affirmative reply be given to this qusetion, it will be understood that there is no suggestion that this is an ideal state of affairs which corresponds adequately to the demands of the nature of the Church; it is simply a matter of recognizing a *de-facto* situation.

The visibility of the Church rests primarily on the three " structurizing" sacraments: baptism, confirmation and orders, and on the exercise of the offices deriving from them. The hierarchy proposes revelation, supervises the life of the society and administers the sacraments. The faithful, in virtue of baptism, publicly accept the direction and ministry of the hierarchy and bear witness to Christ in Christian action. Confirmation lends an official validity and efficacy to these activities. Clearly only the integral sacramento-juridical member contributes to the visibility of the Church in an integral manner. There is a radical difference, as far as visibility is concerned, between such a person and all those who, whatever degree of sacramental life may be theirs, do not openly acknowledge the Vicar of Christ. It is this difference which justifies the denomination of "separated" applied to all who are not known as Roman Catholics. It still remains true that for the eye of faith the mystical body of Christ, and therefore the Church, is revealed in all baptized believers. The vision of faith extends beyond the area of Christians to which the apologete must necessarily confine his attention. An element of conjecture enters into all judgments affirming the membership of individuals, for faith and charity are not subject to certain observation; but, just as we can say that one who professes integral Roman Catholicism contributes to the integral visibility of the Church, so we can add that all the baptized, because they have received the sacrament of initiation into the unique society of Christ on earth, thereby professing at least implicit submission to the Roman hierarchy, and because their lives bear the mark of Christian teaching, give at least partial visibility to the mystery of Christ and consequently to the society which he founded. It must never be forgotten that our concept of a human society, with its clearly-defined circle of membership, is no more than an analogy for understanding the Church. We have to correct our juridical categories by taking into account the mystery of faith and charity.

If the non-baptized also are members of the Christian society their membership too, by reason of the nature of the Church, must be in some fashion visible. That their activity may be judged by an observer to be directed by principles which we recognize as Christian might be said to lend a certain visibility to their membership; but a sacramental visibility is necessary for membership of the Church. For this recourse must be had to the Eucharist, cause and symbol of mental membership of Christ and of the Church. It may be objected that this is to stretch the concept of visibility to such an extent that it no longer corresponds to the plain meaning of the term. Again we must appeal to analogy. In terms of purely human association it is nonsense to suggest that a person who has never applied for membership, or perhaps has never heard of the existence of the society in question, could be considered a visible member. But the primary element of the Church is grace, not what is juridically verifiable; and this fact must modify our concept of visible membership. The membership of the non-baptized believer is in no way juridically verifiable; but the Eucharist makes it visible, not, certainly, in such fashion that we can point to an individual and to his visible affiliation to the Church, but visible in a manner consonant with the mystery of the Church. We might term it a sacramento-objective visibility, contrasting this with subjective visibility which requires at least personal reception of the sacrament of baptism.

The Roman Catholic Church, accordingly, is the visible and unique Church of Christ. The apologete is interested in its visibility insofar as it enables the enquirer to distinguish the true Church from innumerable other societies making a like claim. But the visibility which is a property of the Church of the Incarnate Word is integrally achieved only in a restricted section of humanity; vestiges or incipient traces of it may be discovered wherever men belong to Christ.

B. *Unity*

As with the problem of visibility our approach to that of unity must be guided, not only by an abstract concept of the Church, but also by a recognition of a factual situation. And since we have argued that the Church, though always visible, is not integrally visible by reason of defects in individuals' membership, we are compelled by logic to admit that the unity of the Church has not, at the present moment in the history of salvation, been integrally realized. Once again, this is not at all the same thing as denying the unity of the Church as it is exposed in apologetics.

The note of unity, a manifestation of the true Church through community in faith, worship and organization, is realized in the unifying action of the hierarchy and in the faithful who publicly accept their ministrations. The question may

be asked, however, whether the integral unity thus achieved
among those known as Roman Catholics may not be extended
in non-integral fashion to all those who are members of Christ.
The very fact that the existence of members not known as
Roman Catholics is admitted, necessitates an affirmative reply.

Whereas the apologete is compelled to consider unity as it
appears externally, St. Thomas, taking for granted the conclusion of apologetics, is concerned to analyze the property of
unity itself. He sees it to be a property of the primary element of the Church, that is, of faith and charity. That the
secondary elements—those externals which primarily occupy
the apologete—are causes, conditions and consequences of
unity, he admits; but precisely by indicating that they are
secondary he supplies the principle for accounting theologically for the unity which can exist among all Christians.

The principal place to be consulted is the question on the
sin of schism, II-II, q. 39. After noting that in moral affairs
the formal aspect is to be discovered in the intention (*id quod
est intentum est per se*), he goes on to define the sin of schism
as "the intention to separate oneself from that unity which is
made by charity (*quam caritas facit.*)" Charity unites, not
only individuals, but as well " the whole Church in the unity
of the spirit [*or* Spirit] "; and it is sin against the latter which
is primarily meant by schism. Then follows:

The unity of the Church is to be sought in two things: namely, in
the mutual connection of the members of the Church; and further
in the ordination of all the members of the Church to one head.
[*Col.,* 2:18-19]. Now this head is Christ himself; and his place is
taken in the Church by the Supreme Pontiff. Accordingly schismatics are those who refuse to submit to the Supreme Pontiff and
who are unwilling to live in communion with the members of the
Church who are subject to him.[126]

The two elements of unity thus described are the effect of
charity; but the nature of the Church requires that they be
expressed in external communion with others, not only by

---

[126] *Summa theol.,* II-II, q. 39, a. 1.

works of charity, but in all those actions which characterize the Roman Catholic Church. But, given what is primary, unity is not wholly prejudiced by imperfections in external communion. Faith and charity ensure that the social obligations imposed through revelation are accepted in their entirety, even if, in greater or less degree, implicitly. Unity is established; but, in respect of the secondary elements of the Church, it is partial, not integral. The separated Christian who possesses charity is moved by God in the same way, essentially, as the Roman Catholic in grace; the spirit of unity animates both. The difference lies only in the external situation in which each—through no fault or merit of his own—finds himself. In one case the knowledge and opportunity required for developing all the potentialities of charity are given; in the other case knowledge is given, but only as implicit in faith, and opportunity is given in limited fashion only. Since without explicit knowledge and full opportunity, integral unity, extending to all the secondary elements in the Church, is not realized, the mystical body on earth suffers, not disunion, but imperfect union. The Church is involved in history and in temporal development because of its secondary elements; and this necessarily affects, though indirectly, the primary element. Unity, like everything that stems from virtue in the Church, is at once possessed and in need of development and perfection. The perfection which through Christ belongs to the Church must be developed in the life of each member.

It is a necessary consequence of these principles that the Roman Catholic sinner is not in perfect union with Christ or with the Church; he is, says St. Thomas, " separated by merit from the unity of the Church," though not, " by number." [127] Only a narrowly juridical view of the Church, which fails to take account of the full mystery, will prompt a denial of this. A very real participation remains, unless excommunication should intervene to forbid the use or benefit of the secondary

[127] *Ibid.*, II-II, q. 39, a. 1, ad 2; *I ad Cor.*, cap. 11, lect. 7 (M. n. 691).

elements of the Church to the sinner. But all sinners—Catholic, non-Catholic or non-baptized—who retain infused faith preserve a participation, however remote, in the unity of the Church in proportion to each one's interior and exterior bonds.

*   *   *   *

While, then, in the visible structure of the Roman Catholic Church alone is the mystical body integrally visible on earth, and here alone are brought together all the secondary elements of unity, there are to be found incipient elements of visibility in those members of Christ and the Church who have not yet realized actually their implicit submssion to the pope; and there is, in addition, a fundamental unity among all members which finds integral expression only among those known as Roman Catholics and which is symbolized and caused by the sacrament of the true body of Christ, the sacrifice and Communion of the Church. Visibility and unity which are both perfect (charity) and integral (corporeal) will be realized through all members of the Church only after the general resurrection. It is unnecessary to add that the duty of the Church on earth is to bring all members of Christ into that integral union where alone the richness of redemption is made fully available to men.

The attempt to demonstrate the unity of all men of good will in membership of Christ and in acknowledgement of the Vicar of Christ should not be dismissed as a theological *tour de force*. There is a real union which must be explained, a union, however masked by juridical separation and difference of opinion, which became almost palpable during the life and especially at the death of the Pope of Unity, John XXIII.

COLMAN E. O'NEILL, O. P.

Iesus Magister Institute,
Lateran Pontifical University,
Rome, Italy

SCRIPTURE AND TRADITION IN RECENT
CATHOLIC THOUGHT

༄

THOSE who had occasion during the past decade to examine current trends in Catholic theology, especially in French and German literature, were aware of the rapid emergence of an impressive body of new facts and opinions concerning the classic problem of Scripture and Tradition. Between 14 and 20 November last year, the importance, if not the nature, of these rather esoteric developments suddenly acquired wide publicity by reason of their reverberations in the Second Vatican Council. For it seems to have been the chapter on Scripture and Tradition, of the schema presented by Cardinal Ottaviani's Theological Commission that occasioned the first deployment of opposition at the Council along lines of properly doctrinal controversy. The colorful debate that followed issued in a vote that discovered the protesting group to be a large but technically insufficient majority, only to be dramatically confirmed by the Pope's personal intervention, requiring the schema to be withdrawn and submitted for revision to a special committee tantamount to a coalition. While our knowledge of these events and their sequel must remain unofficial and incomplete, quite enough has appeared to show that the question of Scripture and Tradition is not only an insistent but a volatile one for the fathers of the Second Vatican Council. So was it also, of course, for the fathers of the Council of Trent. And yet, for the fathers of the intervening First Vatican Council it had become a neutral issue, considered to have been settled at Trent, and to require no more original treatment than verbatim citation of the Tridentine formula. Only one bishop seems to have proposed an ampler statement on Tradition, and that in the vaguest of terms and without eliciting any sympathetic response.[1] These strikingly different attitudes towards the question of Scripture and Tradition, in the two great modern Councils separated by less than a century are, of course, the result of many factors of several kinds brought to bear during the interval. The brief account that follows will be concerned only with theological factors—most of which happen to be very recent factors—and with these only under their broadest aspects. I hope to indicate the immediately appreciable questions that have been most definitively raised, the literature in which they have been most satisfactorily treated, and the mutual pertinence that they most obviously display; to offer, in other words, an introductory essay, comprising a logical outline and a basic bibliography.

THE SHAPE OF THE PROBLEM

Scripture and Tradition. A Church of Scotland biblical scholar, J. K. S. Reid, expressed what has oftenest been meant by " the problem of Scripture and Tradition " in a way that is concise, and about as accurate as such concision permits:

> There are at least two conceivable relations between tradition and Scripture. The first is that tradition arises out of and is ultimately dependent upon Scripture; the other is that tradition exists as an independent factor alongside of Scripture. Between these two views, out of the Bible or alongside the Bible, the Roman Church has never quite decided.[2]

One critical reflection that is prompted at once by Reid's framing of his dilemma, and which he doubtless means to anticipate by his qualifying " at least," is that it is not strictly complete from a standpoint of disinterested logic. That is to say, whatever one may conclude about a subsequent tradition's arising out of Scripture, it remains a logical possibility, and seems moreover to be an historical fact, that out of ante-

---

[1] See *Mansi* L, 268. Del Valle, Bishop of Huanuco, Peru, proposed that an amplification of the doctrine on Tradition be included in the second chapter of the *Constitutio dogmatica de fide catholica.*

[2] Reid, J. K. S. *The Authority of Scripture* (London, 1957), p. 134.

cedent tradition, and indeed what can fairly be called an ecclesiastical tradition, Scripture itself arose.[3] Although implications drawn from this fact by students of the *Formgeschichte*
school raise problems of a literary historical nature for everyone and of a theological nature more especially for the biblical fundamentalist, such consequences of the fact, unlike the
fact itself, lie outside our present subject. To establish a case
for institutionally controlled tradition as formative of the
rabbinic *torah* in late Judaism, and for its counterpart in the
Apostolic Church as generative of the written Gospel is, to
be sure, refutation of a formidable school of historical thought
that thrived within liberal Protestantism, and had unhappy
resonances in Catholicism. At the same time, it must be
conceded that for Catholics to invoke such considerations
against the substance of Reformation doctrine on the primacy
of Scripture would be to content themselves with scoring verbal points. Contemporary Protestant theologians accept and
develop these findings, predominantly of Protestant scholars,
no less readily than do Catholics, nor does there seem to be
any serious reason derivable from the Reformers why they
should not.[4]

[3] This viewpoint seems to have been distinctly furthered in a recent important
contribution to biblical studies: Gerhardsson, B., *Memory and Manuscript: Oral
Tradition and Written Transmission in Rabbinic Judaism and Early Christianity*
(Lund & Copenhagen, 1961). For a detailed summary and high evaluation of
this work, see: Fitzmyer, J., "Memory and Manuscript: The Origins and Transmission of the Gospel Tradition," *Theological Studies* 23 (1962) 442-457. Fitz-
myers cites the following two passages, which clearly suggest the relevance of
Gerhardsson's work: "By the middle of the 2nd century, the four Gospels had
reached a position in which it began to be natural to quote them as Holy Scripture: a development which later spread very rapidly and which became accepted
in different parts of the Church. But up to this time the Gospels are *holy tradition* rather than Scripture, and function to all appearances mainly orally." p. 202.
" The synoptic tradition was transmitted and written down in the context of a
Church which did not believe Jesus to be a mere earthly teacher . . ." p. 325.
For earlier studies with a similar bearing, see Cerfaux, L., *La voix vivante de
l'Evangile au début de l'Eglise* (Paris, 2nd ed., 1956); also Taylor, V., *The Formation of the Gospel Tradition* (London, 1957).

[4] For example: Aulén, G., *Reformation and Catholicity* (Wahlstrom, E. H., tr.;
Philadelphia, 1961): "In the same way it has often been said in modern times

Tradition and Church. Another consideration invited by the way Reid constructs the problem is that, whereas on first reading it might have appeared to contain only two operative terms whose relationship comes under examination, namely Scripture and Tradition, actually by intimation there are and by rights there ought to be three such terms, Scripture, Tradition, and Church. I would give this point some emphasis, from the conviction that any attempt to analyse the Catholic understanding of Scripture and Tradition will ultimately depend for its effectiveness on the conceptual distinctness of this third term, Church. This distinctness disconcertingly waxes and wanes in many contemporary discussions, resulting sometimes in outright inconsistency, often in unformulated confusion.[5]

The systematic importance of this position of the Church in our problem also entails, and is clearly suggested by, its practical ecumenical importance. This came clearly to view in certain reactions to Pius XII's *Humani Generis* of 1950, when a number of Orthodox and Protestant writers who had been quite sympathetic to a distinction between Scripture and Tradition showed dismay at the prominence and seeming autonomy given by the encyclical to the further distinc-

---

that the New Testament is a compendium of the original, apostolic *tradition.* No real objection can be made against the statement. It is in evident agreement with the facts. But if from one point of view the New Testament may be seen under the aspect of tradition, this in no sense means a downgrading of the authority of Scripture, or an elimination of the problem of the relationship between Scripture and tradition . . . Whether or not we call the New Testament writings primary apostolic tradition is mostly a matter of terminology. That it *can* be so designated does not jeopardize at all the primacy of Scripture in relation to all other tradition in the Church." p. 133.

[5] An instance occurs in the otherwise remarkably lucid writing of Robert McAfee Brown: Brown, R. M. & Weigel, G., *An American Dialogue* (Garden City, 1960). After appropriating words of Leeming, the sole point of which is to emphasize that the Assumption " cannot be known either by historical evidence or by an explicit tradition " whereas " we know it because the Church teaches it," Brown " sees the dogma of the Assumption, then, as a clear-cut and grievous example of what happens in the life of the Church when tradition gains the upper hand over Scripture . . ." pp. 90-91.

tion of Church or, its equivalent in the context, "magis-terium." [6] George Barrois fairly typified this concern.

It looks as if Rome had given up the definition of Trent for all practical purposes. *Humani Generis* discreetly casts a mantle of Noah on the ill-fated concept of unwritten tradition. Instead, it lays the major emphasis upon what it calls "the living teaching authority of the Church" vested in the hierarchy.[7]

It will not be out of place to observe that here still another distinction has rather subtly emerged, and one that may well prove to be the crucial one for the correlative enterprises of controversy and ecumenism. The further distinction is hier-archy. It is interesting in this connection to examine the re-cent ecumenical volume by Gustaf Aulén, a major portion of which is devoted to expounding Lutheran tenets on Tradition with an eye to the relevant Roman positions.[8] He claims full meaningfulness and vitality within his own confession for Scripture, for dependence on tradition in the use of Scripture, and for the inherence of tradition within the Church. To this extent he establishes strong analogy, if not precise agreement, with Rome. But where he represents differences concerning Tradition to be most evident and most abrupt is in the con-text which he designates as *Ordo*, where these differences very closely approximate the pattern of contrast between Lutheran doctrine concerning "ministry" and "priesthood" and Cath-

[6] See *A.A.S.*, XXXXII, pp. 567 f. The passage to be singled out as chief irritant for Protestants seems to be the following: "Una enim cum sacris eiusmodi fonti-bus (in Sacris Litteris et in divina 'traditione' [quotation marks in the original]) Deus Ecclesiae suae Magisterium vivum dedit, ad ea quoque illustranda et enu-cleanda, quae in fidei deposito nonnisi obscure ac velut implicite continentur. Quod quidem depositum nec singulis christifidelibus nec ipsis theologis divinus Redemp-tor concredidit authentice interpretandum, sed soli Ecclesiae Magisterio." (D. 2314) Catholic comment centered rather on the immediately preceding passage, on the decisive doctrinal authority of the "ordinary Magisterium," particularly of papal encyclicals.

[7] Barrois, G. A., "An overlooked Encyclical," *Christian Century* 68 (1951) p. 79. For a survey of response to the encyclical, see: Weigel, G., "Gleanings from the Commentaries on *Humani Generis*," *Theological Studies* 12 (1951) 520-549.

[8] Aulén, G., *op. cit.*, pp. 123-176.

olic doctrine concerning "hierarchy" and "laity." Accordingly, it is entirely possible that for the specifically ecumenical aspect of the problem of Scripture and Tradition, the agenda of the Commission on Lay Apostolate will prove more relevant in the present Council than that of the Commission on Faith and Morals.

Dogma of the Assumption. Tension of the kind precipitated by the objectionable emphasis in *Humani Generis* grew still more acute when, less than three months later, Pius seemed to be suiting action to the word in defining the dogma of the Assumption of the Blessed Virgin Mary. Barrois' comment on the encyclical, cited above, was echoed in Oscar Cullman's reaction to the new definition, likewise typifying a widely-shared Protestant opinion:

Moreover, is not the Catholic Church tending to throw over, if not in theory, at all events in practice, the fiction of a tradition equated with the interpretation of Scripture, when in justifying the dogma proclaimed in 1950, she did not delay over assigning it any Scriptural basis, but relied instead on the Church's consensus? [9]

In *Munificentissimus Deus* the brief account of Scripture as being the "ultimate basis" of the doctrine found in the Fathers and theologians is, in fact, largely unspecified and almost incidental, whereas in the summary of the tradition of the doctrine the only direct witness cited from the whole patristic age is the very last of the Greek Fathers, John Damascene.[10] Faced

[9] Cullman, O., *La tradition: problème exégétique, historique, et théologique* (Neuchâtel, 1953), p. 38. For a survey of Protestant opinion on the whole question, much of it influenced by the Assumption definition, see: Dubarle, A., "Ecriture et tradition à propos de publications protestantes récentes," *Istina* 3 (1956) 399-415, 4 (1957) 113-128. Cullman's criticisms have been dealt with extensively and sympathetically by Jean Daniélou in several journals and many articles. For a summary statement by the latter see: Daniélou, J., "Ecriture et tradition dans le dialogue entre les chrétiens séparés," *Documentation Catholique* 54 (1957) 283-294, and his original reply to Cullman, *Dieu Vivant* 24 (1953) 107-116.

[10] See *A.A.S.*, XXXXII, pp. 761 ff. The document cites, in order, John Damascene, Germanus of Constantinople, Modestus of Jerusalem (?), Amadeus of Lausanne, Anthony of Padua, Albert the Great, Thomas Aquinas, Bonaventure, Bernardine of Siena, Robert Bellarmine, Francis de Sales, Alphonsus, Peter Canisius,

with this unusual sparseness of biblical and other early doctrinal evidence, knowledgeable readers of the encyclical could not but recall that earlier in the same year the distinguished Catholic patrologist Berthold Altaner had concluded an account of prolonged research on the history of the doctrine in these emphatically negative terms:

The definability of the Assumption cannot be upheld from the standpoint of scientific theology. In the first place, there is no scriptural proof, hence no biblical foundation for dogma. An appeal to typology and allegorical exegesis is scientifically valueless. In the second place, no traditional proof can be brought forward to confirm that in some form there exists a tradition extending to the apostolic age. The expressions and texts that are commonly proposed as evidence of tradition do not rest upon historico-theological tradition. Rather are they simply efforts to provide a speculative foundation for Mary's Assumption. The speculative theology of *convenientia* comes into view from the seventh, perhaps even from the fifth century.[11]

Historical and Theological Traditions. The dogmatic definition, which transpired so shortly after this judgment of Altaner's need not, of course, be taken to discredit his scholarship, much less his faith, and in point of fact the excellence of his work has not been seriously challenged. What the defin-

---

and Suarez, concluding: "Haec omnia sanctorum Patrum ac theologorum argumenta considerationesque Sacris Litteris, tamquam ultimo fundamento nituntur; quae quidem almam Dei Matrem nobis veluti ante oculos proponunt divino Filio suo coniunctissimam, eiusque semper participantem sortem." (D 2331) The last consideration is then briefly developed. For commentary attempting to develop it more fully, see Bea, A., "La Sacra Scrittura ultimo fondamento del domma dell' Assunzione," *La Civiltà Catolica* 4 (1950) 547-561; Peinador, M., "De Argumento Scripturistico in Bulla Dogmatica," *Ephemerides Mariologicae* 1 (1951) 27-44; Rivera, A. "El argumento escrituristico en la Bula Munificentissimus," *Estudios Biblicos* 10 (1951) 145-163. For a discussion of the problem of tradition in the light of the definition, see: Bacht, H., "Tradition und Lehramt in der Diskussion um das Assumpta-Dogma," in *Die mündliche Überlieferung* (Schmaus, M., ed.; Munich, 1957). The latter applies to the problem certain ideas on the development of doctrine derived from Rondet, de Lubac, and Rahner.

[11] Altaner, B., "Zur Frage der Definibilität der Assumptio B.M.V.," *Theologische Revue* 46 (1950) p. 19. The entire study occupies three installments in the same journal: 44 (1948) 128-139; 45 (1949 130-142; 46 (1950) 6-20.

ition does seem to impose on Altaner, and on all of us, in view
of the premises of Catholic faith, is a need to distinguish with
some care what is to be understood by " the standpoint of
scientific theology." In that regard, it may prove useful to
contrast with Altaner's summation that of another eminent
Catholic scholar, this time a systematic theologian, Bernard
J. F. Lonergan. It too appeared only a short time before the
definition:

> From the seventh century to the present day the affirmation
> of the Assumption has increased in clarity and unanimity in the
> Church of God. In the Dark Ages there existed doubts about the
> fact of the Assumption and consequent obscurity regarding the
> object of the feast. In the mediaeval period obscurity was removed
> mainly through the influence of St. Albert the Great, while the
> scholarship of the Renaissance removed the grounds of doubt that
> had lingered in the Liturgy from the Dark Ages. As prior to the
> Renaissance the Assumption was not denied, so since it has not
> been doubted. Finally, from 1869 to 1941 vast numbers of peti-
> tions for the definition of the Assumption have been addressed to
> the Holy See. To select the most significant of these petitions,
> namely, those from resident episcopal sees, an incomplete survey
> reveals that from 820 sees, 1332 Patriarchs, Archbishops and Bish-
> ops have sent 1859 petitions asking that Our Lady's Assumption
> be defined as a matter of faith. While this leaves 299 residential
> episcopal sees unrepresented, that is, some 27% of the total, it pro-
> vides very serious ground for expecting the agreement of all the
> rest. Such practically universal agreement and consent both down
> the centuries and throughout the Church provide the theologian
> with sufficient ground for affirming that the Assumption can be
> defined.[12]

It is important to notice that while Lonergan disagrees
clearly enough with Altaner's conclusion, he does not seem to
dispute his data. Altaner simply says that he cannot vindi-
cate historically the existence of a continuous doctrinal tradition from the apostolic Church. Lonergan for his part is

[12] Lonergan, B. J. F., " The Assumption and Theology," in *Vers le dogme de
l'Assomption* (Montréal, 1948). The petitions here referred to have been published
collectively: *Petitiones de Assumptione corporea B. Virginis Mariae in caelum
definienda ad S. Sedem delatae* (Hentrich-Von Moos, ed.; Vatican, 1942).

wholly silent on the first seven centuries, admits doubts until the Middle Ages, and notes confusion until the Renaissance. If anything, the case from history sounds weaker in Lonergan's brisk resumé than in Altaner's deliberate conclusions. But of course the point is that Lonergan's case is not a case from history, but a case from contemporary consensus. His argument is that history finds intimations of the dogma and does not find rejection of it, whereas the Church of his own day appears to bear unanimous witness to its claim on faith. Thus he judges it to be revealed and definable, and therefore to be apostolic and traditional.

Authentication A Posteriori. I have dwelt so long over this one case of the Assumption, not for its own sake, but for the sake of its singular power of illustration. It brings forth with unusual clarity an aspect of the Roman Catholic approach to revelation that Catholics in general find basic to their belief and central to their religious experience, whereas Protestants in general find it especially uncongenial. Catholics, not excluding learned ones, are far more disposed to seek modern consensus as a sign of primitive authenticity, than they are to seek in primitive authenticity a ground for modern consensus. This will appear as either a vicious circle or a begging of the question unless it be viewed in the full light of all that the Church means to the Catholic, a light that is neither wholly nor principally the light of natural reason. Thus Newman in 1837: " How hopeless then it is to contend with Romanists, as if they practically agreed with us as to the foundation of faith, however much they pretend to it! Ours is Antiquity, theirs the existing Church." And thus Newman in 1874: " For myself, I would simply confess that no doctrine of the Church can be rigorously proved by historical evidence: but at the same time that no doctrine can be simply disproved by it."[13]

[13] Newman, J. H., *The Via Media of the Anglican Church* (London, 1841) I, p. 70, and *Certain Difficulties Felt by Anglicans in Catholic Teaching* (London, 1888) II, p. 312. The middle term, so to speak, of Newman's transition of faith, is, of course, the conviction he attached to the celebrated " Securus iudicat orbis terrarum."

Between the younger and the elder man the light of reason remains unaltered; it is a faith that has changed. It will suffice to recall the recurrent suggestion of Protestant critics—one that I came upon most recently is C. S. Lewis—that what the Bible is to the Protestant fundamentalist, the teaching Church is to the Roman Catholic.[14] Like all instructive analogies, this too is inexact. But, reserving the right to some qualifications, one may grant that the judgment is largely, perhaps even profoundly, true.

TOWARDS A SOLUTION — AND NEW PROBLEMS

The Evidence of Dogma. In the light of what has been said, it should be possible to return now to the original statement of our problem, from Reid, with a certain expectation that whatever Catholics are saying about the relationship of content between Scripture and Tradition is going to derive, in the first instance and as far as possible, from the teaching Church. Now, what the Catholic Church has taught immemorially and undeviatingly, and what therefore no instructed Catholic would venture to deny, is the twofold assertion that Holy Scripture is a vehicle of Christ's revelation, and that Tradition is likewise a vehicle of Christ's revelation. But that much, clearly presupposed by Reid's question, is no answer to it. What remains to be asked is whether, from the time when the New Testament canon was complete, the second vehicle has been entirely dependent on the first, and whether or not the revelation as transmitted by each is coextensive with the revelation as transmitted by the other.

The only conceivably decisive pronouncement on the question, and the one to which Catholic theology textbooks have regularly appealed, is the decree of the Council of Trent in its fourth session:

The holy ecumenical and general Council of Trent, duly assembled in the Holy Spirit, under the presidency of the aforementioned

---

[14] Lewis, C. S., *Reflections on the Psalms* (London, 1958), p. 112.

three legates of the Apostolic See, hold this purpose ever in view, that within the Church errors be extirpated and there be preserved the very purity of the Gospel, that in former times was promised through the Prophets in the Holy Scriptures, and first set forth by the very lips of Our Lord Jesus Christ, God's Son, who thereupon commanded that through his Apostles it should *be preached to every creature* (Mt. 28:19f.; Mk. 16:15) as source of every saving truth and moral instruction. They recognized that this truth and this instruction are contained in written books and unwritten traditions which, having been received by the Apostles from Christ's own lips, or having been passed on from the Apostles themselves as it were from hand to hand, by the Holy Spirit's inspiration, have come even to us. Following the example of the orthodox Fathers, they receive and venerate with equal filial devotion and reverence all the books of the Old and New Testaments, since the same God authors both, and also those traditions which relate not only to faith but also to moral conduct, as communicated either by Christ's own lips or by the Holy Spirit, and as preserved through uninterrupted succession in the Catholic Church.[15]

Reassessment of Trent. Until quite recently, this decree was understood or assumed by the majority of Catholic theologians to settle the problem of Scripture and Tradition in favour of two distinct vehicles of revelation emanating from the apostolic Church and not always identical, though largely so and everywhere consistent, in doctrinal content. However, the plausibility of a contrary interpretation has been increasingly acknowledged in response to the efforts chiefly of three theologians: Edouard Ortigues, whose writing on the subject was the briefest but the earliest to appear;[16] Josef Geiselmann, whose

[15] *Mansi* XXXIII, 22, A. The crucial portion of the text runs: " perspiciensque, hanc veritatem et disciplinam contineri in libris scriptis et sine scripto traditionibus, quae ab ipsius Christi ore ab Apostolis acceptae, aut ab ipsis Apostolis Spiritu Sancto dictante quasi per manus traditae ad nos usque pervenerunt, orthodoxorum Patrum exempla secuta, omnes libros tam Veteris quam Novi Testamenti, cum utriusque unus Deus sit auctor, nec non traditiones ipsas, tum ad fidem, tum ad mores pertinentes, tamquam vel oretenus a Christo, vel a Spiritu Sancto dictatas et continuas successione in Ecclesia catholica conservatas, pari pietatis affectu ac reverentia suscipit et veneratur." (D 783) The history of the decree is given at length by Jedin, H., *Geschichte des Konzils von Trient* (Freiburg, 1957), II, pp. 42-82.

[16] Ortigues, E., " Ecritures et traditions apostoliques au Concile de Trente,"

work has remarkable scope both as positive and as speculative theology; [17] and George Tavard, whose publications are
more popularly constructed and probably the most widely circulated.[18] Since these three scholars employ respectively the
French, German, and English languages the diffusion of their
common conclusions, independently arrived at, has been extra-
ordinarily rapid and extensive.

Limiting our consideration to the decree of Trent, the chief
point of agreement in virtue of which these three men can be
said to found a school of thought is that the Council did not
teach that Tradition comprises elements of revelation not
found in Scripture. Their basis for this conclusion is a body
of detailed research, most thoroughly executed by Geiselmann,

Recherches de science religieuse 36 (1949) 270-299. This study seems to have
attracted very little attention before the interpretation it advocates was developed
independently by Geiselmann; since then its priority and originality have come to
be appreciated.

[17] Geiselmann, J. R., " Das Konzil von Trient über das Verhältnis der Heiligen
Schrift und der nicht geschrieben Traditionen," in *Die mündliche Überlieferung*
(Schmaus, M., ed.; Munich, 1959) pp. 123-206. This study, although it could hardly
be described as sketchy, must be read as simply the adumbration of a much larger work which its author has not yet completed. As projected, the whole will
comprise three notable volumes, the first treating the doctrine of Trent with which
we are here concerned, the second tracing the consequences of a pseudo-tradition
founded on the misinterpretation of that doctrine, and the third devoted to the
thought of Joh. Ev. Kuhn considered to recapture the authentic doctrine and to
elaborate it in a satisfactory theological synthesis. Only the third of these volumes
has, to my knowledge, so far appeared, and is referred to below. These volumes
will be in turn part of a larger series, edited by Geiselmann but including work
of other scholars, entitled *Die Überlieferung in der neueren Theologie* (Freiburg,
1959-). The one volume collection just referred to, *Die mündliche Überlieferung*,
can be read as a kind of prospectus to the whole series, and is a helpful introduction to its lines of thought.

[18] Tavard, G., *Holy Writ or Holy Church: The Crisis of the Protestant Reformation* (New York-London, 1959). In the substance of their historical content,
Tavard's work and Geiselmann's are largely complementary, but overlapping at
the sixteenth century. Their common ground thus coincides with Ortigues' work,
and the three are in general agreement about the doctrine of the Council. Tavard's
more distinctive contribution pertains to late scholastic and early Reformation
developments, whereas Geiselmann's focus is on post-Tridentine and nineteenth
century theology. Tavard expresses his positive view of the question, presupposing his historical results, in " The Authority of Scripture and Tradition," in *Problems of Authority* (Todd, J. M., ed.; Baltimore-London, 1962) pp. 27-42.

into the deliberations of the Council and the theological climate in which it was held. It would be impossible to retrace this work here, but one significant factor bearing on the text itself of the fourth session has attracted much attention and should be noted. The official wording, which states somewhat obscurely that the Gospel is "contained in written books and unwritten traditions," represents a substitution for an earlier draft which stated unambiguously that it is contained "partly in written books and partly in unwritten traditions," a change which corresponds to objections raised in the Council by the Servite General, Bonnucci, and Nacchianti, Bishop of Chioggia. Both of these men, without denying the utility or authority of Tradition, strongly contended that the whole truth of the Gospel, not simply a part of it, is contained in Scripture.[19] Whether or not their influence can be thought decisive, the substitution of the noncommittal *"et"* for the determinate *"partim . . . partim"* appears inexplicable if the Council intended to teach that part of the revelation is given only outside of Scripture.

This point of view has already aroused vigorous opposition, and may be expected to arouse more as it becomes more widely known among theologians of a more conservative and less ecumenical temper. The late Heinrich Lennerz, whose last writings were three articles directed particularly against Geiselmann, has developed the most elaborate refutation, concluding as follows:

---

[19] The significance, and also the isolation, of these men's position is brought out by Jedin, *op. cit.*, pp. 59 ff. Thus: " Die weitaus wesentlichsten Einwände brachte der Servitengeneral vor. Die vor ihm Chioggia, verneinte er die Gleichstellung von Schrift und Tradition; die ganze evangelische Wahrheit sei in der Schrift enthalten, nicht nur ein Teil; dei Worte " mit gleich liebevoller Anhänglichkeit (pari pietatis affectu) " dürften sich nur auf die Gleichstellung der geschriebenen und ungeschriebenen Traditionen untereinander, nicht aber mit der Schrift beziehen . . . Der wichtigste Punkt der Kritik Bonnuccios an dem Dekretentwurf war die Ablehnung der partim-partim." Nonetheless: " Es kann nicht zweifelhaft sein, dass die Mehrzahl der in Trient anwesenden Theologen wenn nicht den Ausdruck partim-partim, so doch die Sache billigten, nämlich dass die dogmatische Tradition einen die Schrift ergänzenden Offenbarungsstrom beinhalte." pp. 60 f.

The teaching of the Council (of Trent) seems to be clear: the Gospel which Christ commanded the Apostles to teach as the source of all saving truth and moral instruction has come down to us in two ways, the first way in writing, that is, Holy Scripture, and the second way without writing, that is, the unwritten traditions . . . Obviously the whole Gospel which the Apostles were to preach is not contained in Holy Scripture nor in the unwritten traditions. The whole Gospel is found in the Holy Scripture and those traditions taken jointly. And in this sense the Council clearly teaches the insufficiency of Holy Scripture.[20]

Without venturing to choose sides in this debate, it may be worth noting that on both sides an appropriate distinction seems to enjoy too little prominence, the distinction, namely, between what the assembled fathers in overwhelming majority may have supposed to be the truth of the matter, and what the Council in its magisterial function deliberately defined as dogma of faith. A conciliar definition cannot simply be identified with the presumptions, however general, of the conciliar membership. What is taken for granted in a Council does not determine what is taught by a Council, any more than do the religious prejudices of the faithful at a given time, however prevalent, determine their creed.[21]

---

[20] Lennerz, H., "Sine scripto traditiones," *Gregorianum* 40 (1959) 625-635, p. 635. See also: "Sola scriptura?" *ibid.*, 38-53, "Scriptura et traditio in decreto 4. sessionis Concilii Tridentini," *Gregorianum* 42 (1961) 517-522. Also sceptical of the new trends, though more reticent than Lennerz: Moran, V., "Scripture and Tradition: A Current Debate," *The Australasian Catholic Record* 38 (1961) 14-22.

[21] For a usefully cautionary essay on the criteriology of conciliar interpretation, see: Fransen, P., "The Authority of the Councils," in *Problem of Authority* (Todd, J. M., ed.; Baltimore-London, 1962) pp. 43-78. The following observations are especially to the point here: "More recently it has been noted that for the most part, Councils refuse to explain a revealed truth but content themselves with condemning obvious errors arising from all quarters. It is as though they are defining the limits within which the outlook of our faith remains orthodox, by simply excluding views which have no future." p. 57. "If the bishops have often spent whole months choosing one single word or the correct formula for a conciliar canon, the least we can do . . . is to discover through patient historical research the precise reasons which led them to choose this word rather than any other." "The first rule then is the following. In dogmatic texts only the central assertion in a decree or a canon is defined. Similarly, in the case of reforming decrees, we are only bound by the act of will expressed in the law. All reasoning, all

At all events, in view of this radical difference of considered opinion in the light of the same historical evidence, one may well doubt whether Trent can prove an effective arbiter of the current debate over the relative contents of Scripture and Tradition. The primary contribution of the recent studies appears rather to be their demonstration that Trent leaves the point unsettled. Such, in fact, was the more reflective opinion of Geiselmann himself:

> One thing can be taken for certain, this " *et* " is not to be understood in the same sense as the " *Partim* . . . *partim.*" The substitution of " *et* " for " *partim* . . . *partim* " clearly indicates that the magisterium did not absolutely define the Scripture-Tradition relationship as being one in which each contains only a part of the Gospel. Does the " *et* " indicate, though, that the Council decided in favour of the sufficiency of the content of Scripture? Did it embody the opinion of Nacchianti and Bonnucci? The evidence seems to point that way, and for some time I adhered to that opinion, until it became apparent that the projected " *partim* . . . *partim* " reflected theological tendencies. In view of that circumstance, it appears that the " *et* " was primarily a formula of compromise, striking a balance between two trends.[22]

Fathers and Theologians. Since the facts as now presented are inconclusive, it is natural to seek an answer in the less formal witness of patristic consensus and the common teaching of theologians. The testimony of the Fathers on the point in question has not been scrutinized so closely by Catholic scholars as has the documentation touching the Council of Trent. Nevertheless, a consistently significant pattern does emerge from recent studies, and is the more impressive in that it cuts across lines of initial suppositions

---

glosses or subsequent observations which are used in order to explain, to illustrate or to give the motives for this central assertion, do not have the same authority." p. 61. Further valuable considerations of the criteriology of dogmatic tradition, illustrated from a particular doctrinal history and with explicit application to the Lennerz-Geiselmann controversy, are given in: Rahner, K., " Virginitas in partu," in *Schriften zur Theologie* (Einsiedeln-Zürich-Köln, 1961) IV, 173-208.

[22] Geiselmann, J. R., " Das Missverständnis über des Verhältnis von Schrift und Tradition und seine Überwindung in der katholischen Theologie," *Una Sancta* 11 (1956) pp. 138 f.

and final conclusions. That is to say, writers who do, as well as writers who do not, judge Scripture to contain all the doctrine of revelation make substantially the same accounting of patristic opinion on the point. Thus, for instance, Albert Michel's highly respected article on " *Tradition* " in the *Dictionnaire de Théologie Catholique*, which expressed a final preference for admitting non-scriptural elements within revelation, is in general agreement on patristic doctrine with the later work of Yves Congar, who adopts the contrary view. Non-Catholic work on the same subject is in similar harmony.[23] The main point would seem to be that, whereas the Fathers often allude to and instance traditions which, though non-scriptural, are to be honoured by the faithful, such traditions generally concern matters of liturgical usage or applied morality, rather than articles of faith in the proper sense, as in dogmatic statements. Congar draws from patristic usage a valuable distinction between " *la tradition* " and " *les traditions.*" The plural form corresponds to the strictly extra-biblical traditions of the sort just described, whereas the singular refers to the process whereby the Bible's message is continually transmitted and progressively elucidated in the Church. Here is his statement of general conclusions:

They (the Fathers) admit the sufficiency of Scripture. They reiterate the explanation to the effect that the doctors and the conciliar definitions simply give precise expression to what is said with greater or less clarity in Scripture. They also suppose that God has communicated certain important religious elements in another way. Unwritten traditions do exist. In point of fact, however, these regard mainly, if not exclusively, matters of Christian worship and conduct. They invariably assert when treating of this matter that Scripture is not sufficient of itself to yield up its authentic meaning; it is rightly understood only in the Church and its tradition.[24]

[23] For example: Flesseman-Van Leer, E., *Tradition and Scripture in the Early Church* (Assen, 1954), and Kelley, J. N. D., *Early Christian Doctrines* (New York, 1958) pp. 29-51.

[24] Congar, Y. M.-J., " Traditions apostoliques non écrites et suffisance de l'Ecriture," *Istina* 6 (1959), p. 305. Congar has made this notion the title and, in a

The mediaeval theologians give little reason for delay on the problem of Scripture and Tradition as we have been considering it, inasmuch as their teaching on the point derives from and commonly is even cited from the Fathers. They understood their own function as above all one of lending professional assistance to the Church in its permanent effort to understand the inspired books and thereby to elaborate tradition in Congar's sense of the singular form, " la tradition." That is what they meant to do, and their intention, insofar as it implies their doctrinal premiss, is really all that concerns our present context. In their own view, indeed, the theological enterprise is so much a function of the sacred text that, as P. de Vooght has pointed out, it is rather the distinctness of the two than the connection between them that their habit of thought tended to obscure:

In the view of the (mediaeval) theologians the countless authoritative texts (*auctoritates*) do not constitute a second source of theology alongside the first source. These texts are still the Scripture, only in certain perspectives, within certain limits, subjected to elaboration and explanation. They are the *veritas catholica* or *veritas ecclesiae* which developed, especially during Christianity's first centuries, upon, about, and in articulation with the Scripture. In the eyes of the scholastics, Scripture and theology are one.[25]

Polemics and Doctrinal Bias. If the times of the Fathers and those of the scholastic theologians heard few voices raised

certain sense, the theme, of a more recent work: La tradition et les traditions: *essai historique* (Paris, 1960). The book is a compressed and comprehensive historical survey of the theological understanding of tradition, strongest perhaps on the patristic and early mediaeval periods and, one may say inevitably, weakest for the period just before the Reformation concerning which source material is least accessible. His judgments on the points here considered are in substantial agreement with other representatives of the recent trend. This historical volume is to be followed by a specifically theological study of the subject.

[25] de Vooght. P., *Les Sources de la doctrine chrétienne* (Paris-Bruges, 1954), p. 254. For more specific considerations of the relationship between patristic and scholastic teaching on tradition, see: Grillmeier, A., " Vom Symbolum zur Summa," in *Kirche und Überlieferung* (Betz, J., and Fries, H., edd.; Freiburg-Basel-Wien, 1960) pp. 119-169, and Congar, Y. M.-J., " Tradition und Sacra Doctrina bei Thomas von Aquin," *ibid.*, pp. 170-210.

even to question the comprehensive character of scriptural revelation, the times into which the scholastic middle ages slowly merge are very different. Rising influence of the extreme ultramontane canonists, prodded to greater lengths by the conciliar quarrels, gave rise to a tendency of ascribing undefined, ill-described, at times quite unintelligible doctrinal and jurisdictional powers to the papacy. Tavard, in the book already cited, gives a summary account with some tragi-comic illustrations of this phase of the Church's doctrinal history. It is scarcely feasible to draw upon such a period for consensus concerning the doctrinal content and interrelation of Scripture and Tradition. Objective theological concern over the question was infrequently entertained, and such as there was becomes in historical retrospect all but hopelessly confused with a mass of pro-papal and anti-papal hyperbole.

Much the same has to be said of the period of the Reformation that followed upon, and surely in some measure resulted from this state of affairs. It ushered in an age of controversy in which *scriptura sola* became fighting words, laden with factious connotation. The extreme opposite position to that of the Protestants' scriptural exclusiveness was not without partisans, constituting a school of thought that admitted revelation to originate not only apart from Scripture and in excess of its contents, but even by recurrent accretion subsequent to the apostolic age.[26] Between these radical antitheses were the opinions we saw to have predominated at Trent, as well as vestiges of the earlier understanding of Scripture as a unique source, perpetuated in the Church's Tradition.[27] Whereas the Tridentine decree directly excludes the first extreme position, and strongly, if implicitly, avoids its extreme opposite, it appears equivocal with respect to the intermediate alternative. The history of this pre-Tridentine

---

[26] See: Tavard, G., *Holy Writ* . . ., pp. 151 ff.

[27] See: Murphy, J. L., *The Notion of Tradition in John Driedo* (Milwaukee, 1959). Driedo, whom Geiselmann ranks with the supporters of the majority view at Trent, seems to have vacillated at least in terminology, but more habitually to have entertained the opposite view.

period of our present question, as of Theology and Philosophy generally, remains to be written, and poses an immense but important labour. The distinctiveness of its handling in recent work on Scripture and Tradition, typically in that of Tavard, consists chiefly in the renewed perspective in which its welter of opinions have to be viewed once one has accepted, together with its implications, the current reappraisal of Trent's doctrine.

Counter-Reformation and After. There can be little doubt that after the Council and, barring isolated demurs and uncertain innuendos, almost until the present, it was the conception of two unequal, discontinuous sources, both of the apostolic provenance, that prevailed, and prevailed by the putative sanction of Trent. Geiselmann assigns a decisive initiative in the fixing of this, in his view erroneous, conception to Peter Canisius, closely followed by Robert Bellarmine:

The first great post-Tridentine controversial theologian to champion the *partim-partim* was Peter Canisius . . . With Canisius the *partim-partim* view of the relationship between Scripture and Tradition rested secure. According to him, it is divinely ordained, irreformably by human authority, that by fixed laws, partly (*partim*) written and partly (*partim*) not, but enjoined on us by apostolic tradition, the Church is governed, dogma assured, religion protected, and discipline preserved . . . Bellarmine followed him in basing the Scripture-Tradition relationship on the *partim-partim*. In his *De Verbo Dei*, Bellarmine goes so far as to see in it the distinctive characteristic of Catholics. Thus, he divides opinions regarding the nature of God's word into three classes " Some accept only God's inner word (Schwenkfeld, Coppin, Quintin), others only the external but written word of God (Lutherans, Calvinists), still others the word of God partly written (*partim scriptum*) and partly traditional (*partim-traditum*). And these last are the Catholics." [28]

[28] Geiselmann, J. R., " Das Konzil von Trient . . .," pp. 170 ff. Less clearcut than the position of Canisius and Bellarmine is that of the highly influential Melchior Cano. Geiselmann regards him as having held and helped to establish the *partim-partim* interpretation. The same opinion was previously held, but more recently reexamined and reversed by Tavard; see " Tradition in Early Post-Tridentine Theology," *Theological Studies* 23 (1962) 377-405.

Subsequently, their doctrine became a standard catechetical premiss, and the common presentation, as it still remains, of theology manuals designed for the seminaries.[29] The position seems to have gone unmodified even by speculative theologians throughout two centuries.

A compensatory development is traced by Geiselmann from somewhat paradoxical beginnings late in the eighteenth century with G. E. Lessing who, although he denied a simple sufficiency to Scripture and to that extent abetted the former tendency of Catholics, at the same time summoned attention to the neglected aspect of pre-Scriptural tradition as the sustaining principle of the life of the early Church. With Knüpfel early in the following century, this understanding was retained, while revelation was envisioned as the unique word of God, partly recorded in Scripture but wholly and vitally conveyed as Tradition. Further development by Baader and Möhler tended to unite a classicist emphasis on the preservation of dogma with a romanticist appreciation of its continual vital rejuvenation, conceiving Tradition as living interpretation of the revelation embodied in Scripture. The final and synthetic stage of this development, discovered in the work of Joh. Ev. Kuhn, is the basis of Geiselmann's own position, which identifies the material content of Scripture and Tradi-

---

[29] For a review of theological accounts of Tradition after Trent but before most of the developments with which we are here concerned, see: Burghardt, W. J., "The Catholic Concept of Tradition in the Light of Modern Theological Thought," *Proceedings of the Sixth Annual Convention, C.T.S.A.* (1951) 42-76. The author there observes: "In the eighteenth and nineteenth centuries there are no remarkable insights in regard to the fundamental concept . . ." and "the total Catholic theology of tradition, as it existed at the time of the Vatican Council, is summed up in Cardinal Franzelin," judgments inviting reconsideration in the light of Geiselmann's work. Burghardt's very liberal synthesis of the doctrines he had assembled relating Scripture to Tradition goes only so far as to say that: "In the deposit of tradition, therefore, even written revelation is contained in some way; and if *even* written revelation, then the whole of revelation." pp. 44, 67. This survey, up to date hardly more than a decade ago, provides a useful index of the frequency and importance of developments during the past few years, concerning both the history and the theory of theological tradition.

tion, while seeing the latter as the former vitally unfolding in the Church.[30]

Contemporary Paradox. As must appear from the foregoing survey, especially from a comparison of the first two sections of this paper, the present situation of Roman Catholic thought on our subject has almost as its most prominent aspect a paradoxical one. The paradox exists most conspicuously between the apparent implications of what the recent papacy has been doing in the realm of dogmatic definition, and what recent theologians have been saying about the relationship between Scripture and Tradition. On the one hand, as I have attempted to illustrate from the case of the Assumption, we do have dogma, infallible expression of the revelation, the affirmation of which is not clearly discoverable in Holy Scripture, nor even in an early consensus of the Church's authoritative teachers.[31] On the other hand, as appears from the writings of Congar, Tavard, Geiselmann and others, we also have his-

[30] The foregoing summary is based on Geiselmann, J. R., " Das Konzil von Trient . . ." Part of the more comprehensive project mentioned above, Geiselmann's study of J. E. Kuhn has already appeared: *Die lebendige Überlieferung als Norm des christlichen Glaubens* (Freiburg, 1958). The work exceeds mere critical reporting of Kuhn's contribution, being in fact the author's personal construction of a theology of tradition " dargestellt im Geiste der Traditionslehre von Joh. Ev. Kuhn," in the phrase of its subtitle. It is a work of a large synthetic compass, with important implications for many areas of theology. The gist of its position with regard to our present question may be suggested by the following passage: " Zwei Momente sind es, die den Durchbruch zum neuen Verständnis der Überlieferung herbeigeführt haben. Das eine ist die Unterscheidung von Quelle der Wahrheit und Quelle der Erkenntnis der Wahrheit oder Glaubensquelle, das andere die an der altkirchlichen Theologie, besonders an Irenaeus und Vinzenz von Lerin, ausgerichtete Lehre von der relativ inhaltlichen Vollständigkeit der Heiligen Schrift, von der sufficientia sacrae Scripturae." p. 120. Also noteworthy is: Möhler, J. A., *Symbolik* (Geiselmann, J. R., ed.-com.; Darmstadt, 1961) II, pp. 699-752, Geiselmann's very thorough critique of Möhler's account of tradition (the critical text is given in the first volume, the second confined to commentary).

[31] It is important to bear in mind that this much-criticized dogma was very far from being a definition wrested from the magisterium by any exigencies of doctrinal crisis. Several times, but here especially, subsequent history has given Newman's rhetorical question an answer contrary to his expectations: " When has definition of doctrine *de fide* been a luxury of devotion, and not a stern, painful necessity? " (letter to Ullathorne, 28 Jan. 1870).

torical evidence sufficient to persuade competent theologians that Tradition itself testifies to the doctrinal completeness of Scripture. If one accepts the dogma, as must all Catholics, and at the same time allows the cogency or at least plausibility of this historical conclusion, as do increasingly many Catholics, it follows logically that one at least probably must be able to know that a given doctrine is somehow in Scripture without at the same time being able clearly to locate it there. The Church may be said, in such a view, to interpret Scripture, in the sense that it makes known truths which Scripture contains but does not readily yield to its readers, but it must be confessed that this is to require the word " interpret " to sustain a very special and unfamiliar nuance. The Catholic biblical scholar, John L. McKenzie, has pointed this out candidly in a lecture:

> The interpretation of the Bible by the Church is not exactly exegesis as the word is usually understood. A survey of the treatment of the Bible in dogmatic documents exhibits little or no exegesis. Here the Bible is touched upon only as a rule of faith, and the interpretation takes rather broad lines. Pius XII observed in the encyclical *Divino Afflante Spiritu* of 1943 that the number of texts whose meaning has been defined by the Church is scarcely half a dozen, nor did he specify what these texts might be. The interpretation of the Church consists principally in what is called the " analogy of faith; " this means that the articles of faith proposed by the living teaching authority are a framework within which the meaning of individual books and passages is to be sought. The living teaching authority, then, does not feel itself bound to find biblical evidence for all the articles of the faith which it proposes.[32]

RAMIFICATIONS OF THE PROBLEM

Senses of Scripture. If, then, dogma expresses revelation that is in Scripture, but which literal exegesis, as ordinarily understood, cannot discover there, it is not surprising that some

---

[32] McKenzie, J. L., " The Use of the Bible in Catholic Theology," (an unpublished lecture, delivered at New Haven, 1960).

should feel bidden to admit and employ other modes of exegesis. Thus, Raymond Brown, in a study of the so-called *sensus plenior*, observes:

> There is the exegesis used by theologians and particularly by the Magisterium in the definition of the dogmas of faith. This is especially a problem in the application of texts to our Blessed Lady in the definition of the Immaculate Conception and Assumption . . . In the employment of Marian texts by theologians (or perhaps by the Magisterium) and in the case of some Messianic prophecies, objectively there seems to be an exegesis which is neither strictly literal nor typical.[33]

It may be recalled that slightly more than a decade ago, this problem of providing a scriptural basis for dogma, reenforced by the influential studies of Jean Daniélou and Henri de Lubac of typological and spiritual exegesis among the Fathers, generated an incipient movement among interpreters in favour of reassessing the fuller, spiritual, typical, mystical, allegorical, and other senses of Scripture that exceeded the discoverable intention of its human writers, in order to determine their theological relevance. Thus, Beryl Smalley concluded a study of mediaeval exegesis published about that time by regretfully noting its recrudescence among contemporaries:

> The spiritual exposition, predominant in patristic and mediaeval commentators, had few defenders ten years ago. There was a certain rather tepid admiration for St. Thomas for having defined its limits, but only blame for the extravagance and subjectivism of its exponents. Now the revived interest in mysticism has led certain students to reverse their judgment. Even though the ten-

---

[33] Brown, R., *The Sensus Plenior of Sacred Scripture* (Baltimore, 1955), pp. 74, 76. The 'fuller sense' is a modern coinage, understood as referring to the presence in Scripture of doctrinal statements formulated expressly only later; these the inspired writers recognized, according to one opinion, only vaguely, according to another, not at all. The quest for this elusive sense is even identified with the objective of biblical theology by some, as: Peinador, M., "La integracion de la exegesis en la teologia," in *Sacra Pagina* (Coppens, J., Descamps, A., and Massaux, E., ed.; Paris-Gembloux, 1959), I, pp. 158-179. For a useful preliminary discussion and factual background to the question, see: Dillenschneider, O., *Le sens de la foi et le progrès dogmatique du mystère mariale* (Rome, 1954).

dency is confined to a small circle, it provides a fascinating though alarming example of the way in which the history of exegesis prolongs itself in that of its historians.[34]

Both inside and outside Catholicism, this movement, while still distinctly perceptible, has not thrived among biblical scholars, who have found no way to impose adequately scientific controls upon such elusive and potentially subjective senses of Scripture. It has found warmer hospitality among liturgists, seeking to establish a Christian understanding of biblical passages whose original literal meanings have been modified or supplanted in the course of transfer from a literary to a liturgical context. Some of the latter have gone on to represent the liturgical use of Scripture as normative for the Christian interpretation of the Bible itself, thus threatening to restore the original issue on a new basis, hotly controversial, but not evidently a part of our present subject.

Church Origins and Biblical Inspiration. We have observed that a principal result of recent Catholic speculation, investigation, and experience in the area of tradition has been more closely to associate, even at times perforce to confuse the contemporary message of the Bible with the contemporary message of the Church. This apparently intimate, though at least as yet scarcely analysed interpenetration of ' Holy Writ ' and ' Holy Church ' in their conveying of the revelation through the course of time, is interestingly in harmony with a new orientation that has been given to the theology of biblical inspiration. This trend, inaugurated by Karl Rahner, postulates an essential interpenetration of Bible and Church in their very inception. Rahner has summarized his thesis in his original article on the subject:

In that God wills and fashions the primordial Church, and along with it its constituent elements by a volition that is absolute and predefining, and in accord with salvation-history and escha-

---

[34] Smalley, B., *The Study of the Bible in the Middle Ages* (Oxford, 1952), pp. 359 f. For indications of Catholic scholarly opinion on the question around the same time, see: Cerfaux, L., Coppens, J., Gribomont, J., *Problèmes et méthodes d'exégèse théologique* (Louvain, 1950).

tology, he wills and fashions the Scripture in such a way as to be its inspiring originator and author. In the preceding sentence, the phrase "in that" needs to be precisely understood. It does not mean simply that Scripture came about "on the occasion" or "in the course" of the establishment of the primordial Church. It means rather that God's active, inspiring authorship is an inner moment of the process of formation of the primordial Church, and properly characterized by the fact of being such. God wills Scripture and himself as its author, and brings about both, by means of, because of, and to the extent of his willing himself to be the Church's effective author. Scriptural inspiration is . . . quite simply God's authorship of the Church insofar as this is precisely related to that constituent element of the primordial Church which is Scripture.[35]

Although this formulation of the theory is undeniably terse, and even its fuller elucidation decidedly subtle, it appears clearly enough to be a view of inspiration which, by identifying the coming into being of the Scripture with the coming into being of the Primitive Church, affords a theological analogy favorable to a view of Tradition that consolidates the continuing message of Scripture with the continued teaching office of the Church. Furthermore, if the theory can be sustained, it may be seen as providing a kind of metaphysical insight to accompany a positive historical appreciation of the Church's role in the formation of the Gospel, such as could scarcely be arrived at so long as inspiration is understood simply as a special charism imparted separately to individual human writers. Proponents of the theory do not, however, claim that in its present state of development it is essentially complete or systematically impregnable. What may be a rather substantial deficiency is the theory's failure to circumscribe in any very meaningful way that formative period of the primordial Church to which biblical inspiration is restricted.

[35] Rahner, K., " Über die Schriftinspiration," *Zeitschrift für katholische Theologie* 78 (1956), pp. 157 f. The article was subsequently expanded into a book, recently translated: Rahner, K., *Inspiration in the Bible* (Henkey, C. H., tr.; New York, 1961). Rahner's position is further developed, and some of its difficulties more directly confronted, by: Brinkmann, B., "Inspiration und Kanonizität der Heiligen Schrift in ihrem Verhältnis zur Kirche," *Scholastik* 33 (1958) 208-233.

Development of Doctrine. Although it must be recognized that nearly all the major problems of Scripture and Tradition that have lately come to the forefront of Catholic thinking must seek a large measure of their solution under the distinctively modern heading of " doctrinal development," new positive and original contributions to that very difficult subject are not in evidence. By far the greater number of recent writings on the subject have been restatements, applications, and appreciations of earlier writers, especially Newman and, to a great but lesser extent, Möhler. Among the relatively few recent independent essays on the subject may be found a useful variety of formulations and perspectives, but not, so far as I can determine, any notable advance in understanding beyond these geniuses of the last century.[36] To summarize with the most extreme generality, it may be said that the prevalent concerns of recent writing on development are to admit development as an important and undisguisable fact, to dissuade from explaining development in terms of a formally logical process of derivation, and to relate development to a rejuvenated conception of Christian faith that stresses social, symbolic, and personalistic factors, and to a correspondingly rejuvenated conception of the Church as a living Body of Christ.

[36] Perhaps the most original and enlightening of these recent contributions, but without justifying a reversal of the judgment just expressed, are those of de Lubac and Rahner: de Lubac, H., " Le problème du développement du dogme," *Recherches de science religieuse* 35 (1948) 130-160; Rahner, K., " The Development of Dogma," in *Theological Investigations* (Ernst, C., tr.; Baltimore-London, 1961) I, pp. 39-78 ; *idem,* " Überlegungen zur Dogmentwicklung," in *Schriften zur Theologie* (Einsiedeln-Zürich-Köln, 1961) IV, pp. 11-50; *idem,* " Virginitas in partu," *ibid.,* pp. 173-205. The de Lubac article takes issue with a contemporary representative of the declining school of ' logical ' development, conceived as demanded by the claims of ' scientific ' methodology in systematic theology: Boyer, C., " Qu-est-ce que la Théologie? Reflexions sur une controverse," *Gregorianum* 21 (1940) 255-266. These articles serve to emphasize the mutual involvement of questions concerning the nature of development and those concerning the nature of theology. A contemporary representative of the most conservative theoretical approach to development, reducing it almost to a matter of sheer vocabulary, is: Stephenson, A. A., " The Development and Immutability of Christian Doctrine," *Theological Studies* 19 (1958) 481-532.

In many respects, what may be the most estimable recent contribution to this area of theology is basically a negative one. That is a critical review, historically enlightened and logically acute, by the Anglican ecclesiastical historian Owen Chadwick, of the chief forms of response given to the question of development in the past, examined in the work of some of their purest exponents. Chadwick objectively weighs the respective merits and inadequacies of these approaches, and sees the one taken by Newman as affording the most nearly satisfactory account of the matter. But the problem, however much illuminated, remains, in his view, unsolved:

> Just as the logicians have to be asked the question how their notion of logical development can be regarded as a meaningful use of the word *logical*, so there is a question still to ask about Newman. Nearly all theologians appear to be agreed that, in accordance with the decree of the Holy Office *Lamentabili* in 1907, it is necessary to maintain that revelation ended with the death of the last apostle. This doctrine of revelation excludes Suarez and Lugo. It probably excludes some parts of the *Essay on Development*. The question then for those who think Newman's theology is Catholic, is this: these new doctrines, of which the Church had a feeling or inkling but of which she was not conscious—in what meaningful sense may it be asserted that these new doctrines are not ' new revelation '? [37]

Whereas this question has been much entertained, and purged of a number of false presuppositions tending to accrue to it, it does not seem that in the last analysis it has yet been given a complete, even though hypothetical, answer.

[37] Chadwick, O., *From Bossuet to Newman: The Idea of Doctrinal Development* (Cambridge, 1957), p. 195. The proposition in " Lamentabili " actually states: " Revelatio, obiectum fidei catholicae constituens, non fuit cum Apostolis completa," being one of sixty-five statements which, singly and collectively, Pius X " ceu reprobatas ac proscriptas ab omnibus haberi mandavit." (D 2021, 2065a) Probably the most interesting response to Chadwick's work came, rather uncannily, from Newman himself, in the form of a hitherto unpublished paper written in 1868: Dessain, C. S., " An Unpublished Paper by Cardinal Newman on the Development of Doctrine," *Journal of Theological Studies* 9 (1958) 324-355.

CONCLUSION

It must appear from even this very superficial review that the problem of Scripture and Tradition has been newly illuminated, newly agitated, and newly complicated by contributions and demands from an extrordinary number of quarters: from ecumenism, biblical source-criticism, exegesis, mariological dogma, patrology, scholastic, Reformation, and nineteenth-century history, theory of inspiration, and development of doctrine, as well as from original theological construction. Thus one may take a certain comfort in the epigram of Karl Rahner, that, "if one theological problem can stir up the whole of theology, we may be sure that it has been correctly asked." [38] The predominant new trends of thought are towards admitting, on the one hand, the objective doctrinal sufficiency of Scripture, and towards emphasizing, on the other hand, an intrinsic and essential correlation of Bible, Tradition, and Church. The present mood of Catholic thinking on the question, at once more cautious and more inquisitive than in the past, has generated a gratifying degree of progress in research, originality in hypothesis, and objectivity in controversy. The literature of merely the past dozen years is remarkably abundant, including a substantial amount of more or less original scholarship, together with an immense quantity of derivative writings, chronicles, summaries, criticisms, and popularizations. I have attempted here for the most part to cite only the more significant members of the first category.[39]

[38] Rahner, K., *Inspiration in the Bible*, p. 34.

[39] Two very useful general works on the subject should be noted. An excellent survey volume based on recent literature concerning our subject is: Lengsfeld, P., *Überlieferung: Tradition und Schrift in der evangelischen und katholischen Theologie der Gegenwart* (Paderborn, 1960). A less elaborate scholarly production, more synthetic and of more general scope than the preceding, but with a decidedly French orientation, is: Holstein, H., *La tradition dans l'Eglise* (Paris, 1960). Readers who wish to pursue further reaches of this literature, and especially to examine the results of non-Catholic thought, will find, in addition to abundant references in most of the works here cited, a nearly exhaustive bibliography of the subject for recent years in the "Elenchus bibliographicus" published annually in *Biblica*, currently under the subheading "Hermeneutica biblica."

The question naturally arises of what the Second Vatican Council may be expected to contribute to this rather overwhelming area. Without questioning the objectively limitless scope of its possibilities, it would seem most prudent to hope rather for clearer indication of what lines of inquiry are definitely open to Catholic theologians, rather than for dramatic magisterial solutions to an intricate complex of problems whose very formulation is frankly groping, whose positive data are in process of accumulation, and whose points of insertion into the vast structure of systematic dogma are so numerous, so delicate, and so crucial.

JAMES GAFFNEY, S. J.

Woodstock College
Woodstock, Maryland

THE ONTOLOGY OF THE GOSPEL

∾

HE theological problem of Scripture and Tradition may
be represented as an attempt to solve the Tridentine
equation (Denz. 783) :

$$\text{Gospel} = \text{Scripture} + \text{Traditions} \qquad (1)$$

or in its formulation by the First Vatican Council:

$$\text{Supernatural Revelation} = \text{Scripture} + \text{Traditions} \qquad (2)$$

the equivalence between (1) and (2) resting on the quotation
in Vatican I (Denz. 1787) of Trent.

The attempted solutions ordinarily concern themselves with
the determination of " Tradition (s) " as the unknown variable,
assuming the constancy of the other terms. In what follows,
an attempt will be made to determine the sense of " Gospel,"
in the hope that the other terms of the equation, including the
plus-sign, will then be, if not determined, at least clarified by
the provision of a significant context in which their interpretation may be pursued.[1]

We ask, then, " What is the Gospel? " The sense of the question needs careful determination.[2] (a) The question may be
understood as asking what in detail is contained in the Gospel,
its various teachings; this sense is not directly relevant to the
present inquiry. (b) The question may be understood historically, as asking how in fact the word " Gospel " has been used
at different periods in the history of the Church, and in particular in the Church in its beginnings. (c) The question may be
understood ontologically, as asking what kind of reality is intended by the concept " Gospel," and how this reality is related

[1] It may seem rash to raise this question while it is still under discussion in the
present Council; yet it is in fact still under discussion, and according to reports
at the time of writing no agreement has yet been reached on this topic by the
special Commission under Cardinals Ottaviani and Bea appointed to revise the
schema on the " Sources of Revelation."

[2] I have tried to ask it before in *Blackfriars*, XLIII (1962), pp. 301-13.

to other realities of our experience. It is this third, ontological sense of the question which is the primary one envisaged in this essay, though it goes without saying that no answer could be offered to it without some investigation of the question in its second, historical sense. It does, on the other hand, patently need saying that the question in its historical sense cannot be adequately raised either without some preliminary examination of its ontological presuppositions; for the accustomed techniques of historical scholarship, being confined largely to lexical procedures, frequently fail to observe that different words may refer to the same reality, in that the difference between the terms rests not on a difference in the reality indicated but on the ways in which it is indicated. I shall argue that the reality referred to, say, in the New Testament by the term εὐαγγέλιον is also referred to by other terms in those writings; and that a question (our third, ontological question) then arises which insistently demands an answer. Thus the third sense of the question " What is the Gospel? " will have as its answer a statement about a reality which may for reasons of tradition and convenience be called the " Gospel," but where this term has now become a technical theological term intended to refer to a many-sided reality, one of whose aspects is brought to light in the NT term εὐαγγέλιον (itself multiply significant).[3] The term " revelation " has this technical theological sense, but on the other hand, suffers from the disadvantage of being cut off from its sources; the connection between " revelation " and ἀποκάλυψις is rarely made, and indeed is not particularly significant.

It may be useful here to recall a classical instance of an ontological account of the nature of the Gospel. In the opening of his commentary on St. John,[4] Origen proceeds to what may be called an " analogical " analysis of the notion of " Gospel." He uses the idea of ἀπαρχή, first fruits, as a means of appraising the different realizations of the Gospel: thus the Gospel is

---

[3] Compare for instance the relationship between NT χάρις and the theological " grace."

[4] References by paragraph and page to volume I of the edition by A. E. Brooke, Cambridge, 1896.

the first *fruits* of all the Scriptures, as the Old Testament is their first *growth* (2, p. 4); and all the new Scripture is Gospel, but the Gospels are the first fruits of all these, in virtue of him with a view to whom the Gospel is Gospel (3, p. 5). Of the four Gospels, the Gospel of John is the first fruits, again because of its especially close relation to Jesus (4, pp. 6-7). Since Jesus himself is the Gospel (8, 9, pp. 12-15), " by his sojourning among us and causing the Gospel to be realized in bodily form (σωματοποιηθῆναι), the Saviour has made all things into Gospel " (6, p. 9).

In a general way, everything that provides an account of Christ's sojourn on earth, and prepares for his second coming, and also makes this coming present in the souls of those who desire to receive the Word of God—all this is Gospel (4, p. 8). It is right that the Gospel should be defined in reference to the hearer: for a Gospel tells of the actual presence of something good to the believer or promises that it will be present to him who awaits it (5, p. 8). Jesus himself is all good things, far more than can be contained in the Scriptures (9, pp. 13-14; 10, pp. 14-15). So the Gospel which preaches Jesus is preached throughout the whole world, not only on earth but throughout the universe of heaven and earth (15, p. 19).

We need not endorse every detail of Origen's account of the Gospel to find in it a valuable enlargement of perspective; and we may note for future reference, on the one hand, the ontological concentration of the Gospel in Jesus, and, on the other, the realization of this Gospel in a hearer as anticipated *parousia*, by way of its active or dynamic declaration.

Before beginning a brief examination of the NT evidence, to which we now turn, it may be well to recall certain methodological considerations suggested by Canon Kelly in an outstanding study of certain problems closely related to our own.[5] The essential point for our purposes is that we do not identify a definite body of teaching with a fixed pattern of words, e. g., a " primitive creed," and that this refusal to identify the two does not necessarily involve the rejection of the former, when,

---

[5] J. N. D. Kelly, *Early Christian Creeds*, 2nd ed., London, 1960, pp. 6-14.

as is surely the case, we must reject the latter. For it is the particular situations in the Church's early life which led to the crystallization of fixed patterns and shaped their style, substance and structure. This emphasis on the particular situations of the Church's life, the *Sitz im Leben* or sociological setting of the texts, as we have them, is of the utmost importance. We may suppose that this sociological setting is reflected, not only in the structure of credal formulas, but also in the vocabulary which is used to refer to the body of teaching in each of a variety of situations in the Church's life. It should be noted that the whole *Sitz im Leben* theory, from its origins in Gunkel's work on the Old Testament, is an attempt to correct the excessive literary emphasis due to the inevitable preoccupation of scholars with texts. What perhaps still needs to be recognized is that it is only one aspect of what might be called sociology of knowledge, or simply sociology as such. For whether we appeal to non-literary (e. g., archaeological) evidence or not, what is important is that we should be clear about the object of our inquiry: the life of a community. This life is articulated and shaped in its language, just as the language reveals the life. Consequently the brief survey of NT evidence which follows assumes that there is a life of the early Christian community which took shape in various sociological settings; and that the analogical unity of the life may be grasped in part by reflection on the analogical unity of the numerous expressions used to refer to a " body of teaching " in which the unity of that life found its linguistic projection. This body of teaching is a sociological reality achieving diverse degrees of linguistic articulation in the different situations of the early Church's life.

It is worth considering what these situations might have been. Kelly, with his own special purposes in mind, notes several (p. 13): baptism, catechetical instruction, preaching, day-to-day polemic, liturgy, exorcism, correspondence between Church leaders. In such situations as these, need would often be felt to refer to the " body of teaching " *as a whole*; and it is not unreasonable to suppose that the particular situations

might preselect, or again be shaped by, a special expression by
which that reference might be made, however difficult it may
be to establish unique correlations. The expressions indeed are
so various that it would be extravagant always to try to relate
each to a typical setting. Let us note some of these expressions,
starting with the most obvious one, διδασκαλία, as verbal noun
or as referring to what is taught; this example alone shows how
difficult it is to find some neutral term to refer to the " body
of teaching " apart from its particular realizations. The term
most frequently occurs in the Pastoral Epistles, i. e., in the
setting of a fully-formed Christian community, and has a
characteristic retrospective reference (of the examples outside
the Pastoral Epistles, Mt. 15 : 9, Mk. 7 : 7 and Col. 2 : 22 are
all quotations from LXX; Rom. 15 : 4 contains a reference to
the OT scriptures; Rom. 12: 7 refers precisely to the *office* of
teaching—cf. *didaskalos*—within the body of the community;
cf. Eph. 4: 14), as Bauer-Arndt-Gingrich observe a little
primly (s.v.), " frequently of the teachings of ecclesiastical
Christianity."

Some other terms may be listed, some used much more frequently than others: εὐαγγέλιον, παράδοσις, λόγος, κήρυγμα,
πίστις, παραθήκη, διδαχή, μαρτύριον; the list is not meant to be
exhaustive. No one, I suggest, could wish to maintain that
these different terms (some of them not always used " preg-
nantly ") refer to separate partial unities or sources of " Christian teaching ": they are different ways of referring to the same
reality-in-communication, ways of reference which differ at
least partly because of the different sociological styles of the
communication.

This would seem to be true even of the particularly ticklish
term παράδοσις. In the three texts where it is concerned with
Christian teaching (1 Cor. 11 : 2; 2 Thess. 2 : 15; 3 : 6), it would
be a mistake to try to find differences of content, according as
to whether " doctrine " or " customs " are transmitted: the
essential emphasis is on the style of communication, by a continuous chain deriving from an authority; the continuity thus
made explicit is given as a ground for urging the community

addressed to hold fast to this reality-in-communication. Thus the community addressed is referred to something or someone outside it by way of a chain of communication. The point is even more obvious with the related verbal pair παραδιδόναι and παραλαμβάνειν.

Considerable light has recently been thrown on this pair of terms by a study of the process of communication which they were used to describe in Rabbinic Judaism.[6] The general thesis is this: the material we find in what, since the middle of the second century, we refer to as the Four Gospels, existed from the first in the form of fixed oral traditions transmitted from teacher to pupil by a process of careful memorization as in Rabbinic Judaism; and that these oral traditions of the words and deeds of Jesus were solemnly recited at special reunions of the Christian community, taking place after participation in the synagogue services.[7] In this view the *Sitz im Leben* of the material of the Gospels would no longer be the rather vaguely determined activities of the community suggested by the early form-critics for their atomized pericopes, but the precisely determined assemblies of the early Christian community, presupposing a definite ministerial office of transmission established in the Apostles. Riesenfeld even suggests that the original source of this chain of communication, the first Teacher, was Jesus himself, at least for considerable portions of the material, though not of course for the Passion narratives.

There can obviously be no question of discussing here the well-foundedness of this account; certainly some of its details seem a little far-fetched. Its chief interest for our purposes is that once again our attention is directed to a style of life articulated in a process of communication of a " teaching," in this case what we are accustomed to think of as " the Gospel behind the Gospels." In fact, as we must now briefly try to see, this

---

[6] See, above all, B. Gerhardsson, *Memory and Manuscript*, Uppsala, 1961. Also H. Riesenfeld, " The Gospel Tradition and its Beginnings," *Studia Evangelica*, (T. u. U. LXXIII), Berlin, 1959, pp. 45-65, and printed separately 1957.

[7] This would provide interesting support for attempts to relate the structure of the Gospels to the Jewish lectionary system. Cf. e. g., A. Guilding, *The Fourth Gospel and Jewish Worship*, Oxford, 1960.

last expression is somewhat unsatisfactory, because εὐαγγέλιον in its NT usage does not primarily refer to a kind of abstract of the material of the four Gospels.[8]

It seems clear that the NT usage has as its point of departure the LXX of dt-Isaias. Whether in its verbal or its nominal form, then, we are dealing with an eschatological concept.[9] In its most striking occurrence in the Synoptic Gospels (Mk. 1 : 1), *euaggelion* is followed by a genitive which must be interpreted both objectively and subjectively: Jesus is the content of the *euaggelion* as well as its bearer. It may be that we have in this text a reflection of a semantic development, such that the word, especially in its verbal form, was first used to refer to the announcement of the *basileia*, then after Easter and especially by St. Paul, to refer to the death and resurrection of Jesus as the central content of the *euaggelion*, and finally to refer to all the words and deeds of Jesus as culminating in the events of Easter.

The richness of St. Paul's usage is such as to make brief description impossible. We must note, however, the *active* character of the *euaggelion*, as a " power unto salvation " (Rom. 1 : 16), as a manifestation of the glory of Christ (2 Cor. 4 : 4). It retains throughout its eschatological character as a constantly renewed intervention of God in the history of the individual or the community, through which they are re-inserted into the time of the new birth and the new creation. The *euaggelion* is by definition always new because it is the re-presentation of the definitive end-event; so that it has as its characteristic sociological setting for St. Paul its announcement to the Gentiles: this is the unheard-of novelty which is now shaping the course of history. That is to say, the announcement of the co-heirship of the Gentiles in the promise brings out the

---

[8] For εὐαγγέλιον, see the commentaries and lexica; recently P. Bläser, " Evangelium," *Handbuch theologischer Grundbegrice*, ed. Fries, Munich, 1962, pp. 355-63.

[9] Cf. G. von Rad, *Theologie des alten Testaments*, vol. II, Munich, 1960, pp. 112-37. " Aber da, wo Israel von seinen Propheten aus dem Heilsbereich der bisherigen Fakten herausgestossen wurde und wo sich sein Heilsgrund mit einemal in ein kommendes Gottesgeschehen hinaus verlagerte, da erst wird die prophetische Verkündigung eschatologisch " (p. 132).

intrinsic novelty of the *euaggelion*; the sociological setting of mission-preaching is itself the revelation of what is being revealed. Thus even in the formed Christian community, the co-presence of Jew and Greek is a continual manifestation of the actual presence of the definitive end-event mediated by the *euaggelion*, sustained by the life-in-faith of the community. The " sociological setting " is the expression, the ontological symbol, of the *euaggelion* and hence of the end-event it communicates. The *euaggelion*, the " word of truth " which has come to the Colossians, is bringing forth fruit and growing throughout the whole world, just as it is in them (Col. 1:5-6; cf. 2 Thess. 3:1).

The εὐαγγέλιον is the λόγος τῆς ἀληθέιας (cf. also Eph. 1:13). We should not fail to note the images of growth and life associated with the *logos* in Col. 1:6 (cf. especially Is. 55:10-11; also Ac. 6:7; 12:24; 19:20).[10] For the word is a word of life (Phil. 2:16; 1 Jn. 1 2; cf. Ac. 5:20; 7:38; 1 Pet. 1:23 and Schelkle's commentary (Freiburg 1961) *in loc.*). It is generally agreed today that the original NT use of *logos* in a relevant sense is to refer to the Christian message, and that this very common use provides the background for the unique use of the term in the Prologue of St. John. It seems essential to insist with van den Bussche on the part played in this enrichment of meaning by the element of personal experience (*ervaringselement*). If we read the Prologue as a Logos-hymn, whether one based on an earlier popular hymn (such as 1 Tim. 3:16) or freely composed by St. John himself, we cannot fail to recover that sense of reverent rejoicing which informs it. The *verbum vitae* texts, one of them from the First Epistle of St. John, which we have noticed above, would provide a link between the earlier use referring to the Christian message and the personalized use of the Prologue. It may seem particularly rash to conjecture a

[10] On λόγος, see e. g., R. Schnackenburg, " Logos," *LTK²* VI, col. 112-25; H. van den Bussche, *Het vierde Evangelie* I, *Het boek der tekens*, Den Haag, 1959, pp. 100-17. All practitioners of " biblical theology " should have read James Barr, *The Semantics of Biblical Language*, Oxford, 1961; see pp. 129-40 for an acute criticism of the familiar attempts to magnify the Hebrew *dabar*, thought to " lie behind " *logos*.

sociological setting for this special way of referring to the Christian message as a whole, but we may cautiously suggest that *logos* came more and more to refer to this message as making the risen Christ and his grace and life present to the believer in a unified experienec of Life, Light and Truth, and thus to prepare it for a " cultic " use in a Logos-hymn. Van den Bussche's suggestion that, instead of omitting the last Gospel in some prospective liturgical reform, we should rather sing it as a sort of *Te Deum* has much to recommend it.

Our purpose in examining a few of the words used to refer to the Christian message, the " body of teaching," as a whole, was to indicate a richer content for the Tridentine " Gospel " or the Vatican " Revelation " than is usually assumed in theological discussion, and to suggest various sociological settings in the early Christian community in which this richness of meaning might have been embodied. It is not necessary to our purpose to place much weight on these suggestions, some of which are highly conjectural; the essential point is that the use of the term " Gospel " must implicitly at least include the richness of meaning of all the different terms used in the NT to refer to this reality-in-communication of the message, and imply too the concrete setting of the community in which these terms had their use.

One last reference to NT usage may help to make this point clear. In a profound and fascinating contribution to the Oxford Congress on the Four Gospels,[11] Fr. J. P. Audet, by drawing attention to the formal structure of the Jewish *berakhah* (" benediction ") and comparing it with the NT $\epsilon\dot{v}\lambda o\gamma\dot{\iota}a$-$\dot{\epsilon}\xi o$-$\mu o\lambda\dot{o}\gamma\eta\sigma\iota s$-$\epsilon\dot{v}\chi a\rho\iota\sigma\tau\dot{\iota}a$, was able to suggest a point of view which I may sum up in my own words as follows: the eucharist is a celebration of the Gospel. For in both *berakhah* and eucharist, the *anamnesis* of one of the *mirabilia Dei* is an intrinsic and functional element. The conception is brought out most clearly

---

[11] J. P. Audet, O. P., " Literary Forms and Contents of a normal $E\dot{v}\chi a\rho\iota\sigma\tau\dot{\iota}a$ in the First Century," *Studia Evangelica*, Berlin, 1959, pp. 643-62. See also " Esquisse historique du genre littéraire de la bénédiction juive et de l'eucharistie chrétienne," *RB* 65 (1958), pp. 371-99. His methodological remarks at the beginning of the first study are very much to the point.

in the condensed text of St. Paul (1 Cor. 11:26): "For as often as you shall eat this bread and drink the cup, you proclaim the death of the Lord, till he comes." The proclamation (καταγγέλλειν) of the death of the Kyrios, the conqueror of death, is enacted in the words and deeds of the rite, as a making-present in reality of the *mirabilia Dei* of Jesus' life, death and resurrection, and a pledge of his coming again. The Gospel is reality as well as word, and both reality and word in the enacted life of the Christian community.

We may sum up, then, by saying that the Gospel is revelation-reality as well as revelation-word; [12] and further that it is *revelation-community*. It is revelation-reality in the Logos; it is revelation-word most obviously, though not exclusively, in the Scriptures; for it is both reality and word in the life of faith of the revelation-community. The study of the ontology of the Gospel involves us in seeing it as a reality-in-communication, a being-manifest (*veritas*),[13] in Christ himself, in language, and in the society in which Christ himself is present and which bears witness to this presence in language and rite, and in the lives of its saints. The Gospel is an intelligible (not necessarily *explicitly* intelligible), active presence of eschatological realities in human forms, a presence tied always to the definitive end-event of Christ's death and resurrection and the primary Apostolic community in which that event found its expression.[14]

If the foregoing remarks are in any way acceptable, it is clear

---

[12] I owe this pair of terms to E. H. Schillebeeckx, O. P., *De sacramentele Heilseconomie*, Anvers-Bilthoven, 1952. See also by the same author, "Parole et Sacrement dans l'Eglise," *Lumière et Vie* 46 (1960), pp. 25-45; and K. Rahner, "Wort und Eucharistie," *Schriften zur Theologie* IV, Einsiedeln, 1960, pp. 313-55.

[13] Cf. St. Thomas, IIa-IIae. 5. 3: "Formale obiectum fidei est veritas prima secundum quod manifestatur in Scripturis sacris et doctrina Ecclesiae," a text which I regard as supplying the entire orientation of this essay.

[14] I hope that this will not be read as an escape from theological analysis into a vague mysticism. The appropriate tool for theology here is "sociology," not as a pseudo-science or as pseudo-prophecy, but as a concern for a human community as a bearer of meaning. A key notion would be Wittgenstein's famous dictum, "A language is a form of life." Cf. P. Winch, *The Idea of a Social Science*, London, 1958, and the writings of the Oxford Institute of Social Anthropology (Evans-Pritchard, Lienhardt, Pocock).

that the equations set out at the beginning of this essay require a rather different approach from that which has been usual. If we bear in mind the arithmetical analogy, it seems that all the terms must be of the same type; e. g. we cannot have an equation " 7 apples = 3 oranges + 4 pears." On the other hand, the plus-sign may be misleading, and really stand for a more complicated operation. Some solutions of the equation favour this latter interpretation: " Scripture " is taken for a collection of writings in a vacuum, and " Tradition " (not " traditions ") is held to raise Scripture to the power of the Gospel. This solution seems to me unreal, and obscures the real point of difficulty. For *no* writings, let alone Scripture, are intelligible apart from the community in which they find their use, the " tradition " or convention of their interpretation. Nor again does it seem to me fair to Trent, and to what Trent was trying to say, to make " Tradition " *purely* interpretative, so that it would derive its entire character as Gospel from the Scripture-as-Gospel, the " Holy " Scripture, which it served to interpret.

It would appear, then, that there are two quantities, Scripture-as-Gospel and Tradition-as-Gospel, such that this latter quantity is what is left over when we subtract " Scripture " from " Gospel." Can this quantity, " Tradition-as-Gospel," be identified?

Let us at least be clear that it cannot be simply identified with any of the quantities which have been historically called " Tradition," " *traditiones*," παράδοσις or anything of the kind, any more than " Gospel " can be equated to εὐαγγέλιον or " grace " to χάρις. The quantity which we wish to identify is that reality which is referred to by " Tradition " as a *theological* term, bearing a relationship to historical usages but more inclusive than any one of them. And from what has been said above, it seems to me luminously clear with what this quantity of Tradition must be identified: it is the reality-in-communication, the being-manifest, of the risen Christ, through his death and resurrection and through the original community which expressed it, in the community life-in-faith of the Church. It is quite unnecessary (apart from being in the highest degree implausible) to suppose that this living presence is capable of being itemized in quasi-credal or catechetical forms. The life of any community, not just the Church, is the bearer of an indefinite complex of meanings in a far larger variety of styles of communication than are ordinarily allowed for by scholars or theologians. Nor need we be unduly alarmed by the *theoretical* objection (based of course on the once-for-all completeness of Revelation) as to the danger of contamination of the original purity of the Gospel if it is sustained by a community life so various and so inextricably interwoven with the course of secular history. The danger is not *theoretical* but *practical*, and very real: *sola Scriptura* was and is a mistaken endeavour to establish a kind of sublimated metaphysical purity of the Gospel, but we can appreciate the motive behind the slogan while regretting the attraction which it seems to exert on some modern Catholic theologians. It is the duty of the Church as a whole, and especially of the apostolic institution, to return continually to the purity of the Gospel (though not to Scripture alone). Such a return is not simply " biblical " but " evangelical ": the life of the Gospel may find *more adequate* expression in styles of communication (philosophical, social, poetic, plastic and simply *human*) which are not those of past generations; we need not, for instance, recommend a return to " Semitic thought-forms," or indeed to scholastic ones, however much we should respect both: secular history is not excluded from the scope of divine providence. Each such new expression may form a monument of Tradition, a witness of the Gospel, or again it may be a contamination of its original purity, or more frequently an almost indissoluble amalgam of the two; and it will always have to be the duty of the theologians, of the apostolic institution, and of the great protesting saints (like St. Catherine of Siena), to point the way back to the Gospel, " The Word was made flesh and dwelt among us."

CORNELIUS ERNST, O. P.

Hawkesyard Priory,
  Rugeley, Staffs
    England

TRADITION *

ⱷ

EVEN those who have followed the progress of the Council with a distracted mind, and have gotten their information from the newspapers, could hardly miss the rather lively debate which arose concerning the schema for the decree, " the Sources of Revelation," as well as about the relation between " Scripture and Tradition." A dogmatic decree on the deposit of the faith would necessarily touch on the question of the sources of Christian faith; " that contained in the written books and the unwritten traditions." This had already occurred at the First Vatican Council (Sess. III, chap. 2, Denz. 1787). Without speaking here of the doctrinal and pastoral reasons which led the preliminary Commission to prepare a project on this question, without mentioning again the discussions of which this project was the object throughout six " general congregations " (Nov. 14-21), and without approaching, for its own sake, the problem about the " two sources " and the connections between Scripture and tradition, we could profitably present here a very quick sketch about the origins of the notion of tradition as a *status quaestionis* which could be helpful towards understanding the scope of these debates.[1]

---

* Translated by F. C. Lehner, O. P.

[1] Concerning this debate, one can profitably read, in addition to newspaper reports, Yves M. J. Congar, *Le Concile au jour le jour.* Paris, 1963, pp. 63-71; and René Laurentin, *L'enjeu du Concile.* II. " Bilan de la première session." Paris, 1963, pp. 27-35. It is useful to note that, whatever certain persons thought about the matter, the Fathers who sought to safeguard the vocabulary of the Council of Trent concerning the Gospel as the " sole source of the truth of salvation," did not have the intention of rejecting tradition in order to go back to the Protestant principle about " Scripture alone."

We cannot possibly present even an abridged bibliography on tradition here. Let us only indicate the following recent works: H. Holstein, *La Tradition dans l'Église.* Paris, 1960; Y. M. J. Congar, *La Tradition et les traditions. Essai historique.* Paris, 1960 (The same author is planning to publish a theological study

First of all, it can be said that *tradition (paradosis)*, the living transmission of a truth, is an essential and constitutive element in the religion of Jesus Christ. Of course, the word " tradition " *(paradosis)* is found in the gospels only in the sense of Jewish " traditions," human traditions which the sovereign authority of Jesus' word opposes: " You have heard that it was said to the ancients . . . But *I* say to you . . ." *(Matt. 5:21 etc.)*. And what He says to them is a new tradition, a divine tradition which Jesus wants to substitute for the human traditions in which the Jews had enclosed themselves at the expense of the Word of God. Everything is contained in these few words of Jesus: " All things have been delivered (transmitted, *tradita, paredothen*) to me by my Father " *(Matt. 11:27)*. " All things I have heard from my Father I have made known to you " *(John 15:15)*. " As the Father has sent me, so also I send you " *(John 20:21)*. " Go into the whole world and preach the gospel [good news] to every creature " *(Mark 16:15)*. Jesus is the one who reveals and transmits the secrets of the Father and He sends His apostles to transmit *(tradere)* to the peoples what He Himself has transmitted to them. The Church of Jesus Christ has received the message of revelation to transmit it to men; the apostle in the Church is sent to transmit this message which comes from Christ, the word of God. Thus God's revelation, transmitted to men by Jesus Christ and those He has sent, continues to be transmitted by oral teaching, living in the life of the Church. This transmission is bound up with the apostolic mission, as well as with the living presence of Jesus Christ in His Church and of the Spirit He has promised and sent (Cf., e. g. *Matt. 28:20; John 14:26; 16:13 etc.)*. Revelation, tradition, apostolate, and Church are indissolubly united concepts and realities.

Even St. Paul has some well-crystallized expressions anent these essential realities. He has seen the *Kyrios*, the Lord

---

on the same subject); and, most recently, J. Beumer, " Die mündliche Überlieferung als Glaubensquelle," in *Handbuch der Dogmengeschichte*, by M. Schmaus and A. Grillmeier. Freiburg, 1962.

Jesus raised to His glory; he, too, then, can claim for himself the title of apostle (*I Cor.* 9:1). However, what he teaches he has received by tradition coming from the Lord; he only transmits what he has received (*I Cor.* 11:23; 15:3). These texts are fundamental. Paul congratulates the Corinthians for keeping the *traditions* which he has transmitted to them (*I Cor.* 11:2). These traditions comprise, also, the *kerygma* of salvation and its central point, namely, the Lord's Resurrection, as well as instructions on sacramental practice (the Eucharist), and some advice of a moral or disciplinary order on Christian conduct (Cf. again, for example, *II Thess.* 3:6 etc.). The apostle does not say everything in the letter he sends to the Corinthians, and reserves more precise determinations for the time of his visit with them (*I Cor.* 11:34). Thus he exhorts the Thessalonians to keep a firm grasp on the traditions they have received from him, either *viva voce* or by letter (*II Thess.* 2:15). Tradition, then, can be transmitted orally or in writing. Assuredly, here St. Paul makes allusion to the particular instructions he has given to the Thessalonians, either by his preaching or by his first letter. In these words one finds a very precious indication of the two ways for transmitting the sole tradition, whether it be written or unwritten.

One cannot say absolutely that the apostolic tradition is first and prior to all Scripture. There is the Old Testament, which, for the first Christian generations, is quite simply the *Scripture*. Now the remark that Jesus wrote nothing is trivial: " Jesus Christ wrote only once, and that was on the sand " (M. Blondel). He did not tell His apostles to write, He sent them to preach. His religion is the religion of the Word, not that of the Book. Yet the very circumstances and needs of their apostolate lead the apostles, and especially Paul, to write to the churches they have established. Their catechesis is summarized and established in small books which would later be called " Gospels " (even at the time of St. Justin, they still bear the significative title " Memoirs of the Apostles " [*I Apol.* 67]). St. Luke narrates the history of the first years of the nascent Church; St. John puts into writing his memories and his meditation . . . thus the teaching of the apostles is established in writings which gradually get the rank of *Scripture* alongside the Law and the Prophets. Yet it is important to note that this " Scripture," which does not even contain the *whole* message of Jesus Christ (Cf. *John* 20:13; 21:25), makes its appearance in the current of a living tradition. The famous words of Papias of Hierapolis, disciple of St. John and companion of St. Polycarp, here fall under the pen quite naturally: within the Church, the Church preserves " the living and dwelling word " (in Eusebius, *Hist. Eccl.* III, 39, 4). Although this formula undoubtedly lacks an absolute value, it can express for us the original stature of tradition in the Church.

The second century can be called the Century of Tradition. The false gnostic teachers were the first to claim for themselves " traditions " which, supposedly, came to them by word of mouth, from secret instructions which Jesus reserved for some privileged apostles, including Mary Magdalen. This is the explanation of the abundance of apocryphal " gospels " which appeared in gnostic milieu and which have recently been made known to us by the manuscripts discovered at Nag-Hammadi: *Gospel of Truth, Gospel of Thomas, Gospel of Mary, The Apocryphon of John.*

To this idea of secret revelations and traditions, very contrary to the spirit of Christianity, the Fathers set in opposition *the* tradition of the apostles, the " Tradition of the Church." In this regard, St. Irenaeus is the great teacher of tradition. " There is no gnosis other than the teaching of the apostles " (*Adv. Haer.* IV, 33, 8), which has come to us " by the tradition of the presbyters " (III, 2, 2). After Clement of Rome, " who had seen the apostles themselves, who had friendly relations with them, who still had their preaching in his ears, their tradition before his eyes " (*Adv. Haer,* III, 3, 3), Irenaeus himself is a privileged witness and even, in a certain way, the last witness of this tradition transmitted by the apostles; he had seen and heard Polycarp, who had seen and heard St.

John (in Eusebius, *Hist. Eccl.* V, 20). But John is dead, Polycarp is dead, and Irenaeus will soon die. Where shall we go in search of the authentic tradition of the apostles? To the Churches which they have established and in which the episcopal succession guarantees the fidelity of the doctrinal tradition. " All those who want to see the truth can contemplate, in every church, the tradition of the apostles manifested throughout the world. Moreover, we can enumerate those whom the apostles established as bishops and their successions up to our time. . . . The tradition which has been in the Church since the apostles and the preaching of the truth have come to us in this order and this succession. Furthermore, this is a very adequate proof that this vivifying faith, which has been preserved in the Church since the time of the apostles up to our own time and is transmitted in the truth, is always one and the same " (*Adv. Haer.* III, 3, 1. 3).

By the use of lapidary formulas, Irenaeus can establish the stages of this " tradition," which comes to us from Christ to the apostles, and from the apostles to the Church. We shall cite only one of these formulas: " Such is the preaching of the truth: the prophets have announced it, Christ has established it, the apostles have transmitted it, everywhere the Church presents it to her children " (*Demonstratio*, 98; cf., in almost identical terms, *Adv. Haer.* II, 31, 9; V, praef.). Without having the matter expressly formulated, here one sees the bond existing between tradition and the apostolic succession, between tradition and the magisterium of the Church.

This tradition, which brings the living word of the apostles to us, could, strictly speaking, do without the support of a written text. " If the apostles had not left any Scripture, it would be necessary to follow the order of the tradition which they have transmitted to those to whom they entrusted the churches " (*Adv. Haer.* III, 4, 1). Irenaeus knows barbarous people who cannot read and yet believe in Christ; they carefully guard the ancient tradition; they possess salvation, written by the Holy Spirit, without ink and paper, upon their hearts (*Ibid.* 2; *II Cor.* 3:3).

We shall dwell on these last words, which open very enlightening aspects about what tradition is. It is not merely the preservation and quasi-mechanical transmission of some formulas which have been learned and are recited from memory. The *heart* is what preserves and transmits the deposit of revelation. Thus, like Mary, the Church preserves and meditates in her heart upon the words she has received from Jesus. Through this loving meditation, under the motion of the Spirit present in her heart, she thoroughly examines the deposit of tradition, gradually discovers its profound riches, and thereby draws from the treasure of her heart old and new things. In this way, one sees how dogmatic progress, too, is intimately bound with tradition.

We have said that the gnostics claimed for themselves secret traditions and circulated fantastic " gospels." For his part, Marcion cast aside the whole of the Old Testament and fashioned the New Testament to his liking. Finally, outside heretical circles, there was the circulation, too, of texts which were taken to be " Scripture." At least in certain milieu, this was the case of the *Pastor* by Hermas and the *Epistle* said to be written by Barnabas. Faced with all this literature, how can one distinguish between what one must accept and what one must reject as suspicious or heretical? In final analysis, the criterion to which one refers is the apostolic origin of these writings. But how can one distinguish between what is apostolic and what is not? This is possible because of the tradition of the Church, or, one could say here, the memory of the Church, which, not without some hesitations or gropings, would establish the official list (*canon*) of Scriptures to be accepted or rejected. In this question, which is decisive for the life of the Church, the tradition of the Apostles, kept living in the Church, has played a determinative and normative rôle.

There is another problem, too, which arose during the second century. Scripture should not be taken according to the whim of each person (*II Peter* 1:20). Even at this time St. Peter's

Second Epistle puts its readers on guard against the persons who distort the signification present in Paul's letters, as they do, also, in regard to the other Scriptures (*II Peter* 3:16). The gnostic teachers gave themselves over unrestrainedly to these fantastic exegeses. How can one, then, determine the true meaning of Scripture? Here again, the tradition of the apostles and the Church is the rule and the norm. One must read Scripture " close to the presbyters of the Church, who possess the teaching of the apostles " (*Adv. Haer.* IV, 32, 1). One must be nourished by the Lord's Scriptures in the bosom of the Church (*Ibid.* V, 20, 2). Here one can again take up the text, some words of which we have already cited: " The true gnosis is the teaching of the apostles, the primitive constitution of the Church throughout the whole world, the character of the Body of Christ, [which consists] in the succession of the bishops whereby, through tradition, they have established the Church in each locality, the preservation of the Scriptures, the complete explanation of them which has come down to us without any addition or subtraction, the unfalsified reading of them, their true interpretation . . ." (*Ibid.* IV, 33, 8). Thus, for Irenaeus, the *paradosis* is the explanation of the Scriptures. For Origen, too, whose exegesis can seem rather arbitrary to some persons, it is an important point of " church doctrine," the unanimous conviction of the whole Church that " the Law is spiritual " (*De princ.* I, praef. 8). Scripture can be interpreted only in the tradition of the Church.

We have made an allusion to Origen. Let us cite, also, the following words from his writings: " Since the teaching of the Church, transmitted from the apostles according to the order of succession, has been preserved in the Churches up to the present time, one should accept as truth only what does not depart at all from the ecclesiastical and apostolic tradition " (*De princ.* I, praef. 2). " We should not depart from the ancient tradition of the Church, nor believe anything other than what God's Churches have transmitted to us through [the] succession [of the bishops] " (*In Matt. comm.*, ser. 46).

For the teacher from Alexandria or Caesarea, as for the bishop of Lyons, the source and norm of faith (*regula fidei*) is the tradition of the Church, preserved in and guaranteed by the succession of the Churches.

Other patristic texts enable us to know another aspect of tradition. They are well known, but it is advantageous to recall them here.

In 211, Tertullian wants to prohibit, for Christians, the practice of crowning themselves with flowers. He finds no justification for this severity in Scripture, but he makes reference to the *consuetudo* which has undoubtedly come down in tradition. Moreover, he gives examples of these " observances " which can be used only in the name of tradition and custom: " Thus, beginning with Baptism, before going down into the water, even in church, we obligate ourselves by oath, in the presence of the bishop, to renounce the devil, his pomps and his angels. Then we immerse ourselves three times, answering something which is more than the Lord has determined in the Gospel. Getting out of the water, we taste a mixture of milk and honey, and, from that day, we abstain from taking a daily bath for the whole week. Yet, we receive the sacrament of the Eucharist, which the Lord instituted during the meal and entrusted to us, in assemblies which take place before daybreak, and only from the hands of those who preside. We make offerings for the anniversary of the deceased, as well as that of the birth [of martyrs]. We deem it unlawful to fast and to pray on our knees during the day of the Lord, and we enjoy the same immunity from Easter Sunday until Pentecost. We exercise great care lest any particle of our bread or any portion of [what is in] our chalice should fall on the ground. Whether it is a matter of starting a trip, walking, entering or leaving, dressing ourselves or putting on shoes and stockings, washing ourselves, sitting down for a meal, rising in the morning, going to bed, sitting down, indeed, any activity at all, we mark our forehead with the sign of the cross . . ." (*De cor.* 3).

Much later (375), St. Basil seeking to justify the practice, established in the Church, of glorifying the Father and the

Son *with* the Holy Spirit, makes an appeal, also, to the unwritten tradition. Moreover, the examples he adduces conform to those furnished by Tertullian: "Among the doctrines and definitions preserved in the Church, we hold those of the written teaching and we have collected the other doctrines, transmitted secretly (*in mysterio*), from the apostolic tradition. All these doctrines have the same vigor in relation to piety. No one will disagree with them if one has even very little experience with ecclesiastical institutions; for, if we were to try to put aside the unwritten practices as not having any great vigor, we would unknowingly strike a blow at the Gospel, even as regards essential points. . . . For example, (to recall what first comes to mind and the practice whereof is very common), who has taught us in writing to mark with the sign of the cross those who hope in Our Lord Jesus Christ? What Scripture has instructed us to turn towards the East during prayer? What holy person has left for us, in writing, the words of the epiclesis, pertinent to the moment of the consecration of the bread and the chalice of benediction? We are not content with the words reported by the Apostle and the Gospel; before and after [these words], we pronounce others, received from the unwritten teaching which have a great importance in relation to the mystery. Moreover, we bless baptismal water, the oil for anointment, as well as the baptized person himself. Is this not in virtue of the tradition which has been kept secret and hidden? And what of this! What written word has taught anointment with oil? Whence does the triple immersion come? And everything surrounding Baptism, the renunciation of Satan and his angels, from what Scripture does this come? Is not this the privately and secretly held teaching that our fathers guarded in silence, without anxiety or curiosity, knowing that, by keeping silent, one safeguards the sacred character of the mysteries? . . ." (*De Sp. Sancto*, 27, 66).

These two passages, the convergence of which is the more significant because they come from epochs and regions widely separated from each other, are extremely important for the

history and the theology concerning tradition. One can under-
line two points therein, which really are not expressly formulated in the text, but which are easily disengaged from it in the
light of further developments of theological reflection.

In the first place, one will be led to distinguish *the tradition*
and traditions: the transmission in the Church of the revelation made by Jesus Christ to the apostles, and ecclesiastical
traditions and customs, which, too, can be traced to the practice of the apostles. Thus we have seen Origen justify the
baptism of infants and baptismal anointments. There are, then,
both doctrinal tradition and liturgical or disciplinary traditions.
Their content and their object are different. On the one hand,
it is a matter of the mystery of faith, preached by the apostles, received and transmitted in the Church; and, on the other,
of daily Christian practice and life. Both, however, have " the
same vigor in relation to piety." [2]

Thus, and this is our second observation, these gestures and
rites especially concern the sacramental practice of the Church:
Baptism, Confirmation, the Eucharist (St. Basil particularly
sets this matter in a clear light). An unreasonable historical
criticism will be able to establish that, in fact, one or other
among these rites does not go all the way back to the apostles.
Yet this has little importance in relation to what is essential in
the question. It is always a matter of the practice of the
apostles, transmitted and lived in the Church, of the lived and
living tradition of the Church.

Furthermore, in many cases, these sacramental " traditions "
are inseparable from a doctrinal tradition which establishes and
justifies them. Such is the frequently discussed case of the
baptism of infants. For Origen, this *Ecclesiae observantia*
(*In Levit. hom.* 8, 3) is a tradition which the Church received
from the apostles (*Rom. Comm.* 5, 9). Later, St. Augustine
too would see in this practice the *consuetudo Matris Ecclesiae*,
the apostolic tradition (*De Gen. ad litt.* X, 23, 39). Now, in

---

[2] This text of St. Basil in the Latin canonical collections contains an error in
copying (" affectu " instead of " effectu "). This is the source of the " pari pietatis
affectu " of the Council of Trent. Cf. J. Beumer, *op cit.*, pp. 50-51 and n. 30.

this venerable practice is involved belief in the mystery of original sin. In 418, the Council of Carthage (can. 3) would bring to light the bond between the practice concerning baptism and the dogma of original sin, as it is taught by St. Paul, and " as the Catholic Church, wherever established, has always understood it." These words express two essential characteristics of tradition, namely, that which the Church believes always and everywhere. As the Council of Trent in its turn, would deem this matter, this rule of faith can refer to the " tradition of the apostles " (Sess. V, can. 4).

There is another disciplinary problem involving a dogmatic question: Is it necessary to rebaptize heretics returning to the Church? Cyprian says " Yes ": their baptism is invalid. Pope Stephen says " No," basing his judgment on tradition: " Nihil innovetur, nisi quod traditum est " (in Cyprian, *Ep.* 74, 1), that is, tradition dating back to the apostles (*Ep.* 75, 5). Opposing reason to custom, Cyprian rejects this argument (*Ep.* 71, 3). He fails to see that here custom involves the authority of the Church based upon the tradition of the apostles. Later St. Augustine would put the various aspects of the problem in order and would show that the validity of the sacraments depends, not upon the faith or holiness of the minister, but upon the power of Christ; it is He Who baptizes through Peter, Paul, or Judas (*In Joann.* tr. 5, 18; 6, 7). The theological explanation, however, comes only after the practice, in order to give the reason for a dogmatic truth involved, from the very beginning, in the traditional practice of the Church.

Another question, still quite obscure for the historian, which should be mentioned is the matter of the sacrament of Confirmation. Whence comes the custom of anointing with chrism, which is nowhere witnessed in Scripture? The historian can hesitate, but the theologian, along with Origen, sees therein " the rule transmitted to the Churches " (*typum Ecclesiis traditum*) (*Rom. Comm.* 5, 8). Tradition is the rule, not only for establishing a particular detail in ritual, but also for determining the very matter of the sacrament.

Can one bring this very rapid inquiry to a conclusion? It seems that the principal headings of the outline pertinent to a theology on tradition are already established as early as the patristic period. Tradition is the revelation of Jesus Christ, entrusted by Him to His apostles and left by them to the Church, the column and foundation of the truth solidly established on the apostles and the prophets. This teaching of Jesus and the apostles was soon determined in a Scripture which takes its place beside the Scripture of the Old Testament. Scripture is the source and rule of all the truth concerning salvation: " The Holy Scriptures, divinely inspired," writes St. Athanasius, " are sufficient for the explanation of the truth " (*C. Gentes* 1). In them, St. Augustine adds, " is found everything concerning faith and the rule of life " (*De doctr. christ.* II, 9, 14). Vincent of Lerins would say that it is sufficient to itself (" sibi ad omnia satis superque sufficiens " [*Comm.* 2]). But Scripture is inseparable from tradition, which carries and transmits it, which interprets it authoritatively. We could not correctly understand Scripture, glean its inexhaustible riches, or even know exactly what authentic Scripture (the canon) is, without the authority of tradition. After the text we have just cited, St. Athanasius immediately adds: " Now there are numerous treatises composed by our blessed teachers for this purpose. He who reads them will understand the interpretation of the Scriptures. . . ." Therefore, Vincent of Lerins concludes, to Scripture one must add the authority of the interpretation thereof which the Church gives (" ecclesiasticae intelligentiae auctoritas ") ; one must interpret Scripture " according to the tradition of the universal Church and the rules of Catholic dogma " (*Ibid.* 27). In a few words, faith relies " upon the authority of the divine Law and upon the tradition of the Catholic Church " (*Ibid.* 2). In short, Scripture, Tradition, and the Church are inseparably united—the links of one and the same chain connecting us with the Word of the Living God.

From this one understands that the authority of these

" blessed teachers " comes, not from their personal knowledge,
but from their quality as witnesses of the faith and the tradition of the Church: " They have held what they have found
in the Church; they have taught what they have learned;
they have transmitted to their children what they have
received from their fathers " (Augustine, *C. Julianum*, I, 34;
cf. also *Op. imp. c. Jul.* I, 117: " *Ecclesiae docuerunt, quod
in Ecclesia docuerunt* ") . The Church is the whole believing
community, animated by the Holy Spirit; [3] and, in this community, living daily on tradition, the bishops are eminently
the guardians of the deposit which has been entrusted to
the Church. This is how, for example, St. Hippolytus spoke
at the beginning of the third century: " no one will refute
[these errors] if the Holy Spirit has not been transmitted in
the Church; having first received Him, they have communicated Him to those who had a correct faith. We who are
their successors, who share in the same grace of the priesthood and of teaching, and who are deemed to be the guardians
of the Church, do not close our eyes and do not reduce the
word to silence " (*Philosophoumena* I, pref. 6) .

Moreover, a particular importance is attached to the unanimity of tradition and the universal *consensus* of the Church.
Thus St. Augustine says, " What is held by the universal
Church, what has not been instituted by the Councils, but has
always been maintained, is very deservedly believed to be
communicable only by the authority of the apostles " (*De bapt.*
IV, 31; cf. *Ep.* 54, 1) . This is already the criterion of Vincent
of Lerins: " What is believed everywhere, always, and by all "
(*Comm.* 2) .

Again one will note that the ancient texts do not distinguish
between the apostolic traditio*n* and the ecclesiastical traditio*ns*,
the dogmatic tradition and the liturgical or disciplinary tradi-

---

[3] Here one can recall that St. Thomas speaks of the " familiar instinct of the
Holy Spirit " (*Summa theol.* IIIa, q. 25, a. 3, ad 4um) and the " familiar tradition of the Apostles " (*Ibid.* q. 64, a. 2, ad lum). The revelation of the apostles
is communicated as a family good, as a tradition lived in the Church, under the
action of the Spirit Who dwells in and animates her.

tions. The Council of Trent still speaks only of the unwritten traditions (and yet adds that these traditions concern faith and morals); here there is a point which will become more precise through further theological reflection. This reflection will make a further distinction between objective and subjective tradition, the content of tradition and the one who bears it (*traditio tradita* and *tradita tradens*). Against the unfortunate disjunctions introduced by the Reformation, this reflection will have to establish precise delineations on the relations between "Tradition" and "Scripture"; here again, there must be "distinguishing for the sake of unifying." Again, theology will have to show how tradition is the privileged organ of dogmatic development and to present an exact account of the rôle of the Church in her magisterium, "guardian and mistress of the revealed Word." "Along with the apostolic duty of teaching," she "has received the command to safeguard the deposit" (*Conc. Vat.* I, sess. III, ch. 3 and 4). However, one can be sure, it seems, that the essential was secured from the period of the first centuries.

At the Council of Chalcedon, the bishops very loudly proclaimed their will to uphold the faith of the Fathers, the faith of the Apostles, the faith of Cyril and Leo; and they made a solemn dogmatic decision only "by following the faith of the holy Fathers. . . ." They themselves are the living tradition. The Fathers of the Second Vatican Council, too, are only the voice of Tradition.

THOMAS CAMELOT, O. P.

Le Saulchoir,
Paris, France

MAGISTERIUM OF THE CHURCH AND SACRED THEOLOGY *

ᏬᎯᎧ

I. The Church, Mother and Teacher of Truth

1. *Maternal Magisterium*

THE maternal character of the magisterium of the Church was recognized and praised by Augustine of Hippo, who, during the period of his youth, had been the victim of the deadly lies of the Manichees. Meditating on the Catholic Church, he expresses himself in this way: " If your true and truthful Spouse, from Whose side you have been formed, had not established in His real blood the remission of sins, the whirlpool of the lie would have absorbed me and, once I became earth, the seductive serpent would have irreparably devoured me." [1]

Many men, less endowed than the great Augustine, have not recognized in the magisterium of the Church a source of light and true freedom for the spirit. However, the case is different for those who have inherited that illumination which the First Vatican Council has proclaimed to be the maternal and supremely salutary character of the magisterium of the Church. In fact, in the profession of faith given in the name of the whole Catholic episcopacy at the opening of the Council, the Supreme Pontiff Pius IX said: " I recognize the holy, Catholic, and apostolic Church to be the mother and teacher of all the churches." [2] Moreover, confirming the teaching of the Council of Trent, all the conciliar Fathers declared:

In the questions of faith and morals, with which the edifice of the Christian faith is constructed, that must be held to be the true sense of Holy Scripture which Holy Mother Church has always held

* Translated by C. F. Lehner, O.P.

[1] *Contra Faustum*, Book XV, chap. 3.

[2] *Conc. Oecum. Decreta*, edited by the Centro di Documentazione Instituto per le scienze religiose, Bologna: Herder, 1962, p. 779, 30.

and still holds. She alone has the right to judge the true meaning and the correct interpretation of Sacred Scripture.[3]

2. Authentic and Infallible Magisterium

According to the teachings of the First Vatican Council, which will undoubtedly be the bond uniting the teaching of the Second Vatican Council with traditional doctrine, the magisterium of the Church can be defined as " the right and office which the Church has to teach revealed truth with that supreme authority which all men are obligated to respect with their mind, their heart, their words, and their actions."

The magisterium of the Church is, above all, *authentic,* since it is vested with the same divine authority as that of Jesus Christ, Who instituted this magisterium when He said to His Apostles: " As the Father has sent me, I also send you " (*John* 20:21). In virtue of this divine investiture, which transformed the fishermen of Galilee into ambassadors even of the heavenly Father, the first and eternal truth, Jesus could add: " He who hears you, hears me; and he who rejects you, rejects me; and he who rejects me, rejects him who sent me " (*Luke* 10:16).

Likewise, the magisterium of the Church is *infallible.* In fact, entrusting to His Apostles and, through them, to their lawful successors, the right and duty of teaching all peoples the truths which are indispensable for eternal salvation, Jesus Christ could not refuse to safeguard the members of the teaching Church by His spiritual presence as supreme Master, and therefore, also, with the assistance or *charism* of the Spirit of truth, who would protect the faithful from all error, regarding both the truths to be believed and those concerning practice. This promise was *explicit,* as is evident in the Gospel texts cited previously, and was *repeated* in the discourse of the Last Supper, when the Lord comforted His disciples and said to them: " I will ask the Father and he will give you another Advocate to dwell with you forever, the

[3] *Ibid.,* p. 782, 35-40.

Spirit of truth . . . [who] will dwell and will be in you; the Advocate, the Holy Spirit, whom the Father will send in my name, he will teach you all things, and bring to your mind whatever I have said to you" (*John* 14:16, 26).

On the basis of the promise made directly by Christ, not to all the faithful, but *only* to the Apostolic College and *personally* to Peter, who had been previously named as the foundation of the universal Church, the First Vatican Council has sanctioned the following truths, which have been an undisputed patrimony of the Catholic faith for fifteen centuries:

I am to believe, with an act of divine and Catholic faith, all those things which are contained in the written or transmitted Word of God, and which are proposed for our belief as divinely revealed by the Church, either on the strength of a solemn judgment or through the ordinary and universal magisterium.[4]

In this text there is a clear indication of the existence of a twofold form of authentic and infallible magisterium in the Church: 1) an *extraordinary* magisterium, when solemn or definitive declarations are made; 2) an *ordinary* and *universal* magisterium, when the teaching to be believed or put into practice is concordantly proposed by the Episcopacy to the whole Catholic world. The first type of magisterium pertains to the Ecumenical Council, that is, to the whole Episcopal Body reunited in a general assembly under the presidency of the Roman Pontiff, who alone, by divine right, can convoke Councils, preside over them, approve their *Acts*, and command their promulgation. The second type is exercised by the teaching Church extended throughout the world, as Pius IX had declared, with the Letter " Tuas libenter " of December 21, 1863, to the Archbishop of Monaco.[5]

3. Sacred Magisterium

Because its character is *sacred*, the magisterium of the Church is presented to men as eminently *maternal*, that is,

---

[4] *Ibid.*, p. 873, 25-30.

[5] Denzinger, *Enchiridion Symbolorum*, n. 1683.

able to transfuse salutary and vivifying teachings into their minds. Truly, like Jesus Christ, Whose prerogatives of *Prophet, Priest* and *King* it shares, the sacred hierarchy proclaims that its kingdom is not of this world.[6] Therefore, it is *directly* concerned with matters pertaining to an order of spiritual, supernatural, and eternal realities. Nevertheless, its magisterial power is *indirectly* extended also to terrestial realities, when natural truths or activities have an intimate connection with the spiritual nature of man and his eternal destiny.

In this regard, the teaching of the First Vatican Council is clear.[7] Faithful to this teaching, the Supreme Pontiffs of our time, namely, Leo XIII, St. Pius X, Benedict XV, Pius XI, Pius XII, and John XXIII, have also made pronouncements concerning arguments apparently having only a natural and profane content, such as authority, freedom, matrimony, war, peace, property, the natural sciences, medicine, and the arts. Yet the scope pursued by the Roman Pontiffs has been only that of having the light of the Gospel, of the moral and social doctrine of the Church, radiate on human problems. Their magisterium, then, has been kept *sacred* in its inspiration, scope, and pronouncements; therefore, it merits recognition and attentive consideration.

4. *Living Magisterium*

The liveliness with which the magisterium of the Church is endowed is not the vitality of things subject to physical evolution and, therefore, to continual transformation. Being the echo of the eternal word of God, Who has spoken to men through the prophets, and especially through His Son (Cf. *Heb.* 1), the word of the Church transcends the contingency and changes to which the human spirit, too, is subject in this world. As St. Augustine has already said with regard to divine truth, this word is *always old and always new*, since it is eternal.

---

[6] Cf. Encycl. *Mystici Corporis, AAS* XXXV (1943), 211-212.
[7] *Conc. Oecum. Decreta*, p. 785, 25-30.

In fact, the sacred hierarchy does not limit itself to preserving and defending the deposit of divine revelation, as though it were a matter of dealing with a material treasure. Rather, fully convinced about the perennial vitality and fecundity of God's word, the teaching Church tries to reach the sources or channels of revelation, namely, *Sacred Scripture* and *Tradition*, the infinite divine truth, in the measure which can be better adapted to the intellectual, moral, social, political, and cultural demands of human generations, distinct and diverse in time and space.

Therefore, one commits a serious offense against the sacred hierarchy and, in it, against Christ Himself and His divine Spirit, by pretending to substitute oneself for the sacred hierarchy in its function of faithfully interpreting the teaching of Sacred Scripture and the divine-apostolic Tradition, as though the correct understanding of revealed truth depended more upon the human endowments of mental capacity, culture, and study, than upon the special charism or supernatural light promised by the divine Savior only to His lawful representatives.

In defense of the perennial and irreplaceable value of the authentic magisterium proper to the hierarchy, Pius XII raised his voice in the encyclical *Humani generis*, reminding theologians and all other cultivators of the sacred sciences that:

Along with these sacred sources [Sacred Scripture and Tradition], God has given His Church the *living* magisterium, too, in order to illustrate and develop those truths which are contained only obscurely and, as it were, implicitly, in the deposit of faith. Moreover, the divine Redeemer has entrusted this deposit, for its authentic interpretation, not to each of the faithful, nor even to theologians, but only to the magisterium of the Church.[8]

More than every other Bishop, the Pope recognizes the duty of making his own magisterium ever more *vivid*, in such a way that He may be truly like "a householder who brings

---

[8] Encyl. *Humani generis*, AAS XLII (1950), 569.

forth from his storeroom things new and old " (*Mat.* 13:52). For this providential task, which is very important and obligatory, he is incessantly urged by the Lord's command to His First Vicar: " Strengthen thy brethren " (*Luke* 22:32). Pius XII has offered the following comment:

Immortal words, deeply engraved into the innermost recesses of Our mind, they become even more penetrating whenever, in the exercise of the apostolic ministry, We have to communicate to the Episcopacy and the faithful throughout the world the teachings, norms, and exhortations which are demanded by the fulfillment of the saving mission of the Church and which, without prejudice to their substantial immutability, should always be opportunely adapted to the ever changing circumstances and the varieties of time and place.[9]

On his part, the late Supreme Pontiff John XXIII convoked the Second Ecumenical Council of the Vatican by an act which was truly providential and magnanimous. In his allocution for the solemn opening of the Council (October 11, 1962), he reaffirmed the terms " liveliness " or " vitality " in reference to the magisterium of the Church:

From the renewed, serene, and tranquil adherence to the whole teaching of the Church in its interest and precision, still luminous in the conciliar acts from those of Trent to those of the First Vatican Council, the Christian, catholic, and apostolic spirit of the whole world awaits new strides towards a doctrinal penetration and a formation of consciences in more perfect correspondence of fidelity to the authentic doctrine, even as this is studied and expounded through the forms of investigation and formulation which are characteristic of modern thought. There is a difference between the substance of the ancient teaching of the deposit of faith and the formulation of it as it is stated in new terminology; and this is what must be largely taken into account, with patience if necessary, by measuring everything in the forms and proportions of a magisterium which is especially pastoral in character.[10]

The perennial vitality and, as it were, eternal spring of the

---

[9] Radiomessaggio Natalizio 1948. Cf. Pio XII, *Discorsi e Radiomessaggi*, X, p. 313.

[10] Allocutio *Gaudet Mater*, AAS LIV (1962).

authentic magisterium of the Church, therefore, is simultaneously a fruit of complete fidelity to divine truth, transmitted
from Sacred Scripture and Tradition, and of an interpretation
of the same immutable truths which is always more penetrating, actual, and efficacious—an interpretation to be translated
into a language enriched with the whole patrimony of the
sound philosophical, scientific, literary, and artistic culture of
modern times—so that the word of God might resound in a
way which is understandable, fruitful and pleasing to the ears
of the men of our time. This is the genuine thought of John
XXIII, who, in the same allocution, had said:

Now since such a doctrine reaches the manifold areas of human
activity pertinent to individuals, families, and social life, it is
especially necessary that the Church does not separate herself from
the sacred patrimony of the truth received from the Fathers; and,
at the same time, she must also look at the present, at the new
conditions and forms of life introduced into the modern world
which have opened new paths for the Catholic apostolate.[11]

II. Sacred Theology, Auxiliary of the Divine Magisterium of the Church

1. *The Authentic Organs of the Magisterium of the Church*

These are only the Roman Pontiff and the Bishops in union
with him. This is a fundamental truth of the true Church of
Jesus Christ. In defense of this truth Pius XII deemed it
opportune to make his voice resound in the presence of the
Sacred College of Cardinals and the Catholic Episcopacy
gathered in Rome for the canonization of St. Pius X:

Christ Our Lord entrusted the truth which He had brought from
heaven to the Apostles and, through them, to their successors. In
fact, He sent the Apostles, as He Himself had been sent by the
Father (*John* 20:21), in order that they might teach all peoples
whatever they heard from the Lord (cf. *Matt.* 28:19-20). The
Apostles, then, were constituted doctors and teachers in the Church
by divine right. Therefore, besides the lawful successors of the
Apostles, that is, besides the Roman Pontiff for the universal

---

[11] *Ibid.*

Church and besides the Bishops for the faithful entrusted to their care (cf. CIC, can. 1326), there are no other teachers established by divine right in the Church of Christ.[12]

2. *The Auxiliary Organs of the Magisterium of the Church*

However, even simple priests, and, indeed, the laity can be *auxiliary organs* of the ecclesiastical magisterium. In fact, in the previously cited allocution, Pius XII added the following words:

But either the Bishops or, in the first place, the Supreme Teacher of the Church and Vicar of Christ on earth can call other persons to help them, as collaborators or advisers, in the capacity of teachers to whom they delegate the faculty of teaching (cf. can. 1328). Those who are called to teach, either by special mandate or by reason of an office conferred upon them, fulfill the function of teachers in the Church, not in their own name, nor on the basis of their own theological knowledge, but by reason of the mandate received from the lawful magisterium and, therefore, their capacity always remains subject to the hierarchical magisterium and never becomes their own right, not subject to any power.[13]

Therefore, what grants exegetes and theologians a certain right and authority to teach in the Church officially or publicly consists, not in academic degrees which they have attained or in personal charisms, but only in the *mandate* received from the hierarchy. This mandate, however, does not make the teaching of theologians hierarchical and authentic, since this characteristic is indissolubly bound with the character of the episcopacy; and yet even the teaching of theologians can be *infallible*, when it is in accordance with the hierarchy and the whole teaching Church, in manifesting revealed truths or the teachings which are intimately connected with divine revelation.

3. *Scholastic Theology and the Divine Magisterium of the Church*

There is no mystery in the fact that, in the Second Ecumenical Council of the Vatican, accusations of scholasticism

---

[12] *Discorsi e Radiomessaggi*, XVI, p. 42.　　　[13] *Ibid.*, p. 43.

were levelled against some doctrinal schemata, on the basis
that they adhere too much to the mentality and style of
scholastic theology. What answer can one give to such complaints? One should make a distinction:

a. *Scholastic or scientific theology still enjoys the full rights
of citizenship in the Catholic Church*, without any distinction
among nations and cultures. From history we know that the
accusation of uselessness, and even of danger and loss for the
Catholic faith, as levelled against scholastic theology, is not
a matter only of our time. In the fifteenth century, the Council of Constance and Martin V intervened for the defense of
the ecclesiastical universities against John Wycliffe who held
that they were as useful to the Church " as the devil." [14] In
the eighteenth century, Pius VI condemned those propositions
of the Synod of Pistoia which held that the systems of scholasticism were responsible for the doctrinal and moral decadence of the Church.[15] In the nineteenth century, Pius IX
defended the great masters of scholasticism, St. Thomas and
St. Bonaventure, against accusations (of rationalism and of
complicity with the naturalism and pantheism of modern philosophy) advanced by the followers of Traditionalism against
the scholastic method.[16] Moreover, it was Pius IX who reproved
some German theologians for holding that the method and
principles of the ancient doctors of scholasticism were not suitable for satisfying the intellectual and moral needs of modern
times, and were irreconcilable with progress in the sciences.[17]
In the encyclical " *Aeterni Patris* " (August 4, 1879), whereby
the immortal Leo XIII intended to promote the new flowering
of ecclesiastical studies according to the spiritual needs of the
Church in the nineteenth century, the defense of scholastic
theology is in a positive form and, therefore, even more con-

[14] Denz., *op. cit.*, 609.
[15] Denz. *op. cit.*, 1576, 1579.
[16] *Decretum S. C. Indicis,* June 11, 1855; Denz. *op cit.*, 1652.
[17] Letter to the Archbishop of Monaco, " Tuas libenter " (Dec. 21, 1863); (Denz.
op. cit., 1679); *Syllabus*, proposition 13 (Den. *op. cit.*, 1713).

vincing. Here, in fact, we read: "Once most solid foundations have been laid in this way, there is still a need for the perpetual and manifold use of philosophy, so that sacred theology might receive and take on the nature, habit, and character of a true science." [18] From the whole context of the encyclical, it is clear that the Pope recognizes the value of scientific theology, that is, a more precise and penetrating knowledge of the deposit of the Catholic faith, only in reference to scholastic theology, the only theology which has made a *perpetual* and *manifold* use of rational or perennial philosophy.

Furthermore, even in the twentieth century, the Supreme Pontiffs have defended and praised scholastic theology, especially that of St. Thomas, by repeatedly stating that its *principles*, its *method*, and its doctrinal *patrimony* are the most valid instruments for the defense, illustration, and penetration of the truths of faith. In this regard, the thought of Pius XII in the encyclical " *Humani generis* " is well known. However, it is useful to recall some statements of two other Supreme Pontiffs.

Speaking to the faculties and students of Catholic universities (January 8, 1928), Pius XI said:

They had made excellent deliberation in their decision to be concerned about Thomism and the order of its relations with modern culture. On the one hand, there is in Thomism, as it were, a certain natural Gospel, an incomparably solid foundation for all scientific constructions, since what is especially characteristic of Thomism is its *objectivity*. It has, not constructions or elevations of the spirit which are merely abstract, but constructions and elevations of the mind which follow upon the real content in things. The method of St. Thomas lies in seeing what is seen, what is verified, what is understood in its individuality, and thence rising to what is not seen and not understood. *The value of Thomistic doctrine,* then, *will never be diminished,* since, for this to happen, the value of things would have to be diminished. For this reason, one can easily understand the solicitude of the Church, which has always recognized very great importance in Thomistic doctrine, even by establishing it at the very basis of studies of the sacred sciences.

[18] Leo XIII, *Acta* I (1881), 262.

The young students in the Universities, then, will study Thomistic teaching in relation with modern doctrines. If either of these two parts is known in a rather meagre way, it can only too easily seem to such a student that they are mutually contradictory, whereas, the better they are known, the more splendidly their harmony appears.[19]

In the discourse held on the occasion of the Fifth International Thomistic Congress (September 16, 1960), John XXIII, the Pope of the Second Ecumenical Council of the Vatican, having recommended the study of St. Thomas also to the young members of Catholic Action, concluded:

We strongly desire that the treasure, as it were, of the precepts of St. Thomas be daily uncovered ever more extensively for the very great benefit of the Christian cause, and that, therefore, his writings be ever the more widely diffused among the people, either for the sake of instruction or for advanced teaching, since they are not at all at variance with the mode of thinking pertinent to our times.[20]

It is evident, then, that, even for the compassionate Supreme Pontiff, the method, doctrine, and the very language of St. Thomas have not lost their very great usefulness even for our times.

b. *If used with discretion, scholastic theology can be of very great benefit to the Fathers of the Second Vatican Council.* In fact, although, according to the express intention of John XXIII, the Second Vatican Council should be an eminently pastoral Council,[21] yet it is good to remember that, among pastoral aims, " the increase of the faith " should have the first place and its essential prerequisite. Now this increase necessarily calls for continuity without conservatism, progress without entanglement, the development of the majestic edifice of Catholic dogma without any weakening, as well as a greater consolidation of its rational bases (" praeambula fidei "). However, the only theology which can assure this increase is scho-

---

[19] *Discorsi di Pio* XI. Rome: S. E. I., 1929. Vol. I, pp. 668-69.
[20] AAS LII (1960), 823.
[21] Encycl. *Ad Petri Cathedram*, AAS LI (1959), 511.

lastic theology, since it alone has at its service "ancient and
Christian" philosophy, that is, the perennial philosophy.[22]
Therefore, when John XXIII said that, in the Second Vatican Council, there would be the study and explanation of the
authentic doctrine through the forms of investigation and
formulation pertinent to modern thought, in order that there
might be a Council endowed with a magisterium having an
eminently *pastoral* character, he surely did not intend to propose to, and much less impose upon, the Fathers of the Second Vatican Council a renunciation of the *principles, method,*
and *doctrine* of St. Thomas. Keeping in mind important preceding documents of his magisterium, we must conclude that
John XXIII desired that, along with the use of scholastic
theology (after the example of the Council of Trent and the
First Vatican Council) in the measure required for clarity and
precision in the doctrinal formulations, there should be the
use, also, of the literary apparatus proper to modern philosophical, scientific, and artistic thought, especially in those
constitutions containing eminently practical arguments. It is
vain, then, to expect a formulation of the truths of faith and
morals which would be in ideological contrast to the formulas
already employed in preceding Councils or in the most important documents pertinent to the magisterium of the Roman
Pontiffs. This hope has been excluded by the express will of
John XXIII, who, desiring progress in the formulation of the
truths of faith, still demands that no prejudice be borne
against the immutable ideological content already expressed
with analogous, if not perfect, propriety in the preceding
Councils and in other acts of the magisterium of the Church.
"For one thing is the deposit of Faith, or the truths which
are contained in our venerable teaching; another thing is the
manner wherein these truths are stated, *yet with the same
meaning and the same judgment.*" [23]

---

[22] Pius XII, *Allocutio ad Professores et alumnos Pont. Univ. Gregorianae* (Oct.
17, 1953); AAS XLV (1953), 685.
    [23] Allocutio *Gaudet Mater*, AAS LIV (1962).

c. *The study of St. Thomas Aquinas will help assure greater fruits for the Second Ecumenical Council of the Vatican.* This has been the persuasion of John XXIII, who, in the *Motu proprio* " Dominicanus Ordo," whereby he conferred the title of Pontifical University of St. Thomas Aquinas *in Urbe* upon the International Pontifical College " Angelicum " in Rome (March 7, 1963), indicated the following as the third reason which inspired his benign concession:

We are persuaded that the counsels proposed by the Fathers of the Second Vatican Council will be more happily brought into effect if the study of the doctrine of Aquinas is urged with even greater care and skill.[24]

Really, the following words of the First Vatican Council have more relevance to the theology of St. Thomas than to that of any other ancient or modern Catholic thinker:

And, indeed, reason illumined by faith, when it zealously, piously, and soberly seeks, attains with the help of God some understanding of the mysteries, and that a most profitable one, not only from the analogy of those things which it knows naturally, but also from the connection of the mysteries among themselves and with the last end of man; nevertheless, it can never perceive those mysteries in the manner whereby it perceives the truths which constitute its own proper object.[25]

Moreover, if the Constitutions of the Second Vatican Council will have an eminently pastoral character, they must necessarily deal with arguments which have an intimate connection with the principles and teaching of Catholic faith and morals, which Aquinas has defended, illustrated, and investigated even in their necessary, universal, and immutable conclusions. Therefore, just as the Supreme Pontiffs from Leo XIII to John XXIII, in their encyclicals and other important documents of their magisterium, made considerable use of the thought of the *Doctor Communis* in confronting the arguments which most concern modern society; so too, the

[24] AAS LV (1963), 208-209.
[25] *Conc. Oecum. Decreta*, p. 785, 30-35.

pastors of souls, professors, and lecturers, in explaining the teachings of the Second Vatican Council to the faithful under their care or to their audiences, will be able to have recourse to St. Thomas. They can thus better accomplish the defense, commentaries, and completion of Catholic doctrine which, in the conciliar Constitutions, will necessarily have to be restricted to some rather solemn and programmatic statements.

The theologians who admire and imitate the Angelic Doctor will, in their learning and teaching, know how to unite humility with science, docility to the infallible magisterium of the Church with the attempts to adapt the light of divine revelation to the spiritual needs of modern times and, thereby, to the progress of human thought in every branch of knowledge. They will never appeal to personal *charisms* of the Holy Spirit as a means of proposing for speculative or practical problems those solutions which have been dictated by an existentialist or nominalist philosophy and which, therefore, are in contrast to the solutions already given by the sacred hierarchy. Against the spirit of *modernism*, which even today tempts some exegetes and theologians, all good theologians and especially Thomists are faithful to the oath prescribed by St. Pius X, in which every theologian seeking to remain a Catholic and a suitable teacher in the name of the Catholic Church has the duty of professing the following proposition:

Therefore I most firmly hold the faith of the Fathers and I shall keep it to the end of my life, regarding the *certain* charism of *truth* which is, has been, and will be *in the succession of the episcopacy starting with the Apostles* (Iren. 4, c. 26, 2 [MG 7, 1058C]); not that what is held be better and more aptly seen according to one's culture of any era, but that the absolute and immutable truth preached by the Apostles from the very beginning never be believed or understood in any other way (Tertullianus, *De praescript.*, c. 28 [ML 2, 40]).

In other words, "The divinely instituted magisterium in the Church has a *most special* and *unique* charism, namely, that of giving an authentic interpretation and explanation of the word of God, which has been written and transmitted to us." [26] The mission of the theologian, then, is not to substitute himself for the magisterium of the Church; rather, it is to give his humble services to the magisterium with the conviction that only by serving the truth does the human spirit become free and participate in God's spiritual sovereignty: "To serve God is to rule."

LUIGI CIAPPI, O. P.

Sacro Palazzo Apostolico
Vatican City

---

[26] Card. M. Browne, O. P., "I principali insegnamenti dell'Enciclica 'Humani generis,'" *Sapienza*, 1951.

PRIMACY AND EPISCOPACY:
A DOCTRINAL REFLECTION

∽

THE first Vatican Council defined the primacy of the Roman pontiff. We profess, therefore, that the bishop of Rome is an infallible teacher of the gospel and that he holds universal jurisdiction over the whole Church. The first Vatican Council specified that this jurisdiction is immediate and ordinary, in other words truly episcopal, and hence we are justified in calling the pope the universal bishop of the Church.

At the same time the pope is not the only bishop. In fact, bishops are as essential to the Catholic Church as he is. Despite his primacy, he could never dispense with the episcopal structure of the Church universal and administrate the Catholic people through a system of government more directly under his control. The First Vatican itself made this clear.[1]

This, however, was all that the First Vatican said about bishops in the Church. The original document prepared for the conciliar deliberations included fifteen chapters on the Church and her constitution, but the briefness of the session did not permit the bishops to discuss more than the chapter dealing with papal primacy. Since the council did not deal with the role of bishops in the Church nor define their relationship to the Roman pontiff, the impression was created in many quarters outside the Church that the council had suppressed the episcopal structure of the Catholic Church and introduced a papal government in its stead. The accusations became vocal in terms such as " episcopal jurisdiction has been absorbed into papal," " the pope no longer exercises cer-

---

[1] " Tantum abest, ut haec Summi Pontificis potestas officiat ordinariae ac immediatae illi episcopis iurisdictionis potestati, qua episcopi, qui *positi a Spiritu Sancto* in Apostolorum locum successerunt, tamquam veri pastores assignatos sibi greges, singuli singulos, pascunt et regunt " (Denz. 1828).

tain reserved rights, as he has in the past, but now holds the whole of the bishops' rights in his hands," "the pope has, in principle, taken the place of each bishop."

To reply to these accusations, the German bishops made a collective declaration in 1875 in which they asserted that the episcopal structure of the Catholic Church has remained intact and declared that, despite papal primacy, defined at the council, Catholic bishops continue to teach and rule in their diocese as they always have in the Church.[2] Pope Pius IX expressed his whole-hearted approval of the declaration.

Twenty years later, in his encyclical *Satis Cognitum* (1896) Pope Leo XIII re-asserted the episcopal structure of the Church universal. I shall quote the rather lengthy passage in English:

> But if the authority of Peter and his successor is plenary and supreme, it is not to be regarded as the sole authority. For He who made Peter the foundation of the Church also chose twelve whom he called apostles; and just as it is necessary that the authority of Peter be perpetuated in the Roman pontiff, so the bishops who succeed the apostles must inherit their ordinary power. Thus the episcopal order necessarily belongs to the essential constitution of the Church. Although bishops do not receive plenary, universal or supreme authority, they are not to be looked upon as mere representatives of the Roman pontiffs. They exercise a power truly their own and are ordinary pastors of the people whom they govern.[3]

In these citations dealing with episcopal authority, the principal concern is the role of the bishop in his own diocese, and hence, whatever is said about the relationship of pope and episcopacy really refers to the pope's relationship to the individual bishops. It is now common doctrine that the pope has immediate and ordinary jurisdiction in every diocese of the world, and that, at the same time, the local bishop also has immediate and ordinary jurisdiction in the diocese of

---

[2] (The collective declaration is most easily available in English in the appendix of H. Küng's *The Council, Reform and Reunion* (New York: Sheed & Ward, 1961).
[3] (*Satis Cognitum*, § 52.)

which he is the pastor. These two jurisdictions in the same territory do not conflict with one another; they do not cancel or inhibit one another, but, on the contrary, they are meant to help and re-enforce one another, making hierarchical authority a more efficient service or ministry to the common good of the faithful. The ultimate force which guarantees the harmonious co-ordination of the two immediate and ordinary powers in the same diocese is charity. While papal power is supreme and extends over the bishop as well as his flock, the pope must use this power to build up God's kingdom, to foster the life of the diocese and therefore to safeguard the scope of the bishop in the exercise of his pastoral authority.

Looking upon the relationship between papacy and episcopacy in this individual fashion, very little theological advance was made. No theological formula would represent the relationship adequately. By considering only the relation of pope and individual bishop some problems even seem to become more difficult, especially the question concerning the origin of episcopal jurisdiction. Does a bishop receive his ministerial power to teach and rule directly from Christ, or does he receive it directly from the pope? There can be no doubt that in the Church of our day the individual bishop receives his jurisdiction from the Roman pontiff, receives it, in fact, through papal appointment prior to the sacramental consecration. Limiting the whole question to individual bishops and considering the present practice of the Church, it is certainly true to say that the bishop receives his jurisdiction directly from the pope. This was, in fact, the doctrine taught by Pius XII in *Mystici Corporis* [4]

This approach, however, does not give deep insight into the relation of the pope and the world episcopate. Since, in former ages, jurisdiction was not always passed on to bishops through the successor St. Peter, but also in many other ways specified by law, we must analyse more profoundly the struc-

---

[4] (§ 41): " (Episcopi) ordinaria jurisdictionis potestate fruantur, (quae est) immediate sibi ab eodem Pontifice Summo impertita."

ture of the Church to determine the relation between primacy
and episcopacy. It is, in fact, only when we consider the bishops in their totality that we discover their real place in the
Church of the Lord.

We shall take our lead from canon 228, § 1, of the Code.[5]
Here we learn that the Roman pontiff is not the only one who
exercises supreme authority in the Church as teacher and
ruler, but that the bishops of the Church united to him in
a council also exercise this supreme power. Conciliar power,
moreover, is not derived from that of the pope. According to
the present legislation, it is true, a council must be convoked
and presided over by the pope, and its decrees must have
papal approval, but once they are promulgated, their authority is not papal but properly conciliar. If one were to deny
this, the ecumenical councils of the Church would not hold
supreme authority but simply be consulting boards for the
issuing of papal decrees. It is indeed possible to say that in
a material way the power of the council is derived from the
pope, since, according to present legislation he alone may call
it, dissolve it, and approve its decisions, but formally and
theologically, the power of the council is not derived from
that of the pope.

The recognition that the bishops as a whole, in union with
their head the pope, can act with supreme authority and bear
the charge of the universal Church leads us to the key doctrine determining the relationship between episcopacy and
primacy. This doctrine is referred to as " the collegiality of
the bishops " or " the unity of the episcopal college." According to this doctrine, the bishops of the Church form a body
or college which, as a group, is responsible for teaching and
governing the whole people. To understand the meaning of
this teaching, we must first consider its biblical foundation.

According to the account of the New Testament, Jesus
founded his Church as the new Israel on the twelve apostles
chosen by him. The Twelve were created by Christ as a body.

---

[5] " Concilium Oecumenicum suprema pollet in universam Ecclesiam potestate."

Together they received their instructions,[6] together they received the call to undertake the mission of the world,[7] together they were called to be witnesses to the ends of the earth [8] and together they received the Holy Ghost on the day of Pentecost.[9] We are told that the apostles received the power of the keys as a group [10] and that they are the foundation of the Church.[11] So great was their sense of unity and their realization that as the Twelve they were the Church's rock, that immediately after the defection of the one, they elected another faithful witness to complete their number.[12] They were conscious that as a body they had received the promise of remaining indefectible: " I shall be with you always." [13]

At the same time we also read that Peter, one of the Twelve, was assigned a special place among the apostles. The promises made to the apostles as a group were also made to Peter alone. He is the rock; he holds the power of the keys; his mission is indefectible.[14] He is the head of the apostolic college. But it is within this apostolic body to which he inseparably belongs that his office and prerogative must be understood. In other words, the primacy of Peter does not break the unity of the apostolic college as the foundation of the Church of Christ.

According to Catholic faith, the apostles had successors. These successors were no longer the special instruments of God's self-revelation in Jesus Christ, as were the apostles, but, inasmuch as they preserve, explain and defend the teaching and discipline of the Twelve and, inasmuch as they continue to rule the Church universal, the men who followed the apostles are called their successors.

These successors of the apostles are the bishops. This must not be understood as if each bishop can trace his line of consecration back to a single apostle. What happens, rather, is that the episcopal body as a whole is heir or successor of the apostolic body. The promises which the Lord made to the

[6] (Matt. 10)   [9] (Acts 2:4)   [12] (Acts 1:26)
[7] (Matt. 28: 19)   [10] (John 20:23)   [13] (Matt. 28:20)
[8] (Acts 1:8)   [11] (Eph 2:20)   [14] (Matt. 16: 18, 19)

Twelve and meant to be passed on in his Church are found in the episcopal college as a unit, which is the basic seat of apostolic authority in the Church. The episcopal college, we note, is not the gathering of all Catholic bishops into a single body which sums up the authority which each bishop contributes to it; the episcopal college is, rather, the primary organ of authority in the Church and to be made a bishop means precisely to be integrated into this episcopal college. There, as a member of this college (which as such is the heir of the Twelve), the individual bishop receives his share of apostolic authority to teach and to be a pastor to his flock.

The unity of the episcopal college as heir of the Twelve is the basic theological insight which will solve the questions we have raised in this article. The doctrine is ancient but for a number of reasons it has not been taught for several centuries and hence appears rather new to many of our contemporaries. Though not mentioned in the decrees of the First Vatican Council, it is in perfect harmony with them since the primacy of Peter announces his headship within the unity of the episcopal college. The pope has jursidiction over his brothers, the other bishops, but this supreme jurisdiction does not break the unity of the episcopal body.

This doctrine throws light on the origin of episcopal jurisdiction. We still say that the pope assigns jurisdiction to the individual bishop, but in the total context of apostolic succession the meaning of this sentence can now be defined with some precision. It is clear, first of all, that the jurisdiction of the episcopal body is not mediated through the pope. It comes directly from Christ. As the pope himself is the successor of St. Peter and receives his ministerial power from the Lord, so is the episcopal college as a whole the successor of the Twelve and receives its ministerial power in the same way. According to Catholic faith, this is unalterable. Neither pope nor council could change this structure. To make the assertion that the jurisdiction of the episcopal college was derived from the plenary power of the pope would be tantamount to saying that Christ has put the total ecclesiasical authority into the hands of Peter and that the other eleven apostles receive their share from him. Such a theory would go against the teaching of the Scriptures.

How does the individual bishop receive his jurisdiction? He receives his *sacred authority* by being made a member of the episcopal college. He does not receive authority and is then able to join this college but, on the contrary, by being made a member of this college he then shares in the authority which this college as a unity receives from Christ. According to the present legislation, a new member is joined to the episcopal college through the appointment of the pope. In the past this has not always been so. Often a specified number of bishops was able to receive a member into the episcopal college. This is a question of legislation which has usually been solved in a way most advantageous for the total life of the Church.

But the sacred authority which a bishop receives as a member of the episcopal body is not yet *jurisdiction* in the proper sense, since he must be assigned an area, a territory, or a people in which he can exercise his ministerial authority. The assignment of such an area, a diocese or Church, communicates jurisdiction. Again, according to the legislation of our day, the pope assigns a bishop to a diocese and hence, in this clearly circumscribed sense, we may say that the pope directly imparts jurisdiction to the individual bishop. But he is able to impart this jurisdiction only because the bishop, as a member of the episcopal college, has received a share of the sacred authority which the Twelve have handed on to that body.

The doctrine of episcopal collegiality also throws light on the function of the individual bishop and his relationship to the pope. It is now no longer simply a question of harmonizing in the same diocese two similar jursidictions, one of which is supreme. A bishop has a role in the Church which includes more than being the head of his diocese; as a member of the episcopal college he is, at the same time, co-responsible for the teaching and shepherding of the universal Church. According to the present legislation, this co-responsibility of the bishops does not find much practical application, but as soon as the council was convoked the ancient doctrine of episcopal collegiality became again a living reality. At the council the bishops exercise their office of teachers and legislators for the Church universal in a unique and special manner. Yet we cannot confine this co-responsibility of the bishops for the whole Church to the relatively short periods of ecumenical councils; collegiality is not a privilege bestowed upon the bishops through the pope when calling the council; it is rather a call and duty essentially related to their office.

This understanding of the local bishop may appear new to many. It is, of course, true that the bishop's jurisdiction is confined to his own diocese. But, as a member of the episcopal college, he is concerned with a much vaster part of the Catholic people than his own Church; he is, in fact, concerned with the life of the total Church. His relationship to the pope is not only that of an episcopal subject ruling his diocese in conformity with papal legislation, but as a member of the body of bishops he is an episcopal brother of the pope engaged in dialogue with him.

If the Second Vatican Council wishes to intensify the collegiality of the bishops, a new legislation could create organs through which the co-responsibility we have described could be exercised more freely and more frequently. This could be done, in the first place, through the elevation of episcopal conferences to episcopal assemblies possessing the authority to teach and legislate, subject to the approval of the Holy See. Assigning such power to large groups of bishops would not be an act of legislation inspired simply by pragmatic considerations, but it would correspond profoundly to the very nature of the episcopal office and its collegial coherence. From the most ancient times of the Church it was always believed that the greater the area from which the bishops gathered in councils, the more certain the faithful could be of the Spirit's assistance in their resolutions. To the increasing universality of episcopal councils corresponded an increasing authority attached to them in the teaching of the faith and the imposing of discipline. The general or ecumenical council was the culmination of such episcopal gatherings, and since here the whole episcopate was represented, it was always believed that the Spirit protected his chosen teachers from all error and guaranteed an infallible doctrine.

A second way of intensifying the collegiality of bishops would be the creation of a small council meeting with the pope once a year, a small council composed of bishop-delegates elected by the various regional episcopal conferences, which would deliberate with the supreme head of the Church on matters of teaching and policy. In this way, through their delegates, the bishops of the world would be able to exercise their co-responsibility for the whole Church. Again it should be mentioned that such a small central council would not be a pragmatic institution introduced under the pressure of modern democratic tendencies, but rather an organ of ecclesiastical government corresponding deeply to the divine structure of the Church and revealing the collegial character of episcopacy.

This leads us to the last question we shall consider in this brief article. Can we define more precisely the relationship of pope and episcopacy? We have said so far that the pope holds supreme authority in the Church both as teacher and law-giver; we have also said that the bishops in union with their head the pope, especially as gathered in an ecumenical council, hold the same supreme authority in the Church. Are there then two relatively distinct subjects of supreme authority in the Church, of which the pope acting alone would be one and the pope acting in union with his bishops would be the other? This doctrine of the " subjectum duplex supremae auctoritatis " was indeed taught by many theologians. It was taught by several great 19th century theologians, such as

Kleutgen, Schrader and Scheeben, and from the minutes of the working commission at the First Vatican we know that the definition of papal primacy was not meant to prejudge the doctrine of the "subjectum duplex." [15] In our own day the doctrine of the "subjectum duplex supremae auctoritatis" has found many supporters.

This doctrine has the advantage that it brings to light the dialogue structure within the exercise of supreme authority in the Church. According to this doctrine there is one single and undivided supreme authority granted by Christ to the Church, which is exercised either by the pope alone or, at other times, by the totality of the bishops including their head, the pope. The weakness of the doctrine is, however, that the "either/or" in the exercise of this authority does not bring out the organic character of the Church's unity nor does it show that the supreme authority of the pope leaves intact and serves the unity of the episcopal college. It creates the impression that the pope acting as the supreme head of the Church places himself outside of the episcopal college to which, in fact, he inseparably belongs as the principal member.

Against the accusation, often raised against the teaching of the First Vatican, that the pope's primacy severs him from the rest of the Church and especially from the bishops, and thus makes him an independent and therefore arbitrary ruler, we must assert quite vigorously that the pope acts within the Church and more especially within the body of bishops. Even when defining doctrine "ex sese, non ex consensu Ecclesiae" the pope remains the principal member of this body and exercises his power in the name of, and in favour of, the whole body of bishops to whom Christ has assigned the universal government of the Church.

We prefer not to speak, therefore, of a twofold subject of supreme authority in the Church. Another doctrinal position is at present taught by many theologians and has been adopted

[15] (See J. P. Torrell, *La Theologie de l'Episcopat au premier concile du Vatican*, Paris 1961, pp. 149-58.)

by a great number of bishops, according to which there is *one single* seat of supreme authority in the Church, and this is the episcopal college. As heir of the Twelve (including Peter) it is supreme in teaching and ruling. The exercise of this supreme power may take place in various ways, but each time the whole episcopal college is in some sense involved. Sometimes the bishops exercise their supreme power in union with their head, the pope, at an ecumenical council. At other times the bishops teach or act in union with the pope while remaining dispersed over the world. At other times again, the pope himself teaches or legislates with supreme authority for the universal Church, but when he does so he exercises the supreme authority given to the episcopal body which he, as its head, is able to use *ex sese*, of his own accord. This means that the pope exercising supreme power, while not dependent on the consent of the Church or of the bishops, always acts in the name of the body of bishops and, as it were, for them, in their favour. Without the slightest detriment to the pope's supreme position as defined by the First Vatican, this understanding of the unity and primacy of the episcopal college places papal primacy into an ecclesiological context in which the pope appears more clearly as a member of the Church, a bishop of a diocese, and as head of the whole Church exercising his supreme office as a ministry in the apostolic body of bishops for the good of all the Christian faithful.

GREGORY BAUM, O.S.A.

University of St. Michael's College
Toronto, Ontario, Canada

PRIMACY AND EPISCOPACY: DOCTRINAL
AND PRACTICAL IMPLICATIONS

ൻ

HE collegiality of the bishops and its relation to the
papacy, which the Second Vatican Council is generally expected to set out in its constitution on the
Church,[1] presents a twofold aspect and raises a twofold problem. First, the bishops as pastors of their own dioceses " in
communion with the Apostolic See " are by divine right the
true pastors of their respective flocks, even though the institution of dioceses is part of the organization of the Church,
as this has grown in the course of the centuries, and the assignment of a particular diocese to a particular bishop stems from
an ecclesiastical decision. Bishops rule their dioceses by their
own authority derived from Christ (directly or indirectly);
they do so in communion with the Vicar of Christ and successor to Peter; yet the Pope's universal and immediate jurisdiction in the whole Church in no way impairs but rather
supposes the bishops' ordinary power over their flocks. The
problem here consists in determining and explaining, not
merely the co-existence, but the correlation of these two
powers.

The second aspect of the collegiality of the bishops is their
joint responsibility, in union with and under the authority of
the Pope, for the mission of the universal Church among all
nations. The Pope rules the Catholic Church, not only by
himself or with the assistance of his curia, but with the aid
of his divinely appointed helpers, the college of the bishops,
successor to the college of the Apostles. He does so ordinarily and in common circumstances, when the bishops are dispersed the world over in their dioceses, by their communion
with him and their unanimity with him and among them-

---

[1] Cf. " Collegium Episcoporum," in *The Clergy Monthly* 25 (1961) 183-85; *ibid.*
26 (1962) 259.

selves in doctrinal teaching and pastoral ruling. He does so in an extraordinary manner when the entire Catholic episcopate meets with him in Council. In both cases, there is no Pope without the college of bishops: the Pope is the head of the episcopal college as Peter was the chief of the apostolic college. And there is no college of bishops without the Pope. Here again the relation between the Pope's proper authority and the authority of the body of the bishops under and with him in the universal Church is not a question of mere coexistence but of mutual inclusion and correlation.

All this was accepted and 'lived' doctrine at the time of the First Vatican Council.[2] It was considered not merely as 'theology' but as part of the Church's life and doctrine. That Council was expected to set out the doctrine of the relationship between primacy and episcopacy. It is only the historical accident of a war that interrupted the work of the Council before it could propose its teaching on the episcopacy. It could promulgate only its doctrine on the Pope.

The Second Vatican Council is now to complete the unfinished task of its predecessor. It is expected to propose to the Catholic world the revealed doctrine of the collegiality of the bishops in its relation to the primacy of the Pope. To the two problems mentioned above the Council is to give the answer of our faith, independently of the various theologies of the episcopacy that may be held by Catholic teachers and authors. And it will do so, it may be anticipated, in keeping with the pastoral purpose of the Council so often and definitely stated by Pope John XXIII.[3] This means to say that we must expect not so much an abstract and theoretical statement about the correlation between papacy and episcopacy as a practical expression in rulings about the collaboration of the two powers in the pastoral mission of the Church. Doctrine, in fact, is not only proposed in conceptual formulations but

[2] Cf. G. Dejaifve, S.J., *Pape et évêques au premier concile du Vatican*, Paris 1961; and " Primauté et collégialité au premier concile au Vatican " in EEU quoted below n.4.

[3] Cf. especially his opening address to the Council, October 11, 1962.

also in a manner of living. It will then be the task of theologians, on the basis of the Council's teaching, to construct a theology of the collegiality of the bishops and its relation to the papal primacy.[4]

Meanwhile it may serve both a doctrinal and a pastoral purpose to focus the problems placed before the Council. The basis of our reflexion is twofold: the revealed doctrine that Christ in fact entrusted the Church to the college of the Apostles under Peter, and to its successor the college of the bishops under the Pope;[5] and the fact of the twofold authority in the Church, the papacy and the episcopacy, as it exists today in a concrete historical context—this context developed out of the one-sided teaching of the First Vatican Council which was embodied in the centralization of the Church's government in the Holy See. We should then endeavour to state the two problems as clearly and definitely as possible, and to suggest the theological questions raised by them in the setting of the mystery of the Church. What follows here can be nothing more than an attempt at stating questions rather than solving them.

I. *Pope and Bishops in their Dioceses*

The first problem is this. The Pope's authority in the universal Church, as defined by the First Vatican Council, is the full and supreme power of jurisdiction, both regarding faith and morals, and regarding discipline and government. The Pope has the complete fulness of this supreme power, which

---

[4] Among the recent writings on primacy and episcopacy, we mention here: Y. Congar, O.P. and B. D. Dupuy, O.P. (ed.), *L'épiscopat et l'Eglise universelle*, Paris 1962 (referred to as EEU); J. Hamer, O.P., *L'Eglise est une communion*, Paris, 1962; J. P. Torrell, O.P., *La théologie de l'épiscopat au premier concile du Vatican*, Paris, 1961; K. Rahner and J. Ratzinger, *Episkopat und Primat*, Freiburg, 1961; trans. *The Episcopate and the Primacy*, Edinburgh, 1962; cf. also *Papal Teachings, The Church*, Boston, 1962 (analytical index under Primacy, 876 ff. and the episcopal college, 883 ff.).

[5] For a brief exposition of the scriptural revelation, cf. Archbishop E. Guerry's pastoral on the Council: French text in *Documentation catholique* 60 (1963) 176-79; trans. in *The Clergy Monthly* 27 (1963) 125 ff.

is an ordinary and immediate authority over each and every church, each and every pastor and believer. The bishops' authority, on the other hand, is also ordinary and immediate episcopal power of jurisdiction, by virtue of which the bishops, as successors of the Apostles, guide and govern their respective flocks. There is therefore a twofold ordinary and immediate episcopal power of jurisdiction regarding the faithful: that of the Pope, and that of the bishop. Will these ever enter into conflict? Is there not at least such a danger? The First Vatican Council teaches that the Pope's authority, far from impairing the power of the bishops, rather asserts, confirms and vindicates that power. The two powers, therefore, in the mind of the First Vatican Council, not only coexist but support and strengthen each other.[6] This is a statement of fact. The problem is how this must be conceived and explained doctrinally, and how it works out in practice.

The Doctrinal Problem.—There is, we may assume, a solution to the problem. The very fact that both authorities, that of the Pope and that of the bishops, are of divine right, or in other words, that Christ has entrusted His Church to the college of the Apostles under Peter, and after them to the college of the bishops under His Vicar, is a guarantee that both authorities are required; not only must they exist together, they must also sustain each other.

Yet, the doctrinal difficulty is real. How can there be two ordinary and immediate episcopal authorities, vested in distinct persons, regarding the same subjects? The difficulty would perhaps be without a solution, were the two authorities coordinated. Given human nature as it is, this would be a source of inevitable conflict. But they are not. One is subordinate to the other: the bishop's authority is subordinated to that of the Pope. How then must we understand their

---

[6] Cf. Denzinger, *Enchiridion Symbolorum*, 1831, 1828. Cf. also the statement of the German bishops in answer to Bismarck, and Pope Pius IX's approval, in 1875: texts and presentation by O. Rousseau, O.S.B., "La vraie valeur de l'épiscopat dans l'Eglise d'après d'important documents de 1875," in EEU 709-36.

working together? There seems to be only one way of understanding, *viz.*, that the Pope's authority, for all its being an
ordinary and immediate episcopal power over every flock
and every individual member of the flock, respects the ordinary and immediate authority of the bishops; it does not
replace nor diminish nor annul it in fact. This means that
the exercise of the Pope's authority over the flocks and the
faithful of other bishops will of necessity be limited by that
of the bishops. But when bishops fail to make the proper use
of their authority, then the Pope could and should step in to
supply for the deficiency.[7]

Nor should it be hard to see how the authority of the bishops finds in its dependence on the Pope a basis of security
for its proper exercise. By their communion with the Pope,
the bishops have a divine guarantee that they rule their flocks
after the mind and heart of Christ. Thus the papal charism
of the primacy tends to strengthen the episcopal charism of
the shepherds of the flocks. The latter in a way calls for the
former. Without leaning on the rock of Peter, and the special
assistance promised by Christ to His Vicar on earth, the pastors of the faithful might well feel hesitant and diffident for
a task which is not purely human but supernatural.

Morever, it lies in the nature of the Church, which is both
a visible society and an invisible mystery, that the pastors
of the flocks should not have to depend for their task on the
inner guidance of the Spirit only; they should also find an external support in the visible supreme pastor of the Church.
And the Vicar of Christ, in turn, finds a both human and
supernatural support in the pastors of the dioceses who in
the name of Christ and with the assistance of His Spirit,
guide and rule the flocks entrusted to their care. Papal responsibility for those flocks may be discharged through the responsibility of their own pastors.

The Practical Problem. We can indicate here only briefly

---

[7] On this point cf. G. Thils, " Potestas ordinaria " in EEU 689ff.

how this mutual strengthening of the papal primacy and the episcopal authority works out in practice. The practical problem comes in fact to that of the extension of centralization in the government of the Church. The bishops rule their dioceses on their own authority but in dependence on the Pope. The concrete expression of this dependence consists in the directives from the Holy See and recourse to the Pope's curia in matters beyond their authority. Today the complaint has been made not infrequently that the faculties which the bishops have to obtain from the Holy See entail an unnecessary burden and limitation of their episcopal power. The grievance deserves consideration in the light of the new stress on the status of the bishops in the Church. However, we should also remember the not so rare remark from the Roman curia that bishops apply for sanctions and faculties which they need not ask because these are included in their ordinary powers. The bishops themselves, Rome feels, do not always fully know and use their authority. Both these remarks are symptoms: they reveal a state of mind born from the practice of a centralization which inclines unduly to extend the dependence of the bishops on the papacy. At any rate, the decentralization expected from the Council [8] may put the emphasis on the other aspect of the relation between Pope and bishops, *viz.*, the true pastoral authority of the bishops, and by doing so restore the balance between the two.

Meanwhile, the suggestion of Canon G. Thils,[9] to transpose the text of the First Vatican Council on the primacy in such a manner as first to state the ordinary and immediate episcopal power of the bishops and then to consider the papal primacy in relation to it, may serve as a guiding principle in solving the practical problem synthesizing primacy and episcopacy.

---

[8] On the decentralization that is being prepared by the Council cf., v.g., Cardinal Alfrink, quoted in *The Clergy Monthly* 26 (1962) 291; also the decree on the liturgy, cf. C. Vaggagini, in *Doc. cath.* 60 (1963) 71-78, or *Clergy Monthly* 27 (1963) 131ff.

[9] G. Thils, *art. cit.* 706ff.

II. *Pope and College of Bishops*

More important and more difficult, less studied and far less explicit in the teaching of the Church, is the problem of the relation between the primacy of the Pope and the authority of the college of bishops, not in their own particular dioceses, but in the universal Church. It is here particularly that the relatively new aspect of the collegiality of the bishops comes to its clearest expression.[10] And its significance for a true and renewed understanding of the primacy is important. The following reflections, therefore, are mainly tentative and open to correction and completion.

We may take for a starting point of our reflections the definition of the collegiality of the bishops—as Catholic doctrine, expressing the divine institution of the college of the Apostles and of bishops, and not merely a theological position—which Archbishop E. Guerry proposed recently in a pastoral letter: "the joint responsibility of the entire body of the bishops under the authority of the Pope for the evangelization of the world and the establishment of the Church the world over."[11] The reason for this joint responsibility is that Christ entrusted the Church not only to Peter but to the college of the Apostles under Peter and to its successor, the college of the bishops under the Pope. This collegial and universal authority, Archbishop Guerry states, comes first, before the bishops' responsibility for their own dioceses. They are members of the episcopal college (because they are successors of the Apostles as members of that college) before being in charge of particular dioceses.[12] But their collegial authority also is not independent from the head of the body of bishops, the Pope. Here

---

[10] G. Dejaifve, *op. cit.* shows how this idea of collegiality was active and 'lived,' though not formulated, at the First Vatican Council; cf. also Torrell, *op. cit.*, 135 ff.

[11] Cf. *Clergy Monthly* 27 (1963) 125.

[12] This implies that titular bishops, by the very fact of their consecration (and incorporation into the body of bishops) share in this collegial authority and responsibility; cf. J. Lecuyer, " Orientations présentes de la théologie de l'épiscopat " in EEU 781-811, esp. 792.—We do not enter here further into the theology of titular bishops.

then lies the problem: first, the doctrinal synthesis of this collegial authority with the primacy or 'personal' authority of the Pope; then the practical expression of this collegiality of the bishops in institutions and rulings, dependent on but not absorbed by the Pope's primacy.

The Doctrinal Problem. The doctrinal problem includes mainly two questions: that of the nature of this collegial universal authority of the bishops (with the Pope); and that of its implications for the very nature of the primacy.

First of all, the college of the bishops includes the Pope, as the college of the Apostles included Peter. And the same universal and supreme authority over the universal Church which pertains to the primacy of the Pope is also vested in the college of the bishops. There is therefore a twofold, inadequately distinguished subject of the supreme power in the Church: there is the Pope as head of the college of the bishops, and there is the Pope with the body of the bishops who together make up the college of the bishops. The case is a perfect parallel to that of the infallibility of the teaching Church: the Pope is 'personally' infallible, and the body of the teaching Church (including the Pope) also possesses the same charism of infallibility.[13]

This means, therefore, that the bishops as a body in union with and under the Pope have power of jurisdiction, ordinary and immediate, in the universal Church. Just as by virtue of their episcopal authority they personally guide and rule their own dioceses, so also as a body and as members of that body they share with the Pope in the universal jurisdiction over the entire Church. Together with the Pope and with the whole body of bishops each and every one of them has the power to issue decrees binding on the entire Church. The difference is that here this collegial power is supreme, while their diocesan power is subordinate and dependent on the Pope.

The exercise of this collegial power can be either ordinary or extraordinary. The ordinary manner of its exercise practi-

[13] Cf. Denzinger 1739.

cally coincides with the government of their particular dioceses, or rather is one aspect of that government, viz., the substantial agreement of that government with the government of the entire Church—an agreement that does not exclude but rather postulates particular differences demanded by the different circumstances of various places. The bishops' communion with the Apostolic See guarantees to their government the required conformity with the government of the entire Church and of the whole body of the bishops. This points to the collegial aspect of every diocese, a diocese being not merely an administrative unit in the organization of the Church but the Church as locally present with its full life and full essence.[14]

But it is especially the extraordinary exercise of the collegial authority of the bishops which manifests its complex and exalted nature, namely, the Ecumenical Council. The Ecumenical Council, canon law states, possesses the supreme power over the universal Church (can. 228 § 1). The responsibility for its decrees that are binding on the universal Church does not lie only with the Pope but also with each and every member of the college of the bishops. The bishops in Council with and under the Pope rule the universal Church. They as a body enjoy the special assistance of the Holy Spirit which guarantees the indefectibility of the Church. It is not possible that they would decree what of its nature goes against the holiness and mission of the Church. Accordingly, without in any way detracting from the Pope's supreme authority (the Council's decrees derive their finality from his sanction,[15] because the Pope is head and formal principle of unity of the college of the bishops) the bishops in Council exercise the supreme authority in the universal Church.

The difference, therefore, between the ordinary and extra-

---

[14] On this theology of the local church as local presence of the universal Church, and its meaning for the relation between primacy and episcopacy, cf. K. Rahner, op. cit., 20 ff.

[15] Cf. Can. 227; also the letter of Pope John XXIII, of January 6, 1963, to all the Fathers of the Council, in Clergy Monthly 27 (1963) 107.

ordinary exercise of the bishops' collegial authority is mainly this: in the first case the universal agreement of the bishops is less manifest and is, as it were, only the substantial agreement intended by each and every one of them in the exercise of his episcopal power; in the second case, the concurrence of episcopal authority in the solemn exercise of their collegiality is formally manifest and sanctioned by the Pope's approval of the Council's decrees.[16] These decrees, then, are not merely papal decrees, they are the acts of the collegial supreme authority in the Church.

This particular nature of the collegial authority of the bishops in the Church entails an important consequence regarding the nature of the primacy of the Pope. The supreme authority of the Pope over the universal Church, in essence the same as the episcopal power of the bishops but different in extension and independent of any higher human authority,[17] is essentially the authority of the head of the college of bishops. The authority of the Pope, successor to Peter, is as supreme and universal, not because he is a bishop, but because he is the chief and formal principle of unity of the college of bishops. It is therefore both personal and collegial. Personal, in the sense that it is vested in the person of the bishop who is the head of the Church. Collegial, in the sense that the Pope possesses it as head of the college of bishops. The Pope would not be the primate of the Church, were he not the head of the college of bishops. There could be no Catholic Church without the college of bishops; a Church with only the Pope and the faithful would not be the Church founded by Christ.[18] In other words, the supreme authority in the Church, vested not only in the Pope, but also in the college of bishops under the Pope, can be exercised either by the whole college includ-

[16] Archbishop Guerry, in the above quoted pastoral, shows the actual fact of this collaboration between Pope and bishops in the first session of the Council.

[17] Cf. the title used by the Pope in the convocation bull of the Council, " Ioannes catholicae Ecclesiae episcopus "; cf. *Clergy Monthly* 27 (1963) 99.

[18] Christ has founded the Church on the college of the Apostles under Peter, cf. above n. 5.

ing the Pope, or by the head of the college 'personally' but as head of the college.

This shows that the primacy is of its nature necessarily related to the episcopacy. It includes in its essence and concept the other term of the relation, the college of bishops, just as the college of the bishops endowed with the supreme authority in the Church of necessity includes the Pope or primate of the Church who formally causes its unity. Yet, this necessary relation of the primacy to the collegial authority of the bishops does not mean that papal decrees derive their force from the consent of the bishops.[19] The formal principle of unity does not draw its unity and being from the multiplicity which it unifies, though it cannot be principle of unity without that multiplicity. But it does mean that papal decrees, as distinct from conciliar decrees, are the 'primatial' exercise of the supreme authority in the Church of which conciliar decrees are the 'collegial' exercise. They do, therefore, include an implicit reference to the college of the bishops and intend to state what would be the decision of the college of bishops supposing they were called upon to express their collegial authority. In both cases of papal and of conciliar decrees with universal binding force, the divine assistance is warrant of their rightness.

We cannot detail further here what this essential reference of the primacy to the episcopacy means regarding the government of the universal Church. Only one or other practical implications may be indicated here.

The Practical Problem. The collegiality of the bishops with and under the Pope implies that each and every one of them shares in the responsibility for the Church's mission in the world. This was stated already, in connection with the foreign missions, by Pius XI and Pius XII, in their mission encyclicals.[20] It also prevails for the entire pastoral ministry

---

[19] Compare the definition of the Pope's infallibility, Denzinger 1839.

[20] Pius XI, *Rerum Ecclesiae*, AAS 18 (1926) 68 ff.; Pius XII, *Fidei donum*, AAS 49 (1957) 235ff.

of the Church regarding Catholics and non-Catholics, Christians and non-Christians. Bishops are responsible for the pastoral mission of the Church, not only in their own dioceses, but in the entire world.

Little wonder then that today the new awareness of the collegiality of the Catholic episcopate takes flesh and bone in new institutions. The most typical of these, no doubt, are the national and regional bishops' conferences which are, we may say, an 'incarnation' of this collegiality, of the communion among bishops and of their awareness that their pastoral responsibility extends beyond their own dioceses.[21] The Council is expected to give an official status to these conferences in the organization of the Church. These are expected to become the actual organs for a decentralization in the Church's government or for a more effective participation of the episcopate in the universal government of the Church, which is the practical sequel to the present-day rediscovery of the collegiality of the episcopate.

Another practical symptom of this rediscovery may be seen in the national or regional secretariats for Christian unity which are springing up in several countries, in answer to the Pope's appeals and in imitation of his example, to share in the work for unity among all Christians. In our contemporary ecumenical outlook, this is a natural expression of the bishops' collegiality.

A further practical consequence, with possible far-reaching implications, is that bishops and dioceses may take their share of responsibility for the apostolate in mission lands. A new pattern of the 'sending Church' is in preparation, apparently, in which not only missionary societies and religious institutes but the non-missionary dioceses as well take the responsibility for sending out to mission lands the helpers to

---

[21] On these bishop's conferences, cf. Archbishop Guerry, in *Clergy Monthly* 27 (1963) 127. For a theology of these conferences as expression of the collegiality, cf. P. Fransen, S.J., "Episcopaat and Primaat," *Streven* 16 (1962-63) 346-52, esp. 349ff.

the local hierarchy and clergy still needed for the Church to face up to her task of evangelization.[22]

These few examples may suffice to show the pastoral renewal of the Church's life which the new realization of the collegiality of the bishops is likely to bring about. Nor is it to be feared that this will turn to the detriment of the primacy of the Pope. Rather, if it is true that the actual setting of the primacy is the college of the bishops of which as primate he is the principle of unity, then a deeper realization and 'living' of the collegiality of the episcopate under the Pope cannot but profit the primacy as well. One of the most significant results of this new balance between primacy and episcopacy would be that it levels the road towards Christian unity.

Conclusion: Theology of Primacy and Episcopacy

With all this, hardly anything was said as yet of the theological elaboration required for a deepening of the interrelation between primacy and episcopacy in the renewed theology of the Church as the Mystical Body of Christ. If the above reflections on the doctrine of the faith about primacy and episcopacy seem to be confined to the juridical and external side of the ruling Church, let it be said at once that a transposition of the doctrine from the juridical to the mystical level of the Church is one of the most essential tasks of that theology.

In the light of the mystery of the Church, what is expressed as authority and power, whether of Pope or bishops, is grace and service [23]—charismatic grace attached to the functions which the college of the bishops under the Pope have in the Body of Christ; functions which may go by the name of authority or power but are in their very essence services to the Church, to the whole Christ and to Christ himself. Needless to say, that on the exalted level of the supernatural and myster-

[22] Cf. "The Council and the Missions" in *The Clergy Monthly Supplement* 6 (1962-63) 221 ff.

[23] Cf. Y. Congar, O.P., "La hiérarchie comme service" in EEU 67-99; and P. Fransen, "L'autorité des conciles" in *Problèmes de l'autorité* (Paris, 1962), 59-99.

ious reality of the Church, there can be no clash between the various gifts which the Spirit imparts to the Body of Christ: they all are given for the common good. In their human expression and based upon the evangelical concept of authority as service rather than power,[24] the practical synthesis between primacy and episcopacy can and will be worked out in the charity and humility of which Christ Himself set the example. The servant of the servants of God, servant to his brethren in the episcopate, and these in turn servants to the flocks entrusted to their care and to the whole Church—all of them discharge their respective functions in unison and with the strength of their special charisms, for the building up of the Body of Christ.

P. DE LETTER, S.J.

St. Mary's College,
Kurseong, N.E. Ry., India

---

[24] Cf. Luke 22, 25ff; John 13, 13ff.

THE BISHOP IN HIS OWN DIOCESE *

∾

I. Two Aspects of a Bishop

THE Second Vatican Council was opened October 11, 1962. An imposing cortege of more than two thousand five hundred bishops descended in silent and prayerful procession from the halls of the Vatican Palace and entered the council chamber. The figure of Pope John XXIII, seated on the gestatorial chair, closed the procession. The spectacle, presided over by the Vicar of Christ on earth, was a marvelous image of the living Church. It was the dawn of the Council.

The Church was *felt*, alive and present. The spectacle of countless bishops, congregated around the Pope, the Supreme Shepherd, embodied the words of the Apostle: "The Holy Spirit has placed you as bishops, to rule the Church of God." [1] They are the successors of the Apostles, whom Christ made continuators and ministers of His work.[2] This is what they have always done. It is what they assembled to do, summoned by the Vicar of Christ to an Ecumenical Council.

Nevertheless, no one had previously taken part in an episcopal assembly of this kind, because, as it is well known, the last Ecumenical Council was the First Vatican Council, interrupted in 1870.[3] It was, therefore, the first time they took part in a council. But almost all brought with them their pastoral experience, an experience in knowing how to govern

---

* Translated by F. C. Lehner, O. P.

[1] *Acts* 20:28.

[2] "Christus fuit in lumen et salutem gentium per discipulos suos, quos ad praedicandum gentibus misit" (St. Thomas Aquinas, *Summa theologiae*, IIIa, q. 42, a. 1, ad 1). And in the answer to the second objection, he appraises this fact in the following way: "non est minoris potestatis, sed maioris, facere aliquid per alios, quam per seipsum. Et ideo in hoc maxime potestas divina in Christo monstrata est, quod discipulis suis tantam virtutem contulit in docendo, ut gentes quae nihil de Christo audierant, converterent ad ipsum."

[3] Cf. H. Jedin, *Breve historia de los Concilios.* Barcelona: Herder, 1960, pp. 150-151.

their dioceses, since most of them have spent the best years of their lives at the head of their respective dioceses.

In fact, this consideration makes us logically think about a bishop in two dimensions, namely, the collective and the individual. Both episcopal dimensions can be explained and expressed in the following formulae: (1) *Regere ecclesiam suam,* that is, " his diocese ";[4] and (2) *Regere Ecclesiam Dei,* that is, the entire Church, as regards the members of the college or *corpus episcoporum,* the head of which is the Pope.[5]

This second, or ecumenical and universal, function affects the whole Mystical Body in its earthly and temporal aspect; and a council is the outstanding instance of this greater function. The first, or local and diocesan, function cannot be disassociated from the essence and global life of the Church, but there is no doubt that it has its own unique and proper value within the bounds of the diocese.

The spectator at the inaugural act of the Second Vatican Council intuitively recognized that twofold dimension of the episcopacy. The bishops, congregating around the Pope, manifest the universal dimension of the episcopacy; and yet in their ethnic differences one immediately recognizes the places of their origin, their nationality, their dioceses. In his own diocese, through long years of solicitude and vigilance, the bishop actually fulfills the mission which we have termed " local."

While the Christian world awaits the *Acta* of the Second Vatican Council, we are going to focus our attention on that silent and modest aspect, the role of the bishop. We are going to view and study him in his " local mission," at the head of his particular church or diocese.

The concrete theme about " the bishop in his diocese " implies four elemental questions according to both the methodological and factual meanings of the terms: *What is a diocese? What is the bishop's role? What role does a bishop play in his diocese? Will the Second Vatican Council speak about the*

---

[4] CIC.: can. 329, § 1.
[5] CIC.: can. 223 and 228.

diocese and the role of its own pastors? We shall try to offer brief answers to these questions in the following pages.

II. WHAT IS A DIOCESE?

It is useless to consult the *Code of Canon Law* to learn what a diocese is. The legislator gives laws, not definitions. The *Code* speaks of the " exclusive competence of the supreme ecclesiastical power to establish, change the limits of, divide, unify, or abolish " a diocese; [6] but it does not say what it is. Nevertheless, it is not hard to guess, under the letter of the *Code*, what a diocese is; its definition is a latent concept, implicit in many canons, especially that canon which deals with the bishops who " govern, with ordinary jurisdiction, their particular churches."

The analysis of the etymology of the term " diocese " and the history of its ecclesiastical usage—so closely united to the language and to the typical structures of the Roman Law— are marginal to our study. Any monographic study has abundant data on this point.[7] Our express interest concerns, in the first place, a *simple juridical* definition of " diocese "; and, in the second place, by a penetration into the context, what we might call a *theological* definition of " diocese."

The juridical definition is given to us by a specialist on the subject: " In juridical ecclesiastical law, a diocese is that territory, well defined in its extension and limits, which is governed by a bishop with ordinary authority according to the norms of Canon Law." [8]

But this definition, valid and exact in jurisprudence, tells what a diocese is from the outside, that is, from the aspect of the jurist. The theologian, however, seeks, not the extrinsic or juridical, but especially the formal dimension and vital struc-

---

[6] CIC.: can. 215, § 1.

[7] Cf. A. van Hove, " Diocese," in *The Catholic Encyclopedia*, New York, 1909. V, 1-6; Cl. Bouuaert, " Diocèse," in *Dict. de Droit Canonique*, IV, 1257-1267; P. Fourneret, " Diocèse," in *Dict. de Théologie Catholique*, IV, 1362-1363.

[8] P. Ciprotti, " Diocesi," in *Enciclopedia Cattolica*, Città del Vaticano, 1950, IV, col. 1651.

ture of the diocese. In this sense, he strives for the definition from within, from the inmost nature of the diocese. Theologically considered, then, what is a diocese? In our times, when theologians are focussing their attention on ecclesiology, the question has been approached with unusual emphasis.

According to some contemporary outlines, the primordial ideas pertinent to a theology about the *diocese* are the peculiar condition of the diocese as a " particular or local church " on the one hand, and, on the other, the immediate and ordinary authority which the bishop exercises over it. As a " particular church," the diocese is a true " becoming," that is, the historical and local manifestation of the living Church, enlivened by the Holy Spirit, united by exterior and interior bonds. This " becoming " takes place especially in the celebration of the Eucharist. Consequently, " the local church " is a Church " realization " in the sense that it is not static or a mere portion of the universal Church. It does not arise from the atomizing of the space which the Church as a whole occupies in the world, but is, rather, a concentration of the Church in its own " life essence "; [9] and, as regards the authority which the bishop exercises over it, the diocese relies on his condition of being a

---

[9] K. Rahner, " Primauté et Épiscopat. Quelques réflexions sur les principes constitutionnels de l'Église," in *L'Épiscopat et l'Elise universelle*. Paris: Editions du Cerf, 1962, p. 555. Speaking of the " mystery of the particular Church," he adds: " When the Church as a whole truly becomes an *event* in the fullest sense of the word, she is necessarily the local Church. The whole Church is appreciable in the local Church " (*Ibid.*, p. 551). The Church as an institution would be distinguished from the Church as a becoming: " Thus we distinguish the Church as a simple institution with her permanent social constitution from the Church as a becoming. She especially becomes an actual event appreciable in time and space when she becomes an event as the *communion of Saints, as a society* " (*Ibid.*, p. 552). The Church, whose profound essence is to accomplish the historical presence of Christ in the world and to produce a palpable manifestation of God's plan of salvation, " attained in Christ," is transformed into an *event* through the local celebration of the Eucharist: " in the deepest sense, the Church becomes an event fully only in the local celebration of the Eucharist " (*Ibid.*, p. 554). A local church is equivalent to an episcopal church (Cf. *ibid.*, p. 555), since the local bishop is the proper minister of that celebration. And since the universal Church should be manifested in a determinate place and find its highest fulfillment in the Eucharistic celebration, the existence of the episcopacy is continued by divine right (Cf. *ibid.*, pp. 555-556).

successor of the Apostles, Ministers of the Eucharist in its full sense, etc.

In this *theology* of the diocese, there are some inconvenient elements, as well as elements to be avoided. In the first place, the language is not clear, the formulas employed are very vague. In the second place, instead of showing the subordination of the power of the bishop in the diocese to that of the Pope, it emphasizes an antinomy between these two powers.[10] In the third place, the collective values seem to annul the individual values, in a way similar to that which occurs in " panliturgicism," which, as a communal cult, drowns freedom and drains the efficacy of private piety; that is, the integration of the " particular church " into the universal Church remains very blurred.

It is true that a diocese is not only a juridical prefecture, nor are the bishops merely papal officials. Yet the juridical character cannot be denied. One cannot change the limits of a diocese or eliminate them. The " particular churches " or what were early called, by the use of an expression from Roman law, " dioceses," obey the spatial-temporal character of the Church on earth. Christ founded the Church; Christ instituted the hierarchy. The Apostles are the founders of the " Christian communities " or " particular churches." The Roman Church itself, as a particular church, continues that historical rhythm. Moreover, the ecclesiastical " concentration " must be applied, through analogy with the diocese, to the parish. This, too, is a " particular church," a " Christian community," with its pastor and its " realization," basically connected with the diocese.[11]

---

[10] Cf. *ibid.*, pp. 545-548.

[11] CIC.: can. 216: " Territorium cuiuslibet dioecesis dividatur in distinctas partes territoriales: unicuique autem parti sua peculiaris ecclesia cum populo determinato est assignanda, suusque peculiaris rector, tanquam proprius eiusdem pastor, est praeficiendus pro necessaria animarum cura." " What is a parish in fact? It is the smallest part of the unique and universal flock entrusted to Peter by Our Lord. Under the authority of a responsible priest who has received the custody of souls from his Bishop, it is, in the Church of Jesus Christ, the first community of Christian life, a community humanly adjusted in such a way that the pastor can

One should not forget that the juridical structure and the hierarchical structure of the Church are instruments for accomplishing the mystery of Christ in the world, that is, the redemption; and consequently they are ordered to this supreme aim of salvation.[12] The cellule is not separated from, nor does it live outside of, the whole being. In our case, a parish or a diocese is a cellule or a union of cellules. (Let us never forget the individual Christians who give themselves to the whole living and functioning unity of the Church.) Christ rules and governs His Church,[13] all the others being subordinate hierarchs, His envoys: the Pope, the bishops, the pastors of the parishes. Instead of harsh and crude antinomies between laws, unity must be sought. Instead of clashes among powers, there must be subordination to the very aim and essence of the Church. With a great theological sense, the Angelic Doctor could see this ecclesiastical integration when he stated that the universal Church is a great " parish," the Pope being its rector. On an ascending scale, the simple faithful person finds

know his flock and the flock its pastor. A determinate territory normally marks its limits within the diocese, in such a way that the parish is situated in a concrete part of the territory and fixed in local traditions and with definite horizons. In the very center of this territory, the crowning tower makes it possible to see how the parish church rises, with its baptismal font, its confessional, its altar, and its sacrarium, all constituting a symbol of unity in the faith and, as it were, a center of its spiritual life " (*Letter from the Secretariate of State to the new " Semaine Sociale" in Canada*, July 18, 1953). Cf. *Colección de encíclicas y documentos pontificios*. Madrid, 1962, II, pp. 1356-1357.

[12] Cf. A. Huerga, *La Iglesia de la caridad y la Iglesia del derecho*. Barcelona: Flors., 1960, pp. 42-46.

[13] Pius XII, Encyclical Letter "Mystici Corporis." AAS XXXV, 1943, p. 209. St. Thomas had said: " Interior autem influxus gratiae non est nisi a solo Christo, cuius humanitas, ex hoc quod est divinitati coniuncta, habet virtutem iustificandi. Sed influxus in membra Ecclesiae quantum ad exteriorem gubernationem potest aliis convenire. Differenter tamen a Christo: primo quidem quantum ad hoc quod Christus est caput omnium hominum qui ad Ecclesiam pertinent secundum omnem locum et tempus et statum; alii homines dicuntur capita secundum quaedam specialia loca, sicut episcopi suarum ecclesiarum; vel etiam secundum determinatum tempus, sicut Papa est Caput totius Ecclesiae, scilicet, tempore sui Pontificatus; et secundum determinatum statum, prout scilicet sunt in statu viatorum. Alio modo, quia Christus est caput Ecclesiae propria virtute et auctoritate; alii vero dicuntur capita in quantum vicem gerunt Christi " (*Summa theol.*, IIIa, q. 8, a. 6).

three rectors: the diocesan priests, the bishop, and the Pope.[14] And, in a descending scale, the pastoral responsibility is personified, from higher to lower in an analogous way, in the Pope, the bishop, the pastor.[15]

Summarily: a diocese cannot be defined only through its historical or juridical elements; nor can it do without them. The theological definition is based upon the aspect of the " particular church," of the " living Christian community " inasmuch as the bishop exercises his very special functions. A. Briva says:

We have been reserving the name 'church' to the catholic and universal society which forms the whole Mystical Body of Christ. Nevertheless, the sources of revelation and patristic and medieval terminology apply the word 'church' to the particular communities over which a bishop presides. These particular churches have been designated by the juridical name of 'diocese.' . . . Even though materially the terms 'diocese' and 'particular church' generally coincide, the word 'diocese' has a juridical burden which logically came after the concept of the particular church. Because of the visible nature of man, the Church must necessarily order and organize herself according to, as well as adhere to, the human manner of being and living; but men rely upon some territory. To determine the territorial limits of a particular church, it is necessary to assure the complete spiritual needs of all its faithful, . . . [and] this gives place to the concept of the diocese.[16]

In this sense, the *diocese* as a juridical reality is subject to space and time, that is, to historical variations; as we have said, the legislator can change its limits or simply abolish it.[17] But, as a living reality, as a Christian community or " particular church," the diocese is an unalterable essence, directly related to the Mystical Body or universal Church.

---

[14] " Sed parochianus quisque magis tenetur obedire Episcopo quam presbytero parochiali " (St. Thomas Aquinas, *Contra impugnantes Dei cultum et religionem*, n. 88 [*Opuscula theologica*, II Turin-Rome: Marietti, 1954, p. 26]). " Sacerdos proprius non solum est parochus, sed etiam Episcopus vel Papa " (*Ibid.*, n. 150 [p. 33]).

[15] " Episcopi, qui sunt in superiori potestate constituti, magis habent curam de subditis quam etiam ipsi sacerdotes parochiales " (*Ibid.*, n. 88 [p. 26]; cf. *ibid.*, n. 79 [p. 25]). The reason is even more evident in reference to the Pope.

[16] A. Briva, *Colegio episcopal e iglesia particular*. Barcelona, 1959, p. 43.

[17] Cf. CIC.: can. 215, § 1.

III. The Form of the Flock

Although a bit rapidly, we have so limited the concept of the juridical and theological definition of " diocese " that we can now make an inquiry about the " bishop in the diocese." This problem has two aspects, that is, it is resolved into two specific questions: " What is the bishop in the diocese? " and " What is his role in it? " To be and to do—here is the two-fold question.

We said before that the bishops are a divine institution and that the dioceses are apostolic or ecclesiastical creations. " Christ is the bishop of all souls," the " Eternal Shepherd." [18] The Apostles, bishops themselves, who continue the work of Christ, offer us precious elements for focussing the figure of the bishop at the head of a diocese.

St. Peter uses an exquisite expression: τύποι γινόμενοι τοῦ ποιμνίου, that is, " becoming . . . a pattern to the flock " (" forma facti gregis ").[19] The Petrine formula refers prin-cipally to the bishop.[20]

The word τύποι (form), directly signifies exemplarity or model. But, according to its scholastic usage, it suggests a deeper meaning: the form gives being to and specifies things. Within the realm of sociology, the formal cause of society is usually established in the authority.

At any rate, the bishop is a foundation stone of the diocese. He is its supreme authority, since he is the " instrument " for the fulfillment of the work of saving that portion which has been entrusted to his care. He is that successor of the Apostles who rules, with ordinary and immediate power, over the diocese.[21] He has the obligation to give men the " deposit of the faith " and the " deposit of grace." [22]

---

[18] Cf. *I Peter* 2:25; Benziger, *Enchiridion Symbolorum*, § 1821.

[19] *I Peter* 5:3.

[20] " Haec beati Petri verba praecipue ad Episcopum spectant, utpote qui *Pastoris* munus habeat et gerat " (Pius XII, Allocution of Nov. 2, 1954; AAS. XLVI, 1954, p. 670).

[21] Cf. CIC.: can. 329, § 1.

[22] Cf. Pius XII, " Allocution to the Congress on Pastoral Liturgics in Assisi," Sept. 22, 1956; AAS. XLVIII, 1956, p. 713.

There are few scriptural passages as moving as that in the
Acts of the Apostles where St. Paul, preacher of the Gospel,
founder of innumerable " particular churches," gives his last
instructions to the bishops. Here is St. Luke's narrative:

From Miletus, however, he sent to Ephesus for the presbyters
of the church; and when they had come to him and were assembled
he said to them:

" You know in what manner I have lived with you all the time
since the first day that I came into the province of Asia, serving
the Lord with all humility and with tears and in trials that befell
me because of the plots of the Jews; how I have kept back nothing
that was for your good, but have declared it to you and taught
you in public and from house to house, urging Jews and Gentiles to
turn to God in repentance and to believe in our Lord Jesus Christ.
And now, behold, I am going to Jerusalem, compelled by the
Spirit, not knowing what will happen to me there; except that in
every city the Holy Spirit warns me, saying that imprisonment
and persecution are awaiting me. But I fear none of these, nor do
I count my life more precious than myself, if only I may accomplish
my course and the ministry that I have received from the Lord
Jesus, to bear witness to the gospel of the grace of God.

" And now, behold, I know that you all among whom I went
about preaching the kingdom of God, will see my face no longer.
Therefore I call you to witness this day that I am innocent of the
blood of all; for I have not shrunk from declaring to you the whole
counsel of God. Take heed to yourselves and to the whole flock
in which the Holy Spirit has placed you as bishops, to rule the
Church of God, which he has purchased with his own blood. I
know that after my departure fierce wolves will get in among you,
and will not spare the flock. And from among your own selves men
will rise speaking perverse things, to draw away the disciples after
them. Watch, therefore, and remember that for three years night
and day I did not cease with tears to admonish every one of you.

" And now I commend you to God and to the word of his grace,
who is able to build up and to give the inheritance among all the
sanctified. I have coveted no one's silver or gold or apparel. You
yourselves know that these hands of mine have provided for my
needs and those of my companions. In all things I have shown you
that by so toiling you ought to help the weak and remember the
word of the Lord Jesus, that he himself said, ' It is more blessed to
give than to receive.' "

Having said this, he knelt down and prayed with them all. And there was much weeping among them all and they fell on Paul's neck and kissed him, being grieved most of all at his saying that they would no longer see his face. And they escorted him to the ship.[23]

We could compare this Pauline discourse with his pastoral epistles. The essential doctrine would be the same, practical advice would seem more extended, the " daily pressing anxiety, the care of all the churches " [24] would keep on burning in the breast of the intrepid herald of the Gospel. But there is no doubt that the transcribed discourse has the solemn air of a testament. Those worn, calloused hands of Paul are a testament of his poverty and toil; that voice, short of breath because of the emotion involved in parting, testifies what the episcopal program of the Apostle has been and what it is to be for his successors. A bishop, then, is a successor of the Apostles who must give his life for his sheep.[25]

Numberless ecclesiastical documents give the exact scope of the bishop's pastoral mission, his prerogative as a successor of the Apostles, his powers and his duties.[26] We could say that everything in him implies, in a most direct way, the " form of the flock." In this regard, indicating the twofold episcopal dimension of being and action, Pope Pius XII has said:

Although every bishop is responsible only for that portion of the flock which has been entrusted to his care, the charity pertinent to him as legitimate successor of the Apostles, by divine institution and in virtue of the office he has received, makes him individually and collectively responsible for the apostolic mission of the Church, according to the words of Christ to His Apostles: ' As the Father has sent me, I also send you ' (John 20 : 21). This mission, which must encompass all nations and all times, did not cease with the

[23] Acts 20:17-38.

[24] II Cor. 11:28.

[25] Cf. John 10:11.

[26] Cf. Denzinger, op. cit., §§ 960, 966, 1821, 1826, 1836, 1962 (Leo XIII, Encyclical Letter " Satis cognitum," June 29, 1896; AAS. XXVIII, 1895-1896, p. 723: " nec tamen vicarii Romanorum Pontificum putandi [episcopi], quia potestatem gerunt sibi propriam "); CIC.: can. 108, § 3; 329, § 1; 334, § 1; Pius XII, Encyclical Letter " Mystici Corporis," June 29, 1943; AAS. XXXV, 1943, pp. 211-215, etc.

death of the Apostles; it continues in the person of all bishops in communion with the Vicar of Jesus Christ.[27]

The proper pastor of his diocese, with ordinary and immediate power: this is the synthesis of the bishop's prerogatives as indicated by the *Code*.[28] The bond between the bishop and his concrete flock, his diocese, is so deep and so firm that it basically explains his purpose and demands of him a vigilant and multiple activity. The static figure of the bishop, invested with a supreme hierarchical dignity, acquires a sacred functional dynamism in the service of the supernatural interests of the faithful. This conclusion is reflected, with joyful evidence, in the texts of Scripture, in the teachings and practice of the Holy Fathers, in the liturgy, and in the common teaching of the ordinary and solemn magisterium of the Church.

For example, without taking time to make a minute analysis, we do well to recall the ritual of episcopal consecration. The prayers and rites of this consecration gradually give us a complete and majestic silhouette of the figure of the bishop. Let us take part in the *creation* of a " pontiff " chosen among men and for men as he acquires a dignity of service. The precise and meaningful expression in Sacred Scripture is, " For every high priest taken from among men is appointed for men in the things pertaining to God." [29] The consecration attains its culmination in the imposition of the hands, whereby the transmission of episcopal powers is achieved. The consecrating bishop gives to the consecrated bishop a sacramental ordina-

---

[27] Pius XII, Encyclical Letter " Fidei Donum," April 21, 1957; AAS. XLIX, 1957, p. 237: " Quodsi unusquisque Episcopus portionis tantum gregis sibi commissae sacer pastor est, tamen qua legitimus Apostolorum successor ex Dei institutione et praecepto apostolici muneris Ecclesiae una cum ceteris Episcopis sponsor fit, secundum illa verba quae Christus ad Apostolos fecit: *sicut misit me Pater, et ego mitto vos* (Jo. 20: 21). Haec quae *omnes gentes . . . usque ad consummationem saeculi* (Matt. 28: 19-20) amplectitur missio, cum Apostoli de mortali vita decesserunt, minime decidit, immo in Episcopis, communionem cum Iesu Christi Vicario habentibus, adhuc perseverat."

[28] CIC.: can. 334, § 1: " Episcopi residentiales sunt ordinarii et immediati pastores in dioecesibus sibi commissis."

[29] *Hebr.* 5: 1.

tion which enables him " to rule " his " Church and the people entrusted to " him.[30] The bishop, a high priest, full of grace and virtues, a continuator of the hierarchy, receives the royal investiture and the vestments symbolizing it.[31]

The Angelic Doctor gives a detailed explanation of the symbolism pertinent to the episcopal robes,[32] and adds that, like Christ, the bishop is called the spouse of the Church in a special way.[33] For this reason, the nuptial ring, a sign of his hierarchical supremacy and his fullness of power, shines on his hand.[34]

In addition to the very meaningful rite of episcopal consecration, let us recall, too, how Thomistic theology sees the bishop " ordained " for the diocesan pastoral mission. If the ritual of the consecration puts the " new creature," the bishop, in charge of the ministry or pastorate of a flock, Thomistic theology points out the reasons for this. The pastoral mission is the final cause of the episcopacy. " In each obligation the aim of the obligation should be noted. Now the bishop obligates himself to carry out the pastoral function for the salvation of his subjects." [35] In speaking about that sacred and unavoidable duty of the bishop, St. Thomas repeats the terms " principally," " principal," and " final " with importunate insistence. That pastoral mission is what actually turns them into continuators of the apostolic work. According to Aquinas' thought, the exercise of the pastorate is, from another aspect, what raises the " episcopal state " to a " state of perfection." [36]

---

[30] *Manuale e Pontificali Romano . . . de consecrario electi in episcopum.* Rome, 1923, p. 93.

[31] Cf. " L'évêque d'après les prières d'ordination," for the Canons Regular of Mondaye, in *L'Épiscopat . . . ,* o. c., pp. 739-780.

[32] Cf. St. Thomas Aquinas, *in IV Sent.,* d. 14, q. 3, a. 3; d. 24, q. 3, a. 3, ad 6.

[33] Cf. *ibid.,* d. 20, q. 3, a. 2, ad 3.

[34] Cf. *ibid.,* q. 1, a. 4, ad 1; a. 24, q. 3, a. 3, ql. 3.

[35] St. Thomas Aquinas, *Summa theol.* II II, q. 185, a. 5.

[36] Cf. *ibid.,* q. 184, a. 6; *in Matt.* 19; *De perfectione vitae spiritualis,* cap. 21-24; *Quodlibetales* III, q. 6, a. 3.

Finally, the advantage for the flock should be the supreme criterion for the choice or removal of a bishop.[37]

In these four theological reasons, taken in their Thomistic context, the placing of the bishop into a diocese acquires a clear meaning of service, usefulness, and supernatural functionalism. In keeping with the scholastic axiom, " the end, first in intention, last in execution," the final cause makes the whole being of the episcopacy dynamic. That aim presides over and commands ecclesiastical legislation concerning bishops. Here the *Code* seems to be completely transfixed with a powerful internal *theological* and *teleological* current. The salvation of souls is the supreme law in the juridical order of the Church. The group of canons relevant to the episcopacy constitutes an authentic proof. Thus, from the very start, the title " concerning bishops " offers a canon which juridically sketches the bishop. Yet the juridical sketch is none other than the theological and dogmatic sketch. The canon states: " Bishops are the successors of the Apostles and by divine institution are placed over particular churches which they govern with ordi-

---

[37] Cf. St. Thomas Aquinas, *Summa theol.* IIa IIae, q. 185, a. 1; a. 2, ad 1 et ad 2; a. 4; *In I Tim.*, 3, lect. 1. In the first *Quodlibetales* (a. 14), St. Thomas compares " bishops and doctors in theology," who are, " as it were, the principal artisans of the spiritual edifice," with those who exercise a subordinate ministry and are equivalent to " manual artisans."

An interesting question is presented in the *Summa theol.* (IIa IIae, q. 185, a. 3) concerning the candidates for the episcopacy. The solution has a view to the common good and, therefore, " ille qui debet aliquem eligere in episcopum, vel de eo providere, non tenetur assumere meliorem simpliciter . . ., sed meliorem quoad regimen ecclesiae, qui scilicet possit ecclesiam et instruere et defendere et pacifice gubernare." To this passage, in which the solution is full of seriousness and serenity, Cajetan appends a question of a practical type, " Whether the bishop should be learned and a doctor of theology, or of canon law? The answer, touching on the actual historical situation, is in favor of " theologian bishops." Those who defend " canonist bishops," the famous commentator says, " longe aberrant: tum quia officium episcoporum . . . est praedicare—materia autem praedicationis non est ius, sed Evangelium—; tum quia magis tenetur episcopus ad docendum populum servare ea quae ad bonos mores spectant . . . quam docere homines sacros canones, quos non ipse Dominus, sed homines ediderunt. Constat autem quod docere servare mandata Dominica spectat ad theologicam scientiam . . . Et ideo episcopi tenentur omni tempore esse theologi " (*in IIam IIae*, q. 185, a. 3, n. IV).

nary jurisdiction." [38] These are solemn and precise words which are a close version of those other words, of more laborious expression, included in the Dogmatic Constitution *Pastor Aeternus* of the First Vatican Council: " That ordinary and immediate power of episcopal jurisdiction, whereby bishops, who, established by the Holy Spirit, have succeeded to the place of the Apostles, nourish and govern each of the flocks entrusted to each of them as true shepherds." [39]

It could be said that this is the foundation stone upon which the *canonical* figure of the bishop is raised. On that solid and strong foundation rises the hierarchical structure of the Church as a supernatural society in time and in the world. The " power of feeding " [40] the flock of the Lord is rooted in the divine mission of the episcopacy and is concretized in the juridical charge of a diocese.

Without losing sight of this basic structure, the *Code* dedicates a considerable legislative elasticity to the bishop pledged to a *diocesan* pastoral care. The right to the pastorate is correlative with the duty, the dedication.[41] For this reason, the *Code* requires that the person called to the episcopal dignity be gifted with intellectual and virtuous qualities, especially " the zeal for souls," [42] that is, an impatient love of and care for souls. The legislator shares in that impatience in two ways: first, by commanding that the bishop-elect, having received the apostolic letter, not put off his consecration for more than three months and that he takes possession of his diocese

[38] CIC.: can. 329, § 1.
[39] Denzinger, *op. cit.*, § 1828. Time and time again, St. Thomas states that bishops are the successors of the Apostles (Cf. *Summa theol.* IIa IIae, q. 184, a. 6, ad 1; q. 185, a. 5; IIIa, q. 67, a. 2, ad 1; q. 72, a. 11). This is a dogmatic truth about which primitive Christianity was clearly conscious. Cf. the excellent work of A. M. Javierre, " Le thème de la succession des Apôtres dans la littérature chrétienne primitive," *L'Episcopat* . . . . , *op. cit.*, pp. 171-221.
[40] Cf. J. P. Torrell, *La théologie de l'épiscopat au premier Concile du Vatican.* Paris, 1961, pp. 119-130; the explanation given by Zinelli (MANSI LII, 1104) is interesting. Cf. also U. Betti, *La Costituzione Dommatica " Pastor Aeternus" del Concilio Vaticano I.* Rome, 1961.
[41] CIC.: can. 335, § 1.
[42] CIC.: can. 331, § 1.

within a period not exceeding four months; [43] secondly, by peacefully and lovingly controlling the progress of the diocese, for which purpose he establishes prudent norms, such as the "ad limina" visit and the quinquennial reports made by the bishops.[44]

But above all he urges upon them the complete discharge of pastoral duties. The flowering of piety and the Christian life among the faithful depends, in great measure, upon the loving dedication of the bishop to his flock. "They must be vigilant," says one canon, "lest abuses creep into church discipline, especially concerning the administration of the Sacraments, the cult of God and the Saints, the preaching of the word of God, sacred indulgences, the fulfillment of pious wills; and they should take care that the purity of faith and morals be preserved among the clergy and the people." [45] The custody of the flock is like the protection of a living and divine treasure. In order that pastoral care might be more efficacious, the legislator establishes two more concrete duties; the first is the duty of residence, the other is the duty of pastoral visitation. Both duties are inherent to or derived from the august episcopal mission. In the juridical order, both unite the bishop to his diocese with a strong legal bond.

The obligation to reside personally in the diocese is formulated clearly and vigorously: "Even if bishops have a coadjutor, they are bound by law to personal residence in the diocese." [46] The law establishing the obligation of the pastoral

---

[43] CIC.: can. 333.

[44] CIC.: can. 338, § 2; 340; 341. These juridical obligations, regulating the relations of the bishops with the Pope, correspond to the nature of the Church as an organic and perfect society. Nevertheless, the bishops preserve their prerogatives and authority. There is a fundamental text from the encyclical letter "Mystici Corporis" which should be kept in mind because of its clarity and its doctrinal depth: "As regards their own dioceses, bishops feed and govern as true *Pastors*, in Christ's name, the flock entrusted to each of them. Yet, in so doing, they are not completely independent, but are put under the authority of the Roman Pontiff, although they enjoy ordinary jurisdiction, which the same Supreme Pontiff has directly communicated to them. For this reason, they are to be venerated by the faithful as *successors of the Apostles* through divine institution" (AAS, XXXV, 1943, pp. 211-212).   [45] CIC.: can. 336, § 2.   [46] CIC.: can. 338, § 1.

visitation is accompanied by a massive program concerning its aim and the manner in which it is to be carried out: " To preserve sound and orthodox doctrine, safeguard good morals and correct the evil, as well as to promote peace, innocence, piety and discipline among the people and the clergy, and otherwise to provide for the welfare of religion according to the circumstances, bishops are obligated to make a complete or partial visitation of the diocese every year." [47]

These two laws are clearly Tridentine. On this occasion, the famous Council prescinded from the theological debate as to whether " residence " was of " divine right," [48] and amicably settled the indifference of some pastors by a pair of positive dispositions which even today retain vigor and force. For a great part, the Catholic reform was based upon these laws and dispositions.

The bishop is *the form of his flock.* In the foregoing pages, we have tried to delineate the static and dynamic content of the Petrine phrase. The text from the *Epistle to the Hebrews* gave us, too, the human and hierarchical view of the bishop; he is a *pontiff* chosen *from* and *for* men. The great bishop St. Augustine offers us the description of the bishop trembling in the presence of his faithful because of his episcopal dignity and yet joyous in discovering that he is on their level in faith and love: " For I am a bishop for your sake; with you I am a Christian. The former is the title of the office I have received; the latter, the title of salvation." [49] This is the complete image of the bishop as the embodiment of his mission.

---

[47] CIC.: can. 343, § 1; cf. can. 344-346. Already the Venerable Bartolomé de los Mártires spoke, with his characteristic pastoral and doctrinal zeal, about the " most serious duty of visitation " incumbent upon bishops. Cf. *Concilium Tridentinum,* ed. Goerresiana, VIII (Freiburg: B. Herder Co., 1909), p. 419.

[48] Concerning this theme, one can consult: B. Carranza, *De residentia episcoporum* . . . Venice, 1572; L. Castano, " Pio IX e la Curia Romana di fronte al dibattito tridentino sulla residenza," *Miscellanea Historiae Pontificiae,* VII. Rome; 1943; Fr. Garcia Guerrero, *El decreto sobre la residencia de los obispos en la tercera asamblea del Concilio Tridentino.* Cadiz, 1943; P. Damino, *Il contributo teologico di Bartolomeo de' Martiri al Concilio di Trento.* Rome, 1962, pp. 36-60.

[49] St. Augustine, *Serm. 340* (PL XXXVIII, § 1483).

IV. THREEFOLD SERVICE

What we should analyze now is the unfolding of the bishop's power in the diocese. " Each bishop is the center and foundation of the unity in the particular church, this being, in turn, a living part of the whole Church." [50] This center and foundation, however, immediately takes on a dynamic and active character. In the rite of episcopal investiture, the consecrating bishop says: " The bishop must judge, interpret, consecrate, ordain, offer, baptize, and confirm." [51] As expressed in a more schematic formula, the action of the bishop in his diocese embraces a threefold service, namely, teaching, priesthood, and government. The service implies power, which is equally converted into office, duty, and pastoral ministry.

1) *The Right and Service of Teaching:* The Apostles received the mandate: *Teach, preach the gospel to every creature.*[52] In his lucid conscientiousness about the sacred duty concerning the " ministry of the word," St. Paul consecrates the phrase " faith from hearing." [53] His admonitions to the bishops give evidence of his preoccupation that they faithfully carry out the mission of teaching. If we stop for a moment on the texts, we discover that the teaching centres around one theme: the " mystery of Christ." For this, one must adopt two attitudes: that of defending the gospel message against venomous attacks from the enemies of Christ (the " false prophets " and the " false doctors " being harshly anathematized by St. Paul);[54] and that of propagating this mystery.[55] We have,

[50] J. Lecuyer, " Orientations présentes de la théologie de l'Épiscopat," *L'Épiscopat . . .*, op. cit., p. 808.

[51] *Manuale e Pontificali Romano . . . de consecratio electi in episcopum.* Rome, 1923, p. 88.

[52] *Matt.* 28:19; *Mark* 16:15.

[53] *Rom.* 10:17.

[54] Cf. *Acts* 20:29-30; *I Tim.* 1:19; 4:1; *II Tim.* 2:16; 3:1-5; *Tit.* 3:9-11.

[55] *I Cor.* 9:16; *Rom.* 1:14; *Gal.* 1:11-12; *II Tim.* 4:6-7. The same St. Mark, very simple in his narration, ends his Gospel in this way: " But they went forth and preached everywhere, while the Lord worked with them and confirmed the preaching by the signs that followed " (*Mark* 16:20).

then, the theme and the mode of episcopal preaching or teaching. The bishops are the successors of the Apostles; they are most clearly exemplified in the Pauline epistles.

Some persons are amazed that the Church, in its papal magisterium or in the magisterium of the residential bishops, confronts and condemns false doctrines, the errors against faith and morals. This is her obligation. Yet, if the Roman Pontiffs or the bishops were to limit themselves to the " defense " of revealed doctrine, they would fulfill only one part of their teaching office. They are not only " guardians " of orthodoxy; they are also authentic "expounders," " teachers," and " interpreters." This they are exclusively, that is, by proper right; in virtue of this right, they can *delegate* this mission.

Substantially, this is the primary function of the bishop, the first duty. In his broad exercise of the supreme magisterium, Pius XII frequently vindicated the teaching right and office of the bishops of the Church. In one of his discourses we read:

Christ Our Lord confided to the Apostles, and, through them, to their successors, the truth which He had brought from heaven. . . . Thus the Apostles have been constituted teachers, that is, masters of the Church, by divine right. Therefore, besides the legitimate successors of the Apostles, that is, the Roman Pontiff for the universal Church and the bishops for the faithful entrusted to their care, there are no other teachers by divine right in the Church of Christ; although they, and particularly the Supreme Teacher of the Church and Vicar of Christ on earth, can call others as cooperators or advisers in the exercise of the magisterium and delegate the function of teaching to them, sometimes in concrete cases, sometimes by confiding such an office to them.[56]

Thus this delegated ministry should always be faithful to the bishop and, of course, subject at any moment to his inspection.

From this arise the applications which embrace all religious indoctrination. The same Pius XII put his finger on the sore spot of two dangerous tendencies of our time by discovering

---

[56] Pius XII, Allocution of May 31, 1954 (AAS. XLVI, 1954, p. 314).

and condemning them. The first is the tendency of those who
" teach and have very little care about being united with the
living magisterium of the Church and mold neither their minds
nor their intentions according to the common teaching clearly
proposed by this magisterium in one way or other." The
second is the magisterium of the laity, since " here and there a
theology which they call *lay* has recently started to pullulate,"
and its heralds " distinguish its magisterium from the public
magisterium of the Church, and, in a certain way, set the
former in opposition to the latter."

Some are spurred by an eagerness for novelty, by self-con-
fidence, by the infiltrations of non-perennial philosophies;
others, by the false illusion of prophetic charisms, by the spirit
of independence or by an unbridled zeal for the lay apostolate.
In view of these attitudes, the admonition of Pius XII is
definite:

Matters touching upon religion and morals, being truths which
absolutely surpass the order of sensible things, pertain exclusively
to the authority and competency of the Church. Already in Our
encyclical letter *Humani Generis*, we have described the mentality
and spirit of those to whom We have alluded, and at the same
time we have warned that some of the aberrations reprobated there
are due only to the fact that union with the living magisterium of
the Church has been scorned.

Moreover, referring to *lay theology*, he says:

In the Church there has never been, nor is there or ever will be
a legitimate magisterium of lay persons which God has removed
from the authority which has been the guide and vigilance of the
sacred magisterium. Furthermore, the simple fact that this submission is rejected is itself a convincing argument and a sure
criterion that it is not the Spirit of God and of Christ guiding the
laymen who speak and act in this way.[57]

2) *The Right and Function of Sanctifying:* The priestly or
sanctifying function is associated with the teaching mission.
All the activity of the bishop in his diocese is ordered to the

---

[57] *Ibid.*, pp. 315-317.

sanctification of the faithful. Consequently, the bishop is the " High Priest " of his flock, the " Pontiff," the minister and giver of sacred things, the " sacrificer " by antonomasia. All priesthood is essentially " that which offers sacrifice." In the cited text of the *Epistle to the Hebrews* this sanctifying power of sacrifice is underlined: " that he may offer gifts and sacrifices for sins," for the people and for himself.[58]

In the Christian religion, the bishop has full priestly or sanctifying powers; by his own right he is the minister of the Sacraments, the bearers of grace, the minister especially of the Eucharist, and it is he who confers sacerdotal ordination to the diocesan priests,[59] his collaborators in the sanctifying ministry. Addressing bishops, Pius XII explains the priestly right and office in the following way:

For the priest of the New Law, the principal power and reason of his office is offering the unique and very sublime sacrifice of the Highest and Eternal Priest, Christ our Lord, the same as that which the Divine Redeemer offered in a bloody manner on the cross and which He anticipated in an unbloody way during the Last Supper, desiring that it be repeated perpetually, and, therefore, commanding His Apostles: " Do this in remembrance of me " (*Luke* 22 : 19). It was the Apostles, then, and not all the faithful, whom the selfsame Christ made and constituted priests and to whom He gave the power of offering sacrifice.[60]

Obviously the Pope alludes to the so-called " priesthood of the faithful," with which the laicologists are very much preoccupied and about which they speak very often. Although the Pope touched upon this problem in the encyclical letter *Mediator Dei*,[61] here he speaks of it with decisive precision:

Moreover, whatever may be the true and exact meaning of this honorary title and its content, one must hold as very certain that this *priesthood*, common to all Christians, although elevated and hidden, is differentiated, not only in degree, but also essentially,

[58] *Heb.* 5:1-3.
[59] Cf. St. Thomas Aquinas, *IV Contra Gentes*, 76.
[60] Pius XII, Allocution of Nov. 2, 1954 (AAS. XLVI, 1954, pp. 667-669).
[61] Cf. AAS. XXXIX, 1947, pp. 538-539.

from priesthood truly and properly so-called, which consists in the power of accomplishing the sacrifice of Christ Himself by representing the person of Christ, the Highest Priest.[62]

3) *The Right and Function of Rule:* The teaching and priestly functions are backed by the power of jurisdiction. This is a theme about which it is possible, here, to make only slight indications. The Church of wayfarers, that is, the Church here on earth is necessarily hierarchical by reason of its being an ordered multitude, of its being " a prolongation of Christ," and by reason of its sacramental character.[63] Thence is derived the very existence of " sacred power." [64] The bishop's pastoral rule is connected with the supernatural purpose of the Christian community. St. Thomas communicates the idea of dynamism in the Mystical Body by teaching that grace has influence on the members through the conjoined action of Christ and the hierarchy. The " twofold spiritual power " [65] is ordered to this aim of sanctification.

From the very nature of " power " and its object is derived its extension. In connection with some new theories which try to diminish the field of action pertinent to episcopal jurisdiction, Pius XII offers a reminder of the scope and of the matters pertinent to the governing authority of the bishops. As the pastor of his own flock, the bishop has for a field of action of his authority, care, and vigilance, not only strictly religious matters (as, for example, stating the truths of faith, directing pious practices, administering the Sacraments, performing liturgical functions), but also everything concerning man's supernatural end. The Pope refers concretely to the natural law, derived ethical laws, and social problems, since " in social matters, there is no one sole problem; rather there are many

[62] AAS. XLVI, 1954, p. 669.

[63] Cf. A. Huerga, *op. cit.*, pp. 25-29.

[64] Cf. C. Garcia Extremeño, " Iglesia, Jerarquía y Carisma," *Ciencia Tomista*, LXXXVI, 1959, pp. 26-64.

[65] " Duplex est spiritualis potestas: una quidem sacramentalis, alia iurisdictionalis. Sacramentalis quidem potestas est quae per aliquam consecrationem confertur; . . . Potestas autem iurisdictionalis est quae ex simplici iniunctione hominis confertur " (St. Thomas Aquinas, *Summa theol.* IIa IIae, q. 39, a. 3).

and very serious questions, whether they are only social or politico-social, touching upon the moral order, consciences, and the salvation of souls. Therefore, it cannot be said that they are outside the authority and care of the Church." [66] Naturally, if pastoral activity is to be harmonious and fruitful, it reckons with a *church discipline* which regulates and stimulates the religious life of the faithful. Discipline is the hinge of good government for all society. Moreover, " both laymen and priests should know that the Church is competent and legitimate, and that her respective Ordinaries are competent and legitimate—each one for the faithful entrusted to him and within the common limits of the law—for establishing church discipline and obligating subjects to it, that is, for establishing the exterior manner of behavior and action in all matters touching upon the exterior life. . . . Neither the clergy nor the laity can withdraw from this discipline." [67]

As is evident, it is easy to trace the very teaching office or magisterium possessed by the bishop to this power of jurisdiction.[68]

From the whole foregoing analysis, we can already form an idea about the *being* and *action* of the bishop in his diocese. Because of the supernatural and human abundance which it embraces, a biblical image can help us define him: he is the " Good Shepherd." [69] There are few symbols as beautiful as this; few symbols are as full of meaning, of sacred tradition.

V. Bishop, Diocese, Council

A final question would suggest methodological reflection on the theme of the " bishop in his diocese." Will the Second Vatican Council speak or decide anything in relation to the

---

[66] Pius XII, Allocution of Nov. 2, 1954 (AAS. XLVI, 1954, pp. 671-672).

[67] *Ibid.*, pp. 674-675.

[68] Cf. A. Huerga, *op. cit.*, pp. 31, 38-39.

[69] Cf. *John* 10:1-16. The image is familiar in the Orient and especially in Sacred Scripture. Cf. *Gen.* 48:15; 49:24; *Jer.* 23:1-8; *Ezechiel* 34:23; *Zacharias* 11:4-14; *Matt.* 18:12-13; *Luke* 15:4-6. Yet, although it is a simile breathing goodness and pleasant solicitude, it implies authority, too. Cf. L. M. Dewailly, *Envoyés du Père.* Paris, 1960, p. 64, n. 1.

figure and pastoral care of the bishop? Interest in this question can be unfolded in two ways: the *act* and the *theme*; that is, the question is divided into two questions: Will the Council have a treatise on bishops? This is inquiring only about a future act. The other is: What points about the bishop will it consider? This is asking about the thematic.

As regards the *act*, undoubtedly a " revision," in the actual situation of the world wherein the Church lives, teaches and sanctifies, cannot exclude from its broad, generous, and optimistic program, as outlined on various occasions by Pope John XXIII,[70] the " episcopacy," which has the divine mission of giving spiritual instruction to souls and which, with the Pope, forms the Council.

As regards the *episcopal themes* or *problems* which will constitute the object of the conciliar deliberations and decisions, there are obviously two possible directions: one is the dogmatic, that is, the solution of some theological questions which have not been *defined* as yet; the other is the practical or pastoral, that is, that which refers to the " adaptation " of diocesan territory, as well as of the methods of evangelization, to the needs of our time.

In the field of dogma there are some theological problems which, as yet, have not received the *definitive* verdict of " truths of faith," as, for example, those taken up by the First Vatican Council which, having been suspended, did not resolve them. There are those who say that, just as the First Vatican Council was the Council of the " dogmatic " definitions exalting the figure of the Roman Pontiff, so the present council will be the Council of " dogmatic " definitions which will exalt the figure and the ecclesiastical mission of bishops,[71] as, for example,

[70] Cf. John XXIII, " Allocution to the Cardinals in the Basilica of St. Paul," Jan. 25, 1959, wherein he announced the Council (AAS. LI, 1959, pp. 68-69). In the encyclical letter " Ad Petri Cathedram," he explained the purpose of the Council: " ut ad catholicae fidei incrementum et ad rectam christiani populi morum renovationem, utque ecclesiastica disciplina ad nostrorum temporum necessitates rationesque aptius accommodetur " (June 29, 1959; AAS. LI, 1959, p. 511).

[71] Cf. G. Thils, " Parlera-t-on des évêques au Concile? ", *Nouvelle revue théologique*, LXXXIII, 1961, pp. 785-804.

the " sacramentality of the episcopacy " or the relations between " primacy and episcopacy," between " pope and episcopal
college," etc.[72] A symptom of this gyration of hopes and hypotheses is the publication of numerous books and articles concerning the " theology of the episcopacy." As is easily understood, this bibliography reflects a strong episcopological climate.

In the field of pastoral practice (which is our chief interest
here), too, it is easy to suppose great activity in the Council.
One of the commissions designated for the preparation of the
Council brought up this significant title: " On Bishops and
the Rule of Dioceses." In the plenary sessions of the Central
Commission, held in 1962, Cardinal Marella stated the questions concerning the actual situation of dioceses in the Catholic
world; " episcopal conferences," relations between the episcopacy and the Holy See, and, finally, the pastoral ministry of the
bishops. The official communiqués published in *L'Osservatore
Romano* report, with sufficient accuracy, the orientation of the
pre-conciliar work.

Concerning the theme " actual situation of the diocese," the
aforementioned Cardinal keeps within the bounds of the resumé
given by *L'Osservatore Romano*, not by a purely statistical
report, but by delving into the history and finality of diocesan
territories. Historically the demarcation of the dioceses generally coincided with the confines of civil circumscriptions. As
the Church progressed and was extended throughout the world,
there was recourse to the Pope to establish new dioceses with
their determined territorial limits. The " actual situation " of
the dioceses can be submitted to a " revision " with a view to
" adapting " the territories to civil structures or to the number
of Catholics. It is well known that there are countries where
there are a great number of dioceses, others where they are
scarce, and some where the hierarchy has not been established.
Moreover, the Cardinal analyzed the finality which presides

---

[72] The title of the following work indicates certain doctrinal tendencies: T. I.
Jimenez Urresti, *El binomio " Primado—Episcopado ": tema central del próximo
Concilio Vaticano II*. Bilbao: Desclée de Brouwer, 1962.

over this whole canonical arrangement of dioceses: "it puts the bishop, who is the true pastor of the flock, in a better situation to know, love, and save his lambs," since the Church lives in time and uses "earthly means to attain her supernatural aims." [73] These are definitely the criteria which will preside over the decisions of the Council concerning diocesan territories, the possible creation of new dioceses, and the division of other dioceses.

In greater relief is the theme about the "pastoral ministry of bishops." In the respective communiqué of *L'Osservatore Romano*, we read:

The Members and Advisers of the Central Commission today examined, in particular, the new methods and means of the apostolate needed, either to cope with the situations in which there are found special categories of the faithful, such as emigrants, those on the sea, airline employees, nomads, and tourists, or to draw anew to the faith and the practice of the Christian life all those who are usually designated by the generic term "distant."

[And it added] Modern times, with their multiple technical innovations, impose on the Pastors of Dioceses a pastoral ministry which is ever more flexible in its methods and ever broader in its means.[74] In most recent times, when technical conquests constantly enlarge the orbit of human habitation, pastoral care cannot be limited to an anchored geographic territory. Because of "floating cities," the "apostolate of the sea" gives an unsuspected mobility to the flock entrusted to a bishop. As much can be said about travel on land and through space, in such a way that there is already talk about an "apostolate of the heavens."

In any event, as underlined in a foregoing commentary, the Church lives *with* and *for* the men of her time and is obliged to give testimony of the truth and God's plan of salvation in the most varied and contingent situations. Moreover, in their capacity as Teachers, Pastors, and Pontiffs, her bishops proceed

[73] *L'Osservatore Romano*, February 21, 1962, p. 1.

[74] *L'Osservatore Romano*, May 5, 1962, p. 1. For a fuller technical-juridical account, one can consult the documented and delightful description by S. Alvarez-Menendez, "En torno al futuro Concilio Ecumenico," *Revista española de Derecho Canónico*, XVII, 1962, pp. 115-143, 393-425.

in complete communion with Peter's successor, continuators of the work of Redemption in the territories which have been entrusted to their pastoral solicitude.

Times change; existential conditions progress. The Council may take up problems of a practical type and direct its decisions to a greater adaptation and efficacy of the pastoral ministry. Yet, substantially, the figure of the bishop will continue to be what it has always been: Pastor of his diocese.

ALVARO HUERGA, O. P.

Pontifical University of St. Thomas Aquinas in Urbe
   Rome, Italy

THE LAYMAN IN THE CHURCH [1]

ᕠᕣ

THE purpose of this article is modest, to sketch in broad
lines the place of the *layman*, seen theologically, in the
Church. A general view of the limits of what is possible and permissible, of what pertains to the laity and what
does not, will guard us against breaking through dividing lines
and will prevent our committing errors like the one frequently
made, in connection with proposals for the coming General
Council, that the diaconate should be re-established as an independent order and should be considered as the " summit of
the lay apostolate." That the diaconate should be something
more than a stepping-stone to the priesthood is quite justifi-
ably desired by many people; but it is essentially a clerical
state and can, under no aspect, be called lay-apostolate.

THE CHRISTIAN IDEA OF LAYMAN

The Christian Term " Layman "

By reason, not so much of the secularisation of society, as of
the laicist atmosphere in which this secularisation has been
concretely pursued, the term " lay person," as used by non-
Christians, has usually for Catholic ears (in continental countries) an unfavourable connotation. In the period since the
middle of the nineteenth century the sense of the term has
swung from something like " free-thinker " by way of " anti-
clerical " to " non-cleric " and " non-religious " (in the sense
of one who is not a monk or a nun). In the nineteenth century the term " société laïque " and " enseignement laïque "
made their appearance, having the sense of, not simply non-
religious, but rather positively extra-religious, with the impli-

---

[1] Editor's Note: This article in its present form was published in *Doctrine and
Life*, St. Saviour's, Dublin, July and August, 1961. The translation from the Dutch
(*Tijdschrift voor Geestelijk Leven*, 1959, pp. 669-694) was made by Colman
O'Neill, O. P., and checked by the author. In *Doctrine and Life* it was published
with an Editor's Note and a Translator's Note, q. v.

cation of anti-religious. In our own day, at least as far as the term itself is concerned, this unfavourable connotation has disappeared so that now even Christians can be quite ready to accept its use. Consequently, when we find in the new French Constitution intentions that the state as such, is concerned only with secular, "l'Etat est laïque," this means, if we disregard subjective ulterior intentions, that the state as such, is concerned only with secular affairs and, moreover, is in this sphere autonomous. The confusion attached to the notion is such that, as late as 1945, the Italian Parliament witnessed the following exchange between a socialist and a Catholic deputy. To the demand of a socialist that a "lay person" be appointed minister of education, the Catholic, De Gasperi, replied heatedly that there had never been any intention of appointing a cleric to this post. To which the socialist retorted with equal heat that his meaning was being twisted, that he was not concerned about clerics; by "lay person" he understood a non-Catholic.

The sense attached to the term lay person in theology derives very clearly from Scripture. When the Canon Law uses the term "laicus," a lay person, in the sense of "christifidelis," i. e., one who believes, this has a remote basis in the Scriptures themselves. The word "laikos" comes from "laos," people. In profane Greek usage this signifies the people as distinct from the rulers and leaders of the people, thus as distinct from the ruling and intellectual classes. In the Bible this word has a more precise signification, being applied exclusively to the people of God as distinct from the Gentiles. The "laos" is *the* people, God's people, that is, in relation to the Christian era, the Church of Christ. At the same time, nevertheless, the Scripture uses this term also in contrast to the leaders of this people of God, namely, in contrast to the priests, levites and prophets. The people or the "laos" is that part of the Church that is subject to the leadership and control of the Church's hierarchy.

Going on to the word "laikos," from which the words "laicus," "lay person," are derived: this signifies in profane Greek usage a member of the common class, belonging to the people but set apart from the leaders of the people. We do not find the word in this sense either in the Scripture or in the Septuagint, the Greek translation used by the Jews; but it is found in a few ancient Greek translations of the Old Testament. The sense in which it is used is important. *Laikos,* lay, signifies here the profane or unsanctified, that is, what is not consecrated to the worship of God. In contrast to the loaves of proposition, ordinary bread, which is not reserved for worship, is called simply "lay bread." Likewise, the area of the Temple is " sacred " while outside the Temple is "lay." This distinction between " sacred " and " lay " again applies only to things *within* the people of God. But in early Christian writings this word is soon transferred to persons (see Clement of Rome), and so there appears the distinction between the terms "klerikos" and "laikos" or lay person within the community of the Church.

If we bring all these points together again we gain the following result. A *lay person* is 1) a member of the people of God assembled in the Church, 2) but in this community of the Church he is set apart from the hierarchy, being attached to a distinct group, 3) on the side of the laity this separation implies a reference to the profane, to that, namely, which is not directly connected with the mystery of Church worship. With these data we are already in a position to say that Christian semantics, leading us to the significance of the term, "lay person," *suggests* that the laity is characterised both by its *membership in the Church* and by its relation to *secular affairs.*

The Theological Notion of Lay Person and Lay Spirituality

The Church as the " great Sign set up unto the nations invites to her all who have not yet believed " (First Council of the Vatican; Denz. 1794). In another article (in *Tijdschrift voor geestelijk Leven)* we have pointed out that not only the hierarchy but all the faithful constitute an essential element in this great sacramental sign. The Church here on earth makes manifest on the plane of visible historical fact the grace of redemption; and this grace is nothing other than the person of Christ, dead, indeed, but now raised up to heavenly life. Of this mystery of grace the Church is the outward, human form in the shape of a social sign or, more exactly, in the shape of a community which is a sign (" societas-signum ") *(tekengemeenschap)*. Both in her hierarchy and in her community of lay believers the Church is the visible realisation on earth of the redemptive grace of Christ. The hidden union with God in Christ granted by grace is revealed in, and brought about through, the external social sign of a community governed by the rulers of the Church. It follows that lay people in the Church form an essential part of the efficacious sign of grace *(werkzaam genadeteken)* and of Christ, ascended into heaven. This means that the visible and active presence of grace among us is brought about in two-fold fashion: in and through the apostolic office of the Church's hierarchy (institutional, authoritative and charismatic fashion) and through the faithful who bear the characters of baptism and confirmation (fashion determined by the institutional role of lay people and by charisms).

In this complexus the hierarchy of the Church exercises a directive and authoritative function which exists, consequently, for the sake of the community of lay believers: this apostolic office is ministerial, a service of Christ and of the faithful. Nevertheless, the layman, placed though he is in a relation of obedience, based on faith, to the hierarchy of the Church, is, in his quality of Christian layman, truly and in full a part of the Church. He plays his part in supporting the visible and active historical form of redemptive grace in the world. This distinction between *clerics* (those belonging by the nature of their office to the hierarchy, namely, pope and bishops; or those participating in the hierarchy of orders, namely, simple priests or presbyters and deacons) and *lay people* in the Church is not to be explained merely as the result of historical or sociological development; it originates in the will of Christ himself and is not subject to change. This distinction is of the essence of the Church. It follows that one who actually, in one or other fashion, has an inner *participation* in the true apostolic office of the Church's hierarchy is by definition *not a layman*: he belongs to the clergy of the Church (concretely: pope, bishops, priests and deacons). It is true that the derived participations in this apostolic office (namely, priesthood and diaconate) were not directly instituted by Christ. Christ instituted directly the fullness of the priestly (i. e. episcopal) apostolic office. But the Church is conscious of her power to divide this hierarchical office in response to her needs into separate grades, as has been done, for example, for the priesthood and diaconate.

CHARACTERISTICS OF LAY STATUS

In the first place the layman in the Church is a *Christian*, a member of the Church, the people of God, the Kingdom of God on earth, for he, too, bears a personal responsibility. Christ's command: " Be ye perfect as also your heavenly Father is perfect" (*Matt.* 5:48) is directed to all men: pope, bishops, priests, religious and laity. To seek after the Kingdom of God as after a hidden treasure or a pearl of great price, for the sake of which we must, if necessary, despise all things, is as much an obligation of the layman as it is of the priest and the religious. A life lived in communion with the death and resurrection of Christ is the very definition of Christian life and of the Church. Charity, altruistically motivated and self-sacrificing, must necessarily therefore be the heart of a lay life too. In addition, the Christian life or membership of the community of the Church does not consist only in a personal relationship with God in Christ Jesus; it is at the same time, by the very fact, and *within* this dialogue with the living God, essentially apostolic. We are not meant just to *live in* the Kingdom of God; we have imposed on us the task of extending the Kingdom. This must not be misunderstood. As a lay member of the Church, as one, that is, who does not belong to the ecclesiastical hierarchy, the believer has a part in the *apostolate or mission of the Church*, but not in the mission or apostolate *of the hierarchy*. Looked at under the aspect of apostolate, the Church is a community with an apostolic mission, within which, however, is to be found a priestly or " authoritative " form of apostolate side by side with a lay form of mission. Each of these is a particular form or manifestation of the single apostolate of the whole Church. The distinction between these two forms is a consequence of the distinction, established by Christ himself, between the clergy and the laity. This distinction between two forms of the apostolate is, therefore, itself of divine origin. Consequently, the line of demarcation between the two in the Church cannot be permitted to become indistinct. Recognition of the role played by the laity in the Church can never, therefore, acquire the sense that the layman is now to have a part in what formerly pertained exclusively to the clergy.

My only concern here is to clarify the basic principle of lay spirituality and of the lay apostolate in contrast to the apostolate of the hierarchy.

The ecclesiastical difference between the laity and the clergy can be based only upon the internal structure of the supernatural community, the Church. It is precisely because there is a *community* of the faithful, of laymen, a people of God, that leaders of this people are needed in the Church; a hierarchical authority. And since this community is a *communion in grace*, internally united by the supernatural bond of faith, hope and love, as also by the common bond of the same sacraments of the one faith, the authority in this community cannot be of natural origin: it must have authorisation for its task from Christ, together with the charism that is bound up with such a Christ-given mission. As baptized persons, the laity as well as the clergy have therefore an ecclesiastical, sacred task. But the clergy fulfills this task as a principle of authority and leadership in a teaching, governing and sancti- fying priestly activity; whereas the laity must have the same ecclesiastical sense of responsibility for the Kingdom of God, but as God's people, without the function of authority and thus without the official priesthood. Thus the lay community too belongs to the historical, tangible stature in which the grace of redemption appears on earth: the earthly Church. By their incorporation into the Church, that is, by their baptism, the laity consequently receive a share in this real function of the Church: they receive, namely, the charge to give visible stature to the faithful communion with Christ in grace, in and through their whole life. Therefore every baptized person is conjointly responsible for the Church and for its function as a sign in the midst of this world.

Now, it is true indeed that this ecclesiastical responsibility or mission, which the layman receives in virtue of his bap- tism, is given to a *man*, that is, to a person whose task in this world is to give meaning to his own life; to a person, conse- quently, who is also charged with bringing human order into the sphere of worldly life. On this account, through his bap- tism the faithful layman receives at the same time the charge to *integrate* the earthly purpose of his life *into* his communion in grace with God in Christ. Thus the layman's earthly charge becomes part of his entirely God-centered attitude to life. One who is baptized, therefore, must integrate his in- volvement in the affairs of this world into his existence as a believer and member of the Church. In the very nature of the case, this means that the *typical* mark of the Christian lay status will be an apostolate carried on in and through direct concern with secular affairs.

In what does such an apostolate consist?

In order to determine precisely what the lay status is, at least insofar as it is a form of the visible embodiment of the Church in this world, we must always go back to baptism as the sacrament of our incorporation into the Church, and so, in Christ. Now, the Church is the historical and tangible form in which Christ's grace of victory visibly exists in this world. In and through the Church, the grace of God in Christ is present among us as an historical reality that we can grasp: " a sign raised up among the nations." Because of the Incarnation and its continuation in the Church as the earthly " Body of the Lord," this tangible and visible form of existence belongs to the very essence of Christian grace. Grace, wherever it takes on an historical, visible stature, is " the Church."

If incorporation into this visible communion in grace is then the first and direct effect of baptism, the believer receives in and with his baptism the charge to take his part in the essential function of the Church: he receives the charge to give, in and through his earthly life, a visible stature to his communion in grace with God. The life, the entire life of the baptized layman must consequently become the *visibility of grace*; through every given situation and in every moment his earthly life must be a " signum gratiae christianae " (a sign of Christian grace). Only in this way can the responsibility be fulfilled which all who are baptized bear together, for the Church and for its function as a sign in this world.

As a citizen, the layman is situated directly in a context of the worldly concerns (*in de " diesseitige " dimensie*) of this earthly life, but at the same time, as one who has been baptized, namely, as Christian layman in the Church, he has the charge to be " the Church " *in* his worldly situation. In other words, however, the Christian layman is placed in this world, the Church must find its visible manifestations in him: in his occupation, in his relations with his fellow men and in his dealings with things, in his family and its integration in the society and the nation; in short, in the entirety of his secular life. This living, rooted in the world, as a concrete manifestation of his security in God's grace and of his solicitude for the Kingdom of God, is *typical* of the Christian layman. We will analyse this further.

*   *   *   *

The world in which we live, the world of nature and history, goes back ultimately, not simply to the divine Creator, but more exactly to the divine Creator who desires to enter into personal relations with us. Through such personal communication with the living God our life in the world takes on deeper significance. Human freedom, to which God personally addresses himself, has also a creative function in respect of cultural values. Now, the fact is that God addresses us personally in order that we may find him now not merely indirectly, through natural realities and history, in other words, through our existence in the world; but that we may also enjoy direct, as it were vertical and immediate, relations with him in a personal intercourse with him, person speaking to person, even though it must be through the veil of faith without vision. God's personal design for us implies, therefore, that our meeting with God in his self-revelation as personal imposes as a basic requirement the raising of our eyes *from* the things of the world *to* God. It is precisely this elevation which must be given to the direction of our lives that naturally opens up at once the possibility of life in the cloister, side by side with Christian life in the world. (This point will not be developed further here.) For the Christian layman in the world this means that even his orientation towards secular affairs can sometimes involve making sacrifices and that, moreover, the layman as a Christian must anticipate such an occasion and hold himself in readiness to make the sacrifice. His involvement in secular affairs can never have the last word. (Neither is further development of this point undertaken here.) But it is precisely this personal communion with God, who is at the same time the Creator, that requires that the secular occupation of the layman be carried out entirely within the context of this dialogue with the living God. Together with God, with whom the Christian layman has a personal relation in Christ and in the Church, the layman assumes his personal responsibility in the history of this world. In this way his dialogue with the world, his creative effort to make

of the world a truly human dwelling-place, participates in his
entirely God-centered attitude to life, participates in his dialogue with God. We Christians too easily show an inclination to leave to unbelievers the secular ordering of temporal
society. We forget that concern for so-called " profane " affairs, the recognition of mundane realities, is an authentic
component of the entirely God-centered attitude to life. Secularisation or laicising in itself is a process that belongs within
the Christian life, within the Church, a process within the life
of the people of God. There is a certain ambiguity in these
words. Their sense is this: that the believer, *within* his dialogue with God, is led to give loyal recognition to earthly
reality too, with its own characteristically secular institutions.
Christian " secularisation " is thus utterly different from atheistic laicisation, which accepts earthly reality as the definitive
and exclusive horizon of life. Exclusively profane or atheistic
laicisation is objectively a heresy (Gr.: " hairesis "); it is a
tearing away of profane affairs, that is, earthly reality, from
the whole to which they belong. For they find their true
place only *within* the relation of existence and of faith which
binds man to God. Only when it is placed outside this context
is earthly reality " profaned."

This orientation towards secular affairs, what I may briefly
call " secular involvement " (*seculariteit*; Eng.: " secularity "),
is the foundation on which rests the specific character of lay
spirituality and of the lay apostolate in the Church. It implies
that the layman also sanctifies himself precisely in this secular involvement, and that his apostolic activity is carried on
first and foremost through this secular involvement. A mother
is a Christian as the mother of a family, a father as a father,
a teacher as a teacher, and so on. By making his contribution to the work of the world, by co-operating, each in his
own place, in the political, social and economic organisation
of temporal society, as tradesman, scientist or intellectual, the
Christian layman places himself in a personal relationship with
God. In this sense the grace given a layman is " lay " grace,

just as it has female characteristics for women, and male for
men: for it is from within his personal situation that each
stands in personal relationship to God. A mother, for example, is placed in personal contact with God through her very
motherhood too. This motherhood itself has a special significance for her existence as a Christian, just as her existence
as a Christian has significance for her motherhood. With his
whole human entity the layman enters personally into an
encounter with God. Though the layman must raise his eyes
from the world to God if he is to gaze full in his face, this
does not mean that he must forget his earthly task as though
this were an occupation from which God is excluded; on the
contrary, it obliges him to realise consciously the religious
dimension of this earthly task itself. If he does this, his secular task too takes on a Christian and apostolic significance.
It is *man*, after all, who is redeemed by Christ. And the entity of the man is not a naked soul; the entity of the man is
that spiritual, personal being who, through his own corporal-
ity and in communion with other men, exists in this world in
order, in and through the humanisation of the world, to hu-
manise himself also. It is in all his concrete reality that this
being is touched by grace and redeemed by Christ; not only
in the kernel of his soul, therefore, but, beginning from this
center of the person, also in his relations to his fellowmen and,
through them, in his relations to the whole world and to the
history of the world.

But redemption, at the same time, lays a *charge* on us.
In connection with the question which concerns us here, this
means that the mundane task of the Christian acquires a
more profound significance: it is co-redemptive. Through the
ordering of temporal society men are made more receptive to
grace and obstacles to salvation are removed. Further, the
tasks of earthly culture become the incarnation of the Christian commitment, in ordering life in this world to bring it into
harmony with the Kingdom of God. Natural and cultural
values must themselves be redeemed and by a redemption

that is not deferred to the end of time but that enters into the context of their history. To achieve this is the particular charge, within his total existence as a Christian, of the layman in the world. The apostolate carried out through responsibility for secular affairs, as the characteristic charge of the Christian layman, I have called here "*apostolic secular involvement.*" Proceeding from a spirit that is redeemed, it is a conscious commital of life to secular affairs within the dialogue with God; and so, in and through this secular task, it opens the world to receive the good tidings of the Word and, by speaking this Word, incarnates it in the world as a foretaste of the eschatological glorification of the body and of the " new heaven and earth." It is saints of this pattern that our world needs at the present moment. A new form of holiness must spread its light in the Christian layman's responsibility for this world— saints who grasp the dogma of creation in all its concrete significance. For *Church Life* (*kerkelijkheid*) means more than what takes its origin from the ecclesiastical hierarchy. Church life (*kerkelijk leven*) is just as much whatever has its origin in the faithful, the people of God, as the fruit of their eucharistic community of grace with Christ. Secular occupations must share in this life of the Church. Culture and all that human existence in the world embraces is not merely culture, that is, a task for man as such. It is a task for man as he is constituted by God; namely, as a being who, even in his very dealings with this world, comes into contact with grace. The risen Christ has significance for our whole life, including its worldly implications. Just as the religious state of perfection within this world is a sign of the future of the Kingdom of God, so the integral lay state in the world is a sign of how salvation exists *in* this world.

It will be seen that in this Christian conception of the lay state in the world the value of the work of human society is fully acknowledged. This conception liberates us, too, from the heresy of extrinsicism and individualism latent in the idea that one's disposition, a " good intention," makes action good (*de krypto-ketterij van het extrinsecisime en individualisme van de gezindheid of " goede mening ").* The fact that an action proceeds from charity (*het caritasmotief*) is not, of itself, enough. Or, more exactly, business efficiency, expertise and scientific knowledge, a sense of responsibility for the organisation of life in the world, all that the concrete task in temporal affairs essentially demands of us, must be absorbed into this God-centered " good intention." These are the earthly form and incarnation of the motive of Christian charity in the layman. Only in this fashion can the values of the material world be respected within the act of faith in divine creation. Only in this fashion, moreover, will the layman experience no break in continuity between his secular occupation and his Christian personality. It not infrequently happens that Christians think of their daily work, even though it takes up the principal part of their time, as something foreign to their being Christian; and so their state of mind fluctuates between an impression of the falseness of their lives as Christians, and then again of an incompatibility between their professional lives and their Christianity. The result often is that the layman either has only moderate interest in his religious practice, or else he swings to the other extreme and has less sense of responsibility and less professional zeal in work than the non-Christian, in the false belief, only half-consciously expressed, that his poor workmanship takes on Christian value by reason of his being in a state of grace and his so-called " good intention "; not forgetting either that it accumulates merit for heaven. How utterly different genuine Christianity in fact is! One example will suffice: that of nursing or health care. For the Christian lay person who is professionally concerned with it, such health care, which forms part of the general providence of society, is not merely a particular function in the universal process of humanising mankind in this world. Nevertheless, it is precisely in this context that this social service becomes a " sacrament of grace," an instrument of Christian fraternal charity. It gives concrete expression to God's love for men in the temporal and tangible form of skilled medical service to mankind. It is an apostolate carried on through trained care of the sick. The giving of skilled medical care and assistance is itself an incarnate witness to Christ's personal love addressing itself personally to men by way of this care of the sick. Here the technical and scientific equipment of modern medicine with its care and services is placed at the disposal of apostolic charity: it *is* this charity in a visible modern expression.

It goes, then, without saying that when we speak to God personally in prayer our task in the world is not something that must be passed over in silence. On the contrary, it should be a subject of conversation; not with the purpose of discovering in prayer more about the technical aspects of our secular work, as prayer obviously cannot teach us anything about that; but primarily in order, in our personal encounter with God, to realise in detail how this secular occupation fits into the economy of salvation, in order to purify our intention and to arouse our desire of saving others. Whenever, in the course of the day, we are working together with God, we may also speak to God about our work. The layman's life of prayer, which still must be truly *prayer*, acquires in this way a colouring different from that of, for example, the religious. His lay occupation is a form-giving principle of his lay spirituality. Even in his personal encounter with God the layman is not simply a Christian, with all the characterstic interests of a Christian as a member of the Kingdom of God; he is also a *layman*. He stands before God in prayer with all his concern for this world. His desire is certainly to deepen his belief in the Kingdom of God and to draw from prayer the strength to devote himself entirely to the service of this Kingdom; still he must realise that his secular occupation is something which cannot be indifferent to the divine overlordship. It is precisely because the layman *personally shares*, through grace, in God's own creative love for the world, that he becomes conscious—and first of all in his prayer—that his secular occupation has a positive, divine, redemptive sense, a significance in the economy of salvation.

From this lay point of view, taking account, that is, of the laity's orientation towards secular affairs, the general Christian apostolic activities of the layman as *Christian* may also be clarified. Thus the function to be fulfilled *in the Church* by the Christian as one who is baptized, confirmed and strengthened by the eucharistic sacrifice, will also always be determined by the layman's characteristic position in the world. A suggestive example of this is the duty laid on the layman by the sacrament of marriage. In the family the preaching of the word of God, for example, is primarily the duty of the parents by reason of the function given them *in the Church* by their marriage, insofar as it is the marriage of people who are baptized. The layman must also be witness in his characteristically lay fashion, in word and action, to the Word of God. He may even be entrusted with the exposition of the Word of God, as a lecturer in theology, although the true " kerygma " or " ministry of the Word " (Acts 6, 4) does not pertain to him, since it is part of the hierarchy's apostolate. Further, since the layman shares in responsibility for the salvation of the Church and of mankind, he too has a *right to speak*. There is place in the Church, as Pius XII indicated, for " public opinion " and open discussion in which the layman may put forward his own point of view. In whatever concerns the salvation of mankind the layman too has a *right* to intervene by word and by action. This right is based on the mission received from the Church by one who bears the characters of baptism and confirmation; it is based too on the charism of the Holy Spirit given him in connection with this mission from the Church. There can therefore be categories of people who become lay apostles and who devote themselves exclusively by vocation to all kinds of Church apostolate; but this will always be as lay people. Others, meanwhile, will employ only their free time to making themselves useful to the Church in some particular fashion, over and above their general lay apostolate. The hierarchy, as guardian of all that pertains to the life of the Church, has consequently the obligation to respect and encourage the characteristically lay form of Church life. A layman, especially if he is an intellectual or has received some form of higher education, has his own view about several aspects of the Church. Exerting *moral influence,* he can from time to time assert himself vigorously. The very fact that he is a layman opens his eyes to aspects which perhaps escape the notice of the hierarchy. Whenever he complains about the cultural inertia of Catholics, the Church ought to listen and weigh his comments on their merits. But in all this specifically lay Christian activity in the Church the laity never act in an *authoritative* capacity; that is the prerogative of the hierarchy. This implies that the entire lay activity of a Christian in the Church falls under the control of ecclesiastical authority. This means likewise that the entire activity of the layman in the Church and the world can in no respect really participate in the hierarchical functions of teaching, government or pastoral care.

Is not this last statement explicitly contradicted by the various forms of Catholic Action which has been defined as " participation by the laity in the apostolate of the hierarchy "?

This requires close attention. After a first and still tentative period in which, during the pontificate of Pius XI, the phrase " lay *participation* in the hierarchical apostolate " was in fact employed, this terminology later disappeared completely from papal documents on Catholic Action and the lay apostolate. In these there is now mention only of " *cooperatio,*" co-operation, of the laity with the hierarchy. This is not simply a question of words. For lay co-operation or collaboration with the hierarchy alters in no way the lay status of the layman and consequently (the term) points at the same time to the characteristically lay sphere in which such co-operation is to be exercised. It indicates too the limits of this co-operation, making it clear that the layman can co-operate only as a *layman,* and therefore by reason of his specifically lay apostolate; and that, consequently, he can never " play " the lay-pastor or the lay-deacon. *Apostolic secular involvement,*

considered precisely as organised co-operation with the clerical apostolate, remains therefore the specifically lay contribution in this collaboration of the laity and the ecclesiastical
hierarchy. The priesthood and the diaconate alone are genuine *participations* in the apostolic office of the ecclesiastical
hierarchy; but precisely by reason of this participation priests
and deacons are no longer laymen; they are clerics, even if
they wear secular clothes and even in the event of their being
married. (This point of view does not date only from the pontificate of Pius XII; we can find it already explicitly proposed
by, for example, Clement of Alexandria and Origen who make
a clear distinction between the laity on the one hand and the
episcopate, priesthood and diaconate on the other.)

Immediate *co-operation* of laymen, on the contrary, with the
ecclesiastical hierarchy, even when it takes the form of fulltime occupation and consequently requires that a person give
up his secular place in the *world*, remains in the category
of the occupation of the *layman* in the *Church*. (This is contrary to Karl Rahner's opinion on the matter, but is in conformity with Pius XII's address to the last Lay Congress in
Rome.) This category corresponds ultimately to what in the
early Church was the sphere of the minor orders and the sub-
diaconate (at that time a minor order). These orders are of
their nature *lay*, but their functions constitute direct co-operation with the apostolate of the hierarchy (although at the
present time these orders, at least in the Code of Canon Law
which is always subject to change, are considered simply as
steps to the diaconate and priesthood and consequently, *on
this account*, are also called clerical). Such lay functions, carrying with them an obligation to co-operate with the hierarchy, therefore, by their very nature do not require ordination, but simply an ecclesiastical nomination, or mandate,
from the hierarchy. (Up to the early Middle Ages the minor
orders and even the sub-diaconate *were never conferred by an
ordination*; an ecclesiastical nomination sufficed. In later
times, by analogy with the diaconate and the priesthood, this

nomination or mandate was accompanied by an ordination which, consequently, is not a true sacrament but simply a sacramental.)

The desire, expressed by lay people and priests, that laymen who devote their whole lives to such an organised form of apostolate in Catholic Action should also receive an *ordination* is theologically unjustified. It is obvious that laymen who, for example, on the missions *in fact* fulfill the functions which pertain to the apostolate of the diaconate should be made eligible for the order itself and so by ordination should become clerics. But ordination is never just a formality! What we now call Catholic Action is, therefore, nothing other than a *modern* form of the old idea of the " minor orders "; namely, the function in which a lay believer gains competency and mandate to collaborate directly with the activity of the hierarchy. This co-operation can, in accordance with the needs of the Church, take on many shapes; in the course of the Church's history its forms have undergone various changes. The following are some examples: assistance in public worship, acting as sacristan or altar-server, the administration of Church property, keeping Church accounts (this was not infrequently entrusted to subdeacons even in the Middle Ages), acting as secretary to a bishop or priest, as a member of the choir, as a reader at church services when there is no deacon. Besides these, all sorts of new and modern forms can be suggested: lay representation among the officials of the diocesan court, lay agencies which would be commissioned by the ecclesiastical authorities to undertake religio-sociographical studies directed towards achieving better results from the hierarchical apostolate; assistance in governing the Church insofar as this government requires various specialisations: canonical, theological, philosophical, sociological and so forth; (so, for example, a great deal of the work now done exclusively by priests in the Roman Congregations and in all sorts of Church activities and organisations could be handled by laymen); further, organisations of laymen for the formation and instruction of

Christians in view of their own lay apostolate in the world, namely, in the family, in the professions and trades, in the public life of the state, and so on; or again, lay organisations to uphold the rights of the Church in public life, or laymen who act as fulltime leaders even of organisations with a specifically religious purpose, etc., etc. I might be able to formulate it as follows: it is a question, not of lay *participation*, but of lay assistance in the exercise of the apostolic function of the ecclesiastical hierarchy. In other words, it is rendering *lay assistance*, whether to the teaching authority of the Church, or to the governmental functions of the Church, or to the sanctifying and pastoral duties of the priesthood. Lay assistance: this signifies consequently co-operation with the apostolate of the hierarchy *insofar as* the latter necessarily includes *secular involvement*. And this secular involvement penetrates deeply into the apostolate of the hierarchy which must of course direct itself towards contemporary mankind with all its human problems, which become problems too for the apostolate of the hierarchy of the Church.

This whole set of problems can no longer be surveyed without the co-operation of the laity who, with their competence in secular affairs, can throw a great deal of light on these matters. It was to just such lay people, devoting themselves fulltime to this kind of apostolic activity that the minor orders were given in the early Church; that is, such persons were appointed by the Church in this way to their official function. Since it is a question of co-operation with the specifically hierarchical apostolate, clearly the hierarchy, although making an appeal for professional work pertaining properly to the layman's competence, always maintains immediate directive control over this form of the lay apostolate (in contrast to the general lay apostolate). For in such co-operation with the hierarchy lay apostles place themselves in complete dependence on the ecclesiastical hierarchy to the immediate service of which they dedicate their secular skills. We may put it this way: the common general lay apostolate moves in the sphere of the world, but as proceeding from the apostolic spirit of a Christian and a member of the Church; it also moves in the sphere of the Church, but there as proceeding from the lay position of one who is baptized and confirmed. Lay co-operation with the apostolate of the hierarchy, on the contrary, moves in the sphere of the ecclesiastical hierarchy, *at least insofar* as this sphere includes secular involvement, that secular involvement which is the proper sphere of the layman.

So we see that the Christian layman bears responsibility both towards the Church and towards the world, and that his apostolic secular involvement is at the service of both Church and world.

POSSIBLE DANGERS OF THE PRESENT-DAY AWARENESS OF THE CHRISTIAN LAITY

We must accept fully the consequences of this lay spirituality. This growth of awareness demands a certain realignment of mentality also on the part of clerics. *Insight* into the specific role of the layman is not sufficient. It is *said* easily enough that the layman must assume more responsibility, but from the moment that laymen actually do this and put forward an opinion quite different from one held by the clergy the alarm bell is sounded in parish and religious houses. In the light of lay experience certain new emphases will sometimes be laid, perhaps even certain aspects in the faith will be brought to light which formerly were not wholly apparent to the clergy with their specifically clerical experience. Besides all this, from the moment that two Christian adults come into contact with one another in the performance of any task, even if one has a position of authority while the other truly possesses a spirit of obedience based on faith and submission to the Church, then it is in the course of nature that friction can no longer be avoided, just as friction between pastors and their bishops cannot be wholly eliminated. It is naturally true that, by reason of the still brief history of Christian self-awareness of the layman in the Church, the laity do not yet know exactly where the limits of their active function in the Church lie. I should say: they do not know this because the theologians themselves do not yet properly know it and because this whole new experience has not yet been fully thought out on the theological level. In these circumstances it need not surprise us if the layman, conscious that he holds his own place and significance in the Church, will sometimes here and there act as though he were the vicar and successor, perhaps not of Peter, but at least of Paul, the unruly one.

We must give the laity time and room so that they may feel their way, guided by the Church and enlightened by theologians (not necessarily priests), towards their own function in the Church, moved as they are by the charism of the Holy Spirit. Now and again mistakes will be made in one direction or another. The clerics themselves in their attempts to define their precise clerical task, have at times been guilty of thoroughgoing " clericalisation " and so have moved outside their own territory. They must not, then, be waiting to pounce if, in his turn, the layman now and again " laicises," or even tries to " clericalise " himself and act as though he were parish priest. Nevertheless, these are the two principal dangers the layman must be on his guard against: on the one hand, that in his loyal recognition of secular reality, in whatever sphere it may be, he will allow himself to become so absorbed in secular involvement that he will forget the dialogue with God, and through his sympathy for the institutions of the secular order, he will lose his feeling for the breath of the Spirit who sometimes breathes out over all institutions; and on the other hand, the danger (which threatens primarily the second form of lay apostolate) that the layman's collaboration with the hierarchy will lead him to arrogate to himself clerical airs, that he will take up an attitude as though the day of the priest in the Church were now ended and as though he, the layman, were now the one to assume care for the salvation of men and of the Church; the danger, in a word, that the layman will consider himself emancipated from the hierarchy.

All the same that does not mean that the layman is simply an executive of official Church decisions. The layman has his own choice which is itself *of the Church*; he has his own task to fulfill which is of the Church. This is a consequence of the mandate of a baptized, confirmed and married Christian. This mandate, through the eucharistic celebration of the whole Church and hence of the layman himself, is continually stimulated and nourished in charismatic fashion until it is activated in word and action which are the expression of his hidden union in grace with Christ and with the whole Church. It is precisely for this reason that in Canon Law too the special activity of the layman in the Church should be given canonical *protection* just as, for example, the special pastoral activity of a parish priest is protected in the Code against possible abuse of episcopal authority. Until the dogmatic notions of the Christian laity are also given canonical structure the layman remains powerless, and may, after enduring as many conflicts as he can support, throw over the whole enterprise. Such canonical protection does not involve any partial withdrawal of the laity from ecclesiastical authority. On the contrary, it is a canonical, authoritative recognition of the particularly lay form of membership of the Church which belongs to the Christian layman.

Much more should properly be said about the full dimensions of the *Christian-being* of the layman, and about the full range of the *lay-being* of the Christian. Further, we should like to contrast the position of the layman in the world with that of lay people who are in religious orders (not priests) and with that of laymen in secular institutes. But this article was intended simply as a general survey. I should like to conclude by stressing once again the fact that the lay believer also belongs to the " great Sign that has been raised up among the nations," a Sign which reveals to all men something vital in this society which calls itself the Church of Christ, something so intriguing that this society becomes for them a truly irresistible invitation to enter into it themselves or to live in it more fervently and more consistently.

E. H. Schillebeeckx, O. P.

Nijmegen, Holland

THE THEOLOGICAL FOUNDATION OF THE
LAY APOSTOLATE

ॐ

The Theology of the Lay Apostolate: Doctrinal and Experimental

THE theology of the lay apostolate cannot be based exclusively on abstract principles, or more correctly on the objective and normative events of Salvation's history narrated in the Holy Scripture, but it must also take into account the facts of the Christian experiences of today. These facts are nothing else than the continuation of the sacred history in the time of the Church under the guidance of the Holy Spirit. An example might make this clearer: the theology of mystical experience is not simply a deduction of what it should be, given the nature of grace, faith and charity, but also an induction of the phenomena of mystical experiences, as they appear, under varied forms in history. We cannot tell exactly what mystical experience should be without considering what it was in history. In the same fashion we cannot say what the lay apostolate should be without paying attention to its diverse manifestations in our times. Theological investigation here must be at the same time doctrinal and experimental. It must try to obtain an understanding of the mission of the Church and of the participation of the laity in that mission. On the other hand the theological inquiry must consider, recognize and respect the variety and the diversity of the callings, orientations and inspirations present in the community life of the Church. Practically this means that the lay apostolate cannot be reduced to any one formula: Catholic action, the Legion of Mary, or the new secular institutes. There has sometimes been an unilateralism, e. g., social action versus apostolic action, Catholic organizations versus free uninstitutionalized apostolate, Catholic action versus everything else, which does not respect the unity and diversity of the gifts of God.

The central theme

The central theme on which depends the full understanding of the vocation and the mission of laymen is probably the relation between the Church and the World. This theme can be evoked under many names. Fr. Congar in his great book [1] calls it: "The position of the laity, Kingdom, Church and World." Pope Paul VI, when Archbishop Milan, formulated the problem in the II World Congress for the Lay Apostolate in very precise terms. In relation to the distinction between the sacred and the profane:

The mission of the Church is to bring the sacred into a determined relationship with the profane in such a manner that the former will not be contaminated but communicated, and the latter will not be altered but sanctified." [2]

Whatever be the definition of the layman (and it is still rather vague in theology), he is doubtless a Christian who remains engaged in the profane tasks and responsibilities of the world. Therefore the value of his vocation and his action *as* a service to the world is of decisive interest for him. But at the same time his participation in the priestly, prophetical and kingly offices of the Church cannot be forgotten. So that in order to understand the apostolate of the laity, we have to start from the two great aspects of the design of God in mankind: the act of creation and the act of the mission of the Holy Trinity. By the first God communicates being to His creatures and especially to man made in His image. By the second God communicates the very eternal life of the Holy Trinity through the mission of the Son and the mission of the Holy Spirit. It is the

[1] Yves M. J. Congar, *Lay People in the Church, A Study for a Theology of the Laity*, Tr. by Donald Attwater, (Westminster, Maryland: Newman Press, 3rd imp. 1962) Ch. III.

[2] *The Mission of the Church*, in Major Documents on Catholic Action from the Second World Congress of the Lay Apostolate (Rome, Oct. 6-13, 1957), (Notre Dame: National Catholic Action Study Bureau, 1958), p. 51.

two-fold response of the Christian to these divine manifestations which explains the totality of the lay apostolate.

The design of God

In order to organize the various elements which come into
play here, Fr. Congar in his book *Lay People in the Church*
goes back to a fundamental vision which is the design of God
for the world and the successive realization of this divine will.
God's purpose is to constitute his kingdom. " And this his good
pleasure he purposed in him, to be dispensed in the fullness of
the times: to re-establish all things in Christ, both those in
the heavens and those on the earth " (Eph. 1 : 9-10). When
Christ is sent in " the fullness of the times," in the center of
history, everything is already given in his person and his mystery. The last times have come. The spiritual gifts are already
really present and we apprehend them by faith, " the substance of things to be hoped for " (Heb. 11 : 1) ; and by hope,
but in the mystery: " And in him you too, when you had heard
the word of truth, the good news of your salvation, and believed in it, were sealed with the Holy Spirit of the promise,
who is the pledge of our inheritance, for a redemption of possession, for the praise of his glory " (Eph. 1: 13-14). The kingdom is here, " The kingdom of God is in the midst of you "
(Lk. 17 : 21), but it does not yet irradiate all its glory. Redemption does not yet produce all its final and eschatological
effects in the transfiguration of the cosmos. We are still oriented towards a future which is that of the new heaven and the
new earth and we groan in expectation with the whole creation
which " awaits the revelation of the sons of God " (Rom. 8 : 19-
22). Between the first coming of Christ and the end of the
world or the second coming, time does not stand still; there is
still a history. These two stages, present and future, of the
kingdom, these two aspects of the kingship of Christ lead us to
recognize the duality of the Church and the world. In this
actual period of redemption realized, but not yet glorious, time
will appear to us as the time of the in-between: the time of the
Church, the time of the mission and of the expansion of the

kingdom of God to "all nations." The time which is also, as regards our options, the time of freedom, of choice and decision.

In the actual economy sacred or "ecclesial" time does not absorb cosmic time which still goes on as an ambiguous time subjected to, but also offered for, redemption.[3] Therefore the salvation in Christ does not eliminate a permanency of the world as the order of nature, whence illness and suffering; and a permanency of the world as the place of evil, partially submitted to the prince of the world, whence sin. "For the mystery of iniquity is already at work" (2 Thes. 2:7).

The act of Creation

At the same time the world as the creation of God, basically good in itself, has its own relative ends: the achievement of more human civilizations. The creation is also already Christo-logical, because it was made by the Word of God who is the Son (Jn. 1:3; Heb. 1:2) and because it is pre-ordained to and actually assumed by redemption and ultimately oriented to the achievement of the Kingdom of God. This is strongly recognized, but somewhat simplified in the "Christified cosmo-genesis" of Teilhard de Chardin. The time of the in-between remains very complex and obliges us to maintain a distinction between the Church and the world and to discern how the one and the other have a proper and specific relationship to the ulti-mate goal which is the one and unique kingdom of God. Thus the layman, in his specific task which is the "*conservatio mundi*," the bringing of all human works and activities into the sphere of the redeeming power of Christ, refers human history to its ultimate accomplishment in the *Parousia*, if he respects the relative ends of these activities.

The Mission of the Holy Trinity

Let us consider now the mission of the Holy Trinity which is the origin of every mission, office and service in the Church.

[3] Jean Mouroux, *Le Mystère du temps. Approche Théologique* (Paris: Aubier, 1962), Ch. VIII.

The Church is formed not only by the creative act of the omnipotence of God but by a second act which communicates to human persons the very life of God. For the operations *ad extra*, the activity of God in the world, must be attributed in common to the Divine Persons. The Church is therefore, before anything else, a *Corpus Trinitatis*,[4] a body in which the human persons are united in the participation of the life which flows from the Holy Trinity. The structure and the mission of the Church depends therefore on the economy of the divine missions. The eternal act of the Father is the primary origin of the Church. In his first discourse St. Peter relates all the events of Christ to "the settled purpose and foreknowledge of God " (Act 2 : 23), and St. Paul blesses the Father of our Lord Jesus Christ who "chose us in him before the foundation of the world " and "predestined us to be adopted through Jesus Christ as his sons " (Eph. 1 : 3-6). The Father *sends* the Son: "For God so loved the world that he gave his only-begotten Son, that those who believe in him may not perish, but may have life everlasting. For God did not send his Son into the world in order to judge the world, but that the world might be saved through him " (Jn. 3 : 16-17; Mat. 10 : 40; 15 : 24; 21 : 27; Lk. 4 : 43; 9 : 48). The whole industry of Christ depends on that original mission.[5] The risen Lord sends the Holy Spirit, who is his spirit, to be the animating soul of the young and incipient Church. Jesus himself has been baptized into his mission by the unction of the Holy Spirit. The Spirit descends upon him (Lk. 3 : 22), he is "full of the Holy Spirit " (Lk. 4 : 1), he goes to Galilee "in the power of the Spirit " (Lk. 4 : 14), and finally he applies to himself the famous text of Isaia (61 : 1-3) in which His Servant is anointed by the Lord to his messianic mission: "The Spirit of the Lord is upon me because he has anointed me; to bring good news to the poor he

---

[4] "quoniam ubi tres, id est pater et filius et spiritus sanctus, ibi ecclesia quae trium corpus est " Tertullian, *De Baptismo*, VI, 2.

[5] Thus the Son is said to be sent by the Father into the world, inasmuch as he began to exist visibly in the world by taking our nature; whereas *He was* previously *in the world* (Jn. 1:1)," (S. Th. I, q. 43, a. 1).

has sent me, to proclaim to the captives release, and sight to the blind; to set at liberty the oppressed, to proclaim the acceptable year of the Lord " (Lk. 5: 18-19). Similarly in virtue of the absolute authority and power which have been given to Christ, he commissioned his apostles to continue his mission (Mat. 28 : 16-20; Lk. 9:2; Lk. 10 : 1). The mission of the apostles comes from the Father and the Son, as St. Paul proclaims at the beginning of many epistles: " Paul, an Apostle, sent not from men nor by man, but by Jesus Christ and God the Father " (Gal. 1 : 1; 1 Cor. 1 : 1; 2 Cor. 1 : 1; Eph. 1 : 1; 1 Tim. 1 : 1; 2 Tim. 1 : 1).

The unity of the mission coming from God became a traditional doctrine. Tertullian expresses it in a classic manner: " *Ecclesiae ab apostolis, apostoli a Christo, Christus a Deo.*" [6] But this mission must be sustained, nourished, enlightened, strengthened by the presence of the Holy Spirit.[7] The Spirit will bring back to the mind whatever Christ has said (Jn. 14:26), he is the spirit of truth (Jn. 14: 16), he will bear witness to Christ and as a consequence the apostles also will bear witness (Jn. 15:26-27). Actually the first preaching of the Church, and the performance of the prophetical gift that the prophet Joel (3 : 1-2) had foreseen for the sons and daughters of Israel starts with the pentecostal gift of the Holy Spirit (Acts 2 : 4; 2 : 16-18; 2 :33). The unity of the divine mission and the diversity of its aspects depend ultimately on the " *agape* " of God who has loved the world. The purpose and the structure of this mission are thereby manifested and we can draw the obvious consequences for the nature of the Church and of her apostolate.

The reason there is a Church, and one Church, is because the love and the eternal life of God have been communicated to mankind in the death, resurrection and exaltation of Christ, the Head of the Church (Col. 1 : 18-20), the High Priest of

---

[6] *De Prescriptione*, 21, 4 and 37, 1.

[7] Yves M. Y. Congar, *The Mystery of the Church,* tr. by A. V. Littledale (Baltimore: Helicon Press, 1960), Ch. VI, " The Holy Spirit and the Apostolic Body: continuators of the work of Christ."

the new covenant (Heb. 5:1-10), the new Adam of a new
humanity: " the last Adam became a life-giving Spirit " (1 Cor.
15:45; Rom. 5:12-21). The Church is the gathering of divided
mankind into the unity of the love and the life that came from
God. She is the instrument and the sign of the reconciliation
of man to God in Christ, of man with men, of man with himself, and of man with the cosmos. She is already this reconciliation partially and mysteriously achieved, but still growing to
" the mature measure of the fullness of Christ " (Eph. 4:13).
Jews and Gentiles, i. e., all nations, have access through Christ
" in one spirit to the Father." Therefore we are no longer
strangers and foreigners, but we are " citizens with the saints
and members of God's household " (Eph. 2:19; 2:11-22).
Christ has become the peace of the world, he has broken down
" the intervening wall of the enclosure," and therefore he has
made possible for mankind to become in peace and unity the
temple of the Lord and the " dwelling place for God in the
Spirit " (Eph. 2:21-22). We do not know the dimensions of
the temple and many are building it and are part of it invisibly.
" Many," says St. Augustine, " seem to be within who are in
reality without and others seem to be without who are in
reality within." [8]

The Church is also a communion in faith, hope and charity,
which is expressed, signified and realized in the unity of faith
preached and kept by the Church and in the unity of the
sacraments. The creator of this unity is especially the personal
love, which is the Holy Spirit, the soul of the Church.[9] The
communication of the eternal life and the presence of the Holy

[8] *Sermo* 354, 2, 2 (P. L. 39, 1564) quoted with other references of St. Augustine
on the same subject in Yves M. Y. Congar, *The Mystery of the Temple or
The Manner of God's Presence to His Creatures from Genesis to Apocalypse*
(Westminster, Maryland: Newman Press, 1962), p. 197 ff.

[9] " For in one Spirit we were all baptized into one body " (1 Cor. 12:13; 1 Cor.
1:4-11). Cf. Leo XIII, Encyclical *Divinum illud munus*; Pius XII, Encyclical
Mystici Corporis. St. Augustine writes: " quod autem est anima corpori hominis,
hoc est Spiritus Sanctus corpori Christi, quod est Ecclesia " (*Sermo* 267, IV, 4; P. L.
t. 38, c. 1231). St. Thomas compares the role of the Spirit to that of the heart:
" Et ideo cordi comparatur Spiritus sanctus qui invisibiliter Ecclesiam vivificat et
unit " (S. T. III, q. 8, a. 1, ad 3).

Spirit are explicitly creators of unity. This unity is also effected and made visible in the Eucharist. The mission of the Church leads to the Eucharist, because she is realized as the mystical body of Christ in her communion to the real body of Christ.[10] This is the reason why, especially before the eleventh century, the expression " mystical body " was primarily attached to the Eucharist and subsequently passed from the Eucharist to the Church, as from the significant to the signified.[11]

From these deep and inner sources pertaining to the very essence of the Church springs the apostolate and, obviously, its high sacred quality should be respected. The apostolate is not at all like the effort of a human, even a moral, society to increase the number of its members, but is, in fact, the communication of the eternal life and the manifestation of the love of God to mankind. By their very nature the divine realities which constitute the Church are universal. They are valid, significant and necessary for all men, and tend towards actual universality. The design of God, the death and the resurrection of Christ, the communion of the Holy Spirit embrace all men. Nobody is a priori excluded from the meaningful tragedy and triumph in which he has been created to be an actor and a communicant. The energies of the divine life, communicated through Christ in the faith and the sacraments of the Church, originate a movement which is less to bring people from without to within the bond of the Church, than to extend from within the " communion " of the Spirit and the Eucharist to the people who are without,[12] in order to realize with them the reconciled mankind of the new creation as it is willed by God. The mission of the Church is not accidental to her being, it is not a matter of choice; it is her being as the total body of Christ

---

[10] " Res hujus sacramenti est unitas corporis mystici " (S. T. III, q. 73, a. 3). Cf. other references in J. Hamer, *L'Eglise est une communion* (Paris: Cerf, 1962), p. 83 ff.

[11] H. de Lubac, *Corpus Mysticum. L'Eucharistie et l'Eglise au Moyen Age* (Paris: Aubier, 2d ed. 1949), p. 47 ff.

[12] Cf. a good explanation of " the communion " in the introduction of Anne Fremantle to *The Papal Encyclicals in their Historical Context* (New York: New American Library Mentor Books, 4th pr. 1960), p. 22 ff.

in its way towards realization. From this theological point of
view the distinction between the mission of the Church and
the specific missionary activity of preaching the Gospel where
it is unheard of, or of planting the Church where she is unknown, is secondary. All the texts of the New Testament in
which the Church is explicitly commissioned to continue the
ministry of Christ are apostolic and "missionary" (Mt. 28:
16-20; Lk. 24:47-49; Jn. 20:21-24; Acts 1:7-8). There is no
sharp distinction between a pastoral and an apostolic activity.[13] The missionary responsibility is given to the whole
Church, to each particular Church and to each Christian who,
in the Church, is sent to the world: "as thou hast sent me

[13] Such a sharp distinction made by the exponents of "missiology" does not
seem convincing, v. g.: "The ordinary ecclesiastical ministry is twofold: *pastoral*
(for the care of the faithful in the Church), and *apostolic* (for the conversion to
the Church)," Andrew V. Seumois, O. M. I., "The Evolution of Mission Theology
Among Roman Catholics," in *The Theology of the Christian Mission*, ed. by
Gerald H. Anderson, (New York: McGraw-Hill, 1961), p. 130. It is of course
true that we may distinguish different kinds of apostolate and amongst them a
typical missionary activity, as we can distinguish in theology a set of problems
covered by "missiology." Thus we had in recent years: "pastoral," "kerygmatic,"
"catechetic," "lay," etc., theologies. This development has been extremely useful,
because it is also true that: "there was a degree of proud contempt from some
theologians, perhaps very competent in traditional scholastic disputations, who
were not inclined to leave the sphere of speculation in order to devote doctrinal
study to the complex ecclesiological realm of missionary realities" (*Ibid.*, p. 129).
But it should not be forgotten that there is basically one "mission" of the
Church, as there is one theology. The theological and practical fragmentation may
lead to opposite results than those which are pursued. For instance: does an
established and institutionalized local Church cease to be "apostolic" in order
to be "pastoral"? Is the missionary activity the work of a small number of
specialists or a responsibility for every Christian? Does the primary task of the
Church of announcing the Gospel and converting people cease ever to be the
primary task of any Church? The relative failure of the Christian missions and
the relative weakness of the Christian witness before racial segregation, the misery
of underdeveloped countries, the international tensions come from the fact that
these things are left to specialists. They are not felt as a common responsibility
of the whole Christian community in the so-called Christian countries where the
Churches are supposed to be "established" and for that very reason, cease precisely in many instances to be "apostolic," i. e., to feel responsible and concerned
for the unevangelized world. The basic error is that in the fragmentation in so
many "theologies," the true nature of the Church and of her "mission" which are
the same everywhere and for every Christian are not seen any more. It is one
more case of the trees hiding the forest.

into the world, so I also have sent them into the world " (Jn. 17:18). The whole Church is in a perpetual state of mission and of movement. Her mission is identical to her being. A Church which would stop being " sent " would not be a Church anymore. Because she is holy, the Church must communicate holiness; she must sanctify in being the instrumental communication of the dynamic divine realities which are present in her. Because she is one, she is bringing the unity of the love of God to mankind, preserving " the unity of the Spirit in the bond of peace: one body and one Spirit, even as you were called in one hope of your calling; one Lord, one faith, one baptism; one God and Father of all who is above all, and throughout all, and in us all " (Eph. 4:3-6). Because the Church is apostolic, her mission is the continuation of the mission of the apostles and through them of the mission of Christ. Because she is catholic, i.e., universal, the Church needs the world and the different races and cultures to express more fully the mystery of redemption, and the world needs the Church to have its science, its art, its work fully realized and consecrated. It is obvious that the apostolate which springs thus from the essential properties of the Church must retain their quality. The apostolate is not a conquest or a crusade. It is not a kind of spiritual colonialism which destroys the freedom and the human quality of the colonized. It is not animated by a spirit of domination, by an unconscious pharisaical pride, by a pretentious will of power and of influence. The apostolate is not a propaganda or a publicity which can use psychological or sociological pressures. When it ceases to be authentic, i. e., to use means which are on the same level as its end—the communication of the mystery of Christ—the apostolate destroys itself even if it seems to be humanly successful. That kind of success will be paid for later on by a more tragic spiritual failure. It would not be difficult to find examples of this in the past and present history of the Church. The servant is not greater than the master. The apostolate is a kind of invitation, addressed to persons as such. It is the highest interpersonal communication which necessarily awakens the maturity and the responsibility of spiritual decision. The unique motive of the apostolate is an authentic love.

The participation of the layman in the mission of the Church

If the mission of the Church is inseparable from her being, to participate in that mission is the same as being a Christian. The layman is committed to the mission of the Church by faith and the sacraments of faith. Faith normally cannot be divorced from the sacraments, and especially from baptism which is a sort of protestation of faith and is called " the sacrament of faith." [14] There is always in baptism a profession of faith. If it is not made by the adult individual, it is performed by the sponsors or by the Church. St. John Chrysostom even calls baptism a treaty passed with God by faith and the confession of faith.[15] As regards the lay apostolate it is important to notice that the sacrament of Christian initiation not only requires a confession of faith but obviously leads to a further working out of this confession. The new liturgical custom in the Easter liturgy to have the assembly renew their baptismal promises is full of signification. All the effects of baptism, as they are mentioned by tradition: the rebirth of a new creature (Jn. 3 : 5), the participation in the death and resurrection of Christ (Rom. 6 : 3-5), the illumination which transforms every Christian into a light put upon the candlestick that it may shine to all that are in the house, all these effects imply an apostolic dimension. In the last instance of the light, the connection is made by the Evangelist himself: " So let your light shine before men, that they may see your good works, and glorify your Father who is in heaven " (Jn. 1 : 9-12).[16] Furthermore by his baptism, the Christian is incorporated into the body of Christ (1 Cor. 12 : 13; Gal. 3 : 27-29)[17] in order to take part in the building up of that body in love (Eph. 4 : 7-16). This spiritual activity is fostered by the sacramental character which is the indelible effect of the Christian initiation. The

---

[14] S. T., III, q. 66, a. 1, ad 1; III, q. 70, a. 1; III, q. 71, a. 1: "Baptism is the sacrament of faith: since it is a profession of the Christian faith."

[15] Jean Chrysosthome, *Huit Catéchèses baptismales inédites,* ed. Antoine Wenger, a. a. (Paris: Cerf, 1957), Cat. IV, 31.

[16] A. d'Alès, S. J., *Baptism and Confirmation* (St. Louis: Herder, 1929), p. 75.

[17] Without excluding the reference to the personal Christ especially in verse 12,

sacramental character is a participation in Christ's priesthood [18] which gives the faithful a spiritual power to receive the other sacraments and " to be deputed to a spiritual service pertaining to the worship of God." [19] Though St. Thomas calls the baptismal character a " passive " [20] power to receive the sacraments, it is obvious by his comments that this power is a source of action. The character is passive as far as it is a seal: the sign of the consecration and the possession by the Spirit (2 Cor. 1:21-22), the sign of the assimilation to Christ, as the *Epistle to the Hebrews* calls Christ the figure, the " character," the express image of the substance of the Father (Heb. 1:3). But this seal of permanent consecration is also a deputation, a commission to take part, not only in the liturgy of the Church, in the divine worship which is by itself " a certain profession of faith by external signs," [21] but also in the accomplishment of the whole Christian life in love.

In the very first baptism rituals it was stressed that the

---

it is clear that St. Paul speaks also of the Church (1 Cor. 12:27-28), in spite of many different interpretations. Cf. Markus Barth, *Die Taufe ein Sakrament? Ein exegetischer Beitrag zum gespräch über die kirchliche Taufe* (Zürich: Zollikon, 1951), p. 318 ff.; S. T., III, q. 68, a. 1.

[18] " In a sacramental character Christ's faithful have a share in his priesthood; in the sense that as Christ has the full power of a spiritual priesthood, so his faithful are likened to him by sharing a certain spiritual power with regard to the sacraments and to things pertaining to the divine worship " (S. T., III, q. 63, a. 5).

[19] S. T., III, q. 63, a. 1.

[20] S. T., III, q. 63, a. 2.

[21] S. T., III, q. 63, a. 4, ad 3; " A character is a kind of seal by which the soul is marked, so that it may receive, or bestow on others, things pertaining to Divine worship. Now the divine worship consists in certain actions . . ." (S. T., III, q. 63, a. 4); grace is given to those who have received the character: " so that they may accomplish worthily the service to which they are deputed " (*Ibid.*, ad 1).

The activity of the character is well stressed in Colman O'Neill, O.P., " The Role of the Recipient and Sacramental Signification," *The Thomist*, 1958 (Vol. XXI), n. 3, p. 284 ff.; *ibid.*, n. 4, p. 508-540; also James E. Rea, *The Common Priesthood of the Members of the Mystical Body* (Westminster Md.: Newman Bookshop, 1947), p. 193: the passive potency " cannot be interpreted to mean that the faithful are ' inactive ' in the sacraments and in divine worship." These references were kindly communicated to me by my confrere Fr. P. Hanley, O.P., professor at the University of Notre Dame.

catechumens had been anointed with the same chrism with which "the priests and the prophets" had been anointed, sealing them for the service of God and the community: "for the implantation of faith in the robust and beautiful olive tree of Thy Church." [22] Baptism already deputes the layman to the profession of faith and Christian service, but this deputation is increased and perfected and more oriented towards the sharing in the apostolic work of the Church by confirmation. Confirmation is considered as giving a certain fullness in the Spirit, a Christian maturity, in which the faithful "receives the power of publicly confessing his faith by words, as it were *ex officio*." [23] It is for this "office" that the Christian is made perfect by the gifts of the Spirit. To be a witness of Christ depends on the power received from the Holy Spirit.[24] This was the promise of Christ and the apostles carried it on by the laying on of hands on the first converted (Heb. 8:14-20; 19:1-7).[25] This

[22] *Trois antiques rituels du baptême*, ed. by A. Salles (Coll. Sources Chretiennes, n. 59; Paris: Cerf, 1958), p. 49-50.

[23] S. T. III, q. 72, a. 5, ad 2.

[24] "You shall receive power when the Holy Spirit comes upon you, and you shall be witnesses for me in Jerusalem and in all Judea and Samaria and even to the very ends of the earth" (Acts. 1:8).

[25] We cannot enter here in the controversy between Catholics and Protestants, between Anglicans and Anglicans, Anglicans and Protestants, Protestants and Protestants, concerning the differences between Baptism and Confirmation. The situation on this point is confused indeed and very sad, especially since Karl Barth has attacked infant baptism (*The Teaching of the Church regarding Baptism*, London: S. C. M. Press, 1948), without decisive biblical justification (O. Cullmann, *Baptism in the New Testament*, Chicago: Henry Regnery, 1950). Lukas Vischer (*La confirmation au cours des siècles*, Neuchatel: Delachaux, 1959) thinks that the age of baptism should be free and accepts confirmation as an introduction to the holy scene or as a repeated profession of faith. André Benoit (*Le baptême chrétien au second siècle. La théologie des Pères*, Paris: Presses Universitaires, 1953), p. 224, does not find any sign of a confirmation in the Fathers of the II Century. Professor G. W. H. Lampe (*The Seal of the Spirit*, London, 1951) professes that the seal of the Spirit is given exclusively in baptism. L. S. Thornton, C. R., (*Confirmation, Its Place in the Baptismal Mystery*, London: Naere Press, 1954) maintains the validity of confirmation. This Anglican theologian makes a valuable remark against "the strange modern notion that a 'completion' of baptism in confirmation is derogatory to baptism. We might just as well say that the Spirit-history in the Acts is derogatory to the Christ-history in the Gospels! This is the unwholesome idea of completeness which we

does not mean that the Holy Spirit is not already given in baptism, but that there is a completion of the Christian initiation " with a commission to confess Christ officially and publicly, and thus to share Christ's mediatorial office of bringing the truth and the charity of God to others." [26] The fact that confirmation is usually given by the bishop, who is the responsible leader of the apostolic mission, is perhaps a sign that he associates the layman, not to his own power, but to his responsibility.[27]

Baptism and confirmation lead to the Eucharist which is " the end and the consummation of all the sacraments." [28] The Eucharist does not imprint in the Christian a character, a deputation, and at first sight it might seem that it has no apostolic signification. But this would be very odd in the sacrament which is the perfection of Christian life. If the Eucharist does not give a character, it is because " it contains within itself Christ, in whom there is not the character, but the very plenitude of the priesthood." [29] The implicit assumption (in this text of St. Thomas) is that the Eucharist bestows something more than the participation in Christ's priesthood which is given in baptism and confirmation. The real union with Christ himself, the unique and supreme Mediator of all men, necessarily involves the communicant in the work of redemption. Considered as the sacrifice of the Church which repeats sacramentally the unique event of the crucifixion for all men and for all times, the Eucharist commits the participant to the

---

found to be flatly contradictory to the perfection of the triune life in God. As the Persons of the Godhead are complementary to one another, so the dispensation of the Spirit is complementary to the work of the Redeemer. So also our identification with the Christ in his life-history through baptism is crowned by *his* bestowal of the Spirit in confirmation " (p. 183). For a complete account of the controversy and a Catholic solution see Bernard Leeming, S. J., *Principles of Sacramental Theology* (Westminster Md.: Newman Press, 2d ed. 1960), Ch. V and VI.

[26] Bernard Leeming, S. J., *op. cit.*, p. 238.

[27] S. T., III, q. 72, a. 8: " The final completion is reserved to the supreme act or power."

[28] S. T., III, q. 63, a. 6.

[29] *Ibidem.*

offering and the sacrifice for the salvation of the world.[30] In
its celebration the Christian community is proclaiming the
death of Christ as the unique salvific event for the past, the
present and the future. In the actual presence of Christ the
memory of the passion is made effective here and now and the
glory of the future is announced.[31] The Eucharist is the proclamation of the meaning of history in the mystery of Christ:
" For as often as you shall eat this bread and drink the cup,
you proclaim the death of the Lord, until he comes " (1 Cor.
11:26). This perfect sacrament is also the realization of the
Church and of her unity. " Because the bread is one, we though
many, are one body, all of us who partake of the one bread "
(1 Cor. 10: 17).[32] The Eucharist is certainly the end and the
final accomplishment of the apostolate and as such it generates
a desire of this sacrament explicit or implicit, without which
none can receive grace and be incorporated in Christ.[33] But
in the end is the beginning; the Eucharist is also the main
source of the apostolate. As the sacrament of charity and of
unity, it gives to its participants not only the spiritual nourishment for their own journey (3 Kings 19:8), but the impulse
to work in charity for unity.

As Gregory observes in a Homily for Pentecost, *God's love is never
idle; for, wherever it is, it does great works.* And consequently
through this sacrament, as far as its power is concerned, not only
is the habit of grace and of virtue bestowed, but it is furthermore
aroused to act, according to 2 Cor. 5:14: " the love of Christ
impels us.[34]

Starting from these theological principles, what are the different forms of the lay apostolate? It would be of course im-

---

[30] " The Eucharist is the perfect sacrament of our Lord's passion, as containing
Christ crucified " (S. T., III, q. 73, a. 5, ad 2).

[31] " O sacrum convivium in quo Christus sumitur, recolitur memoria passionis
ejus, mens impletur gratia et futurae gloriae nobis pignus datur " (Cf. also S. T.,
III, q. 73, a. 4).

[32] " The reality of the sacrament is the unity of the mystical body " (S. T., III,
q. 73, a. 3); *Ibid.*, a. 2, a. 4.

[33] S. T., III, q. 73, a. 3; III, q. 7, a. 1, ad 1.

[34] S. T., III, q. 79, a. 1, ad 2.

possible to mention all of them, but we can try to enumerate the great categories which have become almost classic in the Church.

The forms of the lay apostolate

The layman, by the sacraments he has received, is committed to an apostolate which is co-extensive or co-terminous with his vocation and his life as a Christian. This is the witness or the confession of faith. In the New Testament the idea of witnessing concerns primarily the Twelve Apostles as eye-witnesses of the historical events of the life of Jesus. But this quality is also applied to St. Paul (Acts 22:15) and to the first martyr Stephen (Acts 22:20). Neither of them is properly speaking an eye-witness in the historical sense but they have a profound knowledge of the mystery of Christ. Stephen is a witness because he is " full of the Spirit " (Acts 7:55). The quality of being a witness, though it belongs in a very special sense to the apostles who have accompanied the Lord Jesus during his life time and have become witnesses of his resurrection (Acts 1:21-22), is extended to other Christians. The original image of the Christian witness is the Crucified himself, who is crucified because of his witness. He is the " faithful witness ' (Ap. 1: 5; 3:14; 1 Tim. 6:13). He came into the world " to bear witness to the truth " (Jn. 18:31).

Christ's witness is confirmed by many other witnesses: those of the Father, the Spirit, the Scripture, John the Baptist, the prophets, the works and the sacraments of Christ (Jn. 5:31-39; 8:12-19; 1:6-9; 1:19; 1:32-34; 1 Jn. 1:1-3, 1 Jn. 5:7-12).[35] Those who believe will come into contact with the Son of God full of grace and truth, and will be made capable of giving their own testimony, not as eye-witnesses of the historical fact, but as believers rooted in the experience of their faith, because they have received in them the testimony of God (1 Jn. 5:7-12). The witness is not a teacher, or even less a propagandist. He has identified himself internally with the truth and there-

[35] Art. *Martus*, in Kittel, *Theologisches Worterbuch zum N. T.*, ed. G. Kittel.

fore will manifest it as if he were translucent. He has "the light of life" in himself (Jn. 8:11; Jn. 3:21). The idea of witnessing is very close to that of the confession of faith.[36] It is the expression of one's faith as enveloping the whole individual, family and social life and is manifested in many ways according to the circumstances. It is correlative to the Christian vocation and the basis of every other form of a more active participation. The Christian witness has no specialized applications or limited grounds. It is given as well in the active participation in the liturgy, in the reception of the sacraments which are a "protestation of faith," in the practice of one's family and professional life, as well as in the commitment to social and economic questions. No Christian is excused from this apostolate which is the Christian life itself lived consciously and seriously with all its consequences in every field.

The second group of apostolic lay activities is hard to define. It seems to include a delegation from the hierarchy, a canonical mission.[37] These are the people who consecrate a great part or most of their time to the service of the Church, especially in the teaching of sacred doctrine from scientific theology to catechism. Often now they are gathered in secular institutes. Pius XII has recognized the " missio canonica " of these helpers of the hierarchy by which they participate in the power to teach. But this participation does not change the nature of the lay apostolate and does not transform it into a "hierarchical apostolate." [38] Even when a layman receives the same mission as a priest, v. g., the teaching of theology, the apostolate of the first is lay and that of the second sacerdotal. Some years ago, Karl Rahner,[39] proposed the hypothesis that the lay people employed full time in the service of the Church, lost their lay

---

[36] Fr. Hamer, op. cit., p. 137 ff. insists much on the "homologia" (Rom. 10:9-10), the confession of faith as the basic concept of the lay apostolate.

[37] Hans Heimerl, Laien im Deuxt der Verkündigung. Laien mit mirkung an der Lehraufgabe der Kirche (Wien: Verlag Herder, 1958).

[38] Pius XII, Discourse to the Second World Congress for the Lay Apostolate (Notre-Dame: NFCCS, 1958), p. 8.

[39] Karl Rahner, Schriften zur Theologie (Einsideln: Benzinger, 1955), II, p. 339-373.

status, to become part of the hierarchical apostolate. But this opinion has been generally rejected by Pius XII and theologians,[40] because a real jurisdiction remains linked to the reception of orders. In other words the layman who is teaching theology or explaining the catechism has the authority of his science and his training, but not the authority of the Church. He has nevertheless a responsibility towards the mission which has been entrusted to him. The clerical theologian is in the same situation which is beneficial for the life and the creativity of Christian thinking. Can the layman receive the power to preach? The proclamation of the word of God in so far as it is an official and public mission in the Church, which is the continuation of the mission specifically given to the Apostles, seems to be the duty of bishops and priests. Preaching then is the privileged and indispensable communication of revelation (Rom. 10:14-15); it is authoritative and normative for the Christian life and is addressed to the obedience of faith. The word of God cannot be dissociated from the giving of the sacraments and appears to require the same kind of special mission. "How are men to preach unless they be sent"? (Rom. 10:15). All the spiritual strength of authentic (and rare) preaching comes from the fidelity of the preacher to the word of God and to the mission he has received from God. The examples of the prophets and the Apostles abound. The personality of the preacher is much less important than the authenticity of his mission and his own faith in it. He must be "under constraint"; in a position to ask with St. Paul: "Do I speak these things on human authority"? (1 Cor. 9:8), and to answer: "It is a stewardship that has been entrusted to me" (1 Cor. 9:17). On the other hand the layman has a right and a duty to give private exhortations. The question is not the size of the audience, the solemnity of the occasion, or the eloquence of the speaker (how desirable though!), but the involvement of the human word in the economy of revelation. Nevertheless this question must be solved in the same line as the teaching

[40] Msgr. G. Philips, *Etudes sur l'apostolat des laics* (Brussels: Etudes Religieuses, 1960), p. 11, n. 11.

of theology. Therefore if a layman was given by his bishop the " mission " to preach, he would do so in virtue of his mission, his knowledge and eventually of his charismatic gift, but not as " having authority." Furthermore the layman is not excluded from the task of presenting the gospel to the world,[41] but he will normally do so according to his own typical functions.

The third group of lay activities is devoted to Catholic Action. Not a few controversies have been aroused in recent years on the precise meaning and role of Catholic Action. Karl Rahner distinguishes between the action of Catholics and Catholic Action. He reacts vigorously against the tendency of identifying every form of apostolate with specialized Catholic Action. Other theologians [42] do not accept the distinction between an apostolate " proper," Catholic Action, and an apostolate of Christian existence, the testimony and the life of the Christian.

Those in favor of the distinction insist mostly on the necessity not to isolate the layman from his natural and human milieu. The layman is mediator, because of his participation in the priesthood of Christ, between the world of grace and the world of concrete existence. This world, in all its aspects: love, marriage, family, profession and work, politics and economics cannot be assumed in ecclesiastical organizations and it is not desirable that the world should be so assumed. The Church must remain the Sacrament of the kingdom of God and not a political establishment.[43] The layman has an apostolic voca-

---

[41] Pius XII (loc. cit., p. 21) wrote: The collaboration of the laity with the Hierarchy "embraces cooperation in the very activities of the Hierarchy itself which can be communicated to the (simply) faithful."

[42] Msgr. Tiberghien, *Une controverse sur l'action catholique. Masses ouvrière*, t. 13, Mars 1957, p. 41-52.

[43] The monumental error of the book of Joseph Comblin, *Echec de l'Action Catholique?* (Paris: Ed. Universitaires, 1961) is to submit the State and all the activities of a civilization to the Church. The author sees the failure of Catholic Action in the spiritual and individual character of its apostolate. It has never reached the mass of the unbelievers; which is true. But the remedy is certainly not to have Catholics as heads of State, so that the temporal power could be used to bring back the people in the Church. The author's nostalgic memories

tion antecedent to the official mandate that he receives in Catholic Action. This is the Christian witness. Karl Rahner calls it: "the apostolate of charity in the 'mundane' situation which belongs to the essence of the layman." Pius XII seems to mention this kind of apostolate when he wrote:

The relations between the Church and the world require the intervention of lay apostles. The *consecratio mundi* is, essentially, the work of the laymen themselves, of men who are intimately a part of economic and social life, who participate in the government and in legislative assemblies.[44]

Those who refuse the distinction between witness and Catholic Action fear that the primary care of the evangelization will be forgotten. They do not like to see evangelization and witness opposed, as if these two aspects of the Christian life were separable.

It obviously would be an error to oppose irreducibly these two modes of action: the action of the Catholic and Catholic Action. It seems nevertheless that they are not identical, but correspond to different realities. "Catholic Action," wrote Pius XII, "must not either claim the monopoly of the lay apostolate, for, along with it, there remains the free lay apostolate."[45] In the view of the Pope, Catholic Action is a "particular form of the lay apostolate." It has "always the character of an official apostolate." It receives a mandate from the hierarchy and expresses itself in movements organized and recognized as such, on the national or international level under the responsibility of the bishops and the Holy See. In order to put an end to the monopoly of Catholic Action and to allow other forms of apostolate to flourish, the Pope has proposed a reform of terminology and of structure. Catholic Action then becomes a generic name which may cover many other forms of apostolate which have their specific names: The Legion of Mary or *Pax Christi*, for instance. Therefore Catholic Action

of the times when the conversion of the king implied the conversion of the whole nation are very typical, and utterly untheological.

[44] Pius XII, *loc. cit.*, p. 11.   [45] Pius XII, *loc. cit.*, p. 12.

becomes a kind of federation of all the Catholic works.[46] This change is not necessarily clarifying the still obscure goal of Catholic Action. The problems also are very different from one country to another, and it is probable that the Council will leave to the bishops and to the national assemblies of Cardinals and bishops the care of solving them. The classic definition of Catholic Action by Pope Pius XI as " the participation of the laity in the apostolic mission of the hierarchy " is applied more and more today to a broader notion of "lay apostolate." [47] If Catholic Action is to have a distinctive goal and specific methods, like the principle of the evangelization of the similar by the similar, it should be distinguished from devotional guilds like the sodality of Mary and from temporal commitments like those of the trade-unionists. This distinction is clearer in Europe than in America and it would be useful in Africa or South America. There always has been an ambiguity in Catholic Action. It has been accused of "institutionalization" because it leaves no room for new inspirations and new adaptations. Clericalism is another criticism, because the direction of the bishops and their appointed chaplains has left no room for the autonomy and the spontaneity of the laity. It was said to be "the organized interference of the clergy in the apostolic mission of the laity." [48] A third reproach is the inefficacy of Catholic Action because it does not correspond to the divided and pluralistic structure of society which is prevalent to-day. It certainly would be useful if the Council could indicate what

[46] Card. Suenens has expressed similar views in *L'unité multiforme de l'Action Catholique*, Nouv. Rev. Théol., t. 80, 1958, p. 3-21.

[47] It is remarkable that in his pastoral letter of 1962, *The Call of the Council*, Card. Cushing does not even mention Catholic Action, but speaks of the holiness of the laity, its commitment to the temporal order, and its share in the missionary and pastoral work of the Church (p. 26-28; 30-33). Fr. Robert A. Graham, *The Laity and the Council*, in *The Second Vatican Council* (New York: America Press, 1962), p. 50, writes: "The term 'lay apostolate' is now current; it is the term most likely to get the sanction of official use in the decrees of the general council. The transitions in vocabulary (Catholic Movement, Christian Democracy, Catholic Action, Lay Apostolate) mark the four phases in the apostolic evolution about to culminate at the Council."

[48] Robert A. Graham, S. J., *loc. cit.*, p. 50.

the precise role of Catholic Action is. Traditionally Catholic Action takes two forms: it pursues a mission of evangelization which may go as far as the presentation of the Christian message in catechetics and instruction. But it also tries to influence the social and economic structures (salaries, housing, conditions of life, segregation, leisure, etc.) in order to create an environment more conducive to a human, moral and spiritual life. But these two aims are the source of a new ambiguity. In places where that social action was most needed like South America and Africa, Catholic Action never succeeded of course to cope with the huge problems of these countries, or even to awaken Catholics to their responsibilities. Nor for that matter did the hierarchy succeed. In more affluent countries, small groups of Catholics working in the slums discovered that they were powerless to change the conditions of life and looked towards a more direct social and political action. But this more direct action involves necessarily the collaboration with non-Catholics and cannot be confined inside Catholic organizations.

In this regard the Encyclicals *Mater et Magistra* and *Pacem in terris* are striking a new note; the second even more explicit than the first. Less emphasis is put on Catholic organizations as such than on the " duty to take an active part in public life, and to contribute toward the attainment of the common good of the entire human family as well as to that of their own political community " (*Pacem in terris*). The great error of the Catholics is " an inconsistency in their minds between religious belief and their action in the temporal sphere " (*Pacem in terris*). The emphasis on temporal commitment involves the collaboration with " all men of good will " that the Pope strongly recommends as was never done before. The commitment to the temporal tasks, which is the fourth kind of lay apostolic activities, is given by Pope John XXIII as a direct consequence of the lay Christian vocation. Inspired by the Gospel, the layman works then in the profane dimension of civilization and human history. This does not exclude, as some theologians have feared, the reference of all human realities to their sacred origin in the creation of God, or the divine meaning of history given in Christ. But the layman, engaged in temporal tasks, is not primarily concerned to bring them in Catholic organizations. He is the anonymous mediator who by his presence, his work and his witness establishes an indirect communication between the sacred world and the profane world.

There is still much thought to be given and much work to be done in the realm of the lay apostolate. But having been inspired by Pope John XXIII, the Ecumenical Council has aroused much hope. Please God that it will not be disappointed.

AUGUSTIN P. LEONARD, O. P.

Visiting Professor
University of Notre Dame
Notre Dame, Ind.

THE LAITY AND ECUMENISM

ᘒ

THE movement for Christian unity known as ecumenical, which has provided the somewhat ugly word " ecumenism " to describe its activities, began within Protestantism over fifty years ago. Today it has caught the attention of the whole Christian world and promises to become a major preoccupation for all of us, Catholics, Protestants, and Eastern Orthodox alike. In thinking about our part in it, it is well to remind ourselves of what the Holy See has done by way of directives in regard to it. In 1949 Rome issued the first official document in which the existence of the ecumenical movement was recognized and its techniques of approach between separated Christians recommended to Catholics. The official name of the document is *The Instruction of the Sacred Congregation of the Holy Office to Local Ordinaries on the Ecumenical Movement (Ecclesia Catholica).*

In this Instruction directives are given to Catholics concerning the part they can and should take in promoting ecumenical action. The Instruction opens by saying that the deep desire for Christian unity that has arisen in the world is the work of the Holy Spirit in answer to the prayers of the faithful. It goes on to commend " reunion " work as a very important part of the Church's apostolate. Clergy and laity alike are to be encouraged to take part in it. General instruction is to be given on this work by bishops in pastoral letters, and centers are to be set up in each diocese, where possible, with a priest expert in ecumenical matters in charge to supervise and guide the progress of the work.

The bishops are exhorted to promote ecumenical activity positively and with prudent encouragement, as well as to guide it in the problems it will encounter. Regulations are laid down for discussion meetings on questions of doctrine between theologians on either side and for collaboration in social problems by lay people. When matters of doctrine come up for debate between Catholics and non-Catholics, as inevitably they do, provision will be made for studying the best method of approach between them in this kind of dialogue, as it is called. In preparation for it, lectures and study groups will have to be organized. Finally, all Catholics are asked, and indeed urged, to pray for this work that it may spread its influence widely. The Instruction was issued thirteen years ago, and at the time little notice was taken of it, at least in English speaking countries.

But, since the election of John XXIII to the Papacy, a rapid change of atmosphere has taken place owing to his vigorous initiatives, both by word and by example. He has emphasized on many occasions that we must make the Church attractive to the outsider not by altering its faith, but by a change of attitude involving a spiritual renewal in charity. We must commend our beliefs in terms non-Catholics can understand—by relating our truths to theirs in non-technical language, by taking away usages and customs which are unessential and which have outgrown their former usefulness and become hindrances to mutual understanding. But we must go further than that. By love and sympathy we must seek to penetrate their minds, to see from their point of view what they think and the way they think, however foreign it may seem at first sight to our ways. We encourage them to do the same. By doing this, we shall prepare the ground for a convergent move towards unity in faith under the impulse of the Holy Spirit. At the same time, we shall find ourselves faced by the problem of ecumenical encounter.

An individual friendship grows with knowledge of each other, love of each other gained by living together and coming to share in understanding of each other's ways of thought. Such a friendship is brought to perfection by unity in faith. So, differing groups of Christians can prepare the ground for a common unity in faith by sharing a spirit of friendship founded on the desire to understand what the differences are that divide them and why they do so. We must grasp as a reality and not just as a notion what we all learn, that God gives, and only God can give, unity in faith. We can prepare the ground for it by our love, and we must not shrink from this preparation even when we realize it is going to be a long and arduous process lasting maybe for generations. That is the very essence of the ecumenical spirit.

How is it to be implemented, and especially how by lay people who will be vitally concerned in bringing it about? At the present moment we are in an interim period waiting for authority to provide new lines of action. The principal authority is, of course, the Pope in Council, the Vatican Council still in progress, with only a small part of its work as yet undertaken and none of it publicly promulgated. But the prospect for new developments and, perhaps, particularly in matters which affect the laity and their apostolate (not only in work which is specifically on behalf of unity) is hopeful and encouraging.

Here in England we have an Episcopal Committee for the promotion of unity work, chosen by our hierarchy to represent them. Its president is Archbishop Heenan of Liverpool. His first action taken two years ago was to organize a conference at Heythrop College in Oxfordshire for the instruction of priests in ecumenical ideas. Each diocese sent representatives to this conference, and all the main religious Orders and Congregations were represented. Cardinal Bea, six of the English bishops, and some seventy priests were present. Many aspects of ecumenism and its applications were thoroughly threshed out in lectures and in discussion commissions. We were told to speak our minds freely, and we did. All suggestions noted, and there were many, were embodied in a report drawn up by Archbishop Heenan, and this has been presented to the hierarchy for their consideration. It is probable that our bishops will be much influenced in their decisions for action by what happens in the Vatican Council when it resumes its sessions.

There was a general agreement at the Heythrop Conference that the most fundamental part of unity work is dialogue between theologians and scholars in other disciplines, Catholic and non-Catholic, at a deep theological level. Our differences are rooted in theology and history. The meetings must be small, hardly more than a dozen or so, in round table conferences. They must be frequent, continuous, regular, and widespread. What goes on at these discussion conferences will be passed gradually to levels lower down. The second important level is encountered within academic and professional standards, including the university student. Here, people who are able to do so will prepare themselves by lectures and group discussions for the organizing and directing of mixed meetings of Catholics and non-Catholics for dialogue in theology, history, Bible study, and sociology. Thirdly comes the parochial level, perhaps the most important of all for educating the laity, not so much in the intellectual approach, as in the underlying spirit of unity, in the encounter of charity, in respect for conscientious churches, and above all in the need for prayer. This last embraces all Catholics: it is universal.

Prayer must be the motive power of all ecumenism. Unless our work is surrounded by it and penetrated through and through with it, we may be certain that it will come to nothing. Ways and means must be found of encouraging people to pray, not just during the official eight days, but continuously, daily or weekly, not only as individuals but corporately. Unity Masses can be arranged with a group attendance or similar arrangements for united prayer before the Blessed Sacrament. In the near future we may hope for the possibility of corporate prayer with non-Catholics. We must wait in patience for the directives of the Council.

Meanwhile it may perhaps be useful to sketch a kind of basic program of preparation or self-training for an apostolate of unity, a program suited to all, from theologians to what we may call the ordinary parishoner. We are apt to say to ourselves, " What can I do? I could pray more fervently and regularly, with more consistency and love, if my prayer could be joined with action. What can an ordinary person do who is occupied all day with earning a living or running a household or both, who hasn't much time for anything but the daily duties of life? "

There is in fact a great deal we can all do. We come into contact in daily life with non-Catholic Christians. We often deeply respect them as good people, mix with them on easy social terms, work with them, or have professional relations with them. But how often do we speak to them on matters of religion, get to know what their religion means to them, or in any way share in their experience at this deep level? This is nearly always a closed book to us, a territory into which we never intrude. And yet they are our brethren in Jesus Christ, separated from us it is true because they are outside the visible boundaries of the divine society, Christ's Mystical Body, the Church, while we are privileged to share in its full fellowship.

Yet they are united with us in their belief in the great central truth of the Christian faith, that Christ died for our sins and rose again for our justification, and *this* unity is something which is more fundamental, more vitally important than anything that divides us. But this is often lost sight of because of our divisions. We forget that we are brethren in Jesus Christ, though separated brethren. We act and speak very often as if, in respect of that which is most important in our lives, we are enemies who can have no dealings with each other. How has this come about? It has come about because the movement of Protestantism in the sixteenth century was a rebellion against the teaching authority of the Church Christ founded. Rebellion is a form of warfare which induces war psychology on both sides.

We all know what that is. The enemy in warfare is always wrong; he is the evil aggressor and we, the innocent who are sinned against. The case is all black on their side, all white on ours. He is unjust, his motives and his actions are malicious. We do not try to understand him and see his point of view. We are hostile to him and want to vanquish him and force him to accept our conditions. But the Reformation happened over four hundred years ago, and Protestants and other non-Catholics are no longer consciously and of set purpose rebels against the authority of the Church. They may even be instinctively seeking what we believe to be their true home and the fullness of truth to be found in it.

But although the spirit of war psychology has largely vanished from our social relationships with non-Catholics, it still holds sway in that inner citadel of the soul where faith resides. And because it does so, we keep studiously away from the inner citadel of non-Catholics and seldom intrude into it. When by chance we do, it is often to argue about religion. When we begin to argue about religion, war psychology inevitably comes to the surface. We are out to marshal our arguments like soldiers going in to attack, ruthless and determined.

We are out to win a victory of mind over mind. We do not stop to consider the arguments of our opponents, really to weigh their value and understand their bearing on the matter in hand. We just argue for victory. The result is that we defeat our own end. We fail to convince and only succeed in confirming our opponent in his beliefs, even if he has been unable to cope with our arguments. We have treated him not as a brother but as an enemy. Yet he is in fact our brother in Jesus Christ. In all probability he has received the sacrament of baptism, with its gift of God's friendship we call grace. Only grave sin can destroy that gift and true sorrow for sin can restore it.

The baptised non-Catholic belongs, of course, to a religious body which is not a part of the true Church. However, he does so, not as an act of conscious rebellion against our Lord, but in good faith, believing that his church is part of the true Church. When he attends the Holy Communion or the Lord's Supper or the Breaking of Bread in his own church, it is not a true sacrament according to the standards which Christ has laid down for us through the mind of his Church. But the non-Catholic using this ordinance according to standards recognized in the religious body to which he belongs, though he is in error, humbly believes he is being obedient to Christ. He humbly desires to receive grace. He is in good faith, and we are fully at liberty as Catholics to believe that in answer to his good faith God gives him the grace he seeks.

By receiving this grace he is united, though invisibly and unconsciously, with Christ in his Mystical Body, which is the Catholic and Roman Church. That is why he is our brother in Christ, though not in a full sense a member of the Church, because he is separated from visible fellowship with us.

The realization of these truths should make us humble and should remove any element of war psychology that may be in us. It should lead us to seek the friendship and understanding of our non-Catholic neighbors. We must not argue with him in any win-a-victory spirit. We must above all look for the truth in what he believes. We must make sure by listening to him carefully whether what he says is really erroneous or only a partially realized truth or a truth expressed in language unfamiliar to us. This is the psychology of peace, and it sets up a spirit of friendship built upon love and the desire to understand.

Let us take a particular situation to illustrate this way of approach. If a Catholic finds himself involved in a discussion with a Protestant about the Blessed Sacrament, his first instinct (we have inherited it from our war psychology) is to concentrate on the supposed fact—that his Protestant friend *denies* the real presence of Christ our Lord in the sacrament he received. So he begins by explaining what Catholics mean by it. He feels instinctively that transubstantiation is a bogey word; nevertheless he makes the attempt and uses it as his starting point. If he does use the formidable word and its accompanying technical terms, he will soon find himself lost in a wilderness of misconceptions. Far better to seek out first what we hold in common, if it is a great deal. Anglo-Catholics, of course, believe almost exactly as we do. Let us take here the case of an evangelical or low church friend, a Baptist or Methodist perhaps, with whom you are carrying on such a discussion.

If you say, " I believe that in the act of Holy Communion Christ our Lord comes to us to be the food of our souls," you are beginning on something you both hold in common. You will find, in all probability, that a good Protestant will answer, " Yes, I believe that, too. Paul talks of Christ living in us and we in him. Jesus gives us his life that way." "Yes," you will answer, "The bread and wine are signs, visible signs, of his presence, ordained by him to be used by us." Your Protestant friend will reply, "Yes, I believe that. As we receive the signs, he enters into our life, our souls, and unites himself with us through the Holy Spirit and we become by his power Christlike. That is what grace means: it is the power, the personal power, of his love in us."

So far, you see, you are in complete agreement on something tremendous. This has deep meaning for both of you. That agreement sets up unity between you, it draws you together and encourages you to listen to each other. It prepares the ground for the differences that are there, too. Sooner or later they will come to the surface. Perhaps your friend will say one day, "Don't you Roman Catholics worship the bread, the Host as you call it?," and if he is very frank he will add "We think that's idolatry, you know." It is a warfare word, of course. You must not get angry though you may be tempted. Now must you embark here on a complete explanation of the bogey word transubstantiation? He's not yet ready for it. Say, "Yes, we do worship the Host, or rather we worship what the Host represents." It sounds very Protestant to use that word, but in fact it is perfectly good theology, because sacraments are outward signs representing the invisible that they signify.

Then go on to say, "We believe that, in a way that is deeply mysterious and belongs not to earth but heavenly things, Christ our Lord in his glorious and risen life identifies himself with the sign, with the bread. It is our offering in the sense that it signifies our life—food and drink that supports life. He makes himself, in the heavenly places, one with it, and so, through it one with us by the power of the Holy Spirit; and in doing so he changes it inwardly. The whole transaction is something that does not belong to this world. Its only connection with this world is the bread and wine and ourselves, they wholly of this world and we partly. What you can see and touch and handle of the bread remains what it was before, but its inner reality has been taken up into the eternal world and transformed, made one with Christ by the power of the Holy Spirit. In Holy Communion Christ gives himself to us in and through the signs. The earthly and the heavenly are joined together, made one. What is visible, tangible of bread and the invisible Christ are united. Our earthly food is inwardly transformed; it becomes heavenly. Though as a sign it remains of the earth, heaven and earth meet in it. In a sense we are taken up with it, too, into the heavenly places, the eternal world, to Christ—to be in Christ, to be filled with Christ, to be made Christ-like."

You have not taught your Protestant friend everything, but you have linked your truth with his truth and that will have given your truth a chance to take root in the soil of what you each hold in common. This illustrates the ecumenical approach by applying it in a single particular instance. It is grounded upon love and understanding brought about by sharing what you both hold dear. As you can see, given time and patience, your discussion will carry you much further. You have shown your friend by implication three mysteries of the faith that in reality are one. (1) The once-for-all sacrifice on Calvary which has redeemed us by Christ's blood-shedding. He deeply believes in that already. (2) The perpetual pleading of this sacrifice by the Risen Christ in the presence of his Father. (3) The Mass-transaction, under the sacramental signs, by which Christ our Lord applies by the Holy Spirit in his own person, sacrament-ally, the divine-human power which derives from the victory of Calvary, the victory of obedience. This is the mystery by which within his Mystical Body, the Church, he makes available to his members his saving power. There is only one sacrifice and it is all sufficient, but its power is given to us by Christ himself from day to day in the Mass, under the signs which represent in the deeply mysterious reality the body broken and the blood shed. Maybe, too, your Protestant friend will have shown you something of that deep, personal, evangelical love for Jesus Christ, which is the common possession of both Catholics and Protestants and is sometimes more conspicuous in the lives of our separated brethren than it is in our own.

By first seeking and honoring the truth in what our neighbor believes, we create the best possible foundation on which to build up the truth we have to give him, truth which as yet he does not possess. We must not be in a hurry. We must not expect to convert him in a matter of hours or days, in weeks or months, or even in years, and perhaps not at all. Very likely, he loves the tradition in which he was born and brought up and values highly customs and usages of religious observance which are not ours and which often seem alien to our way of thinking. We must not seek to tear him roughly and ruthlessly away from his non-Catholic surroundings before God calls on him to sacrifice them. So long as non-Catholic Christians are deeply and conscientiously convinced of the truth of their own way, they are bound in conscience to follow that way and no other. They cannot become Catholics until God gives them the power to do so. There is, therefore, a true place in the scheme of things under God's Providence for the dissident churches until such time as unity of faith in the one Church is attained by them. We are only God's instruments in digging and cultivating the ground. God himself, and only God, is able if he wills to plant the seed of faith in this ground, where it will take root and grow and so extend the faith which the non-Catholic already has into the fullness of the Catholic faith.

If then, we set ourselves to the best of our ability to engage in the apostolate of positive charity and understanding, we shall be working for unity in the most valuable way possible, among the rank and file of non-Catholic Christians. On this foundation of unity in love and understanding and not otherwise, the scholars and theologians will be able to build successfully. In working in this way we shall find that our prayers for unity will become increasingly living, real and fervent, because they will be closely united in our lives with action.

HENRY ST. JOHN, O. P.

Hawkesyard Priory
Rugeley, Staffs, England

THE PLACE OF RELIGIOUS IN THE
APOSTOLATE OF THE CHURCH *

ᴄᴀᴏ

A CTUAL though the problem of the religious state of life
as compared to that of the secular priest may be,[1] this
question is not envisioned here; nor do the states of
perfection need concern us. We refrain as well from the recent
discussions concerning the spirituality of the diocesan clergy.
The points at issue are rather the apostolate of religious and,
in particular, the conditions in which this apostolate is exercised. In their activites the members of a religious institute,
in one way or another, are not subject to the full authority
of the local ordinary: he cannot demand of them just any
sort of activity; nor are they unqualifiedly subject to his disposition. The problem before us concerns the exemption of
religious and of their collaborators in the apostolate. In some
way this problem touches upon all forms of religious life
engaged in apostolic activity. It extends from the monastic
orders exercising a genuine apostolate to congregations of
teaching or nursing brothers. The problem is not limited to
the religious life; societies of the common life (secular institutes) enjoy the same kind of exemption. While many of the
arguments, examples, and points of application in this essay
refer to the sacerdotal life, the total extension of the principles and the universal character of the conclusions should be
kept in mind.

In what does the exemption of religious consist; what are
its traits? We recall first that all institutes of pontifical right
enjoy autonomy as to internal regimen according to the terms

---

* Translated by Thomas C. O'Brien, O.P. from *Nouvelle Revue Théologique*
(March, 1959) 271-281.

[1] Conference to a gathering of religious of different communities, Brussels,
January 13, 1959.

317

of their own form of exemption, plenary or partial.[2] By reason of this legal institution the management of religious subjects belongs solely to their superior. It is he who places them
at the service of diocesan authority, transfers them, or changes
their assignments. This autonomy, of course, does not extend
without qualification to apostolic activity. To exercise the
ministry of preaching to the faithful, the canonical mission of
the residential bishop is required.[3] In the interim between
the foundation of the mendicant orders and the Council of
Trent, the canonical mission of Regulars came from the Pope
through their religious superiors.[4] In the case of the Order of
Friars Preachers, for example, the mission was conferred
through incorporation into the Order.[5] Since the sixteenth
century, this exceptional privilege has been progressively cur-
tailed. Currently, since the Code, apart from the case of the
ministry purely within fully exempt institutes, it belongs to
the head of the local church to confer canonical mission. But
it still remains true that the local ordinary can exercise his
rights solely over religious placed at his disposition by superiors. The exercise of apostolic activity in a diocese is thus
indirectly affected by the internal autonomy of religious.

What is the purpose of exemption? The maintenance and
development of the religious life along its characteristic lines
presupposes the self-sufficiency of the superior and consequently a real independence in regard to internal government.

---

[2] Cf. E. Fogliasso, " Exemption des religieux," dans *Dict. de dr. can.*, t. 5, col.
646-665 (abondante bibliographie); T. Schaeffer, *De religiosis ad normam Codicis
iuris canonici*, 3e éd., Rome, 1940, pp. 789-801.

[3] *Can.* 1328, 1337, 1338. In his discourse on Dec. 8, 1950, Pius XII stated: " The
exemption of religious orders is not in opposition with the principle of the constitution bestowed by God upon the Church: and it is in no way opposed to the
law in virtue of which the priest owes obedience to the bishop. As a matter of fact,
according to canon law, exempt religious depend upon the bishop of the place
insofar as they take part in the fulfillment of the bishop's task and the proper
organization of the spiritual care of souls." (A. A. S., 1951, t. 43, p. 28; *Doc. Cath.*,
1950, col. 1671; cf. N. R. *Th.*, 1951, p. 180).

[4] Cf. E. Feyaerts, " De evolutie van het predikatierecht der religieuzen," *Studia
catholica*, 1950, t. 25, pp. 177-190 et 225-240.

[5] Cf. M.-H. Vicaire, *Histoire de saint Dominique*, Paris, 1957, t. II, p. 72.

In the course of time this liberty, having become exemption, emerged as an instrument of reform. The monastery of Cluny made its associated monasteries profit from the broad immunities which it had obtained.[6] As a safeguard of religious fidelity, exemption became by this very fact the guarantee of unity. The appearance of the mendicant Orders brought more precise characteristics to this autonomy.[7] The concession of more liberties put at the disposal of the Holy See, and thus of the whole Church, apostolic forces which Christianity so urgently needed. Ever since, we see centralized orders under superiors who are in close contact with the Pope. After many historical vicissitudes, such an order of things today still determines the availability of religious institutes for apostolic undertakings.

Study of the elements of pastoral integration is the order of the day; among other things in this study is the planning of better parochial apportionment and improved organization of evangelical activities. This context demands theoretical and practical reflections on the autonomy of religious which would allow religious to be assigned their place with full effectiveness in the complexus of the Church's tasks.

I. EXEMPTION AND SPECIALIZATION

What is the significance of the approval of a religious institute? In the goal proposed by and for a religious society, the Holy See recognizes *the response to a need in the Church*. The ecclesiastical approval permits the pursuit of this end to be organized socially within the Church and offers to those who

[6] Cf. J.-F. Lemarignier, " L'exemption monastique et les origines de la réforme grégorienne," dans A. Cluny, Congrès scientifique (9-11 juillet 1949). Travaux du Congrès, Dijon, 1950, pp. 288-340.

[7] The form of life of the mendicants was to affect all exemption from then on. Exemption was to be no longer local but personal. Historically the change in purpose should be noted. Every one had been progressively set forth in order to prevent interference in the government of monasteries, in the internal life of communities. The privilege of exemption in the case of the mendicants pertains to the organization of their apostolate.

wish to dedicate themselves to this end guarantees of effectiveness and stability. In a word the Holy See recognizes, not merely a service, but *an action of the Church*.

The services are multiple and varied. Institutes vowed exclusively to the contemplative life need not be considered. Those which are directly engaged in apostolic undertakings are difficult to classify. While recognizing the difficulty of drawing a sharp line of demarcation, a way of discerning two general types may still be possible. Every religious institute is characterized at once by its own spirituality and its works.[8] In view of the emphasis placed upon one or other of these contemporary elements, we are confronted by two apostolic groups. The respective character of each is distinguished principally either by a determined type of activity or by a particular spirituality.

These apostolic activities are numerous: preaching, teaching, publication, formation of clergy in seminaries, the Christion education of youth, corporal and spiritual assistance to the sick or destitute, foreign missions, parochial missions, evangelization of the rural or working classes. Such activities are explicitly indicated in the statement of the purpose of some institutes. In other cases, they have been inspired in the course of time by reason of special aptitude and appropriate formation. In the first category a special place must be given to orders and congregations whose objective is the parochial apostolate, the ordinary ministry within the diocesan framework, with an insistence at times upon the communal spirit of the clerical group or upon a concentration of members in populous parishes.

Other institutes, those of the second category, set out in general to live in a certain spirit a religious life that is apostolic, including varied forms determined by the great needs of

---

[8] As a first approach to the problem, the following work will provide valuable assistance: *Dictionnaire des instituts religieux en France*, Centre de documentation sacerdotale, Paris (17, rue de Varenne), 1957. In this volume of 160 pp. there is a brief notice with bibliography on each institute.

the Church. Here the field of apostolate is not limited. Rather it is the form of spirituality that predominates and delineates the spirit of the members and the message to be propagated. The messages are often the great devotions of the Church: The Sacred Heart, the Blessed Sacrament, the Virgin Mary, St. Therese of the Infant Jesus, the patrimony of the French school, and many others. Religious of this group have a great flexibility for adapting to the needs of the moment and for responding to the calls of the apostolate. In addition, their autonomy guarantees their mobility. Thanks to this they can be gathered together at any point where a concentration of apostolic workers is especially required. In today's Church this exceptional availability is a spiritual fund the full value of which must be appreciated and its full resources put to work.

The religious of the first group have a narrower range; they are less easily directed to varied channels. Their higher degree of specialization, however, compensates for a certain lack of adaptability. Of course, opportunities for specialization are open to religious members of all institutes without exception; but we are pointing to apostolic orientations built into the nature of the religious communities as such. Once an order or congregation is vowed exclusively or by special title to the Christian education of youth, to the evangelization of workers, to preaching, to the care and apostolate of the sick, or to foreign missions, then its whole being is pointed in such a direction. Specialization is not merely personal but collective; it marks the entire formation and shapes the life of the community. *The existence of a large body of specialized capabilities is another good for the Church. They are the instruments the Church fashions for itself in order to deal with the needs of the moment and to make provision for the future.*

Such specialized capabilities are not a monopoly of the religious life. The secular clergy is well endowed with them; witness the national chaplaincies of Catholic Action, great interdiocesan works, and general services of the episcopacy. It is important to observe that these specializations, whether under an individual or corporate title, tend toward a kind of prescriptive autonomy which has not yet received juridic consecration, but is at present simply a fact.[9] By a kind of implicit delegation of all the bishops of France, for example, the assembly of Cardinals and archbishops nominate for offices on a national level the chaplains of organizations whose activity embraces an entire territory.[10] This collective appointment *ipso facto* confers a certain autonomy (real, yet difficult to define precisely) in regard to the individual members of the hierarchy. A kind of law of natural necessity emerges. To be exercised these special offices require, in regard to particular authorities, a status of autonomy with direct subjection to higher authorities to whom the care and responsibility of more general projects belong.

II. Specialized Groups and the Service of Catholicity

Whether these groups be secular, religious, or mixed in their composition, they are a vehicle for the exercise of catholicity. Through them the local Church is brought into the broader stream of collective Catholic life. A diocese cannot remain closed within itself. While in the person of its head it has the fullness of the priesthood, still it does not contain all the resources it needs for the full development of the Christian life. Even as it can communicate its own experience to others, so by the same token, it can profit from those who have lived elsewhere. The local diocese, for example, will be the first to profit from sociological studies carried out by the large organizations equipped for such work. Theological and pastoral studies published by individuals or reviews can provide fruit-

---

[9] The *Mission de France* already has its own canonical status of autonomy. See on this point the constitution *Omnium Ecclesiarum*, Aug. 15, 1954, A.A.S., 1954, t. 46, pp. 567-574 et *Doc. Cath.*, 1954, t. 51, col. 1153-1160. There is a commentary in the article by Msgr. J. Denis, " La prélature ' nullius ' de la Mission de France," *L'Anne canonique*, 1954-1955, t. 3, pp. 27-36.

[10] Cf. V.-L. Chaigneau, *L'organization de l'Eglise catholique en France*, Paris, 1956, p. 49.

ful suggestions. Vitality in contacts, in intercommunication, in common enterprises, presupposes the existence of specialized groups. Often it is through them that the broad movements, Roman in inspiration, become operative in the dioceses. Thus, the creative and vital impulse to the biblical and liturgical movements have frequently been given by their effort. As a capacity for the universal and as a permanent force, catholicity is not simply a static fact, but rather it is an activity practiced by all those who exercise a ministry.

Through and in the works of catholicity the Church unceasingly gathers men into her unity, assimilates the infinite variety of human nature into the unity of heart and soul proper to the Christian community (Art. IV, 32). This catholicity is realized on the diocesan level within the framework of the ordinary jurisdiction of the residential bishop. It belongs to him to take care that the community be open to all social classes, all ages, all languages, all cultures, and eventually to all races. Thus he must see that the Christian community be prepared effectively to assimilate this multiplicity and richness. But for the functioning of catholicity on a territorial level, the bishop needs the contribution of instrumentalities not bound to such and such a geographical place.

There is a further dimension to the episcopal responsibility. Specialized supra-diocesan and universal groups must be viewed as a response to the desires and concerns of the bishops who exercise the pastoral office within the limits of a particular Church; even more so, they must be viewed in terms of the concerns of episcopal responsibility seen in its fullness. Beyond the ordinary jurisdiction, bishops have a participated jurisdiction in common with the Vicar of Christ.[11] Possessed collegially, this jurisdiction is not by way of supplement or addition to the supreme and universal jurisdiction of the Pope. It merges with it. The bishop, as he is head of the local

---

[11] On the collegial nature of the episcopacy, see Msgr. A.-M. Charue, évêque de Namur, *Problèms du clergé diocésain*, II, extrait des *Mandements*, t. II, no. 28, pp. 221-223; Ch. Journet, *L'Eglise du Verbe incarné*, t. I, Paris, 1941, pp. 500-511; Y. Congar, *Jalons pour une théologie du laïcat*, Paris, 1953, pp. 386-400.

Church, has by that fact a *Catholic* concern which passes beyond all territorial boundaries. It is hardly necessary to recall here the words of Pius XI spoken à propos of the missions:

It is not only Peter, whose See We occupy, but at the same time, all the apostles, whose successors you are, that the Master has commanded to go throughout the whole world preaching the Gospel to every creature. From this it evidently follows that if the duty of propagating the faith rests upon Us, you must without any possible doubt come to share in Our works and to assist Us in this task to the degree permitted by the fulfillment of your local and personal task.[12]

By reason of the participation of the collective episcopate in the universal pastoral mission of Peter's successor, members of specialized bodies are assured that they represent ecclesial interests which are not disparate from those of residential bishops.

This is true even when the diocesan Church is not directly the beneficiary, as is the case in foreign missions. Thus it is by way of response to a demand internal to the nature of the episcopacy that these specialized bodies bring the broad interests of the universal Church into contact with the local concerns.

III. THE RELIGIOUS STATE AND SPECIALIZED GROUPS

In the discussion of these points we have intentionally set

---

[12] *Rerum Ecclesiae*, 28 février 1926, A.A.S., 1926 t. 18, p. 69.—On April 21, 1957, addressing himself directly to the bishops by the encyclical *Fidei donum*, Pius XII wrote:

" United by the closest bonds to Christ as well as to His Vicar you will desire, Venerable Brothers, to take your part in a spirit of vital charity in this care of all the Churches which weigh on our shoulders. . . . Without doubt it was to the apostle Peter alone and to his successors, the Roman Pontiffs, that Jesus entrusted the whole of his flock. . . . But while each bishop is properly the pastor only of the portion of the flock entrusted to his care, his quality as legitimate succesor of the apostles by divine institution makes him solidly responsible for the apostolic mission of the Church. . . . This mission which must embrace all nations and all time has not ceased with the death of the apostles; it continues in the person of all the bishops in communion with the Vicar of Jesus Christ."

A. A. S., 1957, t. 49, pp. 236-237; *Doc. Cath.*, 157, t. 54, col. 587-588.

aside the question of the religious life as a state of perfection.[13] This in no way implies that the question has no bearing upon the existence and activities of specialized groups. Both seculars and regulars have already demonstrated their aptitude for these special functions. Yet the elements which in the religious life facilitate adaptation to these tasks should be understood. By giving to the pursuit of perfection the character of total and definitive self-donation, the religious state gives to the apostle a connaturality with the message he bears. This is true in general regarding the assignment of the religious to apostolic tasks. But it is of special importance to single out how this state, as it assures a greater stability in one particular concentration and more frequent possibilities for creative initiative, is a preparation for formally specialized functions. There are, it is true, factors built into the religious life, even as into the ordinary sacerdotal life, that create the occasion for numerous changes. It is impossible to keep someone always in the same place. The exigencies of life are opposed to such stability, and stability is not even desirable at all times. The possibility of change is itself a human value which can be profitable. From one day to the next, the professor of theology can become a provincial, or the chaplain of a Catholic Action group can become a master of novices. But the peculiar renunciation imposed by the vows permits restricting such factors of change to a minimum. The superior has the power to employ a religious subject according to his real capacities and the actual condition of his vitality. There is no need to deal with acquired rights, nor to be concerned about honoring seniority or about rewarding meritorious service. For such reasons, and many more which are difficult to spell out, several apostolic ventures of broad scope have been the work of religious. In Belgium, as in France, social action, the apostolate of the cinema, radio, publication, reviews

[13] On the place of the religious state in the mystery of the Church, see the pages devoted to this problem in *Rev. des Sciences phil. et théol.*, 1957, t. 41, pp. 557-559; 1959, t. 43, pp. 336-338.

on the spiritual life, the ecumenical apostolate, youth movements—all these are areas in which the creative action of religious has predominated. This fact is quite universal, with the
exception of specialized Catholic Action in Belgium. Obvious,
as well, is the contribution of religious throughout the world
to ecclesiastical sciences; and this is an influence which has
important bearing on the apostolate.

IV. Diocesan Authorities and Specialized
Religious Groups

Currently diocesan authorities more and more assign secular priests to specialized tasks. This is a bright sign; it is a
response to a necessity of pastoral life. The progress of evangelization in the modern world imposes such a tendency. At
the beginning of the last century, on the heels of the Concor-
dat of 1801, when pastoral work was exercised exclusively on
a territorial level " priests were almost always assigned to
parishes under diverse titles: curés, officiating ministers, priest
administrators . . .; in the parishes of large cities there were
priest catechists, priest organists, even deacons and subdeacons with special offices." [14] The number of priests remaining
under the bishop for administration, for the seminary, and for
certain chaplaincies was small. Contemporary dimensions of
the life of our society demand more and more priests. On a
diocesan level, regional or national, there is need for missionaries for domestic missions; retreat masters; chaplains for
Catholic Action, for the university world, for technical schools;
directors of works, of education; ecclesiastical advisers on theatre, radio, and television; chaplains for factories (as in Italy);
and specialists for the apostolate of the worker and for professional unions.

The deployment of all apostolic forces must be made according to the needs of special missions. This supposes an overall
plan which utilizes to the maximum the already existant spe-

[14] Y. Daniel et G. Le Mouël, *Paroisses d'hier . . . Paroisses de demain*, Paris,
1957, p. 218.

cializations and particularly those religious institutes whose vocation it is to provide workers already equipped for specific tasks. When such a plan is lacking, it usually presents a paradoxical situation. At the same time as the secular clergy assumes the determined tasks for which an order has been approved by the Church, the same order may be asked to assume within the diocese tasks for which it has not been designed. Such a poor utilization of its resources is an anomaly the Church can ill afford.

Honesty requires the recognition that it is not *merely* the want of an over-all plan that determines this situation. There are more profound reasons. Diocesan authorities often have the impression that a religious is never totally engaged by the undertaking they have conferred upon him; that, rather, he is totally dedicated only to the institute whose habit he wears. There is the risk that the religious who renders immense services brings with him his own individuality, a personality a bit complex for the kind of work to which he is called. He comes on the scene not only with the spirituality of his order, always a great form of spirituality of the Church, but with some practices of devotion having a more private character, with an *esprit de corps* expressed sometimes in a policy of privilege-seeking, with the memory of controversy between schools the excesses of which the Holy See has more than once had to censure, and with the concern also for the financial needs of his own institute. In a word, he brings a mentality which has not always been susceptible to openness or service. Another ground for fear on the part of the diocesan authorities is that the religious institute may establish a kind of diocese within a diocese by reason of the complex of personal relations which can create its public churches, its colleges, its third orders, its congregations, its confraternities, its works of all sorts. In addition, the religious appears to them sometimes as a kind of meteor or a free lancer who does not enter into the makeup of the diocese, nor does he concern himself with being informed about the directives given by the bishop of the place,

nor has he any inclination to use the powers received in the
spirit with which they are conceded to him.

We are not pleading a case. There is, then, no necessity of
establishing or of refuting the grounds for such fears. There
is merely a question of recognizing that there are risks involved in the very nature of the situation, and that the psychological reactions described are often verified. No one should
seek to balance off the given value against the specific draw-
backs characteristic of the contribution of the individual religious. But at the same time, neither should anyone deny that
the full force of this value may be blunted by certain questionable attitudes. The impressions we have described, then,
should make us turn to what is essential.

In the Christian community specialized capabilities constitute a service to the Church, a work of catholicity. For a religious order there can be no suggestion of setting out to gain
influential offices or positions of control in order, as it were,
to acquire trophies. There is such a thing as a collective
humility just as there is an individual humility. Both are necessary in the kingdom of God. Our personal contributions
must be those alone which serve to fashion out of human
variety a true totality in Christ. Then He makes us more fit
to enter into the apostolic program of the Church, of which
the Holy Spirit is the effective agent in conjunction with the
apostolic college, as this is continued in today's world by
the college of bishops under the direction of the successors of
Peter.

V. The Need of a Constant Concern for the Proper Character of Religious Institutes

The harmony of catholicity is upset by a failure to respect
proper goals. To ask an institute of teaching brothers to
accept important nursing duties is a procedure ill suited to
the equilibrium of the Church. The formation and pattern of
life which prepares the institute for the one task does not at
all dispose to the other. Rather, the latter increases the risk

of destroying the basic elements constituting the institute's strength. To insist that an exclusively missionary order accept metropolitan parishes is as harmful as putting an institute whose objective is the parochial apostolate into college or university chaplaincies. When the primitive constitutions of the Friars Preachers declare, "We cannot accept churches to which the care of souls is annexed," [15] they are merely expressing negatively the will of St. Dominic to consecrate himself exclusively to the ministry of the Word of God, a choice the more remarkable because St. Dominic is by origin a canon regular. An institute ordered to a precise apostolic task must be treated like a delicate mechanism of a watch the movements of which are closely intermeshed and synchronized.

For institutes whose constitutions do not designate a specialized apostolic field, the situation is not the same. They may more readily and more rapidly enter into the diocesan apostolate. Nevertheless, even here a concern for the proper character of each one is necessary. Their employment in the apostolate should respect a form of religious life which is, with the Church's approval, the collective expression of a devotion, a spirituality, an ascetical practice derived from the Christian heritage. Pastoral planning cannot do violence to such particularized vocations; it *must* respect their distinctive antecedents.

Obviously it is difficult to attain precise delineations within the variety of religious institutes. The distinctions I have proposed in these pages may provide some slight clarification. But in the face of the complexities which remain, it might seem simpler to deal with all religious as an amorphous group only numerically distinguishable. All the same, it is legitimate to inquire whether the evaluation of apostolic resources in these days does not demand something more. Today many Catholic ecumenists are capable of discerning the most delicate nuances separating two protestant denominations. Should

---

[15] *Dist.* II, chap. XXVII, 2.

we do less with regard to the internal organization of the Church in which the problem is in no way so complex.

This respect for their own purposes is incumbent above all on the institutes themselves. In many orders and congregations, under the pressure of events, disparate activities have become annexed to their original works. In the beginning these activities were a temporary measure of expediency; too quickly they have become a condition of life. This results sometimes in a melange of activities in which the outsider has difficulty discerning the fundamental orientation of the institute. To accord full value to its authentic purpose, or to rediscover it after events have obscured it, seems to be the just duty of every religious institute. There is a general conviction on this point. The contacts among major superiors established in Belgium and France cannot but advance this conviction. As long as an institute is isolated, or thinks of itself as isolated, it can easily consider itself obliged to respond to all appeals. Confronted by the presence of other religious orders even of the same nation, however, an institute should become aware that the better service to the Church is to remain faithful to its proper vocation.

A reflection on essential purposes can only result in salutary conclusions. Sometimes it will be necessary to adapt the end to new needs. Some institutes were founded in particular circumstances which no longer prevail. Founded in the thirteenth century for the ransom of captives, the Order of Mercy today still does useful work in the Church because it has courageously rethought its purpose with a view to new needs. Such an eventuality is not to be excluded. But these reflections will result especially in the wise adaptation of means to the end, in the order of the liturgy, in the studies, in the observances, in the rule of life, as well as in the delicate matter of recruitment of vocations. Therefore it is to the interest of religious institutes, in strict accord with their general character, to accept only unquestionable vocations.

Fidelity to purpose remains the principal expression of fidelity to the Holy See. We enter totally into the pastoral design of the Church by meticulously respecting the end for which the Church has given us her approval. The Pope is the proper prelate and supreme superior whom all religious, in virtue of their very vow of obedience, are held to obey.[16] Conformity to our end is one very pure expression of the obedience we owe him.

In the terms of Canon Law the exemption of religious is a "privilege," a negative expression which should signify a positive reality to everyone. It is not a personal advantage to be exploited or to be enjoyed indiscriminately. In the context of the apostolate it is the juridical side of an action of catholicity. It is not a means whereby the religious renders himself untouchable; on the contrary, it is the implement for guaranteeing a more real and effective service.

I am not unaware of the concrete problems. These cannot be resolved other than in a continuing dialogue. But currently, more than ever, conditions have concurred for a serene, lucid, and constructive dialogue. This is first of all true because His Holiness Pope Pius XII, in his *Discourse to Religious*, Dec. 8, 1850, resolved the controversies attendant upon the mere juxtaposition of seculars and religious. Discussions have fulfilled an important role by bringing up and spotlighting the multiple aspects of the problem of spirituality. But they cannot be prolonged indefinitely without damage to the unity of the apostolic effort. Secondly, because all are convinced that no longer is a territorial dimension the sole consideration regulating pastoral endeavor, total remedies must meet the problems in their total new extension. The influence of the large milieu of life—school, factory, army, leisure—imposes, in conjunction with the local structures and subject to controlled effort, apostolic action on a wider and wider scale.

Finally, the correct evaluation of delicate problems by religious and seculars together is advanced by a missionary mentality. In times of diminished apostolic fervor, in a static clim-

---

[16] *Can.* 499, § 1.

ate, relations between religious and seculars readily assume the aspects of rivalry. In a community of charity, in an atmosphere of *mission*, these relations have but one form: a disinterested coordination. And more lasting solutions will be found as good will, enlightened by theology, leads the way, not to some neutral compromise, but to a regard for the authentic nature of the case.[17]

JEROME HAMER, O. P.

Le Saulchoir
Paris, France

---

[17] The problem of the apostolate of religious in its various aspects has been dealt with by R. Kuiters in a recent study: " Over de Verhouding tussen de seculiere en reguliere geestelijkheid," *Tijdschrift voor geestelijk leven*, 1958, t. 14, pp. 245-255, 341-353, 365-376, 456-469.

UNCREATED GRACE—A CRITIQUE
OF KARL RAHNER

◌

M AN speaks God's word in human terms. This is the burden of theology, on one hand an imprint of the divine science itself, on the other a habit and act resident within and elicited by the human intelligence so that it cannot but take upon itself the conditions of the subject wherein alone it exists. Its task is the formulation in human terms of Unalterable Truth with all the inexactitude and mere approximation imposed by the very ineffability of what must always remain mystery. This is what necessitates that the theologian be open to history (without succumbing to the relativism of historicity), that his act be in the nature of a dialogue with other theologians, that theological system not become sectarianism.

This is said somewhat by way of an apology, in these days of welcome emphasis on unity and the exploration of positive meaning, for what might otherwise appear as an overly negative theological venture. These reflections upon one view of the influential Jesuit, Karl Rahner, are presented neither as a mere polemic nor in the spirit of an astringent negativism. Rather, they contain an implicit acknowledgement that perhaps his efforts have opened up a whole new direction to theological speculation on grace, justification, glory, the Incarnation, and the supernatural. And if this be so the contemporary theologian can hardly fail to pursue his richly suggestive line of investigation. However, at the very outset assurance is needed that we do indeed have here an authentic and enriching originality giving new dimensions to our knowledge. Mere innovation, after all, departing from that point of achievement at which theological speculation has already arrived, holds no such promise and indeed may end in impoverishment of the truth. What these pages ask then is whether such assurance, increasingly taken for granted, be warranted.

I. Exposition: Rahner's Theory on Uncreated Grace

1. *The Thesis*

In his one major work thus far translated into English,[1] Karl Rahner presents in the Tenth Chapter his teaching on uncreated grace—a doctrine that already has found many and ardent supporters. Put most simply it is an opinion which sees man's justification as formally constituted by the very presence of divinity to the soul. Sanctity is realized in a seizure and possession of the soul by the personal Spirit of God. Created habitual grace and the other infused gifts of God which energize the soul, though indispensable, are consequences of this prior uncreated grace. The Council of Trent in strong reaction against the extrinsic imputation theories deriving from Protestantism insisted upon the reality of created grace as an effect of God's causal love. It nowise intended to obscure this primary and profounder element in the total grace state.

What is meant here is not the presence of the divine Substance to the soul merely as supernatural agent in the causing of grace. To avoid this misunderstanding Rahner notes with approval the notion of Martinez-Gomez to the effect that, " a logical (not temporal) priority (over) created grace should be ascribed to uncreated grace (*as* given, not just as *to be* given or as *causing* grace) : "[2] Neither is this a reiteration of the position which conceives of God as giving Himself to the soul as immanent term of its supernatural knowledge and love; a presence " sicut cognitum in cognoscente, sicut amatum in amante " in the classical expression of St. Thomas.[3] It is not

---

[1] Karl Rahner, S. J., *Theological Investigations,* Vol. I, God, Christ, Mary and Grace. A translation by Cornelius Ernst, O. P., Helicon Press (Baltimore) and Parton, Longman, and Todd (London), 1961, of *Schriften Zur Theologie,* I.

[2] P. 323, footnote no. 5; italics are those of Fr. Rahner.

[3] *Summa Theol.,* I. q. 43, a. 3.

created grace which in its deepest reachings is formally causative of this union with divinity. Rather it is uncreated grace which calls the latter into being much as a form introduces an ultimate disposition towards itself in the matter to which it is united.

How then are we to conceive of this conjunction of God to the soul? The sole remaining order of causality is formal, and this is precisely what Rahner's theory envisions:

God communicates Himself to the man whom grace has been shown in the mode of *formal* causality, so that this communication is not then merely the consequence of an efficient causation of created grace. Thus . . . the communication of uncreated grace can be conceived of under a certain respect as logically and really prior to created grace: in that mode namely in which a formal cause is prior to the ultimate material disposition. This union in so far as it takes place by way of formal causality, is not simply a consequence of created grace—indeed it precedes the created grace to the extent that this grace, as the ultimate disposition to the union, can only exist when God's formal causality is actually being exercised.[4]

Divine Substance then " informs " or " actuates " the soul. Overtones of De la Taille's theory on the Hypostatic Union as " created actuation by Uncreated Act " are discernible here; the created actuation being, in this context, the created grace itself at least as viewed in one of its formalities. The two teachings have much in common though Rahner acknowledges no direct dependence upon the French Jesuit, and his own theological argumentation (which is our concern here) is developed along somewhat independent lines.

Obviously, no created form (natural or supernatural) will offer a close parallel to what is involved here. The divine " form " must remain immutable, just as this is true of the divine Agent. How exactly the genuine ratio of formal causality is preserved without the inverse affecting of the form by a receiving potency is left somewhat vague. Nevertheless,

[4] Pp. 334 and 335.

because this must be so, the causality in question is given the prefix " quasi ":

One may explicitly draw attention to this metacategorical character of God's abidingly transcendent formal causality by a prefixed ' quasi,' and in cur case then be entitled to say that in the vision of God his Being exercises a *quasi-formal* causality. All this *quasi* implies is that this ' forma,' in spite of its formal causality, which must be taken really seriously, abides in its absolute transcendence (inviolateness, ' freedom ').[5]

Lastly, such a relationship as this of God to creature should not be far removed from theological conceptualization. " For . . . it is indubitably given for every Catholic theologian at least in the special case of the hypostatic union." [6]

2. *Sources of the Teaching*

The origins of Father Rahner's understanding of uncreated grace is in the primary sources of revelation. Scripture and patristic tradition are agreed that the justification of man involves two elements: the communication of the Spirit, and an inner quality inhering in the soul and effecting a transformation of the justified. But the vigorous expressions of God revealing present the latter as a consequence of the former, and as fulfilling a subordinate role in the sanctification of man.

For St. Paul man's inner sanctification is first and foremost a communication of the Personal Spirit of God . . . and he sees every created grace, every way of being πνευματικος, as a consequence and a manifestation of the possession of this uncreated grace. Thus . . . we should say with St. Paul that we possess our pneumatic being (our ' created sanctifying grace ') because we have the personal Pneuma of God.[7]

The same indication is to be found in St. John, although less " explicitly and exclusively." As for the Fathers, especially

---

[5] P. 330. The citation here refers expressly to the beatific vision, but Rahner understands the formal causality as " quasi " in a similar sense where habitual grace is concerned.

[6] *Ibid.*

[7] P. 322.

the Greek Fathers, ". . . They see the created gifts of grace as a consequence of God's substantial communication to justified men." [8]

3. The Theological Argumentation

Presuming from revelation the fact of uncreated grace, it is Rahner's avowed intention to " define the essence of uncreated grace more sharply than has hitherto been the case," and this by " using elements already found within the conceptual equipment of scholastic theology." [9] Reduced to its simplest form the methodology involved is that of using the analogy which prevails between grace and glory, wherein a theological insight traditionally discerned in the latter case is employed " mutatis mutandis " to illumine the nature of grace. To justify the analogy one has only to consider how grace is ontologically the commencement of glory. Their relationship is not merely moral and juridic, but the life of glory is rather seen as the definitive flowering of the life of divine sonship already possessed. Grace is thus an inner entitative principle of the vision of God. Thus there can be, " no objection in principle to applying to an ontology of grace a set of concepts which have proved themselves objectively valid in an ontology of the immediate vision of God . . ." [10]

In the beatific vision God unites Himself to the intellect of the blessed " in ratione speciei." The expression is that of St. Thomas himself,[11] and means that the divine Essence assumes in beatifying knowledge the role of the " species intelligibilis " in knowledge connatural to man. Such species, in intellection as such, is a presentation of the object and so determines the knowledge in a formal way. Prior, however, to the actual

---

[8] *Ibid.*

[9] P. 319.

[10] P. 326.

[11] III *Contra Gentiles,* c. 51: ". . . essentia divina potest comparari ad intellectum creatum ut species intelligibilis qua intelligit . . ." Cf. *De Vertitatis,* 2, 10, a. 11. What is meant here is the impressed species though it is equally true that God also assumes the role of expressed species in the beatific vision.

knowledge which it makes possible and to which it gives speci-
fication, the species *ontologically* determines the knower. This
causality (prior in a non-temporal sense only) can be conceived of only as formal, resulting as it does from the mere
presence of the species, and achieves in the knower an ontological presupposition to cognition.

This ontological determination precedes contact with the
extra-mental reality by way of the species which is conscious
knowledge. At this point Rahner uses language seemingly
originating from sources other than scholastic, yet so revelatory of his concept of knowledge that a somewhat lengthy
citation will not be out of place:

> Knowledge is primarily the being-present-to-itself of an entity:
> the inner illuminatedness of an entity for itself on the basis of its
> determinate grade of being (immateriality). The species must not
> unhesitatingly be conceived of as the ' intentional image ' of an
> object, made present in the mind in a non-real ' mental ' way as
> a copy of the object due to the object's impression upon it. Rather
> it is primarily . . . an ontological determination of the knower as
> entity in his own reality, this determination consequently being
> logically prior to knowledge as consciousness . . . If and in so far
> as the species understood in this way is also the effect of an object
> distinct from the knower and so *entitatively* assimilates the knower
> to the known, the being-present-to-its-own-self (" Beischselber-
> sein ") of the knower as an entity determined by the *species*
> becomes also the knowledge of the object itself . . . [12]

In the case of the beatific vision God unites Himself to
the blessed in such fashion as to effect, by quasi-formal causality, an ontological determination within the intellect of the
" beatus " which precedes and makes possible the eliciting of
the " ipsa visio." What of the created light of glory? It is
here as an ultimate disposition of the soul to such causality,
preceding it as matter does form and introduced into the soul
by the very presence of the form. Now if sanctifying grace
be the homogeneous commencement of glory, an analogously
similar quasi-formal causality should be discernible in the jus-

---

[12] Pp. 328-329.

tification of the wayfarer.[13] This is uncreated grace; it is a ". . . *communication* of the divine Being taking place *by way of formal causality* to the created spirit whch is the *ontological presupposition* of the *visio*." [14] What is achieved here is an immediate entitative union with divinity, prior to and rendering possible the knowledge and love of God through the created gifts of grace in this life, and the " lumen gloriae " in the next. This, in a primary sense, is the justification and sanctification of the soul, both " in statu viae " and " in statu termini."

This in substance is the one basic theological argument upon which Rahner builds his theory of uncreated grace. The metaphysics of intellection illumine for us the nature of God's presence in the intuitive vision of Himself, which in turn reveals to us the essence of the grace state integrally taken. Obviously, it is more an exposition than a demonstration, and so can be evaluated only by an analysis of each of the elements which enter into this construct of analogy. Once the theory be granted certain corollaries follow: 1) it would seem not to be impossible that each Divine Person exercises a distinct and proper influx of the real order in this quasi-formal causality of grace; 2) the words of the Council of Trent on created grace as " causa unica formalis " of justification will admit of interpretation not inimical to this position; 3) hints of this teaching should be discoverable in other theological sources— Rahner expressly mentions Pius XII, St. Thomas, St. Bonaventure, and Alexander of Hales, as well as a host of modern writers.

II. CRITIQUE OF RAHNER'S THEORY

1. *Sources of Revelation*

"Have you received the Holy Spirit," St. Paul asks the new Christians at Ephesus. In this and other vivid expressions

---

[13] Rahner explains that the distinction between the formal casuality in grace and in the " visio " may be either a difference of degree in this causality itself or a difference derived from the material disposition to such communication (p. 336).

[14] P. 335.

Sacred Scripture leaves no doubt that to the just man, over and
above that "seed" and "unction" which is a created quality,
there is given in mysterious fashion the very uncreated substance of God. The Fathers too can very readily be enlisted
in support of this truth.[15] Rahner's contention that uncreated
grace is part of the "given" of revelation, then, is hardly
open to doubt. Further, a certain primacy in the case of uncreated grace seems explicitly to be indicated. And it does
seem true that something more is meant here than God's presence to the Soul as causing grace, for such presence hardly
answers to the notions of "having," of "dwelling in," of
"grace," i.e., gratuitously given. All this is readily admissable
in the revelation itself. But to see this as explicable by some
sort of formal causality is a pure assumption. It can hardly
be said to be revealed even implicitly. The semitic mind and
language were not apt to distinguish clearly the distinct categories of causality. Too many alternate understandings of the
texts suggest themselves—such as a mere primacy of excellence,
one which sees the term of grace (the Inhabitation) as more
significant than its beginning. The suggestiveness that Father
Rahner finds here of uncreated grace being formally constituted by an active quasi-formal causality on God's part can
be no more than a hypothesis. Its verification (as a theory
and not as a meaning of Scripture) must proceed from within
theological science.

2. The Theological Argumentation

Granting the ontological continuity between grace and
glory, in which really but one gift of God exists "inchoative"
in the wayfarer and "consummative" in the blessed; granting
therefore that glory is primarily a change in state allowing for
the manifestation, the full flowering of what must remain hidden in grace, it then follows that a consideration of the con-

---

[15] St. Augustine, for example, writes of the Pentecostal descent upon the Apostles, ". . . it was not only his sacred fragrance—the sacred ointment of His grace
—but His very substance which was poured into their hearts." Sermo CLXXXV,
De Temp.

ditions of that act wherein consists the very essence of consummated supernatural felicity is most apt to yield the inner secrets of grace itself. Of major significance here is the understanding of the beatific vision as perfectly intuitive, so much so that no created species can intervene and achieve the conjunction of intellect and God. This is the express teaching of St. Thomas,[16] and Rahner acknowledges that it is within the system of St. Thomas that he seeks to develop his intuitions. Knowledge without species, however, is not possible;[17] thus the beatific vision is explicable only if the divine Essence so unite Itself to the intellect as to assume the role of an impressed species.[18] But this is obviously only an analogy and we need to ask what precisely is the intelligibility it brings; where, in short, does the similitude end and the much larger area of dissimilation begin. Analogy, after all, is a comparison of diverse things which are only proportionately alike.

(a) *The Intelligible Species in Created Knowledge as Such.*

Here some ontological predetermination of the knower, prior to conscious knowledge does indeed occur. The species has its own " esse reale " as a quality with the passive intellect, and as an accidental form it informs the intelligence—an information previous to the actual " intelligere." The reason for this, however, is that the impressed species is an effect of the knowing subject, something caused by the efficiency of the agent intellect along with the instrumentality of the sense phantasm.[19] It comes to be as an accidental form of the passive intellect in which it inheres; as such it is an ontological determination of the intellect. The same is true of the species in

---

[16] *Summa Theol.*, I, q. 12, a. 2.

[17] Even in God, since knowledge is assimilated, there must be a " species "—one only virtually distinct, of course, from Knower and Known.

[18] Cf. note no. 11.

[19] The instrumentality of the phantasm is objective rather than properly effective since being corporeal it cannot operate towards the production of the immaterial intelligible species except in virtue of a transient spiritual motion deriving from the agent intellect. Cf. Joannis a S. Thoma. *Cursus Phil. Thom.*, Editio Reiser, III, p. 312.

the angelic intelligence; though infused rather than abstracted, they enjoy a real existence in the angelic mind antecedent to actual cognition. In all of this the intellect is looked upon as any other finite entity, as a subject receptive to accidental qualification. When considered formally as intellect the received species now bestows upon it not a new accidental " esse reale " but rather " esse intentionale "; that is, it effects and formally so, another state of " being," one of identification of the intellect with the known object. The identity is not, of course, ontological but of the psychological or representational order. And the species is seen not materially as an entity or accident but formally as a similitude, that is to say it is the very essence of the extra-mental object enjoying an intentional existence within the knower. " Domus in mente est domus in re "—in terms of essence there is identity, it is the two acts of existence that are distinct. In all composed realities existence derives from the form (" forma dat esse "). What then is the existence which the intelligible form gives? It is " intelligere "—the " to be " of knowing.[20] Herein lies the formal causality of the species—the actuation of the intellect, its reduction from potency to act.[21] This is understood in the sense of a *formal* actuation since as the vital operation of the faculty itself intellection is efficiently elicited by the intellect.

Now if I read Father Rahner correctly he would have the species determining ontologically the knower prior to knowledge in a way at least essentially similar to this.[22] But the

[20] Cf. Cajetan, *Comm. in Summa Theol.*, I, q. 12, a. 2, no. XVI: " Quemadmodum enim forma est principium essendi materiae, ita quod idem est esse materiae et formae diversimodi . . . ita species intelligibilis, si actu est in genere intelligibili, est intelligendi principium ita quod intelligere est ut ipsius esse."

[21] There is a parallel in the order of appetition or volition. The causality of the good or end is akin in its own order to that of the true. Final causality is the presence of the end in the appetite (by way of knowledge) effecting love (" prima immutatis appetitus ab appetibile "; I-II, q. 26, a. 2) somewhat as the species is the presence of the object in the cognoscitive faculty effecting, but formally rather than finally, knowledge. In either case the eliciting agency of will or intellect is demanded.

[22] This is not to suggest that Rahner's theory of knowledge is in every sense rec-

very reasons which underlie and imperate such affirmations make impossible any similar conclusions in the case of the beatific vision. Rahner, on the contrary, posits an almost total parallelism.

(b) God as " Species " in the Beatific Vision.

In consummate created knowledge wherein the infinite object is grasped in intuitive vision, the essence of God is present " in ratione speciei." However, as present under this precise formality God does not, indeed cannot, ontologically determine the intellect as a presupposition to its act of vision. Some such determination and elevation is required, but one effected by the divine efficiency in the infusion of the created light of glory. At this point the analogy with lesser knowledge breaks down. The reason quite simply is that here there is no finite form produced by the agent intellect and having existence as a real accident of the passive intellect. The divine object is in the cognoscitive power immediately and in virtue of its own natural (in this case divine) being, and not that accidental being proper to a species. Ordinarily the species has a twofold function: one entitative, the other intentional. In the first way, it is an accident, a quality modifying the soul, a form which in informing is absorbed in the actuation of a

ognizable as that of St. Thomas. There seems implicit in the former's theory a lack of precision in distinguishing between the ontological and intentional orders. He implies that the subject knows his subjective ontological determination by the species first, and then because it is also the effect of an object distinct from the knower " the being present-to-its-own-self . . . of the knower as entity determined by the species becomes also the knowledge of the object." Or again, " The knower and the known do not become one through knowledge (as consciousness); but because they are entitatively one . . . the knower knows the object." (p. 328). If the knowing subject is entitatively one with the object before knowledge this seems to say it takes upon itself the real " esse " of the extra-mental thing. The object however cannot exist in the mind except intentionally. The species has its own " esse reale," it is true, but this is not the species formally considered as similitude, or as it is the object itself with a new (intentional) mode of being. Rahner also cites approvingly the De Veritate, q. 1, a. 1: " assimilatio . . . est causa cognitionis "; but it seems clear that here St. Thomas is not speaking of an assimilation prior to knowledge but rather means that assimilation formally constitutes knowledge.

subject and constitutes with it a new accidental thing. In the
second way, it transcends this function of entitative information (and this due to its spirituality which in turn derives
from the spirituality of the intellect) and without any fusing
with its subject merely actuates or terminates the soul precisely in the line of knowledge. It makes the knower to be
known, to be come identified therewith—but only "intention-
aliter." As quasi "species" in the beatific vision God fulfills
the second of these roles but in nowise the first. St. Thomas'
very language is cautionary when he writes that it is not so
much that the divine essence becomes the form of the intellect as that it holds itself thereto after the fashion of a form.[23]
To perfect only in a terminative way means that the form is
not affected or altered in any way by the subject it perfects;[24]
and this is not mere extrinsicism for God is not only what
(" quod ") is seen, but that whereby (" quo ") He is seen.[25]

One of the more illuminating commentators on St. Thomas
—Sylvester Ferrariensis—has indicated the ultimate reason
on which rests this impossibility of God's determining the intellect ontologically and prior to knowledge, i.e., in the formal
order.[26] It is the identity of essence and existence proper to
Divinity. The divine quiddity cannot be "separated" from its
"esse natural" and given a *distinct* esse within the created
intellect. It is this very separability in the case of things not

[23] *Q. D., Veritate*, q. 8, a. 1: ". . . non oportet quod ipsa divina essentia fit
forma intellectus ipsius, sed quod se habeat ad ipsum ut forma . . ."

[24] Rahner is obliged to maintain that this is so in his own theory, that the
receptivity which is the modification of the creature does not imply any reaction
or determination of the form received. But such mutual determination is involved
unless God actuate merely intentionally or the creature be drawn up into the
uncreated esse proper to a Divine Person. The parallel with efficient causality
that he attempts to draw simply does not hold. It is only accidental to efficiency
as such that the agent undergoes mutation in causing. A purely actual agent whose
causality is his own substance will suffer no alteration whatsoever. But contrawise
the very concept of formal causality, except in the instances above mentioned
where the causality is only reductively formal, involves modification of the form.

[25] St. Thomas, III *Contra Gentiles*, c. 51: ". . . ut sit in tale visione divina
essentia et quod videtur, et quo videtur."

[26] Comm. in III *Contra Gentiles*, c. 51, no. 7.

their own being that makes possible their becoming objects of finite knowledge, at least, in an intuitive and connatural way. Not having any intentional being other than His un-created natural being, God cannot be known (except by anal-ogical inference) unless his very substance be immediately present to the created intelligence. This is the basis for the rejection by St. Thomas of all created species in the vision of glory. In so joining Himself to the creature God formally causes its very "intelligere" and its intentional identity with Himself. St. Thomas refers expressly to this formal actuation, ". . . so the divine essence, which is being itself, is united to the intellect making it to be in act through Himself." [27]

There is a second difficulty attendant upon this concept of a divine quasi-formal causality, apart from its having God enter into composition with the creature. Put simply, it amounts to an obscuring of the distinction between the nat-ural and supernatural orders.[28] Rahner acknowledges that this causality involves a corresponding receptivity on the part of the soul. God is there formally communicating something of His own perfection, which is in turn received by the soul. Presumably this is created and of the accidental order; [29] but certainly it is supernatural (it is described as an ontological presupposition to vision, in the case of glory; and in the case of sanctifying grace would be some sort of analogous prereq-uisite to salvific knowledge and love). But any subject receiv-

---

[27] *Summa Theol.*, I, q. 12, a. 2, ad 3ᵘᵐ: ". . . sicut aliae formae intelligibiles, quae non sunt suum esse uniuntur intellectui secundum aliquod esse quo infor-mant ipsum intellectum et faciunt ipsum in actu; ita divina essentia, quae est ipsum esse, unitur intellectui faciens ipsum in actu per seipsum."

[28] Elsewhere Rahner gives indication of some general misunderstanding of the autonomy of the supernatural order. Cf. his footnote no. 3, p. 333 where he sees, ". . . no difficulty in a created substance from which created grace proceeds con-naturally."!!

[29] How the formal effect of an Uncreated Form can be created and merely acci-dental is another problem implicit in this theory. It points to a confusion of the formal with the efficient order. It might also be noted here that for St. Thomas grace is created *in* the soul and as a supernatural accident thereof (or is educed from the obediential potency of the soul) but it is not created *from* the soul as a subject *out of which* it becomes.

ing a form must bear some proportion thereto and be in potency towards such act. Are we then to conceive of the created soul as having a positive ordination to the supernatural? Does this perfection *formally* proceeding from God, at the same time proceed from a positive potency of the soul in the exercise of genuine material causality? However unintended, this is an implicit denial to glory and grace of any entitative supernaturality.

This is the very reason for the necessity of the " lumen gloriae "—the elevation of the intellect to the point where it is capable of receiving Divinity itself as " species." [30] Precisely because God cannot formally communicate His own uncreated being, He must efficiently bestow a created participation therein, in order to render the vision of Himself possible. Rahner would explain the created light of glory as analogous to the ultimate disposition on the part of matter. But the requisite potency of matter to such a disposition is exactly what cannot be affirmed here of the finite intellect. And once the infused light achieves its elevation, then the intelligence is already in proximate disposition to the terminative actuation by the divine " forma intelligibilis." So conceived this actuation is not so much one the intellect receives as one to which it is elevated.

In the beatific vision the very substance of God cannot be present as a form ontologically determining the creature prior to vision. This being so one cannot argue from the union supposed in such blessed intuition to an analogously similar union as constituting uncreated grace in the wayfarer. The causality in the former case, though indeed formal, only reduces the

---

[30] St. Thomas, *Summa Theol.*, I, q. 12, a. 5: " Respondeo dicendum quod omne quod elevatur ad aliquid quod excedit suam naturam, oportet quod disponatur aliqua dispositione quae sit supra suam naturam . . ." This is reductively material causality. Consequent to the reception of God as " species," the light of glory will make possible the reception of the Divine motion moving the disposed intellect to the " ipsa visio." Thirdly, in the order of efficient causality the " lumen " will operate instrumentally in the intellect's vital eliciting of the vision as its own second actuality.

intellect to act "in genere intelligibilium" and terminates its intuition—none of which is applicable to grace in the way-farer. Any other causality of a formal nature beyond this would be inimical to the perfection of God.

(c) *Quasi-Formal Causality in General and the Analogy with the Hypostatic Union.*

Father Rahner attempts to safeguard his position by insist-ing that the causality here envisioned is only *quasi*-formal that, at least in the case of grace, some such relationship is conceivable if the concept of formal cause be subjected to certain undefined alterations. At least, ". . . the possibility of this must not be put in doubt in virtue of purely rational con-siderations."[31] Three points are offered in defense of this manner of thinking: 1) this quasi-formal causality is meta-categorical in character, 2) what the prefixed "quasi" signifies is that in such union God remains unalterable, just as He re-mains immutable in the exercise of efficiency, and 3) such quasi-formal causality, ". . . is indubitably given for every Catholic theologian at least in the special case of the hypo-static union."[32]

The mind's reach into the mysteries of God must avoid too rigorous an application of mundane concepts. The word of God will not suffer any "a priori" impositions of purely ra-tional categories; of necessity familiar concepts will have to undergo some amplification. In the case of formal causality in the strict sense, the proper concept involved is one of in-trinsic act received in some matter which it determines and specifies—either substantial form determinative of prime mat-ter or accidental form determining second matter—and being in turn determined, limited by that potency. Two elements are involved—perfectivity and receptivity. There are, how-ever, instances of intrinsic act received into potency which are neither substantial nor accidental form, the most obvious case in point being that of existence. Here is not "forma informans, inhaerens" but "forma actuans." As causality, this actuation is formal but only reductively so. Now is there conceivable a third mode of such causality, one wherein the actuality is extended to something other than itself without any corresponding receptivity? Immediately we are outside of the natural order, and are brought in reverence before the mystery of the Incarnation. For this is precisely what occurs in the Hypostatic Union. The Word in virtue of its immediate union to the humanity communicates to it that pure actuality which is the divine Personality and the existence of God as this is proper to the Second Person. This uncreated actuation is true formal causality in an extended sense; it is an analogous mode of formal causality.[33] There seems no objection in referring to it as quasi-formal.

But the question here posed is whether such a causality can be envisioned in the justification of man by way of grace. And the reply is—hardly. The reason lies in understanding exactly what is invloved in such divine formal actuation. Because there is no receiving potency, the communicating act (which can only be Pure Act) will bestow its perfection without limitation, i. e., infinitely. The actuation then will be uncreated.[34] The perfected will be transformed into the perfecting by way of a true identity, i.e., within the area of the perfection communicated since in other respects the perfected will retain its own identity.[35] Since Pure Act does not enter into composi-

---

[33] Cf. Kevin F. O'Shea, C. SS. R., "The Human Activity of the Word," *The Thomist,* April 1959, who refers to such causality as "pure actuation," "*simpliciter perfective* formal causality," and "purely terminative formal cause." He also cites Cajetan in his Commentary on III^a Pars, q. 17, a. 2, no. XVIII. "Nam si de actuare et actuari *infra totam latitudinem suorum modorum* sermo sit non est remotum a philosophia divina Deum posse actuare rem creatam."

[34] Thomists unanimously take exception to De la Taille's *created actuation* by Uncreated Act, for as created the effect must needs be the result of efficiency not formal causality; Cf. T. U. Mullaney, O. P., "The Incarnation: De la Taille vs. Thomistic Tradition," *The Thomist,* January 1954. As remarked earlier, Rahner's conception of quasi-formal causality runs along the line of the French Jesuit's thinking.

[35] The union in the Hypostatic Union is to God as term, thus without composition; yet to a perfective term implying a real, active, physical communication. Cf.

tion with the creature, It suffers no detriment, and by the same token, leaves the creature integral in its own essence and distinct from Itself. The perfected, in short, will become God either ontologically or intentionally. Christ *is* God in the first way, the blessed " become " God in the second. And in both cases the humanity is left integral.

It is impossible that any of this be realized in justification by way of grace. There is no essential transformation of the justified man into the Divine, either ontologically or intentionally. The concept of grace as formal participation in Divinity does imply a transformation, but purely of the accidental order. The divine presence here is not immediate but mediate, i.e., through the mediumship of created effects such as faith and charity. Participation in the divine life is " sub forma gratiae." It is because God Himself is not the pure actuating form of the creature that its elevation to the divine order demands God's supernatural agency in infusing the created

O'Shea, *op. cit.* This however, is not in virtue of anything other than the very union itself. Thus while the Hypostatic Union may be conceived of as a real created *relation* on the part of the humanity to the Word as term, such a relation demands a fundament which is the " ipsa unio," the uncreated identity, the very communication whereby the Word invests and perfects the humanity with His own Personality. Cajetan puts this in a wonderfully lucid phrase: " Est igitur, ut unico verbo dicatur, unio naturarum in Christo relatio creata quaedam, hoc est, consequens earundem unitatem personalem increatam." Comm. in III-a, q. 2, a. 7, no. III. What Thomists are unanimous in rejecting here is any created perfection other than the very humanity itself as through a " mutatio passiva " it is *immediately* joined to the Word. There simply is no other way to avoid assigning to the humanity a material causality exercised over the Word.

Not all Thomists conceive of this " ipsa conjunctio " in the same way. Some are disinclined to see any active and exclusive influence of the Word reducible to the order of formal causality. Cf. J. H. Nicolas, O. P. (*Revue Thomiste*, t. LIII, no. 2, 1953, pp. 421-428; t. LV, no. 1, 1955, pp. 179-183) who prefers to see the Union as merely terminative and perfective only in the sense that the Word " integrates " the humanity. However, the language of Cajetan and John of St. Thomas seems suggestive of something more, and there is a difficulty in seeing how the above position does not reduce the Hypostatic Union to a mere relation. J. M. Ramirez, O. P., without explicitly employing the phrase, seems open to admitting such quasi-formal causality when he writes: ". . . ex parte modi terminandi extremum creatum assumptum . . . Deus perficit creaturam ut forma pure actuans seu terminans, absque ulla informatione." (*De Hominis Beatitudine*, III, Matriti, 1947, p. 497).

form of the wayfarer's sanctity. The "having of the Holy Ghost" attested to in revelation suffers this same mediateness, else how is it to be distinguished from the comprehension of beatitude? And here once again (since grace is the commencement of beatitude) the presence of the Trinity is terminal. The soul now supernaturally energized (primarily in its very essence and derivatively in its powers) reaches to the divine Substance (and Its Three Subsistences) by way of knowledge and love in the exercise of the theological virtues and the gifts.[36] Grace is not yet transfigured into that vision which is to be its consummation.

(d) *A Corollary—Proper Influx on the Part of Each Person of the Trinity?*

Rahner seeks to shed additional light upon the relationship established in grace when he states as a corollary to his theory that, "It is . . . . at least conceivable then that the quasi-formal causality which we have attributed . . . to God and his essence, should also be proper, with regard to the recipient of grace, to the Three Divine Persons in their personal distinction."[37] Seemingly this would follow logically from his teaching. However, it is quite impossible and so throws additional doubt upon his original viewpoint. If the impact of this critique on uncreated grace in general be that it endangers the transcendence of God, the particular objection here is that it is inimical to the unity of God.

In no matter how extended a sense the concept of formal causality be taken, the only communication possible in the case of a divine Person will be that which the Person is in Its

---

[36] Formally considered, the Inhabitation is of the cognitional and affective order. Its ontological character rests upon the fact that God is known and loved not abstractly but in His real and immediate presentiality to the soul (an immediacy which is at once "immediatione virtutis et immediatione suppositi") in the infusion of supernatural life. The knowledge then is quasi-experiential, elicited by charity and the gift of wisdom, and terminates at the divine Personalities as They are already present. It thus takes upon itself the characteristics of a genuine "contuition."

[37] P. 343.

distinct hypostatic character. It can only involve then that whereby a Person stands in relative opposition to the other Two. Should it be something which pertains rather to His identity with the nature, then, by that very fact, it ceases to be proper and becomes common to all three divine Subsistences. This is why it is completely alien to Catholic understanding to attribute any distinct *efficiency* to a divine Person; efficient causality is of the order of operation and it is not activity that is constitutive of divine Hypostasis. In the supposition of quasi-formal causality then, the formal effect communicated could not be a perfection of the order of either essence or existence, for these are necessarily common. There could only be given what is distinct in God; a Relation as it subsists; or a relatively distinct divine Subsistence, for this is what constitutes a divine Personality. All that the soul could receive is the divine Person Itself, and the existence that any concept of personality connotes secondarily—not the " esse " as common to all Persons (this would be a kind of monophysitism) but as proper and exclusive to the distinct Person. This is to say that the only communication possible is one resulting in a union of the hypostatic order. The consequence would be a personification of the humanity, whereby it would be rendered subsistent in each divine Personality. Apart from this, the only other possibility is the purely terminative formation of the glorious intellect by all three divine Persons in vision.

This objection is anticipated by Rahner and he replys by saying that a divine Hypostasis can be communicated in two ways: either in hypostatic union, or ". . . . to the end and only to the end that it can become in virtue of this quasi-formal causality the object of immediate knowledge and love." [38]

---

[38] P. 345. As is consistent with his teaching, Rahner maintains that this causality is of the entitative order, effecting certain ontological presuppositions to knowledge and love. P. de Letter in a very recent article in *The Irish Theological Quarterly*, January 1963, defends, on the other hand, the position that this quasi-formal causality is entirely realised in the intentional order. But this means only to actuate in the sense of causing (formally) the very intellection, and to specify such operation. Were a Divine Person to actuate in this way He would become

Obviously, he doesn't mean the beatific vision, yet for the wayfarer such activity can be rendered possible only by its having essential perfections, i.e., perfections which grant a participation in the divine intellect and will.

For all this Rahner prefers to explain these gifts in the soul as consequences of the pure presence (and resulting personal communications) of a divine Person. The very presence of the first Person, for instance is such as to formally render us His adoptive sons, and so this filiation regards not the Trinity, but the Father alone. The created graces which found such proper relations are not merely to be appropriated to the particular Person. This tendency to dismiss the profound Trinitarian implications of appropriation is somewhat misplaced.[39] If the infused gift of grace be taken formally as appropriated it cannot in the exact same way be appropriated to another Person. It relates the soul to a distinct Person and assimilates it to that Person in His distinct hypostatic character. But this is in virtue of the fact that appropriation must have a real fundament, a basis in reality for the discerned similitude.[40] What is proper is the appropriation ("ipsa appropriatio") and not the grace so appropriated ("appropriatum"); and thus the entire process remains within the cognitional and affective order. It is the very abyss separating created and uncreated which allows for no other possibilities for proper relations save those in appropriation. Created charity, for example, can only be appropriated to the Holy Spirit precisely because charity is distinct in nature from the other gifts of grace while the

an object of immediate vision. Any *formal* effect prior to knowledge would necessarily be outside of the intentional order.

[39] Rahner writes of a kind of pre-Christian monotheism, adding: ". . . and that is what the doctrine of base appropriations in the theology of grace really amounts to . . ." (p. 346).

[40] The adoptive sonship realised in grace regards the entire Trinity, yet at the same time bears an undoubted resemblance to the natural sonship of the Second Person. As so likened to the eternal Son there is accomplished in us an analogical imitation of His relationship to the Father and also the Holy Spirit. It is one thing to see the inner dynamism of the grace state as imitative of the Eternal Origins within the Godhead, and quite another to ascribe this to an *intrinsic* formal causality proper to each Divine Person.

Holy Spirit is nowise different or diverse from Father and Son. The sole distinctness within God is in the line of subsistence. In its own order, a created thing can imitate this. It cannot have the distinct Subsistence itself as its own form or act except in what would be another Incarnation.

3. *Theological Methodology*

Father Rahner has warned us against approaching an understanding of the mysteries of God in too narrow a spirit. And true enough, the analogical leap from finite to infinite will demand purging concepts of all traces of imperfection, rendering them open to the divine. Accordingly, the concept of strict formal causality has been amplified to where it embraces the transformative pure actuation of the creature (in vision and in the Incarnation). But there is a principle of limitation involved here, too. However meta-categorical Rahner's quasi-formal causality be it cannot cease to bear any analogous similitude to formal causality as an ultimate species of cause and still be designated as formal. His theory posits the uncreated " form " as intrinsically received and determinative of the creature in the entitative way, at the same time remaining free of all determination by this reception. This suggests a confusion of formal with efficient cause. And if such imprecision of language is allowable here why may it not be extended to theological usage of such notions as " efficiency," " causality," " actuality," " essence," " existence " etc. The danger here lies in the language of theology becoming equivocal; in the rejection of analogy and the taking of refuge in that practical agnosticism that replaces analogy with mere symbol.[41]

---

[41] How much of a major departure from Catholic Theology this entails can be seen in the theologizing of some contemporary Protestant thinkers. One example would be Paul Tillich who denies that God can be properly called First Cause or Uncreated Substance because these are human terms answering to finite reality. Use of the first results in rationalistic theism; use of the second in a naturalistic pantheism. Thus " it is as atheistic to affirm the existence of God as it is to deny it." For him such terms can be merely religious symbols. Cf. *Four Existentialist Theologians*, edited by Will Herberg, Doubleday, New York, 1958.

In somewhat this same spirit Rahner approaches what he himself recognizes as a difficulty which urges itself against his thinking. This is the teaching of the Council of Trent to the effect that the unique formal cause of justification is grace as an inhering created quality of the soul.[42] This phrase must be interpreted, he maintains, in accord with the intentions of the Conciliar Fathers in giving approval to it. They intended only to do away with any understanding of justification in terms of a mere extrinsic imputation (as, for example, in the teaching of Seripando and certain of the Reformers). They wished to insure the reality of created grace without entering into its relationship with uncreated grace. The "unica causa formalis" does not, in short, mean unique. Even granting that Seripando's position was historically what occasioned this teaching, still this is the dogmatic formula proposed by the Council. What Father Rahner offers is an intepretation, but one that goes against the literal meaning of these words of the magisterium, and there is about it a certain gratuitousness at the very least. And the burden of justifying this reading falls very heavily upon Father Rahner. The procedure suggests that the author has reasoned to a personal opinion highly complex and quite original, and then has been forced to distinguish away an authoritative pronouncement in its defense.

A similar enthusiasm for his theory has led him to seek support from other authoritative sources. To this end he cites the "Mystici Corporis" of Pius XII and finds there in his own favor the two truths: 1) "that between God and man there evidently exists a categorical order which is not that of efficient causality," and 2) "that the doctrine of the 'visio beatifica' should be drawn upon in order to determine the essence of grace. Pius XII is merely echoing long standing tradition and truths fully acknowledged within traditional theology. To see in this any favoring of his own novel teaching is far fetched indeed.

In a section headed "hints of this view in other theologies"

[42] Denz. 799.

he lays claim to inspiration from St. Thomas. This calls for considerable reading into the texts proposed. A passage in the *Third Sentences*,[43] for instance, leads him to remark, " . . . Even St. Thomas once calls the Holy Spirit the *causa formalis inhaerens* of our adoptive sonship." Seen in its full context what St. Thomas does say there is that created charity appropriated to the Holy Spirit is the formal cause of this filiation. And when St. Thomas writes of the divine Persons leaving gifts in the soul by a certain impress or " sigillatio " of Themselves,[44] he is not ascribing to each Person a proper active influx but is referring to a common agent causality resulting in a distinct assimilation to each of the divine Personalities. For he characterizes this " sigillation " as antecedent (not consequent) to " having " a divine Person. The same can be said of the text from the Tertia Pars [45] to the effect that grace is caused by the presence of Divinity. All that is intended there is to show that the grace of union in Christ precedes his created sanctifying grace. True enough, St. Thomas states that created grace stands to uncreated grace " ex parte recipientis vel materiae." [46] but the meaning is made clear when he adds that, on the other side, the Holy Ghost is related to the created grace as Agent and End (" ex parte agentis et finis "). And when in his mature presentation in the *Summa*,[47] St. Thomas writes of sanctifying grace *disposing* the soul to be the recipient of a divine Mission, he is surely not referring to an ultimate disposition introduced by form since the whole point of the article is to conclude that such " having " is only " sicut cognitum in cognoscente, sicut amatum in amante." These are only isolated texts, yet their interpretation is revelatory of how enthusiasm seems here to be impatient of the demands of scholarship.

However wondrous, beyond the telling thereof, be the mys-

---

[43] III *Sent.*, d. 10, q. 2, a. 1, sol. 3.
[44] I Sent., d. 14, q. 2, a. 2, ad 2um.
[45] *Summa Theol.*, III, q. 7, a. 13.
[46] I *Sent.*, d. 14, q. 2, a. 1, sol. 2.
[47] *Summa Theol.*, I, q. 43, a. 3, ad 2um.

tery of man's deification, it cannot be made more than it is without being thereby despoiled. Raised to a formal sharing in that inner-Trinitarian life proper to Diety alone, man is not thus transformed entitatively into God. This is the prerogative of Christ alone; the blessed, too, " become " God but only in the order of knowing and loving. Anything savoring of theological pantheism or a kind of monophysitism ultimately demeans the splendor which is grace. The doctrine of Father Rahner must involve either an unthinkable fusion of God with creature, or a transformation of the creature into the divine by way of hypostatic union or glorious vision. Grace is none of these. The most disquieting feature of this theory (and its variants) is that it is impossible to see that it does not slight the transcendence of God.

Faith is at once a need to understand. The deep things of God suggest a constant dynamism (if not always objective progression) in the striving for such understanding. We should not rest satisfied with mere re-statement of the formulae which arose out of the vitality of the faith in the past. The metaphysics of grace surely can be furthered, rendered more profoundly illumined for us. But the directions which Father Rahner here suggests do seem to break continuity with the rich traditions of the past, even to come close to overstepping the norms of orthodoxy.

WILLIAM J. HILL, O. P.

Dominican House of Studies,
Washington, D. C.

THE SACRIFICE OF THE MASS AS AN ACT OF THE VIRTUE OF RELIGION

A Study in Moral Theology

ᘓᔡᘉ

I N recent years many theologians have shown grave dissatisfaction with the method of presenting and expounding the truth of revelation as it is found in the vast majority (if not indeed in all) of theological manuals. These theologians demand a more vital theology, a more vivid way of presenting divinely revealed truth, a manner more adapted to the mentality and training of the modern man. Such reactions are found among theological writers everywhere and it must be sincerely admitted that they are not altogether without foundation. His Holiness, Pope John XXIII, in his inaugural address to the assembled conciliar fathers, insists that there is urgent need for re-thinking our theology and for expressing it in a new and more modern way. In the same breath, however, he insists that there can be no question whatever of changing in any way the ancient truths, or of "accommodating" them to the whims and fancies of modern man. It is much more a question of presenting the ancient truths in a new garb, as it were, of freeing them from the dust of the past.[1] It is not, I think, out of place to quote the

---

[1] It is not the first time in the history of the Church or in the history of theological discussion that the need of a new formulation of the ancient truths of our faith has been felt, a formulation more suited to the mentality of our adversaries; it is not the first time that such a new expression of divine truth has been urgently called for. We find examples of that in almost every age. Thus we find in the 16th century a renowned theologian, Melchior Cano, who took an active part in the discussions of the Council of Trent on the Blessed Eucharist, the Sacrifice of the Mass and on the Sacrament of Penance, expressing his ideas most candidly on the question. He writes in his famous work, *De Locis Theologicis, Bk XII, chapter 11,* the following: Dixit in Concilio Tridentino vir eloquens sane ac facundus, sed parum theologus tamen, qui id suadere vellet audientibus, adversum haereticos, praesertim Lutheranos, non esse magnum usum scholasticae concertationis, oratorio potius more cum illis disserendum: nostrum enim spinosum esse ac per-

Supreme Pontiff's own words in their full context, for there is an inclination at times to cite his words out of context, and therein lies a grave danger. Here are his solemn words which set down succinctly and clearly the principles governing every theological investigation:

What is needed at the present time is a new enthusiasm, a new joy and serenity of mind in the unreserved acceptance by all of the entire Christian faith, without forfeiting that accuracy and precision in its presentation which characterized the proceedings of the Council of Trent and the first Vatican Council. What is needed, and what everyone imbued with a truly Christian, Catholic and apostolic spirit craves today, is that the doctrine shall be more widely known, more deeply understood, and more penetrating in its effects on men's moral lives. What is needed is that certain and immutable doctrine, to which the faithful owe obedience, be studied afresh and reformulated in contemporary terms. For

molestum. Quae si vera essent, exempla in Theologia disputandi non ab his, quos ante dixi, meliora peterentur. Equidem etsi non sum nescius, quam sit, non scholae dico in disputando mos, sed tota omnino scholae Theologia haereticis invisa, sed eo magis existimo, scholasticam disserendi formam ad haereses refellendas efficaciorem, quo magis haereticis invisa est. Quod si Lutherani academiae subtilitate minime capiuntur, ne oratione quidem ad rhetorum leges artificiose composita capi poterunt, quoniam grandiores sunt et callidiores effecti, quam ut orationis artificio apprehendantur. Verum si eo loco res sit, ut adversum Lutherana dogmata certare cogar, eligant alii (nihil enim impedio) suave orationis genus, quo mollius et familiarius homines istiusmodi ad ecclesiae benevolentiam alliciant, dummodo mihi relinquant scholae ossa servosque ac pressam disserendi soliditatem. . . . . Quum oratorum more quasi torrens fertur oratio, quamvis multa cuiusque modi rapiat, nihil tamen fere teneas, nihil apprehendas. Cum autem ad scholae normam certa via et ratione premitur, contineri amplectique facilius potest. Itaque praeclarum a Divo Thoma accepimus morem disputandi, si eum teneremus. Nemo vero a viro gravissimo orationis delicias quaerat, pigmenta muliebria, fucum puerilem, sed veras gravesque sententias, argumenta solida et propria, sermonem rei, de qua disseritur, accommodatum. . . . Equidem non Divum Thomam modo, sed scholae auctores quosdam alios existimo, si humaniores litteras coluissent, et quae in schola didicerant, eloqui voluissent, ornatissime splendidissimeque potuisse facere; et viros eloquentiae studiosos, si ab scholae instituto non abhorruissent, sed theologiam hanc didicissent et tractare voluissent, gravissime et copiosissime dicere potuisse. . . . *Verum si alterum sit optandum, malim quidem indisertam scientiam, quam inscitiam loquacem.* Nam exempla illa disputationis theologicae suis omnibus numeris absoluta is solum suppeditare potest, qui eloquentiam sapientiae coniunxerit. Age tamen, qualiacumque nostra sunt, et ea ipsi afferamus, quae etsi non meliora erunt quam vetera, erunt tempori fortassis aptiora.

this deposit of faith, or truths which are contained in our time-honored teaching, is one thing; the manner in which these truths are set forth, with their meaning preserved intact, is something else. This then, is what will require our careful, and perhaps too our patient, consideration. We must work out ways and means of expounding these truths in a manner more consistent with a pre-dominantly pastoral view of the Church's teaching office.[2]

When reading much of modern theological writing one gets now and again, unfortunately, the impression that there is an urge to change not only the manner of expressing ancient truths but even of modifying the 'depositum' itself. It is not surprising that the effect of such writing should be felt amongst the young theologians pursuing their theological studies. These frequently show a great lack of sympathy for traditional methods and demand from their professors a more vital, a more *existential* approach to revealed truth. This is true both in the field of dogmatic theology and in that of moral theology. In the domain of moral theology there is a certain amount of confusion of thought in the writings of the moralists themselves and then, of necessity, in the minds of the students. The net result is that the students fail to dis-tinguish between what we may call moral catechesis, that is, simple instruction in the rules governing Christian living as found in the sources of revelation, and formal theological science, which deals with the reality of the supernatural Chris-tian life and strives to expound and analyze scientifically its principles, its structure and its functioning. What the young theologians most often ask for and welcome in this field is a kind of biblical moral theology, which is more immediately applicable in the work of the sacred ministry—preaching and confessional. The reaction here is seen to be double: on the one side, against the casuistical moral teaching of the moral manuals (which most unfortunately reduce all moral theology as such to a science of sin) and on the other side against the speculative moral teaching of St. Thomas and the scholastics.

[2] AAS 1962, p. 791-792.

A very clear example of reaction against the method of the manuals is to be found in the matter of sacramental theology and in this case we are forced to admit that the reaction is most justified indeed. Prof. K. Rahner, for instance, laments the fact that, with the sole exception of the Sacrament of Penance (in which there is an insistence on the acts of the penitent receiving it) "all the sacraments are monotonously discussed according to one and the same pattern" (necessity, institution, structure, that is, matter and form) while "the existential side of the sacrament is given no place by right." [3] In this we agree with him whole-heartedly. Some time ago I had occasion to insist precisely on this point in the context of a series of articles on the role of the sacraments in the Christian life.[4] There I pointed out that the sacraments as used or received by the Christian people pertain to the virtue of religion: they are *external* religious acts. The two fundamental religious movements of the soul are the *movement of giving* to God an oblation of self or our possessions (corresponding to the internal attitude of devotion or devotedness to God, our Creator), and *the movement of receiving from God as suppliants* in humble dependence (corresponding to the internal attitude of prayer or supplication). In our sacramental life we find these very same acts of worship flowing from the Christian and supernatural or infused virtue of religion: the giving to God through Christ, our High Priest and Mediator between us and God the Father, and the receiving of divine life through Christ's sacraments in a spirit of religious submission and deep humility.

In this present article I should like to set down some reflections on the existential character of the greatest of all the external acts of Christian worship, the sacrifice of the Mass. These thoughts have been suggested not so much by a dogmatic study of the sacrament of the Blessed Eucharist as by

[3] Karl Rahner, S. J., *Theological Investigations*, I, p. 18, note 1.
[4] *Doctrine and Life* (Dominican Publications, Dublin, Ireland) 12 (1962) 71-78, 128-137.

a close study of the notion of sacrifice in so far as it is an external act of the virtue of religion, to be placed by all those who either offer or take part in the sacrifice of Christ. And in this I think I am correct in maintaining that I am emphasizing the so-called existential character of the Mass and the vital role it should play in the life of every Christian.[5]

The 22nd Session of the Council of Trent was devoted to the Church's teaching on the sacrifice of the Mass. As it is the most solemn and completely authentic statement we possess on the matter I think it well to quote it in full—in spite of its length—before proposing my theological reflections on its true meaning in the Christian life.

The holy, ecumenical, and general Synod of Trent lawfully assembled in the Holy Spirit with the same legates of the Apostolic See presiding, has decreed that the faith and doctrine concerning the great mystery of the Eucharist in the holy Catholic Church, complete and perfect in every way, should be retained and, after the errors and heresies have been repudiated, should be preserved as of old in its purity; concerning this doctrine, since it is the true and the only sacrifice, the holy Council, instructed by the light of the Holy Spirit, teaches these matters which follow, and declares that they be preached to the faithful.

Since under the former Testament (as the apostle Paul bears witness) there was no consummation because of the weakness of the Levitical priesthood, it was necessary (God the Father of mer-

---

[5] The literature on the Sacrament of the Blessed Eucharist in general and on the Sacrifice of the Mass in particular is immense. However, I should like to quote the following works that have been of special help in the working out of the present essay. Bernhard Durst, O.S.B., " Das Wesen der Eucharistiefeier und des christilichen Priestertums," Herder: Rome, 1953 (*Studia Anselmiana* 32) ; Charles Journet, *La Messe, Présence du sacrifice de la Croix,* Desclée de Brouwer, 1957; Antonio Piolanti, *Il mistero Eucharistico,* Libreria editrice Fiorentina: Florence, 1958; Anton Vorbichler, S. V. D., *Das Opfer auf den uns heute noch erreichbaren ältesten Stufen der Menschheitsgeschichte.* Eine Begriffsstudie, St. Gabriel-Verlag, Mödling b. Wien, 1956; Ansgar Vonier, O. S. B., *A Key to the Doctrine of the Eucharist,* London, 1925) (still one of the best studies on the matter); and the special number of the French review *Lumière et Vie* 7 (1952).

It is of interest to note that Melchior Cano in chapter 12 of Book 12 of the above-mentioned and quoted work, *De Locis Theologicis,* gives a most penetrating theological analysis of the Catholic doctrine on the Blessed Eucharist both as Sacrament and as Sacrifice.

cies ordaining it thus) that another priest according to the order of Melchisedech [Gen. 14:18, Ps. 109:4; Heb. 7:11] arise, our Lord Jesus Christ, who could perfect [Heb. 10:14] all who were to be sanctified, and lead them to perfection. He, therefore, our God and Lord, though He was about to offer Himself once to God the Father upon the altar of the Cross by the mediation of death, so that He might accomplish an eternal redemption for them [edd.: *illic*, there], nevertheless, that His sacerdotal office might not come to an end with His death [Heb. 7.24, 27] at the Last Supper, on the night He was betrayed, so that He might leave to His beloved spouse the Church a visible sacrifice (as the nature of man demands), whereby that bloody sacrifice once to be completed on the Cross might be represented, and the memory of it remain even to the end of the world [I Cor. 11:23 ff] and its saving grace be applied to the remission of those sins which we daily commit, declaring Himself constituted " a priest forever according to the order of Melchisedech " [Ps. 109:4], offered to God the Father His own body and the blood under the species of bread and wine, and under the symbols of those same things gave to the apostles (whom He then constituted priests of the New Testament), so that they might partake, and He commanded them and their successors in the priesthood in these words to make offering: " Do this in commemoration of me, etc." [Luke 22:19; I. Cor. 11:24], as the Catholic Church has always understood and taught. For, after He had celebrated the ancient feast of the Passover, which the multitude of the children of Israel sacrificed [Exod. 12:1 ff.] in memory of their exodus from Egypt, He instituted a new Passover, Himself to be immolated under visible signs by the Church through the priests, in memory of His own passage from this world to the Father, when by the shedding of His blood He redeemed us and " delivered us from the power of darkness and translated us into His kingdom " [Col. 1:13].

And this, indeed, is that " clean oblation " which cannot be defiled by any unworthiness or malice on the part of those who offer it; which the Lord foretold through Malachias must be offered in every place as a clean oblation [Mal. 1:11] to His name, which would be great among the gentiles, and which the apostle Paul writing to the Corinthians has clearly indicated, when he says that they who are defiled by participation of the " table of the devils " cannot become partakers of the table of the Lord [I Cor. 10:21], understanding by table in each case, the altar. It is finally that [sacrifice] which was prefigured by various types of sacrifices, in the period of nature and the Law [Gen. 4:4; 8:20; 12:8; 22; Ex. passim], inasmuch as it comprises all good things signified by them, as being the consummation and perfection of them all.

And since in this divine sacrifice, which is celebrated in the Mass, that same Christ is contained and immolated in an unbloody manner, who on the altar of the Cross " once offered Himself " in a bloody manner [Heb. 9:27], the holy Synod teaches that this is truly propitiatory, and has this effect, that if contrite and penitent we approach God with a sincere heart and right faith, with fear and reverence, " we obtain mercy and find grace in seasonable aid " [Heb. 4:16]. For, appeased by this oblation, the Lord, granting grace and gift of penitence, pardons crimes and even great sins. For, it is one and the same Victim, the same one now offering by the ministry of the priests as He who then offered Himself on the Cross, the manner of offering alone being different. The fruits of that oblation (bloody, that is) are received most abundantly through this unbloody one; so far is the latter from being derogatory in any way to Him. Therefore, it is offered rightly according to the tradition of the apostles, not only for the sins of the faithful living, for their punishments and other necessities, but also for the dead in Christ not yet fully purged. (Denz. 937a-940, trans. R. J. Deferrari).[6]

Such is the Church's official and authentic teaching on the Mass. Every explanation of the Mass, either as a sacrament or as a sacrifice, must take these decisions of the Council of Trent into account and never depart from them. According to this teaching the Mass is: 1) first of all, a real and proper sacrifice; 2) secondly, the same sacrifice as that of Calvary and the Supper Room; 3) differing from Calvary only in the manner of offering the same victim; 4) and fourthly, the only sacrifice of the New Law.

The Mass, then, is a real sacrifice, the only real one of the New Law. That being so, it follows that what is true of sacrifice as such must be true also of the Mass, and what is true of priesthood as such must be true too of our Christian priesthood; and before we can determine how the Christian people should best take part in the sacrifice of the Mass and through it in that of Christ on Calvary, we must first of all under-

[6] In the latest, fully revised edition of Denzinger's *Enchiridion* this text is to be found n⁰ 1738-1743 (Herder: Barcelona 1963).

stand how sacrifice is offered and how one offers or takes part in it. That is the only sound manner of procedure in a theological analysis of the Mass as a sacrifice (and this aspect takes precedence over it as a sacrament) and of the part the faithful should play in the offering of it. Sacrifice is essentially an *external* act of the virtue of religion, and as such it is the sign of an internal sacrifice, of some internal act or attitude of mind of the person who offers it, and in the persons for whom it is offered or in whose name it is offered. This internal sacrifice is nothing else than what theologians call "*devotio*" or devotedness. This is defined by St. Thomas as "a ready will to do what pertains to the service of God." [7] It is the principal *internal* act of the virtue of religion and is an act of submission to God and to God's will in everything. It is a readiness to do God's will no matter what it may be and no matter how it may be made known to us. This complete submission of the creature to God is called by St. Thomas the "interior spiritual sacrifice"; it is the interior spiritual giving or oblation of self. A sacrifice which is offered exteriorly signifies an interior spiritual sacrifice by which the soul offers itself to God.[8] When man submits himself wholly to God he is drawn to manifest this submission in a sensible, tangible way. His nature tells him to offer something to God as a sign of his interior readiness to submit to God in all things.[9] In other words, nature, or better natural reason, tells him to offer some kind of external sacrifice. Now this external sacrifice, which consists essentially in the giving of something to God in a sensible and visible way, in relinquishing ownership of something, presupposes an internal act of giving, an internal "*oblatio*," quite distinct from "*devotio*," while flowing from it and being informed by it. This internal oblation bears directly on the object to be sacrificed, that is, on the object which is to be given over to God. If the external thing to be offered should be oneself (as in the case of self-sacrifice) then this internal oblation could rightly be called an act of self-

---

[7] II-II, 82, 1.   [8] II-II, 85, 2.   [9] II-II, 85, 1.

oblation, and it would be altogether distinct from the act of devotion " *quo anima seipsam offert Deo.*"

Now Christ's sacrifice on Calvary was, in fact, a sacrifice of self, demanded of Him by His Eternal Father for the redemption of sinning mankind. In offering this sacrifice Christ elicited an internal act of self-oblation and carried it into effect by allowing himself to be killed by the Jews. In the Old Law God demanded the killing of an animal, for instance, as a sacrifice (this being the most expressive manner of relinquishing ownership of a living thing and of giving it over to God), that is, an external sign of the people's subjection to and dependence upon Him. In offering this sacrifice the priest of the Old Law, already conscious of his and the people's dependence upon God, had to elicit a special act of giving this thing to God. This internal act, moving to the external action, is essential to sacrifice. Both together make up one complete external human act, the act of sacrifice. In speaking of sacrifice, then, we must be careful to distinguish three elements or acts. 1) First, the act or attitude of " *devotio*," which, as we saw, is a readiness to submit to God in all things, the fundamental act of the religious man, and is signified here by some external action of giving. It is the " *interius spirituale sacrificium*," or the " *principale* " [10] or " *verum* " [11] sacrificium " of which St. Thomas so often speaks. 2) Secondly, there is the internal act of the mind by which the priest relinquishes ownership of some external object and thus gives it over to God, consecrates it or makes it sacred. This is the internal oblation and is an act of the practical intellect.[12] 3) Thirdly, there is the external effective giving of the object to be sacrificed. This is, in the most formal sense of the term, sacrifice: the external carrying into effect of the internal oblation. It is clear that without " *devotio* " sacrifice can have no meaning, since it would then be an empty sign, a sign without anything being

[10] II-II, 85, 3 ad 2.

[11] *Summa contra Gentiles,* III, 120.

[12] Cf. I-II, 102, 3 for the meaning of the different types of sacrifice in the Old Law.

signified. It is clear, too, that the external effective giving or
sacrifice necessarily presupposes the internal oblation just as
every other external human act presupposes an internal act
of the human will, without which the external action would
not even be a human act.

Since the Blessed Eucharist is both a sacrament and a sacrifice we may note here the two main differences between a
sacrament and a sacrifice. 1) Since sacrifice is essentially the
giving of something to God as a sign of our submission it follows that men could institute their own sacrifices, external
signs of their recognition of God's supreme dominion. But a
sacrament is a sign and the cause of some gift given by God
to man. Therefore, only God, from whom the gift comes, can
institute a sacrament.[13] 2) A sacrament of the New Law, instituted by Christ, will, of itself (*ex opere operato*), produce
or increase grace, provided no obstacle be placed in its way
(*non ponentibus obicem*), that is, provided the recipient in
receiving it really places an act of the virtue of religion. Sacrifice, however, of itself, produces no effect, either in the priest
or the assistant unless it be ratified interiorly by them. That
is, it produces its effects according to the devotion and faith
of the offerer, of which devotion and faith it is a sign. Sacrifice is ordained immediately to honouring and placating God
as St. Thomas has shown.[14] Indeed, it is the interior or moral
ratification of the external sacrifice that makes the sacrifice
acceptable to God. It is what reconciles me to God. What
good is it for a person to intercede for me with another person, whom I have offended, unless I sincerely desire to be reconciled to that person, unless I really desire to make amends
for the injury done? We may, of course, deceive our fellowmen, but God we cannot deceive: *Deus intuetur cor.*[15]

In the state of pure nature (that is, had man never been

---

[13] Cf. II-II, 85, 1 ad 3; III, 64, 2.

[14] Est enim hoc proprie sacrificii effectus ut per ipsum placetur Deus: sicut etiam
homo offensam in se commissam remittit propter aliquod obsequium acceptum, quod
ei exhibetur. III, 49, 4.

[15] Cf. III, 83, 4 ad 8.

raised to the supernatural order and had he never sinned) each individual would have been drawn to offer some kind of sacrifice on his own behalf. That is, he would have certainly testified in some tangible and sensible way to the fact that he owed his being and all he had to God, the Creator and sovereign Lord of all. Or, perhaps, he would have deputed others to do it for him, guaranteeing that he would ratify what they did. In this way there would have been instituted a kind of natural priesthood, the deputy (that is, the priest) acting as representative of all the rest in testifying openly and externally to the submission of all. St. Thomas thinks that the honour and dignity of offering sacrifice would have been committed to the first-born of each family.[16] One thing is certain, as experts in the history of religions show, the sacerdotal function has, in fact, always been a social function, the priest acting in the name of many, of the family, of the tribe, of the people. In this state of pure nature, then, man would have decided upon his own sacrifices—their kind, the manner of offering them, etc. But, obviously, the Creator could intervene, should He think fit to do so, and ordain that only such and such sacrifices would be acceptable to Him. He, as Lord and Master of all creation, has the perfect right to do that. And, in fact, in revealed religion, in the Old Law, God (Jahweh) ordained explicitly that certain men (Aaron and his sons) should offer sacrifice to Him on their own behalf and on behalf of the whole Jewish people. They were the priests constituted by Him, His priests. They were thus constituted the mediators between God and the people. God laid down in all detail what precise kind of sacrifices were to be offered. In consequence no others would be acceptable to Him, no others would be regarded as signifying the submission of the people, no others would, in fact, placate Him. The exact ritual of all these sacrifices was also laid down by God, and these ceremonies had to be observed in every detail.

The purpose of all sacrifice as such (which we can deter-

---

[16] Cf. I-II, 103, 1 ad 1 et 3; II-II, 85, 1 ad 1.

mine from a simple analysis of the nature of sacrifice) is fourfold. 1) First, to give honour and glory and praise to the
Creator as the Lord of all being. By sacrifice we wish to show
that we are conscious of our complete dependence upon God.
This is called by theologians the " *finis latreuticus* " of sacrifice. 2) Secondly, to thank the Creator for His goodness to us
in creating us [17] (that is, in giving us a sharing in His Being and
perfections) and in conserving us in being. This is known to
theologians as the " *finis eucharisticus* " of sacrifice. 3) Thirdly,
to implore the Creator never to forsake us, never to withdraw
His aid from us, to beseech Him to continue to look with favour and benevolence upon us. This is called the " *finis impe-
tratorius* " of sacrifice. 4) Fourthly and lastly, in the event
of our having in any way offended the Creator, to make
amends for the injury done and to regain the good-will of God.
In other words to placate His anger. This is termed the " *finis
satisfactorius* or *propitiatorius* " of sacrifice. The first three
ends are essential to all and every sacrifice, even to those that
would be offered to God in the state of pure nature or in the
state of original justice. The fourth is present only when sacrifice is offered by or on behalf of *sinning* creatures.[18]

In the Old Law the people really took part in the sacrifices
in so far as they were present at the actual offering in the
temple. They thus ratified what the priest did in their stead,
while calling forth in their own souls a spirit of submission
(the actualization of the religious attitude of which we spoke
above) to the will of God. This ratification by the people in
the Old Law was obviously a *moral* ratification. They took
no physical part in the actual sacrificial offering, but did share
in the sacrificial meal as symbolic of sharing in the divine
blessing brought on the people by the sacrifice offered.[19] Of

---

[17] St. Thomas often refers to the divine gift of creation for which we must be
ever thankful to the Creator. Cf. II-II, 85; *Summa contra Gentiles*, II, 120.

[18] The whole question of the fourfold purpose or value (Wert) of sacrifice is
brought out extremely well by Bernhard Durst is his work mentioned above in
note 5.

[19] Cf. A. Grail, O. P. in his article, " Le Messe, Sacrament de la Croix, *Lumière*

this submission of the people the external action (external sacrifice) of the priest was a sign, just as much as it was a sign of the priest's own internal submission. Indeed this internal submission (either actualized, or as a state or attitude of mind and soul vis-à-vis of the Creator) is the very soul of sacrifice. Without it, as we saw above, the external action of offering some sensible object to God becomes an empty formula, devoid of meaning because signifying nothing. In that sense, and in that sense only, is the internal sacrifice the "*principale sacrificium*" or the "*verum sacrificium*" and not in the sense that it is the formal constitutive element. It gives meaning to the external rite of sacrifice.

The faithful Jew, assisting in the temple, so associated himself with the sacrifice of the High Priest as to make it his own and apply its fruits to himself personally. He could really and truly say that he personally offered sacrifice, because he offered together with the priest, but subordinated to him. They both offered the same sacrifice, one and the same, numerically identical. There was only one external rite (and that is formally what sacrifice is as an external act of religion), but there were many internal acts of submission to God signified by that one external action. The multiplicity of the internal acts signified does not multiply the sacrifice numerically. This point is of some importance when we come to consider the sacrifice of the Mass in the New Law.[20]

et Vie 7 (1952) p. 25. The same notion is expressed most clearly in the Canon of the Mass in the prayer "Supplices Te Rogamus" after the consecration. It should, however, be remarked that the faithful in the Old Law did not *always* partake of the sacrificial offerings. Such a participation was excluded altogether from the greatest of the Old Testament sacrifices, from the "holocausts." St. Thomas indicates these differences explicitly in his tract on the ceremonial rites of the Old Law (cf. I-II, 102, 3 ad 8) and his teaching is corroborated by modern Old Testament scholars. St. Thomas' theological exposé (I-II, qq. 101-103) of the Old Testament ceremonial law would well repay a careful study.

[20] We shall see that, at Mass, the priest and the faithful unite themselves to Christ, the one High Priest of the New Law, offering Himself in Sacrifice to His Father, in much the same way as the faithful Jew united himself to the priest offering sacrifice in the temple. I say that even with respect to the priests of the New Law: they stand in much the same relation to Christ as the faithful Jew did

In the Old Law the priest offered sacrifice as a principal
agent. He was priest in his own right. He was a priest *sui
iuris*, that is, not sharing in the priesthood of another (Christ),
but just prefiguring Christ's priesthood. He was a priest chosen
from among the people by God. In his own right he offered
the wine or animal or whatever other object was to be offered.
He observed all the prescribed rites in doing so. The people
simply ratified what he did. All these sacrifices were obviously
of a very finite and limited character. They could in no way
give to God all the honour and glory that is His due; alone
he could never hope to satisfy for the sins of all men, sins
which took on an infinite malice because they offended an
infinite being.

When human nature turned away from God by the sin of
Adam God demanded full and complete satisfaction. This we
know from revelation. There infinite satisfaction was asked
for by God. Though this may seem harsh treatment of a poor
finite creature by an All-powerful and infinite Creator, it was
in fact much more a sign of how much God thought of us. Instead of despising us and our sins (or even of annihilating us)
He thought it worthwhile (if I may say so without any irreverence) to make us pay the last cent of our debt to Him. He
considered our self-respect.[21]

But how was this full satisfaction to be paid? Only a God
could have found a means; a means, which in carrying out
the designs of His inexorable justice, was to show forth in a
resplendent way His boundless love for His creature, man.
*Deus, qui humanae substantiae dignitatem mirabiliter condi-
disti et mirabilius reformasti . . .*[22] God decreed that His
Only-begotten Son, His Word, in Whom and by Whom and
through Whom all things (and all men) were made, should
take to Himself a human nature, and in that human nature

to the priest. This in no way derogates from the special dignity of the Christian
priesthood or from its pre-eminence over the priesthood of the Old Law. I hope
to show that later.

[21] Cf. III, 46, 1 ad 3; 47, 3 ad 1.

[22] Prayer at the Offertory of the Mass in the Roman Rite.

(as man) offer the sacrifice of His life in satisfaction for the sins of men to His Eternal Father. The fittingness, or as St. Thomas and other theologians say, the *convenientia*, of this divine plan has often been pointed out. Let it be said, however, that the Word of God, the Logos, is not only the substantial image that God forms of Himself, but is also the image or plan in the mind of the divine Architect of all things made by Him. The Word of God is the living idea of every man, of human nature and all its members, in the mind of God. Man by sin destroyed that plan. It was fitting (*conveniens*, in keeping with the wisdom and goodness of God), then, that all should be put right again by the incarnation of that divine image or idea of us all. Also, since the Word of God is, in that sense, the image of every creature, the Word made flesh could become the real (but mystical) head of a regenerated human nature, just as Adam, by the mere fact of being the *first* man was the physical head of all men.

Having become man the Word of God offered on Mount Calvary the sacrifice of His life to His Eternal Father for *our salvation*. He offered sacrifice in the name of us all, for us all. As a sacrifice, demanded and arranged in every detail by God in His eternal and inscrutable decrees, it gave infinite homage to God; it made infinite amends to His offended majesty; it is infinitely impetratory for us; and it is an infinite act of thanksgiving for the benefits given to all mankind. It was the act of God-Man and, since all actions are the actions of persons, it was the act of a divine Person, and consequently of infinite value. It gave more glory to God and was more acceptable and pleasing to Him than ever was sin, even the greatest, detestable. About 200 years before the Council of Trent the English mystic, Julian of Norwich, penned the following beautiful page:

I stood beholding things general, troublously and mourning, saying to our Lord in my meaning with full great dread: Ah! good Lord, how might all be well, for the great hurt that is come, by sin, to the creature? And here I desired as far as I durst, to have some more open declaring wherewith I might be eased in this matter. And to this our blessed Lord answered full meekly and with full lovely cheer, and shewed that Adam's sin was the most harm that ever was done, or ever shall be, to the world's end; and also He shewed that this (sin) is openly known in all Holy Church on earth. Furthermore He taught that I should behold the glorious Satisfaction: for this Amends making is more pleasing to God and more worshipful, without comparison, than ever was the sin of Adam harmful. Then signifieth our blessed Lord thus in this teaching, that we should take heed to this: for since I have made well the most harm, then it is my will that thou know thereby that I shall make well all that is less.[23]

What good can we draw from Christ's infinite merits? We were not present at Calvary to ratify what He did for us. How can I make His merits mine? How can I make His sacrifice—of honour, praise, thanksgiving, impetration and satisfaction—mine? Seeing that the merits of Calvary are infinite, there is obviously no need for another and different sacrifice. The sacrifices of the Old Law were of finite value. They were many and repeated. In the New Law any sacrifice besides the sacrifice of Calvary would lack a raison d'être. There must be some way in which that which Christ did on Calvary may benefit *me*, may be *my* satisfaction, *my* prayer, *my* thanks, and *my* submission. Well, we make that work of redemption ours through the Mass. Let us see how.

In the Old Law the people derived fruits from the sacrifices offered by ratifying them interiorly, by uniting themselves in interior acts of submission (which include honour, praise, thanks, expiation) to the offerer or priest. How can we unite ourselves interiorly to an act of sacrifice which took place some 2000 years ago? Let it be said right away that we could have ratified (and indeed still can do so) the sacrifice of Calvary in faith, through faith. We could thus ratify and take part in Christ's sacrifice on Calvary morally and reap its fruits interiorly. But God did not wish it to be so intangible. He wished to leave us a means of doing that much more in conformity

[23] Julian of Norwich, *Revelations of Divine Love*, chap. 29, edit. Grace Warrack, p. 60.

with human nature. He wished to leave us a visible sacrifice which should be a sacrament of Calvary and through which we can make present again the sacrifice of Christ and really take part in it, offer it with Christ and apply its merits to ourselves. And this is how: Christ, by His very constitution as God-Man, sent by God the Father to redeem mankind, is essentially Priest and Mediator. As head of His Mystical Body He never ceases to offer Himself for us. "He continueth forever, hath an ever-lasting priesthood, whereby he is able to save forever them that come to God by him: always living to make intercession for us." [24] His act of oblation (self-oblation) is a permanent one in His mind and will. The following should be noted with reference to Christ's sacrifice. a) From the first moment of His existence as man there was "*devotio*" in the mind of Christ. He was always completely subject to the will of His Father. b) There was always in His mind, too, the will to offer sacri-fice, the sacrifice demanded by His Father. But this sacrifice was to be offered in certain determined circumstances, in a certain place and at a certain time: on the cross at Calvary. c) The sacrifice demanded from Him by His Father was the sacrifice of His life, the sacrifice of Himself, for the salvation of mankind. That was His Father's will and Our Lord always gladly accepted it. At the Last Supper Our Lord elicited the *internal* act of self-oblation as bearing on the external giving of Himself to death on the morrow as a sacrificial act. His hour had come and He decided to permit the Jews to take and kill Him. He went to death freely; He accepted the death on the cross as the sacrifice demanded by His Father. This internal act of self-oblation was never withdrawn and did not have to be repeated. Once elicited by Christ it ever remains in His mind and was present actually (virtually!) [25] on Cal-vary, where it was carried into effect *modo cruento et abso-luto*. d) At the Last Supper Our Lord externalized the inter-

[24] Hebr. 7: 24-25.
[25] Cf. Cajetan in I-II, 8, 3; II-II, 24, 10, edit. Leon. n⁰ IV; and Ferrariensis in III C 110.

nal act of self-oblation in another way, in a sacramental or symbolic way. That is, he expressed sacramentally (i.e., in a visible, sensible sign) the effective offering of His life, of Himself, in death. He instituted the s a c r a m e n t of His passion and death. He really offered Himself externally, but sacramentally, to His Father. He said the first Mass. And in the words of St. Peter Canisius:

> The sacrifice of the Mass rightly understood is a holy and living representation of the Lord's passion and of that bloody sacrifice which was offered for us on the Cross, and at the same time an unbloody and efficacious oblation (sacrifice).[26]

Our Lord's internal act of self-oblation is thus externalized sacrificially in two ways: 1) In an absolute and bloody manner on the cross. And this sacrifice on the cross may be called the *absolute* sacrifice of Christ. It was the sacrifice demanded by the eternal decree of His Father in heaven. 2) In a manner (external and accessory) which signifies and represents the absolute manner of offering Himself on the cross; that is, in a sacramental way. But this is no mere commemoration or mere figure or representation of the death on the cross. It is itself also a sacrifice in so far as it really contains Christ the victim offered for us. This is the manner of offering in the Last Supper, and consequently in the Mass.

At the Last Supper He changed bread and wine into His Body and Blood—a fore-presentation of Calvary. In so doing He rendered Himself really present under the species of bread and wine, He who was to offer Himself the next day for many unto the remission of sins. The act of *self-oblation* (His Father demanded and decreed that He offer Himself in sacrifice) in his mind (that is, the complete interior submission, the " *principale sacrificium* " of which we spoke above) never

---

[26] Peter Canisius, *Summa Doctrinae Christianae*, de sacramento Eucharistiae, § VII (edi. Landischuti 1848, p. 95): Missae sacrificium, si rem omnem aeque perpendimus, est revera dominicae passionis, et illius cruenti sacrificii, quod in cruce pro nobis est oblatum, sancta quaedam et viva representatio, atque simul incruenta et efficax oblatio.

changes.[27] He came to do the will of His Father. He was always about His Father's business. The external sacrificial expression of the spirit of submission (and of our submission in and through Him) was made on Calvary in a bloody manner—*modo cruento.* In the Supper Room, the same spirit of submission was represented, or better, fore-presented, in a sacramental, mystical, unbloody, but for all that sensible and visible way—*modo incruento.* He offered Himself just as truly in the Supper Room as He did on Calvary, but in a different manner. The Last Supper was indeed a true sacrifice, offered in a sensible, visible and sacramental way by Christ Himself directly and immediately. It was the very same sacrifice as that of Calvary, it was the offering of Christ Himself by Himself in a visible external way. This act of offering His Body and Blood was an act of His practical human intellect. It was what is called His oblative act. He put this act of giving of self into effect by placing the external signs of death, of His own death, which was to take place the following day. By death a *living* being is given sacrificially to God in the most expressive way possible. These external signs were placed *by His divine power,* by transubstantiation. Transubstantiation itself is not sacrifice.[28] It is external to it. It pertains here

[27] On the permanence of Christ's act of self-oblation and of the possibility of our sharing in it St. Thomas has the following to say: Omnia illa verba quae important comparationem Judaeorum ad Christum et poenam Christi, non dicuntur fieri quotidie. Non enim dicimus quod Christus quotidie crucifigatur et occidatur, quia actus Judaeorum et poena Christi transit. Illa autem quae important comparationem Christi ad Deum Patrem, dicuntur quotidie fieri, sicut offerre, sacrificare et huiusmodi, eo quod hostia illa perpetua est. Et hoc modo est semel oblata per Christum, quod quotidie etiam per membra ipsius offerri possit. (*II Sent.,* dist. 12, exposit. textus, ed. Moos n⁰ 267).

[28] In this connection it must be remembered that the external signs (which pertain to the very essence of sacrifice as an external act of religion) of internal sacrifice were not placed by Christ Himself. But Christ willed that they be placed, that is, he voluntarily allowed Himself to be crucified by the Jews. What the Jews did was not sacrifice and in no way enters into the intrinsic constitution of Christ's sacrifice. And for all that it must be said that Christ's sacrifice consists of the following essential constitutive elements: a) His voluntary dying on the cross, a death willed by Him and ordained by His eternal Father; 2) His internal act of self-oblation in obedience to the will of His Father. —At Mass (and at the Last

only to the mode of sacrifice. But the person Christ transubstantiated in order to offer mystically, really and physically, His human sacrifice. Christ, as Man, offered Himself internally by an internal act of self-oblation. The same person, Christ, as God, implemented this internal offering externally, by His divine power in transubstantiation. This divine power of Christ was brought into play by Christ uniquely in order to externalize His internal oblation of self. It is absolutely inseparable from His act of oblation. Where transubstantiation takes place there also must be Christ's will to sacrifice and Christ's internal oblative act.

Christ offered Himself in the Supper Room, not in order to complete the sacrifice of Calvary, but, as the Council of Trent says, in order to leave His beloved spouse, the Church, a visible sacrifice, as the nature of man demands.[29] In the Last Supper, then, Our Lord really offers Himself to God the Father in an external visible manner, as laid down by God. It is a sacramental way, and it draws all its meaning from the fact that He was to lay down His life in external, physical, natural death on Good Friday. The external sacramental giving or offering of Himself in the Supper Room is essentially a sign of His offering of Himself in natural death on the cross. But since the elements of the eucharistic sacrifice of the Last Supper really and truly contain (by transubstantiation) the Victim to be offered in a bloody manner on the cross the separation of body and blood being signified (as separated from one another) by the double consecration, it follows that the Last Supper is no *mere* sign or symbolic forepresentation of Calvary: it *is* Calvary (that is, the real and external oblation of His own Body and Blood to the Eternal

Supper), Christ's internal will to sacrifice and his oblative act were also externalized in external oblation in so far as, as man, He willed freely the signs symbolic of death as placed by God, by God's divine power either directly and immediately (as at the Last Supper) or indirectly and mediately through the ministry of priests (as at Mass). Here right along the line there is subordination of Christ's human will to the will and power of His Father, who determines in detail the sacrifice He desires from His creatures and the mode of offering it.

[29] Denz. 938.

Father by our Lord Jesus Christ). In other words, the Last Supper is an *efficacious* sign of the cross, just as all the other sacraments of the New Law not only signify grace, but also cause it effectively.

To say that the Mass is a sign of and contains Calvary is another way of saying that the Mass is a sacramental sacrifice. The sacraments of the New Law not only signify but also cause and contain what they signify. In this connection St. Thomas writes:

The sacrifice of the New Law, i.e., of the Eucharist contains Christ Himself, who is the author of sanctification . . . And so this sacrifice is also a sacrament.[30]

If we compare the two, the Mass and Calvary, we see that what was essential in the sacrifice of Christ is to be found identically in both. In the sacrifice of Calvary we find the following: 1) Our Lord offers Himself, Body and Blood, to His Father. He did that sacrificially, that is, externally, as a sign of His internal sacrifice, of His *devotio* and of His internal act of self-oblation in accordance with the will of His Father. Therein is to be found the very essence of His sacrifice, the supreme act of the virtue of religion in the soul of Christ. 2) Secondly, He offered Himself in the manner (mode of sacrifice) laid down by His Eternal Father, to whom He offered the sacrifice of His life. That is, He offered Himself on Calvary by dying a violent death, by allowing Himself to be killed by the Jews. In the sacrifice of the Mass, on the other hand, we find the following: 1) Christ actually offers Himself, Body and Blood, to His Father. This He does externally and sacrificially. This is again the essence of Christ's sacrifice, and it is seen to be identical with the sacrifice of Calvary and also with that of the Last Supper. 2) Secondly, He offers Himself in the manner laid down by God. That is, He offers Himself in sensible signs, under the species of bread and wine. This pertains to the accidental mode of offering sacrifice. And *this mode of offering is essentially representative of the mode of*

[30] I-II, 101, 4 ad 2.

offering on Calvary and only as such is it sacrificial.[31] Hence there is a double consecration in order to symbolize the separation of the Blood from the Body which really took place on Calvary. These are the external signs symbolic of death, of which Pope Pius XII speaks in the encyclical *Mediator Dei.* As Christ offered Himself on Calvary so is He still offering Himself daily on our altars at Mass, but in a different manner, in an external manner, in a sacramental manner.

In the encyclical *Mediator Dei* we read:

Christ our Lord, " priest forever according to the order of Melchisedech," " loved his own that were in the world "; and accordingly, at the Last Supper, on the night on which He was betrayed, He willed to leave to His beloved Bride the Church a visible sacrifice such as the nature of man requires; one by which the bloody sacrifice which was to be enacted once on the Cross should be represented and its memory remain until the end of the world, and its salutary power be applied for the remission of the sins that are daily committed by us. He therefore offered His Body and Blood to God the Father under the appearances of bread and wine, and under the symbols of the same delivered them to be taken by the Apostles; and to them and to their successors in the priesthood He gave command to offer. The august Sacrifice of the altar is therefore no mere simple commemoration of the Passion and Death of Jesus Christ: it is truly and properly the offering of a sacrifice, wherein by an unbloody immolation the High Priest does what He had already done on the Cross, offering Himself to the eternal Father as a most acceptable victim. " One . . and the same is the victim, one and the same is He who now offers by the ministry of His priests and who then offered Himself on the Cross; the difference is only in the manner of offering.[32]

It is sometimes said that the Mass is a *relative* sacrifice merely. If that be the case I cannot see how it can be any

---

[31] In this connection two penetrating and profound texts of Cardinal Cajetan could with profit be read. They are: 1) Chapter 9 of his opusculum *De erroribus contingentibus in Eucharistiae Sacramento*, the title of the chapter being: Quomodo Eucharistiae sacramentum sit sacrificium et in Missa offerri sit institutum a Christo vel ab Apostolis. 2) The second is chapter 6 of his opusculum *De Missae sacrificio et ritu adversum Lutheranos.*

[32] Encyl. *Mediator Dei*, Engl. trans. CTSE, p. 35-36.

more than a "mere simple commemoration of the Passion and Death of Jesus Christ." There is a world of difference between saying that the Mass is a relative sacrifice and saying that it is real, true, proper sacrifice which, however, in the mode or manner of external offering and in that only, is, in the designs of divine Providence, essentially representative of, or relative to, another absolute mode.

We can consider Christ's internal act of offering on Calvary as a theandric action embracing both the preceding Supper and the countless succeeding Masses of ours. We as priests of the New Law do precisely what Christ Himself did at the Last Supper, at His command: " Do this in commemoration of Me." [33] Then were ordained the first priests.[34] Then was first given to men the power to consecrate, that is, to transsubstantiate bread and wine into the Body and Blood of Christ. We consecrate by the power of Christ (by His *divine* power), who at each Mass must *actually* move the priest so that he may be able to perform the stupendous miracle of transubstantiation.[35] Making Christ really and truly present

---

[33] Luke 22:9; I. Cor. 11:24.

[34] Cf. canon of the Council of Trent, Denz. 949.

[35] With regard to the distinction between the essence and mode of sacrifice the following should be noted. Sacrifice is essentially (that is, by definition) an *external* sign of an internal act or state of mind and soul. It is the external offering of something to God. To offer externally and in deed to God is to give over to God absolutely all rights over the object or thing offered. If the thing offered (the objective sacrifice) be a living thing the most expressive manner of offering it to God, humanly speaking, is to kill it. But the actual killing of it is not essential to sacrifice. There are other ways in which it might be made sacred and in that sense given to God sacrificially. In other words, externalization is essential to every sacrifice. But whether in this or that manner (by killing or in any other way that God may decide upon) pertains only to the *mode or manner* of offering. In all this matter it is essential to take into account what God decides, because it is His prerogative to determine the kind of offering and the manner of offering. Consequently no *a priori* rules can be given for judging whether any particular external oblation be sacrificial or not. Everything depends upon what God ordains. Now, Christ offered to God not something that belongs to Him, but Himself, His Body and Blood. Christ willed to offer Himself (interiorly) out of obedience to the decree of His Father. He wished to externalize that will to offer Himself in the manner in which His Father should decide. God, the Father, decreed that Our Lord should offer Himself externally first of all by dying a violent death on the Cross. This

on the altar we (priests) thereby *ratify* in our own human way, by our own personal spirit of devotion or submission, which should flow from our faith and charity, the redemptive sacrifice of Christ. We are swept, as it were, from time into eternity in order to be present again mystically, but really, at Calvary. We make our Lord's sacrifice ours by offering it with Him at Mass, as we would have done had we been present on the first Good Friday on Calvary and had we known what was taking place, namely the sacrifice of our redemption, or as the faithful Jew made the sacrifice of the High Priest his by being present in the temple and by ratifying the action of the priest. Christ is present on our altars actually offering Himself to His Father, and this actual offering is being actually ratified by the priest who consecrates and by all the faithful who unite themselves to him. By consecration the priest places the external signs of Christ's internal oblation of self. These signs represent directly and immediately the will to sacrifice in our Lord's mind. It is defined in the Council of Trent, as we saw above, that the Mass is a real and proper sacrifice, and that it is the sacrifice of Christ by Himself. God willed it so and arranged it so. Pope Pius XII in the Encyclical *Mediator Dei* writes, "The Divine Wisdom has devised a way in which Our Redeemer's sacrifice is marvellously shown forth *by external signs symbolic of death*." [36] They are external signs— and we saw that some kind of externalization is essential to the notion of sacrifice—not by any death, but of Our Lord's

physical natural death of Christ as such is not of the very essence of sacrifice, but in this case it is *the absolute mode* of His sacrifice. God decreed it so. In the Supper Room Our Lord offered Himself (Body and Blood) externally by transubstantiation. Here we have to do with a real, proper and absolute sacrifice. The mode of offering was different to that of the Cross. And this sacramental mode is seen to be essentially relative to and significative of the absolute mode of Calvary. Hence the double consecration. —At Mass Our Lord actually offers Himself externally (in external sacramental signs) through the ministry of the priests. His priests are instruments in His offering of Himself. There the Mass is an absolute sacrifice, but the mode of offering is essentially symbolic of the absolute mode of Calvary.

[36] Ency. *Mediator Dei,* Engl. trans. CTSE, p. 36.

death on Calvary. And these external signs are placed at Mass by Our Lord himself as principal cause and by the priest as instrumental cause, that is, as the minister of Christ. The priests of the New Law are not the successors of Christ but His ministers—*sacerdotum ministerio.*

It should be said that the sacrifice of Calvary is being ratified *officially*, that is, as by one officially constituted to do so in his own name and in the name of the whole Christian people, by the priest at Mass, for he alone has the power to consecrate. In consecrating, the power, the *divine* power, of Christ flows through the priest. This power was used by Our Lord in the first instance (in the Supper Room) for the one and only purpose of placing the external signs of His internal sacrifice, of His internal act of self-oblation. It follows, consequently, that transubstantiation is *in fact* inseparable from the actual will to sacrifice in the mind of Christ. That is an added reason for maintaining, as many theologians do, that Christ, who must actually consecrate in every Mass as principal cause, must also *actually* offer the sacrifice. We might even say that at Mass not only is Christ actually offering sacrifice, He is in a very true sense the o n l y offerer. At Mass Our Lord does exactly what he did at the Last Supper, with this one difference: at the Last Supper He did everything Himself, whereas at Mass He does it through His priests, His ministers. At the Last Supper He gave to His priests the power to consecrate, to transubstantiate. As often as they consecrate they are in physical contact with Christ, who moves them and elevates them to perform the miracle of transubstantiation. Desiring to consecrate, a priest must also wish to offer Christ's sacrifice. He must offer Christ's sacrifice with Him. In this sense, then, we must say that the priest at Mass really offers sacrifice, not as principal cause or offerer, but as an instrumental cause, as a minister. By virtue of his sacerdotal power he can do this as often as he desires to consecrate whether what he does be a sign of his own personal devotion and charity or not, that is, whether he ratifies Calvary morally or not he ratifies it always physically. This is the " *opus oper-atum* " in every Mass. And since the priest offers sacrifice not as a private individual but as the representative of the whole Christian people, it follows that the faithful always derive benefit from every Mass. The faithful have, obviously, their part to play. They are not mere spectators, but are called to take active part in what is taking place at the altar. They must unite themselves to the priest by their own personal acts of submission to the will of God. They must in that way rat-ify what the priest does at Mass, and consequently through the priest they can, in a very human and straightforward way, ratify what Christ did on Calvary and what He is still doing. They, too, through the priest, make Christ's sacrifice theirs, so that their adoration, their thanksgiving, their supplication and their expiation are, as it were, absorbed into the adora-tion, thanksgiving, supplication and expiation of Christ and are offered to God by Our Saviour Himself.

It follows from what has been said that the priest of the New Law stands in much the same relation to our one High Priest, who is Christ, as did the faithful Jew to the priest of the Old Law. The priests of the Old Law offered sacrifices as principal causes or agents. The priests of the New Law do not precisely offer sacrifice: they r a t i f y a sacrifice officially, by virtue of their sacerdotal office. It must be understood that at Mass a real sacrifice is offered to God in a visible, exter-nal but sacramental way. It is offered by Christ. He is the one and only offerer (sacrificant). In the fullest sense of the word, He is the one and only priest. The human priest by his own devotion and in the name of the people (that is, act-ing for them, and from that point of view, much as the priests of the Old Law, a caste apart) ratifies it and thus ap-plies its fruits to himself and to the Christian people. There is no greater difficulty with regard to the relation between the act of oblation in Christ's mind and the priest's act of obla-tion than there was with regard to the relation between the internal sacrifice of the people in the Old Law and the external sacrifice of the priests.[37]

A person, who assists at the sacrifice of a priest and in the manner explained strives to take part in it by seeing to it that it really be the external manifestation of his own internal oblation, can be truly said to offer sacrifice. He offers the sacrifice of the priest, with the priest and subordinated to the priest. In that sense it can be said: he offers sacrifice. In that sense, too, the priest of the New Law can and must be said to offer sacrifice. He offers Christ's sacrifice, with Christ and subordinated to Christ. He is never a principal agent in the actual sacrifice. He offers the Body and Blood of Christ to God the Father (which is quite a different thing from saying that he offers sacrifice to God) by uniting himself to the sacrificial offering of Christ, the one High Priest of the New Law. And in that way Christian priests share in a most marvellous manner in the Priesthood of Christ. And in that precisely consists their dignity and pre-eminence over all the priests of the Old Law. In the encyclical *Ad Catholici Sacerdotii* of Pope Pius XI we read:

And thus the ineffable greatness of the human priest stands forth in all its splendour; for he has power over the very body of Jesus Christ and makes it present upon our altars. In the name of

[37] Two things should be noted carefully here. 1) First, that the sacerdotal power of the New Law consists not precisely in the power to offer sacrifice as such, but in being able to consecrate or transubstantiate with a view to uniting oneself to and making one's own the redemptive act of Calvary. 2) Secondly, that the Sacrifice of the Mass is the Sacrifice of Christ whole and entire, that is, of the Mystical Body of Christ. When the priest consecrates he is never acting as a private individual (whatever his private dispositions may be), but as the representative of the Mystical Body of Christ. Consequently, should the priest not ratify in his own person the sacrifice of Calvary (for instance, by leading a sinful life) the sacrifice of Christ would still be offered because consecration or transubstantiation would still take place. That is, the will to sacrifice in Christ's mind would be really externalized sacramentally. That is, of course, if the priest, however evil personally, wishes to do at least what the Church intends (habet intentionem faciendi quod facit Ecclesia). Should the priest, then, not ratify the sacrifice of Calvary, the people are enabled to do so through his power of consecration.

Christ Himself he offers It a victim infinitely pleasing to the Divine Majesty.[38]

And Pope Pius XII in the encyclical on the Mystical Body of Christ teaches:

Though the Eucharistic sacrifice of Christ Our Lord wished to give special evidence to the faith of the union among ourselves and with our Divine Head, marvellous as it is and beyond all praise. For here the sacred ministers act in the person not only of Our Saviour, but of the whole Mystical Body and of everyone of the faithful. In this act of sacrifice through the hands of the priest, whose word alone has brought the Immaculate Lamb to be present on the altar, the faithful themselves with one desire and one prayer offer It to the Eternal Father, the most acceptable victim of praise and propitiation for the Church's universal needs. And just as the Divine Redeemer, dying on the Cross, offered Himself as Head of the whole human race to the Eternal Father, so in " this pure oblation " He offers not only Himself as Head of the Church to the heavenly Father, but in Himself His mystical members as well. He embraces them all, even the weak and ailing ones, in the tenderest love of His Heart.[39]

In this essay I have consciously avoided entering into the dogmatic discussions concerning the essence of the Blessed Eucharist as making present again the sacrifice of Christ and have touched on them only in so far as they were necessary for my own analysis. Both approaches are obviously intimately connected—the moral and the dogmatic, the approach of the dogmatic and of the moral theologian. I venture to hope that this moral or, as the moderns would have it, existential approach may throw some light on the dogmatic problem of the essence and structure of our Christian sacrifice and in that way also help towards a deeper and more enlightened Eucharistic piety.

CORNELIUS WILLIAMS, O. P.

University of Fribourg
Fribourg, Switzerland

---

[38] Encyl. *Ad Catholici Sacerdotii*, Engl. trans. CTSE, p. 9.
[39] Encyl. *Mystici Corporis Christi*, Engl. trans. America Press, p. 35-36.

THE SACRAMENTAL CHARACTER
AND LITURGY

∾

I N the first chapter of the schema on the liturgy, the Second Vatican Council has provided for an intensification of liturgical thought in the life of the Church in the decades and centuries to come.[1] Part II of the first chapter approved by the Council (though not yet solemnly and definitively) concerns the liturgical formation of the clergy and the people. The liturgy is to be counted among the major disciplines in the seminary curriculum and is to be studied theologically and historically, as well as from spiritual, pastoral, and juridical points of view. Part IV gives directions for promotion of liturgical life in the dioceses and parishes of the world.

The Second Vatican Council has thus set before theologians a challenge for the future. Sacramental theologians in particular must step back from their work, view the sacraments in the context of the whole liturgy, and try to develop a theology which embraces not only the sacraments in their essential matter and form but the whole of the liturgy—the Mass, sacraments, sacramentals, and divine Office. This means finding new principles of greater universality, or new insights into the breadth of familiar principles, in order to have a truly unified theology of the liturgy. Without new principles or new insights into old principles, theology of the liturgy will remain an accidental unity composed of a theology of the sacraments, a theology of sacramentals, and a theology of the divine Office. Needed today and for the future is a theology of the Christian mysteries as the Fathers of the Church understood the term—the whole of the liturgy joining God and man in worship through Christ.

[1] A summary of the first chapter on the liturgy appeared in *L'Osservatore Romano*, December 8, 1962, " I principi generali della riforma liturgica approvati dal Concilio." A complete translation of this article is available in *Worship*, XXXVII (1963), 153-64 under the title " The Approved Chapter One." The points mentioned in text above can be found in this issue of *Worship*, pp. 155, 157, 163.

The purpose of this article is to look at the sacramental characters in the broader context of the liturgy as a whole. Manuals of theology, lectures on theology, and even the commentators on St. Thomas' *Summa Theologiae* often give the impression that the sacramental characters are ordered solely to the essential rites (the matter and form) of the sacraments as causes of grace.[2] This impression is created chiefly by the examples to illustrate the function of the various characters: the character of baptism enables the Christian to receive the other sacraments, the other two characters, and sacramental grace; the sacerdotal character gives the power to consecrate, to absolve from sin, and to administer the sacraments.

The handling of the character of confirmation by some theologians heightens this impression that the characters are ordered to the sacraments in a strict sense as causes of grace.[3] Despite what seems (to me at least) strong evidence that St. Thomas regarded the character of confirmation as ordered actively to public witness and defense of the faith, some theologians, who regard themselves as disciples of Thomas, are loath to admit that ordination of the character. Instead, they attribute the witness and defense of the faith directly to grace, special grace, which is received through the special power or character of confirmation. The reason for this approach seems

---

[2] As an example of this, see Emmanuel Doronzo, O. M. I., *De sacramentis in genere* (Milwaukee: Bruce, 1946), pp. 296-300, 313-315, where the author treats of the character as a potency and as seated in the practical intellect; significantly the author frequently cites Salamanticenses and Gonet. See also Bernard Durst, O. S. B., " De Characteribus sacramentalibus," *Xenia Thomistica*, II (1925), 541-81.

A basis for this judgment is found in St. Thomas. He raises the objection that the sacraments of the Old Law did not confer a character on the soul; therefore, there is no need for the sacraments of the New Law to do so. He answers: " Sacramenta veteris legis non habebant in se spiritualem virtutem ad aliquem spiritualem effectum operantem. Et ideo in illis sacramentis non requirebatur aliquis spiritualis character, sed sufficiebat ibi corporalis circumcisio " (*Summa theol.*, III, q. 63, a. 1, ad 3). But it must be remembered that this is an answer to an objection; it quickly and directly resolves the problem; it does not necessarily follow that this is also a declaration of the total orientation of the character.

[3] For examples, see Emmanuel Doronzo, *De baptismo et confirmatione* (Milwaukee: Bruce, 1947), pp. 350-51; Durst, *op. cit.*, pp. 572-74.

to lie in the prior judgment that the characters are ordered to the sacraments as causes of grace, either to receive the sacraments and their graces or to confer the sacraments and their graces; bearing witness or defending the faith publicly is not the reception or conferral of grace in sacramental action; therefore the character of confirmation cannot be directly ordered to this witness and defense.

I have said that manuals, lecturers, and commentators " give the impression " that the sacramental characters are ordered only to the reception and administration of the sacraments in the strict sense of the word and as causes of grace. Actually, close examination of the texts reveals that they do not close the door altogether to other liturgical actions and even non-liturgical actions with regard to the characters. Nevtheless, the impression is not merely subjective, the result of inattentive reading. There is a preoccupation with the sacraments as causes of grace in reaction to the theology of the reformers; and there is a preoccupation in the conflicts of the schools with the character as being or not being an instance of instrumental causality ordered to the conferral and reception of grace. There is also a neglect of the sacraments as worship. The sacraments are considered as worship in the treatise on the characters; but when the crucial questions of the function and need of the characters come up, the answers are invariably in terms of valid sacraments and the reception or conferral of grace.

In this article we will review briefly the teaching of the Fathers of the Church, St. Thomas, the Council of Trent, and the encyclical *Mediator Dei* of Pope Pius XII in order to see what scope they assign to the sacramental characters— whether they limit their function to the reception and administration of the sacraments in the strictest sense of the word and as conferring grace, whether they extend the function of the characters to other parts of the liturgy, or whether they extend that function even beyond the liturgy.

Both from theoretical and pastoral points of view, it is necessary to determine the scope of the sacramental characters with regard to the liturgy. Theoretically, if the sacramental character is not operative in the entire liturgy, or if it is operative in more than the liturgy, then the liturgy cannot be defined precisely in terms of an activity of the sacramental characters, for the definition would not be convertible with the defined. Pastorally, if the sacramental character is not a principle of the entire liturgy or exclusively of the liturgy, then in preaching and instruction concerning liturgical piety, some other principle more essential and central to liturgical worship should be emphasized.

We shall proceed in the following manner. It will be assumed as generally accepted that the sacramental characters are participations in the priesthood of Christ and empower the Christian to participate in one way or another in Christ's sacrifice and worship.[4] We shall examine the four sources mentioned above to determine more precisely this participation in Christ's priesthood and in the sacrifice and worship which issue from it. First, we shall briefly recall that there is a twofold Christian priesthood, sacrifice and worship—the one spiritual, the other external, visible, ritual. Then we shall examine the sources to see with which priesthood and worship they associate the sacramental characters and to which acts of worship they conceive the characters to be ordered. From this examination a few concise conclusions will be drawn.

The Twofold Christian Priesthood and Worship

A full exposition of the twofold Christian priesthood and worship—one spiritual, the other ritual—is impossible within the limits of this article; we must be content with recalling the

---

[4] Bernard Leeming, S. J. assesses the theological value of this position: " In view of the different manners of speech among the older theologians, it is not more than the theologically probable that the character is strictly a power . . . The view, however, of St. Thomas, that the character gives a share in Christ's priestly power, has become very widely accepted . . ." (*Principles of Sacramental Theology*, [Westminster: Newman, 1956], p. 230).

salient facts to provide a background for the considerations which will follow.[5]

From the moment of his entrance into the world, Christ was moved by the Spirit of God to offer himself interiorly to the Father: " Behold, I come to do thy will, O God " (Heb. 10:2). In virtue of this interior act of charity and devotion, all of Christ's actions assumed a religious, worshipful value. But most especially on Calvary did he give visible manifestation of this spiritual sacrifice, for on Calvary he offered himself as victim according to the will of the Father in a true ritual sacrifice, thus fulfilling and terminating the ritual sacrifices of the Old Law: " Sacrifice and oblation thou wouldst not, but a body thou hast fitted to me " (Heb. 10:5; cf. Eph. 5:2).

St. Peter refers to the Christians of Asia Minor as " a royal priesthood " (I Pet. 2:9), " a holy priesthood, to offer spiritual sacrifices acceptable to God through Jesus Christ " (*ibid.*, 5; cf. Rom. 12:1). St. John in the Apocalypse, greeting the seven churches of Asia Minor, speaks of Christ who " has washed us from our sins in his own blood and made us to be a kingdom and priests to God his Father " (Apoc. 1:6; cf. 5:9-10). The Christian writers to the end of the second century follow this example of the New Testament writers: the truly priestly names *hiereus* and *hierateuma* (" priest " and " priesthood ") are used in Christian contexts only for Christ himself or the Christian people, not for the ministers of the altar, those whom we today designate as priests.[6]

By grace, Christians are members of Christ and share in his grace and the qualities of his grace. But Christ is Priest and his grace is priestly. Therefore, the Christian people by grace are a priestly people. The whole Christian people with their

---

[5] For a thorough study of this subject, see Yves Congar, O. P., *Jalons pour une théologie du laïcat* (Paris: Éditions du Cerf, 1953), pp. 170-246; English translation by Donald Attwater, *Lay People in the Church* (London: Bloomsbury, 1957), pp. 120-80.

[6] Congar, *op. cit.*, pp. 173-74, Eng. trans., pp. 123-24; Emmanuel Doronzo, O.M.I., *De ordine* (Milwaukee: Bruce, 1957), I, 88-90, 277-78.

Head Christ are the fulfillment of the figurative Levitical priesthood of the Old Law. Under the influence of the same Spirit who inspired Christ's offering of himself, Christians too are moved to offer themselves in union with Christ and through him to the Father in heaven. Christians therefore have a spiritual priesthood, sacrifice, worship which are the very core of Christian existence, an existence which is for the glory of the Father.

At the same time, both New Testament and early Christian writers acknowledge a visible, ritual worship with its corresponding visible, external priesthood. The worship here is chiefly " the breaking of bread." [7] the Eucharist,[8] which proclaims the death of the Lord (I Cor. 11:26). This worship is conducted by those who are designated, not by the most proper priestly names mentioned above, but by their functions: *episkopoi* (bishops, overseers), *presbyteroi* (presbyters, elders, advisers) *diakonoi* (deacons, ministers), who receive their office by the imposition of hands.[9] Only those who have been baptized may share in the Eucharistic worship.[10] This ritual sacrifice and the powers and rights to celebrate and partake in it are essentially for the present time: " As often as you shall eat the bread and drink the cup, you proclaim the death of the Lord, until he comes " (I Cor. 11:26); in the heavenly Jerusalem, John saw no temple, symbol of figurative ritual worship, for God and the Lamb are the temple, the fulfillment of ritual worship (Apoc. 21:22).

Though these two priesthoods and their respective sacrifice and worship are distinguishable, they are not isolated, independent realities. The spiritual animates, gives meaning to, the

---

[7] Acts 2:42, 46; 20, 7; I Cor. 10:16; *Didache*, ch. 14; St. Ignatius of Antioch, *To the Ephesians*, 20.

[8] *Didaché*, ch. 14; St. Ignatius of Antioch, *To the Philadelphians*, 4; *To the Smyrneans*, 8; St. Justin Martyr, *Apology*, I, 65-67.

[9] Congar, *op. cit.*, pp. 188-90, Eng. trans., pp. 136-38; for texts, see Doronzo, *De ordine, I*, 221-27 (Scripture), 227-79 (second century tradition, summarized pp. 273-79).

[10] *Didache*, ch. 9 (although it is disputed whether or not this chapter refers to the Eucharist or to an *agape* meal); St. Justin Martyr, *Apology*, I, 66.

ritual priesthood and its activity; the ritual priesthood functions in order to foster the interior; the external sacrifice is the expression of interior sacrifice. However, the fact remains that the Christian may sin, lose the grace of Christ with its priestly quality and cease to offer that spiritual sacrifice of grace spoken of by St. Peter. Yet such a Christian retains his privileges and powers with regard to the valid celebration of visible Christian worship: the sinful ordained minister of the altar can validly offer the Eucharist. The fact of this separation indicates that these two priesthoods and their respective worships are distinguishable realities.

Christian tradition has preserved the notion of the twofold Christian priesthood and sacrifice. Christian writers over the centuries have faithfully reserved the texts of I Peter, Apocalypse, Romans 12:1 and Psalm 50:19 for the Christian faithful. With a constancy that is remarkable these texts have not been applied to the ordained ritual priesthood and its visible worship and sacrifice.[11] Even Trent, which had to combat the Protestant claim that all Christians were equally priests, in its decrees on the priesthood explicitly identifies the subject of its consideration as " the visible and external priesthood " which is associated with the " visible sacrifice " of the New Law, and does not use the texts of Peter, etc. as the Scriptural basis for this priesthood and sacrifice.[12] The Catechism

[11] A sign of this traditional notion is found in the following fact. Paul Dabin, S. J. has collected the texts of the Fathers, the theologians, spiritual writers, and the liturgy, western and eastern, for the whole span of Christian history, in regard to the priesthood of the faithful, in Le sacerdoce royal des fidèles dans la tradition ancienne et moderne (Paris: Desclée, 1950); the Scriptural texts of Peter, etc. continually recur page after page, paragraph after paragraph. Doronzo in De ordine, I, 227-489, collects numerous texts on the ritual priesthood and its function as seen by the Fathers, ecclesiastical writers, liturgy, and councils or synods from Apostolic times to the first part of the fifth century. Except for Tertullian in a semi-Montanist stage (pp. 283, 285), the traditional texts in question are notably absent. This phenomenon is not offered as an argument, but it is not lacking significance.

[12] " Sacrificium et sacerdotium ita Dei ordinatione coniuncta sunt, ut utrumque in omni lege exstiterit. Cum igitur in Novo Testamento sanctum Eucharistiae sacrificium visibile ex Domini institutione catholica Ecclesia acceperit; fateri etiam

of the Council of Trent explicitly distinguishes the exterior priesthood from the interior priesthood of the faithful, and for this latter turns to the scriptural texts mentioned.[13] In our own day we find the tradition faithfully carried on in the encyclical *Mediator Dei* of Pope Pius XII.[14]

With this background of the twofold Christian priesthood in our minds, we can now enter into the heart of this study. To which of these two priesthoods do the sacramental char-

oportet, in ea novum esse *visibile et externum sacerdotium*, in quod vetus translatum est " (Sess. XXIII, Doctrina de sacramento ordinis, cap. 1, Denz. 957, emphasis added). Cf. *ibid.*, cap. 4, Denz. 960; and can. 1, Denz. 961.

[13] " Sed quoniam *duplex sacerdotium* in sacris Litteris describitur, alterum internum, alterum externum; utrumque distinguendum est, ut, de quo hoc loco intelligatur, a Pastoribus explicari possit. Quod igitur ad interius Sacerdotium pertinet, omnes fideles, postquam salutari aqua abluti sunt, Sacerdotes dicuntur, praecipue vero justi, qui spiritum Dei habent, et divinae gratiae beneficio Iesu Christi summi Sacerdotis viva membra effecti sunt. Hi enim fide, quae charitate inflammatur, in altari mentis suae spirituales Deo hostias immolant: quo in genere bonae omnes et honestae actiones, quas ad Dei gloriam referunt, numerandae sunt. [Apocalypse, I Peter, Romans 12:1 and Psalm 50:19 are then quoted.] Quae omnia ad *interius Sacerdotium* spectare facile intelligitur.

" *Externum* vero *sacerdotium* non omnium fidelium multitudini, sed certis hominibus convenit, qui legitima manuum impositione, solemnibusque sanctae Ecclesiae caeremoniis instituti et a Deo consecrati, ad aliquod proprium sacrumque ministerium adscribuntur " (Pars II, cap. 7, quaes. 23 emphasis added).

[14] The encyclical treats extensively of the hierarchical priesthood and its supremacy in the domain of the liturgy, *AAS*, XXXIX (1947), 538-541. In these pages reference is to " adspectabile et externum Iesu Christi sacerdotium " (*ibid.* 538); the traditional texts of I Peter, etc. are not found in this section. Further on in the encyclical, it is explained in what sense the faithful offer the Mass; for this offering to be complete, it ought to be with an interior offering of self as a victim; of this offering the encyclical says: " Quae quidem immolatio ad liturgicum solummodo Sacrificium non reducitur. Vult enim Apostolorum Princeps ut eo ipso quod Christo tamquam lapides vivi superaedificamur, possimus tamquam ' sacerdotium sanctum, offerre spiritales hostias acceptabiles Deo per Iesum Christum ' [I Pet. 2:5]; Paulus autem Apostolus absque ullo temporis discrimine hisce verbis christianos adhortatur: ' Obsecro itaque vos . . . ut exhibeatis corpora vestra hostiam viventem, sanctam, Deo placentem, rationabile obsequium vestrum ' [Rom. 12:1] " (*ibid., 557-58*). We see the traditional texts employed for a Christian priesthood, sacrifice, and worship other than those of the ritual priesthood and its functions. The encyclical continues to show the relationship of these two priesthoods and worships, the ritual serving the spiritual and mediating between the priestly life of Christ and that of his members.

acters belong immediately and to which sacrifice and worship are they directly ordered, the spiritual or the ritual? If they are ordered to the ritual priesthood and worship, are they ordered exclusively to the administration and reception of the sacraments in their essential rites or do they extend beyond this? If beyond this, how far beyond? Beyond the bounds of the liturgy? An answer will be sought for these questions by examining the doctrine of the Fathers, some medieval theologians, chiefly St. Thomas, the Council of Trent and the Catechism of Trent, and *Mediator Dei*. The authority of these sources and their appearance at separated intervals over the course of the whole of Christian history ought to help form a balanced judgment about the orientation of the sacramental characters in the liturgy.

FATHERS OF THE CHURCH

Scripture itself does not say anything explicitly about the orientation of the sacramental characters to the spiritual priesthood and worship or the ritual priesthood and worship. Indeed, Scripture only implicitly reveals the existence of the character as a reality distinct from grace. St. Paul wrote of a sealing of the Christian.[15] From these texts the Fathers developed one of their favorite themes, that of the *sphragis*, the *signaculum*, the seal or brand, the *character*, impressed on the souls of the baptized and perfected in confirmation.

Prior to St. Augustine, the Fathers did not explicitly distinguish between grace and the seal, although no Father said that the seal could be lost, while all admitted grace could be lost; indeed, they affirmed that the character was indelible; it remained in sinners.[16] They considered, moreover, that the seal of baptism was perfected in the second of the rites of initiation, that is, in confirmation. Along with this thinking of the

---

[15] " Now it is God who is warrant for us and for you in Christ, who has anointed us, who has also sealed us and has given us the Spirit as a pledge in our hearts " (II Cor. 1:21-22); cf. Eph. 1:13; 4:30.

[16] For the facts of this and the following paragraph I have followed Leeming. *op. cit.*, pp. 129-250.

Fathers went the practice of the Church of never repeating the rites of baptism and confirmation if validly performed. The Fathers said little about the seal of holy orders, except Gregory of Nyssa,[17] but the practice of the Church with regard to valid ordination was the same as for baptism and confirmation.

St. Augustine, in his controversy with the Donatists, brought out clearly the distinction between grace and the character in baptism and holy orders, a doctrine which naturally applied to the character in confirmation, although Augustine did not explicitly make this application. Augustine also pointed out that the impressing of a permanent character on the soul was the reason why the Church did not repeat these three sacraments once validly conferred.

What purpose or function did the Fathers perceive in the seals fixed on the soul of the baptized and confirmed and in irrevocable consecration of the ordained? What orientation toward priesthood and worship?

What the Fathers saw in the baptismal character (and its confirmational perfection) in the way of function and orientation is not easily pinned down to one thing.[18] By the seal the Christian is made to belong to Christ, shepherd and king. By it the Lord recognizes his own sheep. It is a sign of being made a member of the Christian community, the one flock. It is a protection, a pledge of salvation. It imprints an image of God on the soul. It marks incorporation into the service of the king. Its presence frightens the demons and enables the angels to recognize the Christian. It designates a slave of Christ, a faithful servant. It renders the Christian inviolable

---

[17] P. Pourrat, *Theology of the Sacraments*, (St. Louis: Herder, 1914), pp. 224-25.

[18] This paragraph is based on Jean Daniélou, S. J., *The Bible and the Liturgy* (Notre Dame, Ind.: University of Notre Dame Press, 1956), pp. 54-69; see also Pourrat, *op. cit.* pp. 220-22; Leeming, *op. cit.*, 179-83. What is said of the function of the seal here applies to the confirmational character as well as to the baptismal character (Pourrat, *op. cit.*, p. 222); for a variety of reasons the Fathers did not clearly distinguish between the two characters (Leeming, *op. cit.*, pp. 189-200), but they did recognize a distinction of the two and spoke of the confirmational character as a perfection of the baptismal character (*ibid.*, pp. 201-207).

from hostile forces. It signifies the New Covenant of grace, as circumcision signifies the Old Covenant of the Law. The seal is a sign of God's contract with its possessor to bless him in accord with divine fidelity.

With reason, later theologians spoke of the character as primarily a sign, for the above notions of the function of the character can be reduced to that of signification. If any orientation of the seal is indicated in the above notions, it seems at first to be toward the spiritual priesthood and grace of worship; the anointings in baptism and in confirmation were associated with the indelible consecration of the two sacraments [19] and with the royal priesthood of I Peter and Apocalypse.[20]

But the Fathers recognized the indelibility of the seal: it could not be lost, while grace could. All the privileges and rights implied in the above notions remained in the sinner and also in the schismatics and heretics, though they were unworthy of these privileges and rights, and they possessed them to their damnation as long as they remained unworthy. Besides, if one had the seal of baptism, and only if he had it, he was eligible for the next sacrament, confirmation, essentially a perfection of baptism in the eyes of the Fathers. Initiated into the Christian community by baptism and confirmation, the bearer of the seal could share in the Eucharistic sacrifice, receive other sacraments, such as orders, Christian marriage, ecclesiastical penance, final anointing; he was also a soldier of Christ the King, to bear witness to the faith.

The seal admitted Christians to more than the reception of the sacraments in their essential rites. The Christians of these times did not think of the sacraments in the narrow sense in which we tend to do today. They thought of the Christian mysteries—sacraments in a broad sense of the word—embracing the whole of the liturgy surrounding the sacraments in the narrow sense.[21] If the Christian fell into sin, lost the grace

---

[19] Daniélou, op. cit., pp. 54, 119.

[20] Ibid., pp. 114-17; Leeming, op. cit., p. 234.

[21] For the general sense of "mysterion" and "sacramentum" of the Patristic

of spiritual priesthood and sacrifice, he was still a Christian, still equipped to participate in mysteries validly, though unfruitfully and sacrilegiously; when he returned to grace and truth and unity, he did not need to be sealed again to share in the Christian mysteries.

Thus the seal of baptism and its perfection in confirmation is ordered to visible ritual priesthood and sacrifice in the mysteries. Perhaps it can be said that the Fathers regarded the seals as ordered first to this visible priesthood and worship and through it to the spiritual priesthood and grace of worship; at least that is how they can be interpreted in the light of subsequent theological developments.

As for the character of holy orders, it distinguished the ministers of the Church; it constituted one a representative of the Church and commissioned one to act in the name of Christ.[22] To holy orders belonged the office of teaching and preaching, offering the Eucharistic sacrifice, absolving from sin, administering the other sacraments, blessing, praying in the name of the Church.[23] This priestly power existed fully in the bishop and to a lesser degree in the priest and deacon, and in an even lesser degree in other ministers.

The seal of orders was orientated in part to the visible Christian priesthood with its ritual worship. Indeed, so directly and immediately orientated to this worship was the character seen to be, that sinful, schismatic, or heretical bish-

era see Dom Romanus Rios, O. S. B., "Eucharistic Terms in the Liturgy," *The Clergy Review,* XXVIII (1947), 253-60; C. C. Martindale, S. J., *The Words of the Missal* (New York: Macmillan, 1932), pp. 101-18.

[22] Pourrat, *op. cit.,* p. 230.

[23] The actions mentioned here as well as actions in areas other than worship were attributed by the Fathers to holy orders and, insofar as holy orders involved the character, to the character also. However, we must not read into the association between these acts and the character a significance developed by later theology. That the Fathers did associate a very wide range of actions with holy orders can be seen in the numerous texts of the Fathers and other documents of their time collected by Doronzo, *De ordine,* I, 227-489, 794-918; summaries of the Fathers' ideas on the functions proper to holy orders can be found in this work on pp. 275-77; 372, 487-88, 831, 850-52, 910-13, 916-17.

ops and priests were regarded as capable of performing valid rites, even though they and those to whom they ministered lacked grace, and hence lacked also the spiritual priesthood of grace with its true spiritual sacrifice and worship. This was the very point St. Augustine argued against the Donatists.

From what the Fathers say of the consecrations of baptism, confirmation, and orders, it can be concluded that the characters are ordered immediately to the Christians' status in the visible community of the Church, to their rights, duties, powers in the Church in regard to ritual worship and its mission to teach and bear witness to Christ. Grace is required for personally worthy and fruitful visible worship and testimony to truth; but on the other hand, it is not impossible that grace should be wanting, and yet the visible structure of the Church with its offices, classes, rights, duties, ritual worship, and witness endure. The characters are the basis for this permanence.

There appears to be no basis in the Fathers for saying that the sacramental characters are ordered solely to the administration and reception of the sacraments, in the narrowest sense of the word, and as conferring grace. They are ordered to this, but to much more as well. The priestly consecration is ordered to the whole of the priestly ministry. The confirmational character to the bearing of public witness. The baptismal character to the whole Christian life. But that there is in all of this a special relationship to worship and to the sacraments in a broad sense, Fr. Daniélou suggests when he writes:

The life of ancient Christianity was centered around worship. And worship was not considered to be a collection of rites meant to sanctify secular life. The sacraments were thought of as the essential events of Christian existence, and of existence itself, as being the prolongation of the great works of God in the Old Testament and the New.[24]

St. Thomas

After St. Augustine distinguished the character from grace, not until the thirteenth century was the nature of the char-

[24] Daniélou, op. cit., p. 17.

acter examined more intimately by the theologians. The Fathers had considered the character chiefly as a sign, as *sacramentum*, marking, in conjunction with the external rite, the Christian from the non-Christian, the perfect Christian from the simply baptized, the successor of the Apostles and his associates in the hierarchy from the body of the faithful. St. Augustine had shown that the character is also a thing in its own right, a *res*, which endures after the external rite has ceased and which remains even if grace is lost. The theologians of the thirteenth century, equipped with Greek philosophy and the categories of Aristotle, asked themselves what this thing was in itself. In which category of being was it to be assigned?

Most of the theologians did not succeed in explaining adequately the nature of the character as a thing apart from its nature as a sign. But significantly, some theologians associated the character with various states of faith: the baptismal character marked those who had the faith and lived by it, or should live by it; the confirmational character marked those who had strengthened faith and fought for the faith; the character of orders marked those who were set aside for service of the temple and for the communication of faith to others.[25] What is significant about this association of the characters with the states of faith is that it at least implicitly relates the characters in some way with the activities of the Christian life —living the Christian life as a baptized person, fighting for the faith as confirmed, dispensing the faith to others as ordained. External, visible activity is involved in all of these states, explicitly and principally in the last two, but also very much in the first.

In view of this orientation to activity given to the character by contemporaries, St. Thomas, even though he took quite a different stand on the nature of the sacramental character, was not deviating from the current of theological thought

---

[25] E. g., Albert the Great, *De Sacramentis*, tract. 8, q. 4, a. 3; Bonaventure, *In IV Sent.*, dist. 6, a. 1, q. 4.

about the character. When he defined the characters as instrumental potencies, he was continuing and making more precise the trend of theological thought.[26] This is perhaps the reason why theologians have tended since St. Thomas to follow his lead in this matter (even though brilliant minds have had difficulty with the theory) and have today given his theory wide acceptance.

It is important for us to look closely at St. Thomas' doctrine about the sacramental characters, not so much because of his general theological authority, but because his doctrine represents a kind of quantum-jump in theological thought about the character compared to the doctrine of the Fathers and Thomas' contemporaries, and because his doctrine has become the generally accepted position about the nature of the characters. We ought, therefore, to attend with special care to what his mind was in this matter.

According to Jean Dabin in his classical study *Le sacerdoce royal des fidèles*, cited earlier, St. Thomas identifies the royal priesthood of the faithful with the sacramental character, making the character convertible with participation in Christ's priesthood.[27] Dabin affirms that, ever since St. Thomas, theologians generally have accepted the identification. But there are reasons for saying that Dabin has judged too hastily here, and that if theologians since St. Thomas have accepted this identification, they too have judged too quickly.

A more precise interpretation of St. Thomas is that the sacramental characters are identified immediately with participation (in different ways according to the character in question) in Christ's visible, external, ritual priesthood and worship, which is the means whereby Christians participate by grace in the spiritual royal priesthood and worship of Christ the Priest.

---

[26] Doronzo, *De sacramentis in genere*, pp. 287-88 suggests how St. Thomas' theory draws the other theories together and gives precision and order to all the qualities of the characters.

[27] Quant à son *essence*, le sacerdoce royal s'identifie avec le *caractère* sacramental, défini depuis saint Thomas, par convertibilité avec la participation au sacerdoce du Christ spécialement " (p. 46). Cf. p. 295.

The following facts are the reasons for saying this is St. Thomas' idea:

1) St. Thomas does say that the sacramental character is a participation in the priesthood of Christ, but he never uses the traditional texts of I Peter 2:5, 9, Apocalypse 1:6; 5:9-10, Romans 12:1, and Psalm 50:19 on the royal priesthood and spiritual sacrifice as the Scriptural foundation for this theory.[28] He frequently uses these texts, but always in reference to the spiritual priesthood and grace of sacrifice, never in reference to that participation in Christ's priesthood which he identifies with the sacramental characters.[29] The sacramental characters pertain immediately to the Christian priesthood and worship which is external, visible, ritual.

2) In the *Summa theologiae*, in the treatise on the sacraments, St. Thomas uses two distinct modes of expression when referring to how the sacraments perfect the soul. With regard to the sacraments as causes of grace and with regard to sacramental grace itself, St. Thomas says these perfect the soul for "the worship of God according to the religion of the Christian life."[30] The Christian life of grace is in itself religious.

---

[28] Congar, *op. cit.*, p. 184, Eng. trans., p. 132. This is evident from the passages culled by Dabin from St. Thomas' works, *op. cit.*, pp. 294-302: those texts which mention explicitly the sacramental character do not mention the traditional Scriptural texts.

[29] In one instance, *Summa theol.*, III, q. 82, a. 1, ad 2, St. Thomas even places in contrast the sacramental power of the priest to offer the Eucharist (though he does not use the term "character") and the spiritual priesthood of the faithful to offer spiritual sacrifices, the texts of Scripture being applied to the latter: "Laicus iustus unitus est Christo unione spirituali per fidem et caritatem, non autem per sacramentalem potestatem. Et ideo habet spirituale sacerdotium ad offerendum spirituales hostias, de quibus dicitur in Psalmo 50:19 . . . et Rom. 12:1 . . . Unde et I Petr. 2:5 dicitur: 'Sacerdotium sanctum offerre spirituales hostias.'"

[30] "Gratia sacramentalis ad duo praecipue ordinari videtur, videlicet, ad tollendos defectus praeteritorum peccatorum . . . et iterum ad perficiendam animam in his quae pertinent ad *cultum Dei secundum religionem vitae christianae*" (III, q. 62, a. 5, emphasis added); "Sacramenta Ecclesiae ordinantur ad duo, scilicet ad perficiendum hominem in his quae pertinent ad *cultum Dei secundum religionem christianae vitae*, et etiam in remedium contra defectum peccati" (*ibid.*, q. 65, a. 1, emphasis added).

By faith, hope, and charity the Christian worships God; [31] the principal sacrifice in a proper sense of the word is interior devotion, whereby man offers himself to the service of God; [32] sanctity is the permeation of the moral life by religion.[33] This is the language of spiritual priesthood and worship.

In contradistinction to this, St. Thomas says that the sacramental characters perfect the soul for " the worship of God according to the *rite* of the Christian religion (or Christian life)." [34] Now " rite " implies ceremony, regulated external action, the exterior side of worship. When speaking of the effects of the sacraments, St. Thomas uses this mode of expression involving the word " rite " in the question on the sacramental character; in questions concerning grace itself, St. Thomas uses the other expression without the word " rite." St. Thomas was never careless with words. His terminology here implies that the character is directly associated with the visible Christian priesthood and sacrifice rather than with the spiritual royal priesthood.

One may be unwilling to admit that St. Thomas intended to distinguish two realities or two formalities—" the religion of the Christian life " from " the rite of the Christian religion or life "—and maintain instead that St. Thomas was simply using different phrases for the same thing, namely, Christian worship. Still, his use of the word " *ritus* " is significant. This is so because of the connotations of the word mentioned above —exterior, organized, visible ceremonial action—and because the word is used with apparent deliberation as the context for the sacramental character and not for sacramental grace. The sacramental character pertains to organized ritual worship.

---

[31] *Summa theol.*, II-II, q. 81, a. 5, ad 1.

[32] *Ibid.*, q. 85, a. 4.

[33] *Ibid.*, q. 82, a. 8.

[34] " Sacramenta novae legis ad duo ordinantur, videlicet ad remedium contra peccata, et ad perficiendum animam in his quae pertinent ad *cultum Dei secundum ritum christianae vitae* " (*ibid.*, III, q. 63, a. 1, emphasis added); " Sacramenta novae legis characterem imprimunt inquantum per ea deputantur homines ad *cultum Dei secundum ritum christianae religionis* " (*ibid.*, a. 2, emphasis added).

Now such worship pertains chiefly to the external side of Christian worship; for the interior grace of worship itself is essentially free, the New Law of grace being the perfect law of liberty; whatever " organization " of Christian worship there is, concerns primarily the exterior activity which leads to or issues from the interior life of grace.[35]

Hence a second reason for saying that, according to St. Thomas, the sacramental character is identified immediately with the visible, ritual priesthood and worship, and not with the spiritual royal priesthood and worship, is St. Thomas' association of the character with " the rite of the Christian religion," with emphasis on " rite." [36]

3) St. Thomas affirms that the character is a participation in the priesthood of Christ. The kind of participation to which he refers is very important. The character is not a participation in the order of formal causality, but in the order of efficient causality; not a participation of a form in an exemplar, but of a subordinate mover in the motion of a principal agent.[37] St. Thomas regards the sacramental character as a ministerial potency, as an instrumental force. Through men qualified by the sacramental characters, Christ visibly prolongs his sacerdotal (and kingly) activity in the world, ritually rendering present his sacrifice of the cross and communicating its fruits. The sacramental character makes men like Christ the Priest in the order of action, not in the order of being.

A distinction is made by St. Thomas between being baptized in Christ by conformity to him, which is by grace, and being baptized in Christ by configuration to him, which is achieved by the sacramental character.[38] The royal priesthood

---

[35] *Ibid*. I-II, q. 108, aa. 1 and 2.

[36] Cf. Congar, *op. cit.*, pp. 184-87, Eng. trans. pp. 133-35.

[37] Stephen McCormack, O. P., " The Configuration of the Sacramental Character," *The Thomist*, VII (1944), 469-70.

[38] " Baptizari in Christo potest intelligi dupliciter: uno modo in Christo, id est, in Christi conformitate . . . alio modo dicuntur aliqui baptizare in Christo, in quantum accipiunt sacramentum Christi; et sic omnes induunt Christum per configurationem characteris, non autem per conformitatem gratiae " (*Summa theol.*, III, q. 69, a. 9, ad 1).

of the faithful consists principally in this conformity to Christ the Priest by grace, a participation of a form, grace, in a superior form, the fullness of Christ's grace. Christ's grace is priestly and kingly by its very nature and the grace we receive from him bears the same modalities. Like the grace which is its foundation, the royal priesthood will endure forever and function eternally in praise and thanksgiving.

The participation in the priesthood of Christ by the character consists in configuration to Christ, a participation in the sacramental activity of Christ. This participation, like the sacramental activity itself, is for the time between Christ's pasch and parousia.[39] The character is indeed indelible, not because it is ordered to an everlasting activity, but only for the glory or the shame of those who use it well or badly in this life.[40]

The third reason, therefore, for saying that St. Thomas identified the sacramental character immediately with the visible, ritual priesthood and worship of the Christian life, rather than with the spiritual royal priesthood and its worship, is the kind of participation in the priesthood of Christ which the character is: a participation in the visible priestly activity of Christ.

4) St. Thomas brings up an objection to the indelibility of the character: the exterior cult to which the sacramental character is ordained will not remain in heaven; therefore the sacramental character will not remain perpetually in the soul.[41] In response St. Thomas does not deny the ordination of the

---

[39] " Fideles Christi ad praemium quidem futurae gloriae deputantur signaculo praedestinationis divinae. Sed ad actus convenientes praesenti Ecclesiae deputantur quodam spirituali signaculo eis insignito, quod character nuncupatur " (*ibid.*, q. 63, a. 1, ad 1).

[40] " Quamvis post hanc vitam non remaneat exterior cultus, remanet tamen finis illius cultus. Et ideo post hanc vitam remanet character et in bonis ad eorum gloriam, et in malis ad eorum ignominiam " (*ibid.*, a. 5, ad 3).

[41] " Cessante fine, cessare debet et id quod est ad finem, alioquin frustra remaneret. . . . Cultus autem exterior, ad quem character ordinatur, non remanebit in patria, in qua nihil agetur in figura, sed totum in nuda veritate. Ergo character sacramentalis non remanet in perpetuum in anima. Et ita non inest indelebiliter " (*ibid.*, a. 5, obj. 3).

character to exterior worship; he simply admits that the exterior worship will cease and explains the continued existence of the character as a source of glory or shame for its bearer.[42] What is significant here is the admitted relationship between the sacramental character and exterior worship, the function of visible, ritual priesthood. Significant too is St. Thomas' not assigning any activity of the character for after this life, when the spirit will dominate the body and no need will be had for sensible, sacramental activity.

5) St. Thomas clearly states that the character is a sign of deputation for " actions befitting the Church of the present ";[43] they distinguish the faithful of Christ from the servants of the devil " in relation to the cult of the present Church." [44] St. Thomas refers to holy orders as " the orders of the Church militant." [45] If the sacramental character is ordered to the activity of the present Church militant, then it is ordered immediately to ritual priesthood and worship, for such is the priesthood and worship proper to the Church on earth in time.

It may be objected that this would not rule out the character's being ordered to spiritual priesthood and worship with equal immediacy, because it is this latter which gives meaning and value to external worship. This objection would be valid if the only argument for the character's ordination to visible priesthood and worship were the association of the character with the Church militant. But when we add the admitted relationship of the character to exterior worship, its association with the " rite " of the Christian religion, and its being a participation in Christ's sacramental activity among men in

---

[42] Quoted in note 40 above.

[43] See note 39.

[44] Et similiter character fidelium est quo distinguuntur fideles Christi a servis diaboli vel in ordine ad vitam aeternam, vel in ordine ad cultum praesentis Ecclesiae. Quorum primum fit per caritatem et gratiam . . . secundum autem fit per characterem sacramentalem " (*Summa theol.* III. q. 63, a. 3, ad 3).

[45] " Sed ordines Ecclesiae militantis respiciunt participationem sacramentorum et communicationem, quae sunt causa gratiae " (*ibid.*, Suppl. q. 34, a. 1, ad 3).

time, the picture emerges of the character and its activity forming a part of the peculiar structure of the Church in this world, an essentially " sacramental " structure in the broad sense of the word, a visible sign of God's efficacious love for man.

The conclusion to be drawn from the preceding paragraphs is clear; St. Thomas did not simply identify the spiritual royal priesthood of the faithful with the sacramental character, as Dabin affirms. Rather, continuing the traditional view of a twofold participation in the priesthood and worship of Christ, St. Thomas saw the sacramental character as ordered directly and primarily to the visible, ritual priesthood and worship which forms part of the structure of the sacramental Church on earth.

Now we must ask a crucial question for our study: To which activities in this visible worship of the Church militant did St. Thomas consider the sacramental characters to be ordered? Only to the essential rites of the sacraments as conferring grace or to other actions also?

Without question St. Thomas regards the sacramental characters as ordered to making, dispensing, and receiving the sacraments; he explicitly mentions this order several times.[46] Since St. Thomas carefully distinguishes between sacraments in their essential rites which are of necessity and the solemnities of the sacraments added to the essentials,[47] we can reasonably presume that when he speaks about the order of the characters to the sacraments, he means the sacraments in the strictest sense of the word.

In his Commentary on the Sentences, however, St. Thomas says that the characters are ordered to sacramental actions directly,[48] which implies that indirectly they may be ordered to other actions.

---

[46] In IV Sent., d. 1, a. 1, sol.; a. 2, sol. 1 and ad 3; a. 4, sol. 1 and 3; Summa theol., III, q. 63, a. 5; q. 5, a. 5, ad 2; Supp., q. 34, a. 1, ad 3; a. 2, ad 2; q. 35, a. 2.

[47] Summa theol., III, q. 66, a. 10; q. 84, a. 4, ad 3.

[48] " Cum character sit virtus seu potentia spiritualis ad actiones sacramentales

Far more frequently, St. Thomas' language is very general about that to which the characters are ordered. In his *Commentary on the Sentences*, the characters are said to be ordered to " spiritual things," [49] " spiritual actions," [50] " sacred actions," [51] "hierarchical actions, which are the administration and reception of the sacraments and of other things which pertain to the faithful." [52] In the *Summa theologiae*, St. Thomas' language is different from that in the *Commentary*, but still general; the character is ordered to " those things which belong to divine worship," [53] to receiving and giving "those things which pertain to the worship of God," [54] to " the protestation

ordinata, si ex aliquo quod per nos fiat, imprimi character debeat, oportet quod per sacramenta novae legis imprimatur, et per ea tantum, quia *ad illas actiones tantum directe illa potentia ordinatur*" (*In IV Sent.*, d. 4, q. 1, a. 4, sol. 1, emphasis added here and in the subsequent citations).

[49] " Character est distinctivum signum quo quis ab aliis distinguitur ad *aliquid spirituale* deputatus. Sed ad *spirituale* potest aliquis tripliciter deputari. Uno modo, ut aliquis in se *spiritualia* participet; et ad hoc quis deputatur in baptismo . . . unde character baptismalis . . . est quasi quaedam spiritualis potentis passiva. Alio modo, ut *spiritualia* quis in notitiam ducat per eorum fortem confessionem; et ad hoc deputatur in confirmatione. . . . Tertio modo, ut etiam *spiritualia* credentibus tradit; et ad hoc deputatur aliquis per sacramentum ordinis. Et ideo sicut in baptismo confertur character et in ordine, ita et in confirmatione." (*In IV Sent.*, d. 7, q. 2, a. 1, sol. 1). Cf. *ibid.*, ad 3; sol. 3, ad 3.

[50] " Character datur ad exercendas *actiones spirituales* aliquas simpliciter " (*ibid.*, d. 4, q. 1, a. 3, sol. 3, ad 1). Cf. *ibid.*, a. 1, ad 5; a. 2, sol. 2, ad 2 and ad 5; a. 4, sol. 1, ad 1; sol. 3.

[51] " Signum datur ad duo; ut recipiens configuretur quasi adscriptus ad communicandum divinis sacramentis et *actionibus sacris* . . ." (*ibid.*, d. 4, q. 1, a. 2, sol. 1). *Ibid.*, a. 4, sol. 2 speaks of " doing some sacred spiritual thing ": " Quicumque autem mancipatur ad *aliquid sacrum spirituale exercendum*, oportet quod habeat spiritualem potestatem, et solum talis."

[52] " Hoc signum nihil aliud est quam quaedam potentia qua potest in *actiones hierarchicas*, quae sunt *ministrationes et receptiones sacramentorum, et aliorum quae ad fideles pertinent*" (*ibid.*, d. 4, q. 1, a. 1, sol.). " ' Communio fidei ' " oportet quod recipiatur pro communione in *sacramentis fidei et aliis actionibus quae fidelibus competunt*, ad quas nullus admittatur antequam characterem suscipiat spiritualis potestatis respectu illorum " (*Ibid.*, a. 2, sol. 1, ad 3). Cf. *ibid.*, a. 4, sol. 3.

[53] " Character importat quaedam potentiam spiritualem ordinatam ad *ea quae sunt divini cultus*" (*Summa theol.*, III, q. 63, a. 2, corp.). Cf. *ibid.*, a. 4, corp. ad 1 and ad 3.

[54] " Deputatur quisque fidelis ad recipiendum vel tradendum aliis *ea quae per-*

of faith through exterior signs," [55] and to " divine worship." [56]

If St. Thomas had understood the characters as ordered exclusively to the essential rites of the sacraments, he could very easily have used the word " sacrament " in the places mentioned above; but he did not; in a few cases he refers the characters to the sacraments *and* to these other objects. The logical conclusion is that he did not restrict the sacramental characters to the making, administration, and reception of the sacraments in their essential rites.

That the *ratio* of character as understood by St. Thomas is not by nature restricted to the essential rites of the sacraments is manifested in St. Thomas' consideration of the characters of confirmation and orders.

The sacramental character of confirmation is ordered to the reception of the sacraments, [57] but it is also ordered to "public confession," [58] " courageous confession," [59] " certain sacred actions besides those within the capacity of the baptized," [60] " doing those things which pertain to the spiritual battle against the enemies of faith," [61] " professing publicly the faith

---

tinent ad cultum Dei. Et ad hoc proprie deputatur character " (*ibid.,* a. 3, corp.). Cf. *ibid.,* a. 1, corp. a. 4, ad 1; a. 5, corp.; in this last St. Thomas says the spiritual power regards " sacramentorum *et* earum quae pertinent ad divinum cultum."

[55] " Character ordinatur ad ea quae sunt divini cultus. Quo quidem est *quaedam fidei protestatio per exteriora signa* " (*ibid.,* a. 4, ad 3).

[56] " Sacramenta novae legis . . . ordinantur . . . ad *cultum divinum* " (*ibid.,* a. 6, corp.). Cf. *ibid.,* ad 2; a. 2, corp.

[57] " Sed ad recipientes pertinet sacramentum baptismi . . . Ad idem etiam ordinatur quodammodo confirmatio . . . Et ideo per haec tria sacramenta character imprimitur, scilicet per baptismum, confirmationem, et ordinem " (*ibid.,* a. 6).

[58] " Potestas characteris huius [confirmationis] est potestas activa, non ad conferendum spiritualia, quod est ordinis, sed magis ad *confitendum publice* " (*In IV Sent.,* d. 7, q. 2, a. 1, sol. 1, ad 3).

[59] " Ad spirituale potest aliquis tripliciter deputari . . . alio modo, ut spiritualis quis in notitiam ducat per eorum *fortem confessionem*; et ad hoc quis deputatur in confirmatione " (*ibid.,* sol. 1).

[60] " Et ideo per sacramentum confirmationis datur homini potestas spiritualis ad *quasdam actiones alias sacras, praeter illas ad quas datur ei potestas in baptismo* " (*Summa theol.,* III, q. 72, a. 5, corp.).

[61] " In confirmatione accipit homo potestatem *ad agendum ea quae pertinent ad pugnam spiritualem contra hostes fidei* " (*ibid.*). Cf. *ibid.,* ad 1.

of Christ in words." [62]   By confirmation the Christian is deputed, like the recipient of orders, to a special office, a deputation which is given by the one who has the office of ruler.[63]

Moreover, in the *Commentary on the Sentences*, St. Thomas
explicitly calls the confirmational character an active power,
not for conferring spiritual things on others subject to the confirmed, but for public confession and witness, making known
the faith.[64] In the *Summa theologiae* he does not use the phrase
" active power " of the confirmation character, but the words
he uses and the function he assigns to the character indicate
that he still thought of it as an active power for spiritual battle and for the confession and defense of the faith publicly,
officially, even by word.[65]

From St. Thomas' treatment of the confirmational character a picture emerges of the character and its activity as a
part of the structure of the sacramental Church visibly carrying on Christ's activity through the ages. While Christ
continues his priestly action among men through all three
characters (though in a different way in each character), he
continues his kingly activity through the confirmational character. Christ came into this world as king to bear witness to
the truth (John 18:37); he continues this activity in his
Church through men equipped with the character of confirmation. If St. Thomas had lived to write his own treatise on
the sacrament of orders, he may very well have explicitly
affirmed that the character of orders contains the fullness of
this deputation to proclaim and defend the truth in Christ's
name.[66]

---

[62] " Ita confirmatus accipit potestatem *publice fidem Christi verbis profitendi*,
quasi ex officio " (*ibid.*, ad 2).

[63] " Dicendum quod per ordinem et confirmationem deputantur fideles Christi
ad aliqua *specialia officia*: quod pertinet ad officium principis " (*ibid.*, q. 65, a. 4,
ad 2).

[64] See note 58.

[65] See notes 61-63.

[66] A hint of this is contained in the *Commentary on the Sentences*, where St.
Thomas affirms that one can be deputed to the spiritual in three ways: " uno
modo, ut aliquis in se spiritualia participet; et ad hoc quis deputatur in baptismo:

St. Thomas' view of the character of orders also shows that in his mind the notion of character is not exclusively in terms of the essential rites of the sacraments. The sacerdotal character is necessary, of course, for consecration and immolative offering of the Eucharist, for the remission of sins, and for the conferring of the other sacraments, except for matrimony and, in necessity, for baptism. But the sacerdotal character is a potential whole which is ordered to all those actions which are performed by the priest as well as by the deacon and by those in the other orders,[67] which, in St. Thomas' view, the Church explicated from the divinely established deaconate.[68]

Hence, St. Thomas sees the sacerdotal character ordered not only to consecrating the Eucharist, absolving sins, and conferring other sacraments, but also to praying in the name of the Church, to receiving the offerings of the people, placing them on the altar for the priestly offering, instructing the faithful in preparation for the Eucharist, proclaiming the word of God in the Old Testament and the New.[69] A reading of articles two and four of question thirty-seven of the Supplement (or 4 Sent., d. 24, q. 2, a. 1, qla. 2 and a. 2) leads to one conclusion: when St. Thomas wrote these words he conceived of the sacerdotal character as ordered to all those actions which are necessary in some way for the integral and worthy celebration of the Eucharist; some of these actions are sacraments in the strict sense—baptism, confirmation, penance, and final anointing. Other actions are not sacraments in the strict sense—they are prayers, ceremonies, reading the word of God, preaching, blessings, etc.

To sum up this survey of St. Thomas' thought: St. Thomas

. . . alio modo, ut spiritualia quis in notitiam ducat per eorum fortem confessionem; et ad hoc quis deputatur in confirmatione; . . . tertio modo, ut *etiam spiritualia* credentibus tradat; et ad hoc deputatur aliquis per sacramentum ordinis " (*In IV Sent.*, d. 7, q. 2, a. 1, sol. 1). The " etiam " for orders suggests that the character of orders includes the power of confirmation and adds to it.

[67] *Summa theol.*, Suppl., q. 37, a. 1, ad 2.

[68] *Ibid.*, a. 2, ad 2.

[69] *Ibid.*, a. 4; note in particular the responses to the objections.

considered the sacramental characters as pertaining to the visible, ritual priesthood and ordered to the exterior worship of the Church of the present time. He considered the characters ordered to many more actions in this ritual worship of the Church than the administration and reception of the sacraments in their essential rites. The baptismal character is for the reception of hierarchical actions, be they sacramental or simply " those which pertain to the faithful." Since the confirmational character extends even to public, verbal confession and defense of the faith, no reason exists for restricting it to the essential rites of the sacraments when it functions in those things which pertain to the worship of God. The extent of the sacerdotal character to much more than the essential rites of the sacraments is conveniently demonstrated by the attribution to this character of those varied activities performed by those in major and minor orders.

TRENT AND *Mediator Dei*

The decrees of councils and the encyclicals of popes do not ordinarily enter into the niceties of theology but are content with statements of the fundamental truths of Christianity. This holds true for the Council of Trent and the encyclical *Mediator Dei* with regard to the orientation of the sacramental characters in the liturgy. Close examination of the pertinent texts of the Council [70] and *Mediator Dei* [71] reveals that they do not go beyond the notion of the characters as signs. They both associate the character of holy orders with the visible, external priesthood of Christ; and *Mediator Dei* assigns the baptismal character as part of the reason why the faithful can be said truly to offer, in some sense, the Sacrifice of the Mass. Thus two of the characters are associated with the ritual priesthood and sacrifice, though the association of the baptismal character is not made to appear so closely or exclusively bound to it as the sacerdotal character. As to which

---

[70] Sess. XXIII, Doctrina de sacramento ordinis, cap. 4, Denz. 960.

[71] *AAS*, XXXIX (1947), 538-39, 555.

acts of visible worship the Council and *Mediator Dei* regard the characters to be ordered, the most that can be said is that they do not exclude the characters' being ordered to more than the essential rites of the sacraments.

CONCLUSION

The purpose of the study presented in these pages was to determine whether the sacramental characters as powers, whereby men share in the priesthood of Christ, are ordered only to the essential rites of the sacraments or also to other rites of the liturgy as well. The investigation which followed in pursuit of the answer to this question led to the twofold Christian priesthood and worship, the spiritual and the visible. The sacramental characters were found to be associated most closely with the visible, ritual priesthood and the exterior worship of the Church on earth. The characters of confirmation and holy orders were found to be associated also with the Church's function of proclaiming, witnessing, and defending the truths of faith and thus to be related to Christ's kingly office. The characters were found to be ordered not exclusively to the administration and reception of the sacraments in their essential rites, but to a wide range of activities embracing those acts of worship and witness which pertain to Christians precisely as members of the visible Church and which are the continuation among men in time of Christ's priestly and kingly activity.

Specifically with regard to the liturgy, therefore, it can be concluded that the sacramental characters as participations in Christ's priesthood are ordered to the entire liturgy as the visible worship of the Church militant prolonging Christ's priestly mediation, even though the characters are ordered directly and principally to the sacraments in their essential rites. What each character is in itself, why and how each is operative in the various rites that constitute the entire liturgy, are questions which must be left for another study.

Not restricted to the essential rites of the sacraments, the sacramental characters ought not to be restricted to the liturgy. This is obvious for the characters of confirmation and holy orders, because these characters are participations not only in the priesthood of Christ but also in his kingship, which function is not restricted to the liturgy. But this is true also for the baptismal character. The baptismal character is ordered to those ecclesiastical actions which pertain to the members of the Church as such and by which the influx of Christ's priestly sanctifying power is received and terminated in its effect. The actions of the baptized in active participation in the liturgy fulfill these conditions. But the conditions can be fulfilled outside the celebration of the liturgy, for example, in the use of a sacramental.

The use of a sacramental is not always a liturgical act, for example, the use of a blessed rosary, even though the blessing constituting the sacramental be a liturgical act. The use of a sacramental by a member of the Church, however, is a sensible action proper to members of the Church. Insofar as the prayer of the Church is annexed to the use of the sacramental, the action has an ecclesiastical quality to it. And through the use of the sacramental the Christian receives grace from Christ, though the nature of the causality and the effect differ from the causality and effect of the sacraments.

Hence, although the sacramental characters as participations in the priesthood of Christ are necessary for liturgical worship, they are not restricted to this activity. The liturgy can *not* be defined *solely* in terms of a function of the sacramental characters, even insofar as they are participations in Christ's priesthood.

CHRISTOPHER KIESLING, O. P.

Aquinas Institute, School of Theology
Dubuque, Iowa

PLACE OF THE LITURGY IN CHRISTIAN SPIRITUALITY

∽

T O oppose liturgical prayer and private prayer is a mistake. For the most part, such oppositions have only a rhetorical value in the heads of those who maintain them. Their aim is nearly always to emphasize the need of one form of prayer, wherever this type is forgotten through negligence or exclusion. Now whatever goes without saying, goes even better when it is said; and, after all, it is useful to show that the profound and real content of " devotions " is nothing other than what pertains to actual liturgical rediscoveries. For example, the true cult of the Sacred Heart has only the aim to interiorize the Paschal mystery. It is always necessary to rectify and complete one type of prayer by another. To combat an uncontrolled taste characteristic of individualism, then, it is legitimate to recall the eminent value of the Christian cult, or to point out to the directors of extremely cumbersome chant that true prayer cannot exist without solitude and silence.[1] However, it is no less true that deviations are present in both positions.[2] It is useless to keep

---

[1] Cf. L. Boyer, " *Liturgie et contemplation,* àpropos d'un livre récent de Jacques et Raïssa Maritain," in *La Vie Spirituelle,* April, 1950, pp. 406-9; and P. R. Régamey, " L'orientation contemplative de la prière liturgique," in *La Vie Spirituelle,* May, 1960, especially pp. 478-84.

[2] " Since the end of the fifteenth century, the generalized practice of mental prayer has tended to give an increasing importance to private prayer, and yet there was a notable regression in the use of liturgical forms [of prayer]. In the seventeenth century, Saint-Cyran and Thomassin thought that religious women who did not know Latin were better off in the recitation of the Office, since, in praying, they were not embarrassed by the text. In our own time, a reaction in the inverse sense is starting to occur, inasmuch as, by exalting liturgical prayer, one has minimized the importance of mental prayer in a way which seems to be excessive. Now, if one remembers that every prayer is, in itself, the prayer of the Church, one can ask what is the precise meaning of the term ' private prayer.' One could not be using this term to indicate prayer wherein the member of the faithful is really alone in God's presence, since such a prayer does not exist and,

on reiterating such complaints as " You have become accustomed to talking so much during Mass that you cannot pray any more," etc. There is justice in the remark that praying does not mean showing interior movies with head in hands.

A False Problem

There is something more serious. One may hold, for example, by way of defence of the liturgy, " there is no explicit foundation for mental prayer in the Gospel." The ridiculousness of such a claim, even in the mouth of a professor, is of little importance. Yet such aphorisms open the way for " throwing the baby out with the bath water." All of us are too clever in rationalizing our infidelities. Moreover, one does not need long practice to know that the life of prayer is obtained only with great courage.[3] Thus such statements not only seem stupid; they are also culpable. Besides, we thereby bless the brutality of our age which has the advantage of speaking to us sharply and of obliging us to be true exteriorly, even if faithfulness is lacking. The quality of the dramatic inventions of our time and its genius of renewal in expression have quickly made us recognize the insufficiencies in our liturgical language, as well as made the audacities of the mystagogues seem tame.[4] Furthermore, the taste for psychological verifications and the haste of sociological investigations place us under the obligation of fighting against all spiritual " experiences " which would lead to self reliance rather

at all times, the whole Church is praying in us. We are never alone in prayer, and the dogma of the communion of saints lets us claim that the humblest of our mental prayers unites us with the supplication pertinent to the eternal Church, as also is the case of even the most solemn liturgical office. Any way it is taken, the distinction between public prayer and private prayer concerns only the human actualizations of prayer, without touching upon its very essence " (L. Cognet, " Le prière chrétienne," in La Prière, Paris: Les Éditions du Cerf, 1959, pp. 100-101).

[3] Cf. P. R. Régamey, " La Prière, conditions de sa vérité," in La Vie Spirituelle, February, 1959, pp. 117-136.

[4] One can not be excessive in recommending a rereading of the entreating words of Father Couturier in Art Sacré, especially " Devant l'art profane," January-February, 1950; " Le douloureux problème des arts missionnaires," March-April, 1951; " Théâtres," September-October, 1952.

than to reconciling the soul to the darkness of the faith. Moreover, we have the right to investigate with a view to a better grasp of why the opposition between private prayer and liturgical prayer is a false problem, as well as of the motives whereby we are held to establish our adherence to the prayer of the Church.

I. THE BASIS OF ALL PRAYER: THE PRAYER OF CHRIST

It can never be repeated enough that the first problem is, not whether private prayer or public prayer should be preferred, but, quite simply, whether there is the courage to pray or infidelity; then, whether the prayer is a *Christian* prayer or mere self-seeking.

Really, there is only one prayer since the Incarnation; that which should meet the soul of God's Son. Like public prayer, private prayer is, first of all, Christ's prayer. Prayers are Christian only to the extent that they are prayers of Christ, that is, prayers made *in the Spirit*,[5] or *in the name of Jesus*.[6] St. Augustine goes so far as to say that every other prayer is an anti-prayer and that it turns into sin!

The prayer which is not made in Christ's name, not only cannot take away sin, but itself turns into sin, since it is not made in the name of the mediator of God and men, Jesus-Christ, man and priest for all eternity according to the order of Melchisedech (*Commentary on Psalm 108:9 and 18*).

Whether our prayer is private or public, then, there is the same spirit praying in us, namely, that of Christ. All common liturgy depends upon the personal relation of each of the members of the community to Christ, his head (just as, in a choir, the quality of the group depends upon the intensity of the relation of each singer to the choirmaster).

By prayer, there is gradually effected, as it were, a transformation of our sentiments, our desires, and our sufferings

---

[5] Cf. John 14:13; 16:23-24; 11:41-42; Rom. 8:33-34; Col. 3:16-17; Ephes. 3:11-12; Phil. 2:5; Heb. 9:14; 7:25; I John 2:1; Apoc. 5:4-10; II Cor. 1:20.

[6] Luke 11:13; Ephes. 6:18; Rom. 8:26; II Cor. 13:13; Gal. 4:6.

into the sentiments, desires, and sufferings of Christ. This transformation is comparable to that which is accomplished in the Mass, namely, the transformation of bread and wine into the Body and Blood of Christ. While we truly remain ourselves, a sort of *transubstantiation* is wrought in us through prayer. In a certain way, we acquire a personality which is infinitely superior to our own; we are no longer alone in chanting the psalms or reading the Bible; Christ, our eternal Highpriest, chants and reads God's plan of love in heaven:

> Thus, from these two (Christ and the Church), everything took place as though there were only one person . . . if they are two in one flesh, why not also two in one voice? Let Christ speak, then, since in Christ, the Church speaks; and in the Church, Christ speaks. The Head speaks in the Body, and the Body in the Head (St. Augustine, *Commentary on Psalm 30:4*).

" *Come, Lord Jesus, Come* "

This has led us to discover the first concrete movement governing all Christian prayer, the first appeal with which each of our prayers should open: " Come, Spirit of God," " Come, Lord Jesus, Come," " Lord, teach us to pray." *God alone can form prayer in us*, since, in short, *only the Love of a God can countenance God's Love*. And one could say that a person is a Christian from the time when he can no longer speak to God except with and through Christ, with a recognition of the fact that the only face which God does not resist is that of His Son. " For all of you who have been baptized into Christ, have put on Christ " (*Gal.* 3:27; cf. also *I Cor.* 1:9; *Eph.* 1:5; *Gal.* 4:6). This is the principal movement of prayers in the Mass, namely, the memorial or commemoration of the saving mystery, whereby we speak to God with the very words used by His Son: *Recalling the Passion, Resurrection, and Ascension of Thy Son, we offer Thee the perfect victim . . . and through Him, with Him, and in Him we give glory to Thee.*

Christ, then, is truly our " Highpriest," as He is called in the *Epistle to the Hebrews*, which says that *He lives always to make intercession for men.* St. John says that He is our advocate. What does this mean, other than that Our Lord is the one in heaven who presents to His Father our praise, our adoration, and our petitions? Thus we can say that, in God's presence, He repeats our own words, that He takes up our poor human words by transforming them and making them His own. Our prayer is thereby strengthened and made absolutely efficacious inasmuch as it becomes Christ's prayer.

God could not bestow upon men a more excellent gift than by granting them His Word as their Head, through Whom He has created all things, and by uniting them to Him as His members, so that He would be, at the same time, Son of God and Son of man, one God with the Father, one man with men; so that, offering up our prayers to God, we would not separate the Son from them, and the Body of the Son, offering its prayers, would not be separated from its Head. Thus Our Lord Jesus Christ, the only Savior of His Body, prays for and in us, and receives our prayers. He prays for us as our Priest, He prays in us as our Head, He receives our prayers as our God. Let us recognize, then, that we speak in Him and He speaks in us . . . It is in Him that we recite, and it is in us that He Himself makes this prayer of the Psalm which bears the title " Prayer of David." In hearing these words, then, let none say: " Christ does not speak here at all." Nor let anyone say: " It is not I who speaks." But, if he believes that he is in Christ's Body, let him say: It is Christ Who speaks, it is I who speak." *Never speak without Him, and He will say nothing without you* (St. Augustine, *Commentary on Psalm 85:1*).

On Earth As In Heaven

In this mediation of Christ, let us not see an optional intermediary. It constitutes Christian prayer. This is not for us a recourse which we could omit and which would have only an ephemeral usefulness resulting from the imperfections of our state.[7]

[7] It should be emphasized how many of even the best writings on mystical theology fail to consider this mediation of Christ as what differentiates Christian mysticism. Frequently there is the belief that the mere phenomenological approach of listing mystical " states " alone would enable one to establish the criteria for comparison; but one would thereby run the risk of being led to singular conclusions

Before St. Augustine, St. Paul is decisive on this point, and, with him, the unison of statements in the New Testament:[8] "Whatever you do in word or in work, do all in the name of the Lord Jesus, giving thanks to God the Father through Him" (*Col.* 3:16-17). "All the promises of God find their 'Yes' in him; and therefore through him also rises the 'Amen' to God unto our glory" (*II Cor.* 1:20). "According to the eternal purpose which he accomplished in Christ Jesus our Lord. In him we have assurance and confident access through faith in him" (*Eph.* 3:11-12).

This intermediary is necessary under a twofold title. We cannot be reunited with God without going through Christ. Christ is both the beginning and the end of our prayer.

In fact, in turning towards God, man never forgets that first of all he is a sinner. Man becomes reunited with God only by departing from sin. Every advance here on earth is always an advance from sin; even in heaven, beatitude and grace are the fruits of Christ's priesthood, and the elect are conscious of having come from sin. Moreover, for us, praying is asking for something to which we would have no right, had Christ not merited it. He has merited that God be merciful to us. He alone could reinstate us in grace. Such is the principle or foundation for our prayer. Christ satisfies and prays for us; he prays as man. He does not demand grace as a right which we have, but He asks for it in virtue of the right which He has acquired to ask for it. Furthermore, if all prayer presupposes that one has a certain title to be heard, we can no

and of making a definitive removal of every possibility to establish a comparative study on mysticism. Moreover, it is hard to see how one can fail to take account of the *object* as the decisive criterion involved in the structure of the mystical state, with the understanding that *this object* can be *something no longer perceived.* If, in ecstasy, Christ is no longer apparently present, this has never meant that His mediation is no longer real. To make the matter explicit in a few words, let us say that, from the reality perceived as given exteriorly, He has become light, dwelling in the gaze itself (or as the Scholastics say, from the object "which," He has become the object "whereby"). His mediation is only more decisive, and, after all, that is the ultimate purpose of the Christian life.

[8] Cf. footnotes Nos. 5 and 6.

longer pray without going through Christ. Prayer presupposes that God is accessible. Yet, outside Christs' mediation, God is not accessible for us. Too, through Christ, we truly approach God in such a way that our advances in this approach to God are measured exactly by our advances in our approach to Christ. He is, in the full sense of the words, the *way* and the *term* (Note the relation between the Greek όδός and εἴσαδος, *Jn.* 14:6 and *Heb.* 10:19-22). "Therefore he is able at all times to save those who come to God through him, since he lives always to make intercession for them" (*Heb.* 7:25).

One could as well explain this need for Christ's mediation by examining the purpose of our prayer, namely, sharing the divine nature. How can one pretend to live like God other than as the Son has lived? Moreover, there is no term for our prayer other than the resumption, for our sake, of the dialogue of the Son to the Father: *Thy will be done on earth as it is in heaven.* If Christ has made satisfaction for us and has thereby established the possibility of our prayer, to derive the benefits of this satisfaction, personal application is necessary [9] and this work of satisfaction must be assumed by each person. Now such an application to each person has not been achieved at one single time. Furthermore, our prayer is regulated exactly by the mystery of redemption. We are not only in God's presence, but we must relive the steps involved in the mystery of redemption which Christ, in His glorious state, no longer lives.

[9] "Christ after redeeming the world at the lavish cost of His own Blood, still must come into complete possession of the souls of men. Wherefore, that the redemption and salvation of each person and of future generations unto the end of time may be effectively accomplished, and be acceptable to God, it is necessary that men should individually come into vital contact with the Sacrifice of the Cross, so that the merits, which flow from it, should be imparted to them. In a certain sense it can be said that on Calvary Christ built a font of purification and salvation which He filled with the Blood He shed; but if men do not bathe in it and there wash away the stains of their iniquities, they can never be purified and saved" (Pope Pius XII, *Mediator Dei*, Nov. 20, 1947, Vatican Library Translation, Washington: National Catholic Welfare Conference, § 77).

" I Cannot Read "

To understand the prayer of the Church, then, one must never envisage it outside this prayer of Christ; otherwise it is no longer a question of Christian prayer. This is a matter of faith and does not allow for any exceptions. One can illustrate this truth by a scriptural parallel, which very well expresses this absolute need of Christ's presence in our learning to pray.

And the vision of all shall be unto you as the words of a book that is sealed, which when they shall deliver to one that is learned, they shall say: Read this: and he shall answer: I cannot, for it is sealed. And the book shall be given to one that knoweth no letters, and it shall be said to him: Read: and he shall answer: I know no letters (*Isaia* 29-11-12).

" A man who does not know how to read"—such is our situation as long as, in liturgical prayer, we refuse the very intervention of Jesus in our prayer.

And I wept much, because no one was found worthy to open the scroll or to look thereon. And one of the elders said to me, " Do not weep; behold, the lion of the tribe of Juda, the root of David, has overcome to open the scroll and its seven seals." And I saw, and beheld, in the midst of the throne and of the four living creatures, and in the midst of the elders, a Lamb standing, as if slain, having seven horns and seven eyes, which are the seven spirits of God sent forth into all the earth. And he came and took the scroll out of the right hand of him who sat upon the throne. And when he had opened the scroll, the four living creatures and the twenty-four elders fell down before the Lamb, having each a harp and golden bowls full of incense, which are the prayers of the saints. And they sing a new canticle, saying, " Worthy art thou to take the scroll and to open its seals: For thou wast slain, and has redeemed us for God with thy blood, out of every tribe and tongue and people and nation " (*Apoc.* 5:4-9).

Thus, contrary to what we think, prayer comes *from on high*.[10] That is why it is always accompanied by a conversion.

---

[10] Cf. the provocative study of E. Peterson, *Le Livre des Anges* (Paris: 1954), and even more so that of J. Tyciak, *Maranatha* (Bonn: 1949), which is well worthy of translation into other languages.

It is primarily a matter, not of speaking or unfolding one's desires, but of listening and receiving. God has preceded us; God has anticipated us; and we come first to accept the prayer of the Lamb and make it our own. He alone could open the book; He alone can do it now. And the most basic reason establishing the liturgy and assuring its need is, finally, that God has wanted to give us Christ, His Son, as mediator and priest, the only intermediary worthy enough to pray. *Holy Father, eternal God, we praise Thee through Thy Son Jesus . . . Through Him, with Him, and in Him we give Thee thanks and dare to say: Our Father.* Such are the beginning and the end of the Canon of the Mass, as well as of every prayer worthy of the name " Christian."

" And I Wept Much "

This is not reserved to the author of the *Apocalypse*. Rather, it would be our condition when we want to go to God by our own capacities alone, and whenever we fail to give liturgical prayer its true place in our life. Let us see the exact attention with which Joan of Arc followed the liturgical season and its demands even when war or captivity dispensed her from this care; or the submission of St. Bernard in his sermons to his monks to teach them to pray according to the moment of the mystery of redemption; or again the care of Theresa of Avila in nourishing her interior prayer. None of these persons pretended to have any setting for prayer other than the liturgy.[11] Each one teaches us, in a concrete manner, what the liturgy is: a setting for life, the atmosphere, the living milieu established on earth by Christ's life, in order that this life may be born and developed in man.

[11] See the very explicit texts (as, for example, Relation XX) of St. Theresa of Avila and St. John of the Cross, which it would be good to cite for all those who reduce the rôle of the masters of spirituality to that of mere theorists of a so-called spiritual experience. . . Cf. the numerous texts cited by R. Hoonaert, " Liturgie ou contemplation," in *Études carmélitaines*, April, 1932, pp. 177-215, and especially the excellent and very accurate study of Fr. Lucien-Marie de Saint-Joseph, O. C. D., " Oraison et prière liturgique chez sainte Thérèse d'Avila," in *Carmel*, 2nd trimester, 1960, pp. 92-114.

II. Why Is The Liturgy Necessary?

Every living thing needs room for expansion. And this is not optional. Something which might seem negligible, such as an atmospheric disturbance or a change in temperature, can destroy life. Come a spring frost, extremely low temperature during a night in May, and the crop is lost. This is true also as regards what is most precious and fragile in man, namely, his divine life. He does not, with impunity, breathe any air whatsoever. And there are sunless regions, unheated places which leave only a desert in the soul.

A Region for Life

Every man needs a milieu where his prayer can be born and be developed, a milieu where he can learn to live according to Christ's ways. This milieu is the liturgy, the common prayer of the Church.

Just as man does not invent his life, so he does not invent his faith; he receives it. Likewise, he has not invented his prayer, but receives the prayer of Christ, the prayer born of the Spirit of God and now living in the community of His children. Since I have to learn my prayer, I need an education, a pedagogy. Now this pedagogy has been proposed to me in the most marvelous manner ever: through a living history, a history which does not pass away, which has become eternal because it has been that of the Son of God.[12] In this prayer, I do not at all devise for myself what should be; rather I enter into cooperation in a work which another initiates, I cede to another's desires, I accept participation in a plan, a project which surpasses me and is anterior to me. That is why we all have to be initiated in this project, to receive it from those among God's people who have come before us. Each generation educates the following generation and has it

---

[12] For a Christian, one of the great interests in the history of religions is to see how religions wherein faith is not addressed to a personal God, have difficulty in avoiding the two great devaluations of the mystery about God: an abstract god-idea or a god-idol. Cf. the penetrating analyses of O. Lacombe, *L'Absolu selon le Védanta* (Paul-Geuthner, Paris, 1937).

enter into this movement of prayer arising from Christ and sustained by expectation of Him.

A region is needed for every expansion of life. And here, contrary to what too many presentations (for example, alas, certain movies on religious ceremonies, etc.) would have one readily believe, it is not enough to compare the liturgy with the folklore of a village, the customs of a community, or the traditions of a family or a profession. No, much more is involved, namely, a living milieu, ever the indispensable conditions enabling the person desirous of living to breathe, grow, and be nourished. Moreover, if the milieu disappears, life, too, passes away.[13]

However, living things everywhere are responsible for their milieu. The strong take care of it for the weak. The same is true in the life of prayer.

The meaning of the liturgy, the purpose of a common prayer is, therefore, first summarized in this: the Church proposes the prayer of Christ to me and welcomes me into the living milieu wherein this prayer can flourish. It is no more optional for a " member " to live attached to its organism or to be separated from it, than for a Christian to leave his community. He is a Christian only if he is a member of Christ, and he is a member of Christ only if he lets life come into him by participation in the faith and the prayer of his brethren.

The children of God are the body of God's only Son; and, since He is the head and we are the members, there is only one Son of God. Therefore, he who loves the children of God, loves the Father. And no one can love the Father without loving the Son; and whoever loves the Son should love, also, the children of God . . . and, in loving, he himself becomes a member in union with the Body of Christ, and there will be one sole Christ loving Himself (St. Augustine, *Commentary on the Epistle of John to the Parthinians*, V, 5, 3).

[13] Few more explicit testimonies can be found than those of the seminarians in Algeria in their response to the inquiry of *La Vie Spirituelle*. This response was published in the aforementioned magazine in August-September, 1960, 464.

This is what should be brought to the attention of the person who would doubt the importance of the liturgy.[14] It is the irreplaceable teacher of our prayer in the exact title wherein Christ's prayer is the ultimate law of all prayer for each one of us.

Following Christ's Example

No one can dispense himself from this education in prayer, or from a *permanent* pedagogy which accompanies us during our whole lifetime, as the intermediary which God has selected as a means whereby we might draw close to Him.[15]

Christ Himself has given us the example; He has recognized the cult given to God in the temple (*Lk.* 2:46; *Mt.* 23:21; *Mk.* 11:17; *Jn.* 2:15-17). He takes part in the cult of the Synagogue (*Lk.* 4:14-17; 13:10; *Jn.* 18:20). He agrees to

[14] Perhaps one can rightly regret that this argumentation is too little present in the recent work of Jacques and Raïssa Maritain. And if, in spite of the generosity of the authors, their resolution raises a problem, we do not at all think, as Father Bouyer says (*Le Vie Spirituelle*, April 1960, p. 409), that it is a matter of knowing whether the opposition between the demands of mental prayer and the demands of the liturgy is scholastic or not, and whether the remedy is scholastic or not. One cannot ask "liturgy or mental prayer?" in the name of scholasticism, since *there is no opposition* between them; rather there enters a poor way of understanding them which isolates them, as well as a good way which distinguishes them in order to unite them.

Without our thinking, thereby, that scholasticism is no longer useful (a point remaining to be proved positively), there still remain the problems of discerning what is the rôle of the virtue of religion and technological virtues in the liturgy and mental prayer, of having a precise knowledge about the difference of the moments of Christological mediation, which is necessary in every prayer, and of showing, thereby, the decisive criterion for distinguishing Christian mysticism from mystical experience in general (by taking the object as the point of departure, rather than what is only a moment and an effect of the mystical state, namely, ecstasy).

[15] "Holy Scripture and the liturgy are precious gifts from God to His spouse, the Church: both are sources of divine life, both are sensible expressions of the incarnate Word. But *the less dispensable of the two is the liturgy,* a vital artery of the Mystical Body of Christ. The Church can subsist without Holy Scripture, just as she existed during the first centuries, before the Gospels and the Epistles of the Apostles were redacted; but she cannot exist without the liturgy, which bears her sacramental and sacral life in her" (I. Herwegen, O. S. B., "L'Écriture Sainte dans la liturgie," *Le Maison-Dieu*, no. 5, p. 7).

belong to a true community; He recognizes the customs and traditions of the Jewish cult, as well as the ritual meals of each community, the priesthood, and the liturgical authority. Moreover, it is not a matter of a merely external recognition; Our Lord accepts this cult in its interior significance. The spontaneous reactions in His prayer constantly give evidence of this. The psalms, learned and accepted from the community, are what He cites on each great occasion in His life: at the time of His short-lived triumph (*Mt.* 21:26), during the last solemn announcement about His death (*Jn.* 12:27), at the Last Supper, while He spoke of His betrayal (*Jn.* 13:18), during the last discourse (*Jn.* 15:25) and His final prayer (*Mt.* 26:38; 27:46, etc.) .

In the same way the primitive Christian community would remain associated with the temple (*Lk.* 24:53; *Acts* 2:46; 3:3; 5:25; 5:42, etc.) and would preserve the ensemble of Jewish practices which had finally taken on a definitive meaning since Christ fulfilled them. He condemns himself to misunderstanding Christian prayer, who does not see that it is bound up with a community, with a liturgy, i.e., in its proper sense, " a work-of-a-people," *yet such as Jesus accomplished and lived it in His mystery.* Moreover, it is no longer optional; Christ has made the choice for us. Furthermore, our reticence at common prayer almost always conceals, in addition to laziness or our small and individual well-being, more serious refusals: false angelicism and the illusion of believing that one can do without learning, without receiving the nourishment of prayer, the manna, from others.

III. FOR A CHRISTIAN USE OF SYMBOLS

And yet, in view of the manner in which the liturgical life has been proposed to us, is this reticence always unjustified? One would like to think so. However, the actual evidence of a disaffection towards the liturgy, being more general and growing at a greater rate than one would think, poses a problem. Moreover, it would take considerable clerical illusion to imagine that the battle has been won. One will never say enough as to how beneficial has been the golden age of the liturgy, such as we have known it for the past twenty years.[16] It has decisively helped the spiritual life to rise above secondary psychological complications and subjective illusions, as well as to reestablish the mystery of Christ and His objective proposition as its core. But how many obstacles still remain!

Let us not be astonished. All pedagogy encounters such difficulties. Moreover, if the need for the liturgy is the same as that of intermediaries in the faith, the difficulties, too, are the same. We must see how these difficulties pertain to all pedagogy, as well as how they differ.

The Enlargement of Outlook

Like every other type of pedagogy, the liturgy puts to work a universe of signs or symbols. It utilizes things and actions which are commissioned to transmit a message and a presence. Now very often these things no longer say anything. Moreover, we must make our first start by offering an artificial explanation of what should serve to explain! Here there is truly a struggle for the light. Every professor knows very well how difficult it is to maintain what is essential and avoid what threatens to overburden or confuse the basic meaning of things. Now we must avoid illusion concerning the conditions of the actual existence of the liturgy.

One need only see the miter and crosier appear on the televised news program of a blessing of an ocean liner or Catholic Charity truck to have new evidence about the difference, very often brought to mind by the official teaching of the Church, between the mental universe where the liturgy takes its roots and the real character of our imagination.[17] Furthermore, at

---

[16] As well as some time previous. Cf. Dom. O. Rousseau, *Histoire du mouvement liturgique*, Paris, 1945; as well as, for example, the statements of St. Theresa of Lisieux concerning the influence exercised on her by the family reading of the *Année liturgique* of Dom Guéranger.

[17] Cf. the serious warnings from specialists in religious sociology, as, for example, those of J. Monnerot concerning the laicization of the religious feast in Europe,

times it can be understood why some people relegate this liturgy to the level of dusty folklore.

In fact, those who are responsible for this liturgical universe cannot fail to recognize that, especially in these times, the discovery of other civilizations and other cultural ensembles, as remarkable as our own, constantly make our sensibility more demanding. This has been brought into evidence to explain the revolution of painting during the nineteenth century,[18] namely, that, because of photography, there was the intervention, into the imagination as related to painting, of works to which, previously, there was no access, and each of our contemporaries more or less consciously undergoes the effect of this. The Mediterranean basin, latinity, and the Constantinian age can no longer be our sole cultural landmarks. The movies do have an effect on us in having us gain a penetrating knowledge about volcanoes, the dances of Bali, or the Southern Cross. And from now on we *all* know that the clothing of the Roman prefects in the lower part of the empire, now worn by bishops,[19] is less impressive than the kimonos worn in the Japanese court (as we shall see later, this example is excellent for showing that we must restrict ourselves to what is essential).

. . . And the Violence of Actual Experiences

Now even more demanding of attention than the introduction to other civilizations, which has become an irreversible fact, are the experiences in which our contemporaries take delight. These experiences, however, have such a violence and richness as can threaten to supplant the religious quest.

The modern world can propose veritable *ersazt* celebrations

in " Les Masses," *La Nef*, no. 25; as well as the analyses of P. Duployé, " Préface pour un Congrès," *La Maison-Dieu*, no. 10, pp. 7-38: " A symphonic overture announcing astonishingly rich themes, the quasi-totalitarian perspectives manifested by the discovery of a mysticism concerning the ' day of the Lord.' "

[18] Cf. the masterly analysis of A. Malraux at the beginning of *Les voix du silence*. Paris: N.R.F., 1951, pp. 15 sqq.

[19] Cf. Th. Klauser, *Petite histoire de la Liturgie occidentale*. Paris: Éditions du Cerf, 1956, pp. 40 sqq.

for internal desires, and here we are not thinking primarily
of the movies or the theatre. Let us take another example.
For years we have been attending ski competitions held in
certain mountainous villages otherwise very Christian. We
take these as an illustration since, as yet, they are not contaminated by money and they manifest a certain nobility
by the courage and the serious risks which the participants
accept. Let us not see a mere distraction here. That five thousand persons are willing to spend three hours silently standing
in the snow and a very low temperature in order to watch a
ski-jumping contest, easily proves this point to anyone present.
The competition itself has relatively little importance, and
often one forgets who the winner was. One comes primarily
to seek *the living proof of an excellence*. Fifty men go to risk
even the danger of a serious accident (and these are frequent),
to dominate their fear (always present), in order to conquer
gravity, to show *that, by his power alone, man can escape certain limitations*. None of those present is insensible to this
fact. And the quality of the silence, broken merely by a muffled
murmur of admiration, proves for hours that the myth of
Icarus still lives in human reveries. And how can one fail to
think that, even though many of these men are true Christians, all of them would feel terribly strange towards the liturgy when, not knowing a word of Latin, they assisted at
Mass and, the Saturday before, asked for absolution?

Is the Liturgy a Substitute Theatre?

There is, then, the temptation to conclude: what a shame
it is we cannot make an equally forceful proposal by way of
the liturgy! *Yet this is not the level at which we should make
our first endeavors*, since, undoubtedly in most cases, this procedure would be waste of effort before it started, and more,
a betrayal of what is essential in the liturgy.

Just as Our Lord came, not to replace the bakers and the
physicians by His miracles, but by the use of His signs, to
provoke the attention of His contemporaries for something

which surpassed them, namely, God's intervention, so, too, the rôle of the liturgy is not to take the place of human theatres. The story about the author of fables is well known. A painter produced the picture of a lion and made it so realistic that everyone become fearful before the picture. Well, it must be concluded that that was a very poor painting, since the purpose of a work of art exists at the very moment when it represents to me something which refers me to something surpassing the sensible.

A picture shows me a reality, but, at the same time, it should tell me that it is not this reality. Its rôle is, not to take the place of the object, but to make it present and thereby, while it is representing, the picture should efface itself behind what it proposes.

Music which engenders nothing other than a sort of dizziness and the desire for something else at the time when the phonograph record stops is a very mediocre type of music. Certainly one can replay the record in the hope of finding this " something else." Really the only aim at such a time is to evade the uneasiness and flee from the silence, where, however, there remain the interior chant of the music and the lack of satisfaction always accompanying it.[20] Thus should it be in the case of the preacher from whom one expects, not gossip, no matter how intelligent it may be,[21] but the recall of a kingdom which one has forgotten. So should it be in the liturgy, from which we expect, not that it gratify our senses, but that it lead us to the silence of a presence, namely, that of the Savior come from on high.

In other words, in every reality laden with a message, there

[20] Undoubtedly one would have great difficulty in expressing this matter better than Selma Lagerlöf has done in the astonishing scene of despair involving Gösta Berling and the Cavaliers, in *Gösta Berling*, chap. 21 (Paris: Éditions Je sers, 1940, pp. 281-288).

[21] "Make me be among men like a faceless person and my Word over them soundless like a sower of silence, like a sower of darkness, like a sower of churches.

"Like a sower of God's measure . . .

"Make me be like a sower of solitude, and him who hears my word return home uneasy and heavy-hearted" (Claudel, *Cinq grandes odes. La maison fermée*).

are two things: the reality itself and its rôle as ambassador, that is, its relation of subordination to the thing of which it takes the place. Moreover, one must never forget that this reality interests us because of its rôle as ambassador. The taste of bread is of little importance when I ask it to give me Christ . . .[22]

A New Mythology

The greatness of every sign is going in quest, not of itself, but of that which it has been chosen to serve beyond itself. The purpose of music is not to make me live in noise, even if it is harmonized, but to make me recognize my soul.

We understand, then, that the true problem of the liturgy is, not to multiply the signs, but to *read* those which God has selected, to learn how to go to the mystery, to the reality of which the collection of symbols, stories, and realities engaged are the servants.

The horizontal concern which leads one to become interested primarily in the admiration of the signs is a betrayal. Alas, do we dare to pretend that our efforts have not, only too often, stopped at that stage? Then let us not be surprised about the boredom and refusals which have been attendant upon the liturgy, since one will have merely forgotten to give the light . . . What purpose would be served in enlarging the flag if I do not know what it represents . . . (Let us think of the occasional desire to have permission for certain community, conventual, or concelebrated Masses).

Let us take an example. The prophecies of the Easter Vigil can lend themselves to wonderful poetic flights or liturgical applications . . . But a person does not say anything of value if he does not take the trouble to show that their whole purpose and their unique value lies in distributing to us the action of grace from the soul of Christ. He is the new Adam giving a new name to each being and understanding the truth (much

---

[22] There is the well-known anecdote about St. Augustine reprimanding a woman for having smiled during Communion and the answer which excused her. She had recognized the bread roll she herself had made and brought with her.

stronger in the new creation, and found in the refrain of the
first creature) " It was good." He is the new Moses making
His people accept the exodus and the stripping of the old man,
the drowning of everything which must be left in Egypt, in
order that the liberation through Baptism might be inaugurated. He is the new Isaia calling upon those for whom He
is obliged to provide the purification of the Spirit, and sing-
ing the canticle about God's presence with us. He is, again,
Moses judging the infidelity of those whom He has saved,
leaving them His cross and His law as a testimony and memorial of their salvation. Moreover, we all know that, on the
Vigil of Easter, all these prophecies are fulfilled in a last
thanksgiving: the Canon of the Mass.

Let us be careful. Our contemporaries do not come to ask
that the liturgy be a substitute mythology. Let us not underestimate their aptitude for the poetic or their thirst for the
transcendent. They have sufficiently recognized the taste for
the non-figurative, just as they have also had sufficient experience of the exasperation engendered by experiences which are
only sensible, although these may be esthetic; so that they have
become allergic to the adolescent nourishment provided only
too often by our liturgical restorations. That someone speak
to them about the Exodus or about David and his adulteries
is of little importance to them, if the aim is not to read them
as living parables about men whom God has delivered from
evil, if the aim is not to make an explicit discovery about the
salvation accomplished by Christ in God's name. *What commands the understanding of signs is something beyond them.*
By forgetting, only too often, the primacy of this " something
beyond," one prepares disillusionments and one makes of the
liturgy a very exact system good for those who know nothing
else, until they are no longer content with the universe of
their childhood.[23]

Whoever wants to concern himself about the liturgy will

[23] There are still good days for liturgical efforts, since there is vast barrenness
in too many booklets and commentaries.

never cease demanding of himself *a conversion: that which makes the signified have greater importance than the sign,* that which refuses to speak of a reality without asking what it has to do with the faith. Christ alone, God's witness, can open the " book " sealed for every man. Quite simply, then, the liturgy asks that the normal structure of every phenomenon of signification be respected. What is of special worth, what should command everything here, is the reality. This means that one first gives the light, that one assures the presence of the light which alone permits the reading of the reality. Then one will see that the liturgy and all common prayer presuppose an *interior* prayer,[24] that, without this interior attention, one has already lost the message which they bear, and that, without it, the sacraments themselves would be spoiled. Note this minimum requisite enabling a child to approach Holy Communion. He must be able to read something beyond the bread; he must be able to recognize that this bread has only one interest, namely, Christ. The aim of the liturgy is not to celebrate a Mass in dialogue or to have accomplished a " beautiful " Easter Vigil, but to have been reunited with the soul of Christ in prayer. If, too often, there is too little silence, if so many celebrations remain on the exterior wrapper, on what is unusual and accessory in their unfolding, the basic reason is possibly because one is no longer seeking Christ.[25]

[24] Father Régamey has been very correct in reminding us that a collectivity itself had an interior life, a personality which was not reduced to the smallest common denominator . . . including that of the leader! Cf. *La Vie Spirituelle*, May, 1960, pp. 471, 486-88.

[25] This does not mean that every effort to promote clerical culture is useless. One recalls Claudel's prophetic complaints in his letter to Cingria (in 1919) which would find, alas, points of application other than architecture:

" The causes of decadence in Sacred Art can all be summarized in one: this is the divorce, the painful consummation of which was viewed during the past century, between the propositions of the Faith and those powers of imagination and sensibility which are eminently found in the artist.

" When, after the [French] Revolution, the Church, having temporarily lost its position as teacher, had to appeal to artists to help her restore her losses, she found herself, as it were, on the same footing of competition as the other clients sharing

God Is Before His Ambassadors

However, we must go further, since the liturgy and the common prayer of the Church cannot be restored merely to the case of a habitual pedagogy. Here we must invert the relation between the mystery (the principal reality) and the sign, which serves it as a messenger.

In fact, as in every work of art, not only is the most important, the most real, that which gives meaning to everything, beyond the work itself, but here in liturgical prayer, the reality beyond the sign is a Person, a living Person, Christ, Who is God. Moreover, this Person is an all-powerful master, Who, in creating the second, visible reality, decided that it would be His ambassador. In taking a painting or a symphony as a

in the market. The religious crisis in the nineteenth century was, possibly, not especially a crisis of intelligence, but the crisis of a poorly nourished imagination.

" As regards the Church, in losing the cover of Art, she became, during the last century, like a man stripped of his clothing, that is, this sacred body made by men who were at the same time believers and sinners, was exhibited for the first time to the eyes of all in its nudity and in a kind of permanent exposition and betrayal of its infirmities and wounds. For anyone who dares to look at them, the modern churches have the interest and the pathos of a burdened confession. Their ugliness is the exterior manifestation of all our sins and all our defects, weakness, neediness, timidity in faith and sentiment, dryness in the heart, loathing of the supernatural, the domination exercised by conventionalities and formulas, exaggeration in individual and disordered practices, worldly luxury, greed, boasting, sulkiness, pharaisaism, bombast " (*Positions et Propositions*. *Paris*: Gallimard, 1934. Vol. II, pp. 225-227).

And, in *Contacts et circumstances*: " . . One goes into the cathedral; and when one has finished honoring the black Virgin, one turns and receives a sharp pain in the heart. On each side of the incomparable vase, at the foot of these sublime walls, there are two marble statues, a memorial, it seems, of a recent pilgrimage: St. Joan of Arc and St. Louis.

"Is it really marble? Is it not rather the crumb of bread? Camphor? The pulp from parsnip? Hardly solidified paraffin? One would say that it has not been accomplished on decent matter with the chisel and the hammer, but with strokes of the tongue. Moreover, one is ashamed of the truly imbecile expression on these two sacred faces, thus presented for the veneration of the faithful.

" What, then, is the cause of this almost total eclipse, not only of talent and taste, but also of dignity and true piety, which has been occurring in Christian art for a century? One would say that the body of the most profound and most sublime truths in the world, illustrated by incomparable poets and by an illustrious point of departure, one can take part in beauty or music, yet neither is a person. They have no existence independent from the work of art. They are never anterior to it, they can only coexist with the work which bears them. And never does beauty or music decide to be interpreted in such or such a way.

On the contrary, in the prayer of the Church and in every Christian mystery, God is anterior to His ambassadors. And this changes everything. It is the Spirit of God Who has selected such events and not others to bear His message, to represent Christ's prayer, and therefore our own prayer.

Moreover, it is He and He alone Who can give us the key to the meaning. Here there is an inversion in comparison with all human pedagogies. Only God can give us an eye capable of discerning what there is to learn, since it is He Who decided this order. This is what explains anew that this prayer, even if it be common, should be interior or not exist at all. If, animated by God at each instant, this new glance does not exist, there is nothing further to understand. There is no longer anything to " hold together," in the exact meaning of the word " sym-bol." [26] Our Lord Himself would solemnly affirm this:

lineage of superhuman heroes, is explained to abnormal children by a half-idiotic nurse who makes them stupid . . .

"It would be unjust to blame only the faithful. One must take account also of the clergy, who, for too long a time, kept themselves confined from the world in a frightened and defensive attitude and who thought that art could be separated from sin only by being separated from life. The gesture became ugly because it was empty. And yet the priests spend their life in reading and meditating upon the strongest, most energetic, and boldest poetry in the world, namely, that of the psalms and the prophets. In France they exercise their ministry in generally excellent buildings. Prayer and the contact with the highest spiritual realities and with the most moving human miseries open their heart and their mind to all that is great, good and beautiful.

"Whence, then, comes this aversion for strong expression, for holy and strong reality, such as God has made it, if sin has deformed it? How can one otherwise explain that, during a century which has accounted for so many great artists, such as Rude, Carpeaux, Rodin, Bourdelle, Maillol, and Despiau, the ecclesiastical authority has never had recourse to them, but to tombstone and lavabo cutters, to suppliers of images from which the bones have been removed? " (*Contacts et circonstances*. Paris: Gallimard, 1940, pp. 46-50).

[26] One can only rejoice in seeing theological analysis be attentive on this point again. Among the best studies, let us insistently call attention to those of A. Plé,

" The disciples came up and said to him, ' Why dost thou speak to them in parables? ' And he answered and said, ' To you it is given to know the mysteries of the kingdom of heaven, but to them it is not given . . . seeing they do not see, and hearing they do not hear " (*Matt.* 13:11, and *Luke* 8:10). St. John Chrysostom makes the following commentary on this:

I hear that Christ has been crucified and at once I admire His love for men; the infidel hears it, too, and deems that it is mere folly . . . Knowing baptism, the infidel thinks that it is only water; not considering only what I see, I contemplate the purification of the soul achieved by the Holy Spirit. The infidel deems baptism to be a mere ablution of the body; I believe that it also makes the soul pure and holy, and I think of the burial, the resurrection, sanctification, justice, redemption, the adoption of the children the heavenly inheritance, the kingdom of heaven, the gift of the Holy Spirit.[27]

Thanks to the actual and interior distribution from the Spirit of God, then, it is a matter of holding together the mystery which is given to me and yet disguised by the sensible reality which I see. If the Church has dared to add two words (" mystery of faith ") to the formula of consecration, this is only to remind us that faith alone gives us a hold on the true reality present here. And is it necessary to deem that Christ's words (" Seeing they do not see ") and the corresponding words from Chrysostom apply only to unbelievers? Are not our celebrations of Mass frequently tainted with a practical atheism, a certain absence of God?

" Pour une mystique des mystères," in *Supplément de La Vie Spirituelle*, November, 1952, no. 23, pp. 377-396; " Les mystères de Dieu," in *La Vie Spirituelle*, April 1945, pp. 209-226; " Un mystère de Dieu: le prochain," in *La Vie Spirituelle*, October, 1945, pp. 225-241.

And, among many others, especially: A. M. Roguet, *Le Sacrements, Somme théologique* of St. Thomas, French translation, 1945, " Notes doctrinales," pp. 255-377; and I. Dalmais, *Initiation à la liturgie*. Paris: Desclée de Brouwer, 1958, pp. 21 sqq. Among the non-ecclesiastical works, in preference to the well-known works of Mircéa Eliade, E. Cassirer, Cl. Lévi-Strauss, etc., we suggest the grating, but very provocative work by R. Barthes, *Mythologies*. Paris: Seuil, 1957 (as long as the reader modifies more than one conclusion contained therein).

[27] St. John Chrysostom, *In I Cor.*, Homil. I, no. 7 (Cf. Migne, *Patrologia Graeca*, Vol. 61, col. 65).

A Twofold Conclusion

Far from judging the quality of the liturgy on the basis of the exterior, we discover that it has value only on the basis of the interiority presiding therein. Here there is no longer the question of a facile euphoria found in a common excitement, or of the ardor due to the novelty of a popular fad. . . .

> The whole matter consists in uniting every prayer in the heart of Jesus and, when you cannot do more, in being content with opening your void to the Lord so that He might fill it with His own prayer. But we submit to being empty only with great difficulty! Everyone always wants to have something to give. Even in prayer, perfection consists in knowing how to receive everything in one's destitution.[28]

The first phase of common prayer is rigorously identical with the conversion which inaugurates all private prayer: learning to receive, to listen, and to leave problems in another's hands, to His attention, in all matters. Divine Office exists, not just for some sensible or spiritual satisfaction (although there can surely be some wonderful satisfactions therein), but because it concerns God and the encounter with God.

Reciprocally, the same interiority commands every act of private prayer and gives it its necessary collective value, if it is Christian. The Spirit cannot have me pray except in the communion of Saints. He Who led Christ into the desert and directed His ineffable dialogue with the Father, has taught us about the presence of His brethren as involved in this dialogue. It is enough to reread the sacerdotal prayer.[29] In contemplating His Father, Christ was brought back to those

---

[28] R. Voillaume, *Au coeur de masses*, Paris, 1950, p. 90.

[29] In a striking way, this manifests to us a truth which it is always good to remember, namely, how false and useless it is to have the primacy of the common good over the particular good intervene to prove the superiority of a collective act over an interior act. For *the truly interior act is never confined within the limits of the individual*, but, at the summit of personal activity, it is open to the whole community of spirits.

whom the Father had given Him, " What my Father has given me is greater than all " (*Jn.* 10:29).

We can thereby understand the basic originality of liturgical prayer. Human pedagogies, especially of the intellectual order, alas, do not necessarily accomplish what they teach. To be intelligent, it is not enough to pursue courses. A professor can be very precise in producing an excellent disposition of the media, so that each student might approach the light by his own efforts. But the originality of the Christian mysteries comes from the fact that the realities bearing the message can produce what they say.

Christ's physical presence in a living manner testified to, and accomplished for those whom He encountered, the message of His Father's mercy. One could touch His garment and be healed, look at Him and be freed from spiritual blindness, ask Him and be saved from sin.

The Sacraments pursue this energetic presence. If man does not place any obstacle, they will accomplish the salvation of the person who receives them. (There are nuances concerning requisite attention, which is very slight and passive in certain cases, and yet God's power will have worked.)

Thus is it also in the case of the liturgical and common prayer of the Church. It has the true power to accomplish something which surpasses its exterior and visible appearance. As the Sacraments it has, in its own way, the mission to give salvation genuinely. This is the ultimate reason which, contrary to what we are most habituated to do in our liturgical efforts, should urge us not to pass judgment on the exterior result, as well as not to have an exclusive and primary concern about what is visible, since what is truly effected cannot be seen. Here we have an added motive for not reducing the liturgy to a theatrical production, as well as to clearly differentiate it from all non-Christian cult. Surely many other liturgies can be more striking in dramatic expression, as, for example, the Mexican initiations, Bantu circumcisions, or the crowning of a queen! But, no matter how poor it seems on certain days, only the Christian liturgy can say: " Christ is there; God, Who saves us and takes care of our lives, is there." And this is true. In fact, it should not be forgotten that the liturgy has its value more by what it accomplishes than by what it manifests in a sensible way. The whole value of our cult primarily comes, not from its capacity to signify, magnificent as this is, but from its efficaciousness. In the Christian order, the sign is related to cult more because it is efficacious, because it causes Christ's presence, than by what it signifies immediately. In the concentration camps, the cult was present especially by the Mass; and yet recall the conditions in which it was celebrated. If negligence is not involved, the offering of Christ's Body can take place in the dust, and what is essential in the cult will have been attained.

What is no less true is that, if Christ had not been present as a sign, as the visible sign of God, Mary Magdalen, the paralytic, and the man born blind would not have been healed and pardoned. Likewise, our liturgy can cause or accomplish something pertinent to the mystery only if there is a visible sign.

Now this sign can no longer be the humanity of Christ. At the time when Our Lord lived among men, this humanity was the sign summing up all divine presence. Since the Ascension, the physical Christ is no longer the sign of God for us, since He is no longer there, since we no longer see Him. But there is His " mystical " body. Henceforth all the saving signs would be proposed to us by His mystical body. The signs of salvation are now entrusted to the assembly of men who pray in the name of His Son and are responsible for the Eucharist. Moreover, the saving signs can have real power only if there is this assembly. No matter how reduced it may be, this assembly has become indispensable, so that I cannot confer baptism or absolution upon myself, or celebrate the Eucharist all alone.

In this " community " condition of the Christian cult, let us not see a mere, more or less agreeable, complement surviving after an attempt at private prayer. We have previously said that it is the living milieu needed for the very existence of all prayer. The significative value of the community is filled with the mystery of God. The assembly of my brethren is the sacrament which henceforth takes the place of Christ's physical presence. This assembly is what transmits belief in the celebrated mystery, by safeguarding and regulating the tradition of this faith. This assembly is what assures the conversion, by obligating the individual to a true attention towards " the other," whoever it may be. This assembly is what assures us of our reconciliation with God, by offering us the strength of this pardon which is capable of uniting men. This assembly is what raises the human act of giving thanks, by declaring that love has been stronger than every division. This assembly is what will accomplish the final human justice, by consecrating to God even that which arises from the external activity of men, as a decisive sign of their interior prayer.

*   *   *   *

Let no one, then, try any more to establish an opposition between private and common offering in prayer. The existence of each demands such an interiority that the unaided powers of man cannot assure it. And yet, when this interior presence is lacking, all prayer is only self-seeking, dramatics, or egoism.

Christ alone takes upon Himself all prayer, and by one sole mean, namely, our fidelity to His Spirit living in the community of Saints. Henceforth, this is His own mystical body.

BERNARD BRO, O. P.

Editions du Cerf
   Paris, France

AN OBSERVER LOOKS AT THE SCHEMA
ON THE LITURGY

∼

THE invitation issued by Pope John XXIII to that part of Christendom not in communion with Rome to send observers to the Second Vatican Council was received by the world with great joy as an indication of the Holy Father's concern for Christian Unity. The Ecumenical Movement has, for many years, absorbed much of the time and interest of large numbers of Christians; and plans for bringing together some of the divided parts of Christendom have been discussed and even (as in South India) brought into being. But hitherto the Roman Catholic Church has felt obliged to stand aside from these discussions and negotiations. Her particular doctrine of the Church makes it impossible for her to enter the arena of ecumenical debate, with the result that the rest of the Christian world has had to go its own way, realising that the unity for which it was working could be only incomplete and partial since more than half of those baptised into the Name of the Lord Jesus would remain outside it. In the Upper Room Christ prayed for unity, not for duality; and no true unity can be achieved until *all* are one.

The fact that the Church of Rome has now ventured a little into the field of ecumenical discussion is, therefore, of the greatest significance, and has aroused much hope in the minds of men, both believers and non-believers. The setting up of a Secretariat for Promoting Christian Unity, the sending of observers to the General Assembly of the World Council of Churches in New Delhi, and now the invitation to other Churches to send delegate-observers to the Vatican Council have taken the ecumenical movement into a new sphere, a new dimension.

440

Although the Pope has made it clear that the *ultimate* objective of the Council is unity, he realises as well as anyone else that this goal is a long way off. He has therefore set before the Council an *immediate* objective which will set the Church on the path which, it is hoped, will lead in the right direction. This *immediate* objective is renewal of the Church's life, out of which will come better understanding, and so a greater desire for co-operation and unity. In the *Schemata* on which the debates in the Council are based, and in many of the speeches made there, these two objectives have been constantly referred to. Although the meetings of the Council are private and confidential, the observers are allowed to be present, and every one of the fathers who gets up to speak knows that his words will be noted by us and perhaps even quoted in the reports which we send in from time to time to the heads of our respective Churches. There is no doubt that the presence of thirty to forty observers has had a considerable influence on the way in which the Council has progressed, and will continue to do so in the months which lie ahead.

The divisions of Christendom are nowhere more apparent than in the sphere of worship. In the English country town where I live, with a population of 10,000 souls, there are six places of worship. There is the cathedral (the old church founded by St. Wilfrid in the seventh century and containing part of the original structure) and a nineteenth century church, both of which belong to the Church of England. There are also a Roman Catholic church, two Methodist churches, and a building where the Assembly of God worships. This means that the Christians in Ripon are divided into at least four different groups and are unable to worship together. The same pattern would apply to any other English town. In the United States there would probably be even more independent places of worship. To the outsider this seems ridiculous —a fantastic waste of opportunity and of resources. Why, then, cannot we all sink our differences and worship God together in one building?

We all know that there are many answers to these questions. Each " church " has its own form of worship, its own customs, its own history. But these are largely the *results* of division. The divisions themselves rest upon much deeper issues than that, though they are reflected in the forms of worship. The *lex orandi* is closely connected with the *lex credendi*: a man worships according to what he believes. That is why John Selden could write in his *Table Talk*: " To know what was generally believed in all ages, the way is to consult the liturgies, not any private man's writing. So, if you would know how the Church of England serves God, go to the Common Prayer Book, consult not this or that man."

As worship is nowadays a divisive influence among Christians, so it is one of the first things that must be considered when we look forward towards the goal of unity. It was perhaps for this reason that the first subject to be discussed by the Vatican Council was that of the Liturgy. It was a long debate which lasted a whole month, and many suggestions were made to the Liturgical Commission for its consideration. The *Schema* on the Liturgy is a remarkable document. As a student of history, and, to some extent, a traveller in Europe, I know something about Roman Catholic worship, and I was delighted to see how far the *Schema* was prepared to go in reforms which, to an Anglican like myself, seem so much to be desired. Not all the proposals in the *Schema* will receive the approval of the Council; but if only some of them are accepted, it will bring the worship of the Roman Catholic Church far more into line with that of other parts of Christendom. Renewal, in the field of worship, is clearly desirable. Most Christian communions now have some sort of " liturgical movement " which is affecting their life and paving the way towards Christian unity. So far as the Anglican Communion is concerned, our worship is in many ways much closer to that of the Roman Church than is that of any other body. Thomas Cranmer did not " compose by himself " the Book of Common Prayer (as stated by Archbishop Jaeger of

Paderborn in *The Ecumenical Council, the Church and Christendom*, p. 153). A very large percentage of the Prayer Book is the language of the Missal, the Breviary and the Pontifical, translated into English. But Cranmer worked on certain principles, adapting his material to make it consistent with what he believed about God, the Church and Christian worship.

When I read the *Schema* on the Liturgy, I realised that many of the proposals which were to be put before the Council were in fact points which we ourselves had accepted four hundred years ago. These would include greater simplicity, the use of the vernacular, more reading of Scripture, more preaching and catechising, the part assigned to the laity in the Mass, the possibility of administering the Sacrament under both kinds. As I read this *Schema* I was reminded of a notable figure in English life some years ago—Arnold Dolmetsch. Dolmetsch was a musician with a great knowledge of, and love for, the music of the sixteenth and seventeenth centuries. He hated the pianoforte, as a coarse modern invention, and devoted much of his time to making virginals, clavichords and harpsichords, on which his beloved music could be played. But he was always trying to improve on his instruments, with the result that people used to say that if he went on improving the harpsichord long enough he would one day triumphantly invent the pianoforte. In reading the *Schema* on the Liturgy, I could not help thinking that if the Church of Rome were to carry out all the reforms proposed they would one day find that they had triumphantly invented the Book of Common Prayer!

The fact that on line 4 of the Proemium to the *Schema* on the Liturgy there is already mention of the "separated brethren" shows that those who drew up this schema were bearing in mind the wishes of the Holy Father that the Council should keep in mind the goal of Christian unity. The proposals which are made are consequently of the utmost interest to us who can look at them, as it were, from outside. There are five propositions on which I would like to comment.

(1) *The plea for more and varied use of Scripture in the Liturgy.* This was one of the principles underlying the compilation of the Book of Common Prayer in 1549 and subsequent years. The result is that the Anglican liturgy is heavily impregnated with material from the Bible. This is particularly noticeable in our daily offices of Matins and Evensong, where something like ninety percent of the material is taken straight from the Bible. In the course of a year an Anglican priest in saying his daily offices reads through the Old Testament once and the New Testament twice. This is a heavy assignment; but it means that his teaching and preaching, and his whole attitude to life, are bound to be deeply and fundamentally influenced by the Scriptures. This is fully in accordance with his ordination vows when the Bishop asks him:

Are you persuaded that the Holy Scriptures contain sufficiently all doctrine required of necessity for eternal salvation through faith in Jesus Christ? And are you determined, out of the said Scriptures, to instruct the people committed to your charge, and to teach nothing, as required of necessity to eternal salvation, but that which you shall be persuaded may be concluded and proved by the Scripture?

To which he replies: " I am so persuaded, and have so determined, by God's grace."

But the daily offices were meant for the laity as well as the clergy, and in fact are said by a number of devout lay men and women each day, either in church or at home. In the preface to the Prayer Book (1549) we find it stated that the purpose of such planned and comprehensive Bible-reading was the edification of the people and the encouragement to right-living. Thus it states that the intention is not only that the clergy should be " stirred up to godliness themselves, and be more able to exhort others by wholesome doctrine and to confute them that were adversaries to the truth"; but also "that the people (by daily hearing of Holy Scripture read in the Church) might continually profit more and more in the knowledge of God, and be the more inflamed with the love of his true religion."

I cannot, of course, quote from the *Schema* on the Liturgy now before the Vatican Council, but there is much in it to show that the fathers wish to increase the amount of Bible-reading in the worship of the Church, as well as to test what is said in church by the standards of Scripture. All this is of intense interest to the observers, most of whom come from communions where Bible-reading and biblical theology are at the very centre of their religious life.

(2) *The place of the Laity in the Worship of the Church.* The title of our Anglican manual—the Book of *Common Prayer*—is a constant reminder that when the priest and congregation meet together for worship they are engaged in a corporate action in which all have a part to play. But Roman Catholic worship, with its emphasis upon the Sacrifice of the Mass, is bound to separate the priest, to some extent, from the people. To the outsider, the Mass often appears to be an act of worship performed by the priest on behalf of the congregation. The congregation can " assist " in various ways— they can pray with the priest, they can be " spiritually co-operative " at every point of the service, they can add their prayers to those of the celebrant and so swell the volume of praise which ascends to the throne of grace. But there is inevitably a " great divide " between priest and people, so that, at times, the priest must go ahead (silently) with his prayers, while the congregation occupy their minds as well as they can, by saying the Rosary or using some other form of devotion.

In most Christian communions there is a desire to make the liturgy more of a corporate act, as it clearly was in the primitive Church. We have all heard of the " dialogue Mass," of the efforts to bring the congregation more and more into the action of the liturgy, to give them certain rights and responsibilities. All this is now becoming much more feasible since, at any rate in the West, the vast majority of the worshipping community are not illiterate peasants, but educated people fully capable of playing an active and intelligent part in the worship of the Church.

It is clear from the *Schema* that the Liturgical Commission is very anxious to pursue this idea. Phrases such as "worshipping with the mind as well as with the voice," "simplicity and clarity," "corporate worship rather than private Masses" all point in the same direction, and are of great interest to the observers most of whom come from Churches where such phraseology has long been familiar.

We Anglicans have always been committed to the idea of a "dialogue Mass." Our Prayer Book was composed at a time when education was spreading in England, and it envisaged an increasingly literate congregation. Our Eucharist is essentially a dialogue, in that there are sixteen points at which the congregation is directed to break in. These include saying with the priest the Nicene Creed, the Gloria, the Lord's Prayer and the Sanctus, and joining in a general Confession and in certain versicles and responses. Besides this, there has been in recent years an attempt, in many parishes, to bring the laity more and more into the liturgy by saying together with the priest the Collect for Purity (with which our Eucharist begins), the Prayer of Humble Access immediately before the Consecration Prayer, and parts of the Prayer of Oblation or of Thanksgiving which come after the distribution of the Elements. Further efforts to make the Eucharist more of a *corporate* offering have been the adoption of the westward position by the priest at the altar, the "offertory procession" in which members of the congregation bring up the bread and wine and hand them to the priest to offer them on the altar, and inviting a layman to read the Epistle.

All this, of course, goes a good deal further than anything suggested in the *Schema*. But the principle behind the liturgical movement in the Anglican Church and in the Roman Catholic Church is the same: to enhance and deepen the *corporate* action of the liturgy. How far the bishops will be prepared to go along these lines is hard to say; but of the speeches which were made when this *Schema* was under discussion, many were clearly pointing in this direction. There was constant emphasis on the pastoral needs of the people. Reference was made to the drift from religion and from worship, to the sense of remoteness, of not being wanted, which so many feel. Even in the Mass there was the danger that people would think that, so long as the sacrifice was offered, it did not matter very much whether they were present or not. Frequently the cry for greater simplicity was uttered. Of course not all the fathers spoke with the same voice; but, as an observer, I sensed all through this long debate that the need for much greater simplicity and co-operation was deeply felt.

The demand for simplicity and co-operation naturally led to one suggested reform, which many would like to see. This was (3) *the Use of the Vernacular*. To the observers, most of whom were accustomed to a Vernacular form of worship, this was naturally of great interest. Just because we lay so much emphasis upon *corporate* worship, so we would never contemplate the use of a language which the congregation as a whole would not understand. (Provision is made in the Church of England for services to be said in Latin, but only in the universities and colleges where it would, presumably, be understood).

The use of the vernacular was one of the major reforms which came about in the sixteenth century. The reformers were all convinced that, if the people were to be taught to *worship*, they must be able to follow the service. As the Preface to the Book of Common Prayer says:

Whereas St. Paul would have such language spoken to the people in the Church, as they might understand, and have profit by hearing the same; the Service in this Church of England these many years hath been read in Latin to the people, which they understand not; so that they have heard with their ears only, and their heart, spirit, and mind, have not been edified thereby.

In any attempt towards liturgical reform the use of the vernacular would seem, at first sight, to be an obvious advantage. But the problem is not quite so simple as it looks. One bishop from Central Africa pointed out that, of course, it was absurd that the Mass should be said in Latin in his part of the world. Latin meant nothing to them and had no connection with their history or the origins of their language. But, he said, in his diocese there were many different languages. The only language they could all hope to understand was Latin! This would apply perhaps only to certain parts of the mission field; but even in the West, Latin can sound strangely different when spoken by an Italian, a German and a New Yorker—as many people listening to the debates in St. Peter's discovered. There is also the difficulty that a vernacular language tends to get out-of-date. The language of our Book of Common Prayer is the language of educated English people in the sixteenth century. We are now constantly being told that it is unintelligible to people of the twentieth century, who find phrases such as " sore let and hindered " or " regenerate and grafted into the body of Christ's Church " quite meaningless.

Although the Council fathers were by no means agreed about the use of the vernacular, there was a general feeling that it might well be employed in all the didactic parts of the Mass, while keeping Latin for the Canon. This would appear to be a satisfactory interim proposal, and would show that the pastoral and corporate nature of worship was being recognised. But I think the observers as a whole felt that, eventually, the worship of the Church ought to be conducted entirely in the language of the people if they were really to be brought in as fellow-worshippers. As an American cardinal said to me one day in Rome: " A man prays best in the language he learned at his mother's knee."

(4) *The need of more preaching.* If the laity are to play a bigger part in the worship of the Church, then they must be instructed, and this means more preaching. The dual ministry of Word and Sacrament is something which we are always trying to preserve, though in fact there is always a tendency to separate them. The great preachers of the fifteenth cen-

tury normally made their sermon an appendage to the Mass; but since then, in both Catholic and Protestant traditions, the Eucharist has not been considered the best time at which to preach long sermons—though it is significant that in our Prayer Book the only place where a sermon is ordered is at the Eucharist or at an Ordination; there is no rubric requiring a sermon at Morning or Evening Prayer. In the past, the tendency in the Roman Church has been for the main instruction of the people to be given outside the liturgical worship. But there seems now to be a movement to bring the two together again. The Church is saying to people: "We want you to understand and follow what is taking place in the liturgy. This is *your* worship as well as that of the priest. He wants to carry you with him: he wants to teach you about God— His nature and His will—he wants your worship to strengthen you to bear witness to your faith in a world which has so largely forgotten God." This pastoral concern is wholly in keeping with the Pope's wishes for the Council. It is also in line with what we are trying to teach our people about the meaning of worship and about the mission of the Church.

(5) *Communion under both kinds.* In New Testament times and for many centuries after that it was customary to communicate the laity in both kinds. Cardinal Bona, writing in 1671, said: "The faithful always and everywhere, from the very beginning of the Church even to the twelfth century, communicated under the form of bread and wine." We now know that this statement is not strictly accurate, and that there were occasions when Communion was given to people under the form of the bread only. But the general practice was to administer the chalice to the laity until the promulgation of the doctrine of Transubstantiation in the thirteenth century. From then onwards the chalice was generally withheld from the laity in the Western Church. But this met with some opposition, first from the Utraquists in Bohemia and then from the sixteenth-century reformers who had no doubt that the commands of Christ clearly meant that all communicants

should receive both the bread and the wine, nor were they impressed by the theory of concomitance put forward by the Council of Trent. It is now the custom in all parts of Christendom, including the Eastern Churches of the Roman Communion to communicate the laity under both kinds, as we saw for ourselves in St. Peter's when one of the Eastern rites was being celebrated.

The administration of the Sacrament under both species presents many problems, as those of us who practise it fully realise. There is the danger of mishap or of irreverence; there is the fact that it takes time; there is the fear of spreading contagious diseases. But against all these we have to weigh the words of our Lord: " Unless you eat the flesh of the Son of man and drink his blood, you have no life in you " (Jn., vi, 53: R.S.V.). Because of this clearly expressed intention of Christ, we of the reformed churches feel that there is no room here for argument. In spite of all the difficulties and dangers we cannot ignore what our Lord has said. The Church of Rome has for long felt able to interpret these words in a different sense. But the fact that suggestions are now being put forward for the restoration of the chalice to the laity, under certain conditions and on certain specified occasions, is naturally a matter of great interest to the rest of Christendom.

I have dealt with five of the proposals upon which the Vatican Council will have eventually to make up its mind, because these seem to me to be of particular interest to the non-Roman Catholic world and to have special significance in the cause of Christian unity. It is not for me to speculate on how the fathers of the Council will vote on these things. All I can say is that if the Council turns its back on all these suggestions and fights for the preservation of the *status quo*, it will inevitably drive the Roman Catholic Church back into isolation from the rest of Christendom and so frustrate the wishes of the Holy Father that the Council shall make a real contribution towards that unity of all His disciples for which our Blessed Lord prayed.

JOHN MOORMAN, D.D.

Bishop of Ripon
Ripon, Yorkshire, England

THOMISM AND THE COUNCIL

❧

POPE JOHN XXIII in convoking the Second Vatican Council encouraged a spirit of renewal in the Church today. The late Holy Father had in that same spirit and context encouraged the study of Thomism:

The other matter that We want to propose for your consideration seems more urgent and more important to Us because We are looking forward to the celebration of the Second Vatican Council, and We have been devoting a great deal of attention to making proper preparations for it: the fact that the treatment and solution of moral questions according to the imperishable principles of Aquinas is of great help in bringing about agreement and unity among those interested in truth and charity. This fact is bound to produce a great deal of the very richest fruit in the form of peace for the Catholic Church and for the whole world.[1]

Obviously, a consideration of the Council should include a discussion of Thomism in the Church; in fact, if the hopes of John XXIII are to be realized, the study of Thomism is " first," " necessary," and to be done "carefully ":

But if all these things that We desire so ardently are to come about, the *first* thing *necessary* is to study the works of St. Thomas *carefully*. And so we are very interested in seeing a steady growth in the number of people who find enlightenment and learning in the works of the Angelic Doctor.[2]

A moment's reflection will urge other important reasons for a consideration of Thomism in the Church. If the spirit of the Church is to be renewed and revitalized in our day, then the study of Thomism, which for centuries has been so much a part of the spirit of the Church, must be approached anew. Certainly, this has been the desire of all the Popes of the

---

[1] Pope John XXIII, Allocution to the Fifth International Thomistic Congress, Sept. 18, 1960. Tr. from *The Pope Speaks*, 6 (1960) 326.

[2] *Ibid.*, 327.

451

modern era. The veritable mountains of documents suggesting, urging, directing the study and use of St. Thomas to meet modern problems, and the number of admonitions to and corrections of those scholars who have neglected or wandered from the principles and method of St. Thomas are sufficient evidence that the Church does not consider Thomism a relic of the past.[3] The " bringing up to date " of the life of the Church in no way implies a neglect of the wisdom of the Common Doctor; on the contrary, such a spirit demands a deeper study of Thomism and a revitalization of its doctrine.

We would be very happy to see what We might term the " treasure " of the precepts of St. Thomas " unearthed " in greater measure each day, to the great benefit of Christianity, and also see his writing reach a much wider public in a language and form perfectly suited to the spirit and temper of our times.[4]

Another, and perhaps the most important, aspect of Thomism in the Church today is the consideration of Thomism in the Church tomorrow. The revitalization of the life of the Church which is enkindled today must be kept burning through the sound theological learning of priests and seminarians. Pope John has also pointed out his interest in seeing especially that the young find " enlightenment and learning in the works of the Angelic Doctor," and " not only priests or scholars but also people interested in the liberal arts. Above all we would like to see this path followed by more of the young people chosen for the work of Catholic Action and holding higher degrees." [5]

If the work of the council is to bear lasting fruit it must be especially concerned with the education of clerical and lay leaders of tomorrow. It is, without doubt, the glory of Thomism that as a system it can sustain the quality of revitalization

---

[3] See S. Ramirez, O. P., " The Authority of St. Thomas," *The Thomist*, XV (1952), 1-109. This is a complete study of the authority of St. Thomas supported by numerous quotations from Papal documents.

[4] Pope John XXIII, *loc. cit.*

[5] *Ibid.*

with lasting strength, but it is also a challenge to Thomistic philosophers and theologians—not a challenge to fight, but to grow. This challenge presents itself to those devoted to the study of St. Thomas, for revitalization must come from within Thomism.

The fact is that the challenge is perhaps even greater today than in the time of Pope Leo XIII because new obstacles have arisen to impede the spirit of Thomism. Father Fabro, recalling Pope Leo XIII's restoration of the philosophy of St. Thomas and founding of the Pontifical Roman Academy of St. Thomas, says significantly:

The Academy, which the generous Founder wishes dedicated above all to the defense and diffusion of the philosophical principles of the Aquinate, today has broadened into three sections . . . nevertheless it has no less maintained its original program which today presents itself, by a sort of historical paradox, as somehow *even more urgent* than at its inception.[6]

At the time of Pope Leo XIII's restoration, Thomism was merely being neglected; now, however, there is a definite and vocal anti-Thomism stirring among Catholic intellectuals which weakens appreciation for the very principles and method which are its foundation.[7]

Another impediment to a genuine Thomism arises from the historical development within the school itself. The restoration initiated by Pope Leo XIII eventually took a direction which did not always adequately represent the authentic Thomistic tradition. The methodology of the manualists, especially, has created for some moderns a distorted notion of Thomism.

Certainly the recent anti-Thomism is related to the false but popular notion of " scholasticism " derived from some of the manualists. But the complaints against Thomism cannot be sustained by harking back to the manualists, for today the effort among Thomists is not simply to re-echo the manualists,

---

[6] C. Fabro, " L '80° della Aeterni Patris," *Osservatore Romano*, Aug. 6, 1959.
[7] This will be discussed in the second part of the paper, pp. 459 ff.

but rather to recover the " total Thomas." The problem of anti-Thomism actually goes much deeper. It has its roots in a new philosophy rather than in a simple complaint against the " late Thomism."

The modern question of the status of Thomism is fundamentally a question of the adequacy of Thomism to meet present needs. Must Catholic philosophers, and consequently theologians, accept the inevitability of pluralistic philosophy and concede that to update the formulations of doctrine new philosophies must be employed to create a new theology? This question is being raised by sincere Catholic intellectuals. While a Thomist might be tempted to dismiss it as patently absurd because of his respect for the unique authority granted to St. Thomas by the Church or because of his understanding of the intrinsic value of Thomism, still it is a question which must be answered before a genuine Thomistic renewal can be widely effected.

An adequate answer is not being attempted here; however, we do wish to investigate these problems and in the course of the discussion suggest some approaches to their solution which might lead to a revitalization of Thomism both in philosophy and theology. We will review briefly 1) the attitude of the Church toward Thomism; 2) the anti-Thomistic attitude in recent Catholic thought; and 3) the role of Thomism in the renewal of the spirit and life of the Church.

I. The Attitude of the Modern Church toward the Doctrine of St. Thomas

The unique place of Thomism in the modern Church cannot be appreciated without considering the major statements of all the modern popes from the time of the encyclical of Leo XIII, *Aeterni Patris*, to the recent *Motu Proprio* of Pope John XXIII, " *Dominicanus Ordo*." [8]

[8] See footnote 3. The following is but a sampling of Papal documents referring to the place of St. Thomas in the Church:

However, we do not wish this discussion of the place of St. Thomas in the Church to focus on the extrinsic canonical and magisterial authority of the Church, but rather on the reasons intrinsic to Thomism which have motivated the juridical support and magisterial endorsement by the Church. Except for Canon 1366 # 2, seldom has there been an encyclical, exhortation, directive or decree on Thomism which has not at the same time given the intrinsic reasons for such pronouncements. And the Church has incomparable credentials to judge of the intrinsic value of philosophy and, of course, theology. The Church not only makes a judgment of various philosophies as any historian of philosophy might, but more, she is a living witness of all the philosophies that have been devised and proposed in the Christian era. The Church has witnessed the

Pope Leo XIII
> Encyclical *Aeterni Patris* (1879), *Acta Leonis XIII*, ed. Bonne Presse s. d., I, 50.
> Brief *Cum hoc sit* (1880), Acta, I, 112.
> Encyclical *Officio Sanctissimo* (1887), Acta, I, 234.
> Brief *Gravissime Nos* (1892), cf. Berthier, LVII, 246-248.

Pope St. Pius X
> Motu proprio *Sacrorum Antistitum*, A.A.S. 2 (1910), 256-257.
> Motu proprio *Doctoris Angelici*, A.A.S. 6 (1914), 336-341.
> Motu proprio *In praecipuis* (Jan. 23, 1904), *Acta Pii X*, ed. Bonne Presse, I, 24.

Pope Benedict XV
> Motu proprio *Sacrae Theologiae*, A.A.S. 6 (1914), 690-691.
> Letter to Cardinal Bisleti, A.A.S. 8 (1916), 412-414

Pope Pius XI
> Apostolic Letter *Officium Omnium*, A.A.S. 14 (1922), 454-456.
> Encyclical *Studiorum Ducem*, A.A.S. 15 (1923), 309-324.
> Apostolic Letter *Unigenitus Dei Filius*, A.A.S. 16 (1924), 144-145.
> Apostolic Constitution *Deus Scientiarum Dominus*, A.A.S. 23 (1931), 253.

Pope Pius XII
> Letter *Quandoquidem*, A.A.S. 34 (1942), 96-97.
> Encyclical *Humani Generis*, A.A.S. 42 (1950), 561-578.
> Allocution Third International Thomistic Congress, A.A.S. 42 (1950), 734-735.
> Exhortation *Menti Nostrae*, A.A.S. 42 (1950), 657-704.

Pope John XXIII
> Allocution Fifth International Thomistic Congress, Sept. 18, 1960, tr. *Pope Speaks* 6 (1960), 325-328.
> Motu proprio *Dominicanus Ordo*, Osservatore Romano, March 7, 1963.

birth and suffered from the errors of false philosophies; in turn, she has seen the last agony of dying philosophies while preserving all that is true. From this continual flow of philosophies over the centuries she has singled out Thomism with special approval. The Church does not make Thomism a sound, safe and true philosophy by approving and prescribing it, but she approves and prescribes it because Thomism possesses certain qualities which make it a total and adequate philosophy capable of aiding and supporting sound theology.

The qualities which a philosophy must possess in order to serve theology are reducible to five. First, it must be based on principles which are universal in scope and absolute in character, otherwise that philosophy cannot encompass reality nor distinguish truth from error. Secondly, it must utilize a philosophical methodology, i. e., an objective scientific procedure which is capable of sustaining a causal investigation of all aspects of reality on various levels of being, of determining the natures of things from proper principles, and through such principles of attaining a knowledge of the ultimate cause of being, of truth, of goodness, of order. Thirdly, from its first principles and scientific investigation, philosophy must establish an ordered body of knowledge about the universe and its causes. Fourthly, it must incorporate a reflective process enabling it to be self-critical of its conformity with the reality from which its philosophical process began. Fifthly, an adequate philosophy must be open to new data and discoveries as these are encountered in human experience.

The universal validity of its principles, the soundness of the method of investigation and proof, the conformity of its doctrine to the real order—these are the criteria of a sound and safe and true philosophy. These are intrinsic to the philosophical system itself, and a system stands or falls upon its intrinsic character.

The Church has provided abundant witness that Thomism contains these five qualities: (1) By reason of its principles Thomism has a solid foundation and universal extension, not limited to one age but adaptable to the needs of all times.[9] Moreover, these principles have been drawn from the most eminent philosophers and doctors of the Church and tested through long reflection and application.[10] " Sound reason cannot neglect such wisdom, nor can religion suffer it to be diminished in the slightest." [11] (2) By reason of its method Thomism has the power to penetrate objectively the meaning, causes, and nature of the universe. There is in the philosophy of St. Thomas

so to speak a certain natural Gospel, an incomparably solid foundation for all scientific construction since the chief characteristic of Thomism is its objectivity. Its constructions or elevations are not those of a mind cut off from reality, but are constructions of a spirit which follows the real nature of things.[12]

(3) St. Thomas presents an ordered body of knowledge about the universe.

[9] " This is the outstanding point about his doctrine, that, being based upon and arranged according to principles which have the widest extension, it is not limited to one period only but is adaptable to the needs of all times " (Leo XIII, *Cum hoc sit, loc. cit.*, 112).

[10] " Moreover, if we speak of these principles of Thomas in general and as a whole, we must declare that his doctrine contains only those principles which the most eminent philosophers and Doctors of the Church discovered through prolonged reflection and discussion regarding the particular reasons determining human knowledge, the nature of God and creation, the moral order, and the pursuit of the goal of human life. Such brilliant patrimony of wisdom which he inherited from those before him he perfected and augmented by the almost angelic quality of his mind. Then he applied it to prepare, illustrate and protect sacred doctrine in the minds of men. Sound reason cannot neglect such wisdom, nor can religion suffer it to be diminished in the slightest " (Pius X, *Doctoris Angelici, loc. cit.*, 337). Also see *In praecipuis, Acta Pii X*, ed. Bonne Presse, I, 24.

[11] Pius X, *Doctoris Angelici, loc. cit.*, 338.

[12] Pius XI, Allocution to University Students, Feb. 1927, in M. Cordovani, " San Tommaso nella parola di Pio XI," *Angelicum*, 6 (1929), 10.

Also on the question of method in St. Thomas, " The question of method is of capital importance. In order for science to be strict and luminous, method is all important. When the method is erroneous and the path is lost, progress is impossible; and therefore a guide is necessary. Thomas is the guide, the *Dux in via* " (Pius XI, Allocution to professors and students, Angelicum, Nov. 12, 1924, cf. *Xenia Thomistica*, III, 600-601, Rome, 1925).

There is no part of philosophy which he [St. Thomas] does not handle with acuteness and solidity. He wrote about the laws of reasoning; about God and incorporeal substances; about man and other things of the sense; and about human acts and their principles. What is more, he wrote on these subjects in such a way that in him not one of the following perfections is wanting: a full selection of subjects; a beautiful arrangement of their divisions; the best method of treating them; certainty of principles; strength of argument; perspicuity and propriety in language; and the power of explaining deep mysteries.[13]

(4) Thomism can be self-critical through mature reflection without discarding its heritage. It can be enhanced with a richer language, strengthened with more precise distinction, divested of less useful scholastic aids, enriched with the advances of modern scholarship,[14] " but never may it be overthrown or poisoned with false principles or be regarded as a great, but obsolete relic." [15] (5) Thomism can be open to new data and experience which will advance theological learning without diminishing its contents. The Church praises theologians who develop Thomism through learned commentaries and investigations of new points developed within Thomism or discovered in the light of modern scholarship.[16] But she cautions against imprudent haste in accepting new ideas.

[13] Leo XIII, *Aeterni Patris, loc. cit.*, 60. Also consider the following: " His doctrine is so inclusive that he has embraced within himself as in a sea all the wisdom flowing from the ancients. Whatever truth was spoken or discussed by pagan philosophers, by the Fathers and Doctors of the Church, by great men who lived before him, he not only thoroughly investigated, but augmented, perfected and disposed with such a clear penetration of ideas, such an accurate system of argumentation . . . that he appears only to have left the power to imitate but not to excel " (Leo XIII, *Cum hoc sit, loc cit.*, 112).

" . . . those especially who study him in philosophy and theology, and specifically students divinely called to the priesthood . . . ought to follow Thomas as leader and master, recalling that there is an *innate* excellence in Thomistic doctrine and a singular force and power to cure the evils which afflict our age " (Pius XII, Letter to Fr. Gillet, March 7, 1942, A.A.S. 34 [1942] 97).

[14] Pius XII, *Humani generis, loc. cit.*, 572.

[15] *Ibid.*; See also Pius X, Motu proprio *In praecipuis*, Jan. 23, 1904, *loc. cit.*

[16] " We entirely approve and commend the measuring, where necessary, of new discoveries in studies, with ancient wisdom. It is perfectly legitimate to investi-

In regard to new questions which modern culture and progress have brought to the forefront, [Catholic scholars] should submit them to careful research, but with the necessary prudence and caution. They should not think, indulging in false irenism, that the dissident and erring can happily be brought back to the bosom of the Church if the full truth found in the Church is not sincerely taught to all without any corruption and diminution.[17]

All this may be summed up in the words of Pope Pius XII:

As the experience of many centuries proves, the method and doctrine of Aquinas is singularly preeminent for teaching students and for investigating obscure truths. His doctrine is in wonderful harmony with divine revelation and is most effective for safeguarding the foundations of the faith as well as reaping usefully and safely the fruits of sound progress.[18]

II. Anti-Thomism in Recent Catholic Thought

A. *A New Philosophy*

If one views only the unqualified support which the Church has given Thomism in recent decades, it might seem strange that an almost violent anti-Thomism should arise among Catholic intellectuals. Yet, it might well be said that the history of anti-Thomism began at the first public lectures of St. Thomas at the University of Paris in 1252. Every age since has seen both the approval of St. Thomas by the Church and in some degree or another a stirring of anti-Thomism. The seeds of this present attitude were germinating in the nineteenth century. But here we are not so much concerned with a detailed study of the historical development leading up to the

gate freely those matters upon which well known interpreters of the Angelic Doctor usually dispute; new findings from history should be applied for fuller understanding of the texts of Aquinas." Pius XII, Discourses to Seminarians at Rome, May 24, 1939. Also, " We did not disapprove, indeed, of those learned and able men who bring their learning and industry and the riches of new discovery to the aid of philosophy: for we clearly see that such a course tends to the increase of learning " (Leo XIII, *Aeterni Patris, loc. cit.*, 62).

[17] Pius XII, *Humani generis, loc. cit.*, 578.

[18] *Ibid.*, 573.

recent attitude, as with an understanding of the content of the present attitude and the philosophy embodying it and making it attractive to the modern mind.

Existentialism

A key to understanding the radical rejection of Thomism is found in the philosophy of existentialism. As most philosophical movements, existentialism was born of a need. The need as Soren Kierkegaard saw it in his own nineteenth-century Denmark was for a return to a full Christian life. Kierkegaard's polemic was meant to restore a living faith in the hearts of Christian people in place of the exaggerated formalism and secularism supported by a rationalistic Hegelian philosophy. Kierkegaard emphasized subjectivity, the living of doctrine, over objectivity, the knowing of doctrine.

While some scholars believe that Kierkegaard himself respected the objectivity of doctrine, this is not true of many who were to follow him. After the First World War, nineteenth-century rationalism was rapidly declining in favor among many Europeans. And just as there was a foment in social and political relationships which was to lead to World War II, so too, there was a foment of ideologies which was to lead to a battle against philosophical systems including those of Kant, Hegel, Engels and Marx. By the end of World War II Western Europe was ready to espouse a new philosophy. The opportunity had already been presented with the rediscovery of Kierkegaard, especially in France. The direction existentialism was to take, however, was hardly that contemplated by Kierkegaard. Breaking with the philosophical systems which were discredited, existentialism was free to delve into the subjective, and it was soon divided into almost as many branches as there were philosophers. Breaking also with any vestige of Christian faith, it became a new atheism. What had begun as a Christian movement with Christian hope in Kierkegaard degenerated into an atheistic cry of despair in Sartre and of rebellion in Camus.

To define existentialism as a philosophy is almost impossible because of divergencies and inconsistencies among those claiming the title, as well as among those who apparently fall within its ambit but disclaim its title.[19] The thought of Kierkegaard and Marcel, for example, for whom Christianity is the focal point of any true existentialism, is radically different from that of Sartre and Heidegger, for whom atheism is integral to existentialist thought. This does not mean that existentialism can be adequately divided simply by distinguishing Christian and atheistic forms. Great gulfs separate individual existentialists and various admixtures of phenomenology, personalism, and vitalism further complicate the picture.

" Existentialism " is used here in its widest signification. Charlesworth has offered a broad definition which touches the core of the matter:

The essence of existentialism, we may say, lies in its insistence upon the *primacy of subjectivity*. First, in the speculative order, . . . this primacy of subjectivity means the rejection of all systematic thought—of the abstract and the necessary and the universal—for the sake of the individual and singular, and unique and ineffable experience of the subject. . . . . Secondly, in the practical or moral order, the order of moral action and choice, this primacy of subjectivity means the rejection of any *a priori* morality and the affirmation of the complete freedom, the complete gratuitousness of the liberty of the subject.[20]

In its almost complete dedication to the subjective, the psychological awareness of experience, in its emphasis on the unique and particular ethical situation, in its practical concern for the good rather than the true, existentialism has made some acute observations about man and his existence.

Its intense subjectivity has yielded reliable insights into the conditions of human existence.[21]

---

[19] J. Marías, "Ortega and the Idea of Vital Reason," *Dublin Review*, Winter (1949), 51.

[20] Charlesworth, " The Meaning of Existentialism," *The Thomist*, XVI (1953) 473.

[21] Vincent Martin, O. P., *Existentialism*, Compact Study, 1962, Washington: Thomist Press, 44.

Existentialism has spotlighted the human condition, and especially the evils which individual men suffer in the present human situation, and the need for a personal commitment to the practical, ethical life to do something about it. A child with indigestion will cry of pain and knows something should be done to relieve it, but he can tell neither why it hurts nor what should be done. Existentialism in much the same way has served to point out some of the ills in man and society, but it has neither carefully analyzed the causes nor offered an adequate remedy.

However valuable the existential insights into the human condition may be, they do not constitute a philosophy of man, of the world, of divinity; nor do they eliminate what has been solidly established in the past concerning God, man and the universe; nor do they substitute for a total synthesis of philosophy in the present. Existentialism's rejection of systematic philosophy, its disgust with the metaphysical, its scorn for the speculative processes of the human mind, its skepticism even in the physical sciences, its neglect of objective truth, its denial of lasting values—all these divest it of the tools with which to cope with the whole of reality and thus plunge it into absurdity and despair. As Fr. Vincent Martin has observed:

It has not provided a balanced and totally human orientation of man to the universe in which he lives, to his fellowman with whom he dwells, or to God to whom he is ultimately ordained—in short, to objective reality.[22]

The vision of existentialism is too limited, its approach too subjective, its cure too radical to be of lasting value. The intellectual crime of existentialism is not that it concentrates on the subjective elements of the human condition—this is simply a matter of a thinker's choice—but that it insists that this inwardness is an adequate philosophical enterprise which can neglect the wisdom of the past and render systematic philosophy both meaningless and useless. When Gabriel Marcel

[22] *Ibid.*

said: " We do not study problems of philosophy, we are those problems," he touched a truth more than he realized. Existentialism, rather than offering a solution, has in reality posed a problem and a challenge to philosophers and theologians— a challenge to re-evaluate and further investigate the subjective, psychological, ethical experiences of man, but to do this according to the very principles which existentialism rejects, the principles of systematic philosophy and theology. The rise of the " new theology " was due to the fact that the challenge was not met, and precisely because the principles of the perennial philosophy were neglected.

B. *A New Theology*

The atmosphere in which the New Theology was created

The " new theology," as it has come to be known,[23] was not simply the adoption of existentialism with a Catholic label, nor a slavish imitation of existentialist thought. Yet it was born in the same ideological atmosphere and was deeply influenced by the same attitudes. The motives of the new theologians were quite Catholic, but their methods were existentialist. The motives in fact were apologetic; the leaders in the movement were seriously and sincerely engaged in trying to save the Catholic faith amidst the political, social, intellectual and religious confusion of pre-War and post-War Europe.

The war stopped theorizing, but it influenced the French theologians, many of whom through the resistance movement were thrown into contact with non-Catholics. This encounter convinced them that the only way non-Catholics could be attracted to the Church was by presenting her in terms of the vital and existential.[24]

This of course was the time of ascendancy of French existentialism, with its subjectivism and rejection of systematic

---

[23] Pope Pius XII termed the movement we are discussing here a " new theology " in an allocution to the Jesuit General Congregation, A.A.S. 38 (1946), 384-388.

[24] G. Weigel, S. J., " The Background of *Humani Generis*," *Theological Studies*, XII (June, 1951), 217.

theology and philosophy. The " new theologians," anxious to
contact existentialist philosophy on its own terms and sympathetic with its opposition to the " rationalistic formulations of
decadent scholasticism," compromised orthodoxy. Louis Charlier denied the scientific validity of human reason working on
matters of faith.[25] D. A. Greenstock summarized the position of
Charlier thus:

The strict theological deduction as the result of a scientific use of
human reason is therefore impossible. Theology, as such, is therefore reduced to a simple explanation of revealed truth in terms
which need not necessarily have a permanent value, but which
can, and indeed should, change with time and according to the
demands of circumstances. This doctrine was far too dangerous
to pass unchecked, and in 1942 the Holy Office banned the writings
in which it appeared.[26]

After the work of Charlier was banned,[27] the approach was
modified. No longer was the validity of human reason denied.
In fact the value of human reason, and even of scholastic
method, was accepted. Turning to an historical argument,
however, the new theologians again rejected scholasticism, not
because of its being contrary to the faith, but because of its
being antiquated and of no use to the faith in modern times.

It is quite evident, indeed, that scholastic theology is out of contact with these categories [historicity and subjectivism]. The world
of scholastic theology is the immobile world of Greek thought,
wherein its mission was to make incarnate the Christian message.
This conception does retain a permanent truth which is always
valid, at least in so far as it consists in affirming that the free
decision of man or man's transformation of his own conditions of
life are not a sort of absolute beginning, through which man
creates himself, but are rather his response to a vocation of God
of which the world of essences are the expression. Yet scholastic
theology makes no place for history. Furthermore, since it affirms
reality to be in essences more than in subjects, it has nothing to

---

[25] L. Charlier, *Essai sur le problème théologique*, 1938.

[26] D. Greenstock, " Thomism and the New Theology," *The Thomist*, XIII,
(1950), 570-571.

[27] A.A.S. 34 (1942), 37.

do with the dramatic world of persons, of the concrete universals which transcend all essences and are not distinguished save through existence, which is to say, not according to the intelligible and understanding, but rather according to value, love and hate.[28]

By 1946 the destruction of scholastic philosophy and theology had taken on the proportion of a victorious crusade. M. de Gaudillac confirms the definitive passing of " neo-Thomism." [29] Hans von Balthasar wrote an epitaph for St. Thomas and the Fathers of the Church:

" A great teacher, esteemed, celebrated, held sacred, canonized and buried." (Péguy)

One ought not to imagine that others are, in our eyes, capable of resisting better such treatment. We turn toward a past further removed, without believing, however, that we give back life to a dying past, that it suffices to exhume the " Greek fathers " and adapt them—for what it is worth—to the needs of the modern soul. We do not have the candor to prefer to a " neo-scholastic theology " one that is " neo-patristic." No historical situation is ever absolutely like any of the others which have gone before. Therefore no situation can furnish its own solutions as a sort of pass-key which would be apt for solving our actual problems.[30]

Ortega y Gasset was moved to say to an audience packed into the Barceló cinema, Madrid, practically on the eve of the encyclical *Humani generis:*

I am able to announce to you that the Roman, Catholic, Apostolic Church is about to relinquish both Aristotelianism and Thomism, and that a new theology is being forged which has close relationship with that of the Greek Fathers.[31]

Although the recognized leaders of the " new theology " movement did not intend to introduce novelty into Catholic doctrine, it was inevitable that this would happen because of some of the approaches adopted. Our purpose here is not to

---

[28] P. Danielou, " Les orientations présentes de la pensée religieuse," *Etudes* (April, 1946), 14.

[29] M. de Gaudillac, *Dieu vivant*, III, 123 ff.

[30] H. von Balthasar, *Présence et pensée*, 1942, viii.

[31] Ortega y Gasset, reported in *YA* (Madrid), Nov. 24, 1949.

investigate doctrinal aberrations which did occur. An adequate
literature exists.[32] Rather, the aim here is to identify the fundamental causes of the errors, for while the " new theologians " did
disavow the particular unorthodox doctrines,[33] they did not
remove the underlying causes. These causes are reducible to
an implicit acceptance of the basic tenets of existentialism,
i. e., the primacy of subjectivity and the rejection of systematic
philosophy and theology. From the existentialist viewpoint,
the world is in constant flux and so also the philosophy which
studies the changing world. The Catholic, therefore, must
" baptize " whatever is current and discard the perennial philosophy as useless for meeting the changing human condition.
Since there is no stable and enduring philosophy, the subjective experience of human life and religious phenomena is the

---

[32] " Among the doctrines proposed as novel mention must be made of the denial
or at least the doubt of the possibility that human reason without the help of
revelation and grace can prove the existence of a personal God by arguments
drawn from the created universe ; the denial that the world had a beginning; the
affirmation that creation of the world is necessary in that it proceeds from the
necessary liberality of divine love; the denial of God's eternal and infallible foreknowledge of the free actions of man; the denial of the transmission of original
sin from the one Adam to all men . . . ; the asserted theory of polygenism;
perversion of the Catholic doctrine of sin . . . ; the doctrine of free elevation of
human nature to the supernatural order; denial of transubstantiation and of the
Real Presence . . . being reduced to pure and simple symbolism; grave doubt
whether matter and spirit differ; the acceptance without any discretion of the
philosophical doctrine of existentialism and evolutionism. All these points Pius XII
condemned in his encyclical *Humani Generis,* and other recent documents and
decreed that they are forbidden in Catholic Schools " (S. Ramirez, O.P., *op. cit.,*
103-104).

An account of tendencies associated with the new theology can be found in
T. Deman, O.P., "Tentatives francaises pour un renouvellement de la théologie,"
Revue de l'Université de l'Ottawa, 20 (1950), 129-167; also, cf. Donnelly, S.J.,
Theological Studies, Sept., 1947 to Sept. 1950; M. Labourdette, O.P., "La théologie
et ses sources," *Revue Thomiste,* xlvi (1946), 353-371; P. Hamell, " *Humani Gen-
eris:* Its Significance and Teaching," *Irish Ecclesiastical Record,* lxxv (1951), 289-302.

[33] " De Lubac, who is certainly one of the best-known names connected with the
phenomenon, hated the word ' new theology,' and he insisted that he and his
friends were not rejecting an ' old theology,' to substitute for it a ' new' one."
G. Weigel, S.J., " The Background of *Humani Generis,*" *Theological Studies,* XII
(1951), 220.

ultimate criterion of truth in any given personal situation or historical circumstance.

Eclecticism which resulted

Existentialism did not offer the Catholic a system of philosophy, but it did create an attitude and approach to sacred doctrine which opened the door to the influence of other new philosophies. Doctrinal deviations of the last thirty years are not all traceable to existentialism and the new theology, but they are the result of the eclecticism created by the primacy of subjectivity and the rejection of perennial philosophy. By 1950 the theological picture was not simply a portrait of a "baptized" existentialism but an impressionist portrait of eclecticism.

In this portrait a multitude of philosophical approaches can be discerned; they include phenomenology, evolutionism, vitalism, personalism, and historicism. Pluralistic philosophy was taken for granted. Any attempt to form a new philosophy and create a new theology, however subjective, unscientific, or limited, was applauded prematurely and without critical analysis. The wisdom of the past was discarded in an effort to meet the unique "existential" problems of contemporary man.[34]

[34] "Today those problems have assumed such dimensions and caused such a multiplicity of tragic conflicts (some already existing, other imminently threatening), that the whole of human thought, and not merely Catholic thought, is profoundly affected by them. The effect is shown in our contemporary confusion and unbalance. . . . All that is essential in man's life and being is under challenge: his liberty, his personality. Every slightest development, political, social, or economic, has ideological implications; and the ideologies influence enormous masses to action and mutual opposition. . . .

"In the situation I have outlined above the attitude of thinkers is revolutionary; they make haste, as though to catch up with the course of events, if possible, to influence it. Such precipitation, whose generosity is not always equalled by ponderation of thought, too frequently ends in a confusion or even a distortion of values and a misunderstanding of their essential hierarchy. In this tendency one notes, first of all, a savage and deliberate break with the past. There is an increasing recession from the living sources of our traditional culture . . . and above all, an almost panic fear of not appearing to be up to date, of appearing to be reac-

New Pastoral Movements

In the midst of this intellectual turmoil, however, other movements were taking shape which were later to prove beneficial to the life of the Church. Social, economic, political upheavals, especially influenced by atheistic communism and existentialism, were turning man's mind from religion. The Church had suffered great losses both in her intellectual influence on the minds of men and in her pastoral care of souls. Theologians were desperately trying to reawaken the life and spirit of the Church in a world torn by two wars, ideologically divided, and struggling toward reconstruction in an atmosphere of secularism, atheistic marxism and existentialism. The practical problem of recapturing the minds and hearts of men in this atmosphere can hardly be appreciated in the United States, which has not been physically, socially, politically, ideologically mutilated by two major wars. But this was the atmosphere in which the Church struggled throughout Europe, with courageous efforts being made in apologetics and pastoral care to bring the Christian life to troubled souls.

Interest in the Bible had increased with the advances of modern scripture scholarship. Catholic thought turned toward its source and a vital reawakening to the works of God among men. In teaching and preaching, the truths of faith were not presented in terms of scientific theology; this, as a highly developed form of sacred doctrine, would not reach the widest audience. Rather these truths were presented in terms of the " good news " of the gospel, introducing the minds of the unskilled to the faith and drawing the hearts of the indifferent to a Christian life. Here were the seeds of renewal, of the modern kerygma, salvation history, and the new catechesis. The needed emphasis on the pastoral care of souls was served by a developing liturgical movement which would draw the

tionaries; and hence an anxiety to jettison *a priori* any modes of thought which are considered traditional, and which are examined less to see whether or not they are valid than whether they are contemporary." Gaëtan Bernoville, " Contemporary Trends in Catholic Thought in France," *Dublin Review*, 224, Fourth Quarter (1950), 13-14.

laity into more vital participation in the solemn mysteries of the Church of Christ; by a renewed concern for sacramental theology with special stress on the role of the recipient; by a renewed emphasis on homilectics; by a fuller realization of the organic unity of the faithful through the doctrine of the Mystical Body; by the opening of a dialogue with other Christians to strengthen the religious spirit and promote unity as a more powerful force in a secularist world. All these movements, today bearing fruit, developed under the influence of conflicting ideologies and with the uncertainty of " first steps " taken, unfortunately, without the aid of systematic theology.

Humani generis

This was the scene at the time *Humani generis* was issued. Many good movements within the Church had been undertaken by zealous theologians anxious to serve the faith in trying circumstances, but these movements, and the theorizing behind them, were weakened by doctrinal deviations resulting from the rejection of systematic philosophy and theology. The underlying commitment to inwardness, the exclusion of objective norms, and the resulting eclecticism all deprived the theoretical efforts of solid, safe, doctrinal foundations and the pastoral movements of prudent, balanced action. The warning of Pope Leo XIII had not been heeded:

But since man is drawn by imitation, we have seen these novelties lay hold of the minds of some Catholic philosophers, who, undervaluing the inheritance of ancient wisdom, have chosen rather to invent new things than to extend and perfect the old by new truths, and that certainly with unwise counsel, and not without loss to science; for such a manifold kind of doctrine has only a shifting foundation, resting as it does on the authority and will of individual teachers. For this reason it does not make philosophy firm and strong and solid, like the old philosophy, but, on the contrary, makes it weak and shallow.[35]

The very heart of the difficulty, the reason for the confusion and loss of proportion and balance in the " new theology " was

---

[35] Leo XIII, *Aeterni Patris, loc. cit.,* 62.

the rejection of the wisdom of the past, especially Thomism. This was pointed out by M. Labourdette in 1946.[36] Pope Pius XII focused on the essence of the problem in two allocutions that same year.[37]

[36] " We do not belong to the company of those who think that the theological wisdom of St. Thomas will be shattered by this contact [with communism, existentialism] or that, met by types of reflexion which are altogether different . . . it will become somewhat dispossessed of the place it has come to own in the Church . . .

" What we regret, however, among many of them [new theologians] is that the bringing to light of the riches of the patristic tradition or the endeavor to find a formulation with life are joined to an evident depreciation of scholastic theology. Far from being opposed to this latter, either in the amplitude of its traditional data or in the essays of a renewed presentation . . . we think for our part that very precisely in the form given it by St. Thomas, scholastic theology represents the truly *scientific* state of Christian thought. This does not imply any disdain for that which went before. This can never be emphasized too much; and the Thomistic synthesis was the first to benefit from it. Neither does this imply that the teaching of St. Thomas ought simply to be repeated word for word: it is obvious that in such circumstances it would be inaccessible to many; and it is quite certain that one would be depriving himself of beautiful and authentic progress due to the further work of Christian (and non-Christian) thinkers. It remains true, however, that this progress must be built on previously laid foundations—at the risk of destroying its own basis. It [the progress] continues the work but does not destroy it; neither does it replace it. It is the prolongation of a synthesis, not a complete overhaul, recomposing according to the categories of modern thought a new "representation" of the world, since all those which have gone before have become irremediably old. Yes, a lot of things are old; . . . but what we do not admit is that theological wisdom is borne away by the wave of impermanence and that what has been determined cannot be held as definitive—and this is not the same as saying closed and not susceptible of being perfected. It implies on the contrary their capacity to assimilate progressively new results of reflexion." M. Labourdette, O. P., "La Théologie et ses sources," *Revue Thomiste,* 56 (1946), 360.

[37] Pius XII, Allocution to the Jesuit General Congregation, A.A.S. 38 (1946), 384 f.; Allocution to the Dominican General Chapter, *ibid.*, 387.

In the latter Pius XII said, . . . " The very foundations of our perennial philosophy and theology are being called into question. . . . Men argue about science and faith, their nature and mutual relations. . . . They talk about truths revealed by God, and question whether the mind with all its acumen can penetrate into them and can deduce further truths from them. Briefly, this is at stake: whether the structure which St. Thomas Aquinas erected beyond and above all time, by putting into an orderly synthesis elements supplied by those who in all ages have cultivated Christian wisdom, stands upon solid rock; whether it is still flourishing and valid; whether it can still defend and protect the deposit of Catholic

Humani generis, issued by Pope Pius XII in August 1950, was a confirmation and elaboration for the whole Church of what he had said in these two allocutions, one to the electors of the Society of Jesus and the other to the delegates to the General Chapter of the Dominican Order. The purpose of *Humani generis* was to clear up the confusion which surrounded the first efforts of the new theologians.[38] In the Encyclical, Pius XII not only pointed out specific errors which had arisen, but indicated the causes of the errors and directed the remedy to be applied. The causes may be summarized briefly as flowing from evolutionism and existentialism, from contempt for scholastic theology and philosophy, and from an uncritical eclecticism.[39] By way of remedy the late Holy Father required that no new opinions be accepted without weighing them with painstaking care, and that the principles, method, and doctrine of St. Thomas be the guide for bringing truth to light and reaping " safely and usefully the fruits of sound progress." [40]

faith and can, even in our day, serve to orientate the further progress of theology and philosophy. *The Church certainly answers in the affirmative."* (Emphasis added.)

[38] J. Levie, S. J., " L'Encyclique 'Humani generis,' " *Nouvelle revue théologique,* LXII (1950), 788.

[39] " The fictitious tenets of this evolution which repudiate all that is absolute, firm and immutable, have paved the way for the new erroneous philosophy which, opposing itself to idealism, immanentism and pragmatism, has assumed the name of existentialism, since it concerns itself only with the existence of individual things and neglects all consideration of their immutable essences. . . .

" They allege . . . that our perennial philosophy is only a philosophy of immutable essences, while the contemporary mind must look to the existence of things and to life, which is ever in flux. While scorning our philosophy they extol other philosophies of all kinds, ancient and modern, oriental and occidental, by which they seem to imply that any kind of philosophy or theory, with a few additions and corrections if need be, can be reconciled with Catholic dogma. *No Catholic can doubt how false this is,* especially where there is question of those fictitious theories they call immanentism, or idealism, or materialism, whether historic or dialectic, or even existentialism, whether atheistic or simply the type that denies the validity of reason in the field of metaphysics. . . . They reproach this philosophy taught in our schools for regarding only the intellect in the process of cognition, while neglecting the function of the will and the emotions. *This is simply not true* " (Pius XII, *Humani generis, loc. cit.,* 573-577). (Emphasis added.)

[40] *Ibid.,* 573.

It should be noted that the movements which were taking shape were not condemned. In fact, efforts to "prudently enrich" philosophy and theology by "building truth upon truth" were warmly encouraged. This important Encyclical looked forward to the renewal being fostered today.

The Pope is not eager to condemn persons; he desires but to halt the spread of errors. His eyes are not turned to the past but to the future. He is concerned, not with fixing the responsibilities of yesterday, but with definitely marking out the positions that have to be held so as to guarantee the healthy condition of Catholic thought.[41]

Effectiveness of Humani generis

Humani generis was an effective instrument of correction and guidance at a critical time, especially with regard to the errors which were explicitly mentioned. No theologian of renown who had been identified with the "new theology" persisted in teaching any specific doctrine declared to be erroneous and false. A tacit, yet genuine, tribute to these theologians is that immediately after the encyclical no individual resisted, nor were any writings banned. Zealous servants of truth and devoted sons of the Church, "they so modified their language as to free their assertions of unorthodox meaning." [42]

Far from stultifying enthusiasm and zeal for the new movements within the Church *Humani generis*, we believe, has served the present renewal most effectively, insofar as it did check unorthodox doctrines associated with the early development of these movements. Released from the grip of doctrinal aberrations, the apologetic and pastoral movements, begun in confusion, were able to take more definitive shape within a framework of orthodoxy. Competent theologians, some earlier involved in questionable opinions, now turned to more careful and scholarly efforts to provide the liturgical, kerygmatic, sacramental, ecumenical movements with more solid doctrinal foundations and with wiser direction. The further clarification of issues and more prudent approach has stimulated a wider

---

[41] J. Levie, *loc. cit.*   [42] Weigel, *op. cit.*, p. 220.

interest in the pastoral and ecumenical movements and paved the way for renewal in the life of the Church so ardently desired and energetically promoted by Pope John XXIII.

Pope Pius XII had forestalled the development of the " new theology." It had never really formulated a body of doctrine, and it is doubtful that an organized theology could have resulted from such a subjective, relativistic, eclectic approach. In its incipient stages only scattered and disparate doctrines were treated from the new approach. The dissolution of such a weak theological body devoid of internal structure and organization was quickly effected by *Humani generis*.

Though the body of the " new theology " readily succumbed to the wise judgments in *Humani generis*, the subjectivism and anti-scholastic spirit underlying the new doctrines still lingered on " in younger addicts to the movements who did not possess the learning and intelligence of the leaders." [43] The spirit of revolution dies slowly, especially when it can subtly associate itself with genuine renewal.

Influence of new theology in the last decade

Certainly some of the excessive existentialist positions and related eclectic novelties had been checked by *Humani generis*. Yet Pope Pius XII realized that the spirit dies hard and he warned, " But we know also that such new opinions can entice the incautious." Since he wrote these words the influence of the new theology has been more disguised, subtle, and difficult to discern. Yet a careful study of recent literature reveals that a harmful subjectivism, with its contempt for scholasticism in the speculative order and its voluntarism in the practical order, still enjoys currency. The spirit which was clearly discernible, but limited to a few thinkers, has now filtered down to a more general audience, including many of the laity, and in countries previously unaffected. Its influence is more extensive, if perhaps less radical, than it was in 1942. For example, sub-

---

[43] *Ibid.* Fr. Weigel was pointing out here that this was a danger. We have averred that his warning has not been heeded.

jects explicitly treated by *Humani generis* such as evolutionism, historicism, existentialism have become issues of general interest and intensive theological discussion only in the last ten years in the United States. Often these subjects are discussed as if *Humani generis* were already archaic and simply not up with recent developments, even when the " recent " developments are merely translations of some previous works or wider distribution of the thought contained in them.

To evaluate accurately the influence of the " new theology " on recent Catholic thought is a difficult undertaking. Certain subjectivist and voluntarist attitudes traceable to the " new theology " have a voice in almost every theological discussion, and certainly in every Catholic movement of our day. This is not to say that the majority of theologians have been so influenced, but sufficient numbers have been affected so as to cloud basic issues. The harmful intrusion often takes place within the context of scholasticism and, as it were, under the very title of Thomism. Without a complete system of his own, the existentialist theologian works within an established system, being satisfied merely to engage in a subtle attrition against basic principles of traditional philosophy and theology. Further, the difficulty of making an evaluation is compounded by the fact that individual authors are affected in different degrees and various ways; thus no general statement is verified uniformly of such authors. Their works do not possess a clear, determined, theological position and, consequently, the influence defies definition.

However, focusing on the point of interest in this article, the attitude toward Thomism, we find a reflection of the contempt that characterized the " new theology." The approach is indeed modified, with the suggestion of a " new theology " being for the most part conscientiously avoided, but subtler devices are now being directed against Thomism. Sometimes the call is for a " new philosophy " [44] to replace Thomism; this,

[44] E. Foye, " Is Thomism the Only Answer? ", *The Catholic World* (Sept. 1960), 355-361. Mr. Foye maintains that the prescription of the Church to teach Thomism

of course, presupposes pluralistic philosophy.[45] Historical and critical methods, supposedly lacking in St. Thomas, are now said to justify a synthesis different from scholasticism.[46] Sometimes an "excessive Aristotelianism" in the system of St. Thomas falls under the scorn of the moderns.[47] The complaint that Thomism is too essentialist and lacks interest in the existing subject is still common,[48] although this complaint was dismissed as false by *Humani generis*.[49] Basic principles of Thomism are declared to be useless or harmful, or to be rejected in the light of modern science or existential insights. Hylomorphism, which could hardly be called incidental to Thomistic philosophy, has been thus disposed of,[50] and this

in her schools should not be taken to mean a rigid Thomism or to discourage attempts to develop a new philosophy as a complete and adequate substitute for Thomism.

[45] "Does not the interpretation we have presented imply an acceptance of 'philosophical pluralism,' i. e., that more than one philosophy can validly present itself as 'true,' and actually be 'true?' Philosophical pluralism is here accepted as theoretically plausible." *Ibid.*, 360.

[46] "What I find lacking in the Thomistic synthesis . . . and in speculative theology as a whole—are historical and critical methods and approach. In modern education and in modern intellectual world these have a place in the training of the educated man which they did not have in the thirteenth century. . . . The historical and critical attitude exhibited by St. Thomas . . . does not meet the standards of modern historians and critics. . . . For this a theology of the layman, as it is now called, different from the scholastic synthesis as it is currently taught in seminaries, seems necessary." J. L. McKenzie, S. J., "Theology in Jesuit Education," *Thought* (Autumn, 1959), 353-354.

[47] See note 53.

[48] " . . . the Thomistic line of thought shows a certain lack of interest in the existing subject, in the concrete existent. The object holds the field. The trouble is (and this is the basic quarrel of modern existentialism with Thomism) that as soon as we make existence an object it vanishes as the existence of a subject. It is no longer existence, but thing, *chose;* no longer dynamic, but static." G. Tavard, A. A., "Christianity and the Philosophies of Existence," *Theological Studies*, 18 (March, 1957), 6.

[49] See note 39; also cf. note 37.

[50] "The demands of knowledge that is certain may force a rejection of a particular Thomistic doctrine, as in our day hylomorphism has come under fire as a result of discoveries in the physical realm." E. Foye, *op. cit.*, 359. Also, "Schillebeeckx's distinction of a double moment in sacramental structure has released the theology of the sacraments from the state of petrification in which scholastic

in spite of the fact that pope, philosopher, and scientist find it useful and enlightening in scientific research.[51] The " classical notion of ' sign ' " is found to be quite useless in a renewed sacramental theology,[52] while " instrumental causality " can be dispensed with unless we choose to think in Aristotelian categories.[53] Another way of rejecting Thomism is to engage in a theological investigation of a problem which is allegedly so new that all the wisdom of the past had missed its point, or of a problem which traditional principles and methodology supposedly can no longer approach; this procedure is simply to ignore the fruits of the past.[54] It is hardly theological scholarship, or, as Pius XII has urged, " building truth upon truth."

hylomorphism had sealed it." G. C. Smit, " The Moment of Transubstantiation," *Theology Digest*, VIII, 1 (Winter, 1960), 41.

[51] " The theory of matter and form . . . is capable of illuminating the requirements of modern science with a light which closely agrees with the results of experimentation." Pius XII, Address to International Thomistic Congress, Sept. 14, 1955, tr. *The Pope Speaks*, II (1955), 220-221.

" The discoveries and theories of the passing centuries have not overturned that doctrine, but rather look to it to introduce intelligibility and order into the confused maze of modern facts and theories." M. Glutz, C. P., " Order in the Philosophy of Nature," *The Thomist*, XXIV (1961), 275.

" The great quantum physicist [Heisenberg] . . . urges a return to the Aristotelian concept of primary matter, such as espoused by Thomas Aquinas, to clarify present obscurities in interpretations of quantum theory." W. A. Wallace, O. P., *Einstein Galileo, and Aquinas*, Compact Studies, 1963, Washington: The Thomist Press, 32.

[52] " The classical notion of ' sign,' as used in our manuals of sacramental theology was derived by the medieval scholastics from a small philosophical work of St. Augustine: a sign is something which, once it is known, leads us to the knowledge of another reality. This is in fact a very poor philosophy of ' sign ' or, as we from now on prefer to call it, symbol. It is quite useless." P. Fransen, S. J. " Sacraments: Signs of Faith," *Worship*, XXXVII (Dec. 1962), 39.

[53] " If our line of reasoning is correct, we could henceforth dispense with the notion of ' instrumental causality,' which, as it seems to us, has done so much harm, and is doing so still. We concede, however, that the notion of ' instrumental causality,' so long as it is correctly explained, would seem to be the key-concept in this chapter of sacramental theology *if* we choose to think in scholastic and Aristotelian categories." *Ibid.*, 42.

[54] C. Williams, O. P., alleges that Karl Rahner has proceeded in this fashion in his *Theological Investigations*, Vol. I. Cf. review of this book in *The Thomist*, XXV (July, 1962), 450.

A more common approach, though just as subtle, involves the selective use of the words of St. Thomas to support a position quite alien to Thomism,[55] or to intimate an extreme position in a polemic.[56]

This is only a sampling of the manner in which the "new theology," especially with regard to its anti-Thomistic bias, influences modern theological and philosophical writing. Granted that care is taken to avoid the errors explicitly outlined in *Humani generis*, still the same spirit prevails. The same harmful effects flow from anti-Thomism, whether it is the extreme position which totally rejects the validity of reason in matters of faith, or the mitigated position which simply suggests that Thomism is useless in the modern world.

Harmful effects of the influence of the "new theology"

Several harmful effects flow from the influence of the "new theology."

First, if the existential suggestions of modern theologians are followed, Catholic theology will be deprived of fundamental principles, the scientific character of its methodology will be destroyed, and the total synthesis—its sapiential vision of the whole of sacred doctrine, the understanding of its elements according to their own proper principles, and the intrinsic relation of its parts—will be lost. In short, the principles, method, and doctrine which the Church to this day has adopted for her own will be discarded and we will be left with that toward which existential influence, whether knowingly or unknowingly, is moving, namely, subjective voluntarism.

The second harmful effect, which follows immediately from the first, is an eclecticism which chooses from ancient and modern alike without concern for the development of doctrine through its entire history. The great theological works are employed only when a selected quotation supports the new

[55] " St. Thomas, almost as if he were presenting the Lutheran heresy, stated the fundamental principle on this matter very clearly." Fransen, *op. cit.*, 48.

[56] " In connection with this St. Thomas developed a parallel of his own which might be called ' existential.' " *Ibid.*, 35.

subjective polemic. Scholasticism is openly scorned and, under the guise of historical criticism, the formulations of the councils and the monumental contributions of the medieval Church can be explained away. The result is the rejection of traditional formulae which the Church has always employed in defining doctrine.[57]

The third harmful effect is the weakening of the Church's authority. Pius XII pointed out this danger in these words:

Now contempt for the terms and the concepts used by scholastic theologians leads naturally to the weakening of speculative theology, which they consider to be devoid of all true certainty since it rests on theological reasons. Unfortunately these advocates of novelty easily pass from despising scholastic theology to the neglect of and even contempt for the Teaching Authority of the Church itself, which gives such authoritative approval to scholastic theology.[58]

Father Gustave Weigel, S. J., elaborated the same point twelve years ago,[59] and went on to show two other ways in which the authority of the Church can be weakened:

They [the authorities] can still be accepted by the simple device of interpreting their edicts in the light of an existential theology. Second they [the existentialist theologians] will reflect that all authority in human society is necessarily conservative, reluctant to change. This inevitable shortcoming of authority will have to be patiently born by the Catholic but it will not perturb him. . . . Such a theory, obviously never expressed in so many words, makes the position of those in authority somewhat uncomfortable; for their authority is revered and never denied, but their instructions will not be obeyed.[60]

---

[57] Pius XII warned of this harmful effect as early as 1946. "Much has been said, not always with sufficient realization of the implications involved, about a new theology which goes on evolving with the constantly evolving universe, so that it is always progressing without ever arriving anywhere. If such a view is to be admitted, what is to become of Catholic dogmas that can never change, what is to become of the unity and stability of the faith?" Pius XII, Allocution to the Jesuit General Congregation, A.A.S. 38 (1946), 384 ff.

[58] Pius XII, *Humani generis, loc. cit..* 567.

[59] Weigel, op. cit., 228.

[60] *Ibid.*

The fourth harmful effect flowing from a selective eclecticism is the impression that any theological insight, no matter how limited in scope or applicability, can be the basis for constructing a totally new and complete synthesis of Catholic theology. The theologian who becomes enraptured with one aspect of theology, who lacks a total and integrated vision of sacred doctrine, is quite likely to attempt to construct a theology based on his limited vision. The result will be a distorted and poorly proportioned sum of theology.

The fifth harmful effect is what might be called the " cult of ambiguity." For many enthusiasts, the condition of theology in the Church today is to be praised because so many new ideas, new approaches, are being discussed and pursued. Theological activity is taken for theological development, intellectual excitement is taken for progress, and mere curiosity is taken for studiosity. Serious thinkers, however, are disturbed by the condition of theology in the Church today, insofar as much effort is being wasted and great minds are pursuing avenues dangerous to the health of the Church. Certainly those theologians who reject scholasticism to pursue eclecticism, who engage in reconstructing a theology divorced from the heritage of scholasticism or Thomism, are contributing more confusion than light. Without the solid foundation and integrated structure of a theological synthesis, their insights cannot find due place or proper proportion in the total theological vision. Their introduction of new terminology prevents evaluation or critical analysis. Thus, one truth seems to contradict another. Old ideas are clothed with new terms to update theological expression, while new ideas are clothed in old terms to disguise innovation. The greatest theological need today becomes one of clarification.

III. The Role of Thomism in the Renewal of the Spirit and Life of the Church

Such clarification can only be effected by a careful self-examination undertaken both by Thomists and their modern critics. The Thomist cannot *a priori* reject all criticism of Thomism as it has been presented in modern times; nor can he deny the value of recent advances in historical criticism, empirical sciences, and positive theology; nor can he neglect the pastoral need of our times. To do any of these would be to betray the spirit of St. Thomas which he should be revitalizing. The modern critic cannot *a priori* reject a genuine Thomistic philosophy and theology because he may have some legitimate complaints about manuals; nor can he deny the value of a scientific synthesis of sacred doctrine according to the principles and method of St. Thomas; nor can he neglect the theological foundations of the pastoral renewal. To do any of these would be to destroy the renewal he wishes to foster.

A Moderate Approach to Revitalization

Unfortunately, present labels serve only to promote a divisive spirit. We hear of " conservatives " and " liberals " doing theological battle. No room is left for the moderate. To the " liberal," the moderate is an enemy in the opposition camp; to the " conservative," the moderate is a " liberal " to be condemned. In a negative way the Council has served to focus attention on the division, the dichotomy, between " liberals " and " conservatives "; but in a positive way it has provided the opportunity for an objective theological reassessment that would seek truth, and consequently theological balance, unity and advancement. Pope John XXIII clearly indicated a moderate approach in his opening address to the Council. The late Holy Father's statement balances his appeal for " updating " with a clear demand for preserving the traditional doctrine " undiluted." [61]

---

[61] We give but one example here. Speaking of the Council the Holy Father says, " Its intention is to give to the world the whole of that doctrine which, notwithstanding every difficulty and contradiction has become the common heritage of mankind—to transmit it in all its purity, undiluted, undistorted. . . . And our duty is not just to guard this treasure, as though it were some museum piece and we the curators, but earnestly and fearlessly to dedicate ourselves to the work that needs to be done in this modern age of ours, pursuing the path which the

Theologians should adopt this spirit of moderation so manifest in the statement of Pope John to the Conciliar Fathers. A lasting contribution will be made only by those who undertake theological investigations in a spirit of moderation, who are " conservative " enough to understand and appreciate a total scientific synthesis and can, therefore, judge wisely the proper place and due proportion of new proposals, and who are " liberal " enough to support and promote them within the limits of sound principles. A theologian must be " conservative " enough to weigh new proposals with " painstaking care and a balanced judgment lest he lose or corrupt the truth he already has," [62] and " liberal " enough to build truth upon truth no matter what its source. For the Thomist this means that, while not abandoning the principles, method, and doctrine of St. Thomas, he must consider those features of Thomism which have been more or less neglected in the recent past, namely, self-criticism through mature reflection and openness to new data of experience. His should be a moderate approach to the revitalization of authentic Thomism.

The Scope of Revitalization

In its broadest terms revitalization of theology implies not only the restoration to health and vigor of the body of theological knowledge, but also the application and use of this knowledge in the Church's apostolate. Obviously, restoration and advancement is a work for skilled theologians at institutions of higher learning, especially universities and faculties granting higher degrees in the sacred sciences. But the fruit of this work, the benefits derived from it, should not remain within the walls of these institutions. The life of the Church in the modern world demands that the wealth of theological knowledge be spread abroad, according to the needs of all peoples of the world. The full implication of this can only be

Church has followed for almost twenty centuries." Pope John XXIII, *Gaudet Mater Ecclesia*, Oct. 11, 1962, tr. *The Pope Speaks*, VIII, 212.

[62] Pius XII, *Humani generis*, *loc. cit.*, 572

understood in the light of a distinction we will here make between " theological research " and the " communication of
sacred doctrine." For example, the theological process of constructing an apologetics, a process which one unskilled in theology could not be expected to comprehend, is quite different
from the resultant apologetics which would be designed precisely for the uninitiated to understand. This distinction between " theological research " and " communication of doctrine " is so important for an understanding of the theologian's
role in the renewal of the Church that a few words should be
said about each.

" Theological research " involves intercommunication between scholars on a scientific level demanded by the discipline
itself. Such an interchange requires the use of precise methodology and technical language. In a certain sense such theological investigations take place within a closed circuit, and
must inevitably do so, because most people are neither inclined
nor prepared to follow their intricacies and complexities. The
scientific fraternity is exclusive with regard both to interpersonal associations and communication in scientific journals.
And the same should be true of theologians engaged in theological research. To preserve the scientific character of theology and develop it as a sacred science, the proper method
and mode of theology must be employed. In the progress
and advancement of theology, moreover, modernization and
continued development of method and terminology is necessary.[63] But such modernization and development should take
place within the processes of the science itself and, far from
being a popularization, should proceed in a way that preserves the scientific character of theology.

On the level of " theological research," as just described,
investigations often involve hypotheses and tentative proposals
which are not " teachable " as the dogmatic or moral doctrine
of the Church, or even as sound theological opinion. Scholarship itself demands such investigative procedures, but those

[63] See pp. 490 ff.

engaged in it can and should expect, and even welcome, the criticism of colleagues, together with their challenges to meet the demands of related disciplines. Even here a delineation of legitimate boundaries of research could be useful, but by no means should tentative matters under research be introduced as reliable opinion to undergraduates or popularized for general distribution. Before such " tentative proposals " are incorporated into pastoral communication they should have passed the test of competent critical analysis and enjoy a degree of acceptance among scholars.[64]

The second problem which confronts the theologian today is more far reaching than the revitalization of theology from within. It is the problem of communication in the pastoral context of the Church's teaching office. The precise problem is to discover methods for teaching most effectively the truths of the faith, not only in institutions of higher learning, but with a view to the needs of the whole Church at all levels of instruction.

Schools of higher education are not confronted with so vast a problem because a certain scientific level is required and academic conditions are controlled. Candidates should be firmly grounded in the faith and through formal training in philosophy should be oriented to the science of theology. Such requirements are to be expected in schools granting higher degrees in theology, i. e., universities, seminaries, and also colleges.[65] At these levels, since science itself makes the curricular

---

[64] "Caution must be used when there is . . . question of hypotheses having some sort of scientific foundation, in which the doctrines contained in Sacred Scripture or in Tradition are involved." Pius XII, *Humani generis, loc. cit.,* 575.

[65] " And so, in order that the genuine and entire doctrine of St. Thomas may flourish in our schools . . . and in order that the system of teaching be abolished which depends on the authority and judgment of the individual teacher, and therefore has a changeable foundation whence many diverse and mutually conflicting opinions arise not without great injury to Christian learning (Leo XIII, Letter *Qui te,* June 19, 1866). We will, order and command that teachers of Sacred Theology in Universities, Academies, Colleges, Seminaries and Institutes having the power by Apostolic indult to grant academic degrees and doctorates in that field take the *Summa Theologica* as the text for their lectures. . . . In this way

demands, only those who have the prerequisites need be admitted to such studies. A tightening of academic requirements is necessary to restore and maintain high standards in theological studies and research.

But the Church has the mission to teach the truths she possesses to all men in a manner conformable to their condition. From this pastoral view of the Church's teaching office, theologians, as servants of the Church, should make the fruits of revelation available to all men. Simply handing down conclusions or a dry summary of theology is not enough, whether in dogma, moral, or apologetics.[66] The growing consciousness of the need for theologians to apply their efforts to communication of doctrine in the modern world, urged by all modern popes, has reached its most explicit formulation in the words of Pope John XXIII:

What is needed is that this certain and immutable doctrine, to which the faithful owe obedience, be studied afresh and reformulated in contemporary terms. For this deposit of faith, or truths which are contained in our time-honored teaching, is one thing; the manner in which these truths are set forth (with their meaning preserved intact) is something else.
This then is what will require our careful, and perhaps too our patient consideration. We must work out ways and means of expounding these truths in a manner more consistent with a predominantly pastoral view of the Church's teaching office.[67]

Theologians must not only preserve and advance theology as a science, but also, in view of the needs of the apostolate, design practical ways and means to communicate sacred truths to all men. The emphasis on the pastoral view of the teaching apostolate of the Church reminds the theologian that sacred doctrine is not only a science, but a wisdom; that it is not only

and *in no other way will Theology be restored* to its pristine dignity, and *the proper order and value will be restored to all sacred studies. . . .*" (Pius X, Motu proprio *Doctoris Angelici, loc. cit.,* 340). (Emphasis added.)

[66] This has been the basis of much complaint not only against text books in use in secondary and undergraduate levels but especially in apologetics and missiology.

[67] Pope John XXIII, *Gaudet Mater Ecclesia, loc. cit.*

speculative, but practical; that it does not merely discover truth for its own sake, but provides the insights into divine revelation which can motivate and guide and energize a vital Christian life.

Serious study is necessary to determine appropriate modes for communicating the truths of sacred doctrine at such diverse levels as, for example, primary parochial schools and Catholic colleges, mission schools in pagan lands and classes of Catholic students on secular campuses. Apart from directing such formal instruction, theologians should provide principles and sapiential guidance for movements within the Church, e. g., the homiletic, liturgical, lay apostolic, sacramental and ecumenical movements, all of which are so essential for giving the truths of sacred doctrine vitality in the Church. The scope of revitalization broadens even more when we realize that not only should theologians provide the principles and guidance to these movements, but should prepare popularizations which embody sound doctrine in a manner which is clear and attractive to the Catholic community—and this not only through books but other modern media of communication. The view of theologians must also go beyond the Catholic community to Christians and non-Christians alike. The truly universal apostolate of the Church requires an attempt to understand contemporary philosophies and religions, and to enter into communication with them.

Even such a summary of the two-fold task of theology today gives some idea of the challenge presented by Pope John XXIII when he called theologians to work out ways and means for communicating the truths of sacred doctrine " in a manner more consistent with a predominantly pastoral view of the Church's teaching office." [68] This challenge should give theologians a broader vision of the horizons of theological investigation and application opening up to them in the modern world.[69] No less should it emphasize the need for a theology

[68] *Ibid.*

[69] Cf. C. Davis, " A Modern Reformation: Changing the Face of the Church," *Clergy Review,* 46 (Oct. 1961), 581-583.

with universal extension of principles, an objective methodology, a total synthesis of doctrine, self-critical reflection, and
openness to new data and experience.

Concluding Observations

While making no pretense of outlining the practical steps
which should now be taken, we would offer some observations
about preliminary work which we believe is essential for revitalizing theology. Sound, safe and true progress require first
of all a restoration of authentic Thomism. This is entirely in
keeping with the attitude of the Church considered in the
first part of this article. For a revitalization of Thomism to
be effected, however, Thomists must meet current objections
and counter the anti-Thomist attitude reflected in recent
Catholic literature. They must do this, not by debate, but
by proving the inherent ability of Thomism to be self-critical,
to assimilate and sponsor modern advances, and to support
and promote with sound theology the pastoral movements
beneficial to the life of the Church. We do not imply that this
work has not already been undertaken by Thomists. It has,
and with considerable success. To survey the literature would
take us beyond the limits of this article, but the result of such
a survey suggests some areas remaining open for further development.

1. A fuller appreciation of the dimensions of Thomistic
thought is needed today. If moderns lack an appreciation of
St. Thomas, it is perhaps because they know him only through
secondary sources which present too limited a view of his works.
Sacred doctrine reached a new high when Scripture, tradition,
the magisterium of the Church, the Fathers, liturgy, philosophy, history and science were shaped by St. Thomas into the
scientific structure of theology. A return to St. Thomas would
be a return to an appreciation of the importance and use of
the sources he employed. " The Scriptural Dimension of St.
Thomas " by J. R. Sheets, S. J.[70] and " Patristic Schools in the

---

[70] *The American Ecclesiastical Review*, CXLIV (March, 1961), 154-174.

Summa" by Nicholas Halligan, O. P.,[71] are examples of particular studies in the dimensions of St. Thomas' thought which can broaden appreciation of his wisdom and his relevance in the modern world. Further, studies in the structure and coherence of his synthesis, such as that by M. D. Chenu, O. P.[72] provide insights of value to Thomists today, while penetrating studies in depth of particular tracts reveal the vitality and applicability of Thomistic doctrine for meeting modern needs.[73]

A word should also be said regarding modes of communication. Although St. Thomas' greatest work was in the scientific mode, he taught and wrote in many styles, employing commentary, homily and even poetry. Modes of knowing other than the strictly scientific do have a place in the Church's apostolate, and the place and utility of each should be studied. The suggestion has already been made,[74] but the realization demands yet more effort.

If theology today is to advance scientifically, modernize its mode of communication, and still retain its meaning, the richness of St. Thomas' thought in extension, depth, and mode must be recaptured. To the foundations he has laid must be added the most reliable findings of recent scholarship. The pressing need is a fundamental synthesis which incorporates

[71] *The Thomist*, VII (1944), 271-322, 505-543.

[72] *Introduction a l'Etude de S. Thomas d'Aquin,* Paris: Vrin, 1950. Chapter XI, " La Somme Théologique " has been translated and published under the title *The Scope of the Summa,* tr. R. E. Brennan & A. M. Landry, Compact Studies, Washington: The Thomist Press, 1962. A translation by D. Hughes, O. P. and A. Landry, O. P. of the entire work is now being prepared and will be published by Henry Regnery Co., Chicago, Ill.

[73] S. Ramirez, O.P., *De Hominis Beatitudine* Tractatus Theologicus (Ad I-II, QQ. 1-5) 3 Vol., Salamanticae, 1942: Matriti, 1942-1947, provides not only a restoration of St. Thomas' view of moral theology but an orientation to the advancement of moral studies. We might also mention here that recent works by Thomists in sacramental theology are of tremendous significance to the liturgical renewal.

[74] " Since these two types of knowledge [scientific and connatural] are quite distinct, the methodological problem is to define the precise nature of each, the advantages and limitations of each, and above all the principles and rules that govern transpositions from one to the other." B. Lonergan, S.J., " Theology and Understanding," *Gregorianum,* 35 (1954), 642-644.

the best of modern research. This calls for cooperation among scholars in all specialized branches of sacred study (Scripture, tradition, etc.), scholars sharing with St. Thomas his broad vision of the horizons of sacred doctrine.

2. A re-evaluation and critical analysis of the brand of Thomism come to be known as " traditional " is needed to rectify historical prejudices and apologetic emphases, as well as to eliminate the influence of philosophies alien to an authentic Thomism. In many cases the modern mind has been offered a Thomism which not only does not represent the full dimensions of the Common Doctor's work, but distorts both his methodology and doctrine. The mirror of the manualist fails in many ways to reflect a true image of St. Thomas. An illustration of how Thomists can and should be critical of manualistic Thomism has been given by Fr. T. C. O'Brien, O. P. His study of the treatment of the existence of God in this manual tradition shows that the influence of non-Thomistic philosophies, especially the division of philosophy of Christian Wolff, has weakened the methodology, inverted the order, and impeded an authentic presentation of Thomistic metaphysics in our own day.[75]

Other critical areas have been pointed out, and recent studies and movements within Thomism reveal how valuable such criticisms can be.[76] Yet much of this work has been only intro-

---

[75] T. C. O'Brien, O. P., *Metaphysics and the Existence of God,* Washington: The Thomist Press, 1960.

[76] A. Fernandez-Alonzo, O. P. in his study "Scientiae et Philosophia Secundum S. Albertum Magnum," *Angelicum,* XIII (1963), 24-59 (tr. by Albertus Magnus Lyceum [mimeo] River Forest, Ill., cited here), pointed out the inadequacies of commentators and manualists in treating Thomistic natural philosophy because of their faulty division of the sciences. " Among them must be numbered: Caprolus, Cajetan and Soncinas; for they divided natural philosophy into as many sciences as there are diverse tracts written by Aristotle . . . (p. 10). Perhaps the gravest error of modern scholastics is that they think that natural philosophy understood in the present day sense as restricted to the ultimate causes of natural things, does not absolutely need scientific experience aided by instruments. . . . Nevertheless, according to the truth, the spirit and the letter, this opinion is wholly opposed to the true Aristotelian-Scholastic philosophy (p. 21). . . . On the basis of these suppositions, it will be easy to see how many assertions which are com-

ductory, i. e., constituting a *status questionis* that opens the way for further studies. This being so, a more systematic historico-theological analysis of nineteenth-century Thomism might do much to correct the "image" of St. Thomas in modern thought.

3. Thomists must enter into dialogue with contemporary philosophers and scientists. Such dialogue is necessary for a three-fold reason: a) to discover the truth contained in modern thought and incorporate it into the Thomistic synthesis; b) to correct what is false, misleading or dangerous to the faith; c) to understand the needs of modern man and improve communication with him. Thus, for example, the modern emphasis on the existential, the subjective aspects of the individual, awaits examination for all three reasons; a) the emphasis has provided insights which open up areas for theological investigation; [77] b) it has also resulted in errors which are dangerous to the faith; [78] c) and it has created needs which can only be met through adequate inter-personal communication.

While openness to and assimilation of new data from the positive sciences has been apparent in recent Thomistic thinking, especially in scientific methodology and psychology,[79] the

monly held in modern scholastic philosophy and taught as true doctrine and as altogether tenable and conformable to genuine traditional philosophy, but which rather are wholly foreign to this philosophy and often contrary to it, must be corrected or totally rejected" (p. 15).

This important study inspired the foundation and guides the work of the Albertus Magnus Lyceum. See note 79.

[77] See note 69.

[78] See note 32.

[79] In the field of modern science and its methodology, particularly noteworthy is the work of the Albertus Magnus Lyceum, River Forest, Ill. The recent publication of *The Dignity of Science* (ed. J. A. Weisheipl, O. P., Washington, D. C.: The Thomist Press, 1961) showed the extent of the scholarship stimulated by this group in the history and philosophy of science over the ten years of its existence. In addition, the writing and lecturing of some of its members, including W. H. Kane, O.P., B. M. Ashley, O.P., R. J. Nogar, O.P., J. A. Weisheipl, O.P., and W. A. Wallace, O.P., has stimulated strong interest in the philosophy of science in American philosophical circles. No less influential has been the work of Dr. V. E. Smith as Director of the Philosophy of Science Institute at St. John's University, Jamaica, N. Y. There Dr. Smith has sponsored a continuing lecture series

great moral problems arising in the modern world and affecting every level of human activity and social relationship continue to challenge Thomism. Serious efforts have been made to solve particular problems as they arise, but fundamental problems, reaching to the very basis of natural law [80] and moral methodology,[81] are largely untouched. Until such basic studies are undertaken the continuing task to which Pope John XXIII pointed in his allocution to the Fifth International Thomistic Congress will be ineffective.[82]

4. While we might suggest that a simple return to St. Thomas' own work would result in some " modernization " of method and vocabulary, a more apparent modernization will take place as Thomism develops through self-criticism and direct contact with contemporary trends and needs. The very

and annually published Studies in the Philosophy of Science which extend the influence of the Lyceum over a wider area, including the field of education. In modern psychology the influence of Thomism towards effecting a new synthesis is particularly noteworthy in the work of Noël Mailloux, O. P., at the University of Montreal, Dr. Magda Arnold at Loyola University in Chicago, and Manuel Barbado, O. P., at the University of Madrid. Likewise the relationship of depth psychology to Thomistic philosophy and theology has been given extensive and favorable treatment by Victor White, O. P., and Gerald Vann, O. P., in England, and by E. M. Stock, O. P., and C. J. D. Corcoran, O. P., in the United States. More recently, a team of philosopher-scientists under the sponsorship of the Albertus Magnus Lyceum, and including Albert Moraczewski, O. P., Celestine Walsh, O. P., and Bernard Zusy, O. P., has begun work on the human brain to make a concerted attack on the mind-body problem and the way in which Thomism can contribute to its solution. All of these efforts reveal the continuing interest of Thomists in modern science and an attempt to assimilate recent findings to the synthesis of the Angelic Doctor.

[80] Only recently Chief Justice Earl Warren of the Supreme Court of the United States, appealed for basic studies in " the law behind the law." His suggestion of a school dedicated to the study of moral standards is significant here. " I can conceive of a school dedicated to the purpose of training such professionals [ethical counselors] becoming the center of research in the field of moral standards, trying to resuscitate the glories of Aristotle, of Maimonides, of St. Thomas Aquinas and of Spinoza." Reported in *New York Times*, Nov. 12, 1962, page 1.

[81] Cf. W. A. Wallace, O. P., *The Role of Demonstration in Moral Theology*, Washington: The Thomist Press, 1962.

[82] " . . . the treatment and solution of moral questions according to the principles of Aquinas is of great help in bringing about agreement and unity among those interested in truth and charity." *The Pope Speaks*, VI (1960), 326.

nature of theology demands that it use the most precise methods and clearest terms available. Consequently, as better definitions, divisions, distinctions, and terms are developed, they should be adopted and incorporated, discarding in the process more subtle, vague, ambiguous and less useful apparatus. Perhaps it is too soon to expect headway with this specific problem, but at least it deserves attention. Some recent works seem even to be heading in the opposite direction, violating even the common rules of literary style, arbitrarily coining words and phrases and preferring obscure to clear terminology. Such obscurantism should not be confused with modernization.

5. Popularization of sacred doctrine has become a necessity in our day. Catholic literature has long been presenting popularizations of spiritual and devotional themes, but only recently has lay interest in theology become so common as to require popularizing the whole of sacred doctrine. Educated laymen themselves, to benefit their personal lives and their apostolate, have demanded such popularizations. *The Companion to the Summa* by Walter Farrell, O. P.,[83] grew out of a lecture series on " Theology for the Layman " that was initiated at the request of the laity. Other popularizations of St. Thomas' synthesis have appeared,[84] yet much more remains to be done. The laity must be kept continually informed as Thomism provides intellectual support to pastoral movements within the Church and grapples with modern philosophical, theological, scientific, and moral problems. In other words, when such problems have been studied at the properly theological level, popularizations should communicate the fruits of these studies to all in a manner they can understand and appreciate.

[83] 4 Vol., New York: Sheed & Ward, 1942.

[84] F. Sheed. *Theology and Sanity*, New York: Sheed and Ward, 1946; P. Glenn, *Tour of the Summa*, St. Louis: B. Herder, 1962. We should mention here the need for adequate textbooks of philosophy and theology, especially for the college level. " College Texts in Theology " (ed. F. L. B. Cunningham, O. P., 4 vol. Dubuque: Priory Press, 1959) is an example of a four-year program of theology for college level closely following the Thomistic synthesis. What is said here about " popularization " applies *servatis servandis* to textbooks.

Obviously, the task of theologians today is monumental. Great and demanding though that task be, however, theologians have reason for optimism to the extent that they call upon the wisdom of St. Thomas. When theologians in schools of higher learning restore a total and authentic synthesis of sacred doctrine, devoted to Thomistic principles, method and doctrine, purified of historical deviations, enhanced by the fruits of modern scholarship, and applied to contemporary needs; such a revitalized theology cannot but provide solid foundation and boundless dynamism to the pastoral and ecumenical renewal in the Church.

This confidence was symbolized in an action of Pope John XXIII when, shortly before his final illness on the feast of St. Thomas, March 7, 1963, he visited the Pontifical Anthenaeum " Angelicum " and honored it with a new title " The Pontifical University of St. Thomas Aquinas in Rome." What was symbolized in his action was eloquently confirmed by the words he spoke:

As we have said, we would be very happy to see what we might term the " treasure " of the precepts of St. Thomas " unearthed " in greater measure each day, to the great benefit of Christianity, and also to see his writing reach a much wider public in a language and form perfectly suited to the spirit and temper of our times (A.A.S. 52, 1960, p. 823); because in the final analysis we are convinced that, if the study of the doctrine of Aquinas is promoted with greater care and skill, the result will be that the resolutions proposed by the Fathers of the Second Ecumenical Council of the Vatican will be carried into effect more fruitfully.[85]

ANTHONY D. LEE, O. P.

Dominican House of Studies
Washington, D. C.

---

[85] Pope John XXIII, Motu Proprio, *Dominicanus Ordo, Osservatore Romano,* March 7, 1963.

EXISTENTIAL ETHICS: A THOMISTIC APPRAISAL

တ

A GENERAL problem that calls for discussion, and hopefully will be treated in the deliberations of the Second Vatican Council, is that of the relationship of moral theology to recent innovations in philosophy. Several papal directives and encyclicals have already discussed moral problems and attempted to rectify errors of the " new theology " associated with these innovations, pointing out in the process more fruitful ways toward a renewal of moral theology.[1] Such problems, while not merely of academic interest—affecting as they do the moral life of all Christians—are nonetheless of major concern to those who teach moral theology in universities and seminaries.

A representative teaching in this category which merits examination is that known in German-speaking countries as *Existentialethik* and coming to be known here as " existential ethics." [2] Its importance derives not only from its subject matter but also from the fact that it is cited as a fruitful application of modern knowledge to the development of theological science. In this article we propose to explain this development and evaluate it from the viewpoint of the teacher of moral doctrine.

The seminary professor, and to a lesser extent the professor in a Catholic university, is torn between two extremes. On the one hand, he is committed to transmitting the theological tradition of the Church to those he teaches, a task difficult in

---

[1] For a brief survey, see the preceding article in this volume, " Thomism and the Council," by A. D. Lee, O. P., particularly p. 490.

[2] The title is suggested in a paper by Karl Rahner, S. J., " Ueber die Frage einer formalen Existentialethik," *Schriften zur Theologie*, Vol. 2 (3. Aufl.), (Einsiedeln/ Köln: 1958), pp. 227-246. It is also known as " individual ethics," and in some earlier writings as " situational ethics." See J. Fuchs, *Situation und Entscheidung*, Grundfragen christlicher Situationsethik (Frankfurt: 1952), pp. 69-92.

itself because of the large amount of material to be covered and the relatively short time available. On the other hand, he must be alert to recent developments in his science, and attempt to assimilate these to the tradition he passes on to his students. Such assimilation of new knowledge, however desirable it may be, is not so simple and straightforward as might appear. Innovations in theology frequently call into question theories on which the existing tradition is based. While such questioning is an acceptable procedure in the profane sciences, it is not always so favorably regarded in sacred science. New doctrines, by their very novelty, are open to the charge of unorthodoxy with all the dissatisfaction this implies and the recrimination it often entails.

If theological advance is usually attended by controversy, recent proposals relating to existential ethics are no exception. By some they are welcomed as brilliant and beneficial insights that vitalize a moral theology which has long been dated, living in isolation from contemporary problems.[3] By others they are regarded as an obfuscation of traditional doctrine that could destroy the foundations of moral theology, and lead to a subjective type of morality which the Catholic Church has been combating for centuries.[4] Such evaluations are undoubtedly extreme, but they underscore the controversial aspect of the new development, and the difficulty this poses for analyzing its teachable content.

To facilitate the latter task, we shall first outline the main elements of existential ethics, and then single out for criticism several points that seem to us at variance with the Thomistic theology which constitutes the mainstay of the Church's traditional doctrine. With this we shall be in a position to make some observations about its value and importance as a moral doctrine to be taught in seminaries and universities.

---

[3] See, for example, Franz Böckle, "Bestrebungen in der Moraltheologie," in *Fragen der Theologie heute* (Einsiedeln: 1957), pp. 443-444.

[4] For an early critique, see M. Labourdette, O. P., *Foi catholique et problèmes modernes,* (Tournai: 1953).

Fundamentals of Existential Ethics

The briefest statement of the new doctrine is contained in an essay by Father Karl Rahner entitled *Gefahren im heutigen Katholizismus*.[5] There the author is arguing against an ethical teaching known as situational ethics that has fallen under ecclesiastical condemnation. Although condemned, in Father Rahner's view this teaching contains some elements of truth.[6] He is interested in preserving such elements and attempts to do so by focusing attention, not on the particular situation in which a person finds himself, but rather on the individuality that is proper to the human person. This individuality is so unique that it cannot be comprehended under the type of generalization found in traditional ethical treatises. Thus the first point is that man's personal nature is so individual as not to be contained under the *general* prescriptions of moral law. In Father Rahner's words:

Since the ontological structure of a being is the objective norm of its operation, man is morally obliged to be and become by free choice the individual that he is. As a spiritual and personal nature intended for an immediate union of love with the Triune God, he is so individual as to enjoy an absolutely unique, incommunicable and unclassifiable individuality. While this spiritual and personal individuality is not comprehensible under general norms, laws and rules, it does stand, like all else, under the obliging will of God, Who does not merely give general precepts, or even individual ones that are only instances of the general, but imperatives that proceed immediately from the " I " of God to the particular " thou " of man. Thus there is a realm of individual morality and religion, a region of moral and religious obligation and duty which, without opposing

---

[5] Einsiedeln: Benziger and Co., 1950.

[6] The Austrian Jesuit states this in the essay, " Ueber die Frage einer formalen Existentialethik," as follows: " Wir haben auf die Situationsethik zu Beginn unserer Ueberlegungen nur darum hingewiesen, weil einerseits das, was wir formale Existentialethik nennen wollen, nicht verwechselt werden darf mit der (skizzierten) Situationsethik und weil anderseits diese Existentialethik nach unserer Meinung der Kern der Wahrheit ist, der auch in der falschen Situationsethik steckt."— *Schriften*, p. 230.

the general laws of morality, lies decidedly outside their pale and cannot be prescribed within their general formulations.[7]

Paralleling this ontological condition of man, it appears that there must be an individual ethics concerned with the moral obligations of the individual as such, prescinding from those obligations each person has in common with other men. This thought leads Father Rahner to maintain that there must be an individual ethics obliging the individual in his very uniqueness, and not insofar as he is merely a case subsumable under a general rule.

Though there cannot be, nor ought there be, an individual ethics in which the individual and his rights contravene the general norms of morality, there is an individual ethics and an individual morality which obliges the individual in a way that is uniquely his, and nevertheless cannot be reckoned as a mere " case," a mere instance of the universal, under these general norms of morality. Thus a " private " sphere of the moral-religious life exists which is not only *de facto* not the concern of general laws and their associated executive and legislative apparatus, but basically cannot be reached by them.[8]

---

[7] Wenn die Seinsstruktur eines Seienden die objektiv vorgegebene Norm seines Handelns ist, dann gehört es auch zum sittlichen Sollen des Menschen, jener Einzelne in freier Entscheidung zu sein und zu werden, der er ist. Wenn somit der Mensch als geistig-personales und mit Gott dem Dreipersönlichen in unmittelbarer Liebesgemeinschaft stehendes Wesen wirklich auch in dem Sinn Einzelner ist, dass ihm auch eine absolut einmalige, unvertauschbare, nie fall- und regelhafte Eigentümlichkeit eignet, und wenn diese geistige personale Einmaligkeit, obzwar nicht durch allgemeine Normen, Gesetze und Regeln einfangbar, doch wie alles Seiende unter dem verpflichtenden Willen Gottes steht, der freilich hier nicht auf das Allgemeine und auf den Einzelnen als Fall des Allgemeinen, sondern unmittelbar vom Ich Gottes auf das je einmalige Du des Menschen geht, dann gibt es einen Bereich des Individuell-Sittlichen und Religiösen, einen Bereich sittlicher und religiöser Pflicht und Aufgabe, die, ohne in Widerspruch mit den allgemeinen Gesetzen des Sittlichen stehen zu können, doch entscheidend über diesen Bereich hinausliegt und von allgemein formulierbaren Normen nicht mehr erfasst werden kann.—*Gefahren*, p. 16.

[8] Wohl kann und darf es keine Individualethik geben, in der der Einzelne und sein Recht sich gegen die allgemeinen Normen des Sittlichen erhebt; aber es gibt eine Individualethik und eine Individualmoral, die verpflichtend, als die einmalig seine, den Einzelnen trifft und dennoch nicht als blosser Fall, als blosses Individuum eines Allgemeinen unter die allgemeinen Normen der Sittlichkeit gerechnet werden

Although he justifies such an individual ethics, Father Rahner does not interpret this to mean that the individual may do as he pleases. The individual man, just as humanity in general, is governed by the will of God. Thus he continues:

This private sphere is not in any way one of private choice and freedom, but stands univocally under the morally obliging and holy will of God, and freely so, directly willing the incommunicable and singular unity of the individual person. This uniqueness is not only something real, but it is also something that is free to cope with man's developing problems. It therefore cannot be merely an object of God's will as creator, but is also an object of His morally obliging will, and even must be truly so as an ontological reality.[9]

Having argued to the existence of an individual ethics binding man in all his uniqueness, Father Rahner is faced with the problem of how the individual can know God's will in his regard, or, more precisely, how one is to ascertain the norms that bind the individual. The solution he arrives at identifies conscience as the organ which recognizes such individual prescriptions. This, however, is not conscience as employed in the usual sense. Rather it is conscience understood as having the special function of perceiving the imperatives of a strict individual ethics, similar to the role ascribed to it by some theologians in the charismatic art of discerning spirits. In Father Rahner's words:

Therefore there must also be in man an organ which recognizes this individually obliging norm. When we call this conscience, we must

kann. Es gibt darum eine " private " Sphäre des sittlich-religiösen Lebens um die sich eine allgemeine Gesetzlichkeit und die darin gesetzgeberischen und überwachenden Organe nicht bloss faktisch nicht kümmern, sondern die einer solchen Gesetzlichkeit und deren Organen grundsätzlich nicht zugänglich sein kann.— *Ibid.*, pp. 16-17.

[9] Diese private Sphäre ist darum nicht im geringsten Sphäre privater Willkür und Ungebundenheit, sondern steht eindeutig unter dem sittlich fordernden heiligen Willen Gottes, jenes Willens freilich, der gerade das unvertauschbare und einmalige Eine des einzelnen Menschen will, eine Einmaligkeit, die nicht nur Tatsache, sondern auch frei zu verwirklichende Aufgabe des Menschen ist und darum nicht bloss Gegenstand des Willens Gottes als des Schöpfers, sondern auch Gegenstand seines sittlich fordernden Willens sein kann und als wahre Seinswirklichkeit auch sein muss.—*Ibid.*, p. 17.

distinguish between two functions of conscience: one which compares the *general* norms of ethics and moral theology with man's
subjective knowledge and applies it to his " case," and another
whereby the individual hears the unique call of God which is valid
only for him and is never completely deducible from general norms.
There must therefore be a " technique," or better a τέχνη, an " art "
in the sense of the ancients, for perceiving these imperatives of
strict individual ethics, which is to be clearly distinguished from the
" theory," the ἐπιστήμη of moral philosophy and theology with their
generally valid norms. If we seek a traditional name for this, we
would call it the charismatic art of " discernment of spirits," a
concept which in later centuries has been generally misunderstood,
because this distinction, either explicitly or by tacit agreement, has
been restricted to the casuistic technique for applying theoretical
norms to the individual " case." In its proper nature, however, it is
something quite different, namely, the ability to discern the unique
call of God for the individual as such. . . .[10]

This will serve as a general characterization of individual or
existential ethics as propounded by Father Rahner. Despite
the brevity of the statement, it should be clear that the Austrian theologian does not wish his new proposal to overturn
the foundations of traditional moral theology. Rather he regards it as a refinement of traditional teaching enabling the
individual to become more aware of the obligations God im-

---

[10] Es gibt darum auch ein Organ im Menschen, das diese Individualsittlichkeit
als fordernde Norm erkennt. Wenn wir es Gewissen nennen, dann müssen wir
zwischen zwei Funktionen des Gewissens unterscheiden: derjenigen, die dem sub-
jektiven Wissen des Menschen die *allgemeinen* Normen der Ethik und der Moraltheologie vermittelt und auf seinen " Fall " anwendet, und derjenigen, durch die der
Einzelne den je *einmaligen,* nur ihm geltenden und aus allgemeinen Normen nie
restlos ableitbaren Ruf Gottes hört. Es muss daher eine " Technik " oder besser
eine τέχνη, eine " Kunst " im Sinn der Alten geben, diese Imperative der strengen
Individualethik zu vernehmen, und sie ist klar zu unterscheiden von der " Theorie,"
der ἐπιστήμη, der normenhaften, allgemeingültigen Moralphilosophie und theologie.
Wenn wir für sie einen traditionellen Namen suchen, so würde er heissen: die
charismatische Kunst der " Unterscheidung der Geister " ein Begriff, der in den
letzten Jahrhunderten eigentlich meist missverstanden wird, weil diese Unterscheidung ausdrücklich oder mit stillschweigender Selbstverständlichkeit eingeschränkt
wird als die Fertigkeit der kasuistischen Anwendung der theoretischen Normen auf
den Einzel-" Fall." Sie ist aber in ihrem eigentlichen Kern etwas ganz anderes,
nämlich das Heraushörenkönnen des einmaligen Rufes Gottes an den einmal
Einzelnen als solchen. . . .—*Ibid.,* p. 17.

poses upon him as an individual, i. e., as distinct from the rest of mankind. The innovation, at least on the surface, cannot be charged with unorthodoxy. It is a development by way of refinement, not one by way of rejection of traditional doctrine.

A Thomistic Critique

Yet, implicit in Father Rahner's treatment is a dissatisfaction with moral philosophy and moral theology as these have been taught through the centuries. This dissatisfaction stems from the modern thought with which Father Rahner is in contact, and particularly from recent philosophical notions arising within phenomenology and existentialism. Both of these movements react against systematic philosophies because of the latters' apparent concern with general natures or essences, and their supposed failure to come to grips with concrete, existing, individual problems. The very term Father Rahner adopts for his system, " existential ethics," opposes individualist ethics to one which might be described as merely " essentialist ethics." Father Rahner would employ the terms " essence " and " existence " in their scholastic understanding—an understanding quite different from their existentialist meanings—and urge the complementarity that should exist between essentialist ethics and existential ethics.[11] But the very fact that he must

[11] He makes this clear in a passage in " Ueber die Fragen einer formalen Existentialethik," which reads as follows: " Der Begriff einer " Existentialethik " schliesst dieses Missverständnis aus, er erweist sich eindeutig als Gegen- und Komplementärbegriff zu abstrakt-allgemeiner " Essenzethik." Dennoch bezeichnet diese " Existentialethik " nicht eine wesenlose " Existenzethik " (im Sinne der geläufigen Distinktion von Existenz und Essenz), sondern bezeiht sich—gemäss dem ursprünglichen Sinngehalt des modernen Wortes " Existential "—auf das *materiale Wesen* des Menschen, insofern sich dieses, wenigstens als φύσις, als Prinzip des Auf- und Eingehens in die Aktualität des (geschichtlich-) personalen Handelns, in der Positivität der je vereinzelten, einmalig-einigen Kon-kretion der individuellen Entscheidung konstitutiv vollenden muss, so dass er gerade nicht in einer rein deduktiv erlangten, abstrakt-essentialen Norm- und Ordnungsethik die *allein* hinreichende Bedingung seiner freien sittlichen Selbstverwirklichung haben kann, sondern ebenso unabdingbar (d. h. in der Linie der *Konstitution* des materialen, sittlich-personalen Wesens) eingewiesen bleibt in die unableitbare qualitative Eigenart des einmaligen, nicht adäquat fallhaften, individuellen Aktes.—Eine Analyse dieser " existentialen " Struktur des

introduce this new development to make up for shortcomings in essentialist ethics seems a tacit admission that a philosophy or theology which deals with natures or essences is by that very fact incapable of supplying adequate moral direction to the individual.

Metaphysics and Moral Science

By way of critique, the principal shortcoming in Father Rahner's proposal is that it is based on a misconception of the nature of moral philosophy and theology as a science in the Thomistic sense, and thus attempts to introduce a correction, or refinement, on an understanding of traditional moral doctrine that is itself erroneous. As might be expected of a thinker in the German tradition, where a strong proclivity for rationalism and idealism has been manifest during the past century and where phenomenology is now eagerly embraced as an overdue corrective, Father Rahner identifies traditional doctrine with a neo-scholasticism that is very different from the teaching of St. Thomas Aquinas. Moral philosophy, for Father Rahner, is an essentialist doctrine that is deduced *a priori* from general principles. This he conceives as originating from an ontology that is itself essentialist or rationalist in inspiration. His line of thought in this matter is clear from the following text:

If the individual is merely the limiting " case " of the universal, if, for example, this person is *only* " *a* man," whose positive reality is nothing more than the realization of a universal essence (which is the foundation of an obligation), and therefore is itself inferior to the universal, insofar as the latter not only includes more under it than this individual, but also has greater richness of meaning, in which case the individual appears *merely* as the space-time limitation of the universal, then an obligation that binds the individual can *only* be grounded in a general essence, in a general obligatory

menschlichen Wesens könnte eine genauere *philosophische* Begründung dessen liefern, was wir hier unter einem mehr theologischen Gesichtspunkt entwickelt haben."— *Schriften*, p. 239, fn. 1.

principle or some combination of such, which can be applied to any (no matter how complicated) " case " of the universal. But if the historical concrete individual (at least wherever this individuality is of a spiritual personal kind) is more than a mere case of the universal, where it has a meaningful positiveness, an individuality that is not merely a *limitatio* of the universal, then this individual can be the object and end of an obligation which is not merely a general principle, but is actually an existential individual obligation.[12]

According to this line of reasoning, if one were to hold an essentialist doctrine in ontology, he would be committed to an essentialist ethics, whereas as soon as he became aware of the ontological uniqueness of the individual, he would thereby be led to investigate an existentialist or individual ethics.

Such alternatives, it need hardly be remarked, are foreign to the thought of St. Thomas Aquinas, who did not develop his moral philosophy in direct dependence on his metaphysics or theology, and who was too aware of the primacy of existence to have unwittingly evolved a philosophy that was " essentialist " in character.

It is entirely possible, on the first point, for one nurtured on the manualist tradition to conceive Thomism as a rationalist

---

[12] Ist nämlich das Einzelne *nur* der (beschränkte) " Fall " des Allgemeinen, ist z. B. dieser Mensch *nur* " *ein* Mensch," dessen positive Wirklichkeit sich erschöpft in der Realisation jenes allgemeinen Wesens (das die Grundlage der Sollensprinzipien ist) und somit höchstens weniger als die allgemeine Idee, insofern diese nicht nur zahlenmässig mehr als nur gerade diesen unter sich befasst, sondern auch mehr an möglicher Inhaltsfülle mindestens offenlässt, so dass das Individuum *nur* als raum-zeitpunktliche Eingrenzung des Allgemeinen erscheint, dann kann ein Seinsollen, das sich auf das Einzelne bezieht, *nur* im allgemeinen Wesen gründen, ein allgemeines Sollensprinzip oder die Kombination von solchen sein, die auf einen (wenn auch noch so komplizierten) " Fall " des Allgemeinen angewandt werden. Ist aber das einzelne geschichtlich Konkrete (wenigstens, dort, wo dieses Einzelne geistig-personaler Art ist) mehr als nur Fall des Allgemeinen, hat es eine inhaltliche Positivität, eine Individualität, die nicht nur " limitatio " des Allgemeinen ist, dann kann dieses, von den allgemeinen Wesensnormen als *solches* nicht mehr erreichte, wenn ihnen auch nicht widersprechende (da es ja nicht realverschieden sein kann von der individuellen Realisation des Allgemeinen im Einzelnen), Gegenstand und Ziel eines Sollens sein, das nicht die Geltung allgemeiner Prinzipien, sondern ein existentielles, individuelles Sollen ist.—*Das Dynamische in der Kirche*, (Freiburg: Herder, 1958), pp. 16-17.

system which first studies metaphysical essences, and then applies such " essentialist " knowledge in succession to the existent universe, to man, to God, and finally to human activity. This is the basic scheme elaborated by Christian Wolff, a plan which influenced so many manuals of the nineteenth and early twentieth centuries, and whose order of teaching proceeded from ontology to cosmology, psychology, theodicy, and ultimately to ethics. Such an order of teaching, as is now known, was never that of the Angelic Doctor. Emphatically rejecting the Platonic doctrine of his day, which started from an intuitive knowledge of essences and descended to the world of experience, he adopted instead the a posteriori procedure of Aristotle, who began philosophy with a study of the world of nature, including man and his moral activity, then proceeded to metaphysics, and finally terminated in a theology which contemplates the First Cause of all.[13]

Similarly, current researches on the primacy of existence in the philosophy of St. Thomas leave little doubt that St. Thomas, far from having an exclusive concern for essences, actually elaborated a philosophy of existence adequate to cope with the problem of the individual.[14] Although allowing that essence, or the nature attained in the universal, is the means by which the individual is known, thereby playing a key role in man's knowledge of singulars, he never regarded the individual itself as the mere ontological realization of a pre-existent essence without its own perfection precisely as singular.[15]

[13] For a clear statement of the manner in which St. Thomas elaborated his philosophy, and how this is opposed to the treatment of Christian Wolff, see J. M. Ramirez, O. P., " De propria indole philosophiae sancti Thomae Aquinatis," in Xenia thomistica, Vol. 1 (Romae: 1925), pp. 53-64.

[14] We have in mind the work of Cornelius Fabro in Italy, of Jacques Maritain and Régis Jolivet in France, of Etienne Gilson and his school in Canada, and a host of writers in the United States who take their inspiration from Gilson, among whom may be enumerated Charles Hart, J. F. Anderson, Joseph Owens, Henri Renard, W. N. Clarke, and others.

[15] St. Thomas' explanation of man's knowledge of singulars is sketched briefly in the Summa Theologiae, I, q. 86, a. 1. See also Cont. Gent., I, 65; De Verit., q. 2, aa. 5-6; q. 10, a. 5, etc.

Angels and Individuation

Father Rahner, however, regards his line of reasoning as at least compatible with the theological thought of St. Thomas, and selects the latter's analysis of the angels as a fitting comparison with the doctrine he himself would elaborate. Thus he writes:

For Thomism . . . what Gabriel adds to the Angel Gabriel is so absolutely unique, so unrepeatable, so free from chance duplication, that even God Himself (even though He can fashion many angels) cannot fashion a second " Gabriel," that is, one merely locally and numerically different from the first, but not distinctive in his inner self. One can also think of obligations which Gabriel must fulfill which are only applicable to him, and that have as little meaning for another angel as the possibility itself that there be a second Gabriel. Thomistically speaking no one in good will may deny that individual norms can be given for strict singulars.

This does not mean, from what has been said, that the norm for any situation is actually given only once, depending on an accidental and uniquely occurring collection of circumstances, even though these could themselves be repeated. It rather means that this norm fundamentally can only be applied to *one* case, which therefore ceases even to be a " case." Again this does not mean that for this absolutely individual Gabriel everything is not applicable which applies to " creature," " spiritual person," " angel," and which flows necessarily from these abstract " essences." Even for Gabriel precisely *as* a creature, etc., such principles exist for every individual norm which we refer to as an imperative. But these principles cannot *adequately* tell him his obligations, no matter how exact and no matter how we can conceive of combining them, because " this angel " according to St. Thomas is fundamentally much more than " an angel." [16]

[16] Für den Thomismus z. B. ist dasjenige, was den Engel Gabriel zu Gabriel macht, so absolut einmalig, unwiederholbar, von Fallhaftigkeit frei, dass selbst Gott (obwohl er viele " Engel " schaffen kann) einen zweiten " Gabriel," der vom ersten nur stellen- und zahlhaft, aber nicht in sich selbst verschieden wäre, unmöglich schaffen kann. Es können also Forderungen gedacht werden darüber, was Gabriel zu sein und zu tun hat, die nur für ihn gelten, die so wenig für andere gelten, wie es einen zweiten Gabriel geben kann. Thomistisch kann man also beim besten Willen nicht grundsätzlich leugnen, dass es Individualnormen von strengster Einmaligkeit geben könne. Das bedeutet nach dem Gesagten nicht, dass faktisch wegen einer zufällig nur einmal verwirklichten Konstellation von Umständen (die es aber an sich öfters geben könnte) die Norm für diese Situation nur einmal aktuell wird.

Having said this, Father Rahner continues: "Now, for various reasons which we cannot go into here, we are led to maintain that the same thing holds for men."[17] He then repeats the line of argument already given to show how the individual human being can be "guided by an imperative that is essentially distinct from the obligations imposed on general essences."[18]

When one searches for the reason which permits Father Rahner to apply his reasoning about angels to men, one finds that this is intimately connected with his notion of individuation, and how prime matter functions as an individuating principle. Thus, when explaining the metaphysical basis of existential ethics, he makes the statement:

Man with his spiritual and moral acts cannot be simply a phenomenon of the universal and only in such universality eternal and enduring in the negative extension of space and time. Rather there must be a positiveness in him as an individual. Put in another way, his spiritual individuality, at least in his acts, cannot be a mere limitation of a universal essence through the negativeness of prime matter as the substantial and purely potential principle of spatio-temporality, merely repeating the same essence in different space-time positions.[19]

Es bedeutet vielmehr, dass diese Norm grundsätzlich nur *einen* Anwendungs-"fall" hat, der dadurch eben aufhört, "Fall" zu sein. Das alles bedeutet natürlich nicht, dass für dieses absolute Individuum Gabriel nicht all das gälte, was für ein "Geschöpf," für eine "Geistperson," für einen "Engel" an notwendigen Prinzipien aus diesen abstrakten "Wesenheiten" erfliesst. Da ja Gabriel auch *als* gerade "er" Geschöpf usw. ist, sind natürlich diese Prinzipien innere Momente an jener Individualnorm, die wir einen "Imperativ" nennen. Aber diese Prinzipien können ihn nicht *adäquat* aussagen, so subtil genau und so raffiniert kombiniert sie auch gedacht werden mögen, wenn anders "dieser" Engel nach dem hl. Thomas grundsätzlich mehr ist als "ein Engel."—*Das Dynamische*, pp. 17-18.

[17] Nun—aus den verschiedensten Gründen, die hier nicht darzulegen sind, sind wir berechtigt, dasselbe für den Menschen zu behaupten.—*Ibid.*, p. 18.

[18] Ist er aber mehr, ist ein geistpersönliches Seiendes mehr als bloss der Schnittpunkt allgemeiner Wahrheiten und Sätze, mehr als Einzel-Fall einer Essenz, die wiederholt werden kann, dann kann dieses einmalig Besondere, diese Existenz angerufen werden in einem Imperativ, der wesentlich verschieden ist von den Sollensprinzipien, die sich aus den allgemeinen Wesenheiten ergeben.—*Ibid.*, p. 18.

[19] Der Mensch mit seinen geistigen und sittlichen Akten kann daher nicht bloss die Erscheinung des Allgemeinen und allein in dieser Allgemeinheit "Ewigen" und

Here the implication is clearly made that the scholastic principles of prime matter and substantial form, traditionally used to explain man's nature, give at best a negative notion of his individuality, and are inadequate as explanations of his existent individuality. Yet, for Father Rahner, they are components of some type of " universal essence," which has its corresponding moral obligations, and therefore can be the basis of an essentialist moral philosophy or theology.

Such an explanation is extremely difficult to reconcile with the Thomistic teaching on individuation, particularly as this applies to the human person. St. Thomas was sufficiently aware of the role of matter and quantity in explaining man's corporeal individuality, as well as that of the human soul under its aspect of substantial form in explaining his spiritual individuality, not to entertain the view of individuation refuted by Father Rahner.[20] But the latter's preoccupation with the individuation of spiritual substances reflects a Suarezian mentality with respect to this whole problem which perhaps does labor under serious difficulties. Here is not the place to enter into a comparison of Suarezian and Thomistic doctrine on individuality.[21] Suffice it to mention that according to our analysis the lacunae Father Rahner finds in scholastic doctrine are not to be found in authentic Thomism, even though they do exist in the teaching of many eclectic Thomists of the sixteenth and seventeenth centuries.

Immergültigen in der negativen Dehnung von Raum und Zeit sein. In ihm als dem Einzelnen muss vielmehr eine Positivität gegeben sein, anders ausgedrückt: seine geistige Individualität kann (wenigstens in seinen Akten) nicht bloss die Eingrenzung eines an sich allgemeinen Wesens durch die Negativität der materia prima sein als des substantiellen und rein potentiellen Prinzips der Raumzeitlichkeit, der blossen Wiederholung desselben an verschiedenen Raum-Zeit-Stellen.—Schriften, p. 236.

[20] The fact that there is a considerable Thomistic doctrine on the uniqueness of the individual man can be seen from a work now some twenty-five years old, R. J. Slavin, O. P., Philosophical Basis for Individual Differences, Washington, D. C.: Catholic University Press, 1936.

[21] For a sketch of Suarezian doctrine on individuation, and the way in which this differs from St. Thomas' teaching, see Gallus Manser, O. P., Das Wesen des Thomismus, 3. Aufl. (Freiburg/Schweiz: 1949), p. 670.

Prudence and Conscience

This brief critique of the metaphysical foundations on which existential ethics is built leads naturally to a consideration of the key problem it raises, namely, how there can be an individual ethics which supplies directives proportioned to the human person in all his individuality. St. Thomas, impressed by the highly individual character of personal ethics, carefully elaborated his tract on prudence to explain how this virtue must complement moral theology.[22] Aware of this in a general way, Father Rahner feels obliged to show the inadequacy of this traditional teaching, and in so doing to justify the need for his individual ethics. In his own words:

It is evident that in concrete circumstances one needs prudence, which is the virtue which determines the right thing to do here and now from and in these concrete circumstances. The role that this virtue, almost completely forgotten in later moral theology, plays according to St. Thomas is well known. But the question is: What is the nature of this virtue and to what object does it have reference? If a person is really to answer this question, he must obviously say: It looks first of all to its collection of general principles and then to the concrete circumstances and asks itself which principles or combination of principles should be applied under such circumstances. So far correct. But then the further question presents itself: Are these circumstances only the cases of universal essences? . . . Or are the circumstances surrounding this type of case themselves something absolutely individual, that cannot be arrived at through the application of these universal essences on a concrete, but not thereby absolutely unique, case? And how then does prudence know this? . . . The appeal to prudence therefore offers no solution to the problem facing us, but merely points it out.[23]

[22] The principal locus for St. Thomas' treatment of prudence is the *Summa Theologiae*, II-II, qq. 47-51; see also I-II, q. 57, aa. 4-6.

[23] Selbstverständlich bedarf es in den " konkreten Umständen " der *Klugheit*, die die Tugend ist, aus diesen " konkreten Umständen " und in ihnen das gerade " hier und jetzt " Richtige zu finden. Bekannt ist ja die Rolle, die diese von der späteren Moraltheologie manchmal fast vergessene Tugend bei Thomas spielt. Aber die Frage ist: Welches ist die Natur dieser Tugend und auf welchen Gegenstand bezieht sie sich? Wenn man diese Frage wirklich beantworten will, dann muss man offenbar sagen: sie blickt zunächst einmal auf die Fülle der allgemeinen Prinzipien und dann

As Father Rahner understands prudence, then, it cannot make the transition from universal essences to actual existence. Therefore he rejects it in favor of the conscience of the individual, which we have already shown to furnish his solution to the problem when it functions in a role similar to that attributed to it in the art of discerning spirits.

Regarding this point in Father Rahner's teaching it should be observed that we are here again at a controversial issue which divides the theological tradition. Although paying lip service to St. Thomas' teaching on prudence, Father Rahner first represents this inadequately, then states the problem in a way that demands a solution in terms of a post-Tridentine doctrine which substitutes the voice of conscience for the prudential decision, and finally proceeds to show how the latter doctrine is itself inadequate. Since we have dealt elsewhere with the Thomistic teaching on prudence and its relation to moral theology, casuistry, and existential ethics, we need not elaborate further on this aspect of Father Rahner's exposition.[24]

---

auf die konkreten Umstände und fragt sich, welches Prinzip (welche Kombination von Prinzipien) unter gerade diesen Umständen aktualisiert werden müsse. Das ist richtig. Aber sofort entsteht die Frage wieder: Sind diese Umstände nur die Fälle von allgemeinen Wesenheiten? . . . *auch noch* etwas absolut Individuelles, das durch die eben angedeutete Komplizierung allgemeiner Wesenheiten auf ein Konkretes (aber darum noch nicht eigentlich Einmaliges) hin noch nicht erreicht ist? Und wie erkennt dann die Klugheit dieses? . . . Mit der Berufung auf die Klugheit wird also die hier gemeinte Problematik nicht gelöst, sonder nur angezeigt. —*Das Dynamische*, pp. 22-23.

[24] For the relation of prudence to moral science as conceived by St. Thomas Aquinas, see *The Role of Demonstration in Moral Theology* (Washington; The Thomist Press, 1962), pp. 110-142. A specific treatment of casuistry is given in the same study, pp. 199-202, and of existential ethics on pp. 203-208; for references to St. Thomas' teaching on conscience, see p. 199, fn. 109. Father Rahner differs from St. Thomas in maintaining that conscience is an " organ " (see text cited in fn. 10 of the present article), while for St. Thomas it is not an organ but an act of the habit of synderesis. As such it gives the least refined judgment of practical reason, whereas the prudential judgment touches the existential act not simply by abstract judgment *in actu signato*, but by moving to exercise *in actu exercito*. For a lucid exposition of this, see Cajetan's commentary on the *Prima Secundae*, q. 58, a. 5, n. 8; also *The Role of Demonstration in Moral Theology*, pp. 95-142, particularly p. 131.

Rather we would here comment on his claim to have elaborated in the process a " science " of individual action, and on the way in which he conceives this " science " to be related to the " art " of discerning spirits.

Throughout his writing Father Rahner purposes to give a scientific consideration of individual morality under the designation of individual or existential ethics. Yet how such an ethics is to be scientifically elaborated is never immediately apparent. He does state that it should be concerned with ascertaining the formal structure and fundamental types of knowledge of individual morality, and then goes on:

Just as on the one hand there can be no science of the individual as a really unique singular as such, and nevertheless there can be a general formal ontology of individuals, so in the same sense can there be a formal discipline of existential concretion, a formal existential ethics. Indeed there must be such a discipline.[25]

By way of elaboration, he enumerates a whole series of questions that underscore the difficulty of any knowledge of the singular as such, and the practical impossibility of stating this in terms employing the general concepts of ordinary discourse, only to conclude somewhat disappointingly, " It is clear that we cannot really answer these questions here." [26]

[25] So wie es einerseits keine Wissenschaft vom Individuellen als wirklich individuellen Einzelnen als solchem geben kann und es doch eine allgemeine formale Ontologie des Individuellen gibt, so und in diesem Sinn kann es eine formale Lehre der existentialen Konkretion, eine formale Existentialethik geben und muss es sie geben.—Schriften, p. 240.

[26] Das praktisch dringlichste und schwierigste Problem hinsichtlich einer solchen formalen Existentialethik wäre natürlich die Frage nach der Erkennbarkeit des individuellen Sittlichen und dessen Verpflichtung (wann und wo eine solche Verpflichung vorliegt). Wenn wir sagen: es muss eine Funktion des Gewissens geben, die nicht nur die allgemeinen Normen auf je meine Situation anwendet, sondern die darüber hinaus auch das durch die Situation und die allgemeinen Normen noch nicht eindeutig Erschlossene, gerade je von mir individuell zu Tuende als solches erfasst, dann haben wir zwar eine wesentliche Grundfunktion des Gewissens genannt, die meistens von der üblichen scholastischen Ethik übersehen wird, wir haben aber noch nicht erklärt, wie diese Individual- bzw. Existentialfunktion des Gewissens zustande kommt. Es wäre da zu fragen: Wie weiss der Einzelne überhaupt von sich als dem einmalig Einzelnen? Wie ist eine solche Erkenntnis denkbar, obwohl

In another context, he comes to grips with the problem again and gives an indication of the approach he has in mind. His ontological reasoning, as we have seen, has led him to affirm that a highly individual obligation is uniquely determined for each human being by Almighty God. How can such an individual obligation be scientifically described? Father Rahner states the problem, and then proposes his solution as follows:

One can naturally say, and this objection is to be expected, that when we have this *individuum ineffabile* who is not a mere case of the universal and falls under a particular determined obligation, then this individual, as well as the obligation itself, is conceptually just as *ineffabile*, and therefore cannot be expressed in any kind of imperative, because even imperatives employ universal concepts. But here we must make a distinction. It is true, as the objection states, that an imperative statement cannot direct an individual in his individuality in the way in which concepts and their corresponding regulatory obligations can represent the universal both in itself and as applied to a determined individual. But an imperative, like a gesture pointing to "this here," has a unique relation to the individual as such. . . . Since the imperative actually contains a pointing gesture . . . it can indicate for us an obligation that is in itself unique.[27]

sie grundsätzlich nicht adäquat die Erkenntnis einer gegenständlichen, satzhaften Reflexion sein kann? Wie ist die Frage zu stellen und zu beantworten, wenn und insofern dieses Individuelle nicht die Individualität meines Seins und meines schon frei gewirkten Zustandes ist, sondern die individuelle Einmaligkeit eines von mir erst noch zu Tuenden? Wie kann dieses individuelle Künftige auch als Gesolltes erkannt werden? Wie sieht diese (sittliche) Notwendigkeit aus, die in der Zukommenden Geschichte und an ihr selbst hervortritt? Es ist klar, dass wir hier all diese Fragen nicht wirklich beanworten können.—*Ibid.*, pp. 240-241.

[27] Man könnte natürlich sagen (dieser Einwand ist zu erwarten): Es mag dieses "individuum ineffabile" geben, das nicht blosser Fall eines Allgemeinen ist, es mag sein, dass diesem so verstandenen Einzelnen auch ein gewisser Sollenscharakter zukommt, aber (das ist der Einwand) dieser ist dann begrifflich notwendig ebenso "ineffabile" wie das, dessen Sollenscharakter er ist, und dieser kann dann auch nicht in einem Imperativ ausgesprochen werden, weil auch ein solcher mit allgemeinen Begriffen arbeitet. Hier ist jedoch zu unterscheiden. Richtig an dem Einwand ist, dass auch ein Imperativ das Einzelne und seine Einmaligkeit nicht so direkt ausspricht und anzielen kann, wie Begriffe (und die mit ihnen gebildeten Aussagesätze und Sollensnormen) das Allgemeine in sich und das Allgemeine in einem bestimmten

Such a "pointing gesture," in Father Rahner's opinion, is effected by the internal workings of the Holy Spirit on man, and can be discerned by his conscience if this functions according to the rule for discerning spirits.

The " science " of individual ethics, in this understanding, does not permit a scientific judgment of the morality of an action placed by any individual. All it does is make general, or universal, or " essentialist " statements that are purportedly true of individual cases, and therefore is in precisely the same category as the traditional ethics it proposes to supplant. Scientific knowledge, in Father Rahner's system, does not tell the individual whether his action is morally right or wrong; rather conscience does this, and it does so with assurance only when properly reinforced by an " art." Instead of the emphasis being on prudence, however, as in the Thomist solution to the problem of ethical individuality, this art is now identified as the art of discerning spirits, following the teaching of the *Spiritual Exercises* of St. Ignatius Loyola.[28] Thus Father Rahner's moral theology becomes a mixture of casuistry, with conscience looking to universal and essentialist norms and applying them to individual cases, and a type of mysticism, with conscience harkening to the movements of the Holy Spirit and discern-

---

Einzelnen aussagen können. Aber ein Imperativ hat doch (ähnlich wie eine Geste, ein Hinweis auf ein " Dieses *da* ") eine eigentümliche Beziehung zu dem Einzelnen als solchem. . . . Anders gesagt, weil der Imperativ doch jenen Hinweisegestus an sich hat . . . darum kann der Imperativ uns hier für den Willen und das Sollen des Einmaligen stehen.—*Das Dynamische,* pp. 20-21.

[28] See Father Rahner's essay in *Ignatius,* ed. Friedrich Wulf, (Würzburg: 1956) entitled " Die Ignatianische Logik der existentiellen Erkenntnis," pp. 345-405. The mention of the *Spiritual Exercises* in this context is not to be construed as any kind of disapproval of this masterpiece of spirituality on the part of the present writer. We say this in anticipation of the criticism of some who would note the comparisons here made between St. Thomas, Suarez, and St. Ignatius, and conclude that this study is merely the prolongation of a long-standing feud between Dominicans and Jesuits. To counteract such an attitude we would observe that Father Rahner's thought has been made accessible to English readers largely through the efforts of a Dominican, Father Cornelius Ernst (see pp. 170-181), while the most articulate spokesmen for an authentic Thomism in recent times have been American Jesuits.

ing God's "pointing gestures" as these successively establish its moral imperatives.[29]

As opposed to this understanding, if the discernment of spirits is conceived as something discontinuous with the general norms of moral theology and the virtue of prudence, then the danger of subjectivism becomes serious. How delicate this balance may be is illustrated by a recent study which attempts to apply Father Rahner's theory to discerning vocations to the religious and lay states.[30] Here the author elaborates in detail what appear to him to be the practical consequences of Rahner's position, explaining how awareness of God's "pointing gestures" can be detected by feelings of peace, joy and consolation in the soul, by a "thematic experience of transcendence," and by other internal symptoms.[31] He is at pains to emphasize, moreover, that the individual imperatives which are the major concern of existential ethics cannot be scientifically established, nor even reached by a reasoning process.[32] They must

[29] It might be helpful here to contrast Father Rahner's analysis with that of St. Thomas. For Father Rahner, the rule of practical reason for the individual is his own conscience, whereas God's plan for him is known through the direct action of the Holy Spirit on him which is discerned by conscience as endowed with some type of charismatic art. For St. Thomas, the rule of practical reason for the individual is known by conscience in a preliminary way as the natural power of judgment furnishing the least refined norm of practical reason, while it is known more accurately with the assistance of prudence, both the acquired and the infused virtue. The divine plan for the individual, manifested to him through the Holy Spirit, is known by various charisms or *gratiae gratis datae*, more proximately by the Gift of Counsel, which in this context may be regarded as a supernatural refinement of infused prudence, and also by other Gifts and virtues, principal among which must be enumerated the Gift of Wisdom. St. Thomas, moreover, connects the virtues and the Gifts with the Beatitudes and the Fruits of the Holy Spirit to give a full account of the way in which graces perfect the individual soul in both its moral and its mystical life. This explanation, it seems to us, is not only fuller but also more in accord with the theological tradition of the Fathers than that of Father Rahner. One noteworthy shortcoming under which Father Rahner's theory labors is that in his view of God's "imperatives" the distinction is lost between counsel and precept, and the obligation of law is accorded some type of ontological status that is extremely difficult to account for.

[30] John D. Gerken, S. J., *Toward a Theology of the Layman*, New York: Herder and Herder, 1963.

[31] *Ibid.*, p. 138.   [32] *Ibid.*, p. 131.

be subjectively experienced, can only be known to the one experiencing them, and nonetheless constitute ultimate norms for the actions of the individual.

We can indeed grant with this author that in such personal decisions as those of a vocation in life, the element of personal experience and inclination, and even of the supernatural work of God in the soul, must play a large part in a man's *prudential* decision. Yet this decision remains one of Christian prudence, assisted by gifts of grace. The theology of St. Thomas as traditionally developed was designed to establish a careful balance between objective and subjective elements in the formation of this prudential decision. It is not clear how the author maintains this balance, nor how Father Rahner's analysis provides a sufficient criterion on which such a balance could be based.

DOCTRINAL IMPORTANCE

This then is the innovation that Father Rahner would introduce into traditional moral theology to preserve the good present in situation ethics, and to apply the fruits of phenomenology and existentialism to the development of theological science. The mere statement of the doctrine, not hitherto available for American readers, may provide those engaged in teaching moral theology the opportunity to form their own judgment of its value and importance. To whatever that judgment may be, we should like to add the following reflections by way of personal comment.

Existential ethics, as a serious attempt to investigate the morality of individual action, is not without its value. This value, however, is somewhat qualified, insofar as its importance lies more in the assistance it gives the expert attempting to work out a theology of individual action than it gives the student seeking a general orientation, usually within a particular theological system. With respect to students of theology, moreover, the value of existential ethics in their intellectual formation is relative to their background and various schools with which they are conversant. In German-speaking countries, for example, where a rationalist neo-scholasticism is still dominant and where Thomism is not actively taught in universities and seminaries, the correctives offered by existential ethics to the doctrine currently taught are probably intelligible and even intellectually satisfying to students. In American seminaries and universities, on the other hand, where a resurgence of authentic Thomism has eliminated many of the errors against which existentialism inveighs, the doctrine is correspondingly of limited educational importance.

Furthermore, the general attempt being made on the Continent to cross-breed existentialism and phenomenology with neo-scholasticism offers only a temporary solution to the basic problem. The resulting doctrine, as is clear to those acquainted with the two sources from which it draws inspiration, is acceptable neither to the modern thinker nor to those expert in traditional doctrine. Ultimately it leads to an anti-systematic eclecticism which could in turn reject the fundamentals of moral science taught by the Church.

In this matter, it would seem, the experience of recent history should warn against any such eclectic and arbitrary development of traditional doctrine. In Germany and Austria particularly, attempts have been made continually during the past two centuries to overthrow scholastic syntheses and replace them by something "modern" that would be more acceptable to non-Catholic thinkers. Such an inspiration was behind the efforts of Georg Hermes to apply the rationalism of Kant towards demonstrating the truths of Catholicism, just as it urged Anton Günther to elaborate a Christian Hegelianism by which he hoped to prove the truths of supernatural religion. Both men, motivated by scholarly and priestly zeal though they were, fell into errors which were corrected by the First Council of the Vatican. German higher criticism, as is well known, led to the heresy of modernism as soon as it was applied to traditional doctrines. The "new theology" against which *Humani Generis* was directed is likewise traceable in its intellectual foundations to the existentialism of Kierkegaard and Heidegger.[33]

Against all of these efforts, recent Popes have repeatedly urged a return to Thomism as the safest way to avoid error and to incorporate worthwhile advances in modern thought.[34] But this must be an authentic Thomism which respects source materials and intelligently applies them in a modern context. Where such Thomism has not been zealously pursued, there has been continual ferment and, not infrequently, unorthodoxy resulting in ecclesiastical condemnation. A recent writer, commenting on the program of Thomistic revival farsightedly inaugurated by Leo XIII, remarks on the vicissitudes that this revival has thus far undergone:

Historically speaking, the program of Pope Leo XIII has never been universally implemented in Catholic colleges, universities and seminaries. Not even the ardent efforts of St. Pius X were able to effect this. Until this program is really attempted in a thorough manner, there will always be zealous priests who react against what they only half understand. Reactions against Thomism in the past half century have always been to a pseudo-Thomism, a half understood St. Thomas.[35]

Although such reactions have been common in Europe, on the whole Thomism has been quite successful here in America. In fact, the Church's " coming to age " in the United States has produced a situation where intellectual leadership in Thomistic thought is gradually being assumed in this country. The time seems to have passed, for example, when American students had to learn all of the errors of Kant to pursue a

---

[33] See the foregoing essay in this volume by A. D. Lee, O. P., " Thomism and the Council," pp. 459-479.

[34] *Ibid.*, pp. 469 ff.

[35] James A. Weisheipl, O. P., " The Revival of Thomism: An Historical Survey," *Programmata Scholarum et Status Personalis*, Aquinas Institute of Philosophy and Theology (River Forest, Illinois), 1962-1963, p. 48. Four centuries ago, Cajetan had much the same comment to make: " We must proceed very carefully in this consideration, lest, departing from the excellence of Aristotle and St. Thomas, we should fall victim to our own imaginings, and coin the new because we do not understand the old."—*In Secundam Secundae*, q. 129, a. 1, n. 2.

course in neo-scholastic philosophy. It would be a step backward, in such a situation, to embark on a program of teaching which would reflect the confusing development of rationalism, idealism, phenomenology and existentialism, in order to uncover the small " kernel of truth " present in these doctrines. The substantial progress already made in the United States towards reinstating authentic Thomism would be poorly sacrificed for such dubious intellectual gain.

Some of course will say that to date American theologians have been very sterile, and that most of the new movements in theology are of European origin. Granted that this is true, it does not follow that Americans will become creative simply by adopting new ideas in uncritical fashion. Rather such ideas ought to stimulate them more vigorously to pursue the road pointed out by the Holy See, the renewal of Thomism through concern with contemporary problems and modern science.

The Second Vatican Council will certainly stimulate such efforts. Its work will furnish a sound guide, but the interpretation of its work provided by a press which naturally stresses the elements of innovation, while neglecting the elements of continuity, must be carefully evaluated. This journalism, however, will not be without its influence on university and seminary students. In view of the resulting interest in such innovations, it would be unwise to slight new theories and thereby impose a type of censorship on young, inquiring minds. But it would be an even more serious error to convey to them the impression, for example, that existential ethics represents a great forward advance in moral theology that will eventually supercede traditional doctrine. This innovation, apart from the corrective it offers to a rationalist neo-scholasticism, adds little to a Thomistic understanding of the human act in its existent singularity.

WILLIAM A. WALLACE, O. P.

The New Catholic Encyclopedia
Catholic University of America
Washington, D. C.

FAITH, FREEDOM IN THOUGHT
AND PUBLICATION

༄

"THE act of the believer does not terminate in the article of faith as such but in the reality it expresses." [1] Academically aloof as this statement may sound, its implications bear directly upon the living experience of faith itself and the current lively state of theological thought, discussion, and publication. The statement touches upon the essential nature of faith itself, as well as upon the bearing of human thought on the exercise of faith. One instance of the exercise of human understanding with and under faith is, of course, theology. Taken either as formal, scientific theology or simply as thought about the truths of faith, theology is a consequence of faith. "Actually there can be no question of whether or not theology is necessary. For all men theologize. The only question worth asking is whether the theology that exists is good or bad, true or false, complete or incomplete." [2]

Men, being men, communicate their theology. Publication is a particular form of communication which, because it is both public and permanent, has far-reaching significance in the Church of God. Theological publication may be classified briefly as either technical or general. The first implies the circulation of specialized research of theologians in academic and professional journals. The second refers to works for newspapers, consumer magazines or trade books. This latter form may be quite serious or popularized; it may be done by a professional theologian or by anyone inclined to express himself about the faith.

---

[1] "Actus autem credentis non terminatur ad enuntiabile sed ad rem." *S. T.*, II-II, q. 1, a. 2 ad 2.

[2] Journet, Charles, *The Wisdom of Faith*. (Newman, Westminster, 1952), 45.

From an admirable concern for the spirit of renewal in the Church today, two attitudes regarding communication of Catholic truth have gained wide acclaim and acceptance. One is that the Gospel message cannot be confined nor conveyed within any one conceptual system. The other is that pre-publication censorship of theological writings should be abandoned. Both touch upon the question of faith, its human expression, and its communication; both are a call for a new freedom. These attitudes provide good reason for an examination of the real issues involved in faith's search for understanding and expression.

I. The Essence of Faith

The distinctive character of theological faith is outlined by the First Vatican Council as:

. . . a supernatural virtue by which we believe those things revealed by God to be true, not because of the intrinsic truth of these realities as perceived by the natural light of reason, but because of the authority of God revealing, Who can neither deceive nor be deceived.[3]

In this formulation the twofold orientation of faith is made clear: it terminates in the realities revealed by God; it is motivated by the authority of God revealing. The relationship between the terminative and the motive object of faith is also made clear: faith assents to what God reveals as true, because it is motivated by the authority of God revealing. Thus it is not the intrinsic evidence of that to which faith assents that brings about this termination; it is exclusively the authority of God revealing.

Because the formal motivation of faith's assent and the basis of its certitude is not intrinsic evidence, but solely the

---

[3] " (Hanc vero fidem . . . Ecclesia catholica profitetur), virtutem esse supernaturalem, qua, Dei aspirante et adiuvante gratia, ab eo revelata vera esse credimus, non propter intrinsecam rerum veritatem naturali rationis lumine perspectam, sed propter auctoritatem ipsius Dei revelantis, qui nec falli nec fallere potest." *Conc. Vat. I*, sess. III, c. 3, *Denz.* 1789.

divine authority, the terminative object of faith is neither clearly seen, nor rationally known. Faith as such implies not vision, not science, not understanding, but simple assent. Thus the relationship of faith to its motive object is decisive. As totally supernatural and gratuitous faith confers the basic capacity (*posse*) to adhere to its motive object; it bestows the otherwise unattainable power to elicit a judgment of assent based upon the authority of God revealing. Truly it is the *initium, radix, fundamentum* of the supernatural life.[4] As a supernatural perfection of intelligence, faith has its specific character in the power to adhere to the word of God revealing; it does not make its own motivation evidential: *Credimus Deum et credimus Deo*. Primarily by reason of its motive object, faith is a theological virtue, a virtue uniting man to God directly as its end and object. The motivating object of faith first puts man in contact with God as He is in Himself. Thus this motivating object is itself also terminative. We do believe *God* and thus believe in the things of God. God revealing is the primary termination of faith; assent to the word of God revealing mediates the acceptance of the truths God reveals. So significant, then, is this motivation and primary termination of faith, that one might say, by way of hyperbole, that the content of the purely terminative object is relatively unimportant. An intrinsic order of intelligibilty is, of course, present within and among the truths revealed by God; but this is not faith's first concern, nor its motive. Thus faith does not assent to the mystery of the Blessed Trinity because of the intelligibility of the processions of intelligence and of love, but exclusively because God has revealed a Trinity of Persons. Faith does not treasure the sacramental system because of its consistency with the theme of the Incarnate Redemption, but simply because it is revealed by God.

The primacy of faith's motive object must be emphasized. This, however, does not mean that faith's termination in definite truths is not essential. Faith is the elevation of man's

---

[4] Cf. *Conc. Trid*, sess. VI, c. 8, *Denz*. 801.

intellect; it does involve the exercise of intelligence upon the specific truths revealed. By way of clarification, a twofold exercise of intelligence in connection with faith should be distinguished. One pertains to faith itself; the other proceeds with faith or under faith.

II. Faith and Understanding

The existence and manner in which God has proposed the truths of faith make plain that the exercise of faith involves the human mode of the mind's operation; for God has revealed Himself by employing *human concepts* to communicate and to signify the *divine realities*. It is true that the divine mysteries themselves are not confined within these human terms, nor is their proper intelligibility and intrinsic evidence manifested through such terms. It is true as well that faith assents to the revealed realities as they are in themselves, by reason of its motive object. But the conceptual or verbal expressions of these realities, whether in sacred Scripture or in articulated formulae of the Church, are not excluded from faith. There is mediation here, as there is in other intellectual experiences. Through these concepts and expressions the realities which faith accepts are truly signified. It is because the realities transcend these media that faith is faith, not vision. But faith is concerned with something definite; it must be directed to certain explicit truths.[5] The expression of the realities to which it assents is not totally unrelated to the realities themselves. While faith is supra-rational, it is not irrational; it remains a kind of knowledge and involves some basic thought. The very restlessness and obscurity in the act of faith suggested by St. Augustine's " *Cum assensione cogitare*," indicates that there is a pondering in the exercise of faith. It is a pondering upon the realities as expressed by the concepts and expressions through which they are present to faith's assent. While faith's firmness rests upon its adherence to its unique motive, the experience of faith's obscurity and

[5] Cf. *S. T.* II-II, q. 2, a. 5.

restlessness indicates the exercise of thought upon its term through the inadequate concepts signifying the term. The pondering of faith is characterized by the inadequacies of the concepts involved, not only with respect to the divine realities, but also with respect to their acceptation by the human mind. By the nature of the case the concepts are analagous: open to a variety of levels of understanding, subject to linguistic or historical nuances. There is, then, an exercise of intelligence involved in faith itself; it is not vision or clear understanding, but a kind of groping, a disquieting experience which the intellect seeks to overcome.

III. Understanding With or Under Faith

In addition to the exercise of thought within the dynamics of faith itself, other intellectual experiences are immediately consequent upon faith. These experiences take their particular forms, on the supernatural level, from the divinely constituted magisterium of the Church with its charismatic assistance, and the Gifts of the Holy Spirit perfective of the intellect of the just man; and on the natural level, from theology, whether as a formal habit or simply as reflective acts of the believer.

All of these phenomena look to faith itself as their reason for being. While faith itself consists essentially in its divinely motivated simple assent, it does involve some thought about the truths which are its terminative object. It is through this thought that faith has its experience of obscurity and inadequacy with regard to divine mysteries. Because the connatural orientation of intellect to understanding cannot rest in such obscurity, the mind seeks to go further, to attain some sort of understanding of the truths to which faith assents. The inherent obscurity of faith initiates the quest for understanding; all of the intellectual experiences mentioned above thus arise from the very nature of faith. The existence of these experiences evoke again the question of the delicate balance involved within the core of faith itself.

As any intellectual act, the act of faith terminates, not in its concepts, in its propositions or articles, but in the reality these signify. But faith is a unique kind of knowledge, an infallible assent to truth because of its motive object. It is in no way based upon intrinsic evidence, yet it is absolutely certain. The basic understanding—in the sense of the assent to definite truths—the pondering, the obscurity, the restlessness involved in faith are directed towards its terminative object. Something of the latter is signified in the propositions, yet the evidence of the truths is not made manifest. Within the intrinsic structure of faith, it is the motive object that keeps faith's assent firm; that guarantees its termination in the *truth*; that bestows the certitude proper to adherence to truth. This motivation prevents the obscurity, the connatural discomfort of intellect in the absence of intrinsic evidence, from shaking faith's assent. But as long as the truths of faith stand before the intelligence of man through the propositions signifying them, the quest of intelligence, over and above the simple assent of faith, goes on. Herein lies the problem. If the exercise of intelligence should result in misunderstanding, in misrepresentation, in distortion of the meaning of the divine truths, then the very existence of faith would be threatened. For example, an erroneous explanation of a divine mystery which would present a contradiction to a truth held firmly by reason would jeopardize the foundation of faith. The famous double truth theory of the thirteenth century was itself a false attempt to escape such dilemmas. On the other hand, a misrepresentation of one divine mystery might introduce a contradiction to other divine mysteries, as, for example, the Calvinist explanation of the mystery of predestination. The history of heresy is witness to the possibilities of human intelligence distorting the divine truths of faith, and thus threatening faith's existence. If the terminative object of faith is so understood as to involve contradiction in any way, the faith's adherence to its motive object is in danger. The mind can tolerate the obscurity of mystery but it cannot bear contradiction. While the intrinsic intelligibility of mysteries ever remains obscure, nevertheless these mysteries must be accepted as *truths*. And they are truths guaranteed by the divine veracity; nothing unworthy of God can be introduced into their explanation, without thereby threatening faith. For faith rests upon this: that God can neither deceive nor be deceived.

A. *Supernatural Assistance*

Because faith does engage the energies of intelligence, because of the delicate balance within the structure of faith, certain supernatural guarantees and aids are conferred by God as faith's supports. On a communal level God bestows charismatic graces upon His Church. In regard to the proposition of revelation itself, both prophecy and inspiration are such graces. Both include the divine assistance that guarantees the accurate and truthful communication of the divine mysteries. For the preservation and evolution of the understanding of the truths of faith, charismatic aids are bestowed upon the divinely constituted magisterium. One principal role of the magisterium, connected with the formal motive of faith, is to point out that certain truths are indeed revealed by God.[6] Another is to interpret the meaning of divine revelation as proposed in Sacred Scripture.[7] It pertains also to the magisterium to propose divine mysteries in formulae which are always accurate and adequate expressions of these truths.[8]

Such formulae are, not merely the negative rejection of what is contradictory to divine truth and unworthy of God's revelation, but also the positive expression of something of the intelligibility of divine mysteries.[9] The magisterium exists with its divine assistance to overcome, to the degree possible, the inadequacy of human concepts both with regard to the

---

[6] Cf. *Denz.* 1792.

[7] Cf. *Denz.* 786, 1788.

[8] Cf. *Denz.* 1800.

[9] The formulation and proposal are not always exhaustive nor even, absolutely speaking, most apt; place is left for clarification, development, and expression more appropriate to particular needs of the faithful.

intrinsic divine realities in themselves, and with regard to the variable significance of these concepts to the human mind. Thus by proposing what is truly revealed, by formulating the expression of divine truths, by authentically interpreting the sense of revelation, the magisterium teaches and directs the posture of intelligence towards the terminative object of faith. In all of these functions the charismatic aids remain with the Church in order to guide the exercise of intelligence in such a way as to preserve the truths of faith and the delicate balance between the motive and terminative objects.

On a personal level, the Gifts of the Holy Spirit—wisdom, understanding, knowledge, counsel—provide the just man with the pledge of another kind of assistance to faith. One reason for the existence of such gifts is to overcome the imperfection of faith. This does not mean, of course, that the essential obscurity in faith can ever be removed; nor does it mean that the gifts confer upon man a contact with God, the motive object of faith, that is more perfect than that conferred by faith itself. The imperfection of faith that is overcome is rather that attendant upon the mediation of human concepts in the exercise of faith. Through the gifts the just man is assured of the special assistance of the Holy Spirit in all that is necessary for salvation.[10] The Holy Spirit, according to the gifts of knowledge, moves the just man to value judgments of the transcendence of God over all that can be signified by the human terms in which revelation is proposed or with which faith's assent is involved. The Holy Spirit quells the restlessness and guides the pondering of intelligence with the assurance that the divine mysteries are true, no matter what specious appearances are alleged against them.[11] Thus a guarantee, a direction, a protection is given to the energies of intelligence through the gifts, in order to safeguard and make more effective faith's adherence to God's truth. Unlike the assistance to the Church, however, the experience of the gift's

[10] Cf. *S. T.*, II-II, q. 8, a. 4 ad 1, ad 3; q. 45, a. 5.
[11] Cf. *ibid.*, q. 8, a. 2; a. 4, ad 2.

operations as such is incommunicable; as supernatural, it is not even certifiable by the recipient. But the general purpose of these gifts is an assurance of the special divine assistance for the strengthening of the faith, and points to the necessity of such a safeguard.

B. *Theology*

Theology is the exercise of human intelligence upon the truths of faith. While rooted in faith and proceeding under faith, theology remains entitatively natural. Does this exercise of intelligence have or, indeed, need to have any such guarantees as those bestowed upon the magisterium and upon the just man?

Neither the magisterium itself nor the gifts of the Holy Spirit are irrelevant to this question. The theologian is a member of the Church; he may also be in the state of grace. However, the charismatic assistance promised to the magisterium is not given to the theologian as such, but to the Church teaching, to the supreme pontiff and the college of bishops. Since the principles of theology are the truths of faith, the theologian is guided by the magisterium and thus profits by the assistance given to it. But this assistance is not given formally to his discursive efforts. Moreover, part of the labor of the theologian is to explicate and to weigh the significance of declarations by the magisterium; in this sense the functioning of the magisterium is presupposed to his tasks. In another sense, his task is presupposed to that of the magisterium, in that the elaborations of the theologian dispose the matter, as it were, from which the Church teaching may formally and authoritatively elucidate or explicate the truths of faith.

The theologian may be and, in terms of the nature of the theological enterprise, should be in the state of grace. He thus personally profits from the assistance of the gifts of the Holy Spirit. This may even serve to deepen his personal insight into the principles and application of theology and even to extend his vision to broader and more fruitful insights. But such experiences are purely personal; they are formally incommunicable and they cannot of their nature enter into theological discourse. In themselves they are non-discursive judgments, affective in their base. Before entering into theology their import must be translated into formally discursive terms, into the terms of theological science.

Is there then any guarantee or guide for the theological project as such? That some guide or control upon the exercise of intelligence in theology is necessary, is beyond question, precisely because theology is the pursuit of understanding of the truths of faith. Here too, then, the delicate balance between terminative and motive objects of faith must be respected. Thus the First Vatican Council marks out the conditions of theological endeavor: that it be conducted *sedulo, pie et sobrie*. The earnestness of the theologian's quest rests upon the realization of the gravity of faith's role as the beginning, the root, and the foundation of salvation. Its reverence is imposed by the subject of inquiry, truths as guaranteed by the divine truthfulness. Its disciplined attitude rests upon the awareness of its own nature as a service to faith, thus to the faithful and to the Church. This soberness is more than the discipline inherent in other intellectual pursuits. Theology must be constantly aware of its roots in the principles of faith and of its specifying character as a natural discursive inquiry. From its radication in faith it must realize that the truths of revelation are not only incomprehensible, but that they are of the highest level of intelligibility. Intelligence thus needs purification from the limitations placed upon it by its connatural object, the being of sensible reality. It needs to search also for clarification and penetration of the accurate signification of the terms in which the truths are proposed. From faith itself, as well, theology possesses the consciousness of the effects of sin upon intelligence as well as upon the appetites of man. Thus a further need for purification arises. The pursuit of the

---

[12] Cf. *Denz.* 1796.

theologian must then be sober, guarding against the ever present possibility of anthropomorphizing, of error, of blindness, of dullness, and of a tendency to make self-vindication replace dedication to truth. Theology needs safeguards.

Does this mean that it has no freedom; that the theologian's efforts must be conducted in an atmosphere of suspicion, under the eyes of a grand inquisitor? The safeguard that is proper and proportionate to theology as an intellectual discipline is the certitude of truth itself. Since certitude is the firm adherence of the mind to one part of a contradiction without fear that the opposite might be true, the possession of certitude is the source of freedom proper to the intellectual level. Theology has its principles from faith; its distinctive procedures are the work of human intelligence. Both from its principles and from the validity of human intelligence, theology has its own inherent safeguards, the sources both of its certitude and therefore of its freedom.

IV. FREEDOM OF INQUIRY

A. *Faith and Freedom*

The primary discipline regulative of theological inquiry is that of faith itself, for the principles of theology are the truths revealed by God as true. The basic subjective certitude of the theologian, therefore, corresponds to the objective truths of his principles, as guaranteed by God Himself. This has its ramifications upon the investigatory processes of the theologian. He is absolutely sure that no proposition devised by human intelligence, no demonstration formulated, no experimental fact discovered, can be true and at the same time in contradiction to any truth of faith.[13] From this assurance he has a norm: he knows that he can pursue any line of inquiry, confront any position with the assurance that its relation to divine truth can be discovered or its alleged con-

---

[13] Cf. *S. T.*, I, q. 1, a. 8: ". . . Cum enim fides infallibili veritati innitatur, impossible autem sit de vero demonstrari contrarium, manifestum est probationes quae contra fidem inducuntur, non esse demonstrationes, sed solubilia argumenta."

tradiction resolved by the same power of human intelligence that formulated it. Every objection to the truths of faith is devised by human reason; it is answerable by the same reason.

More positively, from faith's adherence to divine truth, the theologian knows that his inquiry into the objective intelligibility of these truths can be fruitful. His inquiries can do more than remove any contradictory sense from the understanding of the divine mysteries. Because these are truths, they do admit of some true understanding. In the realm of the positive function of theology—exegetical, patristic, historical and the like—the theologian is dealing with the very expression of divine revelation. By faith itself he is assured that such expressions are communicative and expressive of truth. Thus the use of valid critical instruments of inquiry will provide a deeper penetration into the true meaning of the expressions of divine revelation. The effective use of critical instruments of research will bring him closer to the intention and determined sense of the terms in which revelation is proposed in Scripture, transmitted by the magisterium, or witnessed by the Fathers. As to the speculative and properly discursive phases of theology, the theologian knows that because the divine truths are truths they have an ontological consistency and an intelligible content. Even while acknowledging the essential obscurity and incomprehensibility of mystery, he knows that he can seek and hope to attain some valid insight into the intrinsic intelligibility of the mysteries, both in themselves and in their cohesive relationships, as well as valid inferences expressing their ramifications. This confidence, this liberty of inquiry, is rooted in the faith's adherence to the principles of theology as *truths*. To the degree, then, that his researches yield an understanding of these mysteries in terms of valid metaphysical concepts, to that degree the theologian is assured that he attains a valid, even if common and analogical, understanding of the truths of faith. Thus the certitude of faith itself guides the theologian and moves him with confident freedom, not only to reject all understanding of

mysteries contradictory to intelligence, but to accept all verifiable understanding as valid expressions of the divine realities he considers. There is yet another facet of the freedom
of inquiry derived from theology's dependence upon faith's
adherence to the reality of revealed truths. This adherence
implies an awareness in the theologian of inadequacy in all
human expressions of incomprehensible mystery. But such an
awareness should not beget a paralyzing fear leading to inertia, or to a stultifying repetition of formulae. Rather it is a
spur to seek freely within the resources of intellect further
ways of manifesting the inexhaustible riches of mystery. Thus,
for example, while the theologian can adopt no position contradictory to the dogmatic pronouncements of the magisterium, he can do much more than repeat them verbatim. He
can seek, whether through the positive or the speculative resources of theology, to achieve further insights. The current
emphasis on the social implications of the Holy Eucharist is
an instance of the fruitful exercise of such freedom. The exhortation of Pius XII to theologians that they intensify their
investigations into the doctrine of the divine indwelling is
another.[14] Faith's assurance of the wealth of being and intelligibility in the divine mysteries, bestows a liberty of inquiry
and expression. The human articulation of the truths of faith,
even by dogmatic definitions, does not exhaust the reality
enunciated; there is always perfectibility, possibility of new emphasis, and insights; thus unending theological inquiry.

B. *Reason and Freedom*

While faith itself indirectly indicates the validity of the intellect's quest for understanding, the theologian also has a norm
of direction in the power of human reason itself. It is stupid,
and totally incompatible with the very nature of theology, for
any theologian to delude himself into a rationalistic attitude.
But given the faith and thus the assurance of the truth of
mysteries, he can with all security conduct his rational inquir-

[14] Cf. *Mystici corporis*, A. A. S., XXXV (1943), 231.

ies. Part of that confidence can come from the proved effectiveness of the instruments of inquiry he employs, and from the transcendental validity of the first principles of human reason. To the degree in which these resources of intelligence are valid, so are the expressions of divine truth which their use yields. This is not to scale down the Gospel message to the confines of a conceptual system. But neither is the theologian condemned by the transcendence of divine revelation to agnosticism or to subjective relativism. The evidence, the verification, the validity with which he knows the resources of human reason to be endowed, enable him to see their positive value for the positive expressions of absolute truths. It is one thing to speak patronizingly about " schools of theology," or the " manualist approach "; it is quite another to speak of the absolute truths of human reason. The validity of any expression of divine truths by the theologian depends in some measure upon the validity of the resources of human reason he employs. If these means are sound, if they are true, then he has certitude and assurance—no matter what his " school " or his method—that his assertions are valid and true (not merely popular or attractive). Thus in his use of reason, the theologian has this safeguard to observe: the need and the power of human intelligence to attain certitude in its own level, and to be aware of its own vindication. He also has this freedom: the freedom to make any assertion about the divine that is defensible by reason. This is so whether there be ques-of the sapiential procedures of the scholastic function of theology or of the critical research of its positive phases. A valid use of reason under faith in theology yields truth; it is defensible, " self-conscious " of its own verification and justification. Thus the use of reason in theology has at hand a safeguard and at once a source of freedom proper to intellectual enterprise: the freedom to seek truth reasonably and to certify its attainment reasonably.

This is not to say that the theologian has freedom to formulate or express only those positions which are demonstrably certain. Such positions are attainable and are verifiable; but by the nature of the case, much of theology's endeavor deals with opinion, tentative suggestions, probabilities. The security theology enjoys rests in part upon the power of reason to certify its own procedures, to recognize and distinguish between areas of certainty and those of probability or opinion. This self-justifying power enables the theologian to be sure with a reflective certitude of the value of his direct investigations. The use of intelligence under faith has as one of its purposes to show how what is revealed is true.[15] The obligation thus imposed is to use intelligence to the full extent of its validity. This includes a consciousness of its own value and of a gradation in its approach to truth. The theologian is freed from the intellectual despair that is nominalism or relativism. He can avoid the mistake of confusing what is probable with what is firmly established. He thus has confidence in his evaluation of the precise force of reason's discoveries. To the degree in which they approach certitude, to that degree the theologian is sure of the value of his service to the manifestation of the truth of faith.

Although not rigidly interpreted nor notably observed by Catholic theologians, ecclesiastical approval of the method, doctrine and principles of St. Thomas Aquinas remains operative.[16] There is current discomfort with this approval and with this one, so called, " conceptual system." Prescinding from the ecclesiastical approval, the theologian need only employ this caution: that whatever " conceptual system " he uses be true in itself. Then it can serve to express the truth of divine mysteries. To observe this caution is concomitantly to enjoy the freedom conferred upon intellect by self-assurance, by its intrinsic verification of the resources it uses. It is not unthinkable that, independent of juridic approval, the thought of St. Thomas Aquinas possesses such an intrinsic criterion. It is not impossible that other speculative resources of intelligence be verifiable by resolution to basic metaphysical principles. But to be worthy of theology's appropriation to its service,

---

[15] Cf. *Quaestiones Quodlibetales,* Quodl. IX, q. 4, a. 3 (ed. Marietti, p. 87).
[16] Cf. *C.I.C.,* can. 1366, 2.

such a demand on reason's processes is indispensable. Accept-
ability, attractiveness, popularity are not themselves the criterion of truth. Unless the theologian has a properly intellectual justification for his discursive endeavors, then he has
neither a safeguard proper to theology nor the freedom of
self-assurance that such a criterion alone can provide.

V. *Pre-publication Censorship*

The theologian has his own proper safeguards within the
very constitutives of his science; they are also a source of freedom. Yet in the current state of affairs he must submit, prior
to publication, to another check: examination of his writings
by ecclesiastical censors. What seems objectionable to those
who would discard the institution of censorship is the restriction of freedom they see in the submission of the product of
the theologian's intelligence to an authority endowed with the
right to accept or reject it. An emphasis upon the authori-
tarian and juridic status of censorship, either by its opponents or by those who exercise it, leads to a misapprehension
of its intrinsic nature. In itself censorship should not be seen
as alien to theology's own " self-control " nor, consequently,
to its freedom.

That any responsible person should reject the need for discipline in theological procedures is inconceivable. The recognition of the true relationship between terminative and motive
objects of faith, the existence of supernatural aids to the exercise of intelligence upon the terminative object, indicate the
demand for control. The true reason for censorship is simply
the need for such control. If censorship be properly exercised
it will be merely a continuation of the discipline inherent to
theology itself.

Both censors and censored share the sources of theology's
discipline and its freedom: the certitude of faith and the validity of human reason. By reason of the former, both are absolutely convinced of the truths of faith as *truths*. Both also
share in the conviction that any exercise of intelligence has
the manifestation of truth as its objective, and the effective

use of the resources of reason as its means. Thus from this point of view no restriction extrinsic to the theological enterprise itself need be involved in censorship. The theologian whose whole endeavor is rooted and grounded in faith is united by this faith with every other theologian, including the censor. The problem arises rather on the level of the effective use of intellect. Neither the theologian nor the censor as such has the guarantees provided by charismatic or personal graces. Again, both recognize the need for some sort of check upon the use of intelligence with and upon the truths of faith. There are two indications in the functioning of censorship: the *nihil obstat* of the censors themselves; the *imprimatur* of the local ordinary. Both have a view to the intrinsic content of the work, and to the opportuneness of its publication.

With regard to content, both the *nihil obstat* and the *imprimatur* are negative indications; neither constitutes an endorsement. What they say is that the product of the intellectual energies of the theologian contains nothing opposed or dangerous to the true understanding of the faith. The proper grounds for this negative judgment are not extrinsic to the safeguards inherent in theology itself. The censors examine a product of human intelligence, supposedly competent. From their own intellectual competence, they must evaluate the adequacy and the accuracy of the work of another mind. In this task they are not allowed to base their judgment upon personal opinions or tastes; they are directed to judge in terms of accepted Catholic doctrine and sound theological truths. What pertains *per se* to the censorship situation, then, is the submission of the work of the theologian to critical evaluation by other competent theologians. Of course, the threat of personal prejudice or of human defectibility influencing the censors is ever present. Such possibilities are neither proper nor intrinsic to the question of censorship, but common factors in human affairs. This is recognized in the restrictions placed upon the censor, and the right conceded to the author to be informed of the reasons for rejection.[17] In itself the evaluation of content by

[17] Cf. *C. I. C.*, can. 1394, 2.

the censors is the same evaluation to which the theologian must submit himself: a critical evaluation of the devices of intellect and thus of their relationship to and expression of the truths of faith.

But if this criterion is available to the theologian himself, why should its use be duplicated by censors? The answer is obvious. While intelligence has its own source of self-assurance, it is also subject to the fallibility consequent upon both the connatural orientation of the intellect, and upon the condition of intelligence in the state of fallen nature. It is true that submission to censorship involves the submission to other fallible intelligences. But the whole of human experience both in the theoretical and the prudential orders favors the advantages for objectivity, accuracy, verification and control through consultation and concerted application to a problem.

The question of the opportuneness of publication also pertains to censorship. In this regard, as well, censorship should be recognized and exercised in a way consistent with theological freedom. The censorship judgment upon technical works intended for specialized audiences should be quite different from the judgment relative to works for general consumption. In the first case, all that the censor need decide, one might say, is upon the evidence of the competence of the author. Such works are by their nature intended for an audience at least of equals. They are meant for professionals. Often they are tentative and guarded, simply because they are research works or approaches to new problems. They are published with the very purpose of submission to the clarifying process of free exchange among professional theologians. In this very process the possibility of error by the individual theologian is acknowledged; he submits his own thoughts with the desire to secure a more effective evaluation of the validity of his investigations. The common effect of other trained minds upon the same area is an assistance towards clarification, towards correction, towards achieving a better expression or more cohesive elaboration, of the truths of faith. Thus by the nature of the case, the theologian, granted the fundamental allegiance to faith and to theology that unites him to his colleagues, should be allowed the widest latitude. The very existence of the professional journal is itself an acknowledgment of the employment of safeguards proper to theology, the search for certitude, and the freedom that such certitude alone provides.

Historically, even in recent times, there have been excesses in censorship in this area. The value of the cry against pre-publication censorship is its recognition of a need for vitality in the theological quest. That quest is necessary, an exigency of faith itself, and a corollary to the divine mandate to teach all men of all times. Unless the theologian has the opportunity of employing the progressively perfected resources of intelligence, his thought and its presentation will be isolated from the mentality of contemporaries. Especially in professional publications the theologian has the media in which to advance new ideas. The milieu of such expression contains theology's own correctives through the critical evaluation of the author's peers. The censors of such works must be continually aware that their task is but an extension of theology's own proper discipline. They must thus recognize the inadequacy of all human expressions of divine truth and the consequent, ever-present possibility of enriching the understanding of mystery. They must be aware of the freedom which the living magisterium allows to theologians who employ any valid resource of reason to manifest the truth of revelation. They must take into account the reluctance of the Church to settle definitively points of purely academic moment. They must also take into account the theologian's own consciousness and expression of the validity of the positions he advances, whether as certainties, as opinions, or as probabilities. All of this amounts to a restriction of the censor's judgment in this type of publication to a minimal acceptance of the *nihil obstat*. The mutual trust of the censor and the theologian in the sources of theology's own discipline and freedom will assure the progress and vitality of theological inquiry. Distrust or the restrictive abuse of censorship in this area can only be damaging to the progress of theology and the communication of divine truth.

When the issue is a trade book or articles for some general consumer media, the censor's judgment must be stricter. Here he takes into account, not only the intrinsic content of the work, but also the fallibility of the uncritical minds of general readers. Another facet of the pre-publication censorship question arises here. In professional works the focus of attention of the censor is upon the theologian's efforts to overcome something of the inadequacy of human terms relative to divine reality. In works for general consumption, the censor's focus is rather upon the inadequacy of human expressions of the faith relative especially to untrained minds. Perhaps what the opponents of censorship imply is that the faithful need no protection and in the name of freedom should be given none. Perhaps the *desideratum* would be the education of the faithful to such a degree that they could themselves make a critical evaluation of any statement by any mind about any truth of the faith. This is a dubious ideal; its realization seems impossible. The existence of the magisterium with its charismatic assistance and the existence of the gifts of the Holy Spirit point to the divine realism about the condition of the faithful. Graces are not given superflously. The very existence of the professional theologian in the Church is also a witness to the care needed in intellect's exercise regarding the truths of the faith.

If the judgment of opportuneness rests upon grounds less calculable than that concerning content, it is still not a curtailment extrinsic to the theologian's own point of view. When a work of general circulation is involved, the theologian's objective is to communicate some truth of the faith for the benefit of the faithful. No responsible theologian would seek to circulate his own tentative positions, his hypothetical inquiries, his sometimes advanced terminology, to an uncritical audience. The exercise of discretion by a theologian other than the author himself is simply the attempt to achieve the same objective as that of the author. It takes into account the possibility of the author's point of view and interest being limited, as well as the actual condition and needs of the faithful. The true role of censorship is not the imposition of an arbitrary obligation; it is an effective supplement to the theologian's own commitment to communicate the truth, resulting from his primary conviction, the certitude of faith itself.

No higher designation can be bestowed upon the theologian than that of "*catholicae veritatis doctor.*" [18] Especially through publication for the generality of the faithful the theologian exercises this office. Aware as he must be of the nature of the adherence to Catholic truth by divine faith, he must accordingly be aware of the responsibility he has. His own employment of theology's intrinsic safeguards in his effort to discern and to communicate the truth should dispose him to see pre-publication censorship neither as an affront nor as an alien influence. It serves no purpose to trace its historical source to the renaissance pope, Leo X, or to allege abuses of the office of censor. There is a true intrinsic relationship of the work of theology with the work of the censor. Like the intrinsic discipline of theology itself, censorship can and is designed to preserve the balance between the terminative and the motive object of faith, to strengthen faith's adherence to the truth. Such a guarantee is necessary; it can assist theology and the communication of its ideas towards a true freedom: the freedom of self-assurance and certitude.

. . . Holy Scripture itself, even though it advises us to believe these great realities before we understand them, will be of no use if you misunderstand it. Every heretic has acknowledged the authority of Scripture; each of them has persuaded himself that he was following Scripture, though in reality he was following his own errors. Such men are heretics, not because they reject Scripture, but because they have not understood it: . . . (St. Augustine, *The Trinity*, Bk. XV, n. 51, PL. XLII, 1098).

THOMAS C. O'BRIEN, O. P.

Dominican House of Studies
   Washington, D. C.

[18] *S. T.*, I, Prol.

THE COUNCIL AND THE MISSIONS

∽

S INCE the announcement of the convening of Vatican
Council II, many books and articles have appeared dealing with *aggiornamento* of the Church and with the
ecumenical movement for reunion with our separated fellow
Christians. In these writings the focus of attention has been
centered principally upon the life and activity of the Church
in the western world. Very little has been written, except in
passing, about the mission apostolate in Africa and Asia. Yet
Pope John XXIII has declared that one of the most pressing
topics will be the spread of the Catholic faith.[1] Elsewhere
he had written, " We have never ceased to give Our most lively
concern to the missionary problem in all its vastness, beauty
and importance." [2]

How are we to explain this apparent neglect? I say ' apparent neglect ' because I am sure that the relative inattention
to the missions in current literature concerned with the Council
is not due to lack of interest or to a deliberate intent to ignore
them. Rather, I believe, it should be attributed to the difficulty
involved in locating the missions properly and accurately within the Church's apostolate in this transitional period in her
history. Despite this difficulty, and even because of it, I shall
attempt to offer some general guidelines for the orientation of
our thought upon the subject of missions today.

There is need for a considerable readjustment of our thinking with regard to foreign missions to bring it up to date. The
political, social, economic, and cultural changes in recent years
have been more rapid and more radical in Africa and Asia than
in the western world. It has become commonplace to hear that
" the age of the missions " is over and that we have embarked
upon a new and as yet unnamed and uncharted era in world-

[1] Pope John XXIII, *Ad Petri Cathedram.* AAS, LI (1959), 511.
[2] Pope John XXIII, *Princeps Pastorum*, AAS, LI (1959), 834.

wide Christianity. Pope Pius XII pointed this out in a significant passage:

In other days the life of the Church, in its visible aspect, extended
its force—especially in those countries of old Europe from which
she spread—toward what could then be called the limits of the
world; today, on the contrary, she presents herself as an exchange
of life and energy between all the members of the Mystical Body
of Christ upon earth.[3]

The significance of this statement for the missions, and indeed
for the life of the entire Church, is far-reaching in its implications.

Not the least of the problems concerning a proper conception
of the foreign mission apostolate is a semantic one, for " missions " and " missionary " are highly equivocal terms. Since,
however, there is no ready terminology to substitute for them,
we are compelled to use them, ambiguous as they are, in referring both to the international apostolate of the colonial period,
which is now all but a thing of the past, and to its radically
changed modern counterpart. This is one of the reasons for
a growing tendency to avoid the use of the term " missions," a
tendency which is not to be regretted, for the term has little
theological significance. In its plural form it entered into use in
the early seventeenth century without any direct or immediate
reference to the theological notion of " mission."

For the past four centuries the foreign mission apostolate has
been generally regarded as a pastoral activity of a small seg-
ment of the Church. Only rarely, and only by relatively few
even in our day, has the possibility been considered of developing its underlying theory as a section of sacred theology.
Moreover, the missions have commonly been presented in terms
of activity, and greater emphasis has been given in missionary
writings to the external, visible activity designed to establish a
visible Christian community. Less frequently have writers
given attention to the internal, invisible, spiritual and supernatural activity leading toward the *aedificatio Corporis Mystici
Christi*. Granted there is no real opposition between these two

---

[3] Pope Pius XII, *Christmas Radio Address*, AAS, XXXVIII (1946), 20.

types of activity, still there is a considerable difference in the mental image evoked and in one's consequent understanding of and outlook upon missions.

The reader will appreciate the significance of this difference if he will see it as comparable to, say, a presentation of the sacraments which sets forth only the visible, tangible elements, as opposed to one which treats of the underlying spiritual reality as well. So much writing about the missions has highlighted the feeding of hungry children, the care of lepers, the nursing of the sick, the building of chapels, hospitals and schools, etc., that the public is left with the impression that the missions deal principally with these matters. Is this a truly balanced and theologically accurate presentation of the mission apostolate?

In this country particularly, missionary propaganda has laid such emphasis on these external activities in the natural order that there is danger of glossing over the deeper truth, that the mission apostolate is the activity whereby the Mystical Body of Christ extends itself throughout the world, incorporating men into its bosom and regenerating them with the divine life of grace. Expressed in these terms, it is readily apparent that it is an activity which is principally spiritual and religious, and in the supernatural order. It is important to keep this well in mind if we would avoid the danger of conceiving the missions as something on a level with mere human and natural undertakings. The fact is that the mission apostolate is and must ever be a divine undertaking, something entirely supernatural in its source as well as in its end. Its problems, therefore, should not be treated as merely human problems capable of a human solution by specialists in the secular sciences.

An accurate and balanced conception and presentation of the missions ought to give both aspects mentioned above, and in the proper order. Here the question of right order is fundamental in thought and in action, and naturally right thinking must precede right action.

Pope John XXIII began his new encyclical *Pacem in terris* by insisting on the necessity of observing the order laid down by God if we would have peace.[4] The need of right order is a basic need in the organization and formation of the new age upon which we have entered. Similarly, we must observe right order in our entire approach, both conceptual and methodological, to " missions " in this new ecumenical era.

It was in connection with the mission apostolate that Pope Pius XI noted that it is always from the world of ideas that the grand directives of action flow. He went on to say that we are living at a time when, more than ever before, it is obvious that all the heroism and sacrifices which accompany missionary work are not enough. In order to reap the fruits of these sacrifices and efforts, there is need of a science to indicate and illuminate the most direct ways, to suggest the most profitable methods and means. The missions, he concluded, cannot and ought not to ignore this characteristic of our times.[5]

The science which should explain, guide and direct the mission apostolate is the sacred science of theology. But there is need for presenting this apostolate in a more explicitly theological manner than is the case at present. Nothing will offer greater hope for mission success than the development of the theology of the missions.

This statement may appear an exaggeration to some active missionaries whose interest is centered upon practical mission methods. To some, theology may appear essentially theoretical and speculative, remote, therefore, from the field of practical missionary endeavor. Yet many of the practical mission problems are fundamentally theological. Their solution demands decision and action dictated by sound theological principles and judgment. However theoretical and speculative it may be in itself, theology thus becomes by its extension and application a matter not simply of intellectual delight and enjoyment, but also a most practical science.

[4] Pope John XXIII, *Pacem in terris*; from text published in the *Catholic Standard*, Washington, D. C., April 19, 1963.

[5] Pope Pius XI, Statement on the opening of the Vatican Missionary Exposition, as quoted in André Seumois, O. M. I., *Introduction à la Missiologie*, Schöneck-Beckenried, Switzerland, 1952, p. 7.

The relationship between sacred theology and the other sciences, since this is of great practical importance for the mission apostolate, must also be examined. The proper relation of sacred doctrine to other fields of interest is thus explained by St. Thomas:

This science can, in a sense, depend upon the philosophical sciences, not as though it stood in need of them, but only in order to make its teaching clearer. For it accepts its principles, not from other sciences, but immediately from God, by revelation. Therefore, it does not depend upon other sciences as upon the higher, but makes use of them as the lesser, and as handmaidens.[6]

The mission apostolate depends not on the will of man, but on the will of God. Therefore, it pertains to theology to determine its principles and to measure the legitimacy of methodology that is to be followed in missionary practice. It is necessary to stress the priority of theology if error is to be avoided, for the activities of the mission apostolate touch also on other fields of interest. If one neglects the normative character of theology, there is danger of being submerged in these other fields. Obviously, the missions touch on Protestant missiology, various forms of religion, sociology, anthropology, social psychology, etc. If major consideration is given to what is proper to these other interests in such a way as to dominate the approach to the subject, then the character of the subject will be changed.

Let us take sociology and anthropology as examples, since the representatives of these sciences have, quite properly, interested themselves in applying the findings of their science to the problems of the mission world or—and this comes almost to the same thing—to the problems of the developing countries. Since one of the fundamental mission problems today is the confrontation of the Church with non-western, even non-Christian cultures, anthropology can gather certain data and facts which will be of much value in the missionary enterprise of the Church. Likewise, because the Church exists in this world, the

[6] *Summa Theologiae*, I, q. 1, a. 5, ad 2.

fulfillment of its pastoral mission requires that the social realities of the world in which it finds itself be taken into account. The Catholic Church, since it is composed of human beings who are members of human societies and live within specific cultures, must have certain relationships with these societies and cultures.

Nevertheless, the Church herself cannot be contained completely within the framework of sociology or anthropology, because it is a supernatural society. The Church is far superior to all other societies, since it is not only human but also divine. It surpasses all other societies as grace surpasses nature. " The Church in its entirety is not found within this natural order, any more than the whole of man is encompassed within the organism of our mortal body." [7]

It is to theology that we must turn to ascertain the mission of the Church in the world. It is theology that must direct and guide the social sciences in the implementation of practical mission methodology. No one will question the need for applying social science to the solution of the problems facing human beings in the mission regions. What requires at least equal or even greater stress is the absolute need of theological guidance and direction both for a proper conception of the Church's mission apostolate and for the proper determination of mission methods.

For example, anthropology cannot fully comprehend the complicated question of the adaptation of the Church to non-Christian cultures. Culture by its very nature belongs to the temporal sphere; social anthropology is thus also limited to the temporal sphere, whereas the Church exists in both the temporal and eternal realms. Both theology and anthropology are needed in working out the complicated task of adapting the Church to various cultures, but with the proper subordination of the natural to the supernatural science. The problem of adaptation is principally a theological one, and therefore theology should guide the adaptation with the assistance of anthropology.

[7] Pope Pius XII, *Mystici Corporis*, AAS, XXXV (1943), 223.

Perhaps there are those who will think the need for theology to guide and direct the Church's mission apostolate is quite obvious. The fact is, however, that theological investigation of missionary problems is still sadly inadequate. Perhaps nothing more clearly illustrates this than the experience of Father Joseph Schmidlin, who was unable to find a single author who had ever attempted a systematic discussion or investigation of the *finis missionis*. He himself had to blaze a new trail in this matter " of such fundamental importance for all missionary practice." [8] It is a matter for surprise, to say the least, that only in our present century has there been any attention directed *ex professo* to such an obviously important point, especially since all are aware that *finis specificat media*.

In any case, the representatives of the sacred sciences (dogmatic, moral, historical, scriptural, canonical) ought to enlarge their study of the Church to include the Church throughout the world.

The immense enterprise which has traditionally been known as " the foreign missions " began in a period when the word " Christendom " represented a limited and fairly well defined part of the inhabited world, and when for centuries the Church had been almost completely isolated from the other great religions and cultures of the world. Christian theology and the institutions of the Church were shaped by the experiences of this self-enclosed existence in the western world. Christendom was a largely isolated and self-contained enclave of humanity; the foreign missions were a breaking-out of that enclave into a strange new world.

While there was an enormous expenditure of energy, zeal and material resources for the missions, there was little serious attention given to them by theologians. They were mainly concerned with the Reformation and its consequences in Christendom. Even if they had done so, it would still be necessary for theologians today to painfully rethink many things which their predecessors took for granted. This is being realized and acted

[8] Joseph Schmidlin, *Catholic Mission Theory*, trans. Matthias Braun, S. V. D.: Techny, Illinois, 1931, p. 254.

on in the larger field of *human* ecumenism which the mission apostolate implies.

Nothing will suffice save a radical rethinking of the nature of the Church's missions. Such a rethinking must include both a realistic understanding of the new facts with which missions have to deal, and a humble return to the source of the missions in revelation. This would be necessary even if, in the past, theologians had attended sufficiently to the mission apostolate; for it is necessary for the Church " to look to the present, to the new conditions, and new forms of life introduced into the modern world." [9]

What is the mission of the Church? Our Saviour, as He hung upon the cross, not only satisfied the justice of the Eternal Father, but He also won for us an unending flow of graces. It was possible for him personally, immediately, to impart those graces to men; but He wished to do so through a visible Church that would be formed by the union of men. The Church was established precisely for this task, to spread the kingdom of Christ throughout the world and to afford all men a share in His salutary redemption.[10]

The Church's mission is primarily spiritual and religious, a thing of the supernatural order. But the Church's solicitude for the eternal welfare of man implies no indifference to his temporal condition. As Pope John XXIII wrote in *Mater et Magistra*:

Hence, although Holy Church has the special task of sanctifying souls and making them partake of supernatural goods, she is also solicitous for the needs of men's daily life, not merely those having to do with bodily nourishment and the material side of life, but those also that concern prosperity and culture in all its many aspects and historical stages.[11]

Thus, although the Church is, from her divine mission, primarily concerned with the spiritual and not with the temporal,

---

[9] Pope John XXIII, Allocution on opening of Second Vatican Council, AAS, LIV (1962), 794.

[10] Pope Pius XI, *Rerum Ecclesiae*, AAS, XVIII (1926), 65.

[11] Pope John XXIII, *Mater et Magistra*, AAS, LIII (1961), 402.

it nevertheless fosters the temporal prosperity of individuals and society almost as effectively as if it had been instituted for that purpose alone.

Misunderstandings or even erroneous opinions can exist concerning the precise nature of the Church's mission and the role of missionaries. Couturier refers to the temptation by which the missionary may be inclined to explain all the difficulties in his way by attributing them to cultural factors that make the people impervious to Christian teaching. For example, he may deem it impossible to Christianize the people as a whole, or a section of them, as long as they are burdened with this or that institution, whether it is polygamy, or an unsatisfactory wage system, or slum-dwellings. He may imagine therefore that all his efforts should be directed to that one point, and that only after he has overcome this obstacle will he be able to preach the Gospel. It cannot be doubted that " inhuman " conditions of life can hinder access to the Christian life; but that does not justify the conclusion that " humanization " must precede evangelization.[12]

As Maritain points out, we must resist the temptation arising from the lure of temporal advantage to abandon what is eternal; to abandon it, that is to say, if not in theory, at least in practice by allowing ourselves to lose sight of it more or less completely. We should not allow ourselves to be carried away by the flux of *becoming* when in fact we should be mastering it by the spirit.[13]

The restatement of the relationship between the sacred science of theology and the other sciences in reference to the mission apostolate seems useful and indeed even necessary, for we are facing new situations and so have need of clear insight and proper orientation with regard to them. There is need of clarifying basic principles and the whole matter of a proper approach to the study of the missions and to missionary practice.

[12] Charles Couturier, S. J., *The Mission of The Church* (Helicon Press: Baltimore, 1960), p. 105.

[13] Jacques Maritain, *Religion et Culture* (Desclee de Brouwer: Paris, 1946), p. 51.

Aristotle notes that the beginning is thought to be more than half the whole, and by this he meant that the principles of a given science or art are of great importance for its subsequent development.[14] If the principles are erroneous, it follows that the whole subsequent science or art will be erroneous; if the principles are true, then there is solid foundation for what follows. It is essential, therefore, that we adhere firmly to right principles and accept the guidance of the proper science, since this will be of such great importance for the future global apostolate. One cannot be too careful in this, since the least initial deviation is multiplied later a thousandfold, as the Philosopher says.[15]

Theology—and in using the term I am speaking of the sacred science in its modern development as it takes into account the findings of the social sciences as well as new developments in the catechetical and liturgical fields—must have priority in directing the mission apostolate in the future. In the past it has played far too small a role.

What part of theology should undertake the study of the global apostolate? The answer to this has been suggested in what already has been said about the Church and her mission. But because of the manner in which missions were conceived in the past, it might have been difficult for theologians of the past to answer this question. For some centuries the outlook has been a narrow one. On the one hand, there has been the tendency to regard the foreign missions as a fairly isolated part of the Church's mission, existing somewhere out on the periphery of things and undertaken by a minority group of separate, professional missionaries, who were male, clerical, religious foreigners. Until fairly recent times little thought was given to participation in this apostolate by religious women or even by laymen, whether foreigners or indigenous (apart from lay catechists). The purpose of missions, too, was expressed in too narrow a manner: the propagation of the faith and the salvation of souls. It must be conceded that there was little need for further development of theology in the light of this view of

---

[14] *Ethics* (I, 1098b).   [15] *On the Heavens*, I, 271b, 10.

the missions. Perhaps that is why only one theologian ever treated the missions in a major theological work, and he placed them under *De Fide*.[16]

Today, there is an increasingly clear realization that the *mission* (and therefore the "missions") was entrusted to the entire Church, not to religious orders and mission societies, as was largely assumed without challenge in the past.[17] Moreover, it is realized that the mission apostolate must be comprehensive and not merely an apostolate of spiritual conquest. The qualitative aspect of catholicity, so neglected in the past four centuries of mission history, is also beginning to receive the attention it deserves. Some have begun scholarly study of non-Christian cultures, in order that the good and truth contained in them be incorporated into the Mystical Body of Him who holds the kingship and primacy over all creation.

In a word, it has come to be realized that, as the establishment of the Church is the principal factor in missionary practice, so too the Church is central in mission theology. Therefore, ecclesiology is that part of theology which has the closest bearing on the mission apostolate. This is not to be taken in an exclusive sense, however, for the theological foundation of the *mission*, as an essential aspect of the life of the Church, is also to be seen in the revelation of the one true God, in our knowledge of the universal salvific will of God, in the universal redemptive mission of Christ, and so on.

The mission theology, which is emerging, is largely ecclesiological. The present ecclesiology requires considerable development in order to interpret satisfactorily the Church's global apostolate in the light of new and complex circumstances. The post-Tridentine ecclesiology, being too apologetic, too polemical, and hardly at all concerned with the foreign missions, is not sufficient for this purpose.

[16] Brancati, Laurentius Cardinal, *Commentaria in Tertium Librum Sententiarum.* Tomus Tertius, pars 2a, Romae 1673. Disputationes XVII, XVIII, XIX.

[17] That the Church, and not religious orders or societies, has received the divine mandate was strongly emphasized in an Instruction of the Sacred Congregation of the Propagation of the Faith in 1929. Cf. AAS, XXII (1929), 111.

In order to place the mission apostolate in its proper locus, we must revert to first principles and recall that the Church is Catholic, that catholicity is an essential note of the Church. Basically, this connotes the inner dynamism of the Church, the internal striving to expand throughout the world and among all peoples and cultures. It strives to become truly catholic by means of its " missions." Without this striving the Church would not be true to its nature.

It is then easily seen that the " missions " are nothing more and nothing less than the *mission of the Church* extended on a truly global scale. It is an *essential* activity of the Church itself, and it embraces all the activities of the Church. The mission apostolate is simply the apostolate of the Church in those countries of Africa and Asia traditionally referred to as " mission lands." In conceiving of " missions," the accent must always be on the Church, for the mission was given to the Church, the entire Church.

From this it follows that, far from being a work of supererogation, or the special interest of a few, missions are the collective responsibility of all members of the Church. It follows also that the great issue today is not that of Christian ecumenism, but of *human* ecumenism. Much attention is being given to the former in our western world; it is equally pressing to give attention to that absolute form of ecumenism implied in the mission apostolate.

It might be objected that the Vatican Council has a separate Commission for the Missions, and that therefore the missions are something separate and distinct from the Church's mission. It is quite accidental, and not at all traditional, that there should be a separate mission Commission.[18] So recent are the profound changes in the mission regions (especially the important one of the creation of indigenous hierarchies) that there has not been time to relate matters of Church life in those

---

[18] The First Vatican Council was the first ecumenical council in history to have a separate Commission and agenda for the missions. The Council terminated before this agenda could be taken up. Consequently, the present Council's action on missions will be completely novel, not at all traditional.

regions to those in older Christian regions. Also, separate consideration is necessary owing to the different political, social, economic, cultural, and historical factors associated with the Church's apostolate in the mission regions of Africa and Asia. *De facto*, the status of the Church is different in these regions. We can refer to it as the " developing Church " in these regions, as compared with the " developed Church " in Europe and America. The important point to note is that in both areas it is the Church which will be considered.

If one goes through the list of the other commissions, one will find that the Council has commissions for bishops and the governments of dioceses, for discipline of clergy and laity, for religious orders, for the lay apostolate, for sacramental discipline, for sacred liturgy, for studies and seminaries. All the matters to be considered by these various commissions will apply, *mutatis mutandis*, to the mission regions as well. Obviously, the principal changes or modifications in these matters will be dictated by the cultural and historical differences obtaining between the various continents of the world where the Church today is truly established for the first time in history. The matters to be considered by these commissions will apply substantially to the mission regions as well as to the regions of traditional Christendom. Nonetheless, the very existence of a separate Commission for the Missions illustrates the difficulty referred to at the beginning of this paper. Where are the " missions " properly to be located within the Church's apostolate during this transitional period in the history of the Church? Ideally, they should be considered as an integral part of the Church's general mission. This is the only theologically sound manner of regarding them. The circumstances of history prevented the Council from attaining their ideal formulation.

A short paper can at most offer but a few general guidelines pointing out the need for rethinking missions today. I have suggested that it is most important for all who are concerned with missions to approach them primarily from a theological point of view. This is not to minimize the valuable assistance the social sciences can render to the mission apostolate, but rather to lay particular emphasis on that which is more basic and which has been too much overlooked in the past.

I do not wish to imply that nothing has been done along these lines. As a matter of fact, in the past half-century, in Europe, missiology has made considerable progress and has built up a respectable corpus of knowledge regarding the mission apostolate. Unfortunately, this young science is little known in the United States.[19] But as this country commits itself more and more to the global apostolate, there will be more need for missiology.

Missiologists will quite willingly admit that their *corpus scientificum* is still incomplete and imperfect. Nevertheless, the time has arrived when the knowledge they have assembled ought to be integrated into the various ecclesiastical disciplines. For example, it is readily apparent that an integral Church History must include mission history as well; and the same can be said about the other branches of ecclesiastical studies. They have been separate and divided in the past; it would be intolerable to continue this situation in the future. Just as it would be harmful to the unity and catholicity of the Church to perpetuate any harmful division in the Church, so too it would be harmful to perpetuate any arbitrary and artificial division within the theological branches of knowledge. It is necessary, therefore, to strive for the integration of the missiological branches of knowledge into the traditional branches of sacred doctrine. Then—and only then—will the missions be located properly and accurately within the Church's general mission.

RONAN HOFFMAN, O. F. M. Conv.
Catholic University of America
Washington, D. C.

[19] Missiology is the scientific specialization which studies the work of the establishment of the Church in its doctrinal principles, in its practical norms, and in its historical development both past and present. As such, it pertains to theology and has the following branches: scriptural, dogmatic, patristic, pastoral, mission law, mission history, and missiography.

THE CAUSES OF THE WORLD ECUMENICAL
MOVEMENT

∽

Ecumenical Truth

AN understanding of the causes of the ecumenical movement depends on an understanding of ecumenical
truth. Since this truth is one aspect only of the search
for universal truth applied to a particular sector, this search
is essentially objective. The truth is to be sought for its own
sake, irrespective of its utilitarian application or of any pre-
conceived hypotheses of the searcher. Ecumenical truth differs
from the truths open to philosophical research in that it owes
its origin to a divine revelation, and finds its most perfect
expression in a Kingdom which is not of this world; yet, by the
divine-human necessity of the Incarnation, this truth is embodied in a social institution governed by its own officers, involved in the historical process, suffering inevitably as Christ
suffered, and being rent as was His garment. The fact that
ecumenical truth has a finite as well as an infinite horizon means
that Catholics cannot simply present the ecumenical task as a
spiritual problem to be overcome by prayer and self-sacrifice,
though this is indispensable and, it may be, quite enough for
this or that individual member of the Body of Christ. To each
his own particular vocation in the work for reunion, whether
it be spiritual dynamism and inspiration, such as that which
inspires a religious contemplative to offer her life; or the patient
work of prayerful reflection, comparison, research; or simply
attentiveness to the view-point of those with whom we engage
in discussion. As with philosophical truth, we have to create a
climate of informed opinion before we can move forward to new
acts of understanding and co-operation in the ecumenical field.
Even more than in the domain of philosophical truth, ecumenical understanding depends intimately on the quality of life
and personal witness of the searcher. For if every schism, no

551

less than every heresy, is the consequence of human sin impinging at some point on the life of the Mystical Body, it is clear that every advance towards unity will depend on the quality and consistency of the Christian life and witness of those working for reunion.

The Word " Ecumenical "

Dr. Visser't Hooft distinguishes seven meanings of the word " ecumenical." Pertaining to or representing the whole (inhabited) earth or the whole of the (Roman) Empire are meanings encountered in the Greco-Roman world and the New Testament. The life of the Church in the early centuries gave rise to the meaning of referring to or representing the whole of the Church or of that which possesses universal ecclesiastical validity. The remaining three meanings are modern developments: the world-wide missionary outreach of the Church; the relations between and unity of two or more Churches (or Christians of different confessions); and that quality or attitude which expresses the consciousness of and desire for Christian unity.[1] It does seem, however, that many modern writers, Catholic no less than non-Catholic Christians, use the word in several of these ways or even in combinations in the same context. Since the word is so rich in content such a practice is by no means illegitimate provided the context makes the meaning clear or supports the composite usage. The ignoring of this diversity of meaning lay at the basis of some misunderstanding when it was first announced that there would be an Ecumenical Council, designed not merely to edify the Christian people, but to invite separated Christian communities to find within the Catholic Church that unity sought by so many souls from all quarters of the earth. For Catholics, an ecumenical council has a clearly defined canonical meaning. For the great mass of

---

[1] In Appendix I of *A History of the Ecumenical Movement* 1517-1948, ed. R. Rouse, S. C. Neill, S. P. C. K., London, 1954, pp. 735-740, based on a fuller presentation in his book *The Meaning of Ecumenical* (The Burge Memorial Lecture, 1953) London, 1953. The reader is referred to the Rouse/Neill symposium for a fuller examination of the subject of the present article.

Catholics in the world the reality underlying what has come to be known as the ecumenical movement could be attained only through submission to the See of Peter. But for non-Catholic Christians ecumenism already implied an aspiration to Christian unity going beyond denominational loyalties, based upon an even wider aspiration of humanity in the world of today, and stimulated by the increasing consciousness of human solidarity, in spite of the political disputes of national leaders, and their failure to give serious support to movements such as the League of Nations and the United Nations.

The Catholic Perspective Today

The Ecumenical Council was destined to provide such a renewal of life within the Catholic Church that her essentially ecumenical nature would become clearer to the outside world. This would necessarily involve a twofold movement of renewal and re-appraisal. The Church would have to understand more clearly in the design of her founder her privileged role of spreading the Kingdom of God. And she would have to be more lucid in her attitude to the world in which that Kingdom has to be spread. She would have to have a clearer vision of the world's profoundly divided nature owing to man's selfishness; of its effect on the Church herself; and of its partial but real insights into the truths, which, taught by Christ nearly two thousand years ago, are now part of a universal heritage. Unlike Byzantine Christianity, western Christianity whether Catholic or Protestant has always been a missionary Christianity. But, in the last century, the whole meaning and context of the missionary task has radically changed with the technological and communications revolutions, and the evolution of the world's population into two blocs whose standards of living become ever more radically differentiated. The Church's outward movement must now begin with a far deeper and profounder understanding of those whom, under God's Providence, she is destined to save than the too formal and often stereotyped functions comprehended as her mission in the past. The new ecumenical outlook in Catholicism, as well as in Protestanism, finds its primordial cause in the far-reaching missionary change and the consequent pastoral revolution of the modern world. The confrontation with the new missionary and pastoral task obliges the Church to examine afresh the content and quality of her teaching. A clearer comprehension of what constitutes the essentials and what may safely be adapted and changed will follow; in other words, a new ecumenical outlook will emerge. The ecumenical, missionary and pastoral tasks all need reassessing in light of one another. Further, each has important insights to communicate to the other through specialists at work in these fields. The bishops present at the Second Vatican Council have undoubtedly been oriented in the direction of a new ecumenical outlook by what they have learned from each other in very different missionary and pastoral situations. There is something of a parallel here to the rise of Anglican-Protestant ecumenism half a century ago, when the World Missionary Conference at Edinburgh ushered in a new era of ecumenical co-operation under the stimulus of the urgent need for an end to competition in the mission field.

Ecumenism and Mission

At the time of the later Roman Empire, before the barbarian invasions shattered once and for all the trial marriage between an aging imperial order and a youthful Church becoming conscious of its own strength, ecumenism in Church and State coincided. The known world was seen to be included within the Church's missionary purpose: an ecumenical council fulfilled a secular as well as an ecclesiastical function. The rise of the new barbarian nations contributed to the establishment of the papacy as a secular power in the west, and marked it off from the Byzantine Empire, where Church-State relations were in continuity with the late Roman imperial pattern. The conflict over investiture legitimately defended by the papacy against secular monarchs led to an exaggeration of the temporal authority of the popes. Of its very nature this was bound to militate against recognition of her spiritual and universal authority, and proved indeed to be a major factor in the Reformation.

Yet the fact that Christianity and nationality could form a
new syncretism, hindering at once the Church's ecumenical
outlook and her missionary vocation, did not really become
fully evident until after the second world war in 1945. For in
both world wars, national episcopates invoked the Church's
support in their mutually incompatible demands for patriotic
support, nay, for the right to kill and maim enemy nationals,
Catholic, Protestant, Orthodox, in the name of Christ. The
association of Christian missions with political and economic
imperialism has proved a grave obstacle in recent years to the
establishment of native Churches in countries with newly
acquired independence; while the almost exclusive association
of all forms of Christianity with the western world has alienated
the far-eastern and middle-eastern countries against what has
appeared to them to be a hostile cultural and even political
force. It is noteworthy that almost the only successful attempts
at converting the faithful belonging to Islam have been achieved
by the Russian Orthodox in certain of the Asiatic Soviet
Republics.

The Catholic Ecumenical Vocation Today

With the encyclical of the late Pope John XXIII, *Pacem in
Terris*, the ecumenical vocation of the Catholic Church is seen
to be what it should always have been understood to be, an
international and supranational vocation to all mankind—to
all mankind—but first to those who profess and call themselves
Christians, that they may realise to the full their vocation, now
recognized as God-given though outside the social Body of the
Church. The rest of mankind are potentially members of the
Mystical Body, exhibiting already their divine vocation, although in a fragmentary and incomplete manner. They, like
the members of separated Christian communions, need to be
comprehended by those within the Catholic Church. This is
not simply a question of seeing the world as it really is and of
approaching it with Christian comprehension. Nor is it even
the recognition of the need for the right use of the modern
social sciences and the realization of their relevance for the

pastoral situation. Beyond Christian realism and the acceptation of the rôle of modern techniques lies our acknowledgment
of the part we have played in making the world as it is, racked
with war, starvation, ignorance, sickness, waste. The declarations and leadership of the German Catholic episcopate over
the past few years have been at once profoundly missionary
and profoundly ecumenical. In their messages they point to the
responsibility of Catholics for the very conditions which militate against acceptance of the Christian message by people
outside the Church. In their acts they have given recognition
to the solidarity of Catholics with the world's sin and suffering by linking Christian repentance, asceticism, and self-denial,
as it was in the Apostolic Church, with the relief of the
needy, the salvation of the sinful.

The Origins of Ecumenism

The origins of ecumenism, then, must be sought in the perennial vitality of the Gospel and of the community founded by
Christ. The present outburst of ecumenical activity within the
Catholic Church is simply the realization of an ecumenical
vocation she has always possessed but not always realized in
fact. There can be little doubt that the vigour displayed by
the Catholic Church at certain periods in her history—notably
during the counter-Reformation, the nineteenth century, and
since the accession of John XXIII—has astonished Protestants
who have tended to regard her as too concerned with her historical evolution as an institution to be capable of such dynamism. Would it not be equally true to say, however, that
Catholics have, since the Reformation, likewise tended to
underestimate the power of the Christian message preached by
those separated from the historic community centered round
the see of St. Peter, and now find themselves obliged to attempt
an explanation of the phenomenon of the predominantly
Anglican-Protestant world ecumenical movement and to recognize its authentic witness to the Gospel? [2] Yet biblical scholar-

[2] This is not to fail to recognize the early association and co-operation of the
Orthodox, but simply to emphasize that the main inspiration of the world ecu-

ship on both sides would accept as a common source of inspiration the intimate link of the oneness of the Church founded by Christ with the very unity of the Blessed Trinity as expressed by St. John, the most intimate of our Lord's Apostles. It would equally accept the unity in diverseness of the Body of Christ proclaimed in the Pauline teaching, linking the doctrine of the Spirit's mission with that of the essential unity of the different members of that Body. And it would see God's ultimate purpose to be the recapitulation of all creation in Christ, Whose Body is called in some mysterious way to consummate the work of the unification of all mankind begun in Him.

Catholic-Protestant Ecumenical Inspiration

This return to a fuller realization of the ecumenical nature of the Church as a necessary corollary to the facing of the implications of the world's missionary and pastoral situation is probably the most important cause of the ecumenical movement today, and one which, though most evident in the Anglican-Protestant communions, is now almost as true of the Roman Catholic communion. There can be little doubt that the ecumenical cause has been most keenly pressed by Catholics precisely in those countries feeling to the full the impact of the second world war, the Nazi occupation, and the persecution of the Jews. The first world war had already profoundly shaken the inherited assumptions of the Catholic Church in its relations with society. A study of the characteristic movements of thought and action within Catholicism during the period between the wars would appear to show it had not reflected upon the implications of the first world war and the revolutions accompanying it to the same extent as the Anglican-Protestant world. Striking proof of this assertion may be seen in the prophetic " Church, Community and State " Conference at Oxford in 1937, organized by the " Life and Work " Council later fused with the W. C. C.[3] It seems that an even profounder

menical movement now incarnated in the World Council of Churches was Anglican and Protestant.

[3] See below pp. 560 ff.

shock to Catholicism arose out of the events leading up to and during the second world war and from the leading rôles Catholic statesmen and politicians had played either positively or negatively in their genesis. The two important encyclicals of John XXIII, *Mater et Magistra* and *Pacem in Terris*, decisively relate Catholicism to the problems of the modern world in the same fundamental way as the "Life and Work" stream of the Protestant ecumenical movement. Besides their intrinsic value as a declaration of the mind of the Catholic Church, they have therefore an ecumenical dimension in confronting the non-Christian world with an essentially similar Christian witness, and in holding out the possibility of a common Christian action by Catholic and non-Catholic Christians. In other words, the field is now open for Christian co-operation in the domain of the application of Christianity to the problems of the day. Such co-operation, besides demonstrating to a selfish world the essential altruistic nature of Christian faith and life, will furnish an occasion for Christians of different persuasions to get to know each other better. In a climate of fraternal charity the theological problems that will have to be tackled ultimately will be far more patient of a dispassionate and objective discussion. Catholic participation could also help Protestants to examine the doctrinal assumptions of "Life and Work." Past criticisms ill became Catholic theologians who were in any event precluded from actively helping forward what has proved to be a most valuable contribution of the Protestant ecumenical movement to the human community.

Movements with Ecumenical Implications

The past century has seen Biblical and patristic movements accomplished by a catechetical revival common to Catholic and Protestant circles with perceptible ecumenical overtones. But the liturgical movement seems to be more specifically linked with the ecumenical movement; particularly when the fact is recalled that an ecumenical pioneer such as Dom Lambert Beauduin stimulated liturgical renewal on the eve of the first world war. Considerable interplay between the Catholic and

Protestant liturgical movements was apparent especially in the domain of research at the turn of the century. Its orginal inspiration dates from the French Benedictine revival, part of the French Catholic renaissance of the nineteenth century; and also from the Oxford Movement, a source of renewal and worship for the Anglican-Protestant world no less than for the Catholic Church in English-speaking countries.[4] The growing influence of Cardinal Manning and the ultramontanist party gave the Roman Catholic Church in England an increasingly intransigent attitude towards the Anglican Church and tended to obscure the ecumenical ideals of the Oxford Movement. A continuity existed between it and the old High Church Party in the Church of England, which had always emphasized similarities between Anglicanism and Catholicism and considered reunion as at least within the bounds of possibility. Had there been, in the nineteenth century, any approach by the Catholic Church to the communions issued from the Reformation, it could conceivably only have been made through the Anglo-Catholic tendency within Anglicanism and similar tendencies within Lutheranism, since only in this liaison was there allegiance to the Reformed communions joined with sufficient sympathy and historical understanding of Catholicism. The new respect for history in general and the past history of the Catholic Church in particular which accompanied the Oxford Movement, and the growth in mutual acceptation of their historical authorities, paved the way for the present-day recognition by Catholic scholars that responsibility for the schisms dividing the Church is shared. The nineteenth century as a whole was a period of great stirring of ideas within Anglicanism, Catholicism, and Russian Orthodoxy, some of which have not yet sped their course. One has only to read the prophetic voice of Lamennais to realize how the whole tragic dissociation of the Catholic Church from the new proletariat of the Industrial Revolution could have been avoided, or the writings of Soloviev to under-

---

[4] The period of the thirties was also marked by conscious borrowing from the Catholic liturgical renewal, first in Anglican and later on in Protestant circles. This is fairly obvious to ecumenical observers today.

stand how the two great traditions of the east and the west are complementary and not contradictory. The reaction of the Catholic Church to the dangers facing her at the First Vatican Council, however justifiable they might then have appeared to be, postponed for nearly ninety years the possibility of a positive approach to the Reformation communions. Some progress with the historic churches of the Orthodox federation was discernible from the time of Leo XIII, particularly under the pontificate of Pius XI, who was markedly cool towards the Reformed Churches and the World Council of Churches.

The Rise of Protestant Ecumenism

The result of this combination of circumstances was that the Orthodox-Anglican-Protestant World Ecumenical Movement attained full maturity at the third W. C. C. at New Delhi in 1961 apart from direct Catholic influence.[5] Any Catholic tendencies discernible in that movement were certainly due to Anglican influence working from within, and Orthodox statements and positions often adopted despite the prevailing discussions in the World Conference on Faith and Order (subsequently merged with the Universal Christian Council for Life and Work to form the World Council of Churches at Amsterdam in 1948). The influence of Orthodoxy, though real, must be considered to be on the margin of the movement as a whole. The inspiration of that movement must therefore be sought in the Reformed tradition and its various developments since the sixteenth century. Luther lost his early ecumenical concept of the church under political pressure. While Calvin never ceased to view the church in its totality, he always hoped to achieve a European federation of churches on a doctrinal basis that would be explicit without being exclusive. One remark should be made about the Reformed tradition in general. The Protestant Reformation in Europe was a conscious attempt to reform the pre-Reformation Church and there was no consciousness,

---

[5] Certain Catholic theologians and ecumenists have from time to time helped in drawing up programs for W. C. C. meetings, but these contacts were unofficial, otherwise of course they could not have taken place.

at all events in the beginning, of founding a new church or
churches.

In America, on the contrary, right from the outset the Protestant émigrés were conscious they were founding new churches,
or at least, American counterparts of what were seen as new
confessions already founded in Europe from the Reformation
onwards. A second point may be made about geographical distribution. The Protestant and Catholic communities coincided,
roughly speaking, with political boundaries at the conclusion
of the Wars of Religion (Peace of Westphalia, 1648) and this
division tended to give permanence to the religious divisions.
In North America, Catholics were often political émigrés as the
Protestants mostly were. But whatever the cause, American
Protestants seem to have realized the divided nature of their
religious communities more clearly than their European counterparts until the present century when the world upheavals were
more immediately experienced by the European people and
their religious bodies.

The Ecumenical Significance of the Sects [6]

One exception to this lack of consciousness of the need for
unity concerns the left-wing Protestant movements, particularly, in the early stages, those on the continent of Europe.
Some of those were far more alive to the problem than the
numerically larger Protestant denominations. One of the consequences of the present new look at Christian history from an
ecumenical viewpoint is an increased understanding of the sects,
and in particular the pietist current, dismissed too easily and
too univocally until quite recently by Protestant as well as
Catholic writers as " enthusiast." Such an attitude was quite

---

[6] The word "denomination" is used here of those bodies belonging to the
classical Protestant traditions, Anglican, Methodist, Congregationalist, Lutheran,
Calvinist, Presbyterian, and Baptist, while the word "sect" is used for those
religious bodies away from the mainstream of classical Protestantism. This avoids
an equivocal usage based on sociological norms. It is nevertheless true that certain
"sects," particularly those in the anabaptist tradition, developed subsequently into
"denominations," but it seems preferable to keep to norms based on theological
considerations in an ecumenical discussion.

different from the attempt of other Catholics to isolate and point to Catholic affinities in early Methodism, but this attempt was no less doomed to failure.[7] The strength of the appeal of the sects, as of the denominations before they became too institutionalized or where they have since experienced revivals, lies in the call to return to the Gospel teaching and example; for did not our Lord Himself say: "Heaven and earth shall pass away, but my word shall not pass away"?[8] No adequate study has yet been made of the political and ecclesiastical influence of these movements. When such a study has been done, it will perhaps reveal surprising results, both for ecumenical Christianity and for the sources of contemporary political movements and ideals; it will perhaps reveal these movements inspiring both political trends as well as international movements in favor of world peace and brotherhood.

Return to the One Church of New Testament Times

The sects in modern times have been described as responding to the unpaid bills of the Church, while another familiar comparison has put the sects on a par with the religious orders within Catholicism.[9] There can be little doubt that the failure of the various Christian bodies to live out Christianity on a personal and community level will always have repercussions on denominational loyalties, and awaken the desire to found a community in which a smaller number will better correspond to the exigencies of the Gospel. The wheel has now turned full circle, and unity itself is now more and more seen as a primary exigency of the Gospel itself; the process of fission becoming no longer compatible with fidelity to the word of God. A return to the Gospel today would involve for many Protestants a return to the one Church of New Testament times, a Church that Protestant studies more and more see in continuity with

[7] If the early Methodists do exhibit such tendencies, they owe them in the main to the High Church tendency in the Church of England and not to any direct or conscious borrowing from Catholic sources.

[8] St. Mark xiii, 31; St. Luke xxi, 33.

[9] These also lose their original fire and become institutionalized, new orders with fresh Gospel inspiration taking their place.

the Church of the early Fathers. Whereas half a century ago only Anglicans among the Reformed communions would have accepted the first four Ecumenical Councils as *de fide*,[10] an increasing number of non-Anglican Protestant denominations look back to the period of the councils of the undivided Church as authoritative for doctrine, no less than to the New Testament, finding there the model for the "coming great Church."[11] It is in developments of this kind, fruit of a scholarly research which itself depends upon healthy respect for the authorities of every denomination, that the modern tendency towards coalescence which is so marked a feature of contemporary Protestantism must be sought, and not in what has been considered an increasing disregard for the importance of doctrine. Yet on the margin of these denominations, and among the older sects themselves, new sects spring up, usually among the poorer and less favored members of the community, to testify to the failure of traditional Christian bodies to live out the Christian faith in the sphere of community relationships. Here is an ecumenical dimension, characteristic of the primitive Church, in which the traditional Christian bodies, Catholic and Protestant alike, are still to be found wanting.

North American Interdenominational Movements

The missionary expansion of nineteenth-century Protestantism, itself the occasion of the realization of the need for ecumenical co-operation and eventually for re-union between Reformed bodies, was the expression of the need to spread the Kingdom of God derived from the Protestant revivals in Europe and North America in the eighteenth and nineteenth centuries. The revivals in North America were linked with similar movements in the United Kingdom during these periods, and pro-

[10] Some Anglican authorities would say the first six Councils, while the Anglican agreement with the Old Catholics specifies the first seven Councils. The Bonn Agreement, as it is known, was accepted by the Old Catholic Episcopal Synod at Vienna in 1931 and by the Convocations of Canterbury and York of the Church of England in 1932 and forms the basis for intercommunion between the Episcopal Church of the U. S. A. and the Polish National Church.

[11] Phrase which is the title of a book by Wedel.

duced a crop of specifically evangelical voluntary societies on both sides of the Atlantic concerned with home and foreign missions, the distribution of Bibles and tracts, Sunday schools, temperance, peace, and the slave trade. In their predominantly evangelical inspiration and their concern for specific reforms and causes, denominational differences tended to be obscured. This provided something of a counter-balance to the prevailing reproduction on American soil of the European denominations and sects with all their ethnic distinctions, in a climate made favorable for their proliferation by the separation of Church and State and the complete liberty of worship for every individual or group of persons. The American Revolution had forcibly weaned them from direct European influence, though the improvement of Atlantic communications, the exchange of literature in English, and the constant flow of emigrants, tended to renew those links in the course of the nineteenth century. Two other divisive elements at work were the influence of the frontier, with its perpetual challenge to the settled denominations and sects, and the issue of slavery which profoundly divided all Christian bodies. The decline in importance of these divisive factors and of revivalism in the major denominations led to the rise of new movements lacking in the former significantly evangelical and often Calvinist drive. The end of the Civil War and the changeover of the American economy from a predominantly agricultural to rapidly developing industrial economy, depending for its expansion upon hordes of emigrant laborers, produced new conditions and new needs, evoking interdenominational responses such as that of the Y. M. C. A., the Y. W. C. A., and the Student Volunteer Movement. The U. S. branch of the Evangelical Alliance, founded in 1867, was an organization grouping like-minded individuals, which lost its drive with the death of Philip Schaff in 1893. But his appeal for a " federal or confederate union " which would be a " voluntary association of different Churches in their official capacity, each retaining its freedom and independence in the management of its internal affairs . . . but co-operating in general enterprises " presaged directly the formation of the Federal Council

in 1908 and its present-day successor, the National Council
of the Churches of Christ in the U. S. A. in 1950.

Unity as Creed

The pietistic strain in American ecumenism in the nineteenth
century, echoing that of Zinzendorf a century earlier, finds its
most characteristic expression in the appeal of Thomas Camp-
bell and his son, Alexander, who developed his father's ideas
in his plea for the union and co-operation of all Christians in
order to convert the world. Although the movement later split
and is only now being re-united, the Disciples of Christ have
the merit of being the only denomination to put unity at the
forefront of their *credo*. A Lutheran of pietist tendencies, S. S.
Schmücker, attempted to find a consensus of Protestant creeds
as the basis for federal union; while W. R. Huntingdon, an
Episcopalian, was responsible for a union proposal adopted by
the house of Bishops at the general convention of the Episcopal Church in 1886. Somewhat modified, this was accepted by
the 1888 Lambeth Conference Committee as a basis for Home
Reunion; again modified, its became the center of the well-
known Lambeth Conference " Appeal to all Christian People "
of 1920. The four points concerned the Scriptures as the rule
of faith, the historic creeds, the sacraments of Baptism and
the Eucharist, and the historic episcopate, " locally adapted."
Though doubtless intended as a point of departure for ecumenical discussion, they have tended to be regarded as the
minimum terms on which the Anglican communion would
envisage reunion.

It would certainly be wrong not to associate with these ecumenical activities the movement of thought and action known
as " The Social Gospel " which owes so much to the essentially
ecumenical outlook and inspiration of John Frederick Denison
Maurice. The title " Social Gospel " does less than justice to
the catholicity of its original impulse. One of the sources of
inspiration common to Catholic and Protestant in the present
ecumenical movements is the realization that the Gospel must
be proclaimed to the world in terms the world understands,

and this, without dilution of the original Gospel message or of the radical changes this message implies in the heart of man and in his social and political institutions. Finally, the United States was the seed-bed for concern about the unity of mankind as a whole, which undoubtedly owes something to the Christian influence of this stream of thought and which gave birth to the plans for a League of Nations and a United Nations. So profound was this desire for international order and justice that, even while hostilities were still in progress, the Covenant and Charter were put forward as alternatives to the sterile demands for vengeance and total surrender.

The Witness of Anti-Ecumenism

The later pietistic movement associated with the names of Sankey and Moody portrays a flight from, and the fundamentalist movement of the turn of the century to the present represents a reaction to, this ecumenical concern at the most universal level. Both object to the principle of the Church's engagement in the world and to the theological liberalism said to be implicit in attempts at denominational federalism. The shock of the first world war, the slump, the second world war and the continuing rise of communism has exacerbated this antagonism; though the departments of the National Council of Churches and of the different denominational bodies dealing with international and social problems have continued to develop and concentrate on the point where the Gospel shoe pinches most keenly in our own day. Like the World Council of Churches, the National Council has been opposed by para-ecumenical organizations especially created to carry on the struggle against them and to destroy these twin principles of a continuing movement towards Christian unity and Christian engagement. Despite this opposition, the number of mergers between the older denominations with similar confessions or beliefs continues to grow steadily; though the overall number of denominations and sects remains in all probability about the same through the rise and growth of new sects and the continuing development of " holiness bodies " such as the Pentecostals, recruiting their members from among the dissatisfied and dispossessed.

Ecumenism and Christian Witness

It is noteworthy that the chief opposition to the Catholic Church which remains in religious circles today in the United States comes from these same right-wing fundamentalists. An investigation would almost certainly show they were, in general, opposed to American involvement in the United Nations and to the principle of foreign aid. While concern for ecumenical rapprochement is probably stronger among Catholics in some parts of Europe than in others,[12] American public opinion as a whole strongly supports the drawing together of separated Christian communities and realizes instinctively that a Christianity which does not act as a leaven in the lump of the world is a religion doomed to become a historic relic like Buddhism, Islam, even Judaism. It seems, however, that God in His Providence will not allow this to happen but will galvanize His Chosen People into stirring up life in their midst even by permitting scorn, opposition, persecution. In Europe, the level of Church attendance in communist dominated countries is higher than it is in the west, with the possible exception of Holland, because of the anti-God campaigns and the penalization of those faithful to the Church. The opposition of the fundamentalist wing to ecumenism and to anything that savours of a universal view of humanity, which finds a strange echo in some Catholic circles, is itself the product of a syncretism. Religious and secular history here in North America were inextricably involved and American Christianity was subject to the constant pressures of secularism and materialism. In a country of boundless opportunities depending largely upon a man's own efforts to better himself, people are tempted to think that the struggle for material self-advancement is automatically accompanied by spiritual progress. The ecumenical movement here as elsewhere can lead to a purification of the Christian

[12] Stronger in Holland, parts of Germany, France and Belgium.

religion if people, encountering fellow-Christians whose every-day witness constitutes a challenge to them, are led to examine the bases of their belief and its expression in the light of the exigencies of the Gospel. The causes of the ecumenical movement in their purest form cannot be divorced from the movement of prayer and penitence in the Holy Spirit which leads men to seek to renew their lives in Christ. Nor can they be separated from an ever-increasing concern both with the nature of the Mystical Body and the privileged sources of grace within it, a life whose beginning depends upon water and the Spirit; whose perpetuation, upon nourishment by the Body and the Blood; whose healing, upon the saving words committed to the Apostles upon the day of the Resurrection.

The Ecumenical Responsibility of Catholics

Catholics will help their fellow Christians to see more clearly the relation between these two movements of the soul if they assume the responsibilities corresponding to their privilege of having received the totality of the Catholic faith, and assume leadership in the forefront of all movements for the betterment of their fellows in the name of Christ, whether in the domain of social justice or charity at national and international levels. It is a Gospel principle that from him who has much, whether in spiritual or in material goods, much will be expected. With this principle of Catholic responsibility must always go that of Catholic consistency, proclaimed by John XXIII in *Mater et Magistra* and repeated in *Pacem in Terris*. In their relations with non-Catholics, " let the faithful be careful to be always consistent in their actions, so that they may never come to any compromise in matters of religion and morals. At the same time, however, let them be, and show themselves to be, animated by a spirit of understanding and detachment, and disposed to work loyally in the pursuit of objectives which are of their nature good, or conducive to good." [13] There are indeed signs that a new conception of Catholic ecumenism is emerging,

[13] *Pacem in Terris*, Paulist Press Edition, 157.

in which a realization of the indispensable nature of the Chair of St. Peter as the locus of reunion remains, but with a dawning understanding that it is insufficient to look without, as upon an unenlightened world whose ignorance is largely vincible. The Vatican Council will doubtless give a clear and unequivocal lead in the matter of ecumenical initiative. Meanwhile, the presence of observers from the principal Protestant bodies and the Russian Orthodox Church has been the occasion of a leap forward in mutual understanding as well as for actual theological discussion. The primary cause of ecumenism is ever more clearly emerging as a divinely inspired movement within Christianity as a whole of which the Catholic Church, through its Pope and the Ecumenical Council gathered around him, is at once the touchstone and catalyst.

RONALD COWLEY, O. P.

Georgetown University
Washington, D. C.

ECUMENICAL THEOLOGY AND CONVERSIONS

GENESIS OF A PROBLEM: PROSELYTISM VS. ECUMENICAL FELLOWSHIP

ᘛᘚ

ODAY the making of converts has become a kind of hindrance for ecumenical work to quite a number of ecumenically minded men, at least when one Christian church tries to make converts among the members of other Christian churches. These men use the word "proselytism" only in a pejorative sense; they question the right of churches to make converts among members of churches with which they are and know themselves to be in ecumenical relations; they sometimes seem even to want conversions stopped entirely or at least suspended till all the consequences of the ecumenical problems are better thought out. We find such thought among those outside the Catholic Church, chiefly in the World Council of Churches, where the integration of the International Missionary Council into the World Council of Churches (considered by many one of the most important achievements of the recent New Delhi Assembly and by others hailed as the beginning of a new era of ecumenical work) has provoked heated discussions of this problem. Up to now, it has proved impossible to find an unambiguous solution. In Europe more than a few ecumenically oriented Catholics think that ecumenical work ought to have more influence on convert making and that ecumenical theology, at least when better worked out than it is at present,[1] will point out for Catholics also some consequences for the treatment of converts, both before and after their conversion. They insist that even now we should carefully distinguish between the "conversion" of a Christian and the "conversion" of a heathen.

[1] G. Thils, La " Théologie oecuménique," Notion, Formes, Démarches, Louvain: Warny, 1960.

The theology of conversion is still a neglected study among Catholics; in the many books on converts we rarely find a theological analysis of this mysterious process. Individually, converts pose a practical and pastoral problem; in general, converts are able to furnish a kind of argument to apologetics. These two considerations seem to exhaust Catholic thinking on conversion and the problems of converts are therefore relegated to apologetics and pastoral theology. This fact may very well spring from a lack of development of our Catholic theology, but, in the present situation, could prove to be a blessing in disguise. It is easier to move in a vacuum than to have to assail established positions. Some thought on this problem seems necessary; whether Catholic ecumenical thinking must exert its influence on the work of making converts to the Catholic Church, and whether those who give all their time and work to the winning of converts, must at least follow the evolution of the ecumenical movement and of ecumenical thinking.

Up to now the most vehement opposition to proselytizing activities among their members by missionary societies has come from the Eastern Orthodox Churches, and above all from the Church of Greece. These churches have practical, historical and theological reasons for this aversion. On account of a lack of good preachers and good catechists, at least in sufficient number for their needs, and also because of the concentration of religious life entirely on participation in the divine Liturgy, the faithful of the Orthodox Churches are known to be insufficiently instructed in the faith and, therefore, rather helpless against proselytizing activities. The Greek Church has even tried to make the government interdict them. Being national churches in the full sense of that word, bearers of many old national traditions, and conscious of a long history of defending the national cultural heritage against the oppression of the Turks, they think that whoever tries to make converts among their members at the same time tries to alienate a man from the spiritual life of his people and his country.

Also, though they are members of the World Council of Churches, they have often testified for their " Catholic ecclesiology " against the Protestant majority. They hold themselves to be the already existing true Church of Christ, and therefore consider whoever leaves their church an apostate from Christ. Perhaps we can mention another factor: having been barred for centuries by oppression and other historical circumstances from doing any missionary work themselves, they can appreciate only with difficulty the authentic Christian inspiration of the work of proselytizing missionary societies.

In this situation they could be expected to mount a determined opposition to the proposed integration of the International Missionary Council into the World Council of Churches. They argued that this integration would give a kind of official sanction to the proselytizing activities of missionary societies affiliated to this Council. But the backbone of their resistance lies in their contention that all members of the World Council ought to consider their fellow members as " Sister Churches " and therefore, if for no other reason, readily refrain from proselytizing among their members. A few national Missionary Councils have opposed the integration from exactly the opposite point of view, recruiting their members and supporters chiefly from groups with a " Low Church-mentality." With a fundamentalist kind of theology, with only a very weak appreciation for the mystery of the church, and, therefore, with little zeal for the ecumenical ideals, they do not want what they fear would be the unavoidable consequence of this integration: the hampering of their missionary work for ecumenical policy-reasons.

There are at least two easy answers to these arguments. The first is merely factual: The proselytizing activities in the territories of the Eastern churches stem, for the greater part, from the sectarian missionary bodies—from Adventist, Pentecostal and other groups—which belong neither to any national Missionary Council nor to the International Missionary Council so that this integration means neither a sanction

nor a restraint for their activities. The second answer however
touches a question of principle. The famous " Toronto Declaration " of 1950 on the scope and purpose of the World Council of Churches and the meaning, the consequences and the
obligations of membership in it [2] states explicitly: "membership does not imply that each Church must regard the other
Churches as Churches in the true and full sense of the word."
It is of course required that they " recognize their solidarity with
each other, render assistance to each other in case of need, and
refrain from such actions as are incompatible with brotherly
relationships." This cause, however, is already counterbalanced
by the declaration that no church needs to consider the other
churches as true churches. Each may, therefore, feel obliged
to missionary and even to proselytizing work among other
members. But these answers are obviously too easy, too superficial, too " ad hominem." When the integration was proposed
and the Orthodox opposition began to make itself felt, it was
deemed necessary to make a further study of this issue.

The Third World Conference on Faith and Order, held at
Lund in Sweden at a time when proselytism was not yet a
pressing problem (August 15th to August 28th, 1950), devoted
only a short paragraph of its " Report to the Churches " to
the topic:

There is a difference of opinion among us as to whether a Church has
the right to evangelize the members of other Christian Churches.
While some of us deny that such a right exists, others claim that
it is an essential part of their mission. There are forms of pro
tizing however which are sub-Christian and should therefore find
no place among the followers of our Lord.[3]

The Conference was evidently aware of the existence of the
problem but it had its mind on other problems. The qualification, however, of some forms of proselytizing as " sub-Christian " is very interesting and suggestive in the light of the
result of further study and of later reports.

[2] *The Ecumenical Review*, III (1950-1951), pp. 47/51.
[3] *The Third World Conference on Faith and Order*, Ed. O. Tompkins, London:
SCM Press, p. 31.

The Second Assembly of the World Council of Churches, held at Evanston, Illinois, from August 14th to August 28th, 1954, treated the problem of "Evangelism" in its Second Section.[4] In its meeting in Evanston, immediately after the Second Assembly, the Central Committee of the World Council decided that, "in view of the difficulties which had arisen affecting relationships between member Churches of the W. C. C., a Commission should be appointed for the further study of "Proselytism and Religious Liberty." (This title was later revised to read: "Christian Witness, Proselytism, and Religious Liberty in the setting of the World Council of Churches"). After due preparation this Commission met at the theological Academy of Arnoldshain, Germany, on July 17th and 18th, 1956. Its Report was then revised by another Commission of the Central Committee at its meeting at Galyatetö, Hungary, July 28th to August 4th, 1956, and the result was finally approved for submission to the Churches.[5]

The Introduction states: "This report is primarily concerned with relations between member Churches of the World Council of Churches"; it adds, however, "We are not unmindful of its implications for our relations with other churches and religious bodies." It then points out that it is not treating a new problem:

The issues with which this study is concerned have existed within the ecumenical movement from its very beginning. In 1920 the well-known Encyclical of the Oecumenical Patriarchate with its strong plea for cooperation among the churches has asked for a definite cessation of proselytizing activities.

It then mentions the Toronto declaration on the consequences of membership in the World Council of Churches, but it confesses that this declaration failed to "define what is implied in a constructive relationship between the Churches." It says that the problem of proselytism and of its relation to evangelism has not been squarely faced, and adds:

---

[4] *The Evanston Report,* London: SCM Press, pp. 98/112.
[5] The text in *The Ecumenical Review,* IX (1956/1957), pp. 48/56.

It is owing to this uncertainty that the World Council is sometimes accused of representing proselytizing tendencies and sometimes accused of exactly the opposite, namely of being an obstacle to the full exercise of religious liberty.

It finally enumerates eight historical causes behind the issues of proselytism and religious liberty, among which we note but two:

There has been a great increase in the number and activities of Christian groups appealing for individual conversions, but sometimes with very little church consciousness and with little or no interest in cooperation with others [and] due to greatly increased means of communication and mobility, religious communities no longer find it possible to remain closed to outside influences . . . these technological forces are such that they could only be thwarted by forcible repression.

However, after this thoughtful and realistic introduction, the Report tackles the intricate question of terminology, and here the difficulties appear immediately. It notes:

Proselytism has today an almost completely derogative sense; probably no church and no missionary society involved in the ecumenical movement would wish to call itself a "proselytizing body." It does not seem possible, in practice, to restore the good connotation which the word " proselyte " once carried. The true obedience to the Great Commission: " Go therefore and make disciples of all nations " is today called evangelism, apostolate, soul winning (sic!) and chiefly: witness.

About "bearing witness" the Report has three things to say:

It is the essential mission and responsibility of every Christian and of every Christian church. [Its purpose is] to persuade people to accept the supreme authority of Christ, to commit themselves to Him and to render Him loving service in the Fellowship of his Church [and] it seeks a response which contributes to the upbuilding of the fellowship of those who acknowledge the Lordship of Christ.

[The conclusion from these three points is] both witness and response must therefore in the present necessity take place within the existing situation of division of the Church, [because] an individual enters that fellowship by becoming a member of one of the several existing ecclesiastical communities.

[Proselytism furthermore] is not something entirely different from witness; it is the corruption of witness. When cajolery, bribery, undue pressure or intimidation is used to bring about seeming conversions; when we put the success of the Church before the honor of Christ; when we commit the dishonesty of comparing the ideal of our own Church with the actual achievement of another church; when personal or corporate self-seeking replaces love for every individual with whom we are concerned; when we seek to advance our own cause by bearing false witness against another church . . . then witness has been difformed into proselytism.

This section of the Report ends with a strong plea for religious liberty and freedom:

This right [to freedom of thought, conscience and religion] includes the freedom to change his religion and belief, and freedom, either alone or in community with others, and in public or in private, to manifest his religion or belief, in teaching, practice, worship and observance . . ., for such witness churches and individuals should have equality before the law.

In this question, of course, the whole problem of the relation between the church and the state is involved; the problem of a national church looms threateningly in the background, but the Report insists only on liberty and freedom.

In the next section of the Report we find eight " basic considerations," which form the most important part and try to give the solution to the problem.

1) Every Christian Church is not only permitted but required freely and openly to bear its witness in the world, seeking to win adherents to divinely revealed truth.

2) The commandment to bear witness . . . is valid not only in relation to non-Christians, but also in relation to all who are only nominally attached to any Christian Church.

3) Should errors or abuses within a church result in distorting or obscuring the central truths of the Gospel . . ., other churches may be bound to come to the rescue with a faithful witness to the truth thus lost to view.

4) It is not in the interest of the World Council to have mutilated churches as members; on the contrary, it aims to be a Council of whole, real and genuine Churches [meaning that every member church must be able to bear its witness without any hampering].

5) A church which in the light of its own confession must regard certain teachings of another church as errors and heresies and certain of its practices as abuses cannot be compelled to hold back or to withdraw its views because of the churches' common membership in the World Council.

6) It is precisely within the ecumenical fellowship that this exchange should proceed to the fullest extent and without minimizing the difficulty and seriousness of the issues.

7) It should be inconsistent with its membership to deny another member the state of a church, or to regard it as entirely heretical and hopelessly given over to abuses, so that its members could only be helped by being rescued from it.

The last of these fundamental considerations enumerates three ways for " a witness in the ecumenical fellowship ": unofficial discussion and personal encounter between individuals; official discussion between one church and another; and the work of " Inter-Church Aid," when one church helps another church to recover a healthier life of its own, etc.

The Report terminates with a list of "recommendations for continuous consideration by the member churches." Among these we only indicate a suggestion which might be considered by Catholics in the work of making converts to the Catholic Church: " whenever a member of one church desires to be received into the membership of another church, we should seek consultation between the churches involved."

Because we do not intend to write the complete doctrinal history of the integration of the International Missionary Council into the World Council of Churches, but only want to study the genesis of an ecumenical problem which has arisen outside the Catholic Church, we only note from the Report of the Central Committee of the W. C. C. to the Third Assem-

---

⁶ *Evanston to New Delhi*, Report of the Central Committee to the Third Assembly of the World Council of Churches, Geneva: 1961, pp. 239/245.

bly [6] that at the meeting of this Central Committee at Rhodos
in 1959 " it was felt that the churches had not given sufficient
response to guide the Central Committee." The reactions to
the Provisional Report had evidently been disappointing. A
slightly altered version of the Provisional Report was therefore given again to the member churches, both in the Report
of the Central Committee and in the Third Assembly's Work-
book.[7] The altered version contained this important statement:

> Behind the tension between the right and duty of free Christian
> witness on the one hand, and the obligations of an ecumenical fel-
> lowship to manifest the visible unity of the Church as the Body
> of Christ on the other hand, lies the whole ecclesiological problem,
> which is a major concern in our continuous ecumenical association.[8]

At the Assembly itself the integration of the I. M. C. was
formally proposed, voted on and approved with an overwhelming majority; the study of the Provisional Report may not
have elicited sufficient answers from the member churches, but
it had apparently, in conjunction with the influence of other
perhaps non-theological factors, softened their resistance. The
Report of the Assembly's Section on " Witness " did not touch
the problem. Only the future can show whether the tension
between the duties of free witness and of ecumenical fellowship (with the special meaning of manifesting visible unity the
Central Committee attached to it) has really lessened. We will
have to wait till the newly formed Department of World Mission and Evangelism has started its work and revealed its
methods and intentions.

To sum up: an ecumenical problem regarding conversions
has arisen from the ecumenical work, has been seen and
studied, but has not been resolved. As a problem connected
with the life of the World Council of Churches and in the special form it has taken outside the Catholic Church, it must be
resolved in the light of a theology of the World Council, a

---

[7] *Work Book for the Assembly Committees*, prepared for the Third Assembly of
the World Council of Churches, Geneva: 1961, pp. 56/62.

[8] *Evanston to New Delhi*, p. 239.

theology which has still to be fully elaborated;[9] it may take a long time before the task is finished, and the problem may await a definitive solution for many years. Meanwhile the growing influence of the Orthodox in the World Council might render the problem still more difficult. But a study of the problem as it poses itself to the Catholic Church could be a help for the theologians of the W. C. C.

CONVERSION AND ECUMENISM IN THE NETHERLANDS

When investigating the problem whether our apostolate of making converts to the Catholic Church, at least when we try to win converts from the Christian churches, could degenerate into a proselytism in the pejorative sense of that word,[10] we can take as a starting point a certain truth, and we may be tempted to take an apparent truth as the second point. The truth is that the Catholic Church can only accept a verdict of her own ecclesiology, based on the Catholic faith in the One True Church of Christ which she is herself; she cannot be bound by the ecclesiology of the W. C. C. The apparent truth is that the Catholic Church does not have to acknowledge any sister churches as co-members of the same Council of Churches and that she therefore does not have to acknowledge any obligations implied in a fellowship of churches. She may in the future change her attitude towards the Ecumenical Movement, she may join the W.C.C., she may have some day to face the obligations implied in that membership, but now she can move with an absolute liberty. Apparently! Possibly, however, our own ecclesiology may prove the Catholic Church to be in ecumenical relations to all, or at least to some,

[9] M. J. le Guillou O. P., *Mission et Unité*, (Unam Sanctam XXXIII), Paris: Ed. du Cerf. 1960. Livre Premier. Première Partie. Chapitre VI: " Vers une Théologie de l'Église, Communion Missionaire," Vol. I. pp. 81/103. J. Hamer O.P., " Qu'est, théologiquement, à ses propres yeux le Conseil Oecuménique des Eglises?" *Istina*, 1954, pp. 389/407.

[10] It might be argued that the same problem arises when we make converts among orthodox Jews, but we will neglect this complication.

Christian churches, and these relations may imply obligations concerning the Catholic apostolate of making converts from these churches.

It might be said that the problem is already present, though not yet perceived, when in books about conversions we find autobiographical notices by the former Anglo-Catholic author Sheila Kaye-Smith and the former atheist Gretta Palmer, or by the former Orthodox Bishop Paul Melitijew and the former Hindu Chuni Mukerji, without an explicit warning in the introductions to these volumes that theologically these conversions mean something entirely different.[11] Because this could be called an exaggeration we will put this problem in the form of a short report on the development of both the work of making converts and the ecumenical dialogue in the Netherlands since the end of the Second World War. In itself this development is important only for the Catholics in the Netherlands, but it is an example of how this problem has posed itself to European Catholics; for other countries the same could be said. The history of the relations between Catholics and Protestants in the Netherlands is in broad outlines as follows.

The Calvinists were the dominating party in the Republic of the Seven Provinces; till 1795 the Catholics barely managed to struggle on. During the nineteenth century Catholics and Protestants lived together in the same country with hardly any religious contact. Only in the last decades of this century did they learn to collaborate in politics to fight for the rights of their schools. The first religious contacts were established in the beginning of the twentieth century, but only in the form of an apologetic dialogue. In these years the Apologetical Society Petrus Canisius was founded. Between the two World

---

[11] *The Road to Damascus*, London: Allen, 1949, pp. 228/235 and pp. 27/56; and *Sie hörten seine Stimme*, Luzern: Räber and Cie, 1951, pp. 9/28 and pp. 113/129. It would be easy to find instances in all other volumes of this kind. The same can be said of non-Catholic volumes in *Modern Canterbury Pilgrims*, New York: Morehouse-Gorham, 1956, and *These Found the Way*, Philadelphia: Westminister Press.

Wars there was an initial improvement: a dozen priests were regularly occupied in giving conferences on the Catholic faith to non-Catholic audiences. They won over a few converts as a result of their work, but their intention was primarily to remove misunderstandings. Up to 1940 it was therefore possible to take care of the instruction of converts in the existing parishes and convents, but after the Second World War the situation became entirely different. During the war Catholics and Protestants had met in the resistance to Nazism and had discussed the religious motivation of this resistance, which in the Netherlands was very important. After the war old barriers between the confessions were down. Furthermore, the number of people without any religious affiliation had been growing in ominous proportions; while in the nineteenth century everybody was either a Catholic, a Protestant or a Jew, the 1947 census showed 17% of the population declaring affiliation to no church or religious group. Suddenly there was both an opportunity and a necessity for a much more intensified work of instructing and making converts.

Nowadays practically every town in the Netherlands has its own special institute for the instruction of converts. Some priests, helped by several hundred formed lay-catechists, find their daily work in these institutes and have little time for other work. They belong to almost all the religious Orders and Congregations: Franciscans, Capuchins, Jesuits, Dominicans, Carmelites, Augustinian Eremites, Missionaries of the Sacred Heart and of the Holy Family. No diocesan priests are engaged in this apostolate, but in the parishes they instruct other groups of converts, since these institutes have no monopoly. They retain their independence and have found their own methods. Only the Saint Willibrord Society (the more ecumenically oriented successor of the Apologetical Society Petrus Canisius) can act as a meeting point for discussions and clearing house for experience, chiefly because its President is the Bishops' Delegate for all ecumenical affairs and because the Society can furnish funds for the maintenance of these

institutes. The number of converts is growing every year. But
with all due respect to the apostolic work performed in these
institutes we have to face two facts. The majority of the
priests engaged in convert work have no personal experience
of ecumenical work, do not participate in the ecumenical dialogue, and therefore meet only those Protestants who have
asked for instruction and are considering the possibility of
becoming Catholics. So they see no reason to ask whether it
might be necessary to follow a special method when guiding
Protestants. Furthermore about 60% of the non-Catholics who
seek instruction in the Catholic faith want to marry a Catholic. Here a pastoral problem arises: if the instruction fails to
bring about a conversion, there is the danger of a mixed or
even a merely civil marriage. The consciousness of this danger is certainly not enough to turn the instruction into proselytism, but it can result in the application of gentle pressure, in an over-optimistic appreciation of the response to the
instruction, in an abbreviation of the instruction, or in other
things which might savour of proselytism. As to purely ecumenical contacts between Catholics and Protestants in the
Netherlands, there is not, as in Germany, a semi-official dialogue going on between the churches themselves, but there are
at least some twenty groups of priests and pastors (not only
of professors and theologians!) which meet regularly and have
been doing so for more than ten years. Younger people also
meet frequently though irregularly (and pose the well-known
problems of intercommunion!); and there are some common
activities of Catholics and Protestants, chiefly in the field of
dissemination of biblical information. When the Catholic Saint
Willibrord Society in 1960 was publishing a new translation
of the New Testament, the Protestant Netherlands Bible Society helped in every way. But of the some 200 priests who
belong to the discussion groups only a few at the same time
instruct converts. Others will do it only in exceptional cases,
and some purposely refrain from it. These priests have voiced
some criticism of the work of making converts; sometimes

from a purely practical point of view, suggesting only that a priest engaged in this kind of work might be less acceptable to Protestants in the ecumenical dialogue; sometimes from a rather extreme point of view, demanding that all the work of making converts be suspended until the atmosphere will have been cleared through the ecumenical dialogue. But in most cases they ask simply that the conclusions and consequences of ecumenical thinking and ecumenical work be applied to the apostolate of making converts; that the methods and manners of this apostolate be critically analysed and reviewed in the light of the ecumenical situation; that the meaning of a conversion be studied again from the point of view of ecumenical theology; and that therefore regular meetings be arranged between the participants in the ecumenical dialogue and the workers in these institutes for converts. They expect the first result of these meetings to be that converts from one of the Christian churches will be instructed and received into the Catholic Church in a way different from the instruction of persons without religious affiliation.

It was to be expected that some criticism would come from the Protestant side. It came mostly in the form of friendly questions; the Protestants know quite well that there are no special Catholic activities to win converts from the Protestant churches, while there are certain Catholic activities directed to persons without religious affiliation, and they know that among the persons instructed in these institutes converts from Protestantism form a minority. But the problem of the relation between evangelism and proselytism has been treated in a few theological studies, among which we will cite a recent one. Only this year the Reformed (" Vervormde ") pastor J. A. Helby published a book entitled *Proselytism, an Exploration of an Ecumenical Problem*.[12] It is a dissertation to obtain the degree of a Doctor of Divinity at the University of Utrecht, and the influence of Prof. J. C. Hoekendyk, well known

---

[12] J. A. Helby, *Het Proselitisme: Verkenning van een Oecumenisch Probleem*, Boekencehtrum, 's Gravenhage: 1962.

in ecumenical circles, is clearly visible in it. The general conclusion is, " Proselytism is the opposite of Ecumenism." [13]

Once again, these developments and the discussions in the
Netherlands are not very important in themselves. But they
certainly suggest that we Catholics must squarely face the
problem of proselytism and that we cannot simply go on making converts in the present ecumenical situation: this might
seem, and might be, proselytism and a hindrance to ecumenical work.

The Theological Problem of Conversion
to the Catholic Church

The Jesuit theologian Karl Rahner recently began an article " Some Remarks on the Problem of Conversions " [14] with
the following general statement:

The Catholic Church claims to be the True Church of Christ, and
exclusively so. Since conversions to Christianity as a religion of
personal faith are only possible with adults by a free personal decision, the Catholic Church can never give up the claim to be the
true Church of Christ, which every individual man should join by
his own free decision. . . . Ecumenically it is important to recognize that this claim of the Catholic Church looks to all the other
Christians, who are not excepted because they are already Christians. . . . If this Catholic desire for converts is judged to be something unecumenical, non-Catholics have to understand that this
" will to proselytize " is founded in the claim of absoluteness of
the Catholic Church.

Further comment on this general statement does not seem
necessary; it is simply the expression of traditional and well-
known Catholic doctrine. If the right and even duty of free
witness are acknowledged in a formal ecumenical fellowship,
non-Catholics have to accept the fact that the Catholic Church
proclaims her faith in her own place in God's design for the
salvation of the world; that she proclaims herself to be the

---

[13] *Op. cit.*, p. 133.

[14] Karl Rahner, " Einige Bemerkungen über die Frage der Konversionen," *Catholica*, Vierteljahresschrift fur Kontrovers-Theologie, XVI (1962), I, pp. 1/19.

only True Church of Christ, the *Catholica* who is able to unite
all men with Christ and to give all Christians a spiritual home,
the real *Oecumene* who possesses in her *depositum fidei* all
God's gifts to mankind and will never lose them because she
is protected by the Holy Spirit; and that she, simply by bearing this witness about herself, calls every man to conversion.
This faith of the Catholic Church in her own vocation is in
the last analysis the true explanation of the fact we can never
afford to forget in discussions on the Catholic work of making converts: that the Catholic Church, from the first centuries of her history [15] has endeavored to make converts of all
nations, religions and churches, and that this claim of absoluteness has always been considered an offense and a scandal.

Some remarks must be made however to further classify this
general statement.

Father Rahner himself makes two of them. The first is that
merely in virtue of this general principle the Church is not
obliged to pursue the making of converts in all circumstances
with the same intensity. " The Church could let this work of
making converts fall back behind more general ecumenical
activities." [16] This remark of course might provoke discussions
on the apostolic nature of the Church and Professor Hoekendyk, if he were a Catholic, would certainly object to Father
Rahner's remark. But we had better let this pass. Secondly,
Father Rahner points out that the Catholic Church not only
proclaims herself to be the true Church and the *Catholica*, but
also proclaims to be with absolute certainty recognizable as
such: for her place in God's design she has " *signa certissima*
and *omnium intelligentiae accomodata.*" [17] as the First Vatican
has solemnly stated. We have therefore the problem of the good
faith of all these millions of Christians, who know the Cath-

---

[15] A. D. Nock, *Conversion. The Old and the New in Religion*, Oxford: Claren-
don Press, 1933. (Paperback-edition 1961.)

G. Bardy, *La Conversion au Christianisme durant les premiers siècles*, (Collection " Théologie," Paris: Aubert, 1949).

[16] *Loc. cit.*, p. 2.

[17] *Loc. cit.*, p. 4.

olic Church fairly well, who hear her claim and the call to conversion implied in this claim, but who nevertheless reject this pressing invitation. We can doubt the cogency of the traditional apologetical arguments, but we cannot deny that the Church has solemnly proclaimed herself to be recognizable as the *Catholica*. What are we to think right now of the good faith of all those who are inspired—and this by the working of the Holy Spirit, said the Holy Office itself!—by the ideal of the unity of all Christians, who participate with Catholics in the ecumenical dialogue and make many friends among them, who hear this Catholic witness again and again, and who nevertheless feel sure that they will never seek this unity of all Christians in the *Catholica*? Either their good faith or the Catholic claim is at stake!

Here a third remark on the general statement seems to be necessary.

Modern Catholic ecclesiology, alerted by the problems of the ecumenical situation and prompted by the difficulties of the ecumenical dialogue, does not treat catholicity and ecumenicity only as God's gifts to the Bride of Christ or as the visible and wonderful qualities which the Church will always possess and will always show to the world as the certain sign of her place in God's design. This ecclesiology insists that they also constitute a superhuman task for the Church because she has to realise these inalienable gifts in her consciousness; she has to become always more catholic and ecumenical in her faith and her apostolate, therefore in the way she manifests herself to the world. The traditional ecclesiology—we give only one instance to clarify our meaning—thought the *catholicitas facti* most important, chiefly because it contained a beautiful apologetical argument for the Church; but the present ecclesiology will rather insist on the *catholicitas juris*, because it is so important for the ecumenical task of the Church. Again under the influence of the ecumenical situation and the dialogue, modern Catholic ecclesiology has returned to the problem of weakness and sin in the community of the *Catholica*, an aspect of her life neglected by or underestimated by the traditional ecclesiology which for apologetic reasons preferred to insist on the visible holiness of the Church. Finally, the problem of the historicity of the Church began to influence ecclesiology. Historical forces, chiefly the historical forms of the reactions to heresy and schism, could have brought about a narrowing of consciousness in the Catholic community, by which this community became less catholic and less ecumenical than the *Catholica* could and ought to be. In defending divine truth against heresy she could have lost some of the openness the *Catholica* must have and show to the world. By insisting especially on the *dogmata* contested by the heretics she may have lost something of the well-balanced universality which ought to characterize the *Oecumene*.[18] Modern study of Tradition,[19] in which the " *traditio activa* " receives more attention than in an ecclesiology which thought the relation between Holy Scripture and Tradition the paramount problem, has elucidated the way in which such a narrowing of consciousness could steal into the faith of the Church. The eschatological perspective in which the Church is seen in this modern ecclesiology made the existence of some narrowness somewhat more acceptable in the *Catholica*, since she is not yet the "holy city, New Jerusalem, coming down out of heaven from God." [20] But when all these things are thought out and expressed we must still confess that this narrowing is a weakness and a sin, and that it constitutes a scandal to the world. Therefore when in her present condition the *Catholica* claims to be the *Catholica* and the *Oecumene*, and in this claim implicitly or explicitly calls for conversion, the non-Catholic Christians look at her present historical condition and reject both claim and call.

[18] Ferdinand Holböck, and Thomas Sartory, O.S.B., *Mysterium Kirche*, Salzburg: Otto Muller Verlag, 1962.

[19] See Joseph Wodka, *Church History*, I. pp. 438/465. Feiner, [Trütsch] Böckle, *Fragen der Theologie heute*, Einsiedeln: Benziger, 1957. I/III. Joseph Geiselmann, *Tradition*.

[20] Apoc. 21:2.

Now a certain number of Catholic participants in the ecumenical dialogue might be tempted to praise this refusal. They might be inclined not only to contend that this rejection of the *Catholica's* claim is psychologically understandable, but also to contend that the *Catholica* in her present condition has no right to expect that her claim will be accepted. They would probably add that the ecumenical dialogue is the proper way to overcome this narrowness which prevents the Church from manifesting herself in her full catholicity and ecumenicity, and therefore the Church must not even try to make converts till the dialogue has produced its results; otherwise the Church would be really proselytizing. In opposition to this extreme point of view three things must be said: First, it is not at all certain that the dialogue itself is the proper remedy for the Church's weakness and narrowness. It could be argued that the ecumenical dialogue only leads to a renewed meditation on the contents of her *depositum fidei*, to a proper *ressourcement*, and that this meditation, which could have been brought about by factors other than the ecumenical dialogue and even by purely internal factors, is the proper remedy. An Ecumenical Council is such a meditation, even when the non-Catholics are only present as delegate-observers, not as participants in a dialogue. Furthermore, the question could be asked whether the overcoming of this narrowness and of other weaknesses produced by historical forces could not be followed by the emerging of other weaknesses caused by contemporaneous historical forces. The ecumenical dialogue, itself a historical fact, may dispel this narrowness induced by the historical reactions to heresy and schism, and may bring more open-mindedness, but the Catholic Church will never in her history be without weaknesses, and if we were to put off making converts till she is only glorious and radiant, we have to wait till the Parousia. But the main point is this: the Catholic Church is always the *Catholica*, and, even when showing not only wonderful signs of divine origin and nature, but also painful signs of her human weakness, is always recognizable as the *Catholica*. She is, therefore, always rightly claiming to be acknowledged as the *Catholica* and always rightly calling for conversion to her. The work of the Holy Spirit in the souls of non-Catholic Christians can always bring about real conversions and justified conversions, even when all the members of the World Council of Churches would call them the "results of a bad proselytism."

Vestigia Ecclesiae

Modern Catholic ecclesiology leads to a more finely shaded concept of the Catholic Church, which calls all non-Catholics, the members of the Christian churches not excepted, to conversion by claiming to be the One True Church of Christ. It has also thrown some new light on the position of these members of Christian churches in regard to the Catholic Church by elaborating the doctrine of the *vestigia Ecclesiae* in a new and better way.[21] The Church is able therefore from both these points of view to judge whether and in what sense the Catholic apostolate of making converts can rightly be called proselytism. We have already remarked that we Catholics can in this matter only accept the verdict of our own ecclesiology.

This doctrine of the *vestigia Ecclesiae* is not yet fully elaborated and we cannot yet speak of any *communis opinio*, not even with regard to the definition of the *vestigia Ecclesiae*. A few things however seem to be certain. Outside the Catholic Church we find not simply non-Catholics in either good or bad faith. There are validly baptized Christians. We recognize that there are Christians who have a real and a theologically acceptable faith in Jesus Christ as their Saviour, and who have been formed spiritually by reading the Bible as God's message to men. There are validly ordained bishops and priests, and therefore a valid celebration of the Eucharist. These things are living spiritual forces for non-Catholic Chris-

---

[21] Gustave Thils, *Histoire Doctrinale du Mouvement Oecuménique,* Louvain: Warny, 1955, pp. 183/197. Thomas Sartory O. S. B., *Die Oekumenische Beuwegung und die Einheit der Kirche,* Meritingen bei Augsburg: Kyrios Verlag, 1955, pp. 147/193.

tians, who have often fought to retain them. The ancestors of these Christians were not simply apostates and did not simply leave the Catholic Church, but they took with them some of her spiritual wealth. Sometimes they contended that they could only safeguard these treasures by leaving the Church. Nowadays we do not contend that this claim was valid and that they were right in leaving the Church under that pretext, though the question of their guilt is less clear for us than it was for the Catholics of a more apologetically minded period. We contend that we are not finished with the matter when we have called them either heretics or schismatics and that these Christians—but here they will themselves protest most energetically!—simply by retaining these Catholic treasures remain in a certain relation to the Catholic Church. Because these *vestigia Ecclesiae* are living forces in the non-Catholic churches there is, even if it is somewhat tainted and deformed by being intertwined with heresy and schism and if it lacks proper balance on account of its being wrested from the total Catholic synthesis, a Catholic life outside the Catholic Church; in a sense, we can speak of an " *Ecclesia extra Ecclesiam.*"

What is then exactly the spiritual position of the member of a non-Catholic Christian church, who perceives the claims of the Catholic Church, who is called more or less explicitly to conversion to that Church, and who may be the object of some Catholic activity for winning converts? There are of course many differences between the various Christian churches; there are more differences between the individual members of these churches; and there would be still more differences if we had to consider the problems of the sects, too. The following is proposed as a general summary of the situation.

This member of a church is a man of good faith, who in good faith has been staying away from the Catholic Church and even in good faith could consider her the Scarlet Woman. Karl Rahner has pointed out [22] that it can be very difficult

---

[22] *Loc. cit.*, pp. 3/5.

for us to see how he can be of good faith if he knows the Catholic Church with her divine gifts and her wonderful signs fairly well, but we must suppose this till the contrary is proven. By his faith he is open to the work of the Holy Ghost. Second, this Christian is a member of a religious community, of a Christian church in which he feels spiritually at home; in most cases this will be the church of his family and of his youth, his faith in which may never have been shaken. Furthermore by his membership in this church he undergoes the influence of two contrary and always intertwined forces; of the *vestigia Ecclesiae* and of heresy or schism. Moreover he undergoes the influence of the history and the traditions of the church which was more or less opposed to, and perhaps even a very critical adversary of, the Church of Rome. By the influence of the *vestigia* (for example, baptism) he is—but unconsciously!— directed to and in relation with the *Catholica*. Finally he lives with his church and with the whole Christian world in the present ecumenical situation. He may or may not be vitally taken up by ecumenical ideals, but he will certainly be interested in the problems of Christian unity. He will have heard something of the World Council of Churches and of its relations with Rome and he may have formed a conscious judgment concerning the Church of Rome chiefly with regard to the ecumenical situation.

Two remarks must be added to this sketch of a certainly difficult and complex position. Our Catholic ecclesiology cannot yet tell us with certainty whether we Catholics (we have already mentioned the Toronto Declaration of the World Council of Churches) can call the Christian churches real churches in the Catholic meaning of this word. Most Catholic theologians would agree that the Orthodox Churches are real churches, but they would hesitate to do the same with regard to the Protestant churches. This question was broached in the answers to Hans Asmussen's *Five Questions to Catholics on the Lutheran Church*.[23] It proved much easier to say what we

---

[23] H. Fries, *Antwort an Asmussen*, Stuttgart, 1960.

Catholics think of the sacraments and the ministry of a Protestant church than what we think of that church itself. It is therefore very difficult to give a theological appreciation of the influence of a church with its history and traditions on its members. With regard to the *vestigia Ecclesiae* we must remark that they belong to the synthesis of the *Catholica*, and therefore, in their isolated state outside the *Catholica*, they exert a less balanced influence. Notwithstanding that, however, a Protestant who in his spiritual life has concentrated on the Bible as a guide, but by reason of his background only the Bible, might nevertheless be in a position of strength at least with regard to Biblical formation even from the Catholic point of view.

ECUMENICAL CONVERSION

We must conclude that the relation between the Catholic Church and the non-Catholic Christians is not simply the relation between the One True and Holy Church and those who objectively at least live in heresy and schism. We repeat once more that the Catholic Church which is the *Catholica* and the *Oecumene* has always (even when she, through human weakness and by her own fault, cannot manifest the fullness of her catholicity and ecumenicity to the world) both the right and the obligation to call the non-Catholic Christians to conversion. And we must add that whoever has by the grace of the Holy Ghost seen that this Church of Rome is the *Catholica* and the *Oecumene* is obliged by his own conscience to join this Church and to become a Catholic. Consequently the Catholic work of making converts, even when directed to members of the Christian churches, can never by Catholic standards be called in itself proselytism. It now remains to be seen whether and how it could degenerate into proselytism.

One preliminary remark: the ecumenical dialogue itself could degenerate into a kind of proselytism if it were intended or used as a means to make converts. Undeniably quite a few Protestants after having participated in the ecumenical dialogue, and manifestly under the influence of this participation, did become Catholics.[24] Undeniably too, many Catholics, who do not personally participate in the dialogue and do not understand its intention and its methods, still think it is a new and modern method of making converts. And it is also undeniable that the Catholic partners in the ecumenical dialogue bring their witness of Catholic faith and of Catholic claims. In the scope of the dialogue itself they do not bring their witness in order to make converts; they may for tactical reasons hope that no converts will be made, because that would make it difficult to continue the dialogue; but they have no power to prevent the working of the Holy Ghost through their witness. We cannot investigate here the relation between the apostolate of making converts and the ecumenical dialogue; we only state that they are different activities.

Whenever and however the Catholic Church works to make converts she must always be conscious of her factual position and situation. Her claims are not something apart from herself in her historical condition. She has a right and a duty to call for conversions, but she must always remember that in order to make conversions she must manifest herself as the *Catholica* and the *Oecumene*. Does she manifest to the world the openness and the concern implied in being the *Catholica*, and can she honestly declare trustworthiness? As the *Oecumene* she must make it clear to the world that all Christians will find their spiritual home and will feel at home in her community, but is there in her behaviour no foundation for a suspicion that all converts will be streamlined into accepting a spirituality prevailing through a merely historical evolution and will be obliged to partake in devotions which reflect the faith of only a few peoples? The very English gentleman John Henry Newman, who had found a wealth of spiritual treasures in his Anglican community,[25] was obliged to make

---

[24] Giebner/Goethe/Klunder/Schlier, *Bekenntnis zur Katholischen Kirche*, Wurzburg: Echter-Verlag, 1955.

[25] Sermon, " The Parting of Friends," *Sermons on Subjects of the Day*, XXVI. Ed. Longmans, Green & Co. p. 395.

his spiritual home in a community where Irish sentiments and Italian devotions were dominant; he was brought from Canterbury to Rome by his belief in the *Catholica*, but did she manifest herself to him and could she really make him feel at home?

When the Catholic Church proclaims herself the One True and Holy Church of Christ, and calls for conversions, the only answer she expects and she can accept is, "*Credo*." This *Credo* has something absolute: it affirms the absoluteness of the Church and of her membership; it acknowledges the absoluteness of her authority and her teachings; it confesses the divine element in the origin and nature of the Church. And it is an unconditional surrender. By its absoluteness this *credo* is a judgment on everything pertaining to the former life of the convert; on his allegiance to another religious society or church; on his heresy or schism and his personal opinions; on his doubts, scepticism or his fanaticism. Nevertheless this *credo*, a gift of grace, is a human act and it is therefore at the same time a personal *credo*, with personal motivation from personal experiences and personal needs, with a personal accent and stress on some content of the Church's teaching and a personal engagement in some aspects of her life and apostolate. And in this personal aspect the *credo* is an approbation of the former life of the convert in which this personality was formed. Only in this way the Catholic unity in faith can really become a Catholic unity, not a dead and formal uniformity. The members of the churches are not an impersonal mass, but personalities. Therefore the message of the Church and the message of her claim of absoluteness must be offered in such a way that a personal response is possible; only then in the Catholic community, after the unanimous and absolute *credo*, can the internal dialogue or "multilogue" grow, and the faith of every individual Catholic be enriched by the faith of his fellow Catholics.[26]

[26] C. F. Pauwels, O. P., "Preaching the Mystery of the Church," Holböck/Sartory, *Mysterium Kirche*, Salzburg: Otto Muller Verlag, 1962, II. pp. 645/712.

The Holy Ghost has been working in the soul of the Christian convert, both because of his good faith and because of his ecumenical ideal, to show him the way to the *Catholica*. Because he in his former community possessed something of the Catholic Church, it must be supposed, though it can never be proved, that the Holy Ghost has worked in him through these Catholic elements: because he was baptized, because the Bible was his guide in life, because he had given himself by his faith entirely to Jesus Christ, because the liturgy was such an important part of his life. Maybe it gradually dawned on him that to enjoy these gifts in their fullness he would have to enjoy them in the harmonious synthesis of the *Catholica*. Of course, his *credo* was also a judgment on his past: he had to renounce the heresies and schisms intertwined with these Catholic elements, the anti-Roman position of his former community, some of his history and traditions, even something of the ecumenical movement. But he certainly must not be asked simply to forget this past and to start living as if he had always been a Catholic. His conversion is the approbation and coronation of the most important things in it and he has a right, even a duty, to retain a predilection for them. It is important that he believe himself always to have been a baptized Christian, and though it may be inevitable to investigate the validity of this Baptism outside the *Catholica*, it should never be treated as something of little importance. He must never be asked to be less Biblical in his praying and thinking, and though he must be introduced to the splendours of liturgical prayers he must never lose his Biblical spirituality. If he had a great, a maybe somewhat exaggerated reverence for the Lord's Day, it must never be suggested that the sloppy carelessness of many Catholics in their Sunday-observance, though certainly less sinful than he has thought, should be a pattern of conduct for him as a Catholic. And if he complains that he cannot sing any more the dignified and reverent hymns of the Protestant churches, we will have to concede that he has lost something beautiful by his conversion.

A convert to the Catholic Church should integrate all the results of the influence of the Catholic elements during his former life in the fullness of a Catholic life. Only then can he give an important contribution to the internal dialogue in the Catholic community, because then his personal accent in confessing the mysteries of the *credo* will be different from the accent of those who always have been Catholics.

One last thing ought to be noted. Today's converts will generally become Catholics while being animated by the ecumenical ideals; they will often come into the Catholic Church expressly because they believe her to be the *Catholica* and the *Oecumene* for which they have prayed and longed and struggled. It could be said that they are coming too early: the Catholic Church is not yet fully conscious of her catholicity and her ecumenicity and of all the implications and consequences. Some, therefore, might think it prudent not to insist so much on the ecumenical problems when instructing converts. But the converts cannot wait for better times. They know by the light of faith that this certainly not yet perfect Church is really the *Catholica*. And the ecumenical questions cannot be left out of the instructions of converts, because they point to the most important task of the Catholic Church. Having by their conversion already corrected the biggest and most tragic error of the Ecumenical Movement outside the Catholic Church, i.e., that she is not the *Catholica*, converts can make a valuable contribution from their ecumenical experiences to the internal dialogue of the Catholic community on her ecumenical task and possibilities.

CONCLUSION

These remarks say nothing strikingly new. These things have always been known in the work of teaching converts. But in modern Catholic ecclesiology they have been differently evaluated; they have not only practical but theological value.

In this question the Eastern Churches furnish the best indication of the Catholic Church's intentions. There have been times when a conversion of an oriental Christian could only mean his latinization; those were times when Catholics, thinking of the Eastern Churches, thought only of heresy and schism. Since Pope Leo XIII, however, the respect for the traditions of the Christian East has been growing continuously; now it is generally acknowledged that these are the traditions of the great Eastern Doctors whose feasts are celebrated in the Catholic Church and that the reappearance of these traditions in the already too much latinized Catholic community could only be called an enrichment. A slight expurgation of the Eastern liturgies has been necessary, but latinization has stopped. If an Eastern Christian is by his own conscience brought to conversion, he remains an Eastern Christian. The Orthodox may cry " proselytism " when speaking of the Uniate Churches, but they are an expression of the Catholic reverence for old traditions of the Catholic Church.

With regard to converts from Protestantism, the Catholic community has often required a most complete adjustment and adaptation of these converts to the factual spiritual condition of that community, and even then has complained that these converts were still a nuisance, being critical and overzealous and strangers. The "old Catholics" were the member of the One True Church, who were the children of those who had remained faithful to the Church at the time of the Reformation and often had suffered for her, who had never been anything else but Catholic, who therefore should set the pattern for everybody who wanted to join their community; and the convert had better forget or certainly never show that he formerly had been a member of a heretical or schismatical church. This was the inevitable result of a merely apologetical attitude towards other Christian churches; Catholics wanted to see the situation drawn in black and white; they wanted to believe the Holy Church perfect in every respect, only individual sinners excepted, and they could only see the shortcomings of the others.

The presence of the *vestigia Ecclesiae* in the non-Catholic churches is the true foundation of the ecumenical dialogue between Catholics and non-Catholics, which must go on till the unity of all Christians in one visible Church will ultimately be realized. A dialogue is possible and necessary with all men, but an ecumenical dialogue is only possible when on both sides we find Christian faith. Whenever those, having lived spiritually from Catholic elements and having partaken in the ecumenical dialogue between the churches, come to the fullness of the *Catholica*, and especially when they join the community of the *Catholica* in which the fullness is not completely realized, they must certainly first reject whatever the *Catholica* rejects and readjust their Christian life, but then their coming means an enrichment of the interior dialogue of the community. There are aspects of Catholic life and doctrine in which they feel more at home than those who have always been Catholics; so the doctrine of the universal priesthood of all baptized Christians is a point most converts from Protestantism will understand better than many Catholics. But this enrichment is only possible on condition that converts are accepted with their past and that in the Catholic community there is room for their spirituality.

* * *

When the danger of proselytism is mentioned we are almost automatically reminded of the possibility that less than honest intentions and methods might insinuate themselves in the work of making converts, and we are especially reminded of the fact that many conversions are connected with the purpose of marrying a Catholic. When, however, making converts itself is called "proselytism" from an ecumenical point of view, we can only retort that this can never be the point of view of the ecclesiology of the *Catholica*.

Yet if we conduct the apostolate of making converts without thinking of the implications of our own ecumenical theology and ecclesiology, ... perhaps that should be called "proselytism."

C. F. PAUWELS, O. P.

Albertinum, Nijmegen,
The Netherlands

UNITY: SPECIAL PROBLEMS, DOGMATIC
AND MORAL

∽

THE Bishop of Darwin, Australia, is reported to have said, on his way back from the Council, that some modern theologians are turning somersaults backwards in their anxiety to please non-catholics. He pleaded with the orthodox theologians to take up their pens in order to off-set such writings.[1] This statement merely puts into words what so many of us have been thinking—and experiencing—over a number of years, namely, that too many of our modern theologians are trying to bring into being a new ' situation ' theology, to fit modern needs. We are frequently told, either in so many words or by means of the broadest hints, that orthodox theology, especially if it takes the shape of scholasticism, is one of the main obstacles to reunion. The impression is given that, if only we would adapt our theology, both in concept and in language, to ecumenical needs, we would soon discover that the fundamentals of our Catholic position do not differ so very much from those of our separated brethren.

Instead of attacking such statements directly, the present article is an attempt to examine some of the more fundamental dogmatic and moral problems which face both sides in the ecumenical movement and which must be dealt with if we are to hope, one day, to bring back to the unity of the true Church those who are at present outside it. However, before we can deal with these specific problems certain preparatory remarks must be made, even at the risk of giving offence in certain quarters. Not one of us has any doubt about the value of a true ecumenical dialogue. For us, as Catholics, it implies the continuation of the mission entrusted to the Apostles, a mission which will continue to the end of

[1] *Universe and Catholic Times*, Jan. 25th, 1963.

time and which has for its sole object the one fold under the one shepherd.

There should be no need to point out the demand for absolute sincerity in all our dealings with non-catholics and the reunion question. This sincerity implies many things, but two of them are fundamental. We should not raise false hopes by giving the impression that, with a little good will on both sides, reunion is just around the corner. Nor should we give the false impression that such reunion can be attained without complete unity in the faith. It is distressing, to say the least, to notice that some Catholic theologians do not seem to realise the importance of this. I am not accusing anyone of deliberate insincerity, but in certain modern writings there is a lack of appreciation of the fact that sincerity means absolute truth and that it is the truth alone which brings true freedom.[2]

It is interesting to notice that non-catholic writers are becoming daily more aware of the need for this sincerity as identified with truth. There is a growing consciousness among them of the differences *in fundamentals* which separate the various sects from each other and from the Church of Rome, together with a realisation of the importance of the role of theology in the ecumenical dialogue. Some examples of this will not be out of place, since some Catholic writers have not yet caught up with non-catholics in this matter, and seem to have the impression that many of the doctrinal differences of the past have lost much of their actuality nowadays. In fact, the opposite is the truth. The ecumenical movement has brought about a re-affirmation of certain doctrinal positions in non-catholic circles.

We may surely take the word of the President of the Lund Conference for this. Bishop Brilioth of Upsala (Sweden) said in his presidential address:

It is remarkable that the ecumenical movement has had as a parallel, perhaps partly as a result, a great revival of confessional con-

---

[2] Cf: Cardinal Bea's article in *Nouvelle Revue Théologique*, (Feb. 2, 1962) 84.

sciousness . . . a re-affirmation of doctrinal positions which seemed to have lost their actuality.[3]

And Dr. Visser't Hooft used a phrase which might well become a classic description of the present situation, " The only unity we are concerned with is unity in obedience to truth." [4] The old ecumenical saying " service unites but doctrine divides " which once met with almost universal approval, has now been discarded in favour of a frank recognition of doctrinal differences and of their supreme importance in any attempt at reunion. Commenting on this change Fr. Leeming says:

The development seems to take the following directions: a clearer and stronger, though not universal, admission that doctrinal matters are of the first importance and that to attempt to gloss over differences by ambiguous formulas is wrong both in theory and in practice.[5]

As long ago as 1938, Mackenzie quotes V. Demant as saying, " Where dogmas don't matter there are merely collisions in a fog." [6] It is surely not without significance that non-catholics, in the course of their discussions, have lamented the dearth of theologians competent to handle doctrinal questions.[7] This has led to a growing appreciation of the fact that inter-communion implies a certain rejection of one's own doctrinal fundamentals; which is an approximation of the Catholic position so clearly and simply presented by Bishop Brunner of Middlesborough (England), " The way one worships is bound up with what one believes. We believe differently, therefore, we cannot worship together." [8] That is an example

[3] *Report of Lund Conference*, 1952, 101.

[4] *Ecumenical Review*, 1955/6, 18-36.

[5] *The Chronicles and the Church*, (Longmans: London, 1960) 61. No one should attempt to handle ecumenical problems without a serious study of this work, which is a mine of information and a model of erudition.

[6] *Union of Christendom*, Vol. II (London), 1938.

[7] Report of Gen. Sec., *Ecumenical Review*, XI (Oct., 1956) 43.

[8] *Universe and Cath. Times*, Jan. 25, 1963.

of absolute sincerity and simple truth which might well be copied by theologians everywhere. Similar statements have been made by others, including Professor Zander and Fr. Congar, O.P.[9] But there is another and an opposing tendency in both non-catholic and also in some Catholic circles, which is not so healthy, namely, the idea that we have something to learn in matters of worship from non-catholics. In view of what will be said later about inter-communion, the present writer regards this tendency with grave suspicion as to its practical value.[10]

In view of all this it may well be asked what this absolute sincerity implies from the positive dogmatic angle as far as the Catholic theologian is concerned. The question is not an easy one because it has so many facets, but the main outlines of the reply may well include such basic principles as these:

1. Fidelity to the dictates of *Humani Generis*, to begin with; together with a rejection of the temptation to use the ecumenical excuse as a weapon for the destruction of scholasticism and the creation of a new ' situational ' theology.

2. A realisation that there is no basic division between theology and faith. The observation made by one non-catholic theologian to the effect that we agree in faith but differ only in theology, is an absurdity.

3. There is now an even greater need to return to the basic principle of St. Thomas that reason is an instrument by which we can express and deduce the virtual content of revelation.[11] It would be an error of the first magnitude to neglect the development of Neo-Thomism in favor of some vague, new theology, especially now when the study of Thomism has influenced so many Anglican and Presbyterian theologians. We

---

[9] Quoted in the *Inter-communion Report*, 1952, 350-354.

[10] Cf. the article by Ruth Slade, " The Laity and Christian Unity," *Clergy Review*, (London), Jan., 1963.

[11] Cf. the article entitled " *Humani Generis*, Guia del Teologo," *Ciencia Tomista*, 1951, 546 ff.

need only quote Professor H. Taylor and Dr. E. Mascall as typical examples of this influence. It is high time that we all realised the fact that this is a glorious part of our Catholic inheritance. We should make the most of it, because it is our finest instrument for precise thought and for careful definition—both of which are essential if we are to bring the faith to our separated brethren.

The fact that it is possible to write theology along scholastic and Neo-Thomistic lines, while at the same time writing good English is amply demonstrated by Fr. B. Leeming's work, *Principles of Sacramental Theology*, (Longmans: London, 1956). ' Modern ' theologians, in the Bishop of Darwin's sense of the word, have nothing to offer which can compare with this and it should serve as a model of theological writing at the present day.

4. In this connection every theologian would do well to read and digest G. K. Chesterton's *Orthodoxy*. Speaking of the great theological ' wars ' of the past and of the reasons for them, he says:

It is enough to notice that, if some small mistake were made in doctrine, high blunders might be made in human happiness. A sentence wrongly phrased about the nature of symbolism would have broken all the best statues in Europe. A slip on the definitions might stop all the dances, might wither all the Christmas trees or break all the Easter eggs. Doctrine had to be carefully defined within strict limits, even in order that man might enjoy general human liberties. The Church had to be careful, if only that the world might be careless.[12]

We are in much the same position today; one slip now may cost us years of effort.

Chesterton's basic thesis should be applied to all true ecumenical dialogue unless we wish to stultify all efforts at true reunion. The idea that we must first unite in the hope that doctrinal agreement may follow later is only to put the cart before the horse! It is first of all necessary to explain to our

[12] (London, 1908) 166 ff.

separated brethren in simple language the doctrines of the Church, together with the fact that she dare not depart from them by one iota! This may appear hard—and there are not a few theologians who fight shy of doing it for that reason— but we ought to be aware of the fact that only the truth, with all its consequences, will make them free. The whole point of ecumenical dialogue is not to draw to us first of all, but to explain. The reason is a very simple one, but fundamental; the Orthodox and above all the Protestant theologians, are only *now* beginning to read our writings! To think that they study everything we write as much as we watch their writings would be a grave error in judgment, and one for which we would pay dearly.

5. This point gives rise to yet another. We must not give non-catholics the impression that the great Conciliar decrees of the past can be modified or made easier for their acceptance by a new expression of those truths in more modern language. This would imply that such decrees are capable of radical reform—which is untrue. Have we, by any chance learned bad habits from our ecumenical brethren? We know that, among non-catholics, it is no longer the fashion to disagree openly. The modern phrase for it is " to place a different emphasis." Miss Helle Georgiadis says:

The main obstacle to discussion between different Christian groups is that the same terms are used, but these terms, so far as they apply to the Church, have altered their content as a result of historical pressure, in particular that of the Reformation. Moreover, the oecumenical movement has invested many terms which previously had a specific meaning (the word Oecumencial itself for example) with new significance.

Dr. Visser't Hooft, speaking of Fr. Tavard's book, *The Catholic Appeal to Protestanism* (New York, 1955), points out that we are up against a fundamental difficulty. He does so in a trenchant phrase:

Has Fr. Tavard then not learned the simple A.B.C. of ecumenism, that there is no ecumenical language which is completely un-ambiguous for all concerned? [13]

How one wishes that all Catholic theologians would learn this phrase by heart, and not be taken in by apparent agreement in words! There is, of course, only one real answer to it—clear definition of terms! We are forced back to Neo-Thomism in the end!

Reunion, to a Catholic, must mean unity in faith and worship. To imply the opposite is to destroy the truth and to betray Christ. Most Protestant writers are aware of this, but Catholic authors are not so clear on the point as one would like. On the one hand, many of them give the impression of wishing to cast aside the more sober tunic of orthodox theology for the flimsy dress of modern thought; others give the impression that many of our great doctrines of the past are now extremely doubtful in the bright light of ecumenism. Later in this article we hope to show how dangerous this tendency is and how harmful to true ecumenical dialogue.

6. To sum up: the need is for a clear, definite exposition of the true Catholic position, without fear or favor, yet with all due charity, together with a clear recognition of the facts of the position with regard to our separated brethren. We have no right to hide from them or from ourselves the difficulties in the way to reunion, nor must we give them the impression that the Catholic Church is ready to betray her dogmatic mission. In other matters we can be as liberal as possible, but there can be no half-way house from the strictly doctrinal point of view. While on the one hand we must avoid any semblance of witch-hunting, or the mistakes Augustine made in his dealings with the early Christians in Britain, we must also avoid the even graver mistake made by the Anglican Church in its South Indian Reunion scheme.

This is especially important in view of the fact that the present Anglican Church in Britain considers itself to be a

---

[13] *The Ecumenical Review*, VIII, Jan., 1956.

" bridge church," capable of uniting the two extremes, Rome and other denominations. This has always been her ideal and it is very clear in modern ecumenical writings on the subject.[14]

So much for the general principles. Now, how can we apply them to the major dogmatic problems which face us in our ecumenical efforts?

The first and truly fundamental problem is that of the nature of the Church founded by Christ. But since this is the subject of another article in this series, we need to do no more than mention it here. One point which stands out is the need for a drastic reform of the treatise, *De Ecclesia*, in our textbooks of theology—a reform which takes into consideration the modern developments in the history of this dogma and also the new grounds for discussion. Perhaps the best approach to this problem is the one adopted by Monsignor Charles Journet in his monumental work on the subject.[15] In it we see the Church as she really is, as the Bride of Christ.

Although at times they tend to avoid this issue in their writings, it is clear that non-catholics are aware of the importance of it. There can be no successful attempts at reunion until it is dealt with fully.[16] It covers a vast field, every inch of which must be ploughed and cultivated by the Catholic theologian. There must be special emphasis on the apostolic succession in the episcopate, one of the corner stones in the Catholic concept of the Church as a visible entity and a living magisterium. It would be wrong, both in theory and in practice, for us to state anything other than the Tridentine and Vatican I doctrines on this point, even though we may have to re-word them into more modern language. Even a glance at the ecclesiology of a man like Karl Barth will

---

[14] Cf. Dr. James Good, *The Church of England and the Ecumenical Movement* (Burns Oates: London, 1961), an excellent summary of the present position of the Anglican Church with regard to reunion; and also the Bishop of London's book, *What the Church of England Stands For* (Mowbrays: London) 1952.

[15] *The Church of the Word Incarnate* (Sheed and Ward, 1955).

[16] Cf. *Nouvelle Revue Théologique*, Sept.-Oct. 1961, 832 ff. This article also contains an abundant bibliography.

serve to show us what we are up against and how little the Protestants as a whole really understand the nature of the Church of Christ on earth.[17]

The mission of Christ's Church depends on this doctrine of the nature of the Church as a visible entity in the world, and to accommodate the doctrine to make it fit any ecumenical theory would be to wreck the bark of Peter. Underlying every single Council since the beginning of the Church there has been this idea of a living magisterium as a visible witness to the revelation and redemption of Christ. An historical development of this interesting point would not be time wasted at the present moment.[18]

In this matter of reunion and unity I would venture to suggest that the best contribution we can make—and one for which non-catholics would be very grateful—is a clear statement of the Catholic position with regard to these fundamental problems. Above all, there should be no attempt to create a new theology to fit the ecumenical situation or to water down the great dogmas of the Church so that they may become easier to assimilate or more attractive to those outside the fold. This implies no little effort and no mean theological ability. It will not be accomplished by merely negative criticism of certain elements in the Church which are purely accidental to the issue. Instead, the starting point must be a clear realisation of two things, one related to the present and one to the past.

The Catholic theologian must be fully aware of the present-day approach of non-catholics to the problems he is trying to explain. He must have studied their writings at first hand to see where they fit in with true Catholic doctrine and where they do not. Also he must be able to detect the varied meanings they give to expressions which, to him, are house-

[17] Cf. Maurice Schepers, O.P., " The Works of the Holy Spirit: Karl Barth on the Nature of the Church," *Theological Studies,* Dec. 1962.

[18] Cf. " Concile Oecumenique et Catholicité de l'eglise," *Nouvelle Revue Théologique,* Nov., 1959, 916 ff.

hold words. It is all too easy to attribute a fully Catholic meaning to non-catholic writings when they are, in fact, poles apart from Catholicity. Many Catholic theologians have been misled on this point and have hurriedly ' baptised ' a non-catholic writer too soon, much to his indignation!

A case in point is surely Karl Barth, whose writings may reveal the soul of a man who is earnestly trying to discover Christ, but which certainly do not indicate a close proximity to Catholicity. To say, as one Catholic theologian has said, that there is little or no difference between Barth's doctrine of justification and that of the Catholic Church, or that the differences which do exist could scarcely serve today to bring about any division from the true Church is, in reality, a naive confession of ignorance of the Protestant mind and only serves to obscure the evil of such division.

Protestants themselves are well aware of this vague use of terms, together with the synthesis of errors to which it may easily lead. One of their leading theologians, Dr. E. L. Mascall, puts it like this:

When the unity of truth is broken, it often happens that the result is not a number of fragments of the truth, but a number of conceptions which are misleading, erroneous and heretical. We do not arrive at truth by fitting errors together. It is widely assumed that a synthesis can be reached by taking the agreed elements in our " common christianity ' and by omitting matters on which there is deep disagreement. But to do this is to accept our common *distorted* versions of christianity as a basis, without attempting to cure us all of our distortions. From the highest Common Factor of several erroneous quotients we get, not a true solution, but a result more erroneous still.[19]

Statements such as this reveal a deep knowledge of the importance of dogmatic theology and could have come from the pen of a Catholic theologian. The very basis of reunion is truth, as we have said before, not a leaning-over-backwards to please our separated brethren. They will not easily forgive

[19] *Catholicity*, 44.

us if we make that mistake, because it is just what they themselves are trying to avoid. They are fully aware of the fact that for all to unite under the Pope in the hope of reaching doctrinal agreement later is out of the question. However, there are some who are not as yet aware of the fallacy behind the idea that, since we do not know exactly what Christ wanted for his Church, we must get together to find out. In this they require clear guidance and we need have no fear of offending them if we give it with all charity. They need to be shown that one error in doctrine is enough to vitiate the whole edifice and that it is not enough to bring moral qualities to the " united church " which is our ideal.

There are signs that non-catholic theologians are becoming increasingly aware of the fact that the distinctive " witness " of each sect will have to yield to the " common witness " and that the historic tradition of each body will have to give place to the universal tradition. Here it is important for the Catholic theologian not to be taken in by mere appearances. He should not be prepared to diminish the power of the fact that the Catholic Church is not merely the only guardian of that universal tradition in faith and morals, but also the only Church which has preserved it intact and free from all tarnish of error. The danger here, I think, is the temptation to be a " federationist "—to think in terms of a multitude of more or less independent national churches in federation with one another, rather than in terms of organic unity. Fr. Leeming expresses perfectly the obligation of the Catholic theologian when he says:

The Roman Church has a duty to her own members, to dissident fellow-christians and to the world to assert her claim of uniqueness, unity and visibility, and not to allow it to be obscured.[20]

Obviously, this question stands at the very highest dogmatic level and there has been no fundamental change in the attitude of non-catholics to it since the famous remark of

[20] *Op. cit.,* 240.

Archbishop Davidson during the course of the Malines Conversations, when he said:

But prior to all these (other questions) and far outweighing them in importance, stands the fundamental question—Is there, or is there not, a Vicar of Christ upon earth, who possesses *iure divino* a distinctive authoritative position in relation to the whole of Christendom? [21]

The slant of non-catholic arguments against the papal authority and succession may have changed slightly over the years, but the basic difficulty remains the same for all that, a refusal to admit a primacy of jurisdiction over the whole Church. This is clear from the remarks made by Rev. David L. Edwards, in an article first produced in *Esprit* and later in the *Church Times* (Jan. 10, 1962). It would be foolish of us to ignore this or pretend that it did not exist or was of little importance.

Here the Catholic theologian has an obligation which stems from his faith to explain clearly the Catholic position without being led astray from it by historical red-herrings. He must be prepared to prove that unity without difformity needs a central authority, while at the same time he makes it clear that unity does not necessarily mean uniformity.[22]

Closely connected with the Papal claims is the famous question of the authority of the Bishops in union with the Pope and the laity, in one single unity which corresponds to the organic unity of the body. Here, above all, it is necessary for the Catholic theologian to have a firm grasp of what is meant by the term " historic episcopate " when used by non-catholics and of the real issues at stake in the Gallican controversy of Vatican I (with its origins in the Gallican articles of 1682). The fundamental dogmatic issues are the same as those which divide ecumenists today, namely, federation as opposed to

[21] G. K. Bell, *Randall Davidson, Archbishop of Canterbury*, London, 1952.

[22] Cf. D. Attwater, *The Christian Churches of the East*. Vol. 1. *Churches in Communion with Rome*, (Milwaukee, 1948) which shows clearly how much diversity the Church allows and encourages.

organic unity. Here it is all too easy to be led away by side issues, such as Vatican totalitarianism, over-centralization, submission of the intellect to Roman decisions, etc.[23] These things, if they exist at all, are not an obstacle to true ecumenism as such within the Catholic Church, and to spend all our time on a refutation of them and of their implications is to beat the air in vain. They are *not* the main issues at stake, and to make reunion depend on them and on their reform is to deny the efficacy of the Spirit of God and to make reunion a type of federation ideal, which is absurd.

Even a summary examination of the various reunion documents produced by non-catholics leads us to one essential conclusion—that the aim is compromise. Wherever possible, a formula is agreed upon which will be capable of including all opinions and when this is impossible, then each side is ready to sacrifice a little of what it believes, always with the excuse that this is done in Christian charity. As Fr. Hebert truly says, " There is a tendency to a light-hearted acceptance of schemes for reunion, while we murmur that Christian love counts for more than orthodoxy." [24]

We must not be deceived by words. The Lambeth Appeal of 1920 means now what it always meant in Anglican theology—the doctrine of Fundamentalism married to that of the autonomy of national Churches and as such we cannot admit it. This is the present doctrine of Anglicanism with regard to the future " unified " Church, and in it there is an element of modernism which the Catholic theologian would do well to recognize. What is true of Anglicanism is even more true of non-conformity. Dr. Leslie Weatherhead has expressed it thus:

Clearly no unity will ever be possible if it has to depend on everyone believing the same truths in the same sense. Human minds work differently, and two equally sincere religious men can believe ideas which are completely irreconcilable . . . . No, the way

---

[23] Cf. Hans Küng, *The Council and Reunion*, (Sheed and Ward: London, 1961) 196 ff.

[24] *The Form of the Church*, 104, quoted in Good, *op. cit.*, 67.

to unity is not by endless discussions aimed at making men believe the same thing or worship in the same way.[25]

The doctrine of the Mass as a Sacrifice demands the attention of the orthodox theologian for many reasons. A glance at the *Report of the Commission on Doctrine* appointed by the Archbishops of Canterbury and York in 1922 is enough to demonstrate clearly that, so far as the Eucharist is concerned, Anglicans are prepared to admit every opinion from the strict Lutheran to the extreme Anglo-Catholic.[26]

The Lambeth Conference of 1958 confirms this opinion, while at the same time it includes elements which are not conducive to ecumenism. The Catholic theologian must always be aware of the Protestant slant on this question, and the fact that, even from the purely historical point of view, they are in error about the Eucharist, must not be ignored. Their historical grounds for controversy have changed, it is true, and this alone should make us suspect that Anglican theology is ever more aware of its departure from the " universal tradition " and of the need for a " via media " which will secure its continued existence as a world force.[27] The " bridge church " idea is predominant here once again.[28] It is interesting to notice, in this connection that the *Ways of Worship Report*, (London, 1953) is perfectly clear as to the fact that both Luther and Calvin rejected the sacrificial aspect of the Mass.

So far as Catholics are concerned, the Decrees of Trent set the seal of infallibility on the orthodox Catholic doctrine of the time and nothing can change that. It is one of the points which we must be prepared to discuss with our separated brethren in the ecumenical movement, and we must be pre-

---

[25] Cf. Article in the *Sunday Express*, London, Jan. 27, 1963.

[26] Published by S. P. C. K., London, 1938.

[27] Cf. Article in *Theological Studies*, Vol. 23, No. 2 (June, 1962) under the title " Late Medieval Eucharistic Theology: Orthodoxy or Corruption? "

[28] Cf. *What the Church of England Stands For*, by J. Wand, Bishop of London, (Mowbrays, London) 1952.

pared to do so without selling the past. The doctrines of the Mass must be preserved intact, together with the essential decrees of Trent from both the historical and theological points of view. Only harm can come from a tacit admission that the reforming Protestants were really Catholics at heart and were only attacking the aberrations of medieval theologians—which is nonsense! The Mass is now, as it was then, an essential part of the universal tradition, to which all must submit. Any other position is unorthodox, if not heretical.

Now a word or two about the position of the Catholic Church with regard to the separated Oriental Churches. Here there is much confusion of thought and so many things need be said, each of which would demand a separate article. However, with due apologies, we may attempt a synthesis.

Leaving aside the obvious bone of contention, the jurisdictional primacy of the See of Peter, we can say that the main issue which has to be decided between Rome and the East is that of the "economy" theory, of which an admirable summary is given in Dr. Good's book, already quoted. The important factor in this theory is that Orthodoxy does not— and *cannot*—recognise as valid any sacraments which she has not administered herself. However, she is prepared to re-validate those administered by other religious bodies, *provided* they come over to Orthodoxy. The interpretations of Protestant theologians make this quite clear. Thus Mackensie says that the implication is that Anglicanism has all the necessary conditions for the validity of its orders, except that of belonging to the true Church,[29] while Goudge admits that the principle as applied to Anglican Church means that, if it became an 'Orthodox Church,' its ministers would not have to be re-ordained.[30]

It is not generally realised that the attitude of Orthodoxy to Anglican Orders gives us a general picture of some of the doctrinal difficulties which the Catholic Church has to face

[29] *The Confusion of the Churches*, 238.
[30] *The Church of England and Reunion*, 65.

before there can be any hope of reunion between East and West. Here it is a struggle between two Churches, each of which claims to have the whole truth, and therefore each demanding submission on the part of the other.[31]

In such a situation there are bound to be several points on which East and West agree, for example, the doctrine of the Mass, the seven sacraments and Mariology, for which the East has fought no less bravely than the West. This must not lead the Catholic theologian to assume that agreement on so many points will make his task easier. It is true that such writings as that of Francis Dvornik have lightened the historical horizon to some extent, but that is all.[32] There is still an inner antagonism to Catholicism and all it represents which can only be broken down by much patient effort. This situation is not improved by the identification of religion and politics which has been a decisive element in Orthodoxy for so many centuries.[33] Perhaps this explains why the comments of the Orthodox delegates to the first session of the present Council were less enthusiastic and effusive than those of some of the other representatives.[34]

In his approach to Orthodoxy, the Catholic theologian needs to concentrate his attention on the history of dogma rather than on dogmatic reasonings as such. This is especially true of questions such a papal infallibility and jurisdiction, which are already upheld in theory, if not in practice, by some of the writers of the autocephalous churches.[35] There is room for a deeper investigation of the Papal claims, especially as the history of the first seven General Councils present them to us. On those Councils the faith of Orthodoxy is based, and

[31] Cf. "Orthodoxy, Rome and Oecumenism," by Helle Georgiadis, *Eastern Churches Quarterly*, xvi No. 8 (1956) 7: also *Nouvelle Revue Théologique*, Jan., 196 ff.

[32] *The Photian Schism*, Cambridge University Press, 1948.

[33] Cf. K. Algermissen, *Christian Denominations*, (Herder, 1948) pp. 560 ff.

[34] Cf. the article on this subject in *Ecclesia*, Feb. 16, 1963.

[35] Cf. the writings of some of the Russian theologians, such as A. Chomjakoff and S. Bulgakow.

it should lead logically to a recognition of the Papacy. The fact that it has not done so, especially in recent years, seems to be due to many factors, which include the doctrinal sterility of Orthodoxy (admitted even by their own theologians), an unfounded fear of Romanization and, above all, to the influence of political factors. This latter influence is especially strong in the Russian Church, where the policy of communist infiltration into the ranks of the clergy has been in operation for some years now.

Reunion also presents many moral problems from the Catholic point of view. Two of these are of outstanding importance. One is concerned with the obligation to follow an erroneous conscience and whether such an obligation gives rise to a strict right to religious freedom. The other is concerned with certain aspects of marriage. Some brief observations on these problems may be of use to Catholic theologians.

The general moral principles which govern conscience—even an erroneous one—are clearly laid down in all the text books. On that point there is no real difficulty. The question at issue is whether this obligation to follow an erroneous conscience can give rise to a right in the strict sense of that word. To put this in the form of an example may help us all to understand the real difficulty at issue here. A person brought up in a false religion can have the obligation to follow the dictates of his conscience in religious matters, even though, from the point of view of truth, that conscience may be a false one. Has he, therefore a *right*, juridically speaking, to act in accordance with that conscience? The question is no mere academic one, as will be appreciated immediately once we remember that a right, as opposed to a mere obligation, implies objective juridical demands which command respect and non-interference from all who come up against it.

It is well known that there are two opposing opinions with regard to this question, and it is a fertile and most useful field for the theologian from the historical, juridical and dogmatic aspects. Since it is on the agenda for the next session of the Council, the matter is an urgent one.[36]

Marriage in all its aspects presents many obstacles to reunion as things stand at present. This is especially true of the question of mixed marriages from the non-catholic point of view and, most of all, the great problem of its indissolubility. It is not without significance that Canon Bernard Pawley, who was appointed by the Archbishops of Canterbury and York to act as their personal representative at the Council has listed three matters which, as he puts it, "Undoubtedly deface the image of the Roman Church in the eyes of Christian bodies outside her communion." These three matters are the belief that the Catholic Church is a danger to the natural liberties of man, both religious and political; the rules about mixed marriages (!) and the degree of veneration of the Blessed Virgin.[37] In view of the anomalous position of Anglicanism, it need not surprise us to see that there is no mention of the nature of marriage as a sacrament, much less of its indissolubility. Instead there is the obvious desire, expressed by many another non-catholic writer, that the Roman Church will make some concessions in the matter of mixed marriages, although we are not told clearly how far she is expected to go in this matter.

In spite of all this, one gets the impression that the present position of the Anglican Church is stronger on such things as the indissolubility of marriage than one would think. It is unfortunate to say the least that, for so many years, Anglicanism has been forced to submit to a civil legislation on marriage which she has never entirely accepted from the doctrinal point of view, but which has forced her into an equivocal position from which her leaders long to escape. Whether she will be able to free herself from these claims at any price

[36] The speech made by Cardinal Bea at the Unity Octave meeting in Rome and reported in *Ecclesia*, Feb. 2, 1963, represents one of the contrary opinions we have mentioned.

[37] Cf. *Looking at the Vatican Council*, S.CM. Press, 1962.

less than that of dis-establishment is another matter. *A pri-ori*, she would like to hold fast to the theory that marriage is indissoluble, although she has been forced to admit divorce, while at the same time tending to refuse to admit divorced people to a new marriage in Church, at least in theory.[38]

The position of non-conformity in this matter of divorce is far worse than that of Anglicanism.

The task of the Catholic theologian is clear. The sacramental nature of marriage has to be explained and developed in the light of biblical theology, for on that depends the quality of indissolubility. Here we must make a clear distinction between the strictly theological arguments and those from the natural law, since the latter form a special type of logical argument, leading to an inductive rather than a deductive conclusion. Unless this is clearly understood, the Catholic theologian can easily ask too much of his reasoning, with the fatal result that his arguments do not really prove. The juridical, historical and patristic arguments must all be developed with this point in mind, because at times there is a natural law basis for them, at others a strictly theological one. There is room here for a new examination of the classical text-book reasonings, which can only have full force if these principles are kept in mind.

It may be useful to insist once again that the great dogmatic decisions of the Church with regard to the sacrament of matrimony have an eternal force and must not be neglected or diminished. It is not controversy we are seeking, but a simple yet clear explanation of the truth of Christ's teaching with regard to this sacrament. Nothing less than this will do, if we are to be of any help to our separated brethren in their present moment of trial. They are fighting to preserve dogma against sentimentalism and expediency and we can

---

[38] Cf. Dom Peter Flood, O.S.B., *The Dissolution of Marriage* (Burns Oates: London, 1962) for an excellent summary of English Civil and ecclesiastical law as compared with Canon Law. It is especially useful as a proof of the political aspects of Anglicanism since 1857.

only help them in this fight by preserving intact the law of
Christ and giving good reasons for so doing. For this reason
alone it is the opinion of the present writer that there should
be no concessions made in the matter of mixed marriages
until we see how far Protestanism is prepared to go in order
to preserve the basic essentials of the doctrine on Christian
marriage.

Because the Church itself realises only too well that compromise in doctrinal matters leads inevitably, sooner or later
to another compromise between expediency and sentimentalism, we have as our directive in ecumenical matters the clear
and binding Instruction of the Holy Office to local Ordinaries
on the Ecumenical Movement (1950). One passage of that
instruction says:

Catholic teaching is therefore to be set forth and explained whole
and entire and none of its truths must be passed over in silence
or cloaked in ambiguity; for example, the truths concerning the
nature and means of salvation, the constitution of the Church, the
Roman Pontiff's primacy of jurisdiction and the certainty that
true reunion can only come about by return of dissidents to the
one, true Church of Christ . . . . . All this must be stated clearly
and openly since they are seeking the truth and real union will
never be found outside that truth.[39]

To this instruction we must all adhere, and only through a
faithful observance of its principles will we be able to build
up a truly effective ecumenical dialogue. Any other road will
lead to confusion, if not to costly error.

DAVID L. GREENSTOCK, D.D.

Colegio de Ingleses,
  Valladolid, Spain

---

[39] From the translation of the Instruction published in *The Tablet*, March 4,
1950.

NOTES ON OUR CONTRIBUTORS

∽

FERRER SMITH, O. P., S. T. D., recent President of the Catholic Theological Society of America, co-author of *Preface to Happiness,* and contributor to the theological journals, holds the office of Regent of Studies, Province of St. Joseph, and is Professor of Moral Theology at the Dominican House of Studies, Washington, D. C.

CESLAUS SPICQ, O. P., S. T. D., Professor of Exegesis of the New Testament at the University of Fribourg, author of several books on Biblical studies, frequent contributor to scholarly journals including *Revue Biblique,* is a Consultor of the Biblical Commission.

JOHN KING, O. M. I., S. T. D., who teaches Dogmatic Theology at the Oblate College, Washington, D. C. and has contributed studies in the field of Ecclesiology to several theological journals, accompanied Msgr. Vagnozzi, the Apostolic Delegate to the United States, to the first session of the Second Vatican Council and was appointed a *peritus.*

MAURICE SCHEPERS, O. P., S. T. D., Professor of History of Dogma at the Dominican House of Studies, Washington, D. C., Visiting Instructor in the Department of Religious Education at the Catholic University of America, has recently published a volume in the Foundations of Catholic Theology Series entitled *The Church of Christ.*

JAMES EGAN, O. P., S. T. D., whose theological studies have appeared in THE THOMIST, *Cross and Crown, Angelicum,* and other journals, is Chairman of the College Division of the Dominican Educational Association and Professor in the Graduate School of Theology, St. Mary's College, Notre Dame, Indiana.

EMILIO SAURAS, O. P., S. T. D., Professor at the University of Valencia, Valencia, Spain, contributor to the principal Spanish theological journals, and author of two major works on the Mystical Body, was chosen by the Holy See to assist officials at the Council as a *peritus.*

COLMAN O'NEILL, O. P., S. T. D., whose theological studies have appeared in *The Irish Theological Quarterly,* THE THOMIST, *The American Ecclesiastical Review,* is Professor of Dogmatic Theology at the Institute *Jesus Magister* in Rome.

JAMES GAFFNEY, S. J., S. T. L., having attended Holy Cross College, Boston, Massachusetts, continued his philosophical studies at Spring Hill College, Mobile, Alabama, and his theological studies at Woodstock College, Woodstock, Maryland.

CORNELIUS ERNST, O. P., M. A., S. T. L., Professor of Fundamental Theology at the Dominican House of Studies, Hawkesyard Priory, Rugeley, Staffs, England, whose articles have appeared in *Dominican Studies, Clergy Review,* and *Blackfriars,* has recently had published his English translation of Karl Rahner's *Theological Investigations.*

619

THOMAS CAMELOT, O.P., S.T.D., Vice-Rector of the Dominican Faculty of Theology at Le Saulchoir, Etiolles, France, author of numerous articles and several books, including *Les Conciles d'Ephèse et de Chalcédoine*, was a *peritus* at the first session of the Second Vatican Council.

LUIGI CIAPPI, O.P., S.T.D., Master of the Sacred Palace, Vatican City, author of *De Sacramentis in Communi*, among other books, and of scholarly studies appearing in *Angelicum, Sapienza, Marianum*, and THE THOMIST, was a *peritus* assisting at the first session of the Second Vatican Council.

GREGORY BAUM, O.S.A., S.T.D., Director of the Centre of Ecumenical Studies at St. Michael's College, University of Toronto, Canada, editor of *The Ecumenist*, author of several books, the latest of which is *Progress and Perspectives*, and numerous articles in Ecumenism, is a Consultor of the Secretariat for Christian Unity at Rome.

PRUDENTIUS DE LETTER, S.J., Ph.D., S.T.D., author of *The Call to All Nations* and other books, frequent contributor to scholarly journals, such as *Theological Studies, Irish Theological Quarterly, Bijdragen*, and THE THOMIST, is professor at St. Mary's Theological College, Kurseong, N. F. Ry., India.

ALVARO HUERGA, O.P., S.T.D., affiliated with Centro de Estudios de Espiritualidad (University of Salamanca, Spain), Professor at the Pontifical University of St. Thomas Aquinas in Rome, and noted author, was consultor of the Spanish hierarchy at the first session of the Second Vatican Council.

EDWARD SCHILLEBEECKX, O.P., S.T.D., whose book, *De Sacramentele Heilseconomie*, has brought him international recognition among theologians, was advisor for the Dutch hierarchy at the first session of the Second Vatican Council.

AUGUSTIN LÉONARD, O.P., S.T.D., author of *Phenomenology of the Christian Mystics*, and other books, as well as frequent contributor to French and English theological journals, Professor at the Dominican House of Studies, La Sarte, Huy, Belgium, and Visiting Professor at the University of Montreal, College of New Rochelle, and Notre Dame University, will soon publish another book on Catholicism and religious freedom.

HENRY ST. JOHN, O.P., M.A., Provincial of the English Province of the Dominican Order (1958-1962), author of *Christian Unity and Education*, who has written for *Blackfriars, Life of the Spirit, Clergy Review, Worship* and other journals, is presently continuing his research in Christian unity at St. Dominic's Priory, Isle of Wight, England.

JEROME HAMER, O.P., S.T.D., a recognized authority on Protestant theology, author of *Karl Barth* and *L'Eglise est une Communion*, now at Convento Santa Sabina, Rome, was selected as *peritus* for the first session of the Second Vatican Council.

WILLIAM HILL, O.P., S.T.D., staff editor of THE THOMIST and author of *Proper Relations to the Indwelling Divine Persons*, is Professor of Dogmatic Theology at the Dominican House of Studies, Washington, D. C.

CORNELIUS WILLIAMS, O.P., S.T.D., well known for his many theological contributions in the *Irish Theological Quarterly, Bulletin Thomiste, Freiburger Zeitschrift*, and other journals, is Professor of Theology at the University of Fribourg, Switzerland.

CHRISTOPHER KIESLING, O.P., S.T.L., who has written essays on the liturgy for the book *Seeking the Kingdom*, and contributed articles to *Cross and Crown* and

Fonti Vive, is affiliated with Aquinas Institute School of Theology and Mt. St. Bernard Seminary, Dubuque, Iowa.

BERNARD BRO, O. P., S. T. D., Professor of Dogmatic Theology at Le Saulchoir, Etiolles, France, and literary director of Editions du Cerf, contributes frequently to *Bulletin Thomiste* and *La Vie Spirituelle.*

JOHN MOORMAN, Anglican Bishop of Ripon, England, was an Observer Delegate at the first session of the Second Vatican Council.

ANTHONY LEE, O. P., S. T. L., Managing Editor of THE THOMIST and The Thomist Press, co-editor of a series of brief works in theology, philosophy, science, and the arts entitled *Compact Studies,* is assigned to the Dominican House of Studies, Washington, D. C.

WILLIAM WALLACE, O. P., Ph. D., S. T. D., author of *The Role of Demonstration in Moral Theology* and *The Scientific Methodology of Theodoric of Freiberg,* noted lecturer on the relationship of science, philosophy and theology, is Staff Editor of the Philosophy section of *The New Catholic Encyclopedia,* Catholic University of America, Washington, D. C.

THOMAS O'BRIEN, O. P., Ph. D., S. T. D., author of *Metaphysics and the Existence of God,* staff editor of THE THOMIST, and regional editor of the new English translation of the Summa, is a contributor to many scholarly journals and is Professor of Moral Theology at the Dominican House of Studies, Washington, D. C.

RONAN HOFFMAN, O. F. M. Conv., S. T. L., D. Miss., whose studies in Missiology have appeared in many scholarly journals, Assistant Professor of Missiology and Coordinator of College and Mission Studies (C.S.M.C.) at the Catholic University of America, Washington, D. C., is a member of the editorial board of *Worldmission.*

RONALD COWLEY, O. P., Ph. L., S. T. D., who has contributed to the symposium *Le Christ et Les Eglises* and written many articles for scholarly journals, including *Istina* and *Sacra Doctrina,* is a member of the Centre of Studies, *Istina,* Paris, France.

CARL PAUWELS, O. P., S. T. D., Professor of Theology at the Albertinum, Nijmegen, Netherlands, author of many studies on the problem of conversions, represented the Catholic newspaper *De Volkskrant* at the first session of the Second Vatican Council.

DAVID GREENSTOCK, S. T. D., Fellow of the International Institute of Arts and Letters (Kreuzlingen), and member of the Committee of Higher Studies of the Centro Studi e Scambi Internazionali (Rome), is Vice-Rector and Professor of Theology at the Colegio de Ingleses, Valladolid, Spain.